Windows Server® 2012 R2 Inside Out: Configuration, Storage, & Essentials

William R. Stanek

PUBLISHED BY
Microsoft Press
A Division of Microsoft Corporation
One Microsoft Way
Redmond, Washington 98052-6399

Library of Congress Control Number: 2013955709
ISBN: 978-0-7356-8267-2

Printed and bound in the United States of America.

First Printing

Microsoft Press books are available through booksellers and distributors worldwide. If you need support related to this book, email Microsoft Press Book Support at mspinput@microsoft.com. Please tell us what you think of this book at http://www.microsoft.com/learning/booksurvey.

Acquisitions Editor: Anne Hamilton
Developmental Editor: Karen Szall
Project Editor: Rosemary Caperton
Editorial Production: nSight, Inc.
Technical Reviewer: Bob Hogan; Technical Review services provided by Content Master, a member of CM Group, Ltd.
Copyeditor: Kerin Forsyth
Indexer: Lucie Haskins
Cover: Twist Creative • Seattle

To my readers—thank you for being there with me through many books and many years.

To my wife—for many years, through many books, many millions of words, and many thousands of pages she's been there, providing support and encouragement and making every place we've lived a home.

To my kids—for helping me see the world in new ways, for having exceptional patience and boundless love, and for making every day an adventure.

To Anne, Karen, Martin, Lucinda, Juliana, and many others who've helped out in ways both large and small.

Special thanks to my son Will for not only installing and managing my extensive dev lab for all my books since Windows 8 Pocket Consultant *but for also performing check reads of all those books as well.*

—William R. Stanek

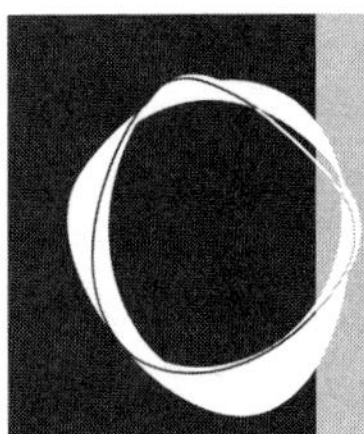

Contents at a glance

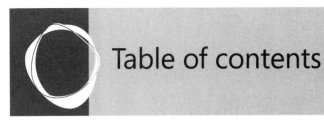

Table of contents

What do you think of this book? We want to hear from you!

Microsoft is interested in hearing your feedback so we can improve our books and learning resources for you. To participate in a brief survey, please visit:

http://aka.ms/tellpress

Introduction

Welcome to *Windows Server 2012 R2 Inside Out: Configuration, Storage, & Essentials*. As the author of many popular technology books, I've been writing professionally about Windows and Windows Server since 1994. Over the years, I've gained a unique perspective—the kind of perspective you can gain only after working with technologies for many years. The advantage for you, the reader, is that my solid understanding of these technologies allowed me to dig into Windows Server 2012 R2 architecture, internals, and configuration to see how things really work under the hood and then pass this information on to you throughout this book.

Anyone transitioning to Windows Server 2012 R2 from Windows Server 2012 may be surprised at just how much has been updated; changes both subtle and substantial have been made throughout the operating system. For anyone transitioning to Windows Server 2012 R2 from Windows Server 2008 R2 or an earlier release of Windows Server, I'll let you know right up front that Windows Server 2012 and Windows Server 2012 R2 are substantially different from earlier versions of Window Server. Not only are there major changes throughout the operating system, but this just might be the first version of Windows Server that you manage using a touch-based user interface. If you do end up managing it this way, mastering the touch-based UI and the revised interface options will be essential for your success. For this reason, I discuss both the touch UI and the traditional mouse-and-keyboard techniques throughout this book.

When you are working with touch UI–enabled computers, you can manipulate onscreen elements in ways that weren't possible previously. You can enter text by using the onscreen keyboard and manipulate onscreen elements in the following ways:

- **Tap.** Tap an item by touching it with your finger. A tap or double-tap of elements on the screen generally is the equivalent of a mouse click or double-click.

- **Press and hold.** Press your finger down and leave it there for a few seconds. Pressing and holding elements on the screen generally is the equivalent of a right-click.

- **Swipe to select.** Slide an item a short distance in the opposite direction of how the page scrolls. This selects the items and might bring up related commands. If pressing and holding doesn't display commands and options for an item, try swiping to select instead.

- **Swipe from edge (slide in from edge).** Starting from the edge of the screen, swipe or slide in. Sliding in from the right edge opens the Charms panel. Sliding in from the left edge shows open apps, and then you can easily switch between them. Sliding in from the top or bottom edge shows commands for the active element.

- **Pinch.** Touch an item with two or more fingers and then move those fingers toward each other. Pinching zooms out.

- **Stretch.** Touch an item with two or more fingers and then move those fingers away from each other. Stretching zooms in.

Who is this book for?

In this book, I teach you how server roles, role services, and features work; why they work the way they do; and how to customize them to meet your needs. Regardless of your job title, if you're deploying, configuring, managing, or maintaining Windows Server 2012 R2, this book is for you. To pack in as much information as possible, I had to assume that you have basic networking skills and a basic understanding of Windows Server and that you are familiar with Windows commands and procedures. With this in mind, I don't devote entire chapters to basic skills or why you want to use Windows Server. Instead, I focus on configuration, security, file systems, storage management, performance analysis, performance tuning, troubleshooting, and much more.

Conventions used in this book

The following conventions are used in this book:

- **Abbreviated menu commands.** For your convenience, this book uses abbreviated menu commands. For example, "Tap or click Tools, Track Changes, Highlight Changes" means that you should tap or click the Tools menu, select Track Changes, and then tap or click the Highlight Changes command.

- **Boldface type.** Boldface type indicates text that you enter or type.

- **Initial capital letters.** The first letters of the names of menus, dialog boxes, dialog box elements, and commands are capitalized. Example: the Save As dialog box.

- **Italicized type.** Italicized type indicates new terms.

- **Plus sign (+) in text.** Keyboard shortcuts are indicated by a plus sign (+) separating two key names. For example, Ctrl+Alt+Delete means that you press the Ctrl, Alt, and Delete keys at the same time.

How to reach the author

Email: williamstanek@aol.com

Web: *http://www.williamrstanek.com/*

Facebook: *https://www.facebook.com/William.Stanek.Author*

Twitter: *http://twitter.com/williamstanek*

Errata & book support

We've made every effort to ensure the accuracy of this book. Any errors that have been reported since this book was published are listed:

http://aka.ms/WSIO_ConfigSE/errata

If you find an error that is not already listed, you can report it to us through the same page.

If you need additional support, email Microsoft Press Book Support at *mspinput@microsoft.com*.

Please note that product support for Microsoft software is not offered through the addresses above.

We want to hear from you

At Microsoft Press, your satisfaction is our top priority and your feedback our most valuable asset. Please tell us what you think of this book at:

http://www.microsoft.com/learning/booksurvey

The survey is short, and we read every one of your comments and ideas. Thanks in advance for your input!

Stay in touch

Let's keep the conversation going! We're on Twitter: *http://twitter.com/MicrosoftPress*.

CHAPTER 1

Introducing Windows Server 2012 R2

Windows Server 2012 R2 is the most powerful, versatile, and fully featured server operating system from Microsoft yet. If you've been using Windows Server operating systems for a while, I think you'll be impressed. Why? For starters, Windows Server 2012 R2 includes a significantly enhanced operating system kernel, the NT 6.3 kernel. Because Windows 8.1 uses this kernel also, the two operating systems share a common code base and many common features, enabling you to apply readily what you know about Windows 8.1 to Windows Server 2012 R2.

In Windows Server 2012 R2, Microsoft delivers a server operating system that is something more than the sum of its parts. It isn't just a server operating system or a network operating system. It is a best-of-class operating system with the foundation technologies necessary to provide networking, application, web, and cloud-based services that can be used anywhere within your organization. From top to bottom, Windows Server 2012 R2 is dramatically different from earlier releases of Windows Server operating systems—so much so that it also has an entirely new interface.

The way you approach Windows Server 2012 R2 will depend on your background and your implementation plans. If you are moving to Windows Server 2012 R2 from an early Windows server operating system or switching from UNIX, you'll find that Windows Server 2012 R2 is a significant change that requires a whole new way of thinking about the networking, application services, and interoperations between clients and servers. The learning curve will be steep, but you will find clear transition paths to Windows Server 2012 R2. You will also find that Windows Server 2012 R2 has an extensive command-line interface that makes it easier to manage servers, workstations, and, indeed, the entire network, using both graphical and command-line administration tools.

If you are moving from Windows Server 2008 or Windows Server 2008 R2 to Windows Server 2012 R2, you'll find the changes are no less significant but are easier to understand. You are already familiar with the core technologies and administration techniques. Your learning curve might still be steep, but in only some areas, not all of them.

You can also adopt Windows Server 2012 R2 incrementally. For example, you might add Windows Server 2012 R2 Print And Document Services and Windows Server 2012 R2 File And

Storage Services to enable the organization to take advantage of the latest enhancements and capabilities without implementing a full transition of existing servers. In most but not all cases, incremental adoption has little or no impact on the network while allowing the organization to test new technologies and roll out features incrementally to users as part of a standard continuance or upgrade process.

Regardless of your deployment plans and whether you are reading this book to prepare for implementation of Windows Server 2012 R2 or to manage existing implementations, my mission in this book is to help you take full advantage of all the features in Windows Server 2012 R2. You will find the detailed inside information you need to get up to speed quickly with Windows Server 2012 R2 changes and technologies; to make the right setup and configuration choices the first time; and to work around the rough edges, annoyances, and faults of this complex operating system. If the default settings are less than optimal, I show you how to fix them so that things work the way you want them to work. If something doesn't function like it should, I let you know, and I show you the fastest, surest way to work around the issue. You'll find plenty of hacks and secrets, too.

To pack as much information as possible into this book, I am assuming that you have basic networking skills and some experience managing Windows-based networks and don't need me to explain the basic structure and architecture of an operating system. Therefore, I won't waste your time answering such questions as, "What's the point of networks?" or "Why use Windows Server 2012 R2?" or "What's the difference between the GUI and the command line?" Instead, I start with a discussion of what Windows Server 2012 R2 has to offer so that you can learn about changes that will most affect you, and then I follow this discussion with a comprehensive, informative look at Windows Server 2012 R2 planning and installation.

Getting to know Windows Server 2012 R2

A primary purpose of Windows Server 2012 R2 is to ensure that the operating system can be optimized for use in small, medium, and large enterprises. An edition of the server operating system is available to meet your organization's needs whether you want to deploy a basic server for hosting applications, a network server for hosting domain services, a robust enterprise server for hosting essential applications, or a highly available data center server for hosting critical business solutions.

Windows Server 2012 R2 is available for production use only on 64-bit hardware. Sixty-four-bit computing has changed substantially since it was first introduced for Windows operating systems. Computers running 64-bit versions of Windows not only perform better and run faster than their 32-bit counterparts but also are more scalable because they can process more data per clock cycle, address more memory, and perform numeric calculations faster. The primary 64-bit architecture Windows Server 2012 R2 supports is based on 64-bit extensions to the x86 instructions set, which is implemented in AMD64 processors, Intel Xeon processors with 64-bit extension technology, and other processors. This architecture offers native 32-bit processing and 64-bit extension processing, allowing simultaneous 32-bit and 64-bit computing.

Inside OUT

Running 32-bit applications on 64-bit hardware

In most cases, 64-bit hardware is compatible with 32-bit applications; however, 32-bit applications typically perform better on 32-bit hardware. Windows Server 2012 R2 64-bit editions support both 64-bit and 32-bit applications using the Windows on Windows 64 (WOW64) x86 emulation layer. The WOW64 subsystem isolates 32-bit applications from 64-bit applications. This prevents file system and registry problems. The operating system provides interoperability across the 32-bit/64-bit boundary for Component Object Model (COM) and basic operations such as cut, copy, and paste from the Clipboard. However, 32-bit processes cannot load 64-bit dynamic-link libraries (DLLs), and 64-bit processes cannot load 32-bit DLLs.

Sixty-four-bit computing is designed for performing operations that are memory-intensive and require extensive numeric calculations. With 64-bit processing, applications can load large data sets entirely into physical memory (that is, random access memory [RAM]), which reduces the need to page to disk and increases performance substantially.

NOTE

In this text, I typically refer to 32-bit systems designed for x86 architecture as *32-bit systems* and 64-bit systems designed for x64 architecture as *64-bit systems*. Support for Itanium 64-bit (IA-64) processors is no longer standard in Windows operating systems.

Running instances of Windows Server 2012 R2 can be in either a physical operating system environment or a virtual operating system environment. To support mixed environments better, Microsoft introduced a new licensing model based on the number of processors, users, and virtual operating system environments. Thus, the four main product editions can be used as follows:

- **Windows Server 2012 R2 Foundation.** Has limited features and is available only from original equipment manufacturers (OEMs). This edition supports one physical processor, up to 15 users, and one physical environment, but it does not support virtualized environments. Although there is a specific user limit, a separate client access license (CAL) is not required for every user or device accessing the server.

- **Windows Server 2012 R2 Essentials.** Has limited features. This edition supports up to two physical processors, up to 25 users, and one physical environment, but it does not support virtualized environments. Although there is a specific user limit, a separate CAL is not required for every user or device accessing the server.
- **Windows Server 2012 R2 Standard.** Has all the key features. It supports up to 64 physical processors, one physical environment, and up to two virtual instances. Two incremental virtual instances and two incremental physical processors are added for each Standard license. Thus, a server with four processors, one physical environment, and four virtual instances would need two Standard licenses, and the same server with eight virtual environments would need four Standard licenses. CALs are required for every user or device accessing the server.
- **Windows Server 2012 R2 Datacenter.** Has all the key features. It supports up to 64 physical processors, one physical environment, and unlimited virtual instances. Two incremental physical processors are added for each Datacenter license. Thus, a server with two processors, one physical environment, and 32 virtual instances would need only one Datacenter license, but the same server with four processors would need two Datacenter licenses. CALs are required for every user or device accessing the server.

NOTE

Windows Server 2012 R2 Datacenter is not available for retail purchase. If you want to use the Datacenter edition, you need to purchase it through Volume Licensing, an OEM, or a Services Provider License Agreement (SPLA).

You implement virtual operating system environments by using Hyper-V, a virtual-machine technology that enables multiple guest operating systems to run concurrently on one computer and provides separate applications and services to client computers, as shown in Figure 1-1. As part of the Hyper-V role, which can be installed on servers with x64-based processors that implement hardware-assisted virtualization and hardware data execution protection, the Windows hypervisor acts as the virtual machine engine, providing the necessary layer of software for installing guest operating systems. For example, you can use this technology to run Ubuntu, Linux, and Windows Server 2012 R2 concurrently on the same computer.

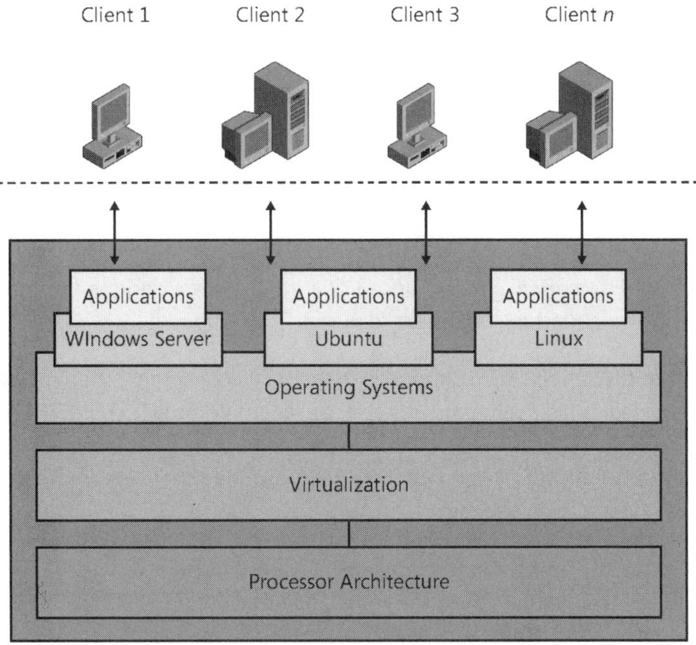

Figure 1-1 A conceptual view of virtual machine technology.

> NOTE
>
> **With Hyper-V enabled, Windows Server 2012 R2 Standard and Windows Server 2012 R2 Datacenter support up to 320 logical processors. Otherwise, these operating systems support up to 640 logical processors.**

For traffic routing between virtual and physical networks, Windows Server 2012 R2 includes Windows Server Gateway, which is integrated with Hyper-V Network Virtualization. You can use Windows Server Gateway to route network traffic regardless of where resources are located, enabling you to support integration of public and private cloud services with your internal networks and integration of multitenant implementations with Network Address Translation (NAT) and virtual private networks (VPNs).

Hyper-V also is included as a feature of Windows 8.1 Pro and Windows 8.1 Enterprise. The number of virtual machines you can run on any individual computer depends on the computer's hardware configuration and workload. During setup, you specify the amount of memory available to a virtual machine. Although that memory allocation can be changed, the amount of memory actively allocated to a virtual machine cannot be otherwise used. Virtualization can offer performance improvements, reduce the number of servers, and reduce the total cost of ownership (TCO).

Windows 8.1 and Windows Server 2012 R2

Like Windows Server 2012 R2, Windows 8.1 has several main editions. These editions include the following:

- **Windows 8.1.** The entry-level operating system designed for home users
- **Windows 8.1 Pro.** The basic operating system designed for use in Windows domains
- **Windows 8.1 Enterprise.** The enhanced operating system designed for use in Windows domains with extended management features

Windows 8.1 Pro and Windows 8.1 Enterprise are the only editions intended for use in Active Directory domains. You can manage servers running Windows Server 2012 R2 from a computer running Windows 8.1 Pro or Windows 8.1 Enterprise by using the Remote Server Administration Tools (RSAT) for Windows 8.1. Download the tools from the Microsoft Download Center (*http://download.microsoft.com*).

Windows 8.1 uses the NT 6.3 kernel, the same kernel that Windows Server 2012 R2 uses. Sharing the same kernel means that Windows 8.1 and Windows Server 2012 R2 share the following components, among others:

- **Automatic Updates.** Responsible for performing automatic updates to the operating system. This ensures that the operating system is up to date and has the most recent security updates. If you update a server from the standard Windows Update to Microsoft Update, you can get updates for additional products. By default, automatic updates are installed but not enabled on servers running Windows Server 2012 R2. You can configure automatic updates by using the Windows Update utility in Control Panel.
- **BitLocker Drive Encryption.** Provides an extra layer of security for a server's hard disks. This protects the disks from attackers who have physical access to the server. BitLocker encryption can be used on servers with or without a Trusted Platform Module (TPM). When you add this feature to a server by using the Add Roles And Features Wizard, you can manage it by using the BitLocker Drive Encryption utility in Control Panel.
- **Remote Assistance.** Provides an assistance feature that enables an administrator to send a remote assistance invitation to a more senior administrator. The senior administrator can then accept the invitation to view the user's desktop and temporarily take control of the computer to resolve a problem. When you add this feature to a server by using the Add Roles And Features Wizard, you can manage it by using options on the Remote tab of the System Properties dialog box.
- **Remote Desktop.** Provides a remote connectivity feature that enables you to connect to and manage a server from another computer. By default, Remote Desktop is installed

but not enabled on servers running Windows Server 2012 R2. You can manage the Remote Desktop configuration by using options on the Remote tab of the System Properties dialog box. You can establish remote connections by using the Remote Desktop Connection utility.

- **Task Scheduler.** Enables you to schedule execution of one-time and recurring tasks, such as tasks used for performing routine maintenance. Like Windows 8.1, Windows Server 2012 R2 makes extensive use of the scheduled task facilities. You can view and work with scheduled tasks in Computer Management.
- **Desktop Experience.** Installs additional Windows 8.1 desktop functionality on a server. You can use this feature when you use Windows Server 2012 R2 as your desktop operating system. When you add this feature by using the Add Roles And Features Wizard, the server's desktop functionality is enhanced, and these programs are installed: Windows Media Player, desktop themes, Video for Windows (AVI support), Disk Cleanup, Sync Center, Sound Recorder, Character Map, and Snipping Tool.
- **Windows Firewall.** Helps protect a computer from attack by unauthorized users. Windows Server 2012 R2 includes a basic firewall called Windows Firewall and an advanced firewall called Windows Firewall With Advanced Security. By default, the firewalls are not enabled on server installations.
- **Windows Time.** Synchronizes the system time with world time to ensure that the system time is accurate. You can configure computers to synchronize with a specific time server. The way Windows Time works depends on whether a computer is a member of a domain or a workgroup. In a domain, domain controllers are used for time synchronization, and you can manage this feature through Group Policy. In a workgroup, you use Internet time servers for time synchronization, and you can manage this feature through the Date And Time utility.
- **Wireless LAN Service.** Installs the Wireless LAN Service feature to enable wireless connections. Wireless networking with Windows Server 2012 R2 works the same as it does with Windows 8.1. If a server has a wireless adapter, you can enable this feature by using the Add Roles And Features Wizard.

In most instances, you can configure and manage these core components in exactly the same way on both Windows 8.1 and Windows Server 2012 R2. Windows 8.1 and Windows Server 2012 R2 have many enhancements to improve security, such as memory randomization and other enhancements to prevent malware from inserting itself into startup and running processes. Windows 8.1 and Windows Server 2012 R2 use address space layout randomization (ASLR) to determine randomly how and where important data is stored in memory, which makes it much more difficult for malware to find the specific locations in memory to attack.

Windows 8.1 and Windows Server 2012 R2 require a processor that includes hardware-based Data Execution Prevention (DEP) support. DEP uses the Never eXecute (NX) bit to mark blocks of memory as data that should never be run as code. DEP has two specific benefits. It reduces the range of memory that malicious code can use and prevents malware from running any code in memory addresses marked as Never eXecute.

If your organization doesn't use an enterprise malware solution, you'll also be interested to know that Windows Defender for Windows 8.1 and Windows Server 2012 R2 has been upgraded to a more fully featured program. Windows Defender now protects against viruses, spyware, rootkits, and other types of malware. Windows Defender is also available on Server Core installations of Windows Server 2012 R2, though without the user interface. If you add Windows Defender as an option on a Server Core installation, the program is enabled by default.

Planning for Windows Server 2012 R2

Deploying Windows Server 2012 R2 is a substantial undertaking, even on a small network. Just the task of planning a Windows Server 2012 R2 deployment can be a daunting process, especially in a large enterprise. The larger the business, however, the more important it is for the planning process to be thorough and fully account for the proposed project's goals and to lay out exactly how those goals will be accomplished.

Accommodating the goals of all the business units in a company can be difficult, and it is best accomplished with a well-planned series of steps that includes checkpoints and plenty of opportunity for management participation. The organization as a whole will benefit from your thorough preparation, and so will the information technology (IT) department. Careful planning can also help you avoid common obstacles by helping you identify potential pitfalls and then determine how best to avoid them or at least be ready for any unavoidable complications.

Your plan: The big picture

A clear road map can help with any complex project, and deploying Windows Server 2012 R2 in the enterprise is certainly a complex project. A number of firms have developed models to describe IT processes such as planning and systems management. For our purposes, I break down the deployment process into a roughly sequential set of tasks:

1. **Identify the team.** For all but the smallest rollouts of a new operating system, a team of people will be involved in both the planning and deployment processes. The actual size and composition of this team will be different in each situation. Collecting the right mixture of skills and expertise will help ensure the success of your project.

2. **Assess your goals.** Any business undertaking the move to Windows Server 2012 R2 has many reasons for doing so, only some of which are obvious to the IT department. You need to identify the goals of the entire company carefully before determining the scope of the project to ensure that all critical goals are met.

3. **Analyze the existing environment.** Examine the current network environment, even if you think you know *exactly* how everything works—you will often find you are only partially correct. Gather hardware and software inventories, network maps, and lists of which servers are providing which services. Also, identify critical business processes and examine the administrative and security approaches that are currently in place. Windows Server 2012 R2 offers a number of improvements, and you'll find it useful to know which ones are particularly important in your environment.

4. **Define the project scope.** Project scope is often one of the more difficult areas to pin down and one that deserves particular attention in the planning process. Defining scope requires prioritizing the goals of the various groups within the organization and then realistically assessing what can be accomplished within an acceptable budget and time frame. It's not often that the wish list of features and capabilities from the entire company can be fulfilled in the initial, or even a later, deployment.

5. **Design the new network environment.** After you have pinned down the project scope, you must develop a detailed design for the new operating system deployment and the affected portions of the network. During this time, you should create documentation describing the end state of the network and the process of getting there. This design document serves as a road map for the people building the testing environment and, with refinements during the testing process, for the IT department later.

6. **Test the design.** Thorough testing in the lab is an often overlooked but critically important phase of deploying a new network operating system. By building a test lab and putting a prototype environment through its paces, you can identify and solve many problems in a controlled environment rather than in the field.

7. **Install Windows Server 2012 R2.** After you have validated your design in the lab and management has approved the deployment, you can begin to install Windows Server 2012 R2 in your production environment. The installation process has two phases:

   - **Pilot phase.** During the pilot phase, you deploy and test a small group of servers running Windows Server 2012 R2 (and perhaps clients running Windows 8.1) in a production environment. You should pick a pilot group that is comfortable working with new technology and for which minor interruptions will not pose significant problems. In other words, this is not a good thing to do to the president of the company or the finance department just before taxes are due.

- **Rollout.** After you have determined that the pilot phase was a success, you can begin the rollout to the rest of the company. Make sure you schedule adequate downtime and allow for ongoing minor interruptions and increased support demands as users encounter changed functionality.

As mentioned, these steps are generally sequential but not exclusively so. You are likely to find that as you work through one phase of planning, you must return to activities that are technically part of an earlier phase. This is actually a good thing because it means you are refining your plan dynamically as you discover new factors and contingencies.

Inside OUT

Getting off to a quick start

People need not be assigned to all these tasks at the beginning of the planning process. If you have people who can take on the needs analysis and research on the current and new network environment, you can get the project underway while recruiting the rest of the project team.

Identifying your organizational teams

A project like this requires a lot of time and effort and a broad range of knowledge, expertise, and experience. Unless you are managing a very small network, this project is likely to require more than one person to plan and implement it. Team members are assigned to various roles, each of which is concerned with a different aspect of the project.

Each of these roles can be filled by one or more persons, devoting all or part of their workday—and beyond in some cases—to the project. No direct correlation exists between a team role and a single individual who performs it. In a large organization, a team of individuals might fulfill each of these roles, whereas in a small organization, one person can fill more than one role.

As with IT processes, a number of vendors and consultants have put together team models, which you can use in designing your own team. Specific teams you might want to use include:

- **Architecture team.** In increasingly complex IT environments, someone needs to be responsible for overall project architecture and providing guidance for integrating the project into existing architecture. This role is filled by the architecture team. Specific deliverables include the architecture design and guidance for the integration solution.
- **Program management team.** Program management's primary responsibility is ensuring that project goals are met within the constraints set forth at the beginning of the

project. Program management handles the functional design, budget, schedule, and reporting. Specific deliverables include a vision or scope document, functional specifications, a master project plan, a master project schedule, and status reports.

- **Product management team.** This team is responsible for identifying the business and user needs of the project and ensuring that the final plan meets those needs. Specific deliverables include the project charter, team orientation guidance and documents for project structure and initial risk assessment.
- **User experience team.** This team manages the transition of users to the new environment. This includes developing and delivering user training and conducting an analysis of user feedback during testing and the pilot deployment. Specific deliverables include user reference manuals, usability test scenarios, and user interface graphical elements.
- **Development team.** The development team is responsible for defining the physical design and feature set of the project and estimating the budget and time needed for project completion. Specific deliverables include any necessary source code or binaries and necessary integrated-solution components.
- **Testing team.** The testing team is critical in ensuring that the final deployment is successful. It designs and builds the test environment, develops a testing plan, and then performs the tests and resolves any issues it discovers before the pilot deployment occurs. Specific deliverables include test specifications, test cases with expected results, test metrics, test scripts, test data, and test reports.
- **Release management team.** The release management team designs the test deployment and then performs that deployment as a means of verifying the reliability of the deployment before widespread adoption. Specific deliverables include deployment processes and procedures, installation scripts and configuration settings for deployment, operations guides, help desk and support procedures, knowledge base, help and training materials, operations documentation, and troubleshooting documentation.

Working together, these teams cover the various aspects of a significant project such as rolling out Windows Server 2012 R2. Although all IT projects have some things in common, and therefore need someone to handle those areas of the project, that's where the commonality stops. Each company has IT needs related to its specific business activities. This might mean additional team members are needed to manage those aspects of the project. For example, if external clients, the public, or both also access some of your IT systems as users, you have a set of user acceptance and testing requirements different from many other businesses.

The project team needs business managers who understand and can represent the needs of the various business units. This requires knowledge of the business operations and a clear picture of the daily tasks staff performs.

Representatives of the IT department bring their technical expertise to the table not only to detail the inner workings of the network but also to help business managers realistically assess how technology can help their departments and separate the impractical goals from the realistic ones.

Make sure that all critical aspects of business operations are covered—include representatives from all departments that have critical IT needs and be sure the team takes the needs of the entire company into account. This means that people on the project team must collect information from line-of-business managers and the people actually doing the work. (Surprisingly enough, the latter escapes many a project team.)

After you have gathered a team, management must ensure that team members have adequate time and resources to fulfill the tasks required of them for the project. This can mean shifting all or part of their usual workload to others for the project duration or providing resources such as Internet access, project-related software, and so on. Any project is easier—and more likely to be successful—with this critical real-time support from management.

Inside OUT

Hiring talent

Sometimes people are not available in-house with all the needed skills, and you must look to consultants or contracted workers. Examine which tasks should be outsourced and exactly what you must receive from the relationship. Pay particular attention to highly specialized or complex areas—the Active Directory Domain Services (AD DS) architecture, for example—and those with a high rate of change.

One-time tasks, such as creating user training programs and documentation, are also good candidates for outsourcing. For areas in which there will be an ongoing need for the lacking expertise, such as security, it might be a better idea to send a staff member to get additional training.

Assessing project goals

Carefully identifying the goals behind moving to Windows Server 2012 R2 is an important part of the planning process. Without a clear list of objectives, you are unlikely to achieve them. Even with a clear set of goals in mind, it is unlikely you will accomplish them all. Most large business projects involve some compromises, and the process of deploying Windows Server 2012 R2 is unlikely to be an exception.

Although deploying a new operating system is ultimately an IT task, most of the reasons behind the deployment won't be coming from the IT department. Computers are, after all, tools business uses to increase productivity, enhance communications, facilitate business tasks, and so on; the IT department is concerned with making sure that the computer environment the business needs is implemented.

Inside OUT

Creating documentation almost painlessly

During the planning process, and as you begin to use the new network environment, you'll be creating numerous documents describing the current state of the network, the planned changes, IT standards, administrative procedures, and the like. It's a good idea to take advantage of all this up-to-date information to create policies and procedures documents, which will help ensure that the network stays in compliance with your new standards and that administration is accomplished as intended.

The same set of documents can also serve as a basis for user guides and administrator and user training and can be made available through the corporate intranet. If the people working on the project, especially those performing testing, take notes about any error conditions they encounter and the resolutions to them, you'll also have a good start on frequently asked questions (FAQs) and other technical support data.

The business perspective

Many discussions of the business reasons for new software deployments echo common themes: enhance productivity, eliminate downtime, reduce costs, and the like. Translating these often somewhat vague (and occasionally lofty) aspirations into concrete goals sometimes takes a bit of effort. It is well worth taking the time, however, to refine the big picture into specific objectives before moving on. An IT department should serve the needs of the business, not the other way around; if you don't understand those needs clearly, you'll have a hard time fulfilling them.

Be sure to ask for the input of people close to where the work is being done—department managers from each business area should be asked about what they need from IT, what works now, and what doesn't. These people care about the day-to-day operations of their computing environment. Will the changes help their staff members do their work? Ask about work patterns, both static and burst—the finance department's workflow is not the same in July as it is in April. Make sure to include all departments and any significant subsets—human resources (HR), finance, sales, business units, executive management, and so on.

You should also identify risks that lie at the business level, such as resistance to change, lack of commitment (frequently expressed as inadequate resources: budget, staff, time, and so on), or even the occasional bit of overt opposition. At the same time, look for positives to exploit; enthusiastic staff can help energize others, and having a manager in your corner can smooth many bumps along the way. By getting people involved, you can gain allies who are vested in the success of the project.

Inside OUT

Talk to the people who will use the technology

Not to put too fine a point on it, make sure that the team members who will be handling aspects of the user experience actually talk with users. The only way to assess adequately what the people doing the work need in critical areas such as usability, training, and support is to get in the trenches and see what they are doing. If possible, have meetings at the user's workstation because it can provide additional insight into daily operations. If passwords are visible on sticky notes stuck to monitors—a far too common practice—you know you have security issues.

Identifying IT goals

IT goals are often obvious: improve network reliability, provide better security, deliver enhanced administration, and maybe even implement a particular new feature. They are also easier to identify than those of other departments—after all, they are directly related to technology.

When you define your goals, make sure that you are specific. It is easy to say you will improve security, but how will you know when you have done so? What's improved and by how much? In many cases, IT goals map to the implementation of features or procedures; for example, to improve security, you will implement Internet Protocol Security (IPsec) and encrypt all traffic to remote networks.

Don't overpromise, either—eliminating downtime is a laudable goal but not one you are likely to achieve on your network and certainly not one on which you want your next review based.

Get to know one another

Business units often seem to have little idea of the IT department's capabilities and operations—or worse, they have an idea, but it is an extremely unrealistic one. This can lead to expectations ranging from improbable to absurd, which is bad for everyone involved.

A major project like this brings together people from all over the company, some from departments that seldom cross paths. This is a great opportunity for members of the various areas of the company to become familiar with IT operations and vice versa. A clearer understanding of both the big picture of the business and the workings of other departments will help smooth the interactions of IT with the rest of the company.

Examining the interaction between IT and business units

A number of aspects of your organization's business should be considered when evaluating your overall IT requirements and the business environment in which you operate. Consider things such as the following:

- **Business organization.** How large is the business? Are there offices in more than one location? Does the business operate across international, legal, or other boundaries? What sorts of departmental or functional boundaries exist?
- **Stability.** Does the business undergo a lot of change? Are there frequent reorganizations, acquisitions, changes, and the like in business partnerships? What is the expected growth rate of the organization? Conversely, are substantial downsizings planned in the future?
- **External relationships.** Do you need to provide access to vendors, partners, and so on? Are there external networks that people operating on your network must access?
- **Impact of Windows Server 2012 R2 deployment.** How will this deployment affect the various departments in your company? Are any areas of the company particularly intolerant of disruption? Are there upcoming events that must be considered in scheduling?
- **Adaptability.** Is management easily adaptable to change? If not, make sure you get every aspect of your plan right the first time. Having an idea of how staff might respond to new technologies and processes can help you plan for education and support.

Predicting network change

Part of planning is projecting into the future and predicting how future business needs will influence the activities of the IT department. Managing complicated systems is easier when it's done from a proactive stance rather than a reactive one. Predicting network change is an art, not a science, but it behooves you to hone your skills at it.

This is primarily a business assessment, based on things such as expected growth, changes in business focus, or possible downsizing and outsourcing—each of which provides its own challenges to the IT department. Being able to predict what will happen in the business and what those changes will mean to the IT department enables you to include room for expansion in your network design.

When attempting to predict what will happen, look at the history of the company. Are mergers, acquisitions, spin-offs, and so on common? If so, this indicates a considerable need for flexibility from the IT department and the need to keep in close contact with people on the business side to avoid being blindsided by a change in the future.

As people meet to discuss the deployment, talk about what is coming up for the business units. Cultivate contacts in other parts of the company and talk with those people regularly about what's going on in their departments, such as upcoming projects and what's happening with other companies in the same business sector. Reading the company's news releases and articles in outside sources can also provide valuable hints of what's to come. By keeping your ear to the ground, doing a little research, and thinking through the potential impact of what you learn, you can be much better prepared for whatever is coming up next.

The impact of growth on management

Many networks start out with a single administrator (or a small team), which makes sense because many networks are small when first implemented. As those networks grow, it is not uncommon for a few administrative tasks to be delegated to others in the company who, although it is not their job, know how to assist the highly limited IT staff. This can lead to a haphazard approach to management, where who is doing what isn't always clear, and the methods for basics (such as data backups) vary from one department to the next, leading to potential problems as time goes by and staff moves on. If this sounds familiar to you, this is a good time to remedy the situation.

Analyzing the existing network

Before you can determine the path to your new network environment, you must determine where you are right now in terms of your existing network infrastructure. This requires determining a baseline for network and system hardware, software installation and configuration, operations, management, and security. Don't rely on what you think is the case; actually verify what is in place.

Project worksheets consolidate information

A large network environment, with a lot of architectural and configuration information to be collected, can require juggling enormous amounts of data. If this is the case, you might find it useful to use project worksheets of some sort. If your company has not created customized worksheets, you can use those created by Microsoft to aid in the upgrade process. Typically, these are available in the operating system deployment kit.

Evaluating the network infrastructure

You should get an idea of what the current network looks like before moving to a new operating system. You will require configuration information while designing the modifications to the network and deploying the servers. In addition, some aspects of Windows Server 2012

R2, such as the sites used in Active Directory replication, are based on your physical network configuration. (A *site* is a segment of the network with good connectivity, consisting of one or more Internet Protocol [IP] subnets.)

For reasons such as this, you want to assess a number of aspects related to your physical network environment. Consider such characteristics as the following:

- **Network topology.** Document the systems and devices on your network, including link speeds, wide area network (WAN) connections, sites using dial-up connections, and so on. Include devices such as routers, switches, servers, and clients, noting all forms of addressing such as computer names and IP addresses for Windows systems.
- **Network addressing.** Are you currently employing Internet Protocol version 4 (IPv4) and Internet Protocol version 6 (IPv6)? What parts of the address space are private, and what parts are public? Which IP subnets are in use at each location?
- **Remote locations.** How many physical locations does the organization have? Are they all using broadband connections, or are there remote offices that connect sporadically by dial-up? What is the speed of those links?
- **Traffic patterns.** Monitoring network traffic can provide insights into current performance and help you identify potential bottlenecks and other problems before they occur. Examine usage statistics, paying attention to both regularly occurring patterns and anomalous spikes or lulls, which might indicate a problem.
- **Special cases.** Do any portions of the network have out-of-the-ordinary configuration needs such as test labs that are isolated from the rest of the network?

Inside OUT

Mapping the territory

Create a network map illustrating the location of all your current resources—this is easier by using tools such as Microsoft Visio. Collect as much detailed information as possible about those resources, starting with basics such as what is installed on each server, the services it's providing, and so on. Additional information, such as critical workflow processes and traffic patterns between servers, can also be very useful when it comes time to consolidate servers or deploy new ones. The easier it is to cross-reference all this information, the better.

Assessing systems

As part of planning, you should inventory the existing network servers, identifying each system's operating system version, IP address, Domain Name System (DNS) names, and the services provided by that system. Collect such information by performing the following tasks:

- **Inventory hardware.** Conduct a hardware inventory of the servers on your network, noting central processing unit (CPU), RAM, disk space, and so on. Pay particular attention to older machines that might present compatibility issues if upgraded. You can use the Microsoft Assessment and Planning (MAP) Toolkit, Microsoft System Center Configuration Manager (SCCM), or other tools to help you with the hardware inventory.
- **Identify operating systems.** Determine the current operating system on each computer, including the entire version number (even if it runs to many digits), in addition to service packs, hot fixes, and other post-release additions.
- **Assess your current Windows domains.** Do you have only Windows domains on the network? Are all domains using Active Directory? Do you have multiple Active Directory forests? If you have multiple forests, detail the trust relationships. List the name of each domain, what it contains (users, resources, or both), and which servers are acting as domain controllers.
- **Identify localization factors.** If your organization crosses international boundaries, language boundaries, or both, identify the localized versions of Windows Server in use and the locations in which they are used. This is critical when upgrading to Windows Server 2012 R2 because attempting an upgrade using a different localized version of Windows Server 2012 R2 might fail.
- **Assess software licenses.** Evaluate licenses for servers and client access. This helps you select the most appropriate licensing program.
- **Identify file storage.** Review the contents and configuration of existing file servers, identifying partitions and volumes on each system. Identify existing distributed file system (DFS) servers and the contents of DFS shares. Don't forget shares used to store user data.

Inside OUT

Where is the data?

Locating file shares that are maintained at a departmental, team, or even individual level can take a little bit of investigation. However, the effort to do so can be well worth it because you can centralize the management of data that is important to individual groups while providing valuable services such as ensuring that regular data backups are performed.

You can gather hardware and software inventories of computers that run the Windows operating system by using a tool such as SCCM. Review the types of clients that must be supported so that you can configure servers appropriately. This is also a good time to determine any client systems that must be upgraded (or replaced) to use Windows Server 2012 R2 functionality. You can also gather this information with scripts or a software management program.

Identify network services and applications

Look at your current network services, noting which services are running on which servers and the dependencies of these services. Do this for all domain controllers and member servers that you'll be upgrading. You'll use this information later to plan for server placement and service hosting on the upgraded network configuration. Some examples of services to document are as follows:

- **DNS services.** You must assess your current DNS configuration. If you're currently using a non-Microsoft DNS server, you want to plan DNS support carefully because Active Directory relies on Windows Server 2012 R2 DNS. If you're using Microsoft DNS but are not using Active Directory–integrated zones, you might want to plan a move to Active Directory-integrated zones.

- **WINS services.** You should assess the use of Network Basic Input/Output System (NetBIOS) by older applications and computers running early versions of the Windows operating system to determine whether NetBIOS support (such as Windows Internet Naming Service [WINS]) will be needed in the new network configuration. If you've removed older applications and computers running early versions of the Windows operating system from your organization, support for WINS is no longer needed. You can remove the WINS Server feature from your servers by using the Remove Roles And Features Wizard. When you remove this feature, the WINS Server service also is removed because it is no longer needed.

- **File shares.** Standard file shares use Server Message Block (SMB), a client-server technology for distributing files over networks. Windows desktop operating systems have an SMB client. Windows Server operating systems also have SMB server technology. Current Windows operating systems support SMB 3.0, which supports end-to-end encryption and eliminates the need for IPsec to protect SMB data in transit. If you've removed all computers running Windows XP and Windows Server 2003 from your organization, neither support for SMB 1.0 nor the Computer Browser service that SMB 1.0 used are needed. You can remove the SMB 1.0/CIFS File Sharing Support feature from your servers by using the Remove Roles And Features Wizard. When you remove this feature, the Computer Browser service also is removed because it is no longer needed.

- **Print services.** List printers and the print server assigned to each one. Consider who is assigned to the various administrative tasks and whether the printer will be published in

Active Directory. Also, determine whether all the print servers will be upgraded in place or whether some will be consolidated.

- **Network applications.** Inventory your applications, creating a list of the applications that are currently on the network, including the version number (and post-release updates and such), which server hosts it, and how important each application is to your business. Use this information to determine whether upgrades or modifications are needed. Watch for software that is never used and thus need not be purchased or supported—every unneeded application you can remove represents savings of both time and money.

This list is only the beginning. Your network will undoubtedly have many more services that you must take into account.

CAUTION

Make sure that you determine any dependencies in your network configuration. Discovering after the fact that a critical process relied on the server that you just decommissioned will not make your job any easier. You can find out which Microsoft and third-party applications are certified to be compatible with Windows Server 2012 R2 in the Windows Server Catalog (*http://www.windowsservercatalog.com/*).

Identifying security infrastructure

When you document your network infrastructure, you will need to review many aspects of your network security. In addition to security concerns that are specific to your network environment, the following factors should be addressed:

- Consider exactly who has access to what and why. Identify network resources, security groups, and assignment of access permissions.
- Determine which security protocols and services are in place. Are adequate virus protection, firewall protection, email filtering, and so on in place? Do any applications or services require older NTLM authentication? Have you implemented a public key infrastructure (PKI) on your network?
- Examine auditing methods and identify the range of tracked access and objects.
- Determine which staff members have access to the Internet and which sorts of access they have. Look at the business case for access that crosses the corporate firewall—does everyone who has Internet access actually need it, or has it been provided across the board because it was easier to provide blanket access than to provide access selectively? Such access might be simpler to implement, but when you look at Internet access from the security perspective, it presents many potential problems.

- Consider inbound access, too; for example, can employees access their information from home? If so, examine the security that is in place for this type of access.

IMPORTANT

Security is one area in which well-established methods matter—pay particular attention to all established policies and procedures, what has been officially documented, and what isn't documented as well.

Depending on your existing network security mechanisms, the underlying security methods can change upon deployment of Windows Server 2012 R2. Windows Server 2003 is the minimum forest and domain functional level Windows Server 2012 R2 supports. When the forest and domain functional levels are raised to this level or higher from a lower level, Kerberos is the default authentication mechanism used between computer systems. This also means that although the Windows NT 4 security model (using NTLM authentication) continues to be supported, it is no longer the default authentication mechanism.

Reviewing network administration

Examining the administrative methods currently in use on your network provides you with a lot of information about what you are doing right and identifies areas that could use some improvement. Use this information to tweak network procedures where needed to optimize the administration of the new environment.

How did you get here?

Some networks are entirely designed—actually considered, discussed, planned, and so forth—but other networks grow. At one end of the spectrum is a formally designed and carefully implemented administration scheme, complete with its supporting documentation set, training, and ongoing compliance monitoring. At the other end is the network for which administrative methods just sort of happen organically—someone did it that way once, it worked, that person kept doing it that way and maybe even taught others to do it that way. Not surprisingly, this occurs most often on small networks. In the middle, and perhaps more typically, is a looser amalgamation of policies and procedures, some of which were formally implemented and some of which were created ad hoc.

Depending on the path that led to your current administrative methods, you might have more or less in the way of documentation, or an actual idea, of the detailed workings of day-to-day administration. Even if you have fully documented policies and procedures, you should still assess how management tasks are actually performed—you might be surprised at what you learn.

Network administrative model Each company has its own type of approach to network administration—some are very centralized, with the IT department making even the smallest changes, whereas others are partially managed by the business units, which control aspects such as user management. Administrative models fit into these categories:

- **Centralized.** Administration of the entire network is handled by one group, perhaps in one location, although not necessarily. This provides a high degree of control at the cost of requiring IT staff for every change to the network, no matter how small.
- **Decentralized.** This administrative model delegates more of the control of day-to-day operations to local administrators of some sort, often departmental. A central IT department might still manage certain aspects of network management in that a network with decentralized administration often has well-defined procedures controlling exactly how each administrative task is performed.
- **Hybrid.** On many networks, a blend of these two methods is used. A centralized IT department performs many tasks (generally the more difficult, delicate operations and those with the broadest impact on the network) but delegates simpler tasks (such as user management) to departmental or group administrators.

Disaster recovery The costs of downtime caused by service interruption or data loss can be substantial, especially in large enterprise networks. As part of your overall planning, determine whether a comprehensive IT disaster recovery plan is in place. If one is in place, this is the time to determine its scope and effectiveness and verify that it is being followed. If one isn't in place, this is the time to create and implement one.

Document the various data sets being archived, schedules, backup validation routine, staff assignments, and so on. Make sure there are provisions for offsite data storage to protect your data in the case of a catastrophic event such as a fire, earthquake, or flood.

Examine the following:

- **Systems and servers.** Are all critical servers backed up regularly? Are secondary servers, backup servers, or both available in case of system failure?
- **Enterprise data.** Are regular backups made of core enterprise data stores such as databases, Active Directory, and the like?
- **User information.** Where is user data stored? Is it routinely archived? Does the backup routine get all the information that is important to individuals, or is some of it stored on users' personal machines and thus not archived?

CAUTION

Whatever your current disaster recovery plan is, make sure it is being followed before you start making major changes to your network. Although moving to Windows Server 2012 R2 should not present any major problems on the network, it's always better to have your backups and not need them than the other way around.

Network management tools This is an excellent time to assess your current suite of network management tools. Pay particular attention to those that are unnecessary, incompatible, redundant, inefficient, or otherwise not terribly useful. You might find that some of the functionality of those tools is present natively in Windows Server 2012 R2. Assess the following aspects of your management tools:

- Identify the tools currently in use, which tasks they perform, who uses them, and so on. Make note of administrative tasks that could be eased with additional tools.
- Decide whether the tools you identified are actually used. A lot of software ends up sitting on a shelf (or on your hard disk drive) and never being used. Identifying which tools are truly needed and eliminating those that aren't can save you money and simplify the learning curve for network administrators.
- Disk-management and backup tools deserve special attention because of file-system changes in Windows Server 2012 R2. These tools are likely to require upgrading to function correctly under Windows Server 2012 R2.

Inside OUT

Think about compatibility issues early

Dealing with compatibility issues can take a lot of time, so examine them early in the process. The time needed to determine whether your current hardware and software will work and what changes must be made to allow them to work with Windows Server 2012 R2 can be lengthy. When you add to that the time necessary to requisition, obtain, install, and configure new software—especially if you must write custom code—you can see why you don't want to leave this until the end of the project.

Defining objectives and scope

A key aspect of planning any large-scale IT deployment of an operating system is determining the overall objectives for the deployment and the scope of users, computers, networks, and organization divisions that are affected. The fundamental question of scope is this: What can you realistically expect to accomplish in the given time within existing project constraints such as staffing and budget?

Some of the objectives that you identified in the early stages of the project are likely to change as constraints become more apparent and new needs and requirements emerge. To start, you must identify who will be affected—which organizational subdivisions and which personnel—and who will be doing what. These are questions that map to the business goals that must be accomplished.

You also must identify the systems that will be affected—the WANs, local area networks (LANs), subnets, servers, and client systems. In addition, you must determine the software that will be changed—the server software, client software, and applications.

Inside OUT

Planning for scope creep

Projects grow—it's inevitable—and although the scope of some projects creeps, the scope of others gallops. Here are a few tips to help you keep the project scope to a manageable level:

- **When an addition to the project is proposed, never say yes right away. Think through the consequences thoroughly, examining the impact on the rest of the project and the project team, before agreeing to any proposed changes.**
- **Insist on management buyoff on changes to the plan. In at least some cases, you won't get approval, automatically deferring the requested changes.**
- **Argue for trade-offs in the project when possible—so that adding one objective means removing another—rather than just adding tasks to your to-do list.**
- **Try to defer any noncritical proposed changes to a future project.**

Specifying organizational objectives

Many goals of the various business units and IT are only loosely related, whereas others are universal—everyone wants security, for example. Take advantage of where goals converge to engage others in the project. If people can see that their needs are met, they are more likely to support others' goals and the project in general.

You have business objectives at this point; now they must be prioritized. You should make lists of various critical aspects of projects and dependencies within the project plan as part of the process of winnowing the big picture into a set of realistic objectives. Determine what you can reasonably accomplish within the constraints of the current project. Also, decide what is outside the practical scope of this Windows Server 2012 R2 deployment but is still important to implement later.

The objectives that are directly related to the IT department will probably be clearer—and more numerous—after completing the analysis of the current network. These objectives should be organized to conform to existing change-management procedures within your enterprise network.

When setting goals, be careful not to promise too much. Although it's tempting and sometimes easier in the short run to try to do everything, you can't. It's unlikely that you will implement every single item on every person's wish list during the first stage of this project, if at all. Knowing what you can't do is as important as knowing what you can.

Inside OUT

Gauging deployment success

You'll find it difficult to gauge the success of a project without having clearly defined goals. Make sure that you define specific, measurable goals you can use to determine when each portion of the project is complete. Everyone on the project team, particularly management, should agree on these milestones *before* the rollout gets underway.

Some goals should map to user functionality (for example, "The XYZ department is able to do ABC"), whereas others will correspond to administrative tasks. Be granular in your goals. For example, "Security policies will be followed" is difficult to quantify; however, "Virus definition files are updated daily" or "Operating system updates will be installed within 48 hours of release" is easy.

Setting the schedule

You should create a project schedule, laying out the timeline, tasks, and staff assignments. Including projected completion dates for milestones helps you keep on top of significant portions of the project and ensures that dependencies are managed.

You must be realistic when considering timelines—not just a little bit realistic, but *really realistic*. This is, after all, your time you are allocating. Estimate too short a time, and you are likely to spend evenings and weekends at the office with some of your closest coworkers.

A number of tasks will be repeated many times during the rollout of Windows Server 2012 R2, which should make estimating the time needed for some things fairly simple: a 1-hour process repeated 25 times takes 25 hours (unless it's automated). If, for example, you are building 25 new servers in-house, determine the actual time needed to build one and then do the math.

When you have a rough idea of the time required, do the following:

- Assign staff members to the various tasks to make sure you have adequate staff assistance to complete the project.
- Add some time to your estimates—IT projects always seem to take more time than you thought they would. This is the only buffer you are likely to get, so make sure you build in some extra time from the start.
- As much as possible, verify how long individual tasks take. You might be surprised at how much time you spend doing a seemingly simple task, and if your initial estimate is significantly off, you could end up running significantly short on time.
- Develop a schedule that clearly shows who is doing what and when they are doing it.
- Get drop-dead dates, which should be later than the initial target date.
- Post the schedule in a place where the team, and perhaps other staff, can view it. Keep this schedule updated with milestones reached, changes to deliverable dates, and so on.

NOTE

You might want to use a project-management tool, such as Microsoft Project, to develop the schedule. This sort of tool is especially useful when managing a project with a number of staff members working on a set of interdependent tasks.

Shaping the budget

Determining the budget is a process constrained by many factors, including but not limited to IT-related costs for hardware and licensing. In addition to fixed IT costs, you also must consider the project scope and the non-IT costs that can come from the requirements of other departments within the organization. Thus, to come up with the budget, you need information and assistance from all departments within the organization, and you must consider all aspects of the project.

Many projects end up costing more than is initially budgeted. Sometimes this is predictable and preventable with proper research and a bit of attention to ongoing expenses. As with timelines, pad your estimates a little bit to allow for the unexpected. Even so, it helps if you can find out how much of a buffer you have for any cost overruns.

In planning the budget, also keep in mind fiscal periods. If your project is crossing budget periods, find out whether next year's budget for the project is allocated and approved.

Budget for project changes

Keep in mind that there are likely to be changes as the project is underway. Each change probably has a cost associated with it, and you might have to fight to have additional funds budgeted or go back to the department or individuals who want the change and ask them to allocate money from their budget to cover the requested change.

Allowing for contingencies

No matter how carefully you plan any project, it is unlikely that everything will go exactly as planned. Accordingly, you should plan for contingencies. By having a number of possible responses to unforeseen events ready, you can manage the vagaries of the project better.

Start with perhaps the most common issue encountered during projects: problems getting the assigned people to do the work. This all-too-common problem can derail any project or at least cause the project manager a great deal of stress. After all, the ultimate success of any project depends on people doing their assigned tasks. Many of these people are already stretched pretty thin, however, and you might encounter times when they aren't quite getting everything done. Your plan should include what to do in this circumstance—is the person's manager brought in, or is a backup person automatically assigned to complete the job?

Another possibility to plan for is a change in the feature set being implemented. If such shifts occur, you must decide how to adjust to compensate for the reallocated time and money required. To make this easier, identify and prioritize the following:

- Objectives that could slip off this project and be placed in a later one if the need arises
- Objectives that you want to slip into the project if the opportunity presents itself

Items on both of these lists should be relatively small and independent of other processes and services. Avoid incurring additional expenses; you are more likely to be given extra time than extra funding during your deployment.

In general, ask yourself what could happen to cause significant problems along the way. Then, more important, consider what you would do in response. By thinking through potential problems ahead of time and planning what you might do in response, you can be prepared for many of the inevitable bumps along the way.

> **Inside OUT**
>
> ***Padding project estimates***
>
> Many consultants pad their project estimates, primarily as a means of ensuring that the inevitable project scope creep isn't problematic later. After all, it's preferable to have a client who is happy that the project came in early and under budget than one who is unhappy at the cost and time overruns. You might want to use this approach by adding a little extra time and not allocating quite all the available money. If you come in early and under budget, so much the better—but you probably won't.

Finalizing project scope

You have goals, know the timeline, and have a budget pinned down—now it's time to get serious. Starting with the highest-priority aspects of the project, estimate the time and budget needed to complete each portion. Work your way through the planned scope, assessing the time and costs associated with each portion of the project. This helps ensure that the time and budget are sufficient to complete the project successfully as designed.

As you finalize the project plan, each team member should review the final project scope, noting any concerns or questions he has about the proposal. Encourage the team to look for weak spots, unmet dependencies, and other places where the plan might break down. Although it is tempting to ignore potential problems that are noted this late in the game, you do so at your own peril. Avoiding known risks is much easier than recovering from unforeseen ones.

> **Inside OUT**
>
> ***Get management approval for your plan***
>
> Executive business management and IT management should approve the deployment plan, especially if they are not on the planning team. This executive sign-off on the plan should occur at a number of points along the way. After the project team agrees on the initial goals is a good time to get approval, as are critical junctures such as after the plan has been validated in the lab and again after a successful pilot. In any case, make sure you have management sign-off before you perform *any* installations in a production environment.

Defining the new network environment

When you have determined the overall scope of your Windows deployment project and the associated network changes, you must develop the technical specifications for the project, detailing server configuration, changes to the network infrastructure, and so on. As much as possible, describe the process of transitioning to the new configuration. Care should be taken while developing this document because it will serve as the road map for the actual transition, much of which is likely to be done by staff members who were not in the planning meetings.

In defining the new (updated) network environment, you must review the current and projected infrastructure for your network. Analyze the domains in use on your network and evaluate the implications for security operations and network performance.

If you are implementing Active Directory for the first time, designing the domain architecture will probably take a substantial amount of work. Businesses already using Microsoft Windows Server 2008 or Windows Server 2008 R2 to manage their network, however, will probably not have to change much, if they change anything at all. Also, consider whether you will be changing the number of domains you currently have. Will you be getting rid of any domains through consolidation?

Impact on network operations

You also must assess the impact of the projected changes on your current network operations. Consider issues such as the following:

- Will network traffic change in ways that require modifications to the network infrastructure? Assess additional loads on each network segment and across WAN links.
- Do you need to make changes to network naming or addressing schemes? Are new DNS namespaces needed and, if so, have the DNS names been registered?
- Will you use read-only domain controllers (RODCs) in remote offices? If so, will you also use read-only DNS (RO DNS) zones?
- Can you phase out NetBIOS and WINS reliance completely? If so, will you use Link Local Multicast Name Resolution (LLMNR) and DNS global names?

Identify security requirements

This is a good time to review seriously the security measures implemented on your network. Scrutinize the security devices, services, protocols, and administrative procedures to ensure that they are adequate, appropriate, well documented, and adhered to rigorously.

Security in Windows Server 2012 RTM and Windows Server 2012 R2 are not the same as in early versions of Windows Server operating systems—the security settings for the default (new) installation of Windows Server 2012 RTM and Windows Server 2012 R2 are much tighter than in those early versions. This might mean that services that were functioning perfectly prior to an upgrade don't work the same way afterward. Some services that were previously started by default are now disabled when first installed.

Assign staff members to be responsible for each aspect of your security plan and have them document the completion of tasks. Among the tasks that should be assigned are the following:

- **Applying regular updates of antivirus software.** Antivirus software is only as good as its virus definition files, so make sure yours are current. This means checking the vendor site every day, even on weekends if possible. Many antivirus packages can perform automatic updates, but you should verify that the updates are occurring.
- **Reviewing security alerts.** Someone should read the various sites that post security alerts on a regular basis, receive their newsletters and alerts, or do both. The sites should include Microsoft (*http://technet.microsoft.com/security/*), vendors of your other security software (for example, *http://www.symantec.com/*), network device vendors (for example, *http://www.cisco.com/*), and at least one nonvendor site (such as *http://www.SANS.org/*).
- **Checking for system software updates.** IT staff should consider implementing the Windows Server Update Services (WSUS) to help keep up to date on security updates, service packs, and other critical updates for both servers and clients. Administrators can use WSUS to scan and download updates automatically to a centralized server and then configure Group Policy so that client computers get automatic updates from WSUS.
- **Checking for hardware firmware updates.** It is important for the various devices on the network, especially security-related ones such as firewalls, to have up-to-date firmware.

Changing the administrative approach

While you are rolling out Windows Server 2012 R2 is an excellent time to fine-tune your administration methods and deal with any issues introduced by the growth and change in the project scope. Well-designed administrative methods with clearly documented procedures can make a huge difference in streamlining both the initial rollout and ongoing operations.

Active Directory provides the framework for flexible, secure network management so you can implement the administration method that works best in your environment. There are mechanisms that support both centralized and distributed administration; Group Policy options offer centralized control, and selected administrative capabilities can be securely delegated at a highly granular level. The combination of these methods allows administration to be handled by using the method that works best for each business in its unique circumstances.

IMPORTANT

Make sure that all administrative tasks and processes are clearly defined and that each task has a person assigned to it.Some administrative changes will be required because of the way Windows Server 2012 R2 works. You might find that existing administration tools no longer work or are no longer needed, so be sure to question the following:

- **Whether your existing tools work under the new operating system. A number of older tools are incompatible with Windows Server 2012 R2—management utilities must be Active Directory–aware, work with NTFS, and so on.**
- **Whether current tools will be needed after you move to Windows Server 2012 R2. If a utility such as PKZIP, for example, is in use now, it might not be required for operations under Windows Server 2012 R2, which has incorporated the functionality of ZIP into the operating system. Eliminating unneeded tools could well be one goal of the Windows Server 2012 R2 deployment project, and it will have a definite payoff for the IT department in terms of simplified management, lower costs, and so forth.**

Select and implement standards

You will also want to select and implement standards. If your IT department has not implemented standards for naming and administration procedures, this is a good time to do so. You'll be gathering information about your current configuration, which will show you the places where standardization is in place and the places where it would be useful.

Make sure that any standards you adopt allow for likely future growth and changes in the business. Using an individual's first name and last initial is a very simple scheme for creating user names and works well in a small business. Small businesses, however, don't necessarily stay small forever—even Microsoft initially used this naming scheme, although it has been modified greatly over the years.

You can also benefit from standardization of system hardware and software configuration. Supporting 100 servers (or clients) is much easier if they share a common set of hardware, are similarly configured, and have largely the same software installed. This is possible, of course, only to a limited degree and depends on the services and applications that are required from each system. Still, it's worth considering.

When standardizing server hardware, keep in mind that the minimum functional hardware differs for various types of servers—that is, application servers have very different requirements than file servers. Also, consider the impact of the decisions the IT department makes on other parts of the company and individual employees. There are some obvious things to watch for such as unnecessarily exposing anyone's personal data—surprising numbers of businesses and agencies still do this.

Inside OUT

Personal information is private!

The amount of personal information that businesses have about individuals is something that should give us all pause. What's even more alarming is the casual disregard with which much of this information is treated.

Consider the use of Social Security numbers in the United States; they show up as student ID numbers (and are posted on professors' doors) and health insurance policy numbers (and are printed on dozens of things, from insurance cards to driver's licenses), to name two of the more common and egregious misuses. If that weren't enough, portions of your Social Security number are used as the default secret PIN for some accounts at financial institutions. That's the same Social Security number that you give to several people each time anyone in your family seeks medical care. How secret!

All IT departments, not just those in the medical industry, would be well served by an inspection of which sorts of personal information they are managing and how they are protecting it.

Change management

Formalized change-management processes are very useful, especially for large organizations and those with distributed administrative models. By creating structured change-control processes and implementing appropriate auditing, you can control the ongoing management of critical IT processes. This makes it easier to manage the network and reduces the opportunity for error.

Although this is particularly important when dealing with big-picture issues such as domain creation or Group Policy implementation, some organizations define change-control mechanisms for every possible change, no matter how small. You have to determine for which IT processes you must define change-management processes and find a balance between managing changes effectively and overregulating network management.

Even if you're not planning to implement a formal change-control process, make sure that the information about the initial configuration is collected in one spot. By doing this, and by collecting brief notes about any changes that are made, you will at least have data about the configuration and the changes that have been made to it. This will also help later, if you decide to put more stringent change-control mechanisms in place, by providing at least rudimentary documentation of the current network state.

Final considerations for planning and deployment

If you are doing a new installation—perhaps for a new business or a new location of an existing one—you have a substantial amount of additional planning to do. This extends well beyond your Windows Server 2012 R2 systems to additional computers (clients, for a start), devices, services, applications, and so on.

The details of such a project are far beyond the scope of this book; indeed, entire books have been written on the topic. If you have to implement a network from the ground up, you might want to pick up one of those books.

You must plan the entire network, including areas such as the following:

- Infrastructure architecture (including network topology, addressing, DNS, and so on)
- Active Directory design
- Servers and services
- Administration methods
- Network applications
- Clients
- Client applications
- Client devices (printers, scanners, and the like)

This is a considerable undertaking and requires educated, dedicated staff, adequate time, and other resources.

Inside OUT

Good news, bad news

Having the responsibility for deploying a new Windows-based network is both a good thing and a not-so-good thing:

- **The not-so-good part is straightforward: it can be a staggering amount of work.**
- **The good thing—and it is a very good thing—is that you are starting with a clean slate, and you have a chance to get it (at least mostly) right the first time. Many a network administrator would envy the chance to do a clean deployment: to start fresh with no existing problems, no previous hardware or applications to maintain, and no kludges or workarounds.**

If you are faced with creating a new network, take advantage of this opportunity and do lots of research before you touch the first computer. With the abundance of technical information available, you should be able to avoid most problems and quickly resolve the few you encounter.

Thinking about server roles and Active Directory

When planning for server usage, consider the workload of each server: which services it is providing, the expected user load, and so on. In small network environments, it is common for a single server to act as a domain controller and provide DNS and Dynamic Host Configuration Protocol (DHCP) services and possibly even additional services. In larger network environments, one or more standalone servers might provide each of these services rather than aggregating them on a single system.

Active Directory is an extremely complicated and critical portion of Windows Server 2012 R2, and you should plan for it with appropriate care. The following section discusses, in abbreviated form, some high-level aspects of server usage and Active Directory that you must consider. The section is meant to offer a perspective on how various server roles, including domain controllers, fit in the overall planning picture, not to explain how to plan for a new Active Directory installation.

Planning for server usage

Windows Server 2012 R2 employs a number of server roles, each of which corresponds to one or more services. Your plan should detail which roles (and additional services) are needed and the number and placement of servers and should define the configuration for each service. When planning server usage, be sure to keep the expected client load in mind and account for remote sites that might require additional servers to support local operations.

Key Windows Server 2012 R2 server roles are as follows:

- **Domain controller.** Active Directory domain controllers are perhaps the most important type of network server on a Windows network. Domain controllers are also one of the most intensively used servers on a Windows network, so it is important to assess the operational requirements and server performance realistically for each one. Remember to take into account any secondary Active Directory–related roles the server will be performing (such as global catalog, operations master, and so on). Keep the following questions in mind:
  - How many domain controllers are required, and which ones will fulfill which roles?
  - Which domains must be present at which sites?

- Where should global catalogs be placed?
- What remote offices (if any) will use RODCs?

- **DNS server.** DNS is an integral part of a Windows network, with many important features (such as Active Directory) relying on it. Accordingly, DNS servers are now a required element of your suite of network services. Plan for enough DNS servers to service client requests, with adequate redundancy for fault tolerance and performance, and plan to have them distributed throughout your network to be available to all clients. Factor in remote sites with slow links to the main corporate network and those that might be only intermittently connected by dial-up. Be sure to do the following:
  - Define both internal and external namespaces.
  - Plan the name-resolution path (forwarders and so on).
  - Determine the storage of DNS information (zone files, Active Directory–integrated application partitions).
  - Determine whether you need read-only DNS services at remote offices with RODCs.
  - Determine whether you need DNS Security Extensions (DNSSEC).

NOTE

Microsoft DNS is the recommended method of providing domain name services on a network with Active Directory deployed, although some other DNS servers provide the required functionality. In practice, however, the intertwining of Active Directory and DNS, along with the complexity of the DNS records Active Directory uses, has meant that Microsoft DNS is the one most often used with Active Directory.

NOTE

DNS information can be stored in traditional zone files, Active Directory–integrated zones, or application partitions. An application partition contains a subset of directory information a single application uses. In the case of DNS, this partition is replicated only to domain controllers that are also providing DNS services, minimizing network traffic for DNS replication. There is one application partition for the forest (ForestDnsZones) and another for each domain (DomainDnsZones).

- **DHCP server.** DHCP simplifies the management of the IP address pool both server and client systems use. A number of operational factors regarding the use of DHCP should be considered:
  - Determine whether DNS servers will act as DHCP servers also and, if so, whether all of them or only a subset of them will be used in this way.

- Define server configuration factors such as DHCP scopes and the assignment of scopes to servers in addition to client settings such as the DHCP lease length.
- Determine whether failover scopes are needed to increase fault tolerance and provide redundancy.

- **WINS server.** First, determine whether you still need WINS on your network. If you have legacy applications in your network environment, WINS might be required to translate NetBIOS names to IP addresses. If so, consider the following questions:
  - Which clients need to access the WINS servers?
  - What WINS replication configuration is required?
- **Network Policy And Access Services.** Network Policy And Access Services provides integrated protection, routing, and remote-access services that facilitate secure, protected access by remote users. Consider the following questions:
  - Do you need protection policies?
  - Do you need to provide routing between networks?
  - Do you want to replace existing routers?
  - Do you have external users who need access to the internal network?
- **Hyper-V server.** Hyper-V provides infrastructure for virtualizing applications and workloads. Use Hyper-V to:
  - Consolidate servers and workloads onto fewer, more powerful servers and reduce requirements for power and space.
  - Implement a centralized desktop strategy by combining Hyper-V technology with Remote Desktop Virtualization Host technology.
  - Create a private cloud for shared resources that you can adjust as demand changes.
- **Application server.** A Windows Server 2012 R2 application server hosts distributed applications built using ASP.NET, Enterprise Services, and .NET Framework.
- **File and storage services.** The File And Storage Services role provides essential services for managing files and the way they are made available and replicated on the network. A number of server roles require some type of file service.
- **Print and document services.** The Print And Document Services role manages printer operations on the network. Windows Server 2012 R2 enables publishing printers in Active Directory and connecting to network printers by using a Uniform Resource Locator (URL), and it provides enhanced printer control through Group Policy.

- **Remote desktop services.** The Remote Desktop Services role supports virtual desktops, enabling a single server to pool virtual desktops centrally and, in this way, host network access for many users. A client with a web browser, a Windows thin client, or a Remote Desktop client can access the Remote Desktop server to gain access to network resources.
- **Web server.** Web servers host websites and web-based applications. Websites hosted on a web server can have both static content and dynamic content. You can build web applications hosted on a web server by using ASP.NET and .NET Framework.

> Inside OUT
>
> *Servers with multiple roles*
>
> **It is common for a single server to fill more than one role, especially on smaller networks. When selecting which roles to put on a single server, try to select ones with different needs. For instance, putting one processor-intensive role (for example, an application server) and a role (such as a file server) that does a lot of network input/output (I/O) on a single system makes more sense than putting two roles that stress the same subsystem on the same machine.**

Designing the Active Directory namespace

The Active Directory tree is based on a DNS domain structure, which must be implemented prior to, or as part of, installing the first Active Directory server in the forest. Each domain in the Active Directory tree is both a DNS and a Windows domain, with the associated security and administrative functionality. DNS is thoroughly integrated with Active Directory, providing location services (also called *name resolution services*) for domains, servers, sites, and services and constraining the structure of the Active Directory tree. It is wise to keep Active Directory in mind as you are designing the DNS namespace, and vice versa, because they are immutably linked.

> NOTE
>
> **Active Directory trees exist within a *forest*, which is a collection of one or more domain trees. The first domain installed in an Active Directory forest functions as the *forest root*.**

The interdependence of Active Directory and DNS brings some special factors into play. For example, if your organization has outward-facing DNS servers, you must decide whether you will be using your external DNS name or another DNS domain name for Active Directory. Many organizations choose not to use their external DNS name for Active Directory unless they want to expose the directory to the Internet for a business reason, such as an Internet service provider (ISP) that uses Active Directory logon servers.

Within a domain, another sort of hierarchy exists in the form of container objects called *organizational units* (OUs), which are used to organize and manage users, network resources, and security. An OU can contain related users, groups, or computers and other OUs.

IMPORTANT

Designing the Active Directory namespace requires the participation of multiple levels of business and IT management, so be sure to provide adequate time for a comprehensive review and sign-off on domain architecture.

Managing domain trusts

Domain trusts allow automatic authentication and access to resources across domains. Active Directory automatically configures trust relationships so that each domain in an Active Directory forest trusts every other domain within that forest.

Active Directory domains are linked by a series of such transitive trust relationships between all domains in a domain tree and between all domain trees in the forest. By using Windows Server 2012 R2, you can also configure transitive trust relationships between forests.

Understand explicit trust relationships

Explicit trusts between domains can speed up authentication requests. An explicit trust relationship allows authentication queries to go directly to the domain in question rather than searching the domain tree, forest, or both to locate the domain in which to authenticate a user.

Identifying the domain and forest functional level

Active Directory now has multiple domain and forest functional levels, each constraining the types of domain controllers that can be in use and the available feature set.

The domain functional levels are as follows:

- **Windows Server 2003 mode.** When the domain is operating in Windows Server 2003 mode, the directory supports domain controllers running Windows Server 2003 and later. A domain operating in Windows Server 2003 mode can use universal groups, group nesting, group type conversion, easy domain controller renaming, update logon time stamps, and Kerberos KDC key version numbers. This functional level also supports passwords for InetOrgPerson users. InetOrgPerson users are a special type of user.

- **Windows Server 2008 mode.** When the domain is operating in Windows Server 2008 mode, the directory supports Windows Server 2008 and later domain controllers. Windows Server 2003 domain controllers are no longer supported. A domain operating in Windows Server 2008 mode can use additional Active Directory features, including the DFS replication service for enhanced intersite and intrasite replication and Advanced Encryption Services (AES) 128-bit or AES 256-bit encryption for the Kerberos protocol. This level also supports the display of the last interactive logon details for users and fine-grained password policies for applying separate password and account lockout policies to users and groups.

- **Windows Server 2008 R2 mode.** When the domain is operating in Windows Server 2008 R2 mode, the directory supports Windows Server 2008 R2 and later domain controllers. Windows Server 2003 and Windows Server 2008 domain controllers are no longer supported. A domain operating in Windows Server 2008 R2 mode can use Active Directory Recycle Bin, managed service accounts, Authentication Mechanism Assurance, and other important Active Directory enhancements.

- **Windows Server 2012 mode.** When the domain is operating in Windows Server 2012 mode, the directory supports Windows Server 2012 and Windows Server 2012 R2 domain controllers. Windows Server 2003, Windows Server 2008, and Windows Server 2008 R2 domain controllers are no longer supported. Active Directory schema for Windows Server 2012 includes many enhancements, but only the Kerberos with Armoring feature requires this mode.

- **Windows Server 2012 R2 mode.** When the domain is operating in Windows Server 2012 R2 mode, the directory supports only Windows Server 2012 R2 domain controllers. Domain controllers running earlier versions of Windows Server are no longer supported. Active Directory schema for Windows Server 2012 R2 includes incremental enhancements.

The forest functional levels are as follows:

- **Windows Server 2003.** Supports domain controllers running Windows Server 2003 and later

- **Windows Server 2008.** Supports domain controllers running Windows Server 2008 and later

- **Windows Server 2008 R2.** Supports domain controllers running Windows Server 2008 R2 and later

- **Windows Server 2012.** Supports domain controllers running Windows Server 2012 and Windows Server 2012 R2

- **Windows Server 2012 R2.** Supports domain controllers running Windows Server 2012 R2

When a forest is operating at the Windows Server 2003 or higher functional level, key Active Directory features, including the following, are enabled:

- **Replication enhancements.** Each changed value of a multivalued attribute is now replicated separately—eliminating the possibility for data conflict and reducing replication traffic. Additional changes include enhanced global catalog replication and application partitions (which segregate data and, thus, the replication of that data).
- **Schema.** Schema objects can be deactivated, and dynamic auxiliary classes are supported.
- **Management.** Forest trusts allow multiple forests to share resources easily. Active Directory domains can be renamed; thus, the Active Directory tree can be reorganized.
- **User management.** Last logon time is now tracked, and enhancements to InetOrgPerson password handling are enabled.

However, to take advantage of the latest Active Directory features, your forests must operate at the Windows Server 2008 R2 or higher functional level. Selecting your domain and forest functional levels is generally straightforward. Ultimately, the decision regarding the domain and forest functional levels at which to operate mostly comes down to choosing the one that supports the domain controllers you have in place now and expect to have in the future. In most circumstances, you will want to operate at the highest possible level because it enables more functionality. Also, keep in mind that all changes to the functional level are one-way and cannot be reversed.

Defining Active Directory server roles

In addition to serving as domain controllers, a number of domain controllers fulfill special roles within Active Directory. Some of these roles provide a service to the entire forest, and others are specific to a domain or site. The Active Directory setup routine assigns and configures these roles, although you can change them later.

The Active Directory server roles are as follows:

- **Operations masters.** A number of Active Directory operations must be carefully controlled to maintain the integrity of the directory structure and data. A specific domain controller serves as the operations master for each of these functions. That server is the only one that can perform certain operations related to that area. For example, you can make schema changes only on the domain controller serving as the schema master; if that server is unavailable, no changes can be made to the schema. There are two categories of operations masters:

- **Forest-level operations masters.** The schema master manages the schema and enforces schema consistency throughout the directory.

The domain-naming master controls domain creation and deletion, guaranteeing that each domain is unique within the forest.

- **Domain-level operations masters.** The RID master manages the pool of *relative identifiers* (RIDs). (A RID is a numeric string used to construct security identifiers [SIDs] for security principals.)

The infrastructure master handles user-to-group mappings, changes in group membership, and replication of those changes to other domain controllers.

The PDC emulator is responsible for processing password changes and replicating password changes to other domain controllers. The PDC emulator must be available to reset and verify external trusts.

- **Global catalogs.** A global catalog server provides a quick index of Active Directory objects, which a variety of network clients and processes use to locate directory objects. Global catalog servers can be heavily used, yet they must be highly available to clients, especially for user logons because the global catalog provides membership information for universal groups. Accordingly, each site in the network should have at least one global catalog server, or you should have a Windows Server 2003 or later domain controller with universal group caching enabled.

- **Bridgehead servers.** Bridgehead servers manage intersite replication over low-bandwidth WAN links. Each site replicating with other sites usually has at least one bridgehead server, although a single site can have more than one if that's required for performance reasons.

NOTE

Active Directory replication depends on the concept of *sites*, which are defined as a collected set of subnets with good interconnectivity. Replication differs, depending on whether it is within a site or between sites. Intrasite replication occurs automatically every 15 seconds; intersite replication is scheduled and usually quite a bit slower.

Planning for availability, scalability, and manageability

The enterprise depends on highly available, scalable, and manageable systems. *High availability* refers to the ability of the system to withstand hardware, application, or service outages while maintaining system availability. *High scalability* refers to the ability of the system to expand processor and memory capacity as business needs demand. *High manageability* refers to the ability of the system to be managed locally and remotely and the ease with which components, services, and applications can be administered.

Planning for high availability, high scalability, and high manageability is critical to the success of using Windows Server 2012 R2 in the enterprise, and you need a solid understanding of the recommendations and operating principles for deploying and maintaining high-availability servers before you deploy servers running these editions. You should also understand the types of hardware, software, and support facilities needed for enterprise computing. These concepts are all covered in this chapter.

> NOTE
>
> **The discussion that follows focuses on achieving high availability, high scalability, and high manageability in the enterprise. Smaller organizations or business units can adopt similar approaches to meet business objectives, but they should determine the appropriate scope with budgets and available resources in mind.**

Planning for software needs

Software should be chosen for its ability to support the high-availability needs of the business system. Not all software is compatible with high-availability solutions such as clustering or load balancing. Not all software must be compatible, either. Instead of making an arbitrary decision, you should let the uptime needs of the application determine the level of availability required.

An availability goal of 99 percent uptime is usual for most noncritical business systems. If an application must have 99 percent uptime, it might not need to support clustering or load balancing. To achieve 99 percent uptime, the application can have about 88 hours of downtime in an entire year or, put another way, 100 minutes of downtime a week.

To have 99.9 percent uptime is the availability goal for highly available business systems. If an application must have 99.9 percent uptime, it must support some type of high-availability solution such as clustering or load balancing. To achieve 99.9 percent uptime, the application can have less than 9 hours of downtime in an entire year or, put another way, less than 10 minutes of downtime a week.

Inside OUT

Clustering support alone isn't enough

Applications that support clustering are said to be *cluster aware*. SQL Server and Exchange Server are examples of applications that are cluster aware. Although both applications can be configured to provide high availability in the enterprise, they don't achieve high availability through cluster support alone. High-availability applications must support online backups and be tested for compatibility with Windows Server 2012 R2. Support for online backups ensures that you don't have to take the application offline to back up critical data. Compatibility testing ensures that the software has been thoroughly evaluated for operation with Windows Server 2012 R2.

To evaluate the real-world environment prior to deployment, you should perform integration testing on applications that will be used together. The purpose of integration testing is to ensure that disparate applications interact as expected and to uncover problem areas if they don't. During integration testing, testers should look at system performance, overall system utilization, and compatibility. Testing should be repeated prior to releasing system or application changes to a production environment.

You should standardize the software components needed to provide system services. The goal of standardization is to set guidelines for software components and technologies that will be used in the enterprise. Standardization accomplishes the following:

- Reduces the total cost of maintaining and updating software
- Reduces the amount of integration and compatibility testing needed for upgrades
- Improves recovery time because problems are easier to troubleshoot
- Reduces the amount of training needed for administration support

Software standardization isn't meant to limit the organization to a single specification. Over the life of a data center, new application versions, software components, and technologies will be introduced, and the organization can implement new standards and specifications as necessary. The key to success lies in ensuring that there is a standard process for deploying software updates and new technologies. The standard process must include the following:

- Software compatibility and integration testing
- Software support training for personnel
- Predeployment planning

- Step-by-step software deployment checklists
- Postdeployment monitoring and maintenance

The following checklist summarizes the recommendations for designing and planning software for high availability:

- Choose software that meets the availability needs of the solution or service.
- Choose software that supports online backups.
- Test software for compatibility with other applications.
- Test software integration with other applications.
- Repeat testing prior to releasing updates.
- Create and enforce software standards.
- Define a standard process for deploying software updates.

Planning for hardware needs

Sound hardware strategy helps increase system availability while reducing total cost of ownership and improving recovery times. Windows Server 2012 R2 is designed and tested for use with high-performance hardware, applications, and services. To ensure that hardware components are compatible, choose only components that are certified as compatible, such as those that are listed as certified for Windows Server 2012 R2 in the Windows Server Catalog (*http://www.windowsservercatalog.com/*).

> NOTE
>
> **All certified components undergo rigorous testing, with a retest for firmware revisions, service pack updates, and other minor revisions. After a component is certified through testing, hardware vendors must maintain the configuration through updates and resubmit the component for testing and certification. The program requirements and the tight coordination with vendors greatly improve the reliability and availability of Windows Server 2012 R2. All hardware certified for Windows Server 2012 R2 also is fully supported in Hyper-V environments.**

You should standardize on a hardware platform, and this platform should have standardized components. Standardization accomplishes the following:

- Reduces the amount of training needed for support
- Reduces the amount of testing needed for upgrades

- Requires fewer spare parts because subcomponents are the same
- Improves recovery time because problems are easier to troubleshoot

Standardization isn't meant to restrict a data center to a single type of server. In an *n*-tier environment, standardization typically means choosing a standard server configuration for the front-end servers, a standard server configuration for middle-tier business logic, and a standard server configuration for back-end data services. The reason for this is that web servers, application servers, and database servers all have different resource needs. For example, although a web server might need to run on a dual-processor system with limited hardware redundant array of independent disks (RAID) control and 4 gigabytes (GBs) of RAM, a database server might need to run on an eight-way system with dual-channel RAID control and 64 GBs of RAM.

Standardization isn't meant to limit the organization to a single hardware specification, either. Over the life of a data center, new equipment will be introduced and old equipment likely will become unavailable. To keep up with the pace of change, new standards and specifications should be implemented when necessary. These standards and specifications, like the previous standards and specifications, should be published and made available to you.

Redundancy and fault tolerance must be built into the hardware design at all levels to improve availability. You can improve hardware redundancy by using the following components:

- **Clusters.** Clusters provide failover support for critical applications and services.
- **Standby systems.** Standby systems provide backup systems in case of total failure of a primary system.
- **Spare parts.** Spare parts ensure that replacement parts are available in case of failure.
- **Fault-tolerant components.** Fault-tolerant components improve the internal redundancy of the system.

Storage devices, network components, cooling fans, and power supplies all can be configured for fault tolerance. For storage devices, you should be sure to use multiple disk controllers, hot-swappable drives, and redundant drive arrays. For network components, you should look well beyond the network adapter and consider whether fault tolerance is needed for routers, switches, firewalls, load balancers, and other network equipment.

A standard process for deploying hardware must be defined and distributed to all support personnel. The standard process must include the following:

- Hardware compatibility and integration testing
- Hardware support training for personnel

- Predeployment planning
- Step-by-step hardware deployment checklists
- Postdeployment monitoring and maintenance

The following checklist summarizes the recommendations for designing and planning hardware for high availability:

- Choose hardware that is listed on the Hardware Compatibility List (HCL).
- Create and enforce hardware standards.
- Use redundant hardware whenever possible.
- Use fault-tolerant hardware whenever possible.
- Provide a secure physical environment for hardware.
- Define a standard process for deploying hardware.

If possible, add these recommendations to the preceding checklist:

- Use fully redundant internal networks, from servers to border routers.
- Use direct peering to major tier-1 telecommunications carriers.
- Use redundant external connections for data and telephony.
- Use a direct connection with high-speed lines.

Planning for support structures and facilities

The physical structures and facilities supporting your server room are critically important. Without adequate support structures and facilities, you will have problems. The primary considerations for support structures and facilities have to do with the physical environment of the servers. These considerations also extend to the physical security of the server environment.

Just as hardware and software have availability requirements, so should support structures and facilities. Factors that affect the physical environment are as follows:

- Temperature and humidity
- Dust and other contaminants
- Physical wiring
- Power supplies

- Natural disasters
- Physical security

Temperature and humidity should be carefully controlled at all times. Processors, memory, hard drives, and other pieces of physical equipment operate most efficiently when they are kept cool; between 65 and 70 degrees Fahrenheit is the ideal temperature in most situations. Equipment that overheats can malfunction or cease to operate altogether. Servers should have multiple, redundant internal fans to ensure that these and other internal hardware devices are kept cool.

> IMPORTANT
>
> **You should pay particular attention to fast-running processors and hard drives. Typically, fast-running processors and hard drives can become overheated and need additional cooling fans—even if the surrounding environment is cool.**

Humidity should be kept low to prevent condensation, but the environment shouldn't be dry. A dry climate can contribute to static electricity problems. Antistatic devices and static guards should be used in most environments.

Dust and other contaminants can cause hardware components to overheat or short out. Servers should be protected from these contaminants whenever possible. You should ensure that an air-filtration system is in place in the server room or hosting facility. The regular preventive maintenance cycle on the servers should include checking servers and their cabinets for dust and other contaminants. If dust is found, the servers and cabinets should be carefully cleaned.

Few things affect the physical environment more than wiring and cabling. All electrical wires and network cables should be tested and certified by qualified technicians. Electrical wiring should be configured to ensure that servers and other equipment have adequate power available for peak usage times. Ideally, multiple dedicated circuits should be used to provide power.

Improperly installed network cables are the cause of most communications problems. Network cables should be tested to ensure that their operation meets manufacturer specifications. Redundant cables should be installed to ensure the availability of the network. All wiring and cabling should be labeled and well maintained. Whenever possible, use cable management systems and tie wraps to prevent physical damage to wiring.

Ensuring that servers and their components have power is also important. Servers should have hot-swappable, redundant power supplies. Being hot swappable ensures that the power supply can be replaced without having to turn off the server. Redundancy ensures that if one power supply malfunctions, the other will still deliver power to the server. You should be aware that having multiple power supplies doesn't mean that a server or hardware component has redundancy. Some hardware components require multiple power supplies to operate. In this case, an additional (third or fourth) power supply is needed to provide redundancy.

The redundant power supplies should be plugged into separate power strips, and these power strips should be plugged into separate local uninterruptible power supply (UPS) units if other backup power sources aren't available. Some facilities have enterprise UPS units that provide power for an entire room or facility. If this is the case, redundant UPS systems should be installed. To protect against long-term outages, gas-powered or diesel-powered generators should be installed. Most hosting and collocation facilities have generators. Nevertheless, having a generator isn't enough; the generator must be rated to support the peak power needs of all installed equipment. If the generator cannot support the installed equipment, brownouts (temporary outages) will occur.

Protect equipment against earthquakes

To protect against earthquakes, server racks should have seismic protection, which should be extended to other components and to wiring. All cables should be securely attached at both ends and, whenever possible, should be latched to something other than the server, such as a server rack.

CAUTION

A fire-suppression system should be installed to protect against fire. Dual gas-based systems are preferred because these systems do not harm hardware when they go off. Water-based sprinkler systems, however, can destroy hardware.

In addition, access controls should be used to restrict physical access to the server room or facility. Use locks, key cards, access codes, or biometric scanners to ensure that only designated individuals can gain entry to the secure area. If possible, use surveillance cameras and maintain recorded tapes for at least a week. When the servers are deployed in a hosting or collocation facility, ensure that locked cages are used and that fencing extends from the floor to the ceiling.

The following checklist summarizes the recommendations for designing and planning structures and facilities:

- Maintain the temperature at 65 to 70 degrees Fahrenheit.
- Maintain low humidity (but not dry).
- Install redundant internal cooling fans.

- Use an air-filtration system.
- Check for dust and other contaminants periodically.
- Install hot-swappable, redundant power supplies.
- Test and certify wiring and cabling.
- Use wire management to protect cables from damage.
- Label hardware and cables.
- Install backup power sources such as UPS and generators.
- Install seismic protection and bracing.
- Install dual gas-based fire-suppression systems.
- Restrict physical access by using locks, key cards, access codes, and so forth.
- Use surveillance cameras and maintain recorded tapes (if possible).
- Use locked cages, cabinets, and racks at offsite facilities.
- Use floor-to-ceiling fencing with cages at offsite facilities.

Planning for day-to-day operations

Day-to-day operations and support procedures must be in place before you deploy mission-critical systems. The most critical procedures for day-to-day operations involve the following activities:

- Monitoring and analysis
- Resources, training, and documentation
- Change control
- Problem escalation procedures
- Backup and recovery procedures
- Postmortem after recovery
- Auditing and intrusion detection

Monitoring is critical to the success of business system deployments. You must have the necessary equipment to monitor the status of the business systems. Monitoring enables you to be proactive in system support rather than reactive. Monitoring should extend to the hardware, software, and network components but shouldn't interfere with normal systems operations—that is, the monitoring tools chosen should require only limited system and network resources to operate.

NOTE

Keep in mind that collecting too much data is just as bad as not collecting any data. The monitoring tools should gather only the data required for meaningful analysis.

Without careful analysis, the data collected from monitoring is useless. Procedures should be put in place to ensure that personnel know how to analyze the data they collect. The network infrastructure is a support area that is often overlooked. Be sure you allocate the appropriate resources for network monitoring.

Inside OUT

Use monitoring to ensure availability

A well-run and well-maintained network should have 99.99 percent availability. There should be less than 1 percent packet loss and a packet turnaround of 80 milliseconds or less. To achieve this level of availability and performance, the network must be monitored. Any time business systems extend to the Internet or to WANs, internal network monitoring must be supplemented with outside-in monitoring that checks the availability of the network and business systems. With outside-in monitoring, you use external systems rather than internal systems for your checks.

Resources, training, and documentation are essential to ensuring that you can manage and maintain mission-critical systems. Many organizations cripple the operations team by staffing minimally. Minimally staffed teams will have marginal response times and nominal effectiveness. The organization must take the following steps:

- Staff for success to be successful.
- Conduct training before deploying new technologies.
- Keep the training up to date with what's deployed.
- Document essential operations procedures.

Every change to hardware, software, and the network must be planned and executed deliberately. To do this, you must have established change-control procedures and well-documented execution plans. Change-control procedures should be designed to ensure that everyone knows what changes have been made. Execution plans should be designed to ensure that everyone knows the exact steps that were or should be performed to make a change.

Change logs are a key part of change control. Each piece of physical hardware deployed in the operational environment should have a change log, which should be stored in a text document or spreadsheet or, ideally, a ticketing system that is readily accessible to support personnel. The change log should show the following information:

- Who changed the hardware
- What change was made
- When the change was made
- Why the change was made

Establish and follow change-control procedures

Change-control procedures must take into account the need for both planned changes and emergency changes. All team members involved in a planned change should meet regularly and follow a specific implementation schedule. No one should make changes that aren't discussed with the entire implementation team.

You should have well-defined backup and recovery plans. The backup plan should specifically state the following information:

- When full, incremental, differential, and log backups are used
- How often and at what time backups are performed
- Whether the backups must be conducted online or offline
- The amount of data being backed up and how critical the data is
- The tools used to perform the backups
- The maximum time allowed for backup and restore
- How backup media is labeled, recorded, and rotated

Backups should be monitored daily to ensure that they are running correctly and that the media are good. Any problems with backups should be corrected immediately. Multiple media sets should be used for backups, and these media sets should be rotated on a specific schedule. With a four-set rotation, there is one set each for daily, weekly, monthly, and quarterly backups. By rotating one media set offsite, support staff can help ensure that the organization is protected in case of a disaster.

The recovery plan should provide detailed, step-by-step procedures for recovering the system under various conditions, such as procedures for recovering from hard disk drive failure or troubleshooting problems with connectivity to the back-end database. The recovery plan should also include system design and architecture documentation that details the configuration of physical hardware, application-logic components, and back-end data. Along with this information, support staff should provide a media set containing all software, drivers, and operating system files needed to recover the system.

> NOTE
>
> **One thing administrators often forget about is spare parts. Spare parts for key components—such as processors, drives, and memory—should be maintained as part of the recovery plan if budgeting allows.**

You should practice restoring critical business systems by using the recovery plan. Practice shouldn't be conducted on the production servers. Instead, the team should practice on test equipment with a configuration similar to the real production servers. Practicing once a quarter or semiannually is highly recommended.

You should have well-defined problem-escalation procedures that document how to handle problems and emergency changes that might be needed. Some organizations use a three-tiered help desk structure for handling problems:

- Level 1 support staff forms the front line for handling basic problems. They typically have hands-on access to the hardware, software, and network components they manage. Their main job is to clarify and prioritize a problem. If the problem has occurred before and there is a documented resolution procedure, they can resolve the problem without escalation. If the problem is new or not recognized, they must understand how, when, and to whom to escalate it.

- Level 2 support staff includes more specialized personnel who can diagnose a particular type of problem and work with others to resolve a problem, such as system administrators and network engineers. They usually have remote access to the hardware, software, and network components they manage. This enables them to troubleshoot problems remotely and send out technicians after they've pinpointed the problem.

- Level 3 support staff includes highly technical personnel who are subject-matter experts, team leaders, or team supervisors. The Level 3 team can include support personnel from vendors and representatives from the user community. Together, they form the emergency-response or crisis-resolution team that is responsible for resolving crises and planning emergency changes.

All crises and emergencies should be responded to decisively and resolved methodically. A single person on the emergency response team should be responsible for coordinating all changes and executing the recovery plan. This same person should be responsible for writing an after-action report that details the emergency response and resolution process used. The after-action report should analyze how the emergency was resolved and the root cause of the problem.

In addition, you should establish procedures for auditing system usage and detecting intrusion. In Windows Server 2012 R2, auditing policies are used to track the successful or failed execution of the following activities:

- **Account logon events.** Tracks events related to user logon and logoff
- **Account management.** Tracks tasks involved with handling user accounts such as creating or deleting accounts and resetting passwords
- **Directory service access.** Tracks access to the Active Directory Domain Services (AD DS)
- **Object access.** Tracks system resource usage for files, directories, and objects
- **Policy change.** Tracks changes to user rights, auditing, and trust relationships
- **Privilege use.** Tracks the use of user rights and privileges
- **Process tracking.** Tracks system processes and resource usage
- **System events.** Tracks system startup, shutdown, restart, and actions that affect system security or the security log

You should have an incident-response plan that includes priority escalation of suspected intrusion to senior team members and provides step-by-step details on how to handle the intrusion. The incident-response team should gather information from all network systems that might be affected. The information should include event logs, application logs, database logs, and any other pertinent files and data. The incident-response team should take immediate action to lock out accounts, change passwords, and physically disconnect the system if necessary. All team members participating in the response should write a postmortem report that details the following information:

- What date and time they were notified and what immediate actions they took
- Whom they notified and what the response was from the notified individual
- Their assessment of the issue and the actions necessary to resolve and prevent similar incidents

The team leader should write an executive summary of the incident and forward this to senior management.

The following checklist summarizes the recommendations for operational support of high-availability systems:

- Monitor hardware, software, and network components 24/7.
- Ensure that monitoring doesn't interfere with normal systems operations.
- Gather only the data required for meaningful analysis.
- Establish procedures that let personnel know what to look for in the data.
- Use outside-in monitoring any time systems are externally accessible.
- Provide adequate resources, training, and documentation.
- Establish change-control procedures that include change logs.
- Establish execution plans that detail the change implementation.
- Create a solid backup plan that includes onsite and offsite tape rotation.
- Monitor backups and test backup media.
- Create a recovery plan for all critical systems.
- Test the recovery plan on a routine basis.
- Document how to handle problems and make emergency changes.
- Use a three-tier support structure to coordinate problem escalation.
- Form an emergency-response or crisis-resolution team.
- Write after-action reports that detail the process used.
- Establish procedures for auditing system usage and detecting intrusion.
- Create an intrusion response plan with priority escalation.
- Take immediate action to handle suspected or actual intrusion.
- Write postmortem reports detailing team reactions to the intrusion.

Planning for deploying highly available servers

You should always create a plan before deploying a business system. The plan should show everything that must be done before the system is transitioned into the production environment. After a system is in the production environment, the system is deemed operational and should be handled as outlined in "Planning for day-to-day operations" earlier in this chapter.

The deployment plan should include the following items:

- Checklists
- Contact lists
- Test plans
- Deployment schedules

Checklists are a key part of the deployment plan. The purpose of a checklist is to ensure that the entire deployment team understands the steps the members need to perform. Checklists should list the tasks that must be performed and designate individuals to handle the tasks during each phase of the deployment—from planning to testing to installation. Prior to executing a checklist, the deployment team should meet to ensure that all items are covered and that the necessary interactions among team members are clearly understood. After deployment, the preliminary checklists should become part of the system documentation, and new checklists should be created any time the system is updated.

The deployment plan should include a contact list that provides the name, role, telephone number, and email address of all team members, vendors, and solution-provider representatives. Alternative numbers for cell phones and pagers should also be provided.

The deployment plan should include a test plan. An ideal test plan has several phases. In Phase I, the deployment team builds the business system and support structures in a test lab. Building the system means accomplishing the following tasks:

- Creating a test network on which to run the system
- Putting together the hardware and storage components
- Installing the operating system and application software
- Adjusting basic system settings to suit the test environment
- Configuring clustering, network load balancing, or another high-availability solution if necessary

The deployment team can conduct any necessary testing and troubleshooting in the isolated lab environment. The entire system should undergo burn-in testing to guard against faulty components. If a component is flawed, it usually fails in the first few days of operation. Testing doesn't stop with burn-in. Web and application servers should be stress tested. Database servers should be load tested. The results of the stress and load tests should be analyzed to ensure that the system meets the performance requirements and expectations of the customer. Adjustments to the configuration should be made to improve performance and optimize the configuration for the expected load.

In Phase II, the deployment team tests the business system and support equipment in the deployment location. Team members conduct similar tests as before, but in the real-world environment. Again, the results of these tests should be analyzed to ensure that the system meets the performance requirements and expectations of the customer. Afterward, adjustments should be made to improve performance and optimize as necessary. The team can then deploy the business system.

After deployment of the server or servers, the team should perform limited, nonintrusive testing to ensure that the system is operating normally. After Phase III testing is completed, the team can use the operational plans for monitoring and maintenance.

The following checklist summarizes the recommendations for predeployment planning of mission-critical systems:

- Create a plan that covers the entire testing-to-operations cycle.
- Use checklists to ensure that the deployment team understands the procedures.
- Provide a contact list for the team, vendors, and solution providers.
- Conduct burn-in testing in the lab.
- Conduct stress and load testing in the lab.
- Use the test data to optimize and adjust the configuration.
- Provide follow-on testing in the deployment location.
- Follow a specific deployment schedule.
- Use operational plans after final tests are completed.

CHAPTER 2

Deploying Windows Server 2012 R2

Microsoft Windows Server 2012 R2 supports only 64-bit architecture. You can install the operating system only on computers with 64-bit processors. You are likely to find yourself installing Windows Server 2012 R2 in various circumstances—a new installation for a new system, an upgrade of an existing Microsoft Windows installation, or perhaps even a new installation into a multiboot environment. You might need to install just a few systems, or you might need to deploy hundreds—or even thousands—in a diverse network environment.

In this chapter, I discuss the things you should know to help you prepare for and perform installations. The way you deploy Windows servers will depend on your objectives and requirements. Windows Server 2012 R2 supports both interactive and automated setup processes, providing flexibility in how you install and configure the operating system. You can even fully automate the installation of a basic or fully configured operating system on a brand-new computer to ease the administrative burden in large deployments, and an automation tool such as System Center Configuration Manager 2012 R2 can help you do that.

Getting a quick start

To install Windows Server 2012 R2, you can boot from the Windows distribution media, run Setup from within your current Windows operating system, perform a command-line installation, or use one of several automated installation options.

In performing the installation, there are two basic approaches to setting up Windows Server 2012 R2: interactively or as an automated process. An interactive installation is what many people regard as the regular Windows installation—the kind in which you walk through the setup process and enter a lot of information. It can be performed from distribution media (by booting from the distribution media or running Windows Setup from a command line). The default Windows setup process when booting from the retail Windows Server 2012 R2 DVD is interactive, prompting you for configuration information throughout the process.

There are several types of automated setup, which actually have administrator-configurable amounts of user interaction. The most basic form of unattended setup you can perform is an unattended installation using only answer files. To take unattended setup a step further, you can use your unattended answer files with Windows Deployment Services (WDS). In either case, the answer file contains all or part of the configuration information usually prompted for during a standard installation process. You can author unattended answer files by using Windows System Image Manager (SIM).

Windows Deployment Services supports installation of desktop and server systems by using Windows Imaging (WIM) and Virtual Hard Disk (VHD) images. VHD images can be formatted using either fixed .vhd files or dynamically expanding .vhdx files. For full automation, you can use System Center Configuration Manager 2012 R2.

The standard Setup program for Windows Server 2012 R2 is Setup.exe. You can run Setup.exe from within the Windows operating system to upgrade the existing operating system or to install Windows Server 2012 R2 to a different partition. The command-line switches on the Windows Setup programs offer you additional options for configuring the installation process. The general installation parameters include the following:

- **Setup */addbootmgrlast*.** The */addbootmgrlast* option adds the Windows Boot Manager as the last entry in the Unified Extensible Firmware Interface (UEFI) firmware boot order. This option is supported only on computers with UEFI running Windows Preinstallation Environment (PE) 4.0 or later.
- **Setup /m:*folder_name*.** The */m:folder_name* option sets an alternate location for files to be used by Setup during the installation process—during setup, the alternate location is searched first, and files in the default location are used only if the installation files are not found in the specified alternate location.
- **Setup */noreboot*.** The */noreboot* parameter prevents the rebooting of the system upon completion of the file copy phase. This option is used to allow other commands or operations to be performed after the files have been copied, but it's used prior to further Setup phases.
- **Setup /tempdrive:*drivepath*.** The */tempdrive:drivepath* parameter designates the hard disk drive location where the temporary installation files will be placed.
- **Setup /unattend:*answer_file_path*.** The */unattend:answer_file_path* parameter, when used with an answer file, instructs Setup to do an unattended new installation (a fresh installation as opposed to an upgrade) based on the values specified in the answer file. The answer file can contain all or part of the configuration information for which the installation process normally prompts the user.

Product licensing

As discussed in Chapter 1, "Introducing Windows Server 2012 R2," in the "Getting to know Windows Server 2012 R2" section, there are four main editions of Windows Server 2012 R2: Foundation, Essentials, Standard, and Datacenter. Although the Windows Server Foundation and Windows Server Essentials editions are for small businesses, the Windows Server Standard and Windows Server Datacenter editions are for any organization that needs a full-featured server.

Licensing for Windows Server 2012 R2 has two aspects: server licenses and client access licenses (CALs). Each installation of Windows Server 2012 R2 on a computer requires appropriate server licensing.

Each server license can be assigned to only a single physical server, and licensing requirements are based on the number of physical processors installed and the number of virtual instances the server runs. All the physical processors on a server must be licensed with the same version and edition of Windows Server 2012 R2.

Windows Server Foundation can be used only with a server that has a single physical processor and allows up to 15 users without a need for separate CALs. Windows Server Essentials can be used on servers with up to two physical processors and allows up to 25 users without a need for separate CALs.

Each Windows Server Standard or Windows Server Datacenter license covers up to two physical processors. Although each Windows Server Standard license covers up to two virtual instances, a Windows Server Datacenter license covers an unlimited number of virtual instances. Thus, a server with four physical processors would require either two Windows Server Standard licenses or two Windows Server Datacenter licenses.

In addition to ensuring that you have the required licenses for Windows Server 2012 R2, you must decide on the client access licensing scheme you will use before installing Windows Server 2012 R2. With Windows Server Standard and Windows Server Datacenter, your choices are as follows:

- **Per server.** One CAL is required for each concurrent connection to the server. This usually means one CAL for every connection to that server.
- **Per device or per user.** A CAL is purchased for each user or device connecting to the server; this usually corresponds to one CAL for every user or computer that will access the server.

Your licensing program determines how you handle both the product key and product activation. Table 2-1 describes how each type of licensing affects installation. Open License and

Windows Server Migration tools might be able to help you migrate your server. These tools are available on computers running Windows Server 2012 R2.

Determining which installation type to use

Windows Server 2012 R2 supports three installation types:

- **Full Server.** Full Server installations, also referred to as Server With A GUI installations, have the Graphical Management Tools And Infrastructure and Server Graphical Shell features (which are part of the User Interfaces And Infrastructure feature) and the Windows on Windows 64 (WOW64) Support framework installed.
- **Minimal Server Interface.** Minimal Server Interface installations, also referred to as Server With Minimal Interface installations, are Full Server installations with the Server Graphical Shell removed. Although this option is not available when installing Windows Server 2012 R2, you can convert to a Minimal Server Interface later.
- **Server Core.** Server Core installations have a limited user interface and do not include any of the User Interfaces And Infrastructure features or the WOW64 Support framework. This is the default installation option.

IMPORTANT

When performing an upgrade, you also must ensure that the language and build type for the current installation and the new installation are the same. You cannot upgrade from one language to another or from one build type to another. In addition, you cannot switch from one installation mode to another as part of the upgrade. Thus, you cannot select an installation type of Server With A GUI on a server that currently is using Server Core mode or vice versa.

TROUBLESHOOTING

Server Core limits installable roles and role services

With a Full Server installation, you have a complete working version of Windows Server 2012 R2 you can deploy with any permitted combination of roles, role services, and features. With a Minimal Server Interface installation, you also can deploy any permitted combination of roles, role services, and features. However, with a Server Core installation, you have a minimal installation of Windows Server 2012 R2 that supports a limited set of roles and role combinations. The supported roles include AD CS, AD DS, AD LDS, DHCP Server, DNS Server, File Services, Hyper-V, Media Services, Print And Document Services, Routing And Remote Access Server, Streaming Media Services, Web Server (IIS), and Windows Server Update Services. In its current implementation,

a Server Core installation is not a platform for running server applications. That said, you can run Hyper-V on Server Core and use it to host virtual machines that run server applications, such as SQL Server, Exchange Server, and Microsoft SharePoint.

Although all three installation types use the same licensing rules and can be managed remotely using any available and permitted remote-administration technique, Full Server, Minimal Server Interface, and Server Core installations are completely different when it comes to local console administration. With a Full Server installation, you're provided with a user interface that includes a full desktop environment for local console management of the server. With a Minimal Server Interface installation, you have only Microsoft Management Consoles, Server Manager, and a subset of Control Panel available for management tasks. Missing from both a Minimal Server Interface installation and a Server Core installation are File Explorer, taskbar, notification area, Internet Explorer, built-in help system, themes, desktop apps, and Windows Media Player.

Unlike earlier releases of Windows Server, you can change the installation type of any server running Windows Server 2012 R2. This is possible because a key difference among the installation types relates to whether the installation has the following User Interfaces And Infrastructure features:

- Graphical Management Tools And Infrastructure
- Desktop Experience
- Server Graphical Shell

Server Core installations have none of these features. Minimal Server Interface installations have only the Graphical Management Tools And Infrastructure feature, and Full Server installations have both the Graphical Management Tools And Infrastructure feature and the Server Graphical Shell feature.

Full Server installations also might have Desktop Experience, which provides Windows desktop functionality on the server. Windows features added include Windows Media Player, desktop themes, Video for Windows (AVI support), Disk Cleanup, Sync Center, Sound Recorder, Character Map, and Snipping Tool. These features enable you to use a server like a desktop computer, but they also can reduce the server's overall performance.

When you know that Windows automatically installs or uninstalls dependent features, server roles, and management tools to match the installation type, you can convert from one installation type to another just by adding or removing the appropriate User Interfaces And Infrastructure features. For more information on converting the installation type, see the "Postinstallation tasks" section later in this chapter.

Using Windows Update

Windows Update is a convenient way of ensuring that the most recently updated driver and system files are always used during server installation. Windows Update connects to a distribution server containing updated files used during Windows installation. The files in Windows Update include setup information files, dynamic libraries used during setup, file assemblies, device drivers, and system files.

NOTE

During setup of the operating system, the Windows Update process does not provide new installation files; rather, it supplies only updated files that replace existing files used during setup. Windows Update might, however, provide device drivers that are not replacements for device drivers existing on the distribution media (in-box device drivers) but are new device drivers supplying additional support for devices or system hardware.

The Windows Update files can be obtained by using two methods:

- Windows Update files can be obtained directly from the Windows Update site during setup, ensuring that the absolute latest setup files are used during the installation.
- Windows Update files can be downloaded to a server on your local network and then shared to provide clients with access to a consistent local copy of the files.

Getting Windows Update files from the update site online is recommended for consumers and small businesses that do not have a full-time Windows administrator. Otherwise, your organization probably should centralize the functionality locally by using Windows Server Update Services (WSUS) in a client/server configuration. WSUS is available as an optional download for Windows Server 2012 R2. Hosting Windows Update files on a local network provides you with additional security and the advantage of ensuring that important operating system updates are applied to all systems within your network environment.

Inside OUT

Using Windows Server Update Services

WSUS is available as an installable role in Window Server 2012 R2. WSUS has both a server component and a client component. The client component is built into Windows client operating systems. Each managed client requires a Windows Server CAL. The WSUS server component uses a data store that runs with Microsoft SQL Server Desktop Engine (MSDE), Microsoft SQL Server Desktop Engine for Windows (WMSDE), or SQL Server. With SQL Server, every device WSUS manages requires a SQL Server CAL or a per-processor license.

WSUS requires Internet Information Services (IIS). The WSUS server component uses IIS to obtain updates over the Internet by using HTTP port 80 and HTTPS port 443. WSUS can also use IIS to update client computers automatically with the necessary client software for WSUS.

For performance and network load balancing, large enterprises might want to have an extended WSUS environment with multiple WSUS servers. In a multiple WSUS server environment configuration, one WSUS server can be used as the central server for downloading updates, and other WSUS servers can connect to this server to obtain settings and updates to distribute to clients.

Preinstallation tasks

You will want to assess the specifics of an installation and identify any tasks that must be done prior to installation. The following is a partial list—a general set of pointers to the installation-related tasks that must be performed:

- Check for firmware updates.
- Check requirements for the operating system version.
- Review the release notes on the operating system media.
- Determine whether to upgrade or perform a clean installation.
- Check your system hardware compatibility.
- Configure how the target computer boots.
- Determine the installation type: interactive or automated.
- Determine the license mode.
- Choose the installation partition.
- Determine the network connectivity and settings.
- Identify domain or workgroup membership account information.
- Disconnect the uninterruptible power supply (UPS).
- Disable virus scanning.

NOTE

When performing a clean installation on old hardware, check to see whether an operating system exists. If one does exist, check the event or system logs for hardware errors, consider using multiboot, uncompress the drives, and resolve any partition upgrade issues.

Plan for Windows Update

Hosting Windows Update on a local network server—as opposed to downloading updates directly from Microsoft each time you install the operating system—can speed up the updates and ensure the consistency of driver versions across the network environment. On desktops running Windows on which updates are applied automatically, Windows Update might restart the computer if this is required to complete important updates. If a restart is necessary, Windows caches the credentials of the user who is signed in to the console, restarts the computer, and then uses the cached credentials to sign the user back in. After signing in with the user's cached credentials, Windows restarts applications that were running previously and then locks the session by using Secure Desktop.

You must also assess your installation requirements and plan the configuration of the drives and partitions on the target computers. If you must create a new partition, modify the system partition, or format the system partition before installation, you can use configuration tools such as the DiskPart, Format, and Convert commands to manage partitions (prior to beginning the automated installation).

Installing Windows Server 2012 R2

For many situations in which you're about to install Windows Server 2012 R2 onto a new computer system—a bare-metal or a clean installation to a computer you can sit in front of—booting from the Windows Server 2012 R2 distribution media is certainly the simplest approach. You need only configure the server to boot from the DVD-ROM by setting the boot device order in the firmware and provide information when prompted. The exception to this is when you must specify command-line switches or run the command line from within Setup. Alternatively, if you work in an environment that maintains standing images of operating systems in use, you can do an interactive installation from a deployment share on the network.

The way you install a server depends somewhat on its firmware interface. As discussed in detail in Chapter 3, "Boot configuration," computers can be either Basic Input Output System (BIOS)–based or Extensible Firmware Interface (EFI)–based. Although BIOS-based computers normally use the master boot record (MBR) disk type for boot and system volumes, EFI-based computers normally use the GUID partition table (GPT) disk type for boot and system volumes. These two disk types are very different.

NOTE

Computers based on x64 use UEFI wrapped around BIOS or EFI. Having UEFI as the firmware architecture is a requirement for hardware to be certified for Windows Server 2012 R2.

Installation on BIOS-based systems

When you are working with Windows Server 2012 R2 on BIOS-based systems, you should be aware of the special types of drive sections the operating system uses:

- **Active.** The active partition or volume is the drive section for system cache and startup. Some devices with removable storage might be listed as having an active partition.
- **Boot.** The boot partition or volume contains the operating system and its support files. The system and boot partition or volume can be the same.
- **Crash Dump.** This is the partition to which the computer attempts to write dump files in the event of a system crash. By default, dump files are written to the %SystemRoot% folder, but they can be located on any partition or volume you choose.
- **Page File.** This is a partition containing a paging file the operating system uses. Because a computer can page memory to multiple disks, according to the way you configure virtual memory, a computer can have multiple page-file partitions or volumes.
- **System.** The system partition or volume contains the hardware-specific files needed to load the operating system. As part of software configuration, the system partition or volume can't be part of a striped or spanned volume.

NOTE

Partitions and volumes are essentially the same thing. The term used varies at times, however, because you create partitions on basic disks, and you create volumes on dynamic disks. Keep in mind, however, that a primary partition on a basic disk is a volume, and a logical drive in an extended partition is also a volume. On a BIOS-based computer, you can mark a partition as active using the Disk Management console or from the DiskPart utility.

Yes, the definitions of *boot partition* and *system partition* are the opposite of what you'd expect. The boot partition, in fact, does contain the \Windows directory—that's just the way it is.

Although these volumes or partitions can be the same, they are required nonetheless. When you install Windows Server 2012 R2, the Setup program assesses all available hard disk drive resources. Typically, Windows Server 2012 R2 puts the boot and system volumes on the same drive and partition and marks this partition as the active partition. The advantage of this configuration is that you don't need multiple drives for the operating system and can use an additional drive as a mirror of the operating system partitions.

Installation on EFI-based systems

A globally unique identifier (GUID) partition table (GPT)–based disk has two required partitions and one or more optional (original equipment manufacturer [OEM] or data) partitions (up to 128 total):

- EFI system partition (ESP)
- Microsoft Reserved (MSR) partition
- At least one data partition

Although EFI-based computers can have both GPT and MBR disks, the computer must have at least one GPT disk for booting.

Planning partitions

Now that you know how Windows Server 2012 R2 uses disks on both BIOS-based and EFI-based computers, consider carefully how you want to partition the hard disk drives. The boot and system files require about 10 GBs of space. To allow for flexibility, you should create a partition for the operating system with at least 40 GBs. This allows for the addition of service packs and other system files later. Don't forget that you should also have enough disk space for the page file and crash dump; I recommend reserving additional disk space equivalent to twice the installed RAM for this purpose.

Although a server could have a single hard disk with a single partition, it sometimes is better to have multiple partitions, even if the computer has only one drive. By using multiple partitions, you can separate operating system files from application data, which might be a recommended best practice for the application. Although this permits the use of services that require installation on nonsystem partitions, it could make migrating to a future operating system more difficult.

For systems with multiple disks, this is a good time to think about whether you want to use a redundant array of independent disks (RAID) to add fault tolerance for the operating system. RAID can be performed at the hardware level or at the operating system level. You will find that the hardware-based RAID provides the best performance and is the easiest solution.

Create additional partitions

If you plan to create multiple partitions, you don't have to worry about doing it when installing the operating system. You can configure the Windows operating system to use a partition of the correct size, such as 40 GBs or more, and then create the other partitions that you want to use after the installation is finished.

Increasingly, enterprises are using storage arrays. If your servers are allocated storage from storage arrays, keep in mind that each logical unit number, or LUN, assigned is a virtual disk and that the virtual disk likely is spread across multiple physical disks (also called *spindles*). Here, hardware-based RAID is configured within the storage array, and you might not need additional software-based RAID. That said, several software-based RAID options are available, and administrators often will want to implement one of these options as an additional safeguard, including:

- **Traditional software RAID.** This is the software-based RAID technology built into the operating system and available in earlier releases of Windows.
- **Storage Spaces.** This is a resilient storage solution available for Windows 8.1 and Windows Server 2012 R2 that uses virtual disk technology. Storage Spaces are preferred over traditional software RAID.

RAID options are discussed in Chapter 12, "Storage management essentials," and include the following:

- Disk striping (RAID 0)
- Disk mirroring or duplexing (RAID 1)
- Disk striping with parity (RAID 5)

Software-based RAID is implemented by using dynamic disks. For a bare-metal installation, the disks on the computer should be formatted as basic disks, and then after installation, you could upgrade to dynamic disks so that you can implement software-based RAID. On existing installations, the computer might already have dynamic disks, which could be the case if a computer is currently using Microsoft Windows Server and you are performing a new installation of Windows Server 2012 R2. Keep in mind, however, that dynamic disks are deprecated for all usages except mirrored boot volumes. If you want to mirror the volume that hosts the operating system, you might want to use dynamic disks because this is one of the best approaches.

IMPORTANT

Deprecated means that dynamic disks might not be supported in future releases of Windows, so you might not want to use dynamic disks on new Windows deployments. It doesn't mean that you can't use dynamic disks. Dynamic disks continue to be available in Windows 8.1 and Windows Server 2012 R2.

For resilience, virtual disks that you create as part of a server's Storage Spaces can also use mirroring or parity. As part of software configuration, you cannot use RAID 0 with system or boot volumes. More typically, operating system files are mirrored, and application data is striped with parity. If you plan to mirror the operating system, you will need two disks. If you plan to create a RAID 5 volume for your data, you'll need at least three disks.

Naming computers

It is surprising how few organizations take the time to plan the names they'll use for their computers. Sure, it is fun to have servers named Lefty, Curly, Moe, Ducky, Ruddy, and Aardvark, but just what do the names say about the role and location of those servers? You guessed it—nothing, which can make it difficult for users and even other administrators to find resources they need. Not to mention the management nightmare that happens when your six cutely named servers grow to number 50 or 500.

Rather than using names that are cute or arbitrary, decide on a naming scheme that is meaningful to both administrators and users—and this doesn't mean naming servers after the seven dwarfs or the J. R. R. Tolkien characters in *Lord of the Rings*. Okay, it might be cool—way cool—to have servers named Bilbo, Gandalf, Frodo, and Gollum. However, pretty soon, you'd have Galadriel, Boromir, Theoden, Eowyn, and all the rest of the cast. At that point, you'd better be ready to field lots of questions, such as, "How do you spell Aeyowin, anyway?" or "What's Thedding, and where is it again?"

To help users and ease the administrative burden, you might decide to use a naming scheme that helps identify what the computer does and where it is located. For example, you could name the first server in the Engineering department EngServer01 and the first server in the Technical Services department TechServer01. These names identify the computers as servers and specify the departments in which they are located. You might also have servers named CorpMail01 and CorpIntranet01, which identify the corporate mail and intranet servers, respectively.

Although naming conventions can be helpful, don't go overboard. The names EngServer01, TechServer01, CorpMail01, and CorpIntranet01 help identify computers by role and location, but they aren't overly complex. Keeping things simple should help ensure that the computer names are easy to remember and easy to work with. Stay away from overly complex names, such as SeattleSrvBldg48DC17 or SvrSeaB48F15-05, if at all possible. Overly complex names are unnecessary in most instances and probably contain information that most users don't need. For example, users won't care that a server is in building 48 or that it is on floor 15. In fact, that information might be too specific and could actually help someone who wants to break into or sabotage the corporate network. Instead of putting exact mapping information in the computer name, keep a spreadsheet that maps computer locations for administrative use and include only general information about the location or department in the computer name.

While we're talking about security, keep in mind that some organizations use server names with arbitrary character strings on purpose. They want to make the network infrastructure difficult to discover and navigate for anyone trying to gain unauthorized access. Thus, they might use computer names like Srv4Wg8th3kb12a or Tkl82jeb4j2e9pz. Here, the organization is using random 15-character strings as computer names, giving up ease of use and reference with the goal of enhancing overall security.

Finally, keep in mind that computer names must be unique in the domain and must be 64 characters or fewer in length. The first 15 characters of the computer name are used as the pre–Windows 2000 computer name for Network Basic Input/Output System (NetBIOS) communications and also must be unique in the domain. Further, for Domain Name System (DNS) compatibility, the name should consist of only alphanumeric characters (A–Z, a–z, and 0–9) and the hyphen.

Network and domain membership options

During installation, you must decide on several important network and domain membership options, such as the following:

- Which protocols the server will use
- Whether the server will be a member of the domain
- What networking components will be installed

Protocols

The primary networking protocols that Windows Server 2012 R2 installs by default are Transmission Control Protocol/Internet Protocol version 4 (TCP/IPv4) and Transmission Control Protocol/Internet Protocol version 6 (TCP/IPv6). Throughout this book, I'll refer to TCP/IPv4 and TCP/IPv6 collectively as TCP/IP. To install TCP/IP correctly, you must decide whether you want to use static IP addressing or dynamic IP addressing. For static IP addressing, you need the following information:

- IP address
- Subnet mask/subnet prefix length

- Default gateway
- Preferred DNS server

For dynamic IP addressing, the IP information is assigned automatically by an available Dynamic Host Configuration Protocol (DHCP) server. If no DHCP server is available, the server will autoconfigure itself. Autoconfigured addressing is typically nonroutable, so you must correct this issue after installation.

Domain membership

Just about every server you install will be a member of a domain rather than a member of a workgroup (with some exceptions, of course). You can join a computer to a domain after installation. If you want to do that, you should have a computer account created in the domain (or create one while joining the domain by using an account with Administrator or Account Operator rights). A computer account is similar to a user account in that it resides in the accounts database held in Active Directory Domain Services (AD DS) and is maintained by domain controllers.

If a server is a member of a domain, users with domain memberships or permissions can access the server and its resources—based on, of course, their individual rights and permissions—without having to have a separate logon. This means that users can log on once to the domain and work with resources that they have permissions to access, and they won't be prompted to log on separately for each server they work with. In contrast, if a server is a member of a workgroup, users must log on each time they want to work with a server and its resources.

Networking components

During installation, you have the opportunity to install networking components. The common networking components for servers are selected automatically. They include the following:

- **Client for Microsoft Networks.** Allows the computer to access resources on Windows-based networks
- **File and Printer Sharing for Microsoft Networks.** Allows other Windows-based computers to access resources on the computer (required for remote logon)
- **Internet Protocol version 4 (TCP/IPv4).** Allows the computer to communicate over the network by using TCP/IPv4
- **Internet Protocol version 6 (TCP/IPv6).** Allows the computer to communicate over the network by using TCP/IPv6

- **QoS Packet Scheduler.** Helps the computer manage the flow of network traffic and prioritize services
- **Link-Layer Topology Discovery Mapper I/O Driver.** Allows the computer to discover and locate other computers, devices, and networking components on the network
- **Link-Layer Topology Discovery Responder.** Allows the computer to be discovered and located on the network by other computers

You can install additional clients, services, and protocols too, including Microsoft LLDP Protocol Driver and Reliable Multicast Protocol. However, try to keep additional component installation to a minimum. Install the components that you know must be installed. Don't install components you think you might need because they might use system resources that would otherwise be available for other services to use.

Performing a clean installation

To perform a clean installation of Windows Server 2012 R2, complete the following steps:

1. Start the Setup program using one of the following techniques:
   - For a new installation, turn on the computer with the Windows Server 2012 R2 distribution media in the computer's disc drive and then press any key when prompted to start Setup from your media. If you are not prompted to boot from the disc drive, you might need to select advanced boot options and then boot from media rather than hard disk, or you might need to change the computer's firmware settings to allow booting from media.
   - For a clean installation over an existing installation, you can boot from the distribution media, or you can start the computer and log on using an account with administrator privileges. When you insert the Windows Server 2012 R2 distribution media into the computer's disc drive, Setup should start automatically. If Setup doesn't start automatically, use File Explorer to access the distribution media and then double-tap or double-click Setup.exe.

   NOTE

   When you try to install Windows Server 2012 R2 using a DVD, you might find that your computer doesn't recognize the installation media. If the media is damaged, you'll need to obtain replacement media. Otherwise, make sure that the DVD drive is configured as a startup device and that you are inserting the media into the appropriate DVD drive.

TROUBLESHOOTING

Using the Rollback Wizard during setup

If Windows Setup encounters a problem during installation, you can select Rollback on the boot menu to start the Rollback Wizard (x:\sources\rollback.exe). You can use this wizard subsequently to restore the previous version of Windows. If the Rollback Wizard is successful, the previous version of Windows is completely restored. If the Rollback Wizard is unsuccessful, the server typically is left in an unbootable state, and you must either perform a full restore of the previous installation or a clean installation of Windows Server 2012 R2.

2. If you started the computer by using the distribution media, choose your language, time, currency formats, and keyboard layout when prompted. Only one keyboard layout is available during installation. If your keyboard language and the language edition of Windows Server 2012 R2 you are installing are different, you might see unexpected characters as you type. Be sure that you select the correct keyboard language to avoid this. When you are ready to continue with the installation, tap or click Next.

3. On the next Setup page, select Install Now to start the installation.

4. If you are starting the installation from an existing operating system and are connected to a network or the Internet, choose whether to get updates during the installation. Tap or click either Go Online To Get The Latest Updates For Setup or Do Not Get The Latest Updates For Setup.

5. With volume and enterprise licensed editions of Windows Server 2012 R2, you might not need to provide a product key during installation of the operating system. With retail editions, however, you'll be prompted to enter a product key and then tap or click Next to continue. Keep the following in mind:

   - When entering the product key, be sure to enter a key for the server edition you want to install. You don't need to worry about using the correct letter case or entering dashes. Setup enters all letters you type in uppercase. When a dash is needed, Setup enters the dash automatically.
   - On the Type Your Product Key For Activation page, the Next button is available for tapping or clicking only when the Product Key box is empty or when you've entered all 25 of the required characters. If you want to enter a product key, you must type the full product key before the Next button is available for tapping or clicking. If you don't want to enter a product key at this time, leave the Product Key box blank and then tap or click Next.
   - The Activate Windows When I'm Online check box is selected by default to activate the operating system automatically the next time you connect to the Internet. Windows Server 2012 R2 must be activated within the first 30 days after

installation. If you don't activate Windows Server 2012 R2 in the allotted time, you see an error stating that "Your activation period has expired" or that you have a "non-genuine version of Windows Server 2012 R2 installed." Windows Server 2012 R2 will then run in a reduced functionality mode. You need to activate and validate Windows Server 2012 R2 as necessary to resume full functionality mode.

6. If you enter an invalid product key, Setup will continue to display the Type Your Product Key For Activation page. To let you know there's a problem with the product key, Setup displays the following warning in the lower portion of the page: "Your product key cannot be validated. Review your product key and make sure you have entered it correctly." Before you can continue, you need to change the product key so that it exactly matches the product key sticker. If you don't see the discrepancy causing the problem, you might want to delete the previously entered product key and then retype the product key. After you reenter the product key, tap or click Next to continue. As long as you enter a valid product key, you'll continue to the next page. Otherwise, you have to repeat this step.

7. If you did not enter a product key, you'll then see the warning prompt, asking whether you want to enter a product key at this time. If you tap or click Yes, you'll return to the Type Your Product Key For Activation page. If you tap or click No, you'll be allowed to continue with the installation without entering a product key.

8. You need to choose whether to perform a Server With A GUI installation or a Server Core installation. If you selected to continue without entering a product key, you'll next need to select the edition of Windows Server 2012 R2 to install, too. Although Setup will allow you to choose any edition, it is important to choose the edition that you purchased. If you choose the wrong edition, you will need to purchase that edition or reinstall the correct edition.

   NOTE

   If you enter a product key, and the server edition you want to install is not listed, tap or click the back arrow and enter the correct product key for that server edition. Keep in mind that you can continue without entering a product key, and this will allow you to choose any available edition. However, if you choose the wrong edition, you will need to purchase that edition, reinstall the correct edition, or upgrade to the correct edition.

9. The license terms for Windows Server 2012 R2 have changed from previous releases of Windows. When prompted, review the license terms. Select the I Accept The License Terms check box and then tap or click Next.

10. On the Which Type Of Installation Do You Want? page, you need to select the type of installation you want Setup to perform. Because you are performing a clean installation to replace an existing installation completely or configure a new computer, select

Custom (Advanced) as the installation type. If you started Setup from the boot prompt rather than from within Windows itself, the upgrade option is disabled. To upgrade rather than perform a clean install, you need to restart the computer and boot the currently installed operating system. After you log on, you then need to start the installation.

11. On the Where Do You Want To Install Windows? page, you need to select the disk or disk and partition on which you want to install the operating system. Windows Server 2012 R2 requires between 10 and 40 GBs of disk space for installation. Keep the following in mind:

    - When a computer has a single hard disk with a single partition encompassing the whole disk, the whole disk partition is selected by default, and you can tap or click Next to choose this as the install location. With a disk that is completely unallocated, you need to create the necessary partition for installing the operating system as discussed in "Creating, deleting, and extending disk partitions during installation" later in this chapter.
    - When a computer has multiple disks or a single disk with multiple partitions, you need either to select an existing partition to use for installing the operating system or to create one. You can create and manage partitions as discussed in "Creating, deleting, and extending disk partitions during installation" later in this chapter.
    - You might see a warning message stating, "This computer's hardware may not support booting to this disk." This can occur if the disk has not been initialized for use or if the firmware of the computer does not support starting the operating system from the selected disk. To resolve this problem, create one or more partitions on all the hard disks that are not initialized.
    - You cannot select or format a hard-disk partition that uses FAT or FAT32 or has other incompatible settings. To work around this issue, you might want to convert the partition to NTFS. Because the inability to select a disk or partition could also be due to a problem with the drivers for the hard disk, you might need to install the device drivers required by a hard disk.
    - When working with this page, you can access a command prompt to perform any necessary preinstallation tasks, to remove a disk partition forcibly that is locked, or to load device drivers to support hard disks that aren't listed as available but should be available. To learn more, see "Performing additional administration tasks during installations" later in this chapter.

12. If the partition you selected contains a previous Windows installation, Setup provides a prompt stating that existing user and application settings will be moved to a folder named Windows.old and that you must copy these settings to the new installation to use them. Tap or click OK.

13. Tap or click Next. Setup starts the installation of the operating system. During this procedure, Setup copies the full disk image of Windows Server 2012 R2 to the location you selected and then expands it. Afterward, Setup installs features based on the computer's configuration and detected hardware. This process requires several automatic restarts. When Setup finishes the installation, the operating system will be loaded and you'll see the logon screen. After you enter and confirm a password for the Administrator account, you can log on.

14. Perform initial configuration tasks by using Server Manager, such as setting the computer name and administrator password.

Use a strong password for the Administrator account

A strong password uses a combination of uppercase letters, lowercase letters, numbers, and special characters. If your administrator password does not meet the Windows Server criteria for strong passwords, a dialog box explaining the criteria for the administrator password appears, and you are given the opportunity to change the password or continue with it as is. The use of a strong password for the Administrator account is a security step well worth taking. Weak passwords remain one of the more significant ways by which the security of a Windows network is compromised, yet they are one of the easiest problems to fix.

Performing an upgrade installation

Although Windows Server 2012 R2 provides an upgrade option during installation, an upgrade with Windows Server 2012 R2 might not be your best option. Why? Not every Windows role, role service, feature, or application can be upgraded. When you start an upgrade, Setup performs compatibility checks to verify that all the components and applications installed on the computer can be upgraded. Identified issues are shown in a compatibility report.

The compatibility report will notify you about identified problems and might include guidance on what you need to do before upgrading the server. If incompatible components and applications are installed, you should stop the upgrade and take any required, corrective actions before continuing with the upgrade. Keep in mind that Setup might not identify every compatibility issue, so there might still be unidentified issues that need to be resolved. In addition, keep in mind that any files that an application cannot locate after the upgrade process might have been moved to the temporary storage directory (%SystemDrive%\$WINDOWS.~Q). Because of the challenges presented with upgrading a server, it often is more efficient to migrate services and applications a server is hosting to other servers and then perform a clean installation.

The steps you perform for an upgrade installation of Windows Server 2012 R2 are nearly identical to those you follow for a clean installation. The key difference is that in step 10, you need to select the installation type as Upgrade. If you started Setup from the boot prompt rather than from within Windows itself, the upgrade option is disabled. To upgrade rather than perform a clean install, you need to restart the computer and boot the currently installed operating system. After you log on, you then need to start the installation.

Because you are upgrading the operating system, you do not need to choose an installation location. During this process, Setup copies the full disk image of Windows Server 2012 R2 to the system disk. Afterward, Setup installs features based on the computer's configuration and detected hardware. When Setup finishes the installation, the operating system will be loaded, and you can complete the installation.

When Setup finishes the installation, you'll see the logon screen. After you log on, you can perform initial configuration tasks.

Activation sequence

After you install Windows Server 2012 R2, you should configure TCP/IP networking. If the type of licensing you are using requires product activation after installation, you have 10 days to complete online activation. If you don't, the evaluation period begins and runs for 180 days. During the evaluation period, a notification is displayed on the desktop, telling you the number of days remaining in the evaluation period (except in Windows Server 2012 R2 Essentials). You can also run **slmgr.vbs /dlv** from an elevated command prompt to see the time remaining.

You have several activation options, including activating over the Internet, by telephone, and by various automated activation techniques.

TROUBLESHOOTING

Identifying an elapsed evaluation period

During the evaluation period, the server is fully functional but cannot be booted to Safe Mode. When the evaluation period elapses, a warning appears on the desktop stating that the Windows license is expired. When you log on to Windows, you are prompted to activate Windows. If you don't activate Windows, the server will shut itself down every hour and the only updates that will be applied are security updates.

Inside OUT

Converting an evaluation license to a retail license

The evaluation period is different from installing an evaluation version of Windows. When you install an evaluation version of Windows, you also have an evaluation period of 180 days. When that time elapses, you must reinstall the server with another evaluation product or convert the license to a retail license. You can convert Windows Server 2012 R2 Essentials to the full retail version by entering a retail license, volume license, or OEM key by using the slmgr.vbs command.

For other editions, note the current edition or type the following command at an elevated prompt to determine the edition name: **DISM /online /Get-CurrentEdition**. Next, at an elevated prompt, type **DISM /online /Set-Edition:** ***EditionId*** **/ProductKey:*ProdKey* /AcceptEula**, where *EditionId* is either ServerStandard or ServerDataCenter, and *ProdKey* is the full product key including any dashes. The server will restart twice. Although you cannot convert a domain controller to a retail license, you can install an additional domain controller, assign any roles to this server, and then demote the server so that it can be converted.

Activate Windows over the Internet

Although volume-licensed versions of Windows Server 2012 R2 might not require activation or product keys, retail versions of Windows Server 2012 R2 require both activation and product keys. You can determine whether Windows Server 2012 R2 has been activated in Control Panel. To do this, perform the following steps:

1. In Control Panel, tap or click System And Security and then tap or click System.
2. On the System page, read the Windows Activation entry. This entry specifies whether you have activated the operating system.
3. If Windows Server 2012 R2 has not been activated and you are connected to the Internet, select View Details In Windows Activation and then tap or click Activate.

The computer then checks its Internet connection and attempts to activate the operating system. If this process fails, you need to resolve any issues that are preventing your computer from connecting to the Internet and then tap or click Activate again.

Activate Windows by telephone

With activation over the telephone, you can go straight to product activation by performing the following steps:

1. In Control Panel, tap or click System And Security and then tap or click System.
2. If Windows Server 2012 R2 has not been activated, select View Details In Windows Activation.
3. In the Windows Activation dialog box, tap or click Show Me Other Ways To Activate and then tap or click Use The Automated Phone System.
4. Select a geographic or country/region location and then tap or click Next to obtain a telephone number for your area. You will also get an installation ID, which is a very long string of numbers that you will need to enter in the automated customer service phone system.
5. After you call the phone number and give the installation ID, you will get an activation code, which is another long string of numbers that you have to enter on the Activate Windows page before you can continue with the activation.
6. Tap or click Next and follow the prompts to complete activation.

Using Managed Activation

You also can perform volume activation by using Key Management Service (KMS) or Active Directory. Both technologies use a client/server architecture and require you to install the Volume Activation Services role on a server running Windows Server 2012 R2 and then use Volume Activation Tools to enable and configure the technology.

With KMS, you use Volume Activation Tools to install Generic Volume License Keys or KMS client product keys, and you must specifically configure computers for KMS activation. However, Active Directory–based activation enables you to activate computers automatically, using only their domain connection. Any computer running Windows 8.1 or Windows Server 2012 R2, whether offsite or onsite, can be activated if the computer can join a domain. Activation is performed automatically when a user joins the computer to the domain.

Performing additional administration tasks during installations

Sometimes, you forget to perform a preinstallation task prior to starting the installation. Rather than restarting the operating system, you can access a command prompt from within Setup or use advanced drive options to perform the necessary administrative tasks.

Accessing a command prompt during installation

When you access a command prompt from within Setup, you access the Windows Preinstallation Environment (Windows PE) that Setup uses to install the operating system. During installation, you can access a command prompt at any time by pressing Shift+F10. As Table 2-2 shows, Windows PE gives you access to many of the same command-line tools that are available in a standard installation of Windows Server 2012 R2.

Table 2-2 Commands available in the Windows PE

Command	Description
Arp	Displays and modifies the IP-to-physical address translation tables the Address Resolution Protocol (ARP) uses.
Assoc	Displays and modifies file-extension associations.
Attrib	Displays and changes file attributes.
Cacls	Displays or modifies access control lists of files.
Call	Calls a script or script label as a procedure.
CD/Chdir	Displays the name of the current directory or changes its name.
Chcp	Displays or sets the active code page number.
Chkdsk	Checks a disk for errors and displays a report.
Chkntfs	Displays the status of volumes. It sets or excludes volumes from automatic system checking when the computer is started.
Choice	Creates a selection list from which users can select a choice in batch scripts.
Cls	Clears the console window.
Cmd	Starts a new instance of the Windows command shell.
Color	Sets the colors of the command-shell window.
Comp	Compares the contents of two files or sets of files.
Compact	Displays or modifies the compression of files or sets of files.
Convert	Converts FAT volumes to NTFS.
Copy	Copies or combines files.
Date	Displays or sets the system date.
Del	Deletes one or more files.
Dir	Displays a list of files and subdirectories within a directory.
Diskcomp	Compares the contents of two floppy disks.
Diskcopy	Copies the contents of one floppy disk to another.
Diskpart	Invokes a text-mode command interpreter so that you can manage disks, partitions, and volumes by using a separate command prompt and commands that are internal to Diskpart.

Command	Description
DISM	Services and manages Windows images.
Doskey	Edits command lines, recalls Windows commands, and creates macros.
Echo	Displays messages or turns command echoing on or off.
Endlocal	Ends localization of environment changes in a batch file.
Erase	See the entry for Del.
Exit	Exits the command interpreter.
Expand	Uncompresses files.
FC	Compares two files and displays the differences between them.
Find/Findstr	Searches for a text string in files.
For	Runs a specified command for each file in a set of files.
Format	Formats a floppy disk or hard drive.
Ftp	Transfers files.
Ftype	Displays or modifies file types used in file-extension associations.
Goto	Directs the Windows command interpreter to a labeled line in a script.
Graftabl	Enables Windows to display extended character sets in graphics mode.
Hostname	Prints the computer's name.
IF	Performs conditional processing in batch programs.
Ipconfig	Displays TCP/IP configuration.
Label	Creates, changes, or deletes the volume label of a disk.
Md/Mkdir	Creates a directory or subdirectory.
Mode	Configures a system device.
More	Displays output one screen at a time.
Mountvol	Manages the volume mount point.
Move	Moves files from one directory to another directory on the same drive.
Nbtstat	Displays status of NetBIOS.
Net Accounts	Manages user account and password policies.
Net Computer	Adds computers to or removes computers from a domain.
Net Config Server	Displays or modifies the configuration of the Server service.
Net Config Workstation	Displays or modifies the configuration of the Workstation service.
Net Continue	Resumes a paused service.
Net File	Displays or manages open files on a server.
Net Group	Displays or manages global groups.
Net Localgroup	Displays or manages local group accounts.

Command	Description
Net Pause	Suspends a service.
Net Print	Displays or manages print jobs and shared queues.
Net Session	Lists or disconnects sessions.
Net Share	Displays or manages shared printers and directories.
Net Start	Lists or starts network services.
Net Statistics	Displays workstation and server statistics.
Net Stop	Stops services.
Net Time	Displays or synchronizes network time.
Net Use	Displays or manages remote connections.
Net User	Displays or manages local user accounts.
Net View	Displays network resources or computers.
Netsh	Invokes a separate command prompt that enables you to manage the configuration of various network services on local and remote computers.
Netstat	Displays the status of network connections.
Path	Displays or sets a search path for executable files in the current command window.
Pathping	Traces routes and provides packet loss information.
Pause	Suspends processing of a script and waits for keyboard input.
Ping	Determines whether a network connection can be established.
Popd	Changes to the directory Pushd stores.
Print	Prints a text file.
Prompt	Changes the Windows command prompt.
Pushd	Saves the current directory and then changes to a new directory.
Rd/Rmdir	Removes a directory.
Recover	Recovers readable information from a bad or defective disk.
Reg Add	Adds a new subkey or entry to the registry.
Reg Compare	Compares registry subkeys or entries.
Reg Copy	Copies a registry entry to a specified key path on a local or remote system.
Reg Delete	Deletes a subkey or entries from the registry.
Reg Query	Lists the entries under a key and the names of subkeys (if any).
Reg Restore	Writes saved subkeys and entries back to the registry.
Reg Save	Saves a copy of specified subkeys, entries, and values to a file.
Regsvr32	Registers and unregisters dynamic-link libraries (DLLs).

Command	Description
Rem	Adds comments to scripts.
Ren	Renames a file.
Replace	Replaces a file.
Route	Manages network routing tables.
Set	Displays or modifies Windows environment variables. It's also used to evaluate numeric expressions at the command line.
Setlocal	Begins the localization of environment changes in a batch file.
Sfc	Scans and verifies protected operating system files.
Shift	Shifts the position of replaceable parameters in scripts.
Start	Starts a new command-shell window to run a specified program or command.
Subst	Maps a path to a drive letter.
Time	Displays or sets the system time.
Title	Sets the title for the command-shell window.
Tracert	Displays the path between computers.
Tree	Graphically displays the directory structure of a drive or path.
Type	Displays the contents of a text file.
Ver	Displays the Windows version.
Verify	Tells Windows whether to verify that your files are written correctly to a disk.
Vol	Displays a disk volume label and serial number.
Xcopy	Copies files and directories.

Forcing disk-partition removal during installation

During installation, you might be unable to select the hard disk you want to use. This issue can occur if the hard-disk partition contains an invalid byte-offset value. To resolve this issue, you need to remove the partitions on the hard disk (which destroys all associated data) and then create the necessary partitions by using the advanced options in the Setup program. During installation, on the Where Do You Want To Install Windows? page, you can remove unrecognized hard-disk partitions by following these steps:

1. Press Shift+F10 to start a command prompt. At the command prompt, type **diskpart**. This starts the DiskPart utility.

2. To view a list of disks on the computer, type **list disk**. Select a disk by typing **select disk *DiskNumber***, where *DiskNumber* is the number of the disk you want to work with.

3. To remove the partitions on the selected disk permanently, type **clean**. When the cleaning process finishes, type **create partition primary size=*N***, where *N* is the size of the space you want to allocate to the partition in megabytes.
4. When the create-partition process finishes, tap or click the back arrow button in the Install Windows dialog box. This returns you to the previous window.
5. On the Which Type Of Installation Do You Want? page, tap or click Custom (Advanced) to start a custom install.
6. On the Where Do You Want To Install Windows? page, tap or click the disk you previously cleaned to select it as the install partition. You can then continue with the installation as discussed previously.

Loading mass storage drivers during installation

During installation, on the Where Do You Want To Install Windows? page, you can use the Load Drivers option to load the device drivers for a hard disk drive. Typically, you use this option when a disk drive you want to use for installing the operating system isn't available for selection because the device drivers aren't available.

To load the device drivers and make the hard disk available for use during installation, follow these steps:

1. During installation, on the Where Do You Want To Install Windows? page, tap or click Load Driver.
2. When prompted, insert the installation media or USB flash drive, and then tap or click OK. Setup will then search the computer's removable media drives for the device drivers.
3. If Setup finds multiple device drivers, select the driver to install and then tap or click Next.
    a. If Setup doesn't find the device driver, tap or click Browse to use the Browse For Folder dialog box to select the device driver to load, tap or click OK, and then tap or click Next.

You can use the Rescan button to have Setup rescan the computer's removable media drives for the device drivers. If you are unable to install a device driver successfully, tap or click the back arrow button in the upper-left corner of the Install Windows dialog box to go back to the previous page.

Creating, deleting, and extending disk partitions during installation

When you are performing a clean installation and have started the computer from the distribution media, the Where Do You Want To Install Windows? page has additional options. You can display these options by tapping or clicking Drive Options (Advanced). These additional options are used as follows:

- **New.** Creates a partition. You must then format the partition.
- **Format.** Formats a new partition so that you can use it for installing the operating system.
- **Delete.** Deletes a partition that is no longer wanted.
- **Extend.** Extends a partition to increase its size.

Creating a partition is the key task you need to perform, but you can also delete and extend partitions as necessary. You generally don't need to format partitions because Setup will handle this for you. If the advanced options aren't available, you can still work with the computer's disks by following these steps:

1. Press Shift+F10 to open a command prompt. At the command prompt, type **diskpart**. This starts the DiskPart utility.
2. To view a list of disks on the computer, type **list disk**.
3. Select a disk by typing **select disk *DiskNumber***, where *DiskNumber* is the number of the disk you want to work with.
4. List the existing partitions on the disk by typing **list partition**. You can now do the following:
   - **Create a partition.** Use available space to create a partition by typing **create partition primary size=*N***, where *N* is the size of the space to allocate in megabytes.
   - **Delete a partition.** Select the partition to delete by typing **select partition** followed by the partition number and then delete it by typing **delete partition**.
   - **Extend a partition.** Select the partition to extend by typing **select partition**, followed by the partition number, and then extend it by typing **extend size=*N***, where *N* is the size of the additional space to allocate in megabytes.
5. When you are finished working with disks, tap or click the back arrow button in the Install Windows dialog box. This will return you to the previous window.

6. On the Which Type Of Installation Do You Want? page, tap or click Custom (Advanced) to start a custom install.

7. On the Where Do You Want To Install Windows? page, tap or click the disk you previously cleaned to select it as the install partition. You can then continue with the installation as discussed previously.

Troubleshooting installation

Most of the time, installation completes normally and the Windows operating system starts without any problems. Some of the time, however, installation won't complete or, after installation, the server won't start up, and you must troubleshoot to figure out what's happening. The good news is that installation problems are usually the result of something simple. The bad news is that simple problems are sometimes the hardest to find.

NOTE

For more information about troubleshooting and recovery, see Chapter 21, "Backup and recovery," in *Windows Server 2012 R2 Inside Out: Services, Security, and Infrastructure* (Microsoft Press, 2014). Beyond that, you'll also find troubleshooters in the Help And Support console and in the Microsoft Knowledge Base, which is available online at *http://support.microsoft.com/*. Both are good resources for troubleshooting.

Start with the potential points of failure

Setup can fail for a variety of reasons, but more often than not it's because of incompatible hardware components or the failure of the system to meet the minimum requirements for a Windows Server 2012 R2 installation. With this in mind, start troubleshooting by looking at the potential points of failure and how these failure points can be resolved.

Setup refuses to install or start

If a hardware component is incompatible with Windows Server 2012 R2, this could cause the failure of the installation or a failure to start up after installation. Make sure that Windows Server 2012 R2 is detecting the system hardware and that the hardware is in the Windows Server Catalog or on the Hardware Compatibility List (HCL). As discussed previously, you can perform a compatibility check prior to installing Windows Server 2012 R2.

After you start the installation, however, it's too late. At this point, you have several choices. You can reboot to a working operating system and then restart the installation from the command prompt, using Setup and one of the following debugging options:

- **/1394debug:<*channel*>.** Enables kernel debugging over a FireWire (IEEE 1394) port on a specific channel

- **/debug:<*port*>.** Enables kernel debugging over a COM1 or COM2 port
- **/usbdebug:<*target*>.** Enables kernel debugging over a USB port to a specific target device

These options put Setup in debug mode, which can help you identify what is going wrong. If Setup determines you have hardware conflicts, you can try to configure the hardware and server firmware to eliminate the conflicts. Troubleshooting firmware involves booting the server to the firmware and then completing the following steps:

- **Examine the boot order of disk devices.** You might want to configure the system so that it boots first from DVD-ROM. Watch out, though; after installation, don't keep booting to DVD-ROM thinking you are booting to the operating system—hey, we all get tired and sometimes we just have to stop and think for a moment. If the installation problem is that you keep going back to the installation screen after installing the operating system, you are probably inadvertently booting from DVD-ROM—and you're probably way too tired by now to realize it.
- **Check Plug and Play device configuration and interrupt reservations.** If a system has older components or components that aren't Plug and Play compatible, you might have a device conflict for a hard-coded interrupt. For example, a non–Plug and Play sound card could be hard-coded to use interrupt 13, which is already in use by a Plug and Play device. To work around this, you must configure interrupt 13 under your Plug and Play BIOS settings to be reserved for a non–Plug and Play device. This ensures that Plug and Play does not attempt to use that interrupt and resolves the issue in most cases.

  NOTE

  The only sure way to avoid problems with non–Plug and Play devices is to avoid using them altogether.

Rather than spending time—which could run into several hours—trying to troubleshoot a hardware conflict, you might consider removing the hardware component if it's nonessential—and you might be surprised at what I consider nonessential at this stage. By nonessential, I mean most anything that isn't needed to start up and give you a display for logon. You probably don't need a network card, a sound card, a multimedia controller card, a video coder/decoder (codec), or a removable media drive. If these items are incompatible, you might resolve the problem just by removing them. You can always try to install the components again after installation is complete.

Setup reports a media or DVD-ROM error

When you install directly from the Windows Server 2012 R2 DVD-ROM or perform a network install from a distribution share, you might encounter a media error that causes Setup to fail.

With an actual DVD-ROM, you might need to clean the DVD-ROM so that it can be read or use a different DVD drive. If a computer's sole DVD-ROM drive is the problem, you must replace the drive or install from a distribution share. If you are working with a distribution share, the share might not have all the necessary files, or you might encounter problems connecting to the share. Try using an actual DVD-ROM.

Setup reports insufficient system resources

Windows Server 2012 R2 requires a minimum of 512 MBs of RAM and about 32 GBs of disk space. If the system doesn't have enough memory, Setup won't start. If Setup starts and detects that there isn't enough space, it might not continue, or you might need to create a new partition or delete an existing partition to get enough free space to install the operating system.

Continue past lockups and freezes

If you can get past the potential points of failure, you still might find that the installation locks up or freezes. In this case, you might get a stop error; then again, you might not.

Most stop errors have cryptic error codes rather than clear messages telling you what's wrong. If you get a stop error, write down the error number or code and then refer to the Microsoft Knowledge Base (available online at *http://support.microsoft.com/*) for help troubleshooting the problem. To break out of the stop, you most likely will have to press Ctrl+Alt+Delete (sometimes several times) to get the server to restart. If this doesn't break out of the stop, press and hold the power button on the server until it reboots. Alternatively, disconnect the system power, wait a few seconds, and then connect it again.

The Windows operating system should start up and go directly back to Setup. In some cases, you will see a boot menu. If so, choose Windows Setup to allow the Setup program to attempt to continue the installation. Setup could freeze again. If it does, stay with it and repeat this process—sometimes it takes several tries to get completely through the installation process.

RAM and CPUs can also be the source of problems. Issues to watch out for include the following:

- **Incompatible RAM.** Not all RAM is compatible, and you can't mix and match RAM of different speeds and types. Ensure that all RAM modules are the same type and speed. Further, in some cases, RAM modules from different manufacturers can perform differently (read incompatibly). In such a case, try changing the RAM so that all modules are from the same manufacturer.
- **Malfunctioning RAM.** Static discharges can ruin RAM faster than anything else can. If you didn't ground yourself and use a static discharge wire before working with the RAM modules, you could have inadvertently fried the RAM so that the modules don't work at

all or are malfunctioning. RAM could have also arrived in this condition from the manufacturer or distributor. There are several troubleshooting techniques for determining this. You could update firmware to add a wait state to the RAM so that if the RAM is partially faulty, the system will still boot (but you still must replace the RAM eventually). You can also try removing some RAM modules or changing their order.

- **Incompatible processors.** Not all processors are created equal, and I'm not just talking about their speed in megahertz (which you generally want to be the same for all processors on a server). Some processors might have a cache or configuration that is incompatible with the server hardware or other processors. Check the processor speed and type to ensure that they are compatible with the server. In some cases, you might need to change hardware jumpers, depending on the speed and type of your processors.

- **Misconfigured processors.** Adding processors to a server isn't a simple matter of inserting them. Often, you must change jumpers on the hardware, remove several terminators (one for a power subcomponent and one for the processor—and save them because, trust me, you might find that you need them), and then insert the new components. Check the hardware jumpers (even if you think there aren't any), and ensure that the processors and the power subcomponents you added are seated properly. If you can't get the installation to continue or the server to start up, you might need to remove the components you added. Watch out, though; you probably don't want to continue the installation until the processor issue is resolved—single-processor systems have a different threading and default configuration than multiprocessor systems, meaning this situation might not be a simple matter of adding the processor after installation and making it all work properly.

- **System processor cache problems.** Sometimes, there can be an issue with the system processor cache and its compatibility with Windows Server 2012 R2. Consult the server documentation to determine the correct configuration settings and how the cache can be disabled. If you suspect a problem with this, boot to firmware and temporarily disable the system processor cache, following the server documentation. After the installation is complete, you should be able to enable the cache to avoid a performance hit. Be sure to check both the hardware vendor support site and the Microsoft Knowledge Base to see whether any known issues with your server's processor cache exist.

TROUBLESHOOTING

RAM and CPUs are incompatible

You might be surprised at how common it is for incompatible RAM or CPUs to present problems, especially when installing enterprise-class servers. We had a problem once when we ordered all the components from a single hardware vendor that had verified the compatibility of every element down to the last detail, only to find that the wrong processors and RAM were shipped for the systems ordered. The result was that every

time we added the additional processors and RAM modules, the server wouldn't start up. The only recourse was to continue installation with the minimum processor and RAM configurations shipped or wait until replacements arrived. Electing to wait for replacements added time to the project but ultimately proved to be the right decision. You can bet that we were glad that we padded the project schedule to allow for the unexpected—because the unexpected usually happens.

Most of the time, the installation or setup problem is caused by a compatibility issue with the Windows operating system, and that problem can be fixed by making changes to firmware settings. Sometimes, however, the problem is the firmware, and you'll find that you must upgrade the firmware to resolve the problem.

Check with the hardware vendor to see whether a firmware upgrade is available. If so, install it as the hardware vendor directs. If a new firmware version isn't available, you might be able to disable the incompatible option prior to setup. If this doesn't work, the option you changed wasn't the source of the problem, and you should reenable it before continuing.

NOTE

Reenabling the option might be necessary because some hardware-specific firmware settings cannot be changed after the installation. Thus, the only way to enable the option would be to reinstall the operating system.

Finally, hard-disk-drive settings could also cause lockups or freezes, particularly if you are using Integrated Device Electronics (IDE) drives. When using IDE drives and controllers, you want to ensure that the system recognizes both the drives and the controllers and that both are enabled and configured properly in firmware. You might have to check jumper settings on the drives and the cables that connect the drives. As discussed previously, check for conflicts among the drives, controllers, and other system components. You might need to remove unnecessary components, such as the sound card, temporarily to see whether this resolves a conflict. If a DVD drive is on the same channel as the disk drives, try moving it to the secondary channel and configuring it as a master device. You can also try lowering the data transfer rate for the IDE drives.

Postinstallation tasks

After you've installed a server and logged on, you might be ready to call it a day. Don't do this yet because you should first perform a few final postinstallation procedures. The Tools menu in Server Manager gives you quick access to tools for administration. Using Server Manager as your starting point, you can do the following:

- **Check devices.** Select Device Manager on the Tools menu and then use Device Manager, as discussed in Chapter 7, "Managing and troubleshooting hardware" under

"Viewing device and driver details," to look for undetected or malfunctioning hardware components. If you find problems, you might need to download and install updated drivers for the computer—you can download them from another system and then transfer the files to the new server by using a USB key or by burning the files to a CD/DVD-ROM. If you removed any system hardware prior to installation, you might want to add it back in and then check again for conflicts and issues that must be corrected. You aren't finished with Device Manager until every piece of hardware is working properly.

- **Check the TCP/IP configuration.** When you select the Local Server node in Server Manager, you'll see the server's basic configuration settings. Tap or click the links for the Ethernet settings to open the Network Connections dialog box. Ensure that the TCP/IP configuration is correct and that any additional settings are applied as necessary for the network. Test TCP/IP networking from the command line by using Ping or Tracert and in the Windows operating system by trying to browse the network.

- **Check event logs.** When you select the Dashboard node, you'll see an entry for Local Server. If there are errors or critical events, you can tap or click Events to review them. You also can use the Events panel under Local Server and the Event Viewer to check the Windows event logs. Any startup warnings or errors will be written to the logs. See Chapter 10, "Performance monitoring and tuning," for details.

- **Check disk partitioning.** Select Computer Management on the Tools menu and then use the Computer Management console to check and finalize the disk partitions. Often, you must create the server's application partition or configure software RAID. See Chapter 12 for details.

- **Optimize system configuration.** Follow the techniques discussed in Chapter 4, "Managing Windows Server 2012 R2," for tuning the operating system. For example, you might need to change the display settings, virtual memory pagefile usage, or the Server service configuration. You might also need to add local group and user accounts to the server in accordance with standard IT procedures.

- **Update the server.** Use Windows Update or Windows Server Update Services to ensure that the operating system is up to date and has the most recent updates for stability and security. When Windows Update is configured properly, you can tap or click the Windows Update link on the Local Server node and then tap or click Check For Updates to get updates for the server.

- **Reboot for good measure.** After you configure the server and optimize its settings, perform a final reboot to ensure that (1) the server starts, (2) all the server services start, and (3) no other errors occur. You should reboot even if the changes you made don't require it—it's better to find out about problems now than at 3 A.M. on a Sunday morning.

- **Prepare backup and recovery.** You're almost done. Don't forget about creating an automated recovery disk for the server. You might also want to perform a full backup.

These postinstallation procedures are not only important; they're also essential to ensuring that the server performs as well as can be expected. After these procedures are completed, you should have a server that is nearly ready for its role in a production environment. Don't make the server available to users just yet. To finish the job, you need to install and configure any necessary roles, role services, features, and applications. For certain, configuring these components requires quite a bit of extra work beyond installing the operating system. The installation of these additional components and applications could require one or more reboots or might require several periods during which users are blocked from accessing the server or are requested not to connect to it. Remember, from the users' perspective, it's usually better not to have a resource than to be given one and then have it taken away (even temporarily). Finalize the server and then deploy it, and you'll have happier users.

As discussed earlier in the chapter, you can convert the installation type. To convert a Full Server installation to a Minimal Server Interface installation, you remove the Server Graphical Shell. Although you can use the Remove Roles And Features Wizard to do this, you also can do it at a Windows PowerShell prompt by typing the following command:

```
uninstall-windowsfeature server-gui-shell -restart
```

This command instructs Windows Server to uninstall the Server Graphical Shell and restart the server to finalize the removal. If Desktop Experience also is installed, this feature will be removed also.

To convert a Minimal Server Interface installation to a Server With A GUI installation, you add the Server Graphical Shell. You can use the Add Roles And Features Wizard to do this, or you can type the following command at a Windows PowerShell prompt:

```
install-windowsfeature server-gui-shell -restart
```

This command instructs Windows Server to install the Server Graphical Shell and restart the server to finalize the installation. If you also want to install the Desktop Experience, you can use this command instead:

```
install-windowsfeature server-gui-shell, desktop-experience -restart
```

To convert a Full Server or Minimal Server Interface installation to a Server Core installation, you remove the user interfaces for Graphical Management Tools And Infrastructure. If you remove the WOW64 Support framework, you also convert the server to a Server Core installation. Although you can use the Remove Roles And Features Wizard to remove the user interfaces, you also can do this at a Windows PowerShell prompt by typing the following command:

```
uninstall-windowsfeature server-gui-mgmt-infra -restart
```

This command instructs Windows Server to uninstall the user interfaces for Graphical Management Tools And Infrastructure and restart the server to finalize the removal. Here, a removal of Server-GUI-Shell is implied because this feature depends on the Server-GUI-Mgmt-Infra feature. Because other GUI-dependent roles, role services, and features might be uninstalled along with the user interfaces, run the command with the *–Whatif* parameter first to get details on what exactly will be uninstalled.

If you installed the server with the user interfaces and converted it to a Server Core installation, you can revert to a Full Server installation with the following command:

```
install-windowsfeature server-gui-mgmt-infra, server-gui-shell -restart
```

This command installs the Server-GUI-Shell and Server-GUI-Mgmt-Infra features. As long as the binaries for this feature and any dependent features haven't been removed, the command should succeed. If the binaries were removed, however, or Server Core was the original installation type, you need to specify a source for the required binaries. If you don't do this, the required feature will be downloaded from Windows Update, which could take a long time for some features.

You use the *–Source* parameter to restore required binaries from a WIM mount point. For example, if your enterprise has a mounted Windows image for the edition of Windows Server 2012 R2 you are working with available at the network path \\ImServer18\WinS12EE, you could specify the source as follows:

```
install-windowsfeature server-gui-mgmt-infra, server-gui-shell
-source \\imserver18\wins12ee
```

Although many large enterprises might have standard images that can be mounted using network paths, you can also mount the Windows Server 2012 R2 distribution media and then use the Windows\WinSXS folder from the installation image as your source. To do this, follow these steps:

1. Insert the installation disc into the server's disc drive and then create a folder to mount the installation image by typing the following command: **mkdir c:\mountdir**.

2. Locate the index number of the image you want to use by typing the following command at an elevated prompt: **dism /get-wiminfo /wimfile:e:\sources\install .wim**, where *e:* is the drive designator of the server's disc drive.

3. Mount the installation image by typing the following command at an elevated prompt: **dism /mount-wim /wimfile:e:\sources\install.wim /index:2 /mountdir:c:\mountdir**

/readonly, where *e:* is the drive designator of the server's disc drive, *2* is the index of the image to use, and *c:\mountdir* is the mount directory. Mounting the image might take several minutes.

4. Use Install-WindowsFeature at a Windows PowerShell prompt with the source specified as **c:\mountdir\windows\winsxs**, as shown in this example:

```
install-windowsfeature server-gui-mgmt-infra, server-gui-shell
-source c:\mountdir\windows\winsxs
```

CHAPTER 3
Boot configuration

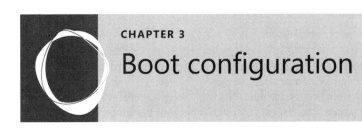

Unlike early releases of server operating systems for Microsoft Windows, Windows Server 2012 R2 doesn't boot from an initialization file. Instead, the operating system uses the Windows Boot Manager to initialize and start the operating system. The boot environment dramatically changes the way the operating system starts, and it is designed to resolve issues related to boot integrity, operating system integrity, and firmware abstraction. The boot environment is loaded prior to the operating system, making it a pre–operating system environment. This ensures that the boot environment can be used to validate the integrity of the startup process and the operating system itself before actually starting the operating system.

Boot from hardware and firmware

At first glance, startup and shutdown seem to be the most basic features of an operating system, but as you get a better understanding of how computers work, you quickly see that there's nothing simple or basic about startup, shutdown, or related processes and procedures. In fact, anyone who's worked with computers probably has had a problem with startup or shutdown at one time or another. Problems with startup and shutdown can be compounded in modern computers because of their extended frameworks for advanced configuration and power management in firmware and hardware.

NOTE

Many administrators install Windows Server 2012 R2 on desktop-class systems without giving careful consideration to how this could affect the operation of the computer. When you install Windows Server 2012 R2 on a desktop-class system, it is critically important for you to understand how computers designed for desktop operating systems handle advanced configuration and power management in hardware and firmware. This will enable you to modify the hardware and firmware settings so that they work better with Windows Server 2012 R2.

Hardware and firmware power states

Before the boot environment is loaded, computers start up from hardware and firmware. Windows desktop operating systems do things a bit differently from Windows Server operating systems when it comes to power-state management features. In Windows desktops, turning off a computer and shutting down a computer are separate tasks. By default, when you turn off a computer running a Windows desktop operating system, the computer enters standby mode. When entering standby mode, the operating system automatically saves all work, turns off the display, and enters a low power-consumption mode with the computer's fans and hard disks stopped. The state of the computer is maintained in the computer's memory. When the computer wakes from standby mode, its state is exactly as it was when you turned off your computer.

You can turn off a computer running a Windows desktop operating system and enter standby mode by tapping or clicking the Settings charm, tapping or clicking Power, and then tapping or clicking Sleep. To wake the computer from the standby state, you can press the power button on the computer's case or a key on the computer's keyboard. Moving the mouse also wakes the computer.

If you install Windows 8.1 or Windows Server 2012 R2 on a mobile computer, the computer's power state can be changed by closing the lid. By default with Windows 8.1, the computer enters the standby state when you close the lid. By default with Windows Server 2012 R2, the computer doesn't change its power state when you close or open the lid, but you can configure the server to shut down when you close the lid.

There are, however, a few gotchas with the power button and the standby state in Windows desktop operating systems. The way the power button works depends on the following:

- **System hardware.** For the power button to work, the computer hardware must support the standby state. If the computer hardware doesn't support the standby state, the computer can't use it, and turning off the computer powers it down completely.
- **System state.** For the power button to work, the system must be in a valid state. If the computer has installed updates that require a reboot or you've installed programs that require a reboot, the computer can't enter the standby state, and turning off the computer powers it down completely.
- **System configuration.** For the power button to work, sleep mode must be enabled. If you reconfigured the power options on the computer and set the power button to Shut Down, the computer can't use the standby state, and turning it off powers it down completely.

You can determine exactly how the power options are configured on a computer running Windows by tapping or clicking the Settings charm, tapping or clicking Control Panel, and tapping or clicking Power Options. The available options depend on the type of computing device.

Diagnosing hardware and firmware startup problems

Whether you are working with a Windows desktop operating system or a Windows Server operating system when trying to diagnose and resolve startup problems, be sure to keep in mind that power-state management capabilities are provided by the hardware but are enabled by the operating system. Because of this, to diagnose and resolve boot issues fully, you must look at the computer's hardware and software, including the following items:

- Motherboard/chipset
- Firmware
- Operating system

To understand the hardware aspects of boot issues better, let's dig in and take a look at Advanced Configuration and Power Interface (ACPI). A computer's motherboard/chipset, firmware, and operating system must support ACPI for the advanced power-state features to work. There are many types of motherboards/chipsets. Although older motherboards/chipsets might not be updateable, most of the newer ones have updateable firmware. Chipset firmware is separate from and different from the computer's underlying firmware interface.

Currently, there are three prevalent firmware interfaces:

- Basic Input Output System (BIOS)
- Extensible Firmware Interface (EFI)
- Unified Extensible Firmware Interface (UEFI)

A computer's BIOS, EFI, or UEFI programming provides the hardware-level interface between hardware components and software. Like chipsets themselves, BIOS, EFI, and UEFI can be updated. ACPI-aware components track the power state of the computer. An ACPI-aware operating system can generate a request for the system to be switched into a different ACPI mode. BIOS, EFI, or UEFI responds to enable the requested ACPI mode.

ACPI 4.0 was finalized in June 2009, and ACPI 5.0 was finalized in December 2011. Computers manufactured prior to this time will likely not have fully compliant firmware, and you will probably need to update the firmware when a compatible revision becomes available. In some cases, and especially with older hardware, you might not be able to update a computer's firmware to make it fully compliant with ACPI 4.0 or ACPI 5.0. For example, if you are configuring the power options, and you don't have minimum and maximum processor-state options, the computer's firmware isn't fully compatible with ACPI 3.0 and likely will not fully support

ACPI 4.0 or ACPI 5.0 either. Still, you should check the hardware manufacturer's website for firmware updates.

ACPI defines active and passive cooling modes. These cooling modes are inversely related to each other:

- Passive cooling reduces system performance but is quieter because there's less fan noise. With passive cooling, Windows lessens power consumption to reduce the operating temperature of the computer but at the cost of system performance. Windows reduces the processor speed in an attempt to cool the computer before increasing fan speed, which would increase power consumption.
- Active cooling allows maximum system performance. With active cooling, Windows increases power consumption to reduce the temperature of the machine. Windows increases fan speed to cool the computer before attempting to reduce processor speed.

Power policy includes upper and lower limits for the processor state, referred to as the *maximum processor state* and the *minimum processor state*, respectively. These states are implemented by using a feature of ACPI 3.0 and later versions called *processor throttling*, and they determine the range of currently available processor performance states that Windows can use. By setting the maximum and minimum values, you define the bounds for the allowed performance states, or you can use the same value for each to force the system to remain in a specific performance state. Windows reduces power consumption by throttling the processor speed. For example, if the upper bound is 100 percent and the lower bound is 5 percent, Windows can throttle the processor within this range as workloads permit to reduce power consumption. In a computer with a 3 GHz processor, Windows would adjust the operating frequency of the processor between 0.15 GHz and 3.0 GHz.

Processor throttling and related performance states were introduced with early Windows operating systems, but these early implementations were designed for computers with discrete-socketed processors and not for computers with processor cores. As a result, they are not effective in reducing the power consumption of computers with logical processors. Beginning with Windows 7 and Windows Server 2008 R2, Windows reduces power consumption in computers with multicore processors by using a feature of ACPI 4.0 called *logical processor idling* and by updating processor-throttling features to work with processor cores.

Logical processor idling is designed to ensure that Windows uses the fewest processor cores for a given workload. Windows accomplishes this by consolidating workloads onto the fewest cores possible and suspending inactive processor cores. When additional processing power is required, Windows activates inactive processor cores. This idling functionality works in conjunction with the management of process performance states at the core level.

ACPI defines processor performance states, referred to as *p-states*, and processor idle sleep states, referred to as *c-states*. Processor performance states include P0 (the processor or core uses its maximum performance capability and can consume maximum power), P1 (the processor or core is limited below its maximum and consumes less than maximum power), and P*n* (where state *n* is a maximum number that is processor dependent, and the processor or core is at its minimal level and consumes minimal power while remaining in an active state).

Processor-idle sleep states include C0 (the processor or core can execute instructions), C1 (the processor or core has the lowest latency and is in a nonexecuting power state), C2 (the processor or core has longer latency to improve power savings over the C1 state), and C3 (the processor or core has the longest latency to improve power savings over the C1 and C2 states).

NOTE

Windows switches processors or cores between any p-state and from the C1 state to the C0 state nearly instantaneously (fractions of milliseconds) and tends not to use the deep sleep states, so you don't need to worry about the performance impact of throttling or waking up processors or cores. The processors or cores are available when they are needed. That said, the easiest way to limit processor power management is to modify the active power plan and set the minimum and maximum processor states to 100 percent.

Windows saves power by putting processor cores in and out of appropriate p-states and c-states. On a computer with four logical processors, Windows might use p-states 0 to 5, where P0 allows 100 percent usage, P1 allows 90 percent usage, P2 allows 80 percent usage, P3 allows 70 percent usage, P4 allows 60 percent usage, and P5 allows 50 percent usage. When the computer is active, logical processor 0 would likely be active with a p-state of 0 to 5, and the other processors would likely be at an appropriate p-state or in a sleep state.

Inside OUT

Processor idling

Logical processor idling reduces power consumption by removing a logical processor from the operating system's list of non–processor affinitized work. However, because processor-affinitized work reduces the effectiveness of this feature, you'll want to plan carefully prior to configuring processing-affinity settings for applications. You can use Windows System Resource Manager to manage processor resources through percent-processor-usage targets and processor-affinity rules. However, both techniques reduce the effectiveness of logical processor idling. Note also that Windows System Resource Manager is deprecated for Windows Server 2012 R2 and will be phased out in future releases of Windows Server.

ACPI 4.0 and ACPI 5.0 define four global power states. In G0, the working state (in which software runs), power consumption is at its highest, and latency is at its lowest. In G1, the sleeping state (in which software doesn't run), latency varies with the sleep state, and power consumption is less than the G0 state. In G2 (also referred to as *S5 sleep state*), the soft off state when the operating system doesn't run, latency is long, and power consumption is very near zero. In G3, the mechanical off state (in which the operating system doesn't run), latency is long, and power consumption is zero. There's also a special global state, known as *S4 nonvolatile sleep*, in which the operating system writes all system context to a file on nonvolatile storage media, allowing the system context to be saved and restored.

Within the global sleeping state, G1, are the sleep-state variations summarized in Table 3-1. S1 is a sleeping state in which the entire system context is maintained. S2 is a sleeping state similar to S1 except that the CPU and system-cache contexts are lost, and control starts from a reset. S3 is a sleeping state in which all CPU, cache, and chipset contexts are lost, and hardware maintains the memory context and restores some CPU and L2 cache configuration context. S4 is a sleeping state in which it is assumed that the hardware has powered off all devices to reduce power usage to a minimum, and only the platform context is maintained. S5 is a sleeping state in which it is assumed that the hardware is in a soft off state, in which no context is maintained, and a complete boot is required when the system wakes.

Table 3-1 **Power states for ACPI in firmware and hardware**

State	Type	Description
S0	ON state	The system is completely operational, fully powered, and completely retains the context (such as the volatile registers, memory caches, and RAM).
S1	Sleep state	The system consumes less power in this state than in the S0 state. All hardware and processor contexts are maintained.
S2	Sleep state	The system consumes less power in this state than in the S1 state. The processor loses power, and the processor context and contents of the cache are lost.
S3	Sleep state	The system consumes less power in this state than in the S2 state. The processor and hardware contexts, cache contents, and chipset context are lost. The system memory is retained.
S4	Hibernate state	The system consumes the least power in this state compared to all other sleep states. The system is almost in an OFF state. The context data is written to hard disk, and no context is retained. The system can restart from the context data stored on the disk.
S5	OFF state	The system is in a shutdown state, and the system retains no context. The system requires a full reboot to start.

Motherboard chipsets support specific power states. For example, a motherboard might support the S0, S1, S4, and S5 states, but it might not support the S2 or S3 states. In Windows operating systems, the *sleep power transition* refers to switching off the system to a Sleep or Hibernate mode, and the *wake power transition* refers to switching on the system from a Sleep or Hibernate mode. The Sleep and Hibernate modes allow users to switch off and switch on systems much faster than the regular shutdown and startup processes.

Thus, a computer is waking up when the computer is transitioning from the OFF state (S5) or any sleep state (S1–S4) to the ON state (S0), and the computer is going to sleep when the computer is transitioning from the ON state (S0) to the OFF state (S5) or sleep state (S1–S4). A computer cannot enter one sleep state directly from another because it must enter the ON state before entering any other sleep state. Sleep and hibernate are disabled in Windows Server.

Resolving hardware and firmware startup problems

On most computers, you can enter BIOS, EFI, or UEFI during boot by pressing F2 or another function key. When you are in firmware, you can open the Power screen or a similar screen to manage ACPI and related settings.

Power settings you might see include the following:

- **Restore AC Power Loss or AC Recovery.** Determines the mode of operation if a power loss occurs and for which you see settings such as Stay Off/Off, Last State/Last, Power On/On. Stay Off means the system remains off after power is restored. Last State restores the system to the state it was in before power failed. Power On means the system turns on after power is restored.

- **Wake On LAN From S4/S5 or Auto Power On.** Determines the action taken when the system power is off and a Peripheral Component Interconnect (PCI) Power Management wake event occurs. You see settings such as Stay Off or Power On.

- **ACPI Suspend State or Suspend Mode.** Sets the suspend mode. Typically, you can set S1 state or S3 state as the suspend mode.

  NOTE

  I provide two standard labels for each setting because your computer hardware might not have these exact labels. The firmware variant you are working with determines the actual labels that are associated with boot, power, and other settings.

Because Intel and AMD also have other technologies to help reduce startup and resume times, you might also see the following power settings:

- Enhanced Intel SpeedStep Technology (EIST), which can be either Disabled or Enabled

- Intel Quick Resume Technology, which can be either Disabled or Enabled

Enhanced Intel SpeedStep Technology (EIST or SpeedStep) allows the system to adjust processor voltage and core frequency dynamically, which can result in decreased average power consumption and decreased average heat production. When EIST or a similar technology is enabled and in use, you see two processor speeds on the System page in Control Panel. The first speed listed is the specified speed of the processor. The second speed is the current operating speed, which should be less than the first speed. If Enhanced Intel SpeedStep Technology is off, the processor speeds will be equal. Advanced Settings for Power Options under Processor Power Management can also affect how this technology works. Generally speaking, although you might want to use this technology with a Windows desktop operating system, you won't want to use it with a Windows Server operating system.

Intel Quick Resume Technology Driver (QRTD) allows an Intel Viiv technology–based computer to behave like a consumer electronic device with instant on/off after an initial boot. Intel QRTD manages this behavior through the Quick Resume mode function of the Intel Viiv chipset. Pressing the power button on the computer or a remote control puts the computer in the Quick Sleep state, and the computer can Quick Resume from sleep when you move the mouse, press an on/off key on the keyboard (if available), or press the sleep button on the remote control. Quick Sleep mode is different from standard sleep mode. In Quick Sleep mode, the computer's video card stops sending data to the display, the sound is muted, and the monitor LED indicates a lowered power state on the monitor, but the power continues to supply vital components on the system such as the processor, fans, and so on. Because this technology was originally designed for earlier Windows operating systems, it does not work in many cases with later Windows desktop operating systems and generally should not be used with Windows Server operating systems. You might need to disable this feature in firmware to enable a Windows desktop operating system to sleep and resume properly.

After you look at the computer's power settings in firmware, you should also review the computer's boot settings in firmware. Typically, you have a list of bootable devices and can select which one to boot. You also might be able to configure the following boot settings:

- **Boot Drive Order.** Determines the boot order for fixed disks
- **Boot To Hard Disk Drive.** Determines whether the computer can boot to fixed disks, and can be set to Disabled or Enabled
- **Boot To Removable Devices.** Determines whether the computer can boot to removable media, and can be set to Disabled or Enabled
- **Boot To Network.** Determines whether the computer can perform a network boot, and can be set to Disabled or Enabled
- **USB Boot.** Determines whether the computer can boot to USB flash devices, and can be set to Disabled or Enabled

As with power settings, your computer might not have these exact labels, but the labels should be similar. You need to optimize these settings for the way you plan to use the computer. In most cases, with server hardware, you'll only want to enable Boot To Hard Disk Drive. The exception is when you use BitLocker Drive Encryption. With BitLocker, you'll want to enable Boot To Removable Devices, USB Boot, or both to ensure that the computer can detect the USB flash drive with the encryption key during the boot process.

Boot environment essentials

Windows Server 2012 R2 supports several processor architectures and several disk partitioning styles. EFI was originally developed for Itanium-based computers. Computers with EFI use the globally unique identifier (GUID) partition table (GPT) disk type for boot and system volumes. Computers based on x86 use BIOS and the master boot record (MBR) disk type for boot and system volumes. Computers based on x64 use UEFI wrapped around BIOS or EFI.

With the increasing acceptance and use of UEFI and the ability of Windows to use both MBR and GPT disks regardless of firmware type, the underlying chip architecture won't necessarily determine which firmware type and disk type a computer uses for boot and startup. That said, generally, BIOS-based computers use MBR for booting or for data disks and GPT only for data disks. EFI-based computers can have both GPT and MBR disks, but you typically must have at least one GPT disk that contains the EFI system partition (ESP) and a primary partition or simple volume that contains the operating system for booting.

With early releases of the server operating system for Windows, BIOS-based computers use Ntldr and Boot.ini to boot into the operating system. Ntldr handles the task of loading the operating system, whereas Boot.ini contains the parameters that enable startup, including the identity of the boot partitions. Through Boot.ini parameters, you can add options that control the way the operating system starts, the way computer components are used, and the way operating system features are used.

However, with early releases of the server operating system for Windows, EFI-based computers use Ia64ldr.efi, Diskpart.efi, and Nvrboot.efi to boot into the operating system. Ia64ldr.efi handles the task of loading the operating system; Diskpart.efi identifies the boot partitions. Through Nvrboot.efi, you set the parameters that enable startup.

Windows Server 2008 and later don't use these boot facilities. Instead, they use a pre–operating system boot environment. Figure 3-1 provides a conceptual overview of how the boot environment fits into the overall computer architecture.

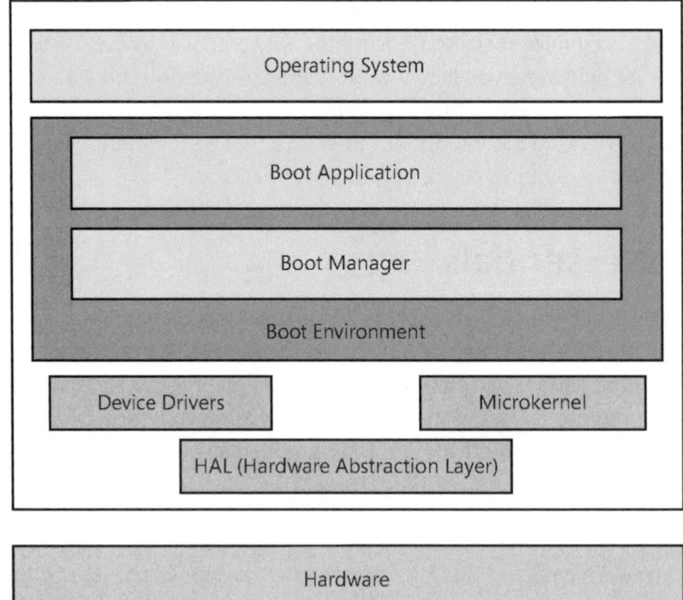

Figure 3-1 A conceptual view of how the boot environment works.

The boot environment is an extensible abstraction layer that allows the operating system to work with multiple types of firmware interfaces without requiring the operating system to be specifically written to work with these firmware interfaces. Within the boot environment, startup is controlled by using the parameters in the boot configuration data (BCD) store.

The BCD store is contained in a file called the *BCD registry*. The location of this registry depends on the computer's firmware:

- On BIOS-based operating systems, the BCD registry file is stored in the \Boot\Bcd directory of the active partition.
- On EFI-based operating systems, the BCD registry file is stored on the EFI system partition.

Entries in the BCD store identify the boot manager to use during startup and the specific boot applications available. The default boot manager is Windows Boot Manager. It controls the boot experience, and you can use it to choose which boot application is run. Boot applications load a specific operating system or operating system version. For example, a Windows Boot Loader application loads Windows Server 2012 R2. Because of this, you can boot BIOS-based and EFI-based computers in much the same way.

Managing startup and boot configuration

You can press F8 during startup of the operating system to access the Advanced Boot Options menu and then use this menu to select one of several advanced startup modes, including Safe Mode, Enable Boot Logging, and Disable Driver Signature Enforcement. Although these advanced modes temporarily modify the way the operating system starts to help you diagnose and resolve problems, they don't make permanent changes to the boot configuration or to the BCD store. Other tools you can use to modify the boot configuration and manage the BCD store include the Startup And Recovery dialog box, the System Configuration utility, and BCD Editor. The sections that follow discuss how these tools are used.

Managing startup and recovery options

The Startup And Recovery dialog box controls the basic options for the operating system during startup. You can use these options to set the default operating system, the time to display the list of available operating systems, and the time to display recovery options when needed. Whether you start a computer to different operating systems or not, you want to optimize these settings to reduce the wait time during startup and, in this way, speed up the startup process.

You can access the Startup And Recovery dialog box by completing the following steps:

1. In Control Panel\System And Security, tap or click System to access the System window.
2. In the System window, tap or click Advanced System Settings in the left pane. This opens the System Properties dialog box.
3. On the Advanced tab of the System Properties dialog box, tap or click Settings under Startup And Recovery. This opens the Startup And Recovery dialog box, as shown in Figure 3-2.

   NOTE

   Open the Advanced tab of the System Properties dialog box directly by typing SystemPropertiesAdvanced.exe in the Apps Search box and pressing Enter.

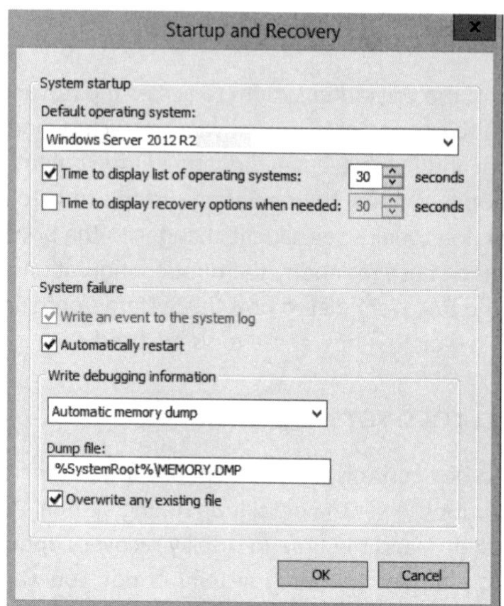

Figure 3-2 Configuring system startup options.

4. On a computer with multiple operating systems, use the Default Operating System list to specify the operating system you want to start by default.

5. Set the timeout interval for the operating system list by selecting the Time To Display List Of Operating Systems check box and specifying a timeout in seconds in the field provided. To speed up the startup process, you might want to use a value of five seconds.

6. Set the timeout interval for the recovery options list by selecting the Time To Display Recovery Options When Needed check box and specifying a timeout in seconds in the field provided. Again, to speed up the startup process, you might want to use a value of five seconds.

7. Tap or click OK to save your settings.

Managing System Boot Configuration

You can use the System Configuration utility (Msconfig.exe) to fine-tune the way a computer starts. Typically, you use this utility during troubleshooting and diagnostics. For example, as part of troubleshooting, you can configure the computer to use a diagnostic startup so only basic devices and services are loaded.

The System Configuration utility is available on the Tools menu in Server Manager. You can also start the System Configuration utility by pressing the Windows key, typing **msconfig .exe** in the Apps Search box, and pressing Enter. As shown in Figure 3-3, this utility has a series of tabs with options.

Use the General tab options to configure the way startup works. Start your troubleshooting and diagnostics efforts on this tab. You can use these options to perform a normal startup, diagnostic startup, or selective startup. After you restart the computer and resolve any problems, access the System Configuration utility again, select Normal Startup on the General tab, and then tap or click OK.

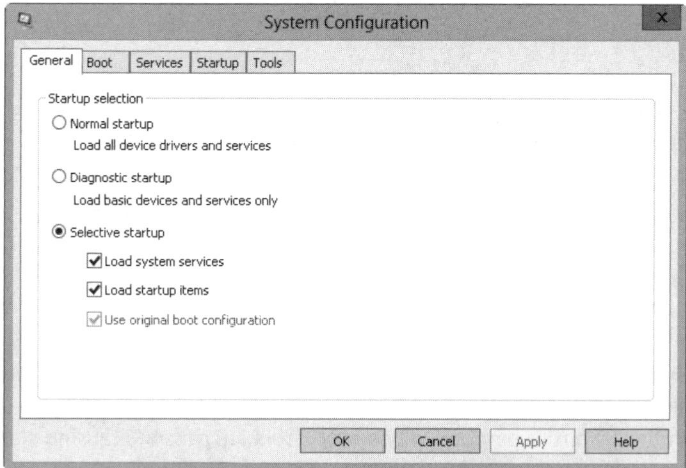

Figure 3-3 Performing a diagnostic or selective startup as part of troubleshooting.

Use the Boot tab options, shown in Figure 3-4, to control the way the individual startup-related processes work. You can configure the computer to start in one of various Safe Boot modes and set additional options, such as No GUI Boot. If after troubleshooting you find that you want to keep these settings, you can select the Make All Boot Settings Permanent check box to save the settings to the boot configuration startup entry.

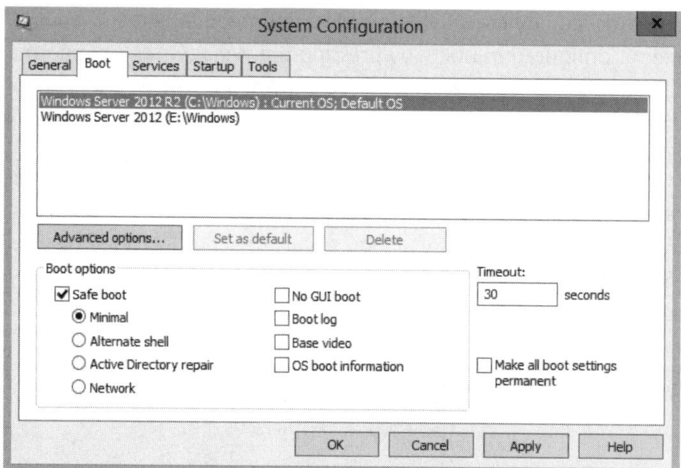

Figure 3-4 Fine-tuning the boot options.

Tapping or clicking the Advanced Options button on the Boot tab opens the BOOT Advanced Options dialog box shown in Figure 3-5. In addition to being able to lock PCI, detect the correct hardware abstraction layer (HAL), and enable debugging, you can use the advanced options to do the following:

- Specify the number of processors the operating system should use. You should use this option when you suspect there is a problem with additional processors you installed in a server, and you want to pinpoint which processors are possibly causing startup problems. Consider the following scenario: a server shipped with two processors, and you installed two additional processors. Later, you find that you cannot start the server. You could eliminate the new processors as the potential cause by limiting the computer to two processors.

- Specify the maximum amount of memory the operating system should use. You should use this option when you suspect there is a problem with additional memory you installed in a server. Consider the following scenario: a server shipped with 4 GB of RAM, and you installed an additional 4 GB of RAM. Later, you find that you cannot start the server. You could eliminate the new RAM as the potential cause by limiting the computer to 4,096 MB of memory.

If you suspect services installed on a computer are causing startup problems, you can quickly determine this by choosing a diagnostic or selective startup on the General tab. After you identify that services are indeed causing startup problems, you can temporarily disable services using the Services tab options and then reboot to see whether the problem goes away. If the problem no longer appears, you might have pinpointed it. You can then permanently disable the service or check with the service vendor to see whether an updated executable is available for the service. As shown in Figure 3-6, you disable a service by clearing the related check box on the Services tab.

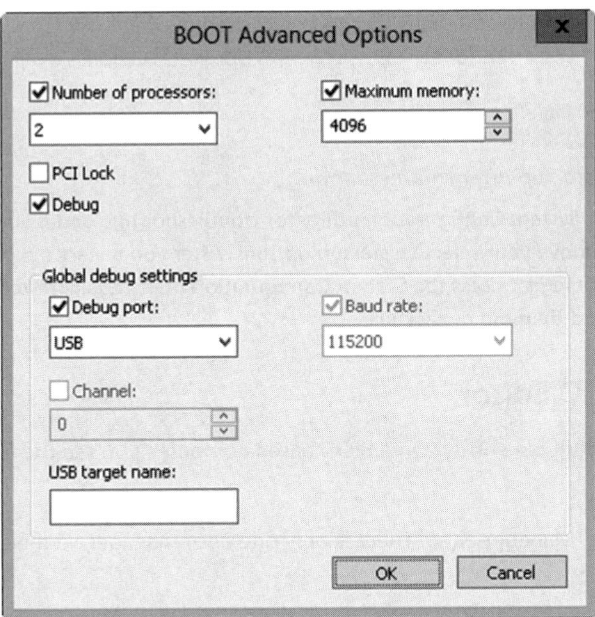

Figure 3-5 Setting advanced boot options as necessary to help troubleshoot specific types of problems.

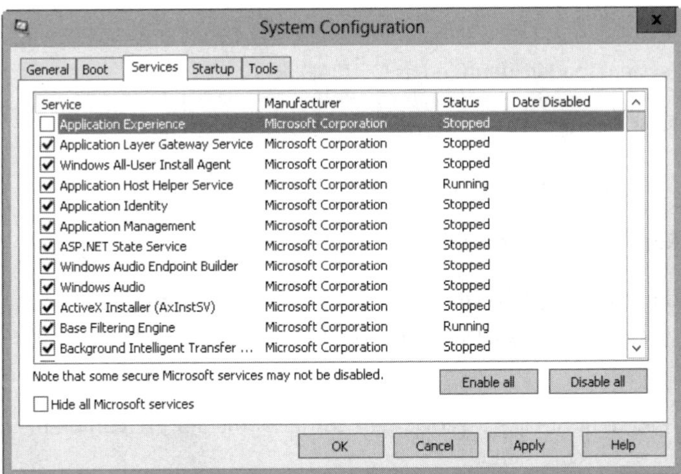

Figure 3-6 Disabling services to pinpoint the source of a problem.

Similarly, if you suspect applications that run at startup are causing problems, you can quickly determine this by using the options on the Startup tab. You disable a startup application by clearing the related check box on the Startup tab. If the problem no longer appears, you might have pinpointed the cause of it. You can then permanently disable the startup application or check with the software vendor to see whether an updated version is available.

TROUBLESHOOTING

Remove selective startup after troubleshooting

If you are using the System Configuration utility for troubleshooting and diagnostics, you should later remove your selective startup options. After you restart the computer and resolve any problems, access the System Configuration utility again, restore the original settings, and then tap or click OK.

Working with BCD Editor

The BCD store contains multiple entries. On a BIOS-based computer, you see the following entries:

- One Windows Boot Manager entry. There is only one boot manager, so there is only one boot manager entry.
- One or more Windows Boot Loader application entries, with one for each version of Windows installed on the computer.

Windows Boot Manager is itself a boot loader application. There are other boot loader applications, including the following:

- Operating system loader, identified as OSLOADER
- Windows Boot Sector Application, identified as BOOTSECTOR
- Firmware Boot Manager, identified as FWBOOTMGR
- Windows Resume Loader, identified as RESUME

You can view and manage the BCD store directly by using BCD Editor (BCDEdit.exe). BCD Editor is a command-line utility. You can use it to view the entries in the BCD store by following these steps:

1. Press and hold or right-click the lower-left corner of the Start screen on the desktop. This displays a shortcut menu.
2. Select the Command Prompt (Admin) to open an elevated command prompt.

3. Enter **bcdedit** at the elevated command prompt.

Table 3-2 summarizes commands you can use when you are working with the BCD store. These commands enable you to:

- Create, import, export, and identify the entire BCD store.
- Create, delete, and copy individual entries in the BCD store.
- Set or delete entry option values in the BCD store.
- Control the boot sequence and the boot manager.
- Configure and control Emergency Management Services (EMS).
- Configure and control boot debugging and hypervisor debugging.

Table 3-2 Commands for BCD Editor

Commands	Description
/bootdebug	Enables or disables boot debugging for a boot application.
/bootems	Enables or disables EMS for a boot application.
/bootsequence	Sets the one-time boot sequence for the boot manager.
/copy	Makes copies of entries in the store.
/create	Creates new entries in the store.
/createstore	Creates a new (empty) boot configuration data store.
/dbgsettings	Sets the global debugger parameters.
/debug	Enables or disables kernel debugging for an operating system entry.
/default	Sets the default entry that the boot manager uses.
/delete	Deletes entries from the store.
/deletevalue	Deletes entry options from the store.
/displayorder	Sets the order in which the boot manager displays the multiboot menu.
/ems	Enables or disables EMS for an operating system entry.
/emssettings	Sets the global EMS parameters.
/enum	Lists entries in the store.
/export	Exports the contents of the system store to a file. This file can be used later to restore the state of the system store.
/hypervisorsettings	Sets the hypervisor parameters.

Commands	Description
/import	Restores the state of the system store by using a backup file created with the /export command.
/mirror	Duplicates a specified entry by mirroring it in the data store.
/set	Sets entry option values in the store.
/store	Sets the BCD store to use. If not specified, the system store is used.
/sysstore	Sets the system store device. Note that this affects only EFI systems.
/timeout	Sets the boot manager timeout value.
/toolsdisplayorder	Sets the order in which the boot manager displays the tools menu.
/v	Sets output to verbose mode.

Managing the boot configuration data store and its entries

BCD Editor (BCDEdit.exe) is an advanced command-line tool for viewing and manipulating the configuration of the pre–operating system boot environment. Although I discuss tasks related to modifying the BCD store in the sections that follow, you should attempt to modify the BCD store only if you are an experienced IT pro. As a safeguard, make a full backup of the computer prior to making any changes to the BCD store. Why? If you make a mistake, your computer might end up in a nonbootable state, and you would then need to initiate recovery.

Viewing BCD entries

Computers can have system and nonsystem BCD stores. The system BCD store contains the operating system boot entries and related boot settings. Whenever you work with the BCD Editor, you will be working with the system BCD store.

On a computer with only one operating system, the BCD entries will look similar to those in Listing 3-1. As the listing shows, the BCD store for this computer has two entries: one for Windows Boot Manager and one for Windows Boot Loader. Here, the Windows Boot Manager calls the boot loader, and the boot loader uses Winload.exe to boot Windows Server 2012 R2.

Listing 3-1 Entries in the BCD store on a single-boot computer

```
Windows Boot Manager
--------------------
identifier              {bootmgr}
device                  partition=F:
description             Windows Boot Manager
locale                  en-US
inherit                 {globalsettings}
bootshutdowndisabled    Yes
```

```
default                 {current}
resumeobject            {fcb757a2-7476-11e1-8312-bd48864d9bf1}
displayorder            {current}
toolsdisplayorder       {memdiag}
timeout                 30

Windows Boot Loader
-------------------
device                  partition=C:identifier            {current}
path                    \Windows\system32\winload.exe
description             Windows Server 2012 R2
locale                  en-US
inherit                 {bootloadersettings}
recoverysequence        {fcb757a2-7476-11e1-8312-bd48864d9bf1}
recoveryenabled         Yes
allowedinmemorysettings 0x15000075
osdevice                partition=C:
systemroot              \Windows
resumeobject            {fcb757a2-7476-11e1-8312-bd48864d9bf1}
nx                      OptOut
```

BCD entries for Windows Boot Manager and Windows Boot Loader have similar properties, which are summarized in Table 3-3.

Table 3-3 BCD entry properties

Property	Description
Description	Shows descriptive information to help identify the type of entry.
Device	Shows the physical device path. For a partition on a physical disk, you see an entry such as partition=C:.
FileDevice	Shows the path to a file device, such as partition=C:.
FilePath	Shows the file path to a necessary file, such as \hiberfil.sys.
Identifier	Shows a descriptor for the entry. This can be a boot loader application type such as BOOTMGR or NTLDR. Or it can be a reference to the current operating system entry or the GUID of a specific object.
Inherit	Shows the list of entries to be inherited.
Locale	Shows the computer's locale setting, such as en-us. The locale setting determines the UI language shown. In the \Boot folder, there are locale subfolders for each supported locale, and each of these subfolders has language-specific UI details for the Windows Boot Manager (BootMgr.exe) and the Memory Diagnostics Utility (MemDiag.exe).
OSDevice	Shows the path to the operating system device, such as partition=C:.
Path	Shows the actual file path to the boot loader application, such as \Windows\System32\winresume.exe.

When you are working with the BCD store and BCD Editor, you see references to well-known identifiers, summarized in Table 3-4, and GUIDs. When a GUID is used, it has the following format, where each N represents a hexadecimal value:

```
{NNNNNNNN-NNNN-NNNN-NNNN-NNNNNNNNNNNN}
```

Such as:

```
{fcb757a2-7476-11e1-8312-bd48864d9bf1}
```

The dashes that separate the parts of the GUID must be entered in the positions shown.

Table 3-4 Well-known identifiers

Identifier	Description
{badmemory}	Contains the global RAM defect list that can be inherited by any boot application entry.
{bootloadersettings}	Contains the collection of global settings that should be inherited by all Windows boot loader application entries.
{bootmgr}	Indicates the Windows Boot Manager entry.
{current}	Represents a virtual identifier that corresponds to the operating system boot entry for the operating system that is currently running.
{dbgsettings}	Contains the global debugger settings that can be inherited by any boot application entry.
{default}	Represents a virtual identifier that corresponds to the boot manager default application entry.
{emssettings}	Contains the global EMS settings that can be inherited by any boot application entry.
{fwbootmgr}	Indicates the firmware boot manager entry. This entry is used on EFI systems.
{globalsettings}	Contains the collection of global settings that should be inherited by all boot application entries.
{hypervisorsettings}	Contains the hypervisor settings that can be inherited by any operating system loader entry.
{legacy}	Indicates that Windows Legacy OS Loader (Ntldr) can be used to start operating systems earlier than Windows Vista.
{memdiag}	Indicates the memory diagnostic application entry.
{ntldr}	Indicates that Windows Legacy OS Loader (Ntldr) can be used to start operating systems earlier than Windows Vista.

Identifier	Description
{ramdiskoptions}	Contains the additional options the boot manager requires for RAM disk devices.
{resumeloadersettings}	Contains the collection of global settings that should be inherited by all Windows resume-from-hibernation application entries.

When additional operating systems are installed on a computer, the BCD store for it has additional entries for each additional operating system. For example, the BCD store might have one entry for Windows Boot Manager and one Windows Boot Loader for each operating system.

When a previous operating system is installed on a computer, the BCD store has three entries: one for Windows Boot Manager, one for Windows Legacy OS Loader, and one for Windows Boot Loader. Generally, the entry for Windows Legacy OS Loader will look similar to Listing 3-2.

Listing 3-2 Sample Legacy OS Loader entry

```
Windows Legacy OS Loader
------------------------
identifier:             {ntldr}
device:                 partition=C:
path:                   \ntldr
description:            Earlier version of Windows
```

Although Windows Boot Manager, Windows Legacy OS Loader, and Windows Boot Loader are the primary types of entries that control startup, the BCD also stores information about boot settings and boot utilities. The Windows Boot Loader entry can have parameters that track the status of boot settings, such as whether No Execute (NX) policy is set for Opt In or Opt Out. The Windows Boot Loader entry also can provide information about available boot utilities such as the Memory Diagnostics utility.

To view the actual value of the GUIDs needed to manipulate entries in the BCD store, type **bcdedit /v** at an elevated command prompt.

Creating and identifying the BCD store

Using BCD Editor, you can create a new, nonsystem BCD store by using the following command:

```
bcdedit /createstore StorePath
```

Here, *StorePath* is the actual folder path to where you want to create the nonsystem store, such as:

```
bcdedit /createstore c:\non-sys\bcd
```

On an EFI system, you can temporarily set the system store device by using the /sysstore command. Use the following syntax:

```
bcdedit /sysstore StoreDevice
```

Here, *StoreDevice* is the actual device identifier store, such as:

```
bcdedit /sysstore C:
```

NOTE

The device must be a system partition. Note that this setting does not persist across reboots and is used only when the system store device is ambiguous.

Importing and exporting the BCD store

BCD Editor provides separate commands for importing and exporting the BCD store. You can use the /export command to export a copy of the system BCD store's contents to a specified folder. Use the following command syntax:

```
bcdedit /export StorePath
```

Here, *StorePath* is the actual folder path to which you want to export a copy of the system store, such as:

```
bcdedit /export c:\backup\bcd.dat
```

To restore an exported copy of the system store, you can use the /import command. Use the following command syntax:

```
bcdedit /import ImportPath
```

Here, *ImportPath* is the actual folder path from which you want to import a copy of the system store, such as:

```
bcdedit /import c:\backup\bcd.dat
```

On an EFI system, you can add /clean to the import to specify that all existing firmware boot entries should be deleted. Here is an example:

```
bcdedit /import c:\backup\bcd.dat /clean
```

Creating, copying, and deleting BCD entries

BCD Editor provides separate commands for creating, copying, and deleting entries in the BCD store. You can use the /create command to create identifier, application, and inherit entries in the BCD store.

As shown previously, in Table 3-4, BCD Editor recognizes many well-known identifiers, including {dbgsettings} used to create a debugger settings entry, {ntldr} used to create a Windows Legacy OS entry, and {ramdiskoptions} used to create a RAM disk additional options entry. To create identifier entries, you use the following syntax:

```
bcdedit /create Identifier /d "Description"
```

Here, *Identifier* is a well-known identifier for the entry you want to create, such as:

```
bcdedit /create {ntldr} /d "Earlier Windows OS Loader"
```

You also can create the following entries for specific boot-loader applications:

- **Bootsector.** A real-mode, boot-sector application, used to set the boot sector for a real-mode application
- **OSLoader.** An operating-system loader application, used to load a Windows Vista or later operating system
- **Resume.** A Windows Resume Loader application, used to resume the operating system from hibernation
- **Startup.** A real-mode application, used to identify a real-mode application

Use the following command syntax:

```
bcdedit /create /application AppType /d "Description"
```

Here, *AppType* is one of the previously listed application types, such as:

```
bcdedit /create /application osloader /d "Windows 8.1"
```

You can delete entries in the system store by using the /delete command and the following syntax:

```
bcdedit /delete Identifier
```

If you are trying to delete a well-known identifier, you must use the /f command to force deletion, such as:

```
bcdedit /delete {ntldr} /f
```

By default, when using the /delete command, the /cleanup option is implied, and this means BCD Editor cleans up any other references to the entry being deleted. This ensures that the data store doesn't have invalid references to the identifier you removed. Because entries are also removed from the display order, this can result in a different default operating system being set. If you want to delete the entry and clean up all other references except the display order entry, you can use the /nocleanup command.

Setting BCD entry values

After you create an entry, you then need to set additional entry option values as necessary. Here is the basic syntax for setting values:

```
bcdedit /set Identifier Option Value
```

Here, *Identifier* is the identifier of the entry to be modified, *Option* is the option you want to set, and *Value* is the option value, such as:

```
bcdedit /set {current} device partition=d:
```

To delete options and their values, use the /deletevalue command with the following syntax:

```
bcdedit /deletevalue Identifier Option
```

Here, *Identifier* is the identifier of the entry to be modified, and *Option* is the option you want to delete, such as:

```
bcdedit /deletevalue {current} badmemorylist
```

> NOTE
>
> **When you are working with options, Boolean values can be entered in several ways. For *true*, you can use *1*, *ON*, *YES*, or *TRUE*. For *false*, you can use *0*, *OFF*, *NO*, or *FALSE*.**

To view the BCD entries for all boot utilities and values for settings, type **bcdedit /enum all /v** at an elevated command prompt. This command enumerates all BCD entries regardless of their current state and lists them in Verbose mode. The additional entries will look similar to those in Listing 3-3 (shown later in the chapter). Each additional entry has a specific purpose and lists values that you can set, including the following:

- **Resume From Hibernate.** The Resume From Hibernate entry shows the current configuration for the resume feature. The pre–operating system boot utility that controls resume is Winresume.exe, which in this example is stored in the C:\Windows \system32 folder. The hibernation data, as specified in the *filepath* parameter, is stored in the Hiberfil.sys file in the root folder on the *osdevice* (C: in this example). Because the resume feature works differently if the computer has Physical Address Extension (PAE)

CHAPTER 3

and debugging enabled, these options are tracked by the *PAE* and *Debugoptionenabled* parameters.

- **Windows Memory Tester.** The Windows Memory Tester entry shows the current configuration for the Windows Memory Diagnostics utility. The pre–operating system boot utility that controls memory diagnostics is Memtest.exe, which in this example is stored in the C:\Boot folder. Because the Memory Diagnostics utility is designed to detect bad memory by default, the *badmemoryaccess* parameter is set to *yes* by default. You can turn this feature off by entering **bcdedit /set {memdiag} badmemoryaccess NO**. With memory diagnostics, you can configure the number of passes by using *Passcount* and configure the test mix as BASIC or EXTENDED by using *Testmix*. Here is an example: **bcdedit /set {memdiag} passcount 2**.

- **Windows Legacy OS Loader.** The Windows Legacy OS Loader entry shows the current configuration for loading earlier versions of Windows. The *Device* parameter sets the default partition to use, such as C:, and the *Path* parameter sets the default path to the loader utility, such as Ntldr.

- **EMS Settings.** The EMS Settings entry shows the configuration used when booting with Emergency Management Services (EMS). Individual Windows Boot Loader entries control whether EMS is enabled. If EMS is provided by BIOS and you want to use the BIOS settings, you can enter **bcdedit /emssettings bios**. With EMS, you can set an EMS port and an EMS baud rate. Here is an example: **bcdedit /emssettings EMSPORT:2 EMSBAUDRATE:115200**. You can enable or disable EMS for a boot application by typing **/bootems** followed by the identity of the boot application with the desired state, such as ON or OFF.

- **Debugger Settings.** The Debugger Settings entry shows the configuration used when booting with the debugger turned on. Individual Windows Boot Loader entries control whether the debugger is enabled. You can view the hypervisor debug settings by entering **bcdedit /dbgsettings**. When debug booting is turned on, *DebugType* sets the type of debugger as SERIAL, 1394, or USB. With SERIAL debugging, *DebugPort* specifies the serial port being used as the debugger port, and *BaudRate* specifies the baud rate to be used for debugging. With 1394 debugging, you can use *Channel* to set the debugging channel. With Universal Serial Bus (USB) debugging, you can use *TargetName* to set the USB target name to be used for debugging. With any debug type, you can use the */Noumex* flag to specify that user-mode exceptions should be ignored. Here are examples of setting the debugging mode: **bcdedit /dbgsettings SERIAL DEBUGPORT:1 BAUDRATE:115200, bcdedit /dbgsettings 1394 CHANNEL:23**, and **bcdedit /dbgsettings USB TARGETNAME:DEBUGGING**.

- **Hypervisor Settings.** The Hypervisor Settings entry shows the configuration used when working with the Hypervisor with the debugger turned on. Individual Windows

Boot Loader entries control whether the debugger is enabled. You can view the hypervisor debug settings by entering **bcdedit /hypervisorsettings**. When hypervisor debug booting is turned on, *HypervisorDebugType* sets the type of debugger, *HypervisorDebugPort* specifies the serial port being used as the debugger port, and *HypervisorBaudRate* specifies the baud rate to be used for debugging. These parameters work the same as with Debugger Settings. Here is an example: **bcdedit /hypervisorsettings SERIAL DEBUGPORT:1 BAUDRATE:115200**. You can also use FireWire for hypervisor debugging. When you do, you must set the debug channel, such as shown in this example: **bcdedit /hypervisorsettings 1394 CHANNEL:23**.

Listing 3-3 Additional entries in the BCD store on a single-boot computer

```
Resume from Hibernate
---------------------
identifier              {fcb757a2-7476-11e1-8312-bd48864d9bf1}
device                  partition=C:
path                    \Windows\system32\winresume.exe
description             Windows Resume Application
locale                  en-US
inherit                 {1afa9c49-16ab-4a5c-901b-212802da9460}
recoverysequence        {fcb757a2-7476-11e1-8312-bd48864d9bf1}
recoveryenabled         Yes
allowedinmemorysettings 0x15000075
filedevice              partition=C:
filepath                \hiberfil.sys
debugoptionenabled      No

Windows Memory Tester
---------------------
identifier              {b2721d73-1db4-4c62-bf78-c548a880142d}
device                  partition=F:
path                    \boot\memtest.exe
description             Windows Memory Diagnostic
locale                  en-US
inherit                 {7ea2e1ac-2e61-4728-aaa3-896d9d0a9f0e}
badmemoryaccess         Yes

EMS Settings
------------
identifier              {0ce4991b-e6b3-4b16-b23c-5e0d9250e5d9}
bootems                 Yes

Debugger Settings
-----------------
identifier              {4636856e-540f-4170-a130-a84776f4c654}
debugtype               Serial
debugport               1
baudrate                115200
```

```
AM Defects
----------
identifier              {5189b25c-5558-4bf2-bca4-289b11bd29e2}

Global Settings
---------------
identifier              {7ea2e1ac-2e61-4728-aaa3-896d9d0a9f0e}
inherit                 {4636856e-540f-4170-a130-a84776f4c654}
                        {0ce4991b-e6b3-4b16-b23c-5e0d9250e5d9}
                        {5189b25c-5558-4bf2-bca4-289b11bd29e2}

Boot Loader Settings
--------------------
identifier              {6efb52bf-1766-41db-a6b3-0ee5eff72bd7}
inherit                 {7ea2e1ac-2e61-4728-aaa3-896d9d0a9f0e}
                        {7ff607e0-4395-11db-b0de-0800200c9a66}

Hypervisor Settings
-------------------
identifier              {7ff607e0-4395-11db-b0de-0800200c9a66}
hypervisordebugtype     Serial
hypervisordebugport     1
hypervisorbaudrate      115200

Resume Loader Settings
----------------------
identifier              {1afa9c49-16ab-4a5c-901b-212802da9460}
inherit                 {7ea2e1ac-2e61-4728-aaa3-896d9d0a9f0e}

Device options
--------------
identifier              {5824ba7c-acee-11e1-ba52-cfa3fef36259}
description             Windows Recovery
ramdisksdidevice        partition=C:
ramdisksdipath          \Recovery\5824ba7b-acee-11e1-ba52-cfa3fef36259\boot.sdi
```

Table 3-5 summarizes key options that apply to entries for boot applications (BOOTAPP). Because Windows Boot Manager, Windows Memory Diagnostics, Windows OS Loader, and Windows Resume Loader are boot applications, these options apply to them as well.

Table 3-5 Key options for boot application entries

Option	Value Description
BadMemoryAccess	When *true*, allows an application to use the memory on the bad memory list. When *false*, applications are prevented from using memory on the bad memory list.
BadMemoryList	An integer list that defines the list of Page Frame Numbers of faulty memory in the system.
BaudRate	Sets an integer value that defines the baud rate for the serial debugger.

Option	Value Description
BootDebug	Sets a Boolean value that enables or disables the boot debugger.
BootEMS	Sets a Boolean value that enables or disables EMS.
Channel	Sets an integer value that defines the channel for the 1394 debugger.
DebugAddress	Sets an integer value that defines the address of a serial port for the debugger.
DebugPort	Sets an integer value that defines the serial port number for the serial debugger.
DebugStart	Can be set to ACTIVE, AUTOENABLE, or DISABLE.
DebugType	Can be set to SERIAL, 1394, or USB.
EMSBaudRate	Defines the baud rate for EMS.
EMSPort	Defines the serial port number for EMS.
GraphicsModeDisabled	Sets a Boolean value that enables or disables graphics mode.
GraphicsResolution	Defines the graphics resolution, such as 1024 by 768 or 800 by 600.
Locale	Sets the locale of the boot application.
Noumex	When set to TRUE, user-mode exceptions are ignored. When set to FALSE, user-mode exceptions are not ignored.
NoVESA	Sets a Boolean value that enables or disables the use of Video Electronics Standards Association (VESA) display modes.
RelocatePhysical	Sets the physical address to which an automatically selected Non-Uniform Memory Access (NUMA) node's physical memory should be relocated.
TargetName	Defines the target name for the USB debugger as a string.
TruncateMemory	Sets a physical memory address at or above which all memory is disregarded.

Table 3-6 summarizes key options that apply to entries for Windows OS Loader (OSLOADER) applications.

Table 3-6 Key options for Windows OS Loader applications

Option	Value Description
AdvancedOptions	Sets a Boolean value that enables or disables advanced options.
BootLog	Sets a Boolean value that enables or disables the boot initialization log.

CHAPTER 3

Option	Value Description
BootStatusPolicy	Sets the boot status policy. It can be *DisplayAllFailures*, *IgnoreAllFailures*, *IgnoreShutdownFailures*, or *IgnoreBootFailures*.
ClusterModeAddressing	Sets the maximum number of processors to include in a single Advanced Programmable Interrupt Controller (APIC) cluster.
ConfigFlags	Sets processor-specific configuration flags.
DbgTransport	Sets the file name for a private debugger transport.
Debug	Sets a Boolean value that enables or disables kernel debugging.
DetectHal	Sets a Boolean value that enables or disables hardware abstraction layer (HAL) and kernel detection.
DriverLoadFailurePolicy	Sets the driver load failure policy. It can be *Fatal* or *UseErrorControl*.
Ems	Sets a Boolean value that enables or disables kernel EMS.
Hal	Sets the file name for a private HAL.
HalBreakPoint	Sets a Boolean value that enables or disables the special HAL breakpoint.
HypervisorLaunchType	Configures the hypervisor launch type. It can be *Off* or *Auto*.
IncreaseUserVA	Sets an integer value that increases the amount of virtual address space that the user-mode processes can use.
Kernel	Sets the file name for a private kernel.
LastKnownGood	Sets a Boolean value that enables or disables boot to last known good configuration.
MaxProc	Sets a Boolean value that enables or disables the display of the maximum number of processors in the system.
Msi	Sets the MSI to use. It can be *Default* or *ForceDisable*.
NoCrashAutoReboot	Sets a Boolean value that enables or disables automatic restart on crash.
NoLowMem	Sets a Boolean value that enables or disables the use of low memory.
NumProc	Sets the number of processors to use on startup.
Nx	Controls No Execute (NX) protection. It can be *OptIn*, *OptOut*, *AlwaysOn*, or *AlwaysOff*.
OneCPU	Sets a Boolean value that forces only the boot CPU to be used.
OptionsEdit	Sets a Boolean value that enables or disables the options editor.
OSDdevice	Defines the device that contains the system root.
Pae	Controls PAE. It can be *Default*, *ForceEnable*, or *ForceDisable*.

You can do this by using the following command:

```
bcdedit /displayorder {16b857b4-9e02-11e0-9c17-b7d085eb0682}
{fcb757a2-7476-11e1-8312-bd48864d9bf1}
```

You can set a particular operating system as the first entry by using /addfirst with /displayorder, such as:

```
bcdedit /displayorder {fcb757a2-7476-11e1-8312-bd48864d9bf1} /addfirst
```

You can set a particular operating system as the last entry by using /addlast with /displayorder, such as:

```
bcdedit /displayorder {fcb757a2-7476-11e1-8312-bd48864d9bf1} /addlast
```

Changing the default operating system entry

You can change the default operating system entry by using the /default command. The syntax for this command is:

```
bcdedit /default id
```

Here, *id* is the operating system ID in the boot loader entry. Thus, you could set the operating system identified in this BCD entry as the default:

```
Windows Boot Loader
-------------------
identifier              {fcb757a2-7476-11e1-8312-bd48864d9bf1}
```

You can do this by using the following command:

```
bcdedit /default {fcb757a2-7476-11e1-8312-bd48864d9bf1}
```

If you want to use a pre–Windows Server 2008 operating system as the default, use the identifier for the Windows Legacy OS Loader. The related BCD entry looks like this:

```
Windows Legacy OS Loader
------------------------
identifier              {466f5a88-0af2-4f76-9038-095b170dc21c}
device                  partition=C:
path                    \ntldr
description             Earlier Microsoft Windows Operating System
```

Following this, you could set Ntldr as the default by entering the following:

```
bcdedit /default {466f5a88-0af2-4f76-9038-095b170dc21c}
```

Changing the default timeout

You can change the timeout value associated with the default operating system by using the /timeout command. Set the /timeout command to the desired wait time in seconds, such as:

```
bcdedit /timeout 30
```

To boot automatically to the default operating system, set the timeout to zero seconds.

Changing the boot sequence temporarily

Occasionally, you might want to boot to a particular operating system one time and then revert to the default boot order. To do this, you can use the /bootsequence command. Follow the command with the identifier of the operating system to which you want to boot after restarting the computer, such as:

```
bcdedit /bootsequence {14504de-e96b-11cd-a51b-89ace9305d5e}
```

When you restart the computer, the computer will set the specified operating system as the default for that restart only. Then, when you restart the computer again, the computer will use the original default boot order.

CHAPTER 4

Managing Windows Server 2012 R2

Systems that run Windows Server 2012 R2 are the heart of any Microsoft Windows network. These are the systems that provide the essential services and applications for users and the network as a whole. As an administrator, your job is to keep these systems running; to do this, you must understand the administration options available and put them to the best use possible. Your front-line defense in managing systems running Windows Server 2012 R2 is the administration and support tools discussed in this chapter.

To run most of the administration tools, you must have administrator privileges. If these aren't included with your current account, you need to provide the credentials for the administrator account when you see the User Account Control prompt. You find detailed information about User Account Control (UAC) in Chapter 9, "Software and User Account Control administration."

Working with the administration tools

Any explanation of how to manage Windows Server 2012 R2 systems must involve the administration and support tools that are included with the operating system. These are the tools you use every day, so you might as well learn a bit more about them.

The one tool you use the most for system administration tasks is Server Manager. It provides setup and configuration options for the local server and options for managing roles, features, and related settings on any remotely manageable server in the enterprise. On servers, Server Manager is pinned to Start and the desktop taskbar by default. This means you can open Server Manager by tapping or clicking the related Start tile or by tapping or clicking the related taskbar button.

NOTE

The executable for Server Manager is ServerManager.exe. If for some reason Server Manager is unpinned from Start and the desktop, you can start Server Manager by using an Everywhere Search. In the Search box, type ServerManager.exe and then press Enter.

Inside OUT

Grant a standard user permission to use Server Manager

You can grant a standard user permission to use Server Manager to view event, service, performance counter, and role and feature inventory data for a remote server. To do this, run Enable-ServerManagerStandardUserRemoting at an elevated Windows PowerShell prompt on the server to which the permission should be granted. Set the *–User* parameter to the account name of the user, in the form of *DOMAIN\AccountName*, *COMPUTER\AccountName*, or *AccountName*. Add the *–Confirm* parameter to eliminate the prompt to confirm. Remove this permission by using the Disable-ServerManagerStandardUserRemoting cmdlet.

Many other utilities are available for administering Windows Server 2012 R2 systems as well. The tools you use the most include the following:

- **Control Panel.** Control Panel is a collection of tools for managing system configuration. You can organize Control Panel in different ways according to the view you're using. A view is simply a way of organizing and presenting options. Category view is the default view; it provides access to tools by category, tool, and key tasks. Icons view is an alternative view that lists each tool separately by name.
- **Graphical administrative tools.** The key tools for managing network computers and their resources are the graphical administrative tools. You can access these tools by selecting them individually on the Tools menu in Server Manager.
- **Administrative wizards.** Wizards are tools designed to automate key administrative tasks. You can access many administrative wizards in Server Manager—the central administration console for Windows Server 2012 R2.
- **Command-line utilities.** You can launch most administrative utilities from the command line. In addition to these utilities, Windows Server 2012 R2 provides others that are useful for working with Windows Server 2012 R2 systems.
- **Windows PowerShell cmdlets.** Windows PowerShell is a full-featured command shell that can use built-in commands called *cmdlets*, built-in programming features, and standard command-line utilities. Use Windows PowerShell for additional flexibility in your command-line scripting.

You can display the desktop by pressing the Windows key+D. You can switch between Start and the desktop by pressing the Windows key. Use the options panel for Start, Desktop, and PC Settings to display charms. You display charms by sliding in from the right side of the screen or by moving the mouse pointer over the hidden button in the upper-right or lower-right corner of the Start, Desktop, or PC Settings screen. Alternatively, just press the Windows key+C.

One of the charms is the Settings charm. Start Settings, Desktop Settings, and PC Settings have nearly—but not exactly—identical Settings panels. The Start Settings panel has a Tiles option that you can tap or click to display an option for adding or removing tiles for the administrative tools on the Start screen. You can display the Settings panel directly by pressing Windows key+I.

Start and Desktop have a hidden menu that you can display by pressing and holding or right-clicking the lower-left corner of the Start screen or the desktop. You also can press the Windows key+X to display this menu. Options on the menu include:

- Command Prompt
- Command Prompt (Admin)
- Computer Management
- Control Panel
- Device Manager
- Disk Management
- Event Viewer
- Power Options
- Programs And Features
- System
- Task Manager
- File Explorer

Although the command prompt and the administrator command prompt are the default options on the shortcut menu, you can change this configuration. The alternative is for the Windows PowerShell prompt and the administrator Windows PowerShell prompt to be displayed on this menu. To configure which options are available, on the desktop, press and hold or right-click the taskbar and then select Properties. In the Taskbar And Navigation Properties dialog box, on the Navigation tab, select or clear the Replace Command Prompt With Windows PowerShell check box as appropriate.

IMPORTANT

On Start, the hidden button in the upper-left corner shows a thumbnail view of the desktop when activated, and tapping or clicking the thumbnail opens the desktop. On the desktop, the button in the lower-left corner shows a thumbnail view of Start when activated, and tapping or clicking the thumbnail opens Start. Pressing and holding or right-clicking the thumbnail displays the shortcut menu.

The following sections provide brief introductions to these administrative utilities. Additional details for key tools are provided throughout this book. Keep in mind that to use these utilities, you might need an account with administrator privileges.

Using Control Panel utilities

Control Panel contains utilities for working with a system's setup and configuration. From Start, you access Control Panel by tapping or clicking the Control Panel tile. From the desktop, you can display Control Panel by accessing the Charms bar, tapping or clicking Settings, and then tapping or clicking Control Panel. When you are working with File Explorer, you can display Control Panel by tapping or clicking the leftmost option button (down arrow) in the address list and then tapping or clicking Control Panel.

Inside OUT

Using the Search box

The Search charm has a Search box that can be focused on Everywhere, Settings, and Files. When it's focused on Everywhere, you can use Search to find installed programs, settings, and files quickly. When it's focused on Settings, you can use Search to find settings and options in Control Panel quickly. When it's focused on Files, you can use Search to find files quickly.

When you are working with Start, you can begin a search just by entering the search text. From the desktop, you must display the Charms bar and then tap or click Search. Because Everywhere Search normally is the default, you also need to tap or click Settings to find settings and options in Control Panel.

Many Control Panel tools and related Properties dialog boxes can be opened directly. On Start, just enter the name of the Control Panel Item with the .cpl extension and then press Enter. In the Windows\System32 folder, these items are listed with the Control Panel Item type. For example, type **inetcpl.cpl** to open the Internet Properties dialog box.

Using graphical administrative tools

Most administration tools are found on the Tools menu in Server Manager. As Table 4-1 shows, dozens of administration tools are available for working with Windows Server 2012 R2. The tool you use depends on what you want to do and, sometimes, on how much control you want over the aspect of the operating system you are seeking to manage. Several tools, including Server Manager and Computer Management, are discussed later in this section. Other tools are discussed later in this chapter or in other appropriate chapters of this book.

Table 4-1 Tools for administration

Administrative Tool	Description
Active Directory Administrative Center	Used to perform many key management tasks for Active Directory.
Active Directory Domains And Trusts	Used to manage trust relationships between domains.
Active Directory Rights Management Services	Used to view and change configuration settings for Active Directory Rights Management Services (AD RMS) clusters in the enterprise.
Active Directory Sites And Services	Used to create sites and to manage the replication of Active Directory information.
Active Directory Users And Computers	Used to manage users, groups, contacts, computers, organizational units (OUs), and other objects in Active Directory Domain Services (AD DS).
Certification Authority	Used to create and manage server certificates for servers and users on the network. Certificates are used to support public key infrastructure (PKI) encryption and authentication.
Computer Management	Used to manage services, devices, disks, and the system hardware configuration. It is also used to access other system tools.
DFS Management	Used to create and manage distributed file systems (DFS) that connect shared folders from different computers.
DHCP	Used to configure and manage the Dynamic Host Configuration Protocol (DHCP) service.
DNS	Used to configure and manage the Domain Name System (DNS) service, which can be integrated with Active Directory.
Event Viewer	Used to view the system event logs and manage event log configurations.
Failover Cluster Manager	Used to manage failover clustering. Clustering enables groups of computers to work together, providing failover support and additional processing capacity.
Fax Service Manager	Used to manage fax services and servers.

Administrative Tool	Description
File Server Resource Manager	Used to manage directory quotas, file screening, and reports.
Group Policy Management	Used to configure and manage Group Policy Objects (GPOs).
Hyper-V Manager	Used to manage Hyper-V and related virtual machine instances.
Internet Information Services (IIS) 6.0 Manager	Used to manage Windows web servers running IIS 6.0.
Internet Information Services (IIS) Manager	Used to manage Windows web servers running IIS 7.0 or later.
iSCSI Initiator	Used to connect to remote Internet Small Computer System Interface (iSCSI) targets and configure connection settings.
Local Security Policy	Used to view and manage settings for local security policy.
MPIO	Used to manage multipath I/O (MPIO) for storage arrays.
Network Load Balancing Manager	Used to manage Network Load Balancing (NLB) configuration settings and clusters.
Network Policy Server	Used to manage Network Access Policy (NAP) client settings, policies, and policy servers.
Print Management	Used to manage Windows print servers and related printers, print queues, printer drivers, and so on.
Remote Access Management	Used to manage DirectAccess and virtual private networking (VPN).
Routing And Remote Access	Used to configure and manage the Routing And Remote Access service, which controls routing interfaces, dynamic Internet Protocol (IP) routing, and remote access.
Security Configuration Wizard	Used to create security policies based on server roles.
Services	Used to manage the startup and configuration of Windows services.
Services for Network File System (NFS)	Used to configure and maintain Services for NFS.
Share And Storage Management	Used to manage network shares and volumes. It also provisions storage for storage area networks (SANs).
System Configuration	Used to perform startup troubleshooting and manage the system startup configuration.
System Information	Used to view information about hardware resources, hardware components, and the software environment.
Task Scheduler	Used to view and manage scheduled tasks.
Volume Activation Tools	Used to install, activate, and manage volume license keys and to configure Key Management Service (KMS).

Administrative Tool	Description
Windows Deployment Services	Used to manage servers, devices, and system images used for deployments.
Windows Firewall With Advanced Security	Used to configure and manage firewall and Internet Protocol Security (IPsec) policies.
Windows Memory Diagnostic	Used to perform diagnostics testing on a computer's physical memory.
Windows Server Backup	Used to manage backup and recovery. You also can use it to schedule automatic backups.
Windows Server Update Services	Used to configure and manage update services.
Windows System Resource Manager	Used to manage resource usage on a per-processor basis (deprecated).
WINS	Used to manage Windows Internet Naming Service (WINS). This service resolves Network Basic Input/Output (NetBIOS) System names to IP addresses and is used with computers running very early versions of Windows and applications written for these very early operating systems that require the Computer Browser service.

Usually, you can use graphical administrative tools to manage the system that you're currently logged on to and systems throughout your Windows domains. For example, in the Event Viewer console, you specify the computer you want to work with by pressing and holding or right-clicking the Event Viewer node in the left panel and then choosing Connect To Another Computer. This opens the Select Computer dialog box shown in Figure 4-1. You can then choose Another Computer and type the name of the computer, as shown.

NOTE

With some tools, such as Event Viewer, you can connect to another server by using alternate credentials. To do this, select the Connect As Another User check box and then tap or click Set User. After you select or type the account name to use in the form of *DOMAIN\UserName*, such as CPANDL\WilliamS, type the account password and then tap or click OK. Keep in mind that remote management of computers is a feature that must be enabled. As discussed later in this chapter, you need to enable inbound rules on the Windows Firewall for each management area you want to work with. For example, you must specifically enable remote management through Event Viewer.

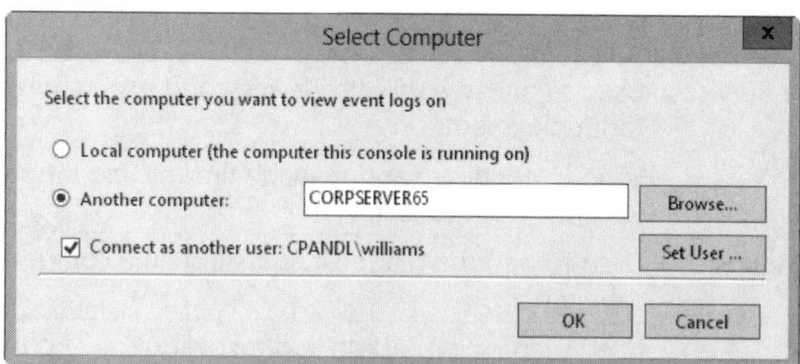

Figure 4-1 Connecting to another computer enables you to manage remote resources.

Which administrative tools are available on a server depends on its configuration. When you add roles, role services, and features, the related management tools are installed on the server. One way remote management is made possible is by installing the Remote Server Administration Tools (RSAT). On servers, you install management tools as features of the operating system by using the Add Roles And Features Wizard.

For remote management from your desktop computer, you can get the Remote Server Administration Tools for Windows 8.1 as a download from the Microsoft Download Center (*http://download.microsoft.com*). Because different versions are available for x64 and x86 systems, be sure to download the version that is appropriate for your desktop computer.

TIP

Beginning with Windows Server 2012 R2, binary source files for roles, role services, and features can be removed to enhance security. If the binaries for the tools you want to use have been removed, you need to install the tools by specifying a source. For more information about role and feature binaries, see Chapter 6, "Configuring roles, role services, and features."

You can install management tools on a server by following these steps:

1. Open Server Manager by tapping or clicking the Server Manager button on the taskbar. Alternatively, from Start, tap or click the Server Manager tile.

2. In Server Manager, select Add Roles And Features on the Manage menu. This starts the Add Roles And Features Wizard. If the wizard displays the Before You Begin page, read the introductory text and then tap or click Next. You can avoid seeing the Before You Begin page the next time you start this wizard by selecting the Skip This Page By Default check box before tapping or clicking Next.

3. On the Select Installation Type page, Role-Based Or Feature-Based Installation is selected by default. Tap or click Next.

4. On the Select Server Destination page, you can choose to install roles and features on running servers or virtual hard disks. Either select a server from the server pool or select a server on which to mount a virtual hard disk (VHD). Keep in mind that only servers that have been added for management in Server Manager are listed. If you are adding roles and features to a VHD, tap or click Browse and then use the Browse For Virtual Hard Disks dialog box to locate the VHD. When you are ready to continue, tap or click Next twice. This skips the Select Server Roles page.

5. On the Select Features page, expand Remote Server Administration Tools and the related subnodes to view the available feature and role administration tools. Select the tool or tools to install. If additional features are required to install a tool you selected, you see an additional dialog box. Tap or click Add Features to close the dialog box and add the required features to the server installation. When you are ready to continue, tap or click Next.

6. If the server on which you want to install the administrative tools doesn't have all the required binary source files, the server gets the files from Windows Update by default or from a location specified in Group Policy. You also can specify an alternate path for the source files. To do this, tap or click the Specify An Alternate Source Path link, type that alternate path in the box provided, and then tap or click OK. For network shares, enter the Universal Naming Convention (UNC) path to the share, such as \\CorpServer41\WS12\. For mounted Windows images, enter the WIM path prefixed with WIM: and include the index of the image to use, such as WIM:\\CorpServer41\WS12\install.wim:4. For a locally mounted image, enter the alternate path for the mounted WIM file, such as c:\mountdir\windows\winsxs.

7. Tap or click Install to begin the installation process. The Installation Progress page tracks the progress of the installation. If you close the wizard, tap or click the Notifications icon in Server Manager and then tap or click the link provided to reopen the wizard.

8. When Setup finishes installing the administration tools you selected, the Installation Progress page will be updated to reflect this. Review the installation details to ensure that all phases of the installation were completed successfully.

Using command-line utilities

Many command-line utilities are included with Windows Server 2012 R2. Most of the utilities you work with as an administrator rely on TCP/IP. Because of this, you should configure TCP/IP networking before you experiment with these tools.

Utilities to know

As an administrator, you should familiarize yourself with the following command-line utilities:

- **Appcmd.** Displays and manages the configuration of IIS.
- **Arp.** Displays and manages the IP-to-physical address mappings Windows Server 2012 R2 uses to send data on the TCP/IP network.
- **Bcdedit.** Displays and manages boot configuration data on the local system.
- **DiskPart.** Displays and manages disk partitions on local and remote systems.

  NOTE

  Windows 8.1 and Windows Server 2012 R2 might be the last versions of Windows to support Disk Management, DiskPart, and DiskRaid. The Virtual Disk Service (VDS) COM interface is being superseded by the Storage Management application programming interface (API). You can continue to use Disk Management and DiskPart to manage storage. These tools cannot be used to manage Storage Spaces, and the cmdlets in the Storage module for Windows PowerShell cannot be used to manage dynamic disks. Dynamic disks also are being phased out in favor of Storage Spaces and might not be available in future versions of Windows.

- **Dnscmd.** Displays and manages the configuration of DNS services.
- **Ftp.** Starts the built-in FTP client.
- **Hostname.** Displays the computer name of the local system.
- **Ipconfig.** Displays the TCP/IP properties for network adapters installed on the system. You can also use it to renew and release DHCP information.
- **Nbtstat.** Displays statistics and current connections for NetBIOS over TCP/IP.
- **Net.** Displays a family of useful networking commands.
- **Netsh.** Displays and manages the network configuration of local and remote computers.
- **Netstat.** Displays current TCP/IP connections and protocol statistics.
- **Nslookup.** Checks the status of a host or IP address when used with DNS.
- **Pathping.** Traces network paths and displays packet loss information.

- **Ping.** Tests the connection to a remote host.
- **Route.** Manages the routing tables on the system.
- **Schtasks.** Displays and manages scheduled tasks on local and remote systems.
- **Tracert.** During testing, determines the network path taken to a remote system.
- **Wbadmin.** Performs backup and recovery operations, including system state recovery and recovery of any type of disk to an alternate location; also gets disk details, including name, globally unique identifier (GUID), available space, and related volumes.
- **Wevtutil.** Displays and manages event logs on local and remote systems.

To learn how to use these command-line tools, type the name at a command prompt followed by **/?**. Windows Server 2012 R2 then provides an overview of how the command is used (in most cases).

Using Net tools

You can more easily manage most of the tasks performed with the Net commands by using graphical administrative tools and Control Panel utilities. However, some of the Net tools are very useful for performing tasks quickly or for obtaining information, especially during telnet sessions to remote systems. These commands include the following:

- **Net Start.** Starts a service on the system
- **Net Stop.** Stops a service on the system
- **Net Time.** Displays the current system time or synchronizes the system time with another computer
- **Net Use.** Connects and disconnects from a shared resource
- **Net View.** Displays a list of network resources available to the system

To learn how to use any of the Net command-line tools, type **net help** at a command prompt followed by the command name, such as **net help start**. Windows Server 2012 R2 then provides an overview of how the command is used.

Using Windows PowerShell

Windows PowerShell, installed by default on Windows Server 2012 R2, is a full-featured command shell that can use built-in commands called *cmdlets* and built-in programming features in addition to standard command-line utilities. Normally, Windows PowerShell is installed by default on Windows Server 2012 R2 and on Windows 8.1 Pro and Windows 8.1 Enterprise. If so, you can run Windows PowerShell by using the following techniques:

- From Start, a quick way to open Windows PowerShell is to type **powershell** and press Enter.
- From Desktop, Windows PowerShell is normally pinned to the taskbar, enabling you to run it just by tapping or clicking the related taskbar button.

NOTE

If Windows PowerShell is not installed, you can install it as a feature of the operating system. In Windows Server 2012 R2, use the Add Features And Roles Wizard. In Windows 8.1, use Control Panel to turn on Windows PowerShell as a feature.

After starting Windows PowerShell, you can enter the name of a cmdlet at the prompt, and it will run in much the same way as a command-line command. You can also execute cmdlets from within scripts. Cmdlets are named using verb-noun pairs. The verb tells you what the cmdlet does in general. The noun tells you what specifically the cmdlet works with. For example, the get-variable cmdlet either gets all Windows PowerShell environment variables and returns their values or gets a specifically named environment variable and returns its values. These are the common verbs associated with cmdlets:

- **Get-.** Queries a specific object or a subset of a type of object, such as a specified mailbox or all mailbox users
- **Set-.** Modifies specific settings of an object
- **Enable-.** Enables a setting or mail-enables a recipient
- **Disable-.** Disables an enabled setting or mail-disables a recipient
- **New-.** Creates a new instance of an item, such as a new mailbox
- **Remove-.** Removes an instance of an item, such as a mailbox

At the Windows PowerShell prompt, you can get a complete list of available cmdlets by typing **get-command**. To get help documentation on a specific cmdlet, type **help** followed by the cmdlet name, such as **help get-variable**.

All cmdlets have configurable aliases as well, which act as shortcuts for executing cmdlets. To list all available aliases, type **get-item –path alias:** at the Windows PowerShell prompt. You can create an alias that invokes any command by using the following syntax:

```
new-item -path alias:AliasName -value:FullCommandPath
```

Here, *AliasName* is the name of the alias to create, and *FullCommandPath* is the full path to the command to run, such as:

```
new-item -path alias:sm -value:c:\windows\system32\compmgmtlauncher.exe
```

This example creates the alias *sm* for starting Server Manager. To use this alias, you just type **sm** and then press Enter when you are working with Windows PowerShell.

Inside OUT

Running Windows commands at the Windows PowerShell prompt

Increasingly, administrators are using Windows PowerShell as their go-to prompt for entering both standard Windows commands and Windows PowerShell commands. Although it is true that anything you can type at a command prompt can be typed at the Windows PowerShell prompt, you need to understand the caveats that apply. Windows PowerShell looks for external commands and utilities as part of its normal processing. As long as the external command or utility is found in a directory specified by the PATH environment variable, the command or utility is run as appropriate. However, keep in mind that a Windows PowerShell execution order could affect whether a command runs as expected. For Windows PowerShell, the execution order is as follows:

1. Alternate built-in or profile-defined aliases
2. Built-in or profile-defined functions
3. Cmdlets or language keywords
4. Scripts with the .ps1 extension
5. External commands, utilities, and files

Thus, when you run a Windows command from the Windows PowerShell prompt, you have to ensure that no element in 1 to 4 of the execution order has the same name as the Windows command you want to run. If an element has the same name, that element will run instead of the expected command.

TROUBLESHOOTING

Resolving passthrough problems

When you are working with the Windows PowerShell prompt, arguments you pass in with commands won't be handled as expected because Windows PowerShell doesn't pass the arguments through in the same way as the command prompt expects them. To resolve this and make it possible to pass in arguments with Windows commands run at the Windows PowerShell prompt, you must enclose the arguments in single quotation marks.

Working with Server Manager

Server Manager is your central management console. You can use it for the initial setup and configuration of roles and features and much, much more. Not only can Server Manager help you quickly set up a new server, the console also can help you quickly set up and maintain your server environment.

Getting to know Server Manager

Normally, Windows Server 2012 R2 starts Server Manager whenever you log on, and you can access Server Manager on the desktop. If you don't want the console to start each time you log on, tap or click Manage and then tap or click Server Manager Properties. In the Server Manager Properties dialog box, select Do Not Start Server Manager Automatically At Logon and then tap or click OK.

> NOTE
>
> **Group Policy can be used to control the automatic start of Server Manager as well. Enable or disable the Do Not Display Server Manager Automatically At Logon policy setting within Computer Configuration\Administrative Templates\System\Server Manager.**

As Figure 4-2 shows, the default view of Server Manager is the Dashboard, which has quick links for adding roles and features to local and remote servers, adding servers to manage, and creating server groups. You find similar options on the Manage menu:

- **Add Roles And Features.** Starts the Add Roles And Features Wizard, which you can use to install roles, role services, and features on the server.
- **Add Other Servers To Manage.** Opens the Add Servers dialog box, which you can use to add servers you want to manage. Added servers are listed when you select the All Servers node. Press and hold or right-click a server in the Servers pane of the All Servers node to display a list of management options, including Restart Server, Manage As, and Remove Server.
- **Create A Server Group.** Opens the Create A Server Group dialog box, which you can use to add servers to server groups for easier management. Server Manager creates role-based groups automatically. For example, domain controllers are listed under AD DS, and you can quickly find information about any domain controllers by selecting the related node.

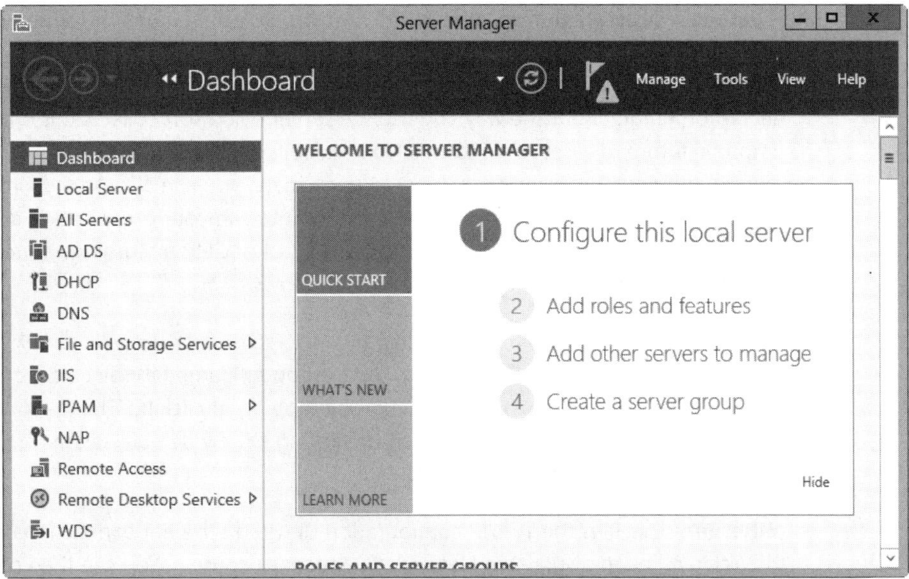

Figure 4-2 Use the Dashboard for general administration.

In the left pane of Server Manager (also sometimes referred to as the *console tree*), you find options for accessing the Dashboard, the local server, all servers added for management, and server groups. When you need to connect to a server by using alternate credentials, press and hold or right-click a server in the All Servers node and then select Manage As. In the Windows Security dialog box, enter your alternate credentials and then tap or click OK. Credentials you provide are cleared when you exit Server Manager. To save the credentials and use them each time you log on, select Remember My Credentials in the Windows Security dialog box. You need to repeat this procedure any time you change the password associated with the alternate credentials.

When you are logged on to a server and select Local Server, you can manage the basic configuration of the server. The Properties panel is where you perform much of your initial server configuration. Properties available for quick management include the following:

- **Computer Name.** Lists the computer name. Tap or click the related link to open the System Properties dialog box with the Computer Name tab selected. You can then change a computer's name by tapping or clicking Change, providing the computer name, and then tapping or clicking OK. By default, servers are assigned a randomly generated name.

- **Customer Experience Improvement Program.** Specifies whether the server is participating in the Customer Experience Improvement Program (CEIP). Tap or click the related link to change the participation settings. Participation in CEIP enables Microsoft to collect information about the way you use the server. Microsoft collects this data to help improve future releases of Windows. No data collected as part of CEIP personally identifies you or your company. If you elect to participate, you can also provide information about the number of servers and desktop computers in your organization and about your organization's general industry. If you opt out of CEIP by turning this feature off, you miss the opportunity to help improve Windows.
- **Domain.** Lists the domain membership (if any). Tap or click the related link to open the System Properties dialog box with the Computer Name tab selected. You can then change a computer's domain information by tapping or clicking Change, providing the domain information, and then tapping or clicking OK. By default, servers are configured as part of a workgroup called WORKGROUP.
- **Ethernet.** Specifies the TCP/IP configuration of wired Ethernet connections. Tap or click the related link to display the Network Connections console. You can then configure network connections by double-tapping or double-clicking the connection you want to work with and then tapping or clicking Properties to open the Properties dialog box. By default, servers are configured to use dynamic addressing for both Internet Protocol version 4 (IPv4) and Internet Protocol version 6 (IPv6). You can also display the Network Connections console by tapping or clicking Change Adapter Settings under Tasks in Network And Sharing Center.
- **Internet Explorer Enhanced Security Configuration.** Specifies the status of Internet Explorer Enhanced Security Configuration (IE ESC). Tap or click the related link to enable or disable IE ESC. If you tap or click the link for this option, you can turn this feature on or off for administrators, users, or both. IE ESC is a security feature that reduces the exposure of a server to potential attacks by raising the default security levels in Internet Explorer security zones and changing default Internet Explorer settings. By default, IE ESC is enabled for both administrators and users.

Inside OUT

Understanding Enhanced Security Configuration

Enabling Internet Explorer ESC reduces the functionality of Internet Explorer but is recommended for both users and administrators. When IE ESC is enabled, security zones are configured as follows: The Internet zone is set to Medium-High, the Trusted Sites zone is set to Medium, the Local Intranet zone is set to Medium-Low, and the Restricted zone is set to High. In addition, the following Internet settings are changed: the Enhanced Security Configuration dialog box is on, third-party browser extensions are off, sounds in webpages are off, animations in webpages are off, signature checking for downloaded programs is on, server certificate revocation is on, encrypted pages are not saved, temporary Internet files are deleted when the browser is closed, warnings for secure and nonsecure mode changes are on, and memory protection is on.

- **NIC Teaming.** Shows the status and configuration of network interface card (NIC) teaming. Tap or click the related link to add or remove teamed interfaces and to manage related options.
- **Product ID.** Shows the product identifier for Windows Server. Tap or click the related link to enter a product key and activate the operating system over the Internet.
- **Remote Desktop.** Opens the System Properties dialog box with the Remote tab selected. You can then configure Remote Desktop by selecting the configuration option you want to use and tapping or clicking OK. By default, no remote connections to a server are allowed. In the Small Icons or Large Icons view of Control Panel, you can open the System Properties dialog box with the Remote tab selected by double-tapping or double-clicking System and then tapping or clicking Remote Settings in the left pane.
- **Remote Management.** Specifies whether remote management of this server from other servers is enabled. Tap or click the related link to enable or disable remote management.
- **Time Zone.** Lists the current time zone for the server. Tap or click the related link to open the Date And Time dialog box. You can then configure the server's time zone by tapping or clicking Change Time Zone, selecting the appropriate time zone, and then tapping or clicking OK twice. You can also open the Date And Time dialog box by pressing and holding or right-clicking the clock on the taskbar and then selecting Adjust Date/Time. Although all servers are configured to synchronize time automatically with an Internet time server, the time synchronization process does not change a computer's time zone.

- **Windows Error Reporting.** Specifies the status of Windows Error Reporting (WER). Tap or click the related link to change the participation settings for WER. In most cases, you want to enable WER for at least the first 60 days following the installation of the operating system. With WER enabled, your server sends descriptions of problems to Microsoft, and Windows notifies you of possible solutions to those problems. You can view problem reports and possible solutions by using Action Center. To open Action Center, tap or click the Action Center icon in the notification area of the taskbar and then select Open Action Center.
- **Windows Firewall.** Lists the status of Windows Firewall. If Windows Firewall is active, this property displays the name of the firewall profile that currently applies and the firewall status. Tap or click the related link to open the Windows Firewall utility. By default, Windows Firewall is enabled. In the Small Icons or Large Icons view of Control Panel, you can open Windows Firewall by tapping or clicking Windows Firewall.
- **Windows Update.** Specifies the current configuration of Windows Update. Tap or click the related link to open the Windows Update utility in Control Panel, which you can then use to enable automatic updating (if Windows Update is disabled) or to check for updates (if Windows Update is enabled). In the Small Icons or Large Icons view of Control Panel, you can display Windows Update by selecting Windows Update.

Other information about the local server is organized into several main headings, each with an associated management panel. The available management panels include:

- **Best Practices Analyzer.** Enables you to run the Best Practices Analyzer on the server and review the results. To start a scan, tap or click Tasks and then tap or click Start BPA Scan.
- **Events.** Provides summary information about warning and error events from the server's event logs. Tap or click an event to display more information about the event.
- **Performance.** Enables you to configure and view the status of performance alerts for CPU and memory usage. To configure performance alerts, tap or click Tasks and then tap or click Configure Performance Alerts.
- **Properties.** Shows the computer name, domain, network IP configuration, time zone, and more. Each property can be tapped or clicked to display a related management interface quickly.
- **Roles And Features.** Lists the roles and features installed on the server in the approximate order of installation.
- **Services.** Lists the services running on the server by name, status, and start type. Press and hold or right-click a service to manage its run status.

When you press and hold or right-click a server name in the Servers pane of a server group or in the All Servers view, you open an extended list of management options. These options perform the corresponding task or open the corresponding management tool with the selected server in focus. For example, if you right-click CorpServer53 and then select Computer Management, Computer Management connects to CorpServer53 and then opens.

Adding servers for management

Before you can use Server Manager to manage remote servers, you must add the servers for management. Any server running Windows Server 2012 R2 can be easily added. Servers running Windows Server 2008 with Service Pack 2 or later and Windows Server 2008 Release 2 with Service Pack 1 or later can be added as well, as long as each server has .NET Framework 4.0 and Windows Management Framework 3.0 and has been enabled for remote management.

You can add a single server to Server Manager by completing these steps:

1. Open Server Manager. In the left pane, select All Servers to view the servers that have been added for management already. If the server you want to work with isn't listed, select Add Servers on the Manage menu to open the Add Servers dialog box.

2. In the Add Servers dialog box, the Active Directory panel is selected by default. Use the options on the Active Directory panel to enter the computer name or fully qualified domain name (FQDN) of the remote server that is running Windows Server. After you enter a name, tap or click Find Now. Alternatively, use the options on the DNS panel to specify a server by computer name or IP address and then tap or click the Search button.

3. In the Name list, double-tap or double-click the server to add it to the Selected list.

4. Repeat steps 2 and 3 to add others servers. Tap or click OK.

Rather than add servers one by one, you can use the Import process to add multiple servers. To do this, follow these steps:

1. Create a text file that has one host name, fully qualified domain name, or IP address per line.

2. In Server Manager, select Add Servers on the Manage menu. In the Add Servers dialog box, select the Import panel.

3. Tap or click the options button to the right of the File box and then use the Open dialog box to locate and open the server list.

4. In the Computer list, double-tap or double-click each server you want to add to the Selected list. Tap or click OK.

Server Manager tracks the services, events, and more for each added server. Servers are listed in the All Servers view by server name, IP address, and manageability status. Server Manager always resolves IP addresses to host names. If a server is listed as Not Accessible, you typically need to log on locally and take corrective action as necessary. For example, you might need to use a console logon to enable remote management.

Creating server groups

When you add servers to Server Manager, the servers are added to the appropriate server groups automatically, based on the installed roles and features. Automatically created server groups make it easier to manage the various roles and features that are installed on your servers. If you select the AD DS group, as an example, you see a list of the domain controllers you added for management in addition to any critical or warning events for these servers and the status of services the role depends on.

You can also create your own server groups to group servers by department, geographic location, or other characteristic. When you create groups, the servers you want to work with don't have to be added to Server Manager already. You can add servers to a group at any time, and those servers are added automatically for management.

You can create a server group by completing these steps:

1. Open Server Manager. Select Create Server Group on the Manage menu to open the Create Server Group dialog box.
2. Enter a descriptive name for the group. Use the provided panels and options to add servers to the group with the following in mind:
   - The Active Directory panel enables you to enter the computer name or fully qualified domain name of the remote server that is running Windows Server. After you enter a name, tap or click Find Now. In the Name list, double-tap or double-click a server to add it to the Selected list.
   - The DNS panel enables you to add servers by computer name or IP address. After you enter the name or IP address, tap or click the Search button. In the Name list, double-tap or double-click a server to add it to the Selected list.
   - The Import panel enables you to import a list of servers. Tap or click the options button to the right of the File box and then use the Open dialog box to locate and open the server list. In the Computer list, double-tap or double-click a server to add it to the Selected list.

- The Server Pool panel, selected by default, lists servers that have been added for management already. If a server you want to add to your group is listed here, add it to the group by double-tapping or double-clicking it.

3. Tap or click OK to create the server group.

Enabling remote management

You can use Server Manager and other Microsoft Management Consoles (MMCs) to perform some management tasks on remote computers as long as the computers are in the same domain or you are working in a workgroup and have added the remote computers in a domain as trusted hosts. You can connect to servers running Full Server, Minimal Server Interface, and Server Core installations. On the computer you want to use for managing remote computers, you should be running either Windows Server 2012 R2 or Windows 8.1, and you need to install Remote Server Administration Tools.

With Windows Server 2012 R2, remote management is enabled by default for applications and commands that use the following:

- Windows Remote Management (WinRM) and Windows PowerShell remote access for management
- Windows Management Instrumentation (WMI) and Distributed Component Object Model (DCOM) remote access for management

You'll find that these types of applications and commands are enabled for remote management because related inbound rules and exceptions for Windows Firewall are enabled. For remote management, Windows Firewall has specific exceptions for Windows Management Instrumentation, Windows Remote Management, and Windows Remote Management (Compatibility). In Windows Firewall With Advanced Security, there are inbound rules that correspond to the standard firewall-allowed applications. For WMI, the inbound rules are Windows Management Instrumentation (WMI-In), Windows Management Instrumentation (DCOM-In), and Windows Management Instrumentation (ASync-In). For WinRM, the matching inbound rule is Windows Remote Management (HTTP-In). For WinRM compatibility, the matching inbound rule is Windows Remote Management - Compatibility Mode (HTTP-In).

You manage these exceptions or rules in either the standard Windows Firewall or Windows Firewall With Advanced Security, not both. Generally, if you want to allow remote management using Server Manager, MMCs, and Windows PowerShell, you should permit WMI, WinRM, and WinRM compatibility exceptions in Windows Firewall.

When you are working with Server Manager, you can select Local Server in the console tree to view the status of the remote management property. If you don't want to allow remote management of the local server, tap or click the related link. Next, in the Configure Remote

Management dialog box, clear Enable Remote Management Of This Server From Other Computers and then tap or click OK.

When you clear the Enable Remote Management Of This Server From Other Computers check box and then tap or click OK, Server Manager performs several background tasks that disable Windows Remote Management (WinRM) and Windows PowerShell remote access for management on the local server. One of these tasks is to turn off the related exception that allows applications to communicate through Windows Firewall, using Windows Remote Management. The exceptions for Windows Management Instrumentation and Windows Remote Management (Compatibility) aren't affected.

You must be a member of the Administrators group on computers you want to manage by using Server Manager. For remote connections in a workgroup-to-workgroup or workgroup-to-domain configuration, you should be logged on using the built-in Administrator account or configure the LocalAccountTokenFilterPolicy registry key to allow remote access from your computer. To set this key, enter the following command at an elevated, administrator command prompt:

```
reg add HKLM\SOFTWARE\Microsoft\Windows\CurrentVersion\Policies\System /v
LocalAccountTokenFilterPolicy /t REG_DWORD /d 1 /f
```

Another way to enable remote management is to type **Configure-SMRemoting.exe –Enable** at an elevated, administrator prompt.

Although these techniques enable basic remote management of computers, you also need to enable rules for these specific management areas:

- **Disks and volumes.** Remote Volume Management must be allowed in Windows Firewall to manage a computer's disks and volumes remotely in Computer Management or Disk Management. In the advanced firewall, several related rules enable management of the Virtual Disk Service and Virtual Disk Service Loader.

  NOTE

  You don't need to enable Virtual Disk Service–related rules to manage Storage Spaces remotely. You manage Storage Spaces in Server Manager, using the options available when you are working with File And Storage Services.

- **Event Log.** Remote Event Log Management must be allowed in Windows Firewall to manage a computer's event logs remotely. In the advanced firewall, several related rules allow management through named pipes (NPs) and remote procedure calls (RPCs).

- **Remote Desktop.** Remote Desktop must be enabled to allow someone to connect to a server by using Remote Desktop. You also must configure access.

- **Scheduled Tasks.** Remote Scheduled Task Management must be allowed in Windows Firewall to manage a computer's scheduled tasks remotely. In the advanced firewall, several related rules allow management of scheduled tasks through RPC.
- **Services.** Remote Service Management must be allowed in Windows Firewall to manage a computer's services remotely. In the advanced firewall, several related rules allow management through NPs and RPCs.

Only Remote Service Management is enabled by default. Remote management is enabled by default on Server Core. You can configure remote management on a Server Core installation of Windows Server 2012 R2 by using sconfig. Start the Server Configuration utility by typing **sconfig**.

Inside OUT

Using Windows PowerShell for remote management

Windows PowerShell provides several ways for you to work with remote computers. One way is to use an interactive remote session. To do this, open an elevated, administrator Windows PowerShell prompt. Type **enter-pssession** ***ComputerName*** **–credential** ***UserName***, where *ComputerName* is the name of the remote computer and *UserName* is the name of a user who is a member of the Administrators group on the remote computer or in the domain of which the remote computer is a member. When prompted to enter the authorized user's password, type the password and then press Enter. You can now enter commands in the session as you would if you were using Windows PowerShell locally. To exit the session, type **exit-pssession**.

Working with Computer Management

Computer Management, shown in Figure 4-3, provides tools for managing local and remote systems. The tools available through the console tree provide the core functionality and are divided into the following three categories, as shown in the accompanying screen:

- System Tools
- Storage
- Services And Applications

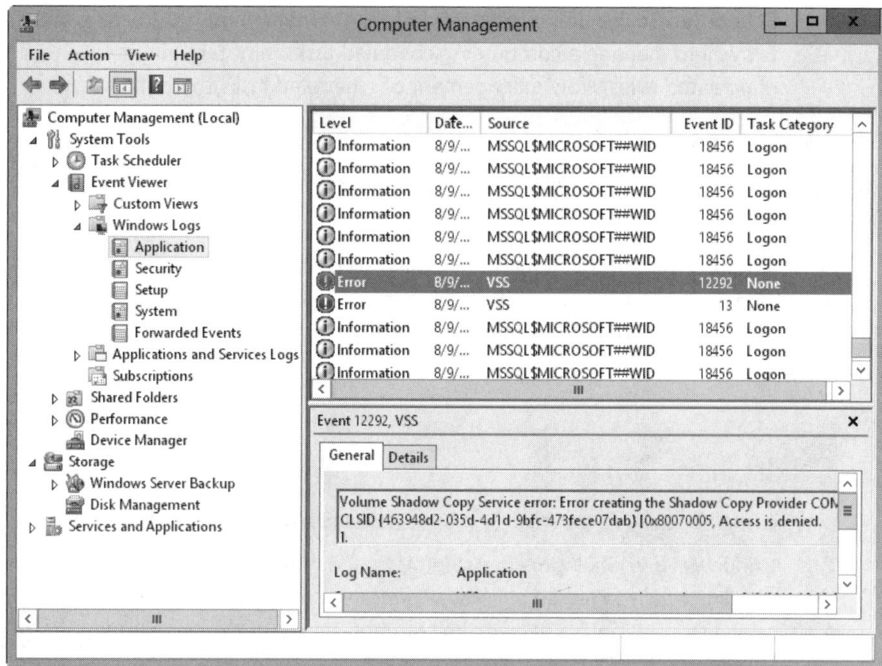

Figure 4-3 Computer Management provides several tools for managing systems.

Computer Management system tools

The system tools are designed to manage systems and view system information. The available system tools are these:

- **Task Scheduler.** Used to view the Task Scheduler Library and to create and manage tasks.
- **Event Viewer.** Used to view the event logs on the selected computer. Event logs are covered in Chapter 10, "Performance monitoring and tuning."
- **Shared Folders.** Used to manage the properties of shared folders in addition to sessions for users working with shared folders and the files the users are working with. Managing shared folders is covered in Chapter 18, "Managing file sharing."
- **Local Users And Groups.** On non–domain controller (DC) computers, used to manage local users and local user groups on the currently selected computer. Local users and local user groups aren't part of Active Directory and are managed instead through the Local Users And Groups view. Domain controllers don't have local users or groups and, because of this, there isn't a Local Users And Groups view.

- **Performance.** Used to monitor system reliability and performance through charts and logs. You can also use this tool to alert users of adverse performance conditions. For more information about performance logging and alerting, see "Performance logging" in Chapter 11, "Comprehensive performance analysis and logging."
- **Device Manager.** Used as a central location for checking the status of any device installed on a computer and for updating the associated device drivers. You can also use it to troubleshoot device problems. Managing devices is covered in Chapter 7, "Managing and troubleshooting hardware."

Computer Management storage tools

The Computer Management storage tools display drive information and provide access to drive-management tools. The available storage tools include the following:

- **Windows Server Backup.** Used to manage backups for server data. You enable backups by adding the Windows Server Backup feature.
- **Disk Management.** Used to manage hard disks and the way they are partitioned. You can also use it to manage volume sets and software-based redundant array of independent disks (RAID) arrays. Disk Management is discussed in Chapter 13, "Configuring disks and storage."

NOTE

Storage Spaces are preferred to software-based RAID and traditional disk-partitioning techniques. Before you implement software-based RAID or partition disks by using Disk Management, you might want to review the options for creating Storage Spaces and allocating storage by using Storage Spaces. See Chapter 17, "Managing Storage Spaces."

Computer Management Services And Applications tools

The Computer Management Services And Applications tools help you manage services and applications installed on the server. Any application or service-related task that can be performed in a separate tool can be performed through the Services And Applications node as well. For example, if DHCP is installed on the currently selected system, you can manage DHCP through the Services and Applications node. You could also use the DHCP tool, which can be accessed on the Tools menu in Server Manager. Either way, you can perform the same tasks.

CHAPTER 5

Windows Server 2012 R2 MMC administration

The Microsoft Management Console (MMC) and the prepackaged administration tools that use it help you more readily manage computers, users, and other aspects of the network environment. The MMC not only simplifies administration but also helps integrate the many disparate tools in the Windows operating system.

The advantages of having a unified interface are significant because after you learn the structure of one MMC tool, you can apply what you've learned to all the other MMC tools. Equally significant is the capability to build your own consoles and customize existing consoles. You can, in fact, combine administrative components to build your own console configuration and then store this console for future use. You would then have quick access to the tools you use the most through a single console.

In this chapter, you learn how to work with and customize the MMC. You also find a discussion of administration tools that use the MMC. You can learn many techniques to help you understand Windows Server 2012 R2 better, and indeed, as mentioned in the previous chapter, you must master the MMC before you can truly master Windows Server 2012 R2.

Using the MMC

The MMC is a framework for management applications that offers a unified interface for administration. It is not designed to replace management applications; rather, it is designed to be their central interface. As such, the MMC doesn't have any inherent management functions. It uses add-in components, called *snap-ins*, to provide the necessary administrative functionality.

Keep in mind that the MMC isn't a one-size-fits-all approach to administration. Some administrative functions aren't implemented for use with the MMC. You configure many system and operating system properties by using Control Panel utilities. Many other system and administrative functions are accessed using wizards. Most administrative tools, regardless of type, have command-line counterparts that run as separate executables from the command line.

The really good news, however, is that you can integrate all non-MMC tools and even command-line utilities into a custom console by creating links to them. In this way, your custom console remains the central interface for administration, and you can use it to access quickly any type of tool with which you routinely work. For more information, see the "Building custom MMCs" section later in this chapter.

For selected snap-ins, the MMC supports the following capabilities:

- **Multiple-item selecting and editing.** These features enable you to select multiple objects and perform the same operations on them, including editing.
- **Drag-and-drop functionality.** This enables you to perform such tasks as dragging a user, computer, or group from one organizational unit (OU) to another in Active Directory Users And Computers.

For the Active Directory Users And Computers snap-in, you can do the following:

- Reset access permissions to the default values for objects, show the effective permission for an object, and show the parent of an inherited permission.
- Save Active Directory queries and reuse them so that you can perform common or complex queries easily.

MMC 3.0 is designed to support snap-ins created for MMC 2.0 and MMC 1.2. You can add these snap-ins to an MMC 3.0 console, and they will run as they do in the versions of MMC for which they were designed. You can use MMC 3.0 to open a console created using MMC 2.0 or MMC 1.2. If you then save the console, you are prompted to save the console in MMC 3.0 format. Doing so will update the console so that it uses the MMC 3.0 framework. However, you will not be able to open the console on computers running previous versions of MMC. The reason for this is that MMC 2.0 and MMC 1.2 do not support MMC 3.0 snap-ins or consoles.

MMC snap-ins

To take advantage of what the MMC framework has to offer, you add any of the available standalone snap-ins to a console. A console is simply a container for snap-ins that uses the MMC framework. Dozens of preconfigured snap-ins are available from Microsoft, and they provide the functionality necessary for administration. Third-party tools from independent software vendors also now use MMC snap-ins.

> NOTE
>
> **The terms *console* and *tool* are often used interchangeably. For example, in the text, I often refer to something as a tool when technically it is a preconfigured console containing a snap-in. Active Directory Users And Computers is a tool for managing users, groups, and computers. Not all tools are consoles, however. The System tool in Control Panel is a tool for managing system properties, but it is not a console.**

Although you can load multiple snap-ins into a single console, most of the preconfigured consoles have only a single snap-in. For example, most of the tools on the Tools menu in Server Manager consist of a preconfigured console with a single snap-in—even the Computer Management tool, as shown in Figure 5-1, consists of a preconfigured console with the Computer Management snap-in added to it.

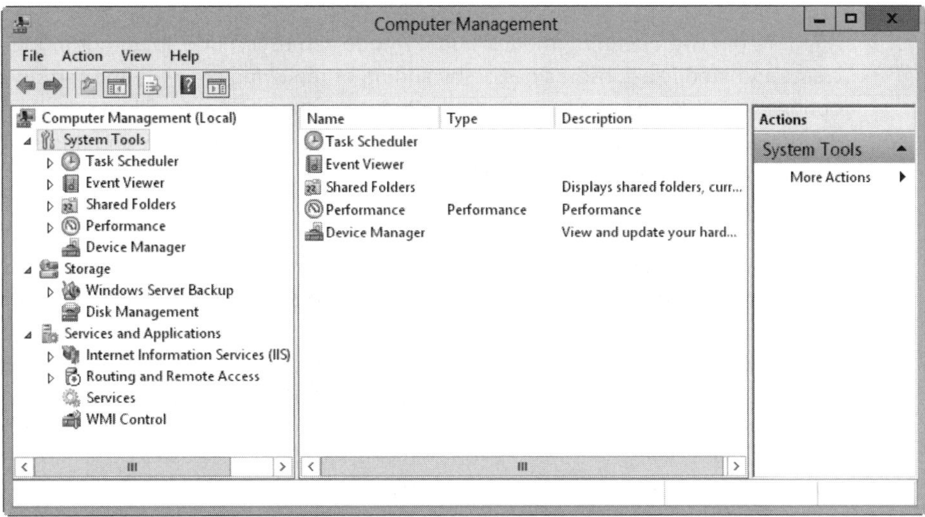

Figure 5-1 This is a preconfigured console with a snap-in added to it.

The many features of the Computer Management snap-in are good examples of how snap-ins can have nodes and extension components. A node defines a level within the console or within a snap-in. Computer Management has a root node, which is labeled Computer Management, and three top-level nodes, which are labeled System Tools, Storage, and Services And Applications. An *extension component* is a type of snap-in that extends the functionality of an existing snap-in. Computer Management has many extensions. In fact, each entry under the top-level nodes is an extension—and many of these extensions can themselves have extensions.

These particular extensions are also implemented as standalone snap-ins, and when you use them in your own console, they add the same functionality as they do in the preconfigured administration tools. You'll find that many extensions are implemented as both extensions and standalone snap-ins. *Many* doesn't mean *all*: some extensions are meant only to add functionality to an existing snap-in, and they are not also implemented as standalone snap-ins.

Keep in mind that extensions are optional and can be included or excluded from a snap-in by changing options within the console when you are authoring it. For example, if you didn't want someone to be able to use Disk Management from within Computer Management, you could edit the extension options for Computer Management on that user's computer to remove the entry for Disk Management. The user would then be unable to manage disks from within Computer Management. The user would still, however, be able to manage disks by using other tools.

MMC modes

An MMC has two operating modes: author mode and user mode. In author mode, you can create and modify a console's design by adding or removing snap-ins and setting console options. In user mode, the console design is frozen, and you cannot change it. By default, the prepackaged console tools for administration open in user mode, and this is why you are unable to make changes to these console tools.

When you open a console that is in author mode, you have additional options on the File menu that help you design the interface. You can use these options to create new consoles, open existing consoles, save the current console, add or remove snap-ins, and set console options. In contrast, when you are working with one of the preconfigured console tools or any other tool in user mode, you have a limited File menu. With user mode, you can access a limited set of console options or exit the console—that's it.

In author mode, you also have a Favorites menu, which you can use to add and organize favorites. The Favorites menu does not appear in user mode.

When you are finished designing a console tool, you should change to user mode. Console tools should be run in user mode, and author mode should be used only for configuring console tools. Three user-mode levels are defined:

- **User mode—full access.** Users can access all window-management commands in the MMC but can't add or remove snap-ins or change console properties.
- **User mode—limited access, multiple window.** Users can access only the areas of the console tree that were visible when the console was saved. Users can create new windows but cannot close existing windows.
- **User mode—limited access, single window.** Users can access only the areas of the console tree that were visible when the console was saved and are prevented from opening new windows.

A console's mode is stored when you save the console and is applied when you open the console. In author mode, you can change the console mode by using the Options dialog box, which you open by selecting Options from the File menu. You cannot change the mode when a console is running in user mode. That doesn't mean you can't change back to author mode, however, and then make further changes as necessary.

To open any existing console tool in author mode, press and hold or right-click the tool's icon and choose Author. This also works for the preconfigured administration tools. Just navigate to the %SystemDrive%\ProgramData\Microsoft\Windows\Start Menu\Programs\Administrative Tools folder, press and hold or right-click the related shortcut, and then choose Author. You will then have full design control over the console, but remember that if you make changes, you probably don't want to overwrite the existing .msc file for the console. So, instead of choosing Save from the File menu after you make changes, choose Save As and save the console with a different name. For best results and easy access to the modified console, be sure to follow the techniques discussed later in the chapter in the "Saving the console tool" section.

Inside OUT

Group Policy settings control authoring and snap-in availability

Remember that at any time, a user with appropriate permissions can enter author mode by pressing and holding or right-clicking the console's shortcut and selecting Author or by running the console tool from the command line with the /A switch. In author mode, users could change the configuration of the tool. One way to prevent this is to restrict authoring in Group Policy.

You can restrict all authoring by users at the local machine, OU, or domain level by enabling the Restrict The User From Entering Author Mode policy setting in User Configuration\Administrative Templates\Windows Components\Microsoft Management Console within Group Policy.

You also can set specific restricted and permitted snap-ins and extensions. One way to do this is first to prohibit the use of all snap-ins by enabling the Restrict Users To The Explicitly Permitted List Of Snap-Ins policy setting in User Configuration\Administrative Templates\Windows Components\Microsoft Management Console within Group Policy. Then specifically enable the snap-ins and extensions that are permitted by using the additional policy settings in the same location. All other snap-ins and extensions would then be prohibited.

Alternatively, you can disable Restrict Users To The Explicitly Permitted List Of Snap-Ins and then explicitly prohibit snap-ins by disabling them using the policy settings under User Configuration\Administrative Templates\Windows Components\Microsoft Management Console within Group Policy. All other snap-ins and extensions would then be permitted.

MMC window and startup

As Figure 5-2 shows, the MMC window consists of the console tree, the main pane, and an optional actions pane. The left pane is the console tree. It provides a hierarchical list of nodes available in the console. At the top of the tree is the console root, which could be specifically labeled Console Root or, as with the preconfigured tools, be simply the snap-in name. Generally, snap-ins appear as nodes below the console root. Snap-ins can also have nodes, as is the case with Computer Management. In any case, if there are nodes below the console root, you can expand them by tapping or clicking the plus sign to the left of the node label or by double-tapping or double-clicking the node.

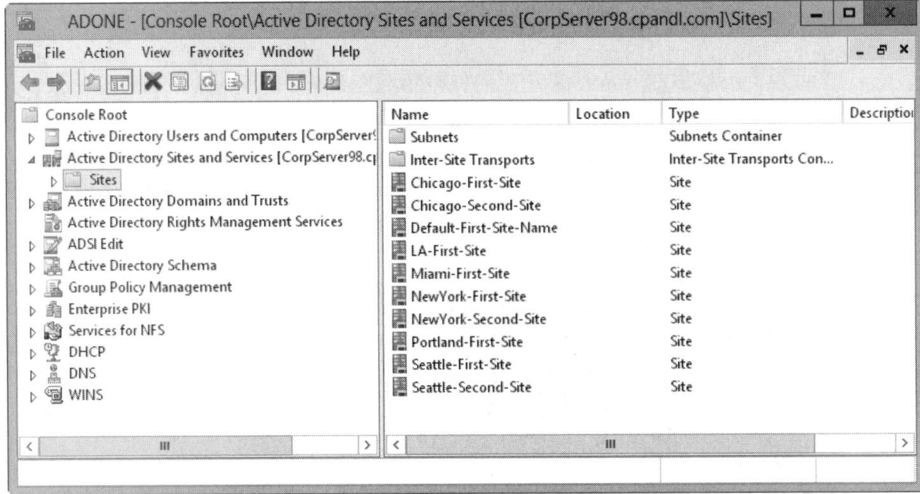

Figure 5-2 MMC windows are customizable.

The main pane is also referred to as the details pane, and its contents change depending on the item you've selected in the console tree. When you are working with one of the lowest-level nodes in the console tree, you'll sometimes have two views to choose from in the details pane: standard or extended view. The difference between the two is that the extended view typically provides quick access links to related, frequently performed tasks and a detailed description of the selected item. These are not displayed in the standard view.

One way to start a console tool is to select it on the Tools menu in Server Manager or double-tap or double-click its icon on the desktop or in File Explorer. You can also start console tools from the Search box, the command prompt, and the Windows PowerShell prompt. The executable for the MMC is Mmc.exe, so you can open the MMC by typing **mmc** in the Search box and then pressing Enter or by entering **mmc** at a command prompt. Either way, you'll end up with a blank (empty) console you can use to design your custom administration tool.

To use an existing console, you can specify the console file to open when the MMC runs. This is, in fact, how the preconfigured tools and any other tools that you create are started. For example, if you press and hold or right-click the shortcut for Computer Management in the %SystemDrive%\ProgramData\Microsoft\Windows\Start Menu\Programs\Administrative Tools folder and then select Properties, you'll see that the target (the command that is run) for the menu item is as follows:

```
%windir%\System32\Compmgmt.msc /s
```

The first part of the target (%windir%\System32\Compmgmt.msc) is the file path to the associated Microsoft Saved Console (.msc) file. The second part of the target (/S) is a command parameter to use when running the MMC. It follows that you can run the MMC by specifying the file path to the .msc file to use and any necessary command parameters by using the following syntax:

```
mmc FilePath Parameter(s)
```

Here, *FilePath* is the file path to the .msc file to use, and *Parameter(s)* can include any of the following parameters:

- **/A.** Enables author mode, so you can make changes to preconfigured consoles and other consoles previously set in user mode.
- **/S.** Prevents the console from displaying the splash screen that normally appears when the MMC starts in earlier versions of the Windows operating system. This parameter isn't needed when running on Windows Server 2008 or later.
- **/32.** Starts the 32-bit version of the MMC, which is needed only if you explicitly want to run the 32-bit version of the MMC on a 64-bit Windows system.
- **/64.** Starts the 64-bit version of the MMC, which is available only on 64-bit versions of Windows.

Inside OUT

Using 32-bit and 64-bit versions of the MMC

The *\/32* and *\/64* parameters for the mmc command are meaningful only on 64-bit Windows versions. The 64-bit versions of the Windows operating system can run both 32-bit and 64-bit versions of the MMC. For 32-bit versions of the MMC, you use 32-bit snap-ins. For 64-bit versions of the MMC, you use 64-bit snap-ins. You can't mix MMC and snap-in versions, though. The 32-bit version of the MMC can be used only to work with 32-bit snap-ins. Similarly, the 64-bit version of the MMC can be used only to work with 64-bit snap-ins. In most cases, if you aren't sure which version to use, don't use

the */32* or */64* parameter. The Windows operating system then decides which version to use based on the snap-ins contained in the .msc file you are opening.

When a console contains both 32-bit and 64-bit snap-ins and you don't specify the */32* or */64* parameter, Windows will open a subset of the configured snap-ins. If the console contains more 32-bit snap-ins, Windows will open the 32-bit snap-ins. If the console contains more 64-bit snap-ins, Windows will open the 64-bit snap-ins. If you explicitly use */32* or */64* with a console that contains both 32-bit and 64-bit snap-ins, Windows will open only the snap-ins for that bitness. On 64-bit systems, 32-bit versions of snap-ins are stored in the %SystemRoot%\SysWow64 folder and 64-bit versions of snap-ins are stored in the %SystemRoot%\System32 folder. By examining the contents of these folders, you can determine when 32-bit and 64-bit versions of snap-ins are available.

Most console tools are found in the %SystemRoot%\System32 directory. This puts them in the default search path for executables. Because there is a file type association for .msc files, specified files of this type are opened using Mmc.exe; you can open any of the preconfigured tools stored in %SystemRoot%\System32 by specifying the file name followed by the .msc extension. For example, you can start Event Viewer by typing **eventvwr.msc**.

This works because of the file association that specifies that .msc files are executed using Mmc.exe. (You can examine file associations by using the ASSOC and FTYPE commands at the command prompt.)

Some console tools aren't in the %SystemRoot%\System32 directory—or the search path, for that matter. For these tools, you must type the complete file path.

MMC tool availability

Generally, the preconfigured MMC consoles available on a server depend on the roles, role services, and features that are installed. As you install additional roles, role services, and features, additional tools for administration are installed, and these tools can be both console tools and standard tools. You don't have to rely on roles, role services, and features installation for tool availability, however. You can, in fact, install the complete administrative tool set on any full-server installation regardless of the roles, role services, or features being used.

Follow these steps to install the complete administrative tool set:

1. In Server Manager, the local server is added automatically for management. If you want to install the admin tools on another server, you need to add the server for management by using Add Other Servers To Manage. Using Server Manager for remote management requires the configuration discussed in Chapter 4, "Managing Windows Server 2012 R2," and a minimum set of permissions.

2. In Server Manager, tap or click Manage and then tap or click Add Roles And Features. This starts the Add Roles And Features Wizard. If the wizard displays the Before You Begin page, read the Welcome message and then tap or click Next.

3. On the Select Installation Type page, select Role-Based Or Feature-Based Installation and then tap or click Next.

4. On the Select Destination Server page, the server pool shows servers you've added for management. Tap or click the server you are configuring and then tap or click Next twice.

5. On the Select Features page, select the Remote Server Administration Tools check box. This selects key tools under the Role Administration Tools and Feature Administration Tools nodes. If you want to select additional tools, expand the tools node and select tools to install as appropriate. If prompted to install required features, tap or click Add Features and then tap or click Next as prompted.

6. Tap or click Install. When the wizard finishes installing the administration tools, tap or click Close.

These tools are then available on the Tools menu in Server Manager and can also be started quickly in the Search box or at the command prompt by typing only their file name (in most cases). At times, you might find it quicker to open consoles from the command line. For example, on a server optimized for handling background services and not programs being run by users, you might find that navigating the menu is too slow. To help you in these instances, Table 5-1 provides a list of the key console tools and their .msc file names. Note that some of the MMCs won't be available even if you install all the Remote Server Administration tools. Tools for certain server roles and features are only available when those roles and features are installed.

Table 5-1 Key console tools and their .msc file names

Tool Name	.msc File Name
Active Directory Administrative Center	dsac.exe
Active Directory Domains And Trusts	domain.msc
Active Directory Rights Management Services	AdRmsAdmin.msc
Active Directory Sites And Services	dssite.msc
Active Directory Users And Computers	dsa.msc
ADSI Edit	adsiedit.msc
Certificate Templates Console	certtmpl.msc
Certificates - Current User	certmgr.msc
Certificates - Local Computer	certlm.msc

Tool Name	.msc File Name
Certification Authority	certsrv.msc
Computer Management	compmgmt.msc
Device Manager	devmgmt.msc
DFS Management	dfsmgmt.msc
DHCP Manager	dhcpmgmt.msc
Disk Management	diskmgmt.msc
DNS Manager	dnsmgmt.msc
Event Viewer	eventvwr.msc
Failover Cluster Management	cluadmin.msc
Fax Service Manager	fxsadmin.msc
Group Policy Management	gpmc.msc
Health Registration Authority	hcscfg.msc
Hyper-V Manager	virtmgmt.msc
Local Group Policy Editor	gpedit.msc
Local Security Policy	secpol.msc
Local Users And Groups	lusrmgr.msc
NAP Client Configuration	napclcfg.msc
Network Policy Server	nps.msc
Online Responder Manager	ocsp.msc
Performance Monitor	perfmon.msc
Print Management	printmanagement.msc
RD Gateway Manager	tsgateway.msc
RD Licensing Diagnoser	lsdiag.msc
Performance Monitor	perfmon.msc
Remote Desktop Licensing Manager	licmgr.exe
Resultant Set Of Policy	rsop.msc
Routing And Remote Access	rrasmgmt.msc
Services	services.msc
Services For Network File System	nfsmgmt.msc
Task Scheduler	taskschd.msc
Trusted Platform Module Management	tpm.msc
Windows Deployment Services	wdsmgmt.msc
Windows Firewall With Advanced Security	wf.msc
Windows Server Backup	wbadmin.msc
WINS Manager	winsmgmt.msc

MMC and remote computers

Some snap-ins can be set to work with local or remote systems. If this is the case, you see the name of the computer with focus in parentheses after the snap-in name in the console tree. When the snap-in is working with the local computer, you see (Local) after the snap-in name. When the snap-in is working with a remote computer, you see the remote computer name in parentheses after the snap-in name, such as (CORPSERVER01).

Generally, regardless of which type of snap-in you are using, you can specify the computer you want to work with in one of two ways. Within the MMC, you can press and hold or right-click the snap-in node in the console tree and then select Connect To Another Computer. This opens the Select Computer dialog box, as shown in Figure 5-3.

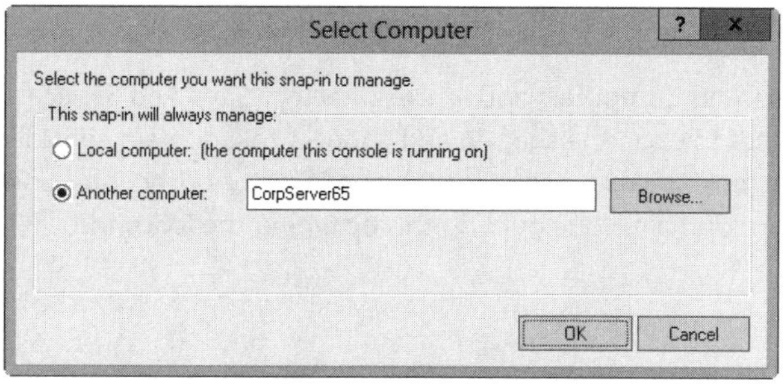

Figure 5-3 Specifying the computer you want to work with.

If you want the snap-in to work with the computer the console is running on, select Local Computer. Otherwise, select Another Computer and then type the computer name or Internet Protocol (IP) address of the computer you want to use. If you don't know the computer name or IP address, tap or click Browse to search for the computer you want to work with.

Some snap-ins that can be set to work with local and remote systems can be started from the command line with the focus set on a specific computer. This is a hidden feature that many people don't know about or don't understand. Set the focus when you start a console from the command line by using the following parameter:

```
/computer=RemoteComputer
```

Here, *RemoteComputer* is the name or IP address of the remote computer you want the snap-in to work with, such as:

```
compmgmt.msc /computer=corpserver01
```

or:

```
services.msc /computer=corpserver32
```

NOTE

For remote management, the appropriate Windows Firewall rules must be enabled on the target computer. Specifically, the inbound rule for COM+ Network Access (DCOM-In) must be enabled in addition to any appropriate rules related to the snap-in you want to work with. For more information, see Chapter 4.

Several hidden options are available with the Active Directory–related snap-ins. For Active Directory Users And Computers, Active Directory Sites And Services, and Active Directory Domains And Trusts, you can use the */Server* parameter to open the snap-in and connect to a specified domain controller. For example, if you want to start Active Directory Users And Computers and connect to the CorpSvr02 domain controller, you could do this by typing the following:

```
dsa.msc /server=CorpSvr02
```

For Active Directory Users And Computers and Active Directory Sites And Services, you can use the */Domain* parameter to open the snap-in and connect to a domain controller in the specified domain. For example, if you want to start Active Directory Users And Computers and connect to the cpandl.com domain, you could do this by typing the following:

```
dsa.msc /domain=cpandl.com
```

Building custom MMCs

If you find that the existing console tools don't meet your needs or you want to create your own administration tool with the features you choose, you can build your own custom console tools. This enables you to determine which features the console includes, which snap-ins it uses, and which additional commands are available.

The steps for creating custom console tools are as follows:

1. Create the console for the tool.
2. Add snap-ins to the console. Snap-ins you use can include Microsoft console tools and console tools from third-party vendors.
3. When you are finished with the design, save the console in user mode so that it is ready for use.

Each step is examined in detail in the sections that follow. Optionally, you can create one or more taskpad views containing shortcuts to menu commands, shell commands, and navigation components you want to include in your custom tool. Techniques for creating taskpad views are discussed in the "Designing custom taskpads for the MMC" section later in this chapter.

Step 1: Creating the console

The first step in building a custom console tool is to create the console you'll use as the framework. To get started, open a blank MMC in author mode. Type **mmc** in the Search box and then press Enter. This opens a blank console titled Console1 that has a default console root, as shown in Figure 5-4.

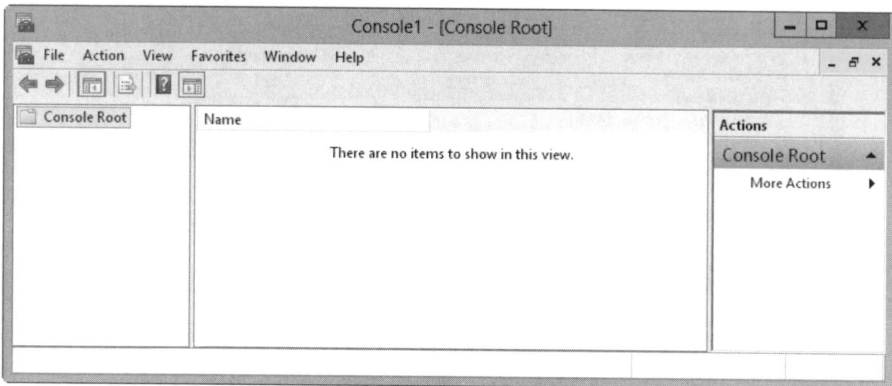

Figure 5-4 Open a blank console with the default console root.

If you want your custom tool to be based on an existing console, you can open its .msc file and add it to the new console. Select Open on the File menu and then use the Open dialog box to find the .msc file you want to work with. As discussed previously, most .msc files are in the %SystemRoot%\System32 directory. Any existing console you choose will open in author mode automatically. Keep in mind that you generally don't want to overwrite the existing .msc file with the new .msc file you are creating. Because of this, when you save the custom console, be sure to choose Save As rather than Save on the File menu.

If you want to start from scratch, work with the blank console you just opened. The first thing you want to do is rename the console root to give it and the related window a more meaningful name. For example, if you are creating a console tool to help you manage Active Directory Domain Services, you could rename the console root Active Directory Management. To rename the console root and the related window, press and hold or right-click the console root and select Rename. Type the name you want to use and then press Enter.

Next, consider how many windows the console tool must have. Most console tools have a single window, but as shown in Figure 5-5, a console can have multiple windows, each with its own view of the console root. You add windows to the console by using New Window on the Window menu. After you add a window, you'll probably want the MMC to tile the windows automatically, as shown in Figure 5-5. You can tile windows by selecting Tile Horizontally on the Window menu. You don't have to do this, however; anytime there are multiple windows, you can use the options on the Window menu to switch between them.

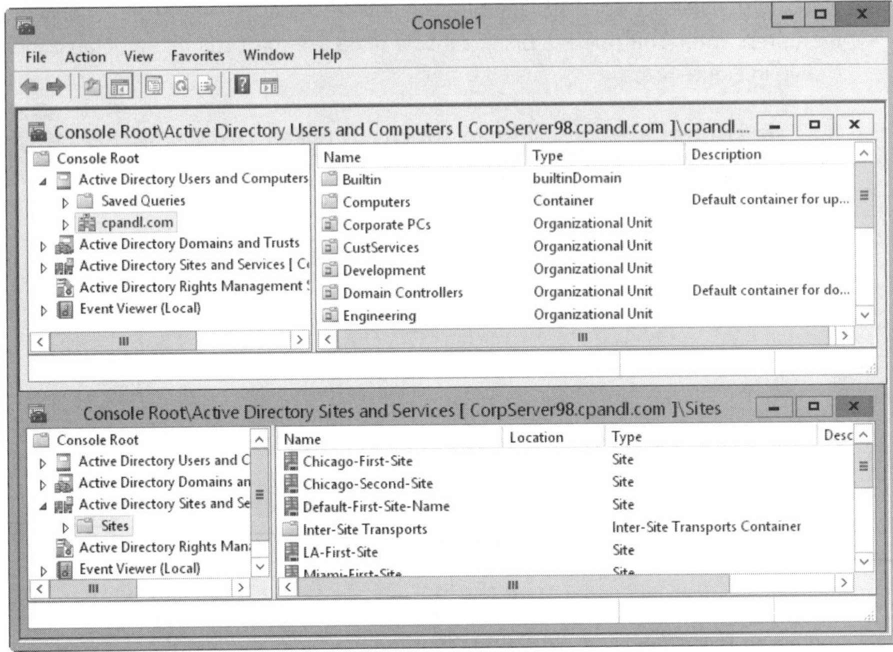

Figure 5-5 Although consoles can have multiple windows, most consoles have a single window.

> **Inside OUT**
>
> ***Using multiple windows in consoles***
>
> **Most console tools have a single window for a good reason: the tool creators wanted to keep the interface as simple as possible. When you introduce multiple windows, you create additional views of the console root, making the interface more complex, often unnecessarily so. Still, there are times when a console tool with multiple windows could come in handy. For example, you might want to have multiple views of the console root in which different areas of the tool are featured, and you could do this by using multiple windows.**

Step 2: Adding snap-ins to the console

While you are thinking about the organization of the tool and the possibility of using additional views of the console root, you should also consider the types of snap-ins that you want to add to the console. Each of the tools listed in Table 5-1 is available as a standalone snap-in you can add to the console. If you've installed any third-party tools on the computer, these tools might have standalone snap-ins you can use. Many other snap-ins are also available from Microsoft.

Again, think of snap-in types or categories, not necessarily specific snap-ins you want to use. You might want to organize the snap-ins into groups by creating folders for storing snap-ins of a specific type or category. For example, if you are creating a console tool for managing Active Directory, you might find that there are four general types of snap-ins you want to work with: General, Policy, Security, and Support. You would then create four folders in the console with these names.

Folders are implemented as a snap-in you add to the console root. To add folders to the console root, follow these steps:

1. In the MMC, choose Add/Remove Snap-In from the File menu in the main window. As shown in Figure 5-6, this opens the Add Or Remove Snap-Ins dialog box.

2. The Available Snap-ins list shows all available snap-ins. Scroll through the list until you see the Folder snap-in. Select Folder and then tap or click Add. The Folder snap-in is added to the Selected Snap-ins list. Repeat this for each folder you want to use. If you are following the example and want to use four folders, tap or click Add three more times so that four Folder snap-ins appear in the Add Or Remove Snap-Ins dialog box, as shown in Figure 5-6.

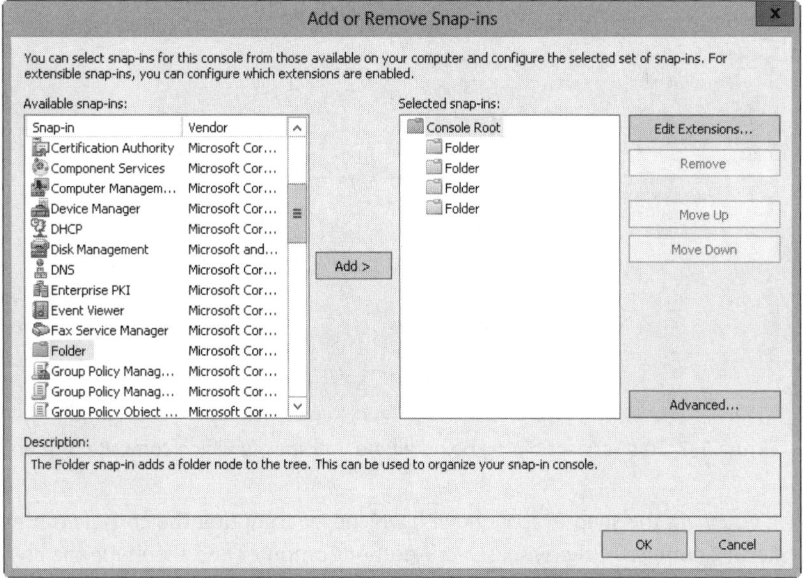

Figure 5-6 Added snap-ins are listed in the Selected Snap-ins list.

3. Now close the Add Or Remove Snap-ins dialog box by tapping or clicking OK and return to the console you are creating.

After you add folders, you must rename them. Press and hold or right-click the first folder and choose Rename. Type a new name and then press Enter. If you are following the example, rename the folders: General, Policy, Security, and Support. When you are finished renaming the folders, follow a similar process to add the appropriate snap-ins to your console.

1. Choose Add/Remove Snap-in on the File menu in the main window. This opens the Add Or Remove Snap-ins dialog box shown in Figure 5-6.
2. Tap or click Advanced. Select the Allow Changing The Parent Snap-in check box. When you tap or click OK, the Add Or Remove Snap-ins dialog box is updated to include a Parent Snap-in drop-down list.
3. In the Parent Snap-in drop-down list, choose the folder to use. In the Available Snap-ins list, choose a snap-in to add as a subnode of the selected folder and then tap or click Add. When you are finished adding snap-ins to the selected folder, repeat this step to add snap-ins to other folders.
4. When you are finished adding snap-ins to folders, tap or click OK to close the Add Or Remove Snap-ins dialog box and return to the console you are creating.

Some snap-ins prompt you to select a computer to manage, as shown in Figure 5-7.

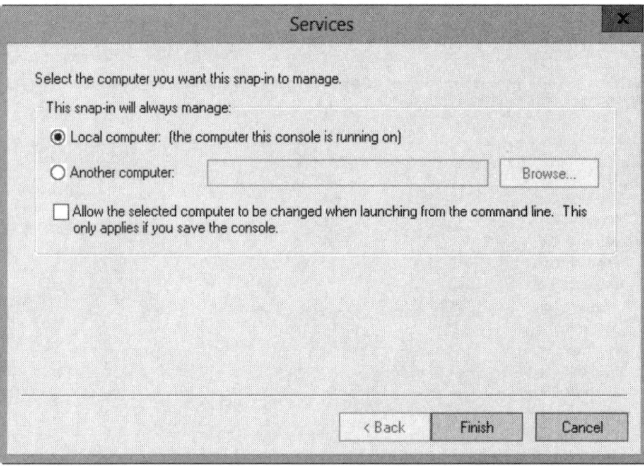

Figure 5-7 This Services dialog box is where you specify which computer a snap-in will manage.

If you want the snap-in to work with whichever computer the console is running on, select Local Computer. Otherwise, select Another Computer and then type the computer name or IP address of the computer you want to use. If you don't know the computer name or IP address, tap or click Browse to search for the computer you want to work with.

Specify which computer to manage

To ensure that you can specify which computer to manage when running the console from the command line, you must select the Allow The Selected Computer To Be Changed When Launching From The Command Line check box. When you select this option and save the console, you can set the computer to manage by using the *Computer*=RemoteComputer parameter.

Some snap-ins are added by using wizards with several configuration pages, so when you select these snap-ins, you start the associated wizard, and the wizard helps you configure how the snap-in is used. One particular snap-in that uses a wizard is Link To Web Address. When you add this snap-in, you start the Link To Web Address Wizard, as shown in Figure 5-8, and the wizard prompts you to create an Internet shortcut. Here, you type the Uniform Resource Locator (URL) you want to use, tap or click Next, enter a descriptive name for the URL, and then tap or click Finish. Then, when you select the related snap-in in the console tree, the designated webpage appears in the details pane.

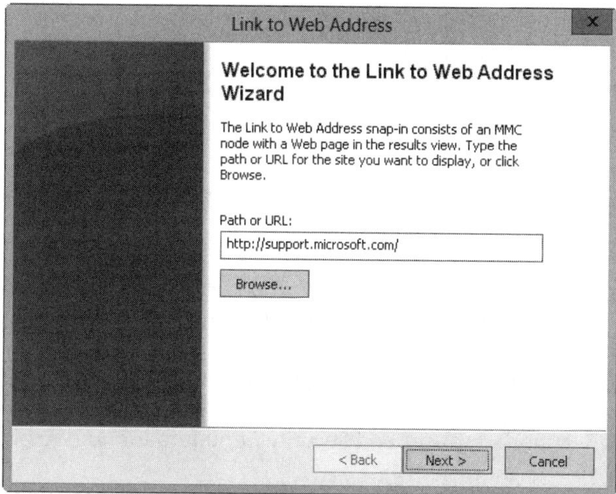

Figure 5-8 You add snap-ins with multiple configuration pages by using a wizard.

While you are adding snap-ins, you can also examine the available extensions for snap-ins. In the Add Or Remove Snap-ins dialog box, choose a previously selected snap-in and then tap or click Edit Extensions. In the Extensions For dialog box, all available extensions are enabled by default, as shown in Figure 5-9. So, if you want to change this behavior, you can select Enable Only Selected Extensions and then clear the individual check boxes for extensions you want to exclude.

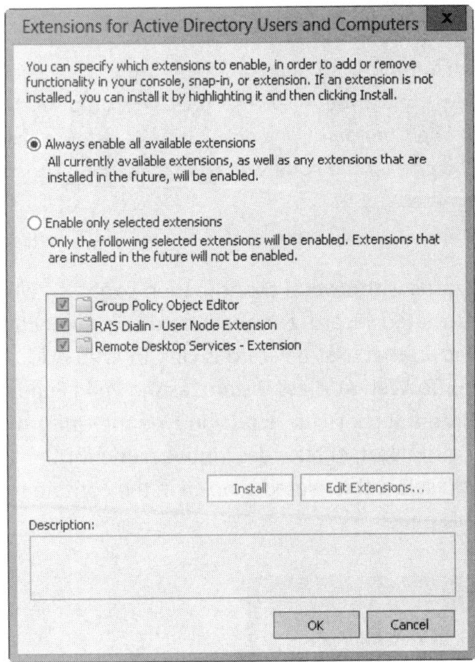

Figure 5-9 You can enable all extensions or selected extensions.

Figure 5-10 shows the example console with snap-ins organized using the previously discussed folders:

- **General.** Contains Active Directory Users And Computers, Active Directory Sites And Services, and Active Directory Rights Management Services
- **Policy.** Contains Group Policy Management and Resultant Set Of Policy
- **Security.** Contains Security Templates and Security Configuration And Analysis
- **Support.** Contains links to Microsoft Knowledge Base, Microsoft Tech Support, and Windows Server Home Page

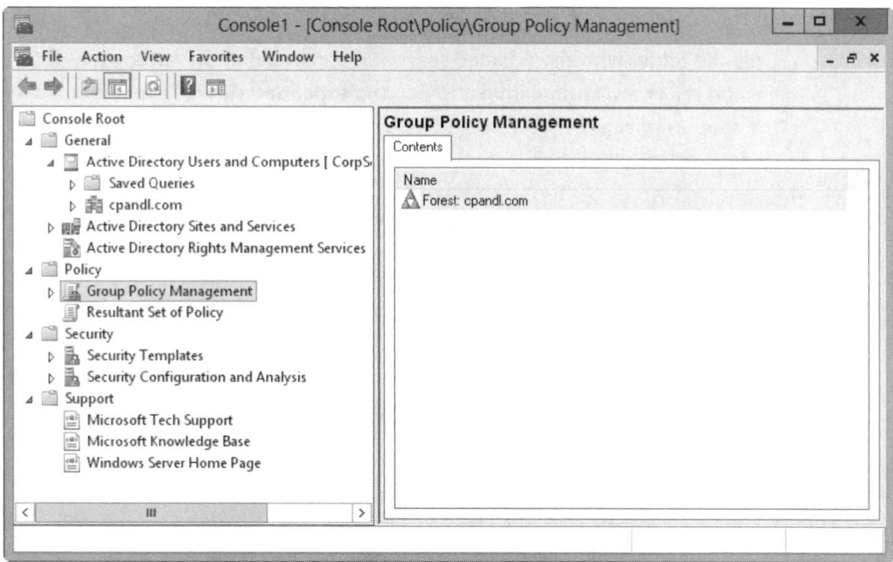

Figure 5-10 A custom console is organized with snap-ins in four folders.

Step 3: Saving the finished console

When you are finished with the design, you are ready to save your custom console tool. Before you do this, however, you should consider a few final design issues:

- What you want the initial console view to be
- Which user mode you want to use
- Which icon you want to use
- What you want to name the console tool and where you want it to be located

Setting the initial console view before saving

By default, the MMC remembers the last selected node or snap-in and saves this as the initial view for the console. In the example tool created, if you expand the General folder, select Active Directory Users And Computers, and then save the console, this selection is saved when the console is next opened.

Keep in mind that subsequent views depend on user selections.

NOTE

Only the folder with the selected snap-in is expanded in the saved view. If you use folders and select a snap-in within a folder, the expanded view of the folder is saved with the snap-in selected. If you expand other folders, the console is not saved with these folders expanded.

Setting the console mode before saving

When you are finished authoring the console tool, select Options on the File menu. In the Options dialog box, as shown in Figure 5-11, you can change the console mode so that it is ready for use.

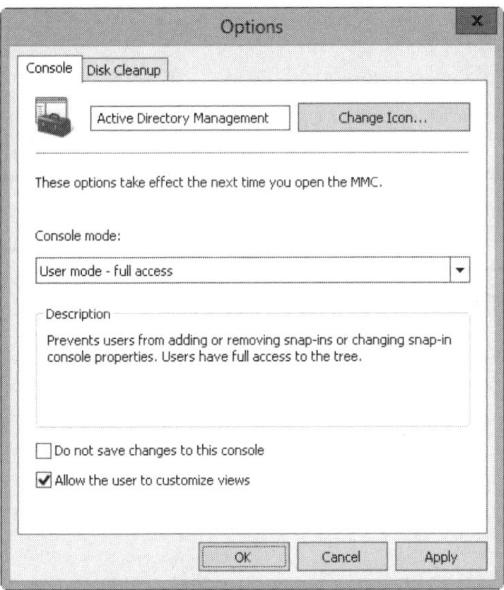

Figure 5-11 On the Console tab of the Options dialog box, you select a console mode and determine whether users can change the console.

In most cases, you'll want to use User Mode - Full Access. Full access has the following characteristics:

- Users have a Window menu that enables them to open new windows; they can also press and hold or right-click a node or snap-in and choose New Window From Here to open a new window.
- Users can press and hold or right-click and choose New Taskpad View to create a new taskpad view.

With user mode set to Limited Access, Multiple Window, the console has the following characteristics:

- Users have a Window menu that allows them to arrange windows; they also can press and hold or right-click a node or snap-in and choose New Window From Here to open a new window.
- Users cannot press and hold or right-click and choose New Taskpad View to create a new taskpad view.

With user mode set to Limited Access, Single Window, the console has the following characteristics:

- Users do not have a Window menu and cannot press and hold or right-click a node or snap-in and choose New Window From Here to open a new window.
- Users cannot press and hold or right-click and choose New Taskpad View to create a new taskpad view.

To prevent user selections from changing the view, you find two handy options when you select Options from the File menu:

- **Do Not Save Changes To This Console.** Select this option to prevent the user from saving changes to the console. Clear this option to change the view automatically, based on the user's last selection in the console before exiting.
- **Allow The User To Customize Views.** Select this option to enable users to add windows focused on a selected item in the console. Clear this option to prevent users from adding customized views.

Setting the console icon before saving

While you are working in the Options dialog box, you might consider setting custom icons for your console tools. All the console tools developed by Microsoft have their own icons. You also can use these icons for your console tools, or you could use icons from other Microsoft programs quite easily. In the Options dialog box (which opens when you select Options on the File menu), tap or click Change Icon. This opens the Change Icon dialog box, as shown in Figure 5-12.

In the Change Icon dialog box, tap or click Browse. By default, the Open dialog box should open with the directory set to %SystemRoot%\System32. In this case, type **shell32.dll** as the File Name and tap or click Open. You should now see the Change Icon dialog box with the Shell32.dll selected, which enables you to choose one of several hundred icons registered for use with the operating system shell. (See Figure 5-13.) Choose an icon, tap or click OK, and then tap or click OK to close the Options dialog box. From then on, the icon will be associated with your custom console tool.

Figure 5-12 You can assign an icon to or change an icon for a console tool.

Figure 5-13 There are many icons to choose from.

Saving the console tool

After you set the user mode, you can save the console tool. It can appear as one of the following:

- **A desktop icon.** Select Save As on the File menu and then navigate the folder structure to %SystemDrive%\Users*%UserName%*\Desktop. Here, *%UserName%* is the name of the user who will work with the tool. After you type a name for the console, tap or click Save.

- **A folder icon.** Select Save As on the File menu and then navigate to the folder where you want the console tool to reside. After you type a name for the console, tap or click Save.
- **An option on the Tools menu in Server Manager.** Select Save As on the File menu and then navigate to the %SystemRoot%\System32 folder. After you type a name for the console, tap or click Save. Tap and hold or right-click the MMC and then select Create Shortcut. By default, you are prompted to save the shortcut on the desktop and tap or click Yes to confirm. Tap and hold or right-click the shortcut and then select Cut. In File Explorer, navigate the folder structure to %SystemDrive%\ProgramData\Microsoft\Windows\Start Menu\Programs\Administrative Tools. In the right pane of File Explorer, tap and hold or right-click and then select Paste.
- **An option on the Tools menu in Server Manager for a specific user.** Select Save As on the File menu and then navigate to the %SystemRoot%\System32 folder. After you type a name for the console, tap or click Save. Tap and hold or right-click the MMC and then select Create Shortcut. By default, you are prompted to save the shortcut on the desktop and tap or click Yes to confirm. Tap and hold or right-click the shortcut and then select Cut. In File Explorer, navigate the folder structure to %SystemDrive%\Users*%UserName%*\AppData\Roaming\Microsoft\Windows\Start Menu\Programs\Administrative Tools. In the right pane of File Explorer, tap and hold or right-click and then select Paste. Here, *%UserName%* is the name of the user who will work with the tool.

Change tool names by using the Options dialog box

By default, the name shown on the console tool's title bar is set to the file name you designate when saving it. As long as you are in author mode, you can change the console tool name by using the Options dialog box. Select Options on the File menu and then type the name in the box provided at the top of the Console tab.

Designing custom taskpads for the MMC

When you want to simplify administration or limit the available tasks for junior administrators or Power Users, you might want to consider adding a taskpad to a console tool. By using taskpads, you can create custom views of your console tools that contain shortcuts to menu commands, shell commands, and navigation components.

Getting started with taskpads

Basically, taskpads enable you to create a page of tasks you can perform quickly by tapping or clicking the associated shortcut links rather than using the existing menu or interface provided by snap-ins. You can create multiple taskpads in a console, each of which you access as a taskpad view. Control Panel is an example of a console that has a taskpad. As with most taskpads, the Control Panel has two purposes: it provides direct access to the commands or tasks so that you don't have to navigate menus, and it limits your options to a set of predefined tasks you can perform.

You create taskpads when you are working with a console tool in author mode. Taskpads can contain the following items:

- **Menu commands.** Menu commands are used to run the standard menu options of included snap-ins.
- **Shell commands.** Shell commands are used to run scripts or programs or to open webpages.
- **Navigation components.** Navigation components are used to navigate to a saved view on the Favorites menu.

Taskpad commands are also called *tasks*. You run tasks just by tapping or clicking their links. In the case of menu commands, tapping or clicking the links runs the menu commands. For shell commands, tapping or clicking the links runs the associated scripts or programs. For navigation components, tapping or clicking the links displays the designated navigation views. If you have multiple levels of taskpads, you must include navigation components to enable users to get back to the top-level taskpad. The concept is similar to having to create a home link on webpages.

Figure 5-14 shows a taskpad created for the Active Directory Users And Computers snap-in that has been added to the custom tool created earlier in the chapter.

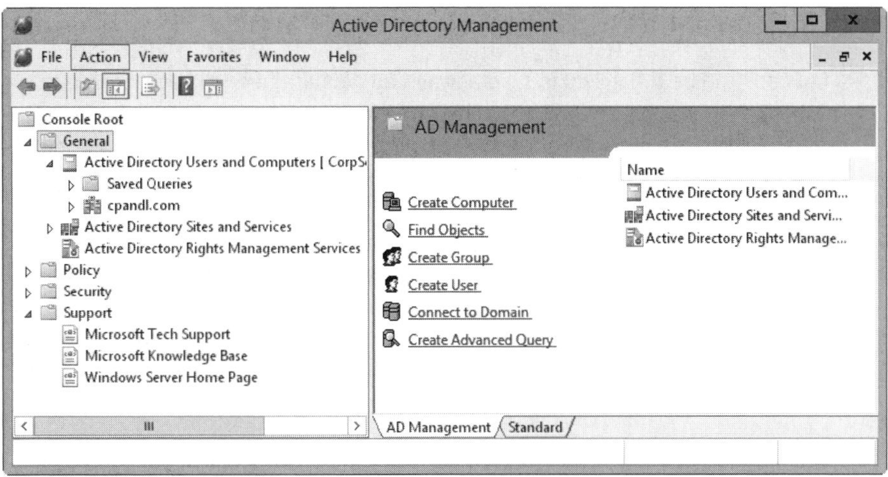

Figure 5-14 This is a custom console with a taskpad that uses a vertical list.

As you can see, the task page view is labeled Active Directory Management, and it provides the following commands:

- **Create Computer.** Used to start the New Object—Computer Wizard
- **Find Objects.** Used to open the Find Users, Contacts, And Groups dialog box
- **Create Group.** Used to start the New Object—Group Wizard
- **Create User.** Used to start the New Object—User Wizard
- **Connect To Domain.** Used to select the domain to work with
- **Create Advanced Query.** Used to define an Active Directory query and save it so that it can be reused

NOTE

You could also add a Connect To Domain Forest option that would be used to select the domain forest to work with. The taskpad hasn't been used to limit the options but rather to provide quick shortcut access to commonly run tasks. In the next section, you learn how to limit user options.

Understanding taskpad view styles

Taskpads can be organized in several ways. By default, they will have two views: an extended taskpad view and a standard view. The extended view contains the list of tasks you've defined and can also contain the console items being managed. The standard view contains only the console items being managed. When you create the taskpad, you have the option of hiding the standard view by selecting the Hide Standard Tab check box.

The extended view of the taskpad can be organized using a vertical list, a horizontal list, or no list. In a vertical list, as shown previously in Figure 5-14, taskpad commands are listed to the left of the console items they are used to manage. This organization approach works well when you have a long list of tasks and you still want users to be able to work with the related snap-ins.

With a horizontal list, as shown in Figure 5-15, the console items managed by the taskpad are listed above the taskpad commands. This organization style is best when you want to display multiple columns of taskpad commands and still be able to work with the related snap-ins.

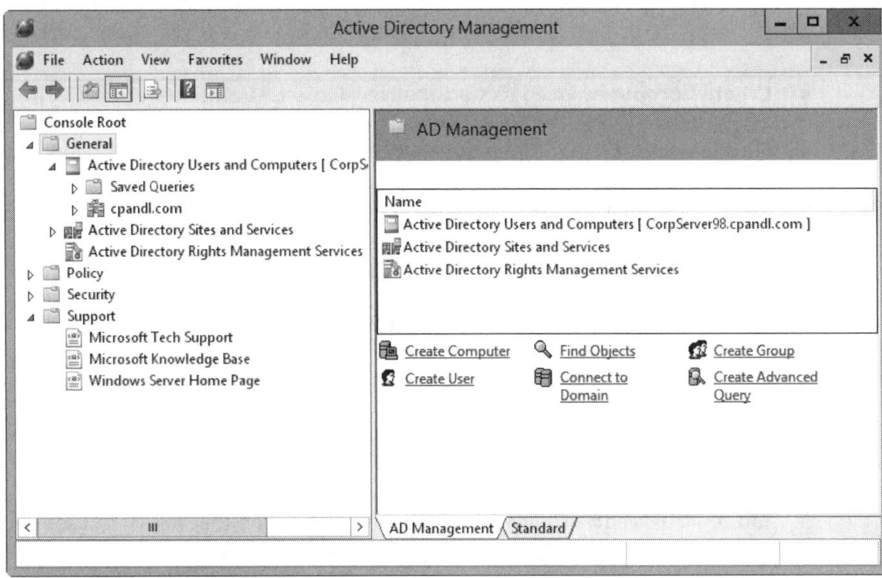

Figure 5-15 A custom console with a taskpad that uses a horizontal list.

In some cases, you might not want to show the console items being managed by the taskpad in the same view as the tasks. In this case, you can specify that no list should be used. When you choose the No List option, the taskpad commands are shown by themselves on the taskpad tab (Active Directory Management in the example), and users can tap or click the Standard tab to access the related console items.

Inside OUT

Limiting user options in taskpads

As discussed, you can limit the options users have in console tools by selecting both No List and the Hide Standard Tab check box. Keep in mind that if the console tool doesn't include a taskpad for a snap-in, users will still be able to manage the snap-in in the usual way. For example, the taskpad shown in Figure 5-15 doesn't define any tasks that manage policy or security, so the snap-ins in these folders will be fully accessible. To prevent users from working with these snap-ins directly, you must define taskpads for those snap-ins or add tasks that use menu commands from those snap-ins to the current taskpad or another taskpad.

When you select the No List option, you can limit users' options to the tasks you've defined and not allow users to access the console items being managed. To do this, you specify that the Standard tab should be hidden. From then on, when working with the console items being managed, users can perform only the tasks defined on the taskpad, such as shown in Figure 5-16.

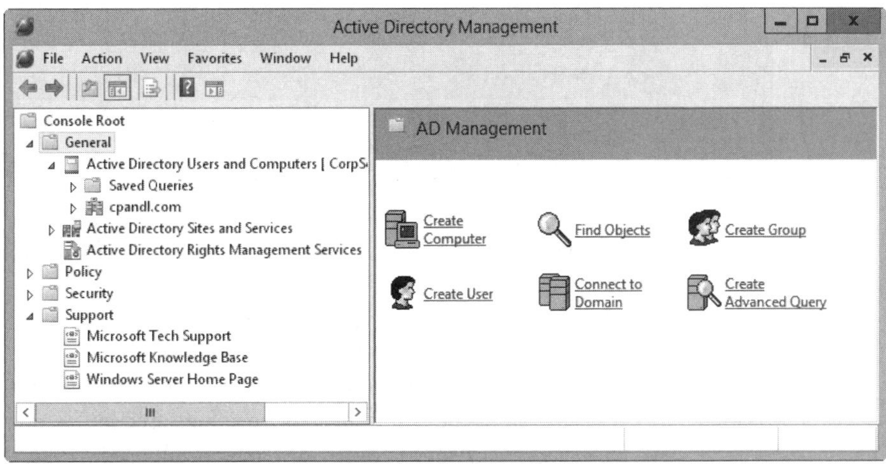

Figure 5-16 By using the No List style and hiding the Standard tab, you can limit user options.

Creating and managing taskpads

Any console tool that has at least one snap-in can have an associated taskpad. To create a taskpad, you must open the console in author mode and then follow these steps:

1. In your custom MMC, press and hold or right-click the folder or console item you want to work with and then choose New Taskpad View to start the New Taskpad View Wizard. Keep in mind that a single taskpad can be used to manage multiple console items.

2. In the New Taskpad View Wizard, tap or click Next and then configure the taskpad display. (See Figure 5-17 for an example.) Select the style for the details page as Vertical List, Horizontal List, or No List and set the task description style as Text or InfoTip. You also can choose to hide the Standard tab (which only limits the tasks that can be performed if you also select the No List style). As you make selections, the wizard provides a depiction of what the results will look like as a finished taskpad. Tap or click Next to continue.

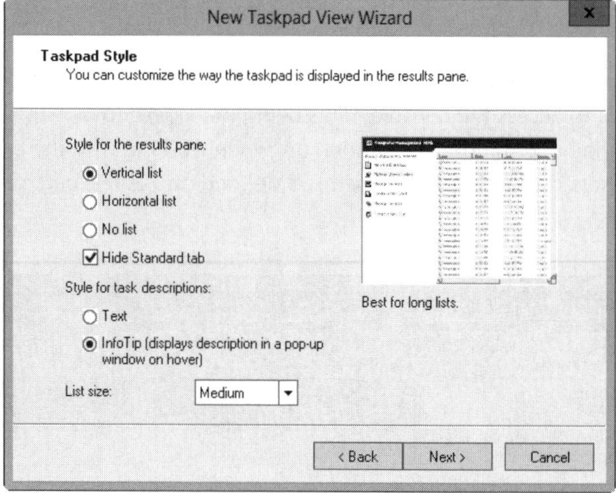

Figure 5-17 Configure the taskpad display in the New Taskpad View Wizard.

3. On the Taskpad Reuse page (shown in Figure 5-18), you must decide whether to apply the taskpad view to the selected tree item only (the item you press and hold or right-click) or to any other tree item of the same type. If you choose the latter option, you also have the option to change the default display for any items used in the taskpad to the taskpad view. Typically, you'll want to do this to standardize the view, especially if you've hidden the Standard tab and don't want users to have other options. Tap or click Next.

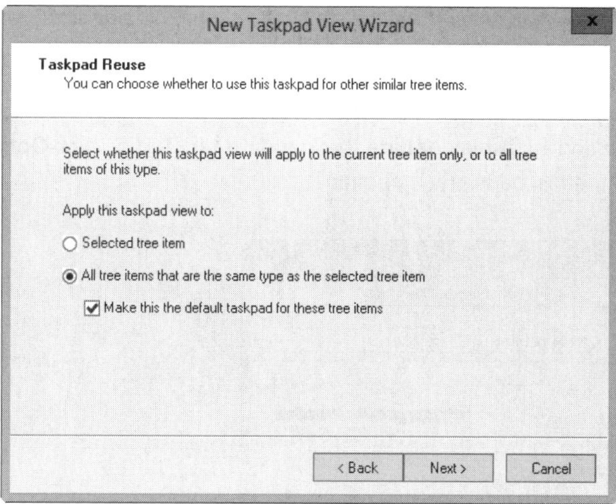

Figure 5-18 Specify a taskpad target.

> NOTE
>
> **Basically, all snap-ins are of the same type, so if you apply the taskpad to any other tree item of the same type, the taskpad view can include any snap-in that you have added to the console.**

4. Next, you set the name and description for the taskpad. The name appears at the top of the taskpad and on the tab at the bottom of the taskpad. The description appears at the top of the taskpad under the taskpad name. Tap or click Next.

5. On the final wizard page, tap or click Finish to create the taskpad. The Add New Tasks To This Taskpad After The Wizard Closes check box is selected by default, so if you tap or click Finish without clearing this option, the New Task Wizard starts and helps you create tasks for the taskpad.

If you want to create multiple taskpads, you can repeat this procedure. For the example console, you might want to have a taskpad for each folder; in that case, you would create three additional taskpads. Any additional taskpads you create can be placed at the same place in the console tree or at a different part of the console tree. You access multiple taskpads placed at the same part of the console tree by using the tabs provided in the details pane.

As long as you are in author mode, any taskpad you created can easily be edited or removed. To edit a taskpad view, press and hold or right-click the item where you defined the taskpad and then select Edit Taskpad View from the shortcut menu. This opens a Properties dialog box containing two tabs:

- **General.** Use the options on the General tab, shown in Figure 5-19, to control the taskpad style and to display or hide the Standard tab. Tap or click Options to specify to which items the taskpad view is applied.

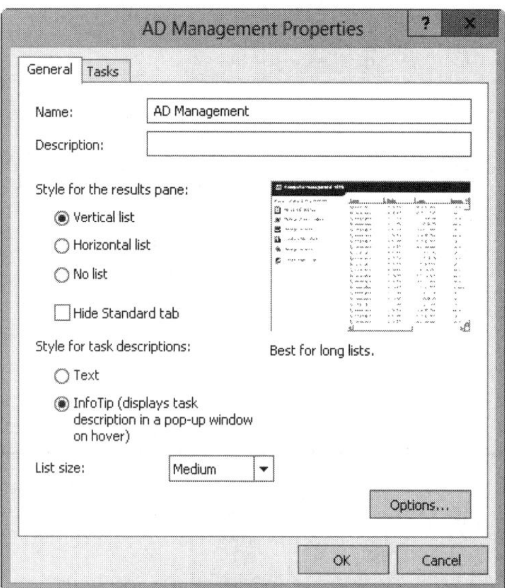

Figure 5-19 Change the view options of a custom taskpad.

- **Tasks.** Use the Tasks tab to list current tasks defined for the taskpad. Use the related options to create new tasks or manage the existing tasks.

Creating and managing tasks

You create tasks by using the New Task Wizard. By default, this wizard starts automatically when you finish creating a taskpad view. You also can start the wizard by using the taskpad Properties dialog box. On the Tasks tab, tap or click New. Alternatively, in your MMC, press and hold or right-click the folder or console item where you defined the taskpad and then select Edit Taskpad View from the shortcut menu.

After the New Task Wizard is started, tap or click Next and then select the command type as follows:

- Choose Menu Command to run the standard menu options of included snap-ins.
- Choose Shell Command to run scripts or programs or to open webpages.
- Choose Navigation to navigate to a saved view on the Favorites menu.

The subsequent screens you see depend on the type of task you are creating.

Creating menu command tasks

After choosing to create a menu command, select a source for the command, as shown in Figure 5-20. You specify the source of the command as a node from the console tree or from the list in the results pane for the item selected when you started the wizard. If you choose Node In The Tree as the source, select a snap-in in the console tree and then choose one of the available commands for that snap-in. The available commands change based on the snap-in you've selected.

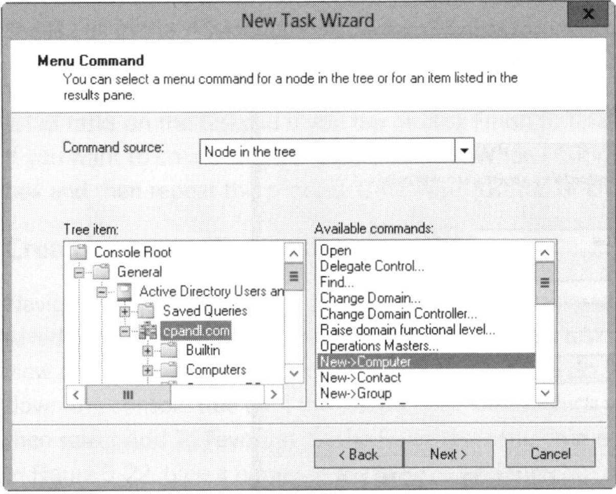

Figure 5-20 Select a command source and then choose from the list of available commands.

Next, you set the name and description for the task. The name is used as the shortcut link designator for the task. The description is displayed as text under the shortcut link or as an InfoTip, depending on the way you configured the taskpad.

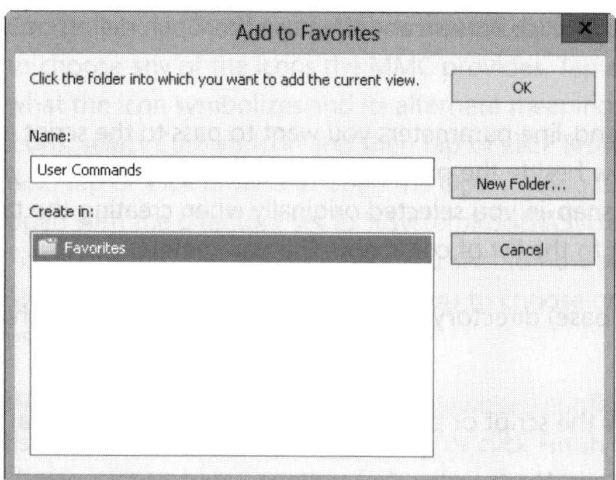

Figure 5-22 Save the current view of the console tool to the Favorites menu.

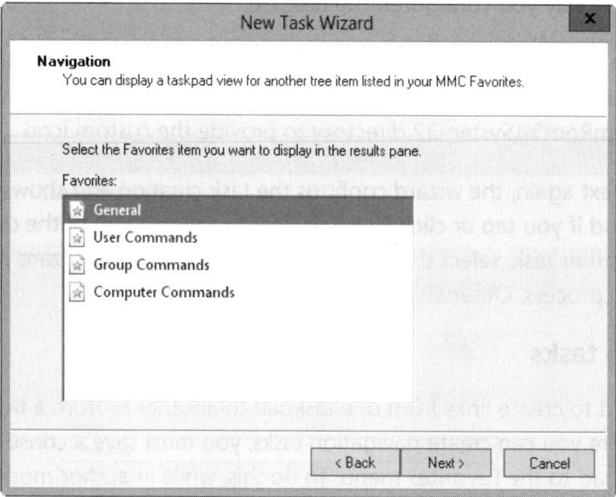

Figure 5-23 Select the previously defined favorite you want to use.

Next, you set the name and description for the task. The name is used as the shortcut link designator for the task. The description is displayed as text under the shortcut link or as an InfoTip, depending on the way you configured the taskpad. If you are creating a link to the main console tool page, you might want to call it Home.

Next, you can choose an icon for the task. As discussed previously, you can select Icons Provided By MMC or Custom Icon. If you created a link called Home, the MMC provides a Home icon to use. If you use custom icons, you probably want to use the Shell32.dll in the %SystemRoot%\System32 directory to provide the custom icon.

When you tap or click Next again, the wizard confirms the task creation and shows a current list of tasks on the taskpad if you tap or click Finish to finalize the creation of the current task. If you want to create another task, select the When I Click Finish, Run This Wizard Again check box and then repeat this process. Otherwise, just tap or click Finish.

Arranging, editing, and removing tasks

As long as you are in author mode, you can edit tasks and their properties by using the task-pad Properties dialog box. To open this dialog box, press and hold or right-click the folder or item where you defined the taskpad and then select Edit Taskpad View from the shortcut menu. On the Tasks tab shown in Figure 5-24, you can do the following:

- **Arrange tasks.** To arrange tasks in a specific order, select a task and then tap or click Move Up or Move Down to set the task order.
- **Create new tasks.** To create a new task, tap or click New and then use the New Task Wizard to define the task.
- **Edit existing tasks.** To edit a task, select it and then tap or click Modify.
- **Remove tasks.** To remove a task, select it and then tap or click Remove.

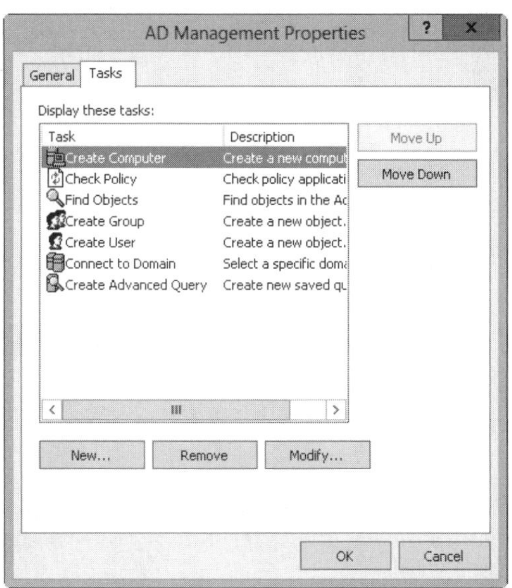

Figure 5-24 Use the Tasks tab in the taskpad Properties dialog box to arrange, create, edit, and remove tasks.

Publishing and distributing your custom tools

As you've seen, the MMC provides a complete framework for creating custom tools that can be tailored to the needs of a wide range of users. For administrators, you could create custom consoles tailored for each individual specialty, such as security administration, network administration, or user administration. For junior administrators or advanced users with delegated privileges, you could create custom consoles that include taskpads that help guide them by providing lists of common commands, and you can even restrict this list so that these individuals can perform only these commands.

Because custom consoles are saved as regular files, you can publish and distribute them as you would any other file. You could put the consoles on a network file server in a shared folder. You could email the consoles directly to those who will use them. You could use Active Directory to publish the tools. You could even copy them directly to the Tools menu in Server Manager, as discussed previously.

In any case, users need appropriate access permissions to run the tasks and access the snap-ins. These permissions must be granted for a particular computer or for the network.

CHAPTER 6

Configuring roles, role services, and features

You prepare servers for use by installing and configuring the following components:

- **Server roles.** Server roles are related sets of software components that enable servers to perform a specific function for users and other computers on networks. A computer can be dedicated to a single role, such as Active Directory Domain Services (AD DS), or a computer can provide multiple roles.
- **Role services.** Role services are software components that provide the functionality of server roles. Each server role has one or more related role services. Some server roles, such as Domain Name Syste m (DNS) and Dynamic Host Configuration Protocol (DHCP), have a single function, and installing the role installs this function. Other roles, such as Network Policy And Access Services and Active Directory Certificate Services, have multiple role services that you can install. With these server roles, you can choose which role services to install.
- **Features.** Features are software components that provide additional functionality. Features, such as Windows Internet Naming Service (WINS) and Windows Server Backup, are installed and removed separately from roles and role services. A computer can have multiple features installed or none, depending on its configuration.

You configure roles, role services, and features by using the Server Manager console. Server Manager's command-line counterpart is the ServerManager module for Windows PowerShell.

NOTE

Although Server Manager enables you to work with a local server, other servers must be added for management, as discussed in "Adding servers for management" in Chapter 4, "Managing Windows Server 2012 R2." For ease of reference in this chapter, I will refer to servers added for management in Server Manager as *managed servers*.

Using roles, role services, and features

Before modifying a server's configuration, you should carefully plan how adding or removing a role, role service, or feature will affect a server's overall performance. Although you typically want to combine complementary roles, doing so increases the workload on the server, so you need to optimize the server hardware accordingly. Also, keep in mind that roles, role services, and features can depend on other roles, role services, and features. When you install roles, role services, and features, Server Manager prompts you to install any additional roles, role services, or features that are required. If you try to remove a required component of an installed role, role service, or feature, Server Manager warns that you cannot remove the component unless you also remove the other role, role service, or feature.

Table 6-1 provides an overview of the primary roles and the related role services that you can deploy on a server running Windows Server 2012 R2. In addition to roles and features that are included with Windows Server 2012 R2 by default, Server Manager enables integration of roles and features that might become available on the Microsoft Download Center as optional updates to Windows Server 2012 R2.

Table 6-1 Primary roles and related role services for Windows Server 2012 R2

Role	Description
Active Directory Certificate Services (AD CS)	AD CS provides functions necessary for issuing and revoking digital certificates for users, client computers, and servers. It includes these role services: Certification Authority, Certification Enrollment Policy Web Service, Certification Authority Web Enrollment, Network Device Enrollment Service, and Online Responder.
Active Directory Domain Services (AD DS)	AD DS provides functions necessary for storing information about users, groups, computers, and other objects on the network and makes this information available to users and computers. Active Directory domain controllers give network users and computers access to permitted resources on the network.
Active Directory Federation Services (AD FS)	AD FS complements the authentication and access-management features of AD DS by extending them to the World Wide Web.
Active Directory Lightweight Directory Services (AD LDS)	AD LDS provides a data store for directory-enabled applications that do not require AD DS and do not need to be deployed on domain controllers.
Active Directory Rights Management Services (AD RMS)	AD RMS provides controlled access to protected email messages, documents, intranet pages, and other types of files. It includes these role services: Active Directory Rights Management Server and Identity Federation Support.

Role	Description
Application Server	Application Server enables a server to host distributed applications built using ASP.NET, Enterprise Services, and Microsoft .NET Framework 4.5. It includes COM+ Network Access, TCP Port Sharing, and other role services.
DHCP Server	DHCP Server provides centralized control over IP addressing. DHCP servers can assign dynamic IP addresses and essential TCP/IP settings to other computers on a network.
DNS Server	DNS Server is a name-resolution system that resolves computer names to IP addresses. DNS servers are essential for name resolution in Active Directory domains.
Fax Server	Fax Server provides centralized control over sending and receiving faxes in the enterprise. A fax server can act as a gateway for faxing and enables you to manage fax resources, such as jobs, reports, and fax devices on the server or on the network.
File And Storage Services	File And Storage Services provides essential services for managing files and storage and the way they are made available and replicated on the network. A number of server roles require some type of file service. It includes these role services and subservices: BranchCache for Network Files, Data Deduplication, Distributed File System (DFS), DFS Namespaces, DFS Replication, File Server, File Server Resource Manager, Services for Network File System (NFS), File Server VSS Agent Service, iSCSI Target Server, iSCSI Target Storage Provider, Server for NFS, Storage Services, and Work Folders.
Hyper-V	Hyper-V provides services for creating and managing virtual machines that emulate physical computers. Virtual machines have separate operating system environments from the host server.
Network Policy And Access Services (NPAS)	NPAS provides essential services for managing network access policies. It includes these role services: Network Policy Server (NPS), Health Registration Authority (HRA), and Host Credential Authorization Protocol (HCAP).
Print And Document Services	Print And Document Services provides essential services for managing network printers, network scanners, and related drivers. It includes these role services: Print Server, Distributed Scan Server, Internet Printing, and LPD Service.
Remote Access	Remote Access provides services for managing routing and remote access to networks. Use this role if you need to configure virtual private networks (VPNs), Network Address Translation (NAT), and other routing services. It includes these role services: DirectAccess and VPN (RAS), Routing, and Web Application Proxy.

Role	Description
Remote Desktop Services	Remote Desktop Services provides services that enable users to run Windows-based applications that are installed on a remote server. When users run an application on a terminal server, the execution and processing occur on the server, and only the data from the application is transmitted over the network.
Volume Activation Services	Volume Activation Services provides services for automating the management of volume license keys and volume key activation.
Web Server (IIS)	Internet Information Services (IIS) is used to host websites and web-based applications. Websites hosted on a web server can have both static content and dynamic content. You can build web applications hosted on a web server by using ASP.NET and .NET Framework 4.5. When you deploy a web server, you can manage the server configuration by using IIS 8 modules and administration tools. It includes several dozen role services.
Windows Deployment Services (WDS)	WDS provides services for deploying computers running Windows in the enterprise. It includes these role services: Deployment Server and Transport Server.
Windows Server Essentials Experience	Essentials Experience provides services previously only available with Windows Server Essentials, including services for deploying workplaces, which are remotely accessible through a web gateway. It requires single-domain installation.
Windows Server Update Services (WSUS)	WSUS provides services for Microsoft Update, enabling you to distribute updates from designated servers. It includes the WID Database, WSUS Services, and Database role services.

Table 6-2 provides an overview of the primary features that you can deploy on a server running Windows Server 2012 R2. Unlike early releases of Windows, some important server features are not installed automatically. For example, you must add Windows Server Backup to use the built-in backup and restore features of the operating system.

Table 6-2 Primary features for Windows Server 2012 R2

Feature	Description
.NET Framework 4.5	.NET Framework 4.5 provides APIs for application development. It replaces .NET 3.5 as the default framework. Only the framework and TCP Port Sharing are installed by default. Other subfeatures include ASP.NET 4.5, HTTP Activation, Message Queuing Activation, Named Pipe Activation, and TCP Activation.
Background Intelligent Transfer Service (BITS)	BITS provides intelligent background transfers. When this feature is installed, the server can act as a BITS server that can receive file uploads from clients. This feature isn't necessary for downloads to clients using BITS. Additional subfeatures include IIS Server Extension and Compact Server.

Feature	Description
BitLocker Drive Encryption	BitLocker Drive Encryption provides hardware-based security to protect data through full-volume encryption that prevents disk tampering while the operating system is offline. Computers that have Trusted Platform Module (TPM) can use BitLocker Drive Encryption in Startup Key or TPM-Only mode. Both modes provide early integrity validation.
BitLocker Network Unlock	BitLocker Network Unlock provides support for network-based key protectors that automatically unlock BitLocker-protected operating system drives when a domain-joined computer is restarted.
BranchCache	BranchCache provides services needed for BranchCache client and server functionality. It includes HTTP protocol, Hosted Cache, and related services.
Client For NFS	Client For NFS provides functionality for accessing files on UNIX-based NFS servers.
Data Center Bridging	Data Center Bridging supports a suite of Institute of Electrical and Electronics Engineers (IEEE) standards for enhancing LANs and enforcing bandwidth allocation.
Enhanced Storage	Enhanced Storage provides support for Enhanced Storage Devices.
Failover Clustering	Failover Clustering provides clustering functionality that enables multiple servers to work together to provide high availability for services and applications. Many types of services can be clustered, including file and print services. Messaging and database servers are ideal candidates for clustering.
Group Policy Management	Group Policy Management installs the Group Policy Management Console (GPMC), which provides centralized administration of Group Policy.
Ink And Handwriting Services	Ink And Handwriting Services provides support for use of a pen or stylus and handwriting recognition.
Internet Printing Client	Internet Printing Client provides functionality that enables clients to use HTTP to connect to printers on web print servers.
IP Address Management Server	IP Address Management Server provides support for central management of the enterprise's IP address space and the related infrastructure servers.
iSNS Server Service	iSNS Server Service provides management and server functions for Internet SCSI (iSCSI) devices, enabling the server to process registration requests, deregistration requests, and queries from iSCSI devices.
LPR Port Monitor	LPR Port Monitor installs the LPR Port Monitor, which enables printing to devices attached to UNIX-based computers.

Feature	Description
Media Foundation	Media Foundation provides essential functionality for Windows Media Foundation.
Message Queuing	Message Queuing provides management and server functions for distributed message queuing. A group of related subfeatures is also available.
Multipath I/O (MPIO)	MPIO provides the functionality necessary for using multiple data paths to a storage device.
Network Load Balancing (NLB)	NLB provides failover support and load balancing for IP-based applications and services by distributing incoming application requests among a group of participating servers. Web servers are ideal candidates for load balancing.
Peer Name Resolution Protocol (PNRP)	PNRP provides Link-Local Multicast Name Resolution (LLMNR) functionality that enables peer-to-peer, name-resolution services. When you install this feature, applications running on the server can use LLMNR to register and resolve names.
Quality Windows Audio Video Experience	Quality Windows Audio Video Experience is a networking platform for audio video (AV) streaming applications on IP home networks.
RAS Connection Manager Administration Kit	RAS Connection Manager Administration Kit provides the framework for creating profiles for connecting to remote servers and networks.
Remote Assistance	Remote Assistance enables a remote user to connect to the server to provide or receive Remote Assistance.
Remote Differential Compression	Remote Differential Compression provides support for differential compression by determining which parts of a file have changed and replicating only the changes.
Remote Procedure Call (RPC) over HTTP Proxy	RPC over HTTP Proxy installs a proxy for relaying RPC messages from client applications to the server over HTTP. RPC over HTTP is an alternative to having clients access the server over a VPN connection.
Remote Server Administration Tools (RSAT)	RSAT installs role-management and feature-management tools that can be used for remote administration of other Windows Server systems. Options for individual tools are provided, or you can install tools by top-level category or subcategory.
Simple Mail Transfer Protocol (SMTP) Server	SMTP Server is a network protocol for controlling the transfer and routing of email messages. When this feature is installed, the server can act as a basic SMTP server. For a full-featured solution, you need to install a messaging server such as Microsoft Exchange Server.

Feature	Description
Simple Network Management Protocol (SNMP) Services	SNMP Services is a protocol that simplifies management of TCP/IP networks. You can use SNMP for centralized network management if your network has SNMP-compliant devices. You can also use SNMP for network monitoring through network-management software.
Simple TCP/IP Services	Simple TCP/IP Services installs additional TCP/IP services, including Character Generator, Daytime, Discard, Echo, and Quote of the Day.
SMB 1.0/CIFS File Sharing Support	File Sharing Support provides support for legacy file shares and clients.
SMB Bandwidth Limit	SMB Bandwidth Limit enables you to limit specific categories of SMB traffic such as Live Migration over SMB.
User Interfaces And Infrastructure	User Interfaces And Infrastructure enables you to control the user experience and infrastructure options (Graphical Management Tools And Infrastructure, Desktop Experience, or Server Graphical Shell). Desktop Experience provides Windows desktop functionality on the server (but these functions can reduce the server's overall performance).
Windows Biometric Framework	Windows Biometric Framework provides the functionality required for using fingerprint devices.
Windows Internal Database	Windows Internal Database enables the server to use relational databases with Windows roles and features that require an internal database, such as AD RMS; Universal Description, Discovery, and Integration (UDDI) Services; Windows Server Update Services (WSUS); Windows SharePoint Services; and Windows System Resource Manager.
Windows PowerShell	Windows PowerShell enables you to manage the Windows PowerShell features of the server. Windows PowerShell and the Windows PowerShell ISE are installed by default.
Windows PowerShell Web Access	Windows PowerShell Web Access enables the server to act as a web gateway for remotely managing servers in a web browser.
Windows Process Activation Service	Windows Process Activation Service provides support for distributed, web-based applications that use HTTP and non-HTTP protocols.
Windows Server Backup	Windows Server Backup enables you to back up and restore the operating system, system state, and any data stored on a server.
Windows Standards-Based Storage Management	Windows Standards-Based Storage Management provides support for managing standards-based storage and includes management interfaces and extensions for Windows Management Instrumentation (WMI) and Windows PowerShell.

Feature	Description
Windows TIFF IFilter	Windows TIFF IFilter focuses on text-based documents, which means that searching is more successful for documents that contain clearly identifiable text (for example, black text on a white background).
WinRM IIS Extension	WinRM IIS Extension provides an Internet Information Services (IIS)–based hosting model. WinRM IIS Extension can be enabled at either the website or virtual-directory level.
WINS Server	WINS Server is a name-resolution service that resolves computer names to IP addresses. Installing this feature enables the computer to act as a WINS server.
Wireless LAN Service	Wireless LAN Service enables the server to use wireless networking connections and profiles.
WOW64 Support	WOW64 Support supports WOW64, which is required on a Full Server installation. Removing this feature converts a Full Server installation to a Server Core installation.
XPS Viewer	XPS Viewer is a program you can use to view, search, set permissions for, and digitally sign XPS documents.

Making supplemental components available

Microsoft designed Server Manager and the underlying framework for managing components to be extensible. This makes it easier to provide supplemental roles, role services, and features for the operating system.

You can make these components available for installation and configuration by completing the following steps:

1. Download the installer package or packages from the Microsoft website. Typically, these are provided as a set of Microsoft Update Standalone Packages (.msu) files.
2. Double-tap or double-click each installer package to register it for use.
3. If Server Manager is running on the server, restart or refresh Server Manager to make the new components available.
4. In Server Manager, use the appropriate wizard to install and configure the supplemental role, role service, or feature.

Installing components with Server Manager

Server Manager is the primary tool you use to manage roles, role services, and features. Not only can you use Server Manager to add or remove roles, role services, and features, but you can use it to view the configuration details and status for these software components.

By default, Server Manager is started automatically. If you closed the console or disabled automatic startup, you can open the console by tapping or clicking the related option on the taskbar. Another way to do this is by pressing the Windows key, typing **ServerManager.exe** in the Apps Search box, and then pressing Enter.

Viewing configured roles and role services

Server Manager automatically creates server groups based on the roles of managed servers. When you select a role-based group in the left pane, the Servers panel shows the managed servers that have this role. As shown in Figure 6-1, the details for the selected server group provide the following information for all servers in the group:

- The status of related system services. You can manage a service (and its dependent services) by pressing and holding or right-clicking and then selecting Stop Services, Start Services, or Restart Services. In many cases, if a service isn't running as you think it should, you can tap or click Restart Services to resolve the issue by stopping and then starting the service.
- Error and warning events the related services and components have generated recently. If you tap or click an event, you get additional information about the event (if available).
- Summary information about the related role services and features, including the number of related role services and features installed and the name and subpath of the related role, role service, or feature in the UI. For example, with Storage Services, the component type is listed as Role Services, and the path is listed as File And Storage Services \Storage Services.

You can refresh the server details manually by tapping or clicking the Refresh Servers button on the toolbar. Otherwise, Server Manager refreshes the details periodically for you. If you want to set a different default refresh interval, tap or click Manage and then tap or click Server Manager Properties. Next, set the new refresh interval in minutes and then tap or click OK.

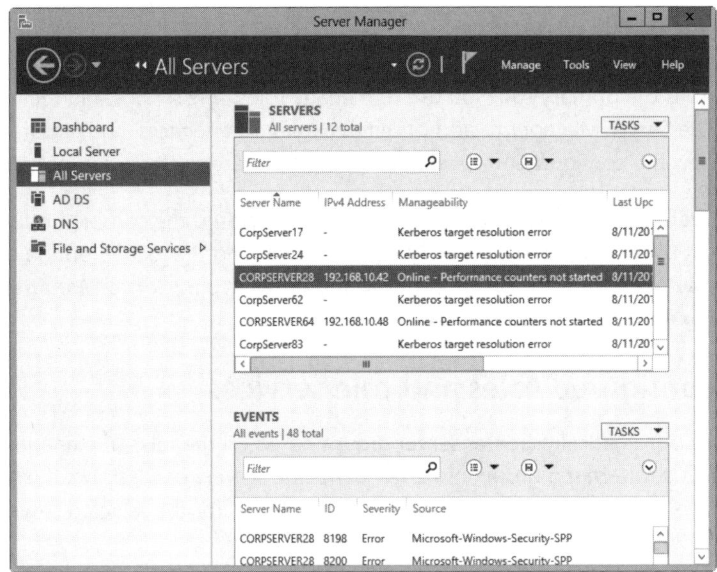

Figure 6-1 View the status details for installed roles.

Managing server roles and features

When you select All Servers in Server Manager, the Roles And Features pane provides details on the current roles and features that are installed on all managed servers. As you set out to add roles to a server, keep in mind that some roles cannot be added at the same time as other roles, and you have to install each role separately. Other roles cannot be combined with existing roles, and you'll see warning prompts about this.

Adding server roles and features

You can add a server role or feature by following these steps:

1. In Server Manager, select Add Roles And Features on the Manage menu. This starts the Add Roles And Features Wizard.

   NOTE

   If the wizard displays the Before You Begin page, read the introductory text and then tap or click Next. You can avoid seeing the Before You Begin page the next time you start this wizard by selecting the Skip This Page By Default check box before tapping or clicking Next.

2. On the Select Installation Type page, Role-Based Or Feature-Based Installation is selected by default. Tap or click Next.

3. On the Select Destination Server page, shown in Figure 6-2, you can choose to install roles and features on running servers or virtual hard disks. Only servers that are running Windows Server 2012 or later and that have been added for management are listed. Either select a server from the server pool or select a server from the server pool on which to mount a virtual hard disk (VHD). If you are adding roles and features to a VHD, tap or click Browse and then use the Browse For Virtual Hard Disks dialog box to locate the VHD. When you are ready to continue, tap or click Next.

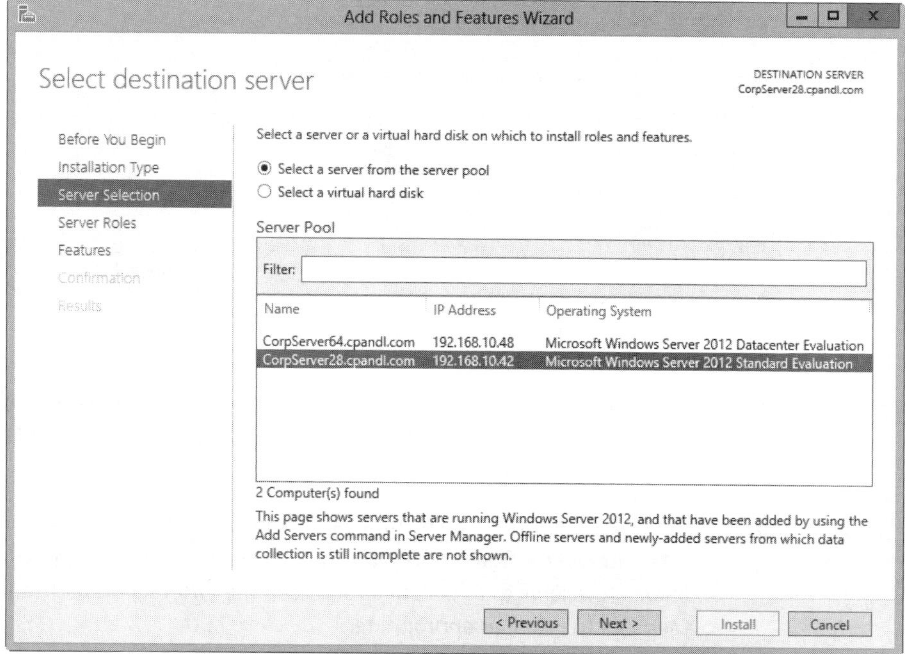

Figure 6-2 Select the server or virtual hard disk to use for the installation.

4. On the Select Server Roles page, shown in Figure 6-3, select the role or roles to install. Some roles cannot be added at the same time as other roles. You have to install each role separately. Other roles cannot be combined with existing roles, and you'll see warning prompts about this. A server running a Server Core installation can act as a domain controller and hold any of the flexible single-master operations (FSMOs) roles for Active Directory.

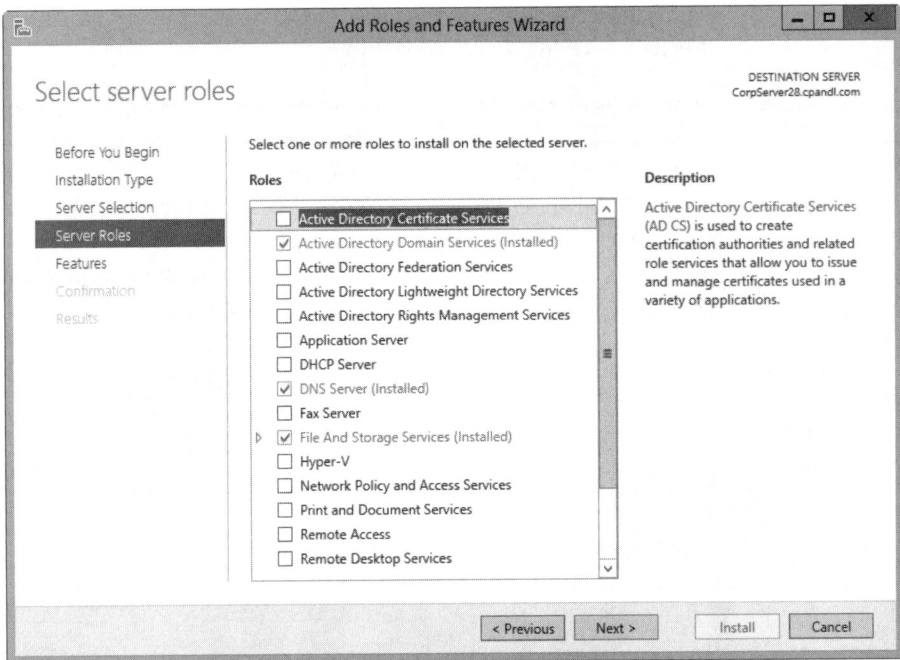

Figure 6-3 Select the roles to install.

5. If additional features are required to install a role, you see an additional dialog box. Tap or click Add Features to close the dialog box and add the required features to the server installation. Tap or click Next to continue.

6. With some roles, you see an extra wizard page, which provides additional information about using and configuring the role. You might also have the opportunity to install additional role services as part of a role. Read the information page and select additional role services to install as appropriate.

7. On the Select Features page, select the feature or features to install. If additional features are required to install a feature you selected, you see an additional dialog box. Tap or click Add Features to close the dialog box and add the required features to the server installation. When you are ready to continue, tap or click Next.

8. On the Confirm Installation Selections page, tap or click the Export Configuration Settings link to generate an installation report that can be displayed in Internet Explorer.

TROUBLESHOOTING

Accessing binary source files

Access to binary source files is required to install server roles, role services, and features successfully. If the server on which you want to install roles or features doesn't have all the required binary source files, the server gets the files from Windows Update by default or from a location specified in Group Policy.

You also can specify an alternate path for the source files. To do this, click the Specify An Alternate Source Path link, type that alternate path in the box provided, and then tap or click OK. If you mount a Windows image and make it available on the local server, you can enter the alternate path as **c:\mountdir\windows\winsxs**. For network shares, enter the UNC path to the share, such as **\\CorpServer36\WS12**. For mounted Windows images, enter the WIM path prefixed with WIM: and include the index of the image to use, such as **WIM:\\CorpServer36\WS12\install.wim:4**.

For information on managing binary source files, see "Managing server binaries" later in this chapter.

9. Restarting the destination server might be required to complete the installation of some roles and features. To restart the destination server automatically if required, select the related check box. If you do not select this check box and a restart is required, you will need to restart the server manually to complete the installation.

10. After you review the installation options and save them as necessary, tap or click Install to begin the installation process. The Installation Progress page tracks the progress of the installation. If you close the wizard, tap or click the Notifications icon in Server Manager and then tap or click the link provided to reopen the wizard.

11. When Setup finishes installing the server with the roles and features you selected, the Installation Progress page will be updated to reflect this. Review the installation details to ensure that all phases of the installation were completed successfully. If any portion of the installation failed, note the reason for the failure. Review the Server Manager entries for installation problems and take corrective actions as appropriate.

Inside OUT

Completing additional installation tasks

Any additional actions that might be required to complete the installation are listed when Setup finishes installing the roles and features you selected. Typically, you have a link you can click to begin these additional tasks. For example, installing a domain controller is a multipart process that begins with installing the components required for the role. After this, you must promote the server and configure directory services—all of which can be done in Server Manager.

If you close the Add Roles And Features Wizard, tap or click the Notifications icon in Server Manager to display a list of recent notifications, as shown in the graphic that follows:

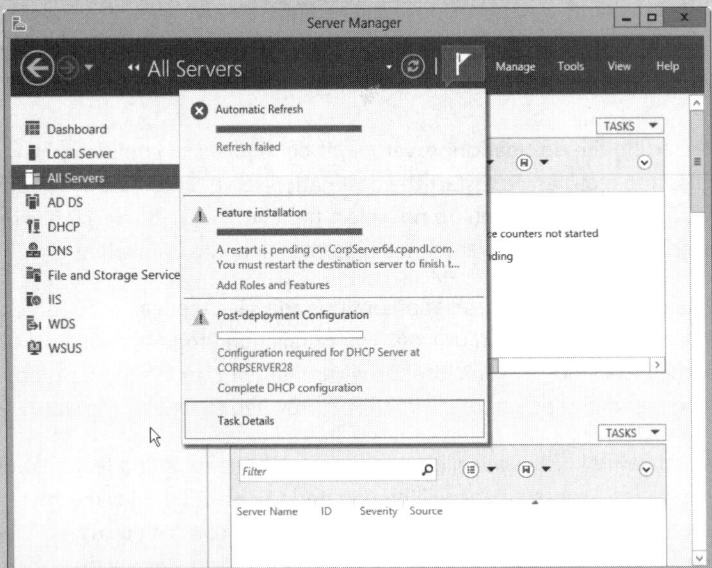

In this example, there are several important notifications:

- The first notification tells you that the automatic refresh of server information failed. This can happen for several reasons, with the most common reason being that one or more of the servers added for management is offline or otherwise inaccessible.

- The second notification tells you that CorpServer64 must be restarted to complete the installation of an added feature. You also could confirm that a restart was required by selecting the All Servers node in Server Manager, where you'd see a status of Online - Restart Pending For CorpServer64 (as long as the server was online and accessible). Finally, tapping or clicking the Add Roles And Features link opens the Add Roles And Features Wizard, where you'd see the Installation Progress page and could note exactly what had been installed to require the restart.
- The third notification tells you that CorpServer64 has a post-deployment configuration task that needs to be performed for DHCP. Tapping or clicking Complete DHCP Configuration opens the DHCP Post-Install Configuration Wizard.

Removing server roles and features

You can remove a server role by following these steps:

1. In Server Manager, select Remove Roles And Features on the Manage menu. This starts the Remove Roles And Features Wizard.

   NOTE

   If the wizard displays the Before You Begin page, read the introductory text and then tap or click Next. You can avoid seeing the Before You Begin page the next time you start this wizard by selecting the Skip This Page By Default check box before tapping or clicking Next.

2. On the Select Destination Server page, you can choose to remove roles and features from running servers or virtual hard disks. Only servers that are running Windows Server 2012 R2 and that have been added for management are listed. Either select a server from the server pool or select a server from the server pool on which to mount a VHD. If you are removing roles and features from a VHD, tap or click Browse and then use the Browse For Virtual Hard Disks dialog box to locate the VHD. When you are ready to continue, tap or click Next.
3. On the Remove Server Roles page, shown in Figure 6-4, clear the check box for the role you want to remove. If you try to remove a role that another role or feature depends on, a warning prompt appears stating that you cannot remove the role unless you also remove the other role. If you tap or click the Remove Features button, Setup removes the dependent roles and features. Note that if you want to keep related management tools, you should clear the Remove Management Tools check box prior to tapping or clicking the Remove Features button and then click Continue. Tap or click Next.

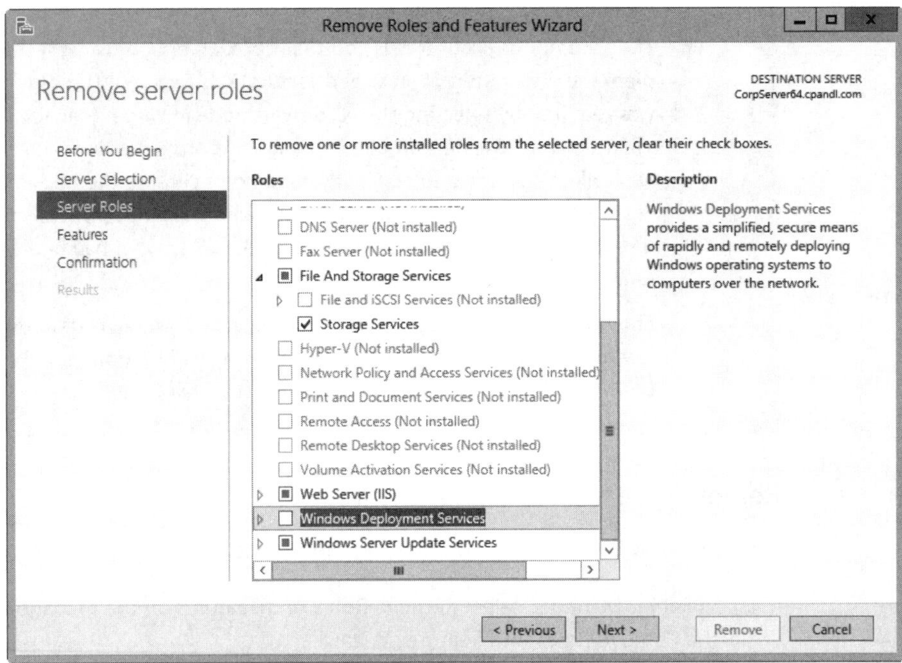

Figure 6-4 Clear selected roles to remove them.

4. On the Remove Features page, the currently installed features are selected. To remove a feature, clear the related check box. If you try to remove a feature that another feature or role depends on, you see a warning prompt stating that you cannot remove the feature unless you also remove the other feature or role. If you tap or click the Remove Features button, Setup removes the dependent roles and features. Note that if you want to keep related management tools, you should clear the Remove Management Tools check box and then click Continue prior to tapping or clicking the Remove Features button. Tap or click Next.

5. On the Confirm Removal Selections page, review the components that Setup will remove based on your previous selections. Restarting the destination server might be required to complete the removal of some roles and features. To restart the destination server automatically if required, select the related check box. If you don't select this check box and a restart is required, you need to restart the server manually to complete the removal.

6. Tap or click Remove. The Removal Progress page tracks the progress of the removal. If you close the wizard, tap or click the Notifications icon in Server Manager and then tap or click the link provided to reopen the wizard.

When Setup finishes modifying the server configuration, you see the Removal Progress page. Review the modification details to ensure that all phases of the removal process were completed successfully. As necessary, note any additional actions that might be required to complete the removal, such as restarting the server or performing additional removal tasks. If any portion of the removal failed, review the Server Manager entries for removal problems and take corrective actions as appropriate.

Managing server binaries

Binaries needed to install roles and features are referred to as *payloads*. With Windows Server 2012 R2, payloads normally are stored in subfolders of the Windows Side-by-Side folder (%SystemDrive%\Windows\WinSXS). However, to enhance security, you can disable roles and features and remove the payload used to install these roles and features. When you remove a payload, servers try to get the required binary files from Windows Update by default. In Group Policy, you can configure an alternative to Windows Update by specifying an alternative download location.

If you want to remove binaries, you use Windows PowerShell to do this and not Server Manager. The ServerManager module for Windows PowerShell is the command-line counterpart of Server Manager.

Inside OUT

Importing the ServerManager module

Generally, when you are logged on to a server running Windows Server 2012 R2, this module is imported into Windows PowerShell by default. If you are working from your management computer running a different operating system, however, you might need to import the module before you can use the ServerManager module's cmdlets. You import the ServerManager module by entering the following command at the Windows PowerShell prompt:

```
import-module servermanager
```

After the module is imported, you can use it with the currently running instance of Windows PowerShell. If the module is not automatically imported, you need to import the module again the next time you start Windows PowerShell. Note also that if the module isn't being imported automatically for you when you start Windows PowerShell, you can add an import statement to your profile and scripts to ensure that the ServerManager module is available, as shown in this example:

```
import-module servermanager
```

The Get-WindowsFeature cmdlet returns a detailed list of a server's current state with regard to roles, role services, and features. When you type **get-windowsfeature** at a Windows PowerShell prompt, you see the state of each role, role service, and feature listed as one of the following:

- **Available.** Meaning the component is available for installation
- **Installed.** Meaning the component is already installed
- **Removed.** Meaning the payload for the component has been removed

As shown in the partial listing that follows, each role, role service, or feature is listed by display name and then by its management naming component:

```
[ ] Active Directory Certificate Services          AD-Certificate           Removed
    [ ] Certification Authority                    ADCS-Cert-Authority      Removed
    [ ] Certificate Enrollment Policy Web Serv...  ADCS-Enroll-Web-Pol      Removed
    [ ] Certificate Enrollment Web Service         ADCS-Enroll-Web-Svc      Removed
    [ ] Certification Authority Web Enrollment     ADCS-Web-Enrollment      Removed
    [ ] Network Device Enrollment Service          ADCS-Device-Enrollment   Removed
    [ ] Online Responder                           ADCS-Online-Cert         Removed
[X] Active Directory Domain Services           AD-Domain-Services           Installed
[ ] Active Directory Federation Services       AD-Federation-Services       Available
  [ ] Federation Service                       ADFS-Federation              Available
  [ ] AD FS 1.1 Web Agents                     ADFS-Web-Agents              Available
    [ ] AD FS 1.1 Claims-aware Agent           ADFS-Claims                  Available
    [ ] AD FS 1.1 Windows Token-based Agent    ADFS-Windows-Token           Available
  [ ] Federation Service Proxy                 ADFS-Proxy                   Available
[X] Active Directory Rights Management Se...   ADRMS                        Installed
```

By using Install-WindowsFeature followed by the management name, you can install a role, role service, or feature and get its binaries if necessary. Use *–includeallsubfeature* when adding components to add all subordinate components. Use *–includemanagementtools* when adding components to add the related management tools.

You can uninstall a role, role service, or feature by using Uninstall-WindowsFeature. If you specify a top-level role with role service and feature subcomponents, the subcomponents are also uninstalled.

To uninstall a role, role service, or feature and then remove the related binaries from the Windows Side-By-Side folder, you use the *–Remove* parameter with Uninstall-WindowsFeature. If you specify a top-level role with role service and feature subcomponents, the binaries for the subcomponents are also removed.

Use *–includemanagementtools* when removing components to remove the related management tools.

In the previous example, Active Directory Certificate Services and its subcomponents were removed. Knowing this, you could retrieve the binaries for the role, subordinate role services, and features and then install these components and the related management tools by entering the following command:

```
install-windowsfeature ad-certificate -includeallsubfeature -includemanagementtools
```

Because adding or removing components requires administrator privileges, you must run this command at an elevated Windows PowerShell prompt.

TROUBLESHOOTING

Performing administrator tasks at a prompt

Whether you are working with the command prompt or the Windows PowerShell prompt, you must open an elevated prompt to perform administration tasks. To open an elevated prompt, press and hold or right-click the shortcut for the prompt on Start, Desktop, or the taskbar and then tap or click Run As Administrator.

If you forget to elevate the prompt and try to perform administration, you typically see an error stating you don't have adequate user rights to make changes. Sometimes, however, the error message won't be as explicit, and command execution simply fails.

By default, when you use Install-WindowsFeature, payloads are restored through Windows Update. You can use the *–Source* parameter to restore a payload from a Windows Imaging (WIM) mount point. For example, if an image for Windows Server 2012 R2 is available at the network path \\ImageServer32\WinServer12R2EE, you could specify the source as follows:

```
install-windowsfeature -name ad-certificate -includeallsubfeature
-source \\imageserver18\winserver12r2ee
```

The path you specify is used only if the required binaries are not found in the Windows Side-By-Side folder on the destination server. You also can mount the Windows Server 2012 R2 distribution media and use the Windows\WinSXS folder from the installation image as your source. To do this, follow these steps:

1. Log on to the server by using an account with administrator privileges. Insert the installation disc into the server's disc drive.
2. Open an elevated command prompt. Create a folder to mount the Installation image by typing the following command: **mkdir c:\mountdir**.
3. Locate the index number of the image you want to use by typing the following command at the elevated prompt: **dism /get-wiminfo /wimfile:e:\sources\install .wim**, where *e:* is the drive designator of the server's disc drive.

4. Mount the installation image by typing the following command at the elevated prompt: **dism /mount-wim /wimfile:e:\sources\install.wim /index:2 /mountdir:c:\mountdir /readonly**, where *e:* is the drive designator of the server's disc drive, *2* is the index of the image to use, and *c:\mountdir* is the mount directory. Mounting the image might take several minutes.

5. Open an elevated Windows PowerShell prompt. Use Install-WindowsFeature with the source specified as c:\mountdir\windows\winsxs, as shown in this example:

```
install-windowsfeature -name ad-domain-services -includeallsubfeature
-source c:\mountdir\windows\winsxs
```

You can use Group Policy to control whether Windows Update is used to restore payloads and to provide alternate source paths for restoring payloads. The policy you want to work with is Specify Settings For Optional Component Installation And Component Repair, which is under Computer Configuration\Administrative Templates\System. This policy also is used for obtaining payloads needed to repair components.

If you enable Specify Settings For Optional Component Installation And Component Repair (as shown in Figure 6-5), you can do the following:

- Set an alternate source file path for payloads as a network location. For network shares, type the UNC path to the share, such as **\\CorpServer82\WinServer2012**. For mounted Windows images, type the WIM path prefixed with WIM: and include the index of the image to use, such as **WIM:\\CorpServer82\WinServer2012\install.wim:4**.

- Restrict downloading payloads from Windows Update. If you enable the policy and use this option, you do not have to specify an alternate path. In this case, payloads cannot be obtained automatically, and administrators will need to specify the alternate source path explicitly.

- Designate Windows Update as the source for repairing components rather than Windows Server Update Services.

TROUBLESHOOTING

Resolving blocked downloads of binaries

Disabling or not configuring Specify Settings For Optional Component Installation And Component Repair doesn't disable component installation and repair. In fact, if you disable or do not configure this policy, Windows uses the standard approach for installing and repairing components, which is to do so through Windows Update. However, if you enable this policy and then specify never to attempt to download payloads from Windows Update, you prevent computers from using Windows Update and require

them to get the payload from a designated alternate source. If you don't specify an alternate source (or if the alternate source is inaccessible), computers are blocked from getting payloads for removed components and payloads for components that need to be repaired. To re-enable automatic component installation and repair, you must change the policy state to either Not Configured or Disabled and then refresh the policy (or wait for the policy to refresh automatically).

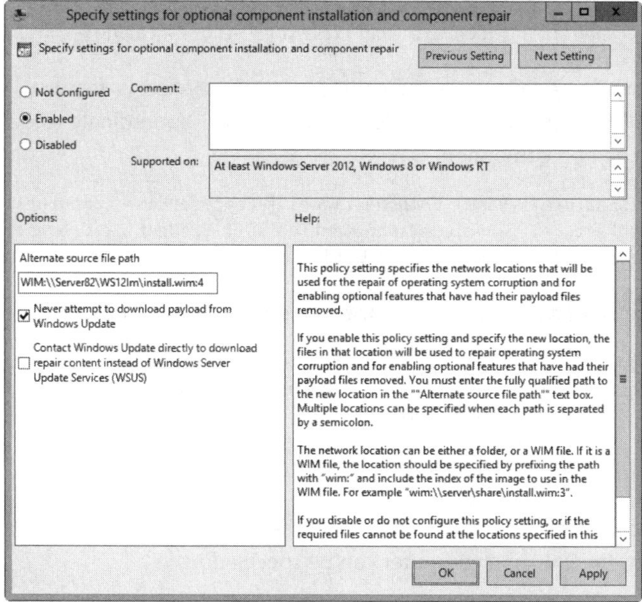

Figure 6-5 Configure component installation and repair through Group Policy.

Installing components at the prompt

Earlier in the chapter, in the "Managing server binaries" section, I discussed using the ServerManager module and its cmdlets. Now it's time to take a closer look at the module and its cmdlets and provide additional examples.

When you want to manage server configuration at a prompt or in a script, you use Windows PowerShell and the ServerManager module. Not only can you use this module's cmdlets to add or remove roles, role services, and features, but you can use them to view the configuration details and status for these software components.

Going to the prompt for Server Management

You manage roles, role services, and features by using the following cmdlets, which are part of the ServerManager module:

- **Get-WindowsFeature.** Lists the server's current state with regard to roles, role services, and features.

```
Get-WindowsFeature [[-Name] ComponentNames] [-ComputerName Computer]
[-Credential Credential] [-LogPath LogFile.txt] [-Vhd VhdPath] [-WhatIf]
```

- **Install-WindowsFeature.** Installs the named role, role service, or feature. The *–IncludeAllSubFeature* parameter enables you to install all subordinate role services and features of the named component.

```
Install-WindowsFeature [-Name] ComponentNames [-ComputerName Computer]
[-IncludeAllSubFeature] [-IncludeManagementTools] [-Credential Credential]
-LogPath LogFile.txt] [-Source SourcePath] [-Restart | -Vhd VhdPath] [-WhatIf]
```

- **Uninstall-WindowsFeature.** Removes the named role, role service, or feature.

```
Uninstall-WindowsFeature [-Name] ComponentNames [-ComputerName Computer]
[-IncludeManagementTools] [-Credential Credential] [-LogPath LogFile.txt]
[-Remove] [-Restart | -Vhd VhdPath] [-WhatIf]
```

When applicable, you can do the following:

- Use the *–ComputerName* parameter to specify the name or IP address of a remote computer to work with. Only one computer can be specified.
- Use the *–Credential* parameter to pass in a credential for authentication. Credential objects are returned by the Get-Credential cmdlet.

  NOTE

  You can specify a user name as the credential by using the "UserName" or "Domain \UserName" format; the quotes are required, such as –Credential "CPANDL\Williams". If you enter a user name, you are prompted for a password.

- Use the *–LogPath* parameter to log error details to a named log file as an alternative to the default logging used. The value you specify sets the path and the name of the log file.
- Use the *–Restart* parameter to restart the computer automatically (if restarting is necessary to complete the operation).

- Use the *–Vhd* parameter to specify the path to an offline VHD, which can be a relative local path on the target computer, such as C:\virt\server12b.vhd, or a network share specified by the UNC path, such as \\server42\curr\server12b.vhd.
- Use the *–WhatIf* parameter to display the operations that would be performed if the command were executed.

Installable roles, role services, and features have a corresponding component name that identifies the component so that you can manipulate it from the Windows PowerShell prompt. This also is true for supplemental components you've made available by downloading and installing their installer packages from the Microsoft website. You specify the list of components to install using the *–Name* parameter. This parameter matches actual component names and not display names. With Get-WindowsFeature, you can use wildcard characters. With Install-WindowsFeature and Uninstall-WindowsFeature, you cannot use wildcards but can use pipelining to get the required input names from another command, such as Get-WindowsFeature.

Understanding component names

Every installable role, role service, and feature has a component name. This name identifies the component so that it can be manipulated from the prompt. Remember, supplemental components are made available by downloading and installing their installer packages from the Microsoft website.

Table 6-3 provides a hierarchical listing of the component names associated with roles, related role services, and related subcomponents. When you are installing a role, you can use the *–IncludeAllSubFeature* parameter to install all the subordinate role services and features listed under the role and the *–IncludeManagementTools* parameter to install the related management tools.

Table 6-3 Component names for key roles and role services

Component Name	Role	Role Service	Subcomponent
AD-Certificate	Active Directory Certificate Services[1]		
AD-Domain-Services	Active Directory Domain Services		
AD-Federation-Services	Active Directory Federation Services[1]		
ADLDS	Active Directory Lightweight Directory Services		

Component Name	Role	Role Service	Subcomponent
ADRMS	Active Directory Rights Management Services		
ADRMS-Server		Active Directory Rights Management Server	
ADRMS-Identity		Identity Federation Support	
Application-Server	Application Server[1]		
DHCP	DHCP Server		
DNS	DNS Server		
Fax	Fax Server		
FileAndStorage -Services	File And Storage Services		
File-Services		File and iSCSI Services	
FS-FileServer			File Server
FS-BranchCache			BranchCache for Network Files
FS-Data-Deduplication			Data Deduplication
FS-DFS-Namespace			DFS Namespaces
FS-DFS-Replication			DFS Replication
FS-Resource-Manager			File Server Resource Manager
FS-VSS-Agent		File Server VSS Agent Service	
FS-iSCSITarget-Server		iSCSI Target Server	
iSCSITarget-VSS-VDS		iSCSI Target Storage Provider	
FS-NFS-Service		Server for NFS	
Storage-Services		Storage Services	
Hyper-V	Hyper-V		
NPAS	Network Policy and Access Services		
NPAS-Policy-Server		Network Policy Server	
NPAS-Health		Health Registration Authority	

Component Name	Role	Role Service	Subcomponent
NPAS-Host-Cred		Host Credential Authorization Protocol	
Print-Services	Print and Document Services		
Print-Server		Print Server	
Print-Scan-Server		Distributed Scan Server	
Print-Internet		Internet Printing	
Print-LPD-Service		LPD Service	
RemoteAccess	Remote Access		
DirectAccess-VPN		DirectAccess and VPN (RAS)	
Routing		Routing	
Remote -Desktop-Services	Remote Desktop Services[1]		
VolumeActivation	Volume Activation Services		
Web-Server	Web Server (IIS)[1]		
WDS	Windows Deployment Services		
WDS-Deployment		Deployment Server	
WDS-Transport		Transport Server	
ServerEssentialsRole	Windows Server Essentials Experience		
UpdateServices	Windows Server Update Services		
UpdateServices-WidDB		WID Database	
UpdateServices -Services		WSUS Services	
UpdateServices-DB		Database	

[1] Indicates that the component has unlisted subordinate components that generally are installed together by adding the *–IncludeAllSubFeature* parameter.

Table 6-4 provides a hierarchical listing of the component names associated with features and related subfeatures. When you are installing a feature, you can use the *–IncludeAllSubFeature* parameter to install all the subordinate second-level and third-level features listed under the feature and the *–IncludeManagementTools* parameter to install the related management tools.

Table 6-4 Component names for key features and subfeatures

Component Name	Feature	Subcomponent
NET-Framework-Features	.NET Framework 3.5 Features[1]	
NET-Framework-45-Features	.NET Framework 4.5 Features	
NET-Framework-45-Core		.NET Framework 4.5
NET-Framework-45-ASPNET		ASP.NET 4.5
NET-WCF-Services45		WCF Services[1]
BITS	Background Intelligent Transfer Service (BITS)[1]	
BitLocker	BitLocker Drive Encryption	
BitLocker-NetworkUnlock	BitLocker Network Unlock	
BranchCache	BranchCache	
NFS-Client	Client for NFS	
Data-Center-Bridging	Data Center Bridging	
EnhancedStorage	Enhanced Storage	
Failover-Clustering	Failover Clustering	
GPMC	Group Policy Management	
Web-WHC	IIS Hostable Web Core	
InkAndHandwritingServices	Ink and Handwriting Services	
Internet-Print-Client	Internet Printing Client	
IPAM	IP Address Management (IPAM) Server	
ISNS	iSNS Server service	
LPR-Port-Monitor	LPR Port Monitor	
ManagementOdata	Management OData IIS Extension	
Server-Media-Foundation	Media Foundation	
MSMQ	Message Queuing[1]	
Multipath-IO	Multipath I/O	
NLB	Network Load Balancing	
PNRP	Peer Name Resolution Protocol	
qWave	Quality Windows Audio Video Experience	
CMAK	RAS Connection Manager Administration Kit (CMAK)	

Component Name	Feature	Subcomponent
Remote-Assistance	Remote Assistance	
RDC	Remote Differential Compression	
RSAT	Remote Server Administration Tools	
RSAT-Feature-Tools		Feature Administration Tools[1]
RSAT-Role-Tools		Role Administration Tools[1]
RPC-over-HTTP-Proxy	RPC over HTTP Proxy	
Simple-TCPIP	Simple TCP/IP Services	
FS-SMB1	SMB 1.0/CIFS File Sharing Support	
FS-SMBBW	SMB Bandwidth Limit	
SMTP-Server	SMTP Server	
SNMP-Service	SNMP Service[1]	
User-Interfaces-Infra	User Interfaces and Infrastructure	
Server-Gui-Mgmt-Infra		Graphical Management Tools and Infrastructure
Desktop-Experience		Desktop Experience
Server-Gui-Shell		Server Graphical Shell
Biometric-Framework	Windows Biometric Framework	
PowerShellRoot	Windows PowerShell	
PowerShell		Windows PowerShell 4.0
PowerShell-V2		Windows PowerShell 2.0 Engine
PowerShell-ISE		Windows PowerShell ISE
WindowsPowerShellWebAccess		Windows PowerShell Web Access
WAS	Windows Process Activation Service[1]	
Search-Service	Windows Search Service	
Windows-Server-Backup	Windows Server Backup	
Migration	Windows Server Migration Tools	
WINS	WINS Server	

Component Name	Feature	Subcomponent
Wireless-Networking	Wireless LAN Service	
WoW64-Support	WOW64 Support	
XPS-Viewer	XPS Viewer	

[1] Indicates that the component has unlisted subordinate components that generally are installed together by adding the *–IncludeAllSubFeature* parameter.

Tracking installed roles, role services, and features

As discussed previously, you can determine the roles, role services, and features that are installed on a server by typing **get-windowsfeature** at a Windows PowerShell prompt. Each installed role, role service, and feature is highlighted and marked as such, with roles and role services listed in the output before features, as shown in the following example:

```
Display Name                                            Name                       Install State
------------                                            ----                       -------------
[ ] Active Directory Certificate Services               AD-Certificate                 Available
  [ ] Certification Authority                           ADCS-Cert-Authority            Available
  [ ] Certificate Enrollment Policy Web Service         ADCS-Enroll-Web-Pol            Available
  [ ] Certificate Enrollment Web Service                ADCS-Enroll-Web-Svc            Available
  [ ] Certification Authority Web Enrollment            ADCS-Web-Enrollment            Available
  [ ] Network Device Enrollment Service                  ADCS-Device-Enrollment         Available
  [ ] Online Responder                                  ADCS-Online-Cert               Available
[X] Active Directory Domain Services                    AD-Domain-Services             Installed

...

[X] .NET Framework 4.5 Features                         NET-Framework-45-Fea...        Installed
  [X] .NET Framework 4.5                                NET-Framework-45-Core          Installed
  [X] ASP.NET 4.5                                       NET-Framework-45-ASPNET        Installed
  [X] WCF Services                                      NET-WCF-Services45             Installed
    [ ] HTTP Activation                                 NET-WCF-HTTP-Activat...        Available
    [ ] Message Queuing (MSMQ) Activation               NET-WCF-MSMQ-Activat...        Available
    [ ] Named Pipe Activation                           NET-WCF-Pipe-Activat...        Available
    [X] TCP Activation                                  NET-WCF-TCP-Activati...        Installed
    [X] TCP Port Sharing                                NET-WCF-TCP-PortShar...        Installed
[ ] Background Intelligent Transfer Service (B...       BITS                           Available
  [ ] IIS Server Extension                              BITS-IIS-Ext                   Available
  [ ] Compact Server                                    BITS-Compact-Server            Available
[ ] BitLocker Drive Encryption                          BitLocker                      Available
```

Because the *–Name* parameter, which enables you to look for components with a specific name, accepts wildcards, you can easily check the installation status and availability of related components. This example returns a list of components with a management name that starts with *NET* or *web*:

```
get-windowsfeature -name net*, web*
```

Technically, you don't need to include *–Name*. The *–Name* parameter is the first expected parameter. Thus, you could perform the previous search by entering the following:

```
get-windowsfeature net*, web*
```

Because you won't always be working with a local computer at the prompt, you can use the *–ComputerName* parameter to specify the name or IP address of the remote computer you want to work with. In this example, you get the status of components on CorpServer18:

```
get-windowsfeature -computername corpserver18
```

For the purposes of documenting a server's configuration, you can save the output in a file as standard text by using the redirection symbol (>) as shown in this example:

```
get-windowsfeature > MySavedResults.txt
```

Here, you save the output to a file named MySavedResults.txt in the current (working) directory.

Installing components at the prompt

You can install roles, role services, and features by typing **Install-WindowsFeature *ComponentName*** at an elevated prompt, where *ComponentName* is the management name of the component to install as listed in Table 6-3 or Table 6-4. In the following example, you install DHCP Server and the DHCP console for managing DHCP Server on CorpServer15:

```
Install-windowsfeature dhcp -ComputerName corpserver15 -includemanagementtools
```

Here, you don't need to include the *–IncludeAllSubFeature* parameter because DHCP Server doesn't have any subordinate role services or features. As Windows PowerShell works, you see a Start Installation progress bar. When the installation is complete, you see the result. The output for a successful installation should look similar to the following:

```
Success Restart Needed Exit Code      Feature Result
------- -------------- ---------      --------------
True    No             Success        {DHCP Server}
```

As you can see, the output specifies an exit code, a list of the exact change or changes made, whether the installation was successful, and whether a restart is needed. The exit code can be different from the Success status. For example, if the components you specify are already installed, the exit code is NoChangeNeeded, as shown in this sample output:

```
Success Restart Needed Exit Code              Feature Result
------- -------------- ---------              --------------
True    No             NoChangeNeeded         {}
```

Here, you see that Install-WindowsFeature was successful but didn't actually make any changes. The Feature Result also shows no changes.

You don't have to name the component or components explicitly that you want to install. Install-WindowsFeature accepts redirected output for component names, enabling you to use another command to get the name or names of the components you want to work with. For example, if you want to install multiple components, such as all .NET components across the multiple .NET frameworks that are available, you could use Get-WindowsFeature to help you do this, as shown in the following example:

```
get-windowsfeature -name NET-* | install-windowsfeature
```

Here, you use Get-WindowsFeature to obtain a list of components with names that start with NET– and then pipe that list to Install-WindowsFeature. The result is that you install all .NET components across all available .NET frameworks.

Component installation doesn't always succeed, and that's a common reason that the server cannot be accessed, as shown in this example with accompanying error text:

```
Success Restart Needed Exit Code      Feature Result
------- -------------- ---------      --------------
False   Maybe          Failed         {}

install-windowsfeature : WinRM cannot process the request. The following error
occurred while using Kerberos authentication: Cannot find the computer
corpserver15. Verify that the computer exists on the network and that the
name provided is spelled correctly.
```

Here, Windows Remote Management (WinRM) couldn't connect to the remote computer. Typically, this occurs because the server is offline or otherwise unavailable. This also could occur if you entered an incorrect server name.

TROUBLESHOOTING

Resolving authentication failure

Less common reasons for authentication failure include improper WinRM configuration or a Kerberos authentication issue:

- **Regarding WinRM, the server might not be enabled for remote management in Server Manager. To resolve this, log on to the server console (either locally or through Remote Desktop), open Server Manager, and then select Local Server Node. If Remote Management is listed as Disabled, click the related link, select Enable Remote Management, and then tap or click OK. For more advanced troubleshooting of WinRM, see "Enabling remote management" in Chapter 4.**
- **Regarding Kerberos, the authentication failure could be related to a disparity between the local computer's date and time and the remote computer's date and time. With Kerberos, authentication fails if the message time stamp is off by more than the allowable time difference. To learn more about Kerberos authentication, see "NTLM and Kerberos authentication" in Chapter 11, "Designing and managing the domain environment" of *Windows Server 2012 R2 Inside Out: Services, Security, and Infrastructure*, (Microsoft Press, 2014).**

Inadequate user rights is another common reason for component installation to fail, as shown in this example, with accompanying error text:

```
install-windowsfeature : You do not have adequate user rights to make changes to
the target computer. If you are already a member of the Administrators group on
the target computer, the changes might have failed because of security restrictions
imposed by User Account Control. Try running Install-WindowsFeature in a Windows
PowerShell session that has been opened with elevated rights (Run as administrator).

Success Restart Needed Exit Code      Feature Result
------- -------------- ---------      --------------
False   No             Failed         {}
```

Normally, when you are using Windows PowerShell for administration, you use an elevated, administrator prompt, and your current credentials pass through to remote computers you work with. However, if your account doesn't have appropriate user rights, you need to provide different credentials; you can do this by using the *–Credential* parameter. You'll be prompted for the user's password if you follow the *–Credential* parameter with a user name, as shown in this example:

```
Install-windowsfeature dns -credential "CPANDL\wrstanek" -includemanagementtools
```

Here, you just type the password and press Enter when prompted to run the command with the named account's permissions. Rather than entering credentials for an account each time you want to perform administration, you can store credentials and then refer to the stored credential, as shown in this example:

```
$cred = get-credential
install-windowsfeature dns -credential $cred -includemanagementtools
```

Here, you use Get-Credential to prompt for a user name and password and then store those credentials in the *$cred* variable. Next, you refer to the stored credentials to install DNS. Because the credentials are stored for the duration of your current Windows PowerShell session, you can refer to them as needed for additional administration.

TROUBLESHOOTING

Understanding stored credentials

Stored credentials are available only in the current Windows PowerShell session. The stored credentials are cleared when you close the Windows PowerShell window. If you have multiple Windows PowerShell windows open, the credentials stored in one window aren't available in another window's session.

To test the installation prior to performing that actual operation, you can use the *–Whatif* parameter, as shown in the following example:

```
get-windowsfeature -name BIT* | install-windowsfeature -whatif
```

If you run this command, you might be surprised to see that BitLocker components are included along with BITS components. To resolve this, you need to be more specific when specifying the component name to match. If you intend to install BitLocker and BitLocker Network Unlock, you can use the following command instead:

```
get-windowsfeature -name bitlock* | install-windowsfeature -whatif
```

If a restart is required to complete an installation, you can have Install-WindowsFeature restart the computer by including the *–Restart* parameter. For planning purposes, especially on highly active production servers, keep in mind that both successful and failed installations could require a restart.

Removing components at the prompt

You can uninstall roles, role services, and features by typing **Uninstall-ServerManager *ComponentName*** at an elevated command prompt, where *ComponentName* is the name of the component to uninstall as listed in Table 6-3 or Table 6-4. Because

Uninstall-ServerManager automatically uninstalls any subordinate role services and features of the specified component, you normally want to test the uninstallation prior to performing that actual operation. To do this, you can use the *–Whatif* parameter, as shown in the following example:

```
uninstall-windowsfeature net-framework-45-features -whatif
```

Here, you want to uninstall .NET Framework 4.5 and related features, which include .NET Framework 4.5 (NET-Framework-45-Core), ASP.NET 4.5 (NET-Framework-45-ASPNET), and multiple subcomponents of WCF Services (NET-WCF-Services45). However, if you want to uninstall only the WCF Services, you enter the following instead:

```
uninstall-windowsfeature net-wcf-services45
```

As with Install-WindowsFeature, you don't have to name the component or components explicitly that you want to uninstall. Uninstall-WindowsFeature accepts redirected output for component names, enabling you to use another command to get the name or names of the components you want to work with. For example, if you want to uninstall multiple components, such as all .NET components across the multiple .NET frameworks that are available, you could use Get-WindowsFeature to help you do this, as shown in the following example:

```
get-windowsfeature -name NET-* | uninstall-windowsfeature
```

To ensure that the command works exactly as expected, you should test the command first by using the *–Whatif* parameter, as shown in the following example:

```
get-windowsfeature -name NET-* | uninstall-windowsfeature -whatif
```

As with installing components, the command output specifies whether a restart is required to complete the task. If a restart is required to complete a removal, you can have Uninstall-WindowsFeature restart the computer by including the *–Restart* parameter.

If an error occurs, and Uninstall-WindowsFeature cannot perform the specified operation, you see an error. Tips and techniques for resolving common errors are discussed in the previous section, "Installing components at the prompt."

CHAPTER 7

Managing and troubleshooting hardware

Unless you've standardized on a particular hardware platform, most servers that you'll work with will have different hardware components. This means different servers will probably have different motherboards, disk controllers, graphics cards, and network adapters. Fortunately, Windows Server 2012 R2 is designed to work with an extensive list of hardware devices. When you install new hardware, Windows tries to detect the device automatically and then install the correct driver software so that you can use the device. If Windows has a problem with a device, you must troubleshoot the installation, which usually means finding the correct device drivers for the hardware component and installing them.

One thing to keep in mind when working with devices is that, like other software, driver software can contain bugs. These bugs can cause a variety of problems on your servers, and not only could the hardware stop working, but the server also could freeze. Because of this, you'll want to monitor routinely for hardware problems and take corrective actions as necessary. You'll also find it helpful to maintain a hardware inventory for servers so that you know which devices are installed and who the manufacturers are.

Understanding hardware installation changes

Hardware installation for Windows Server 2012 R2 hasn't changed much. What has changed significantly, however, are the available options when it comes to hardware devices. All computers can use internal and external hardware devices.

Choosing internal devices

Internal hardware devices are devices you install inside your computer. Typically, you need to power down and unplug your computer and then remove the computer case before you can install an internal device.

Hard drives are the most commonly installed internal devices and, in this area, there are many options. Windows Server 2012 R2 supports both standard format and advanced format hard drives. Standard format drives have 512 bytes per physical sector and are also referred to as *512b drives*. Advanced format drives have 4,096 bytes per physical sector and are also referred to as *512e drives*. 512e represents a significant shift for the hard drive industry, and it allows for large, multi-terabyte drives.

Inside OUT

Working with advanced format hard drives

Hard drives perform physical media updates in the granularity of their physical sector size. 512b drives work with data 512 bytes at a time; 512e drives work with data 4,096 bytes at a time. Having a larger physical sector size is what allows 512e drive capacities to jump well beyond previous physical capacity limits of 512b drives.

Keep in mind, however, that enterprise applications might need to be updated to work efficiently with 512e drives. When there is only a 512-byte write, hard disks must perform additional work to complete the 4,096-byte sector write. For optimal performance, applications must read and write data properly in this new level of granularity (4,096 bytes).

With 512b and 512e, it's not an all-or-nothing proposition. Drive manufacturers have released drives with technology that enables them to transition from 512b to 512e. Seagate drives with SmartAlign Technology are one example.

If you don't know whether a drive is standard format or advanced format, you can easily determine bytes per physical sector by typing the following at an elevated command prompt:

```
Fsutil fsinfo ntfsinfo DriveDesignator
```

Here, *DriveDesignator* is the designator of the drive to check, such as

```
Fsutil fsinfo sectorinfo c:
```

Small Computer System Interface (SCSI) is one of the most commonly used interfaces; there are multiple bus designs for SCSI and multiple interface types. Parallel SCSI (also called SPI), though popular, is giving way to Serial Attached SCSI (SAS). Internet SCSI (iSCSI) uses the SCSI architectural model, but it uses TCP/IP as the transport rather than the traditional physical implementation.

Although many workgroup and enterprise-class server systems continue to use Serial Attached SCSI devices, servers aren't always built using such robust disk systems. Increasingly, for general use, desktop-class computers are being configured with server operating systems, and most of these computers use internal devices with Serial ATA (SATA). That said, for many years, enhanced integrated drive electronics (EIDE), also called Parallel ATA (PATA), was used with desktop-class computers.

EIDE is still in use as of the time this book was written. However, you might find that most newer computers use SATA devices instead. Because SATA cables are significantly smaller than EIDE cables, this results in less clutter inside your computer and improved airflow for better cooling.

Inside OUT

Understanding solid-state drives

Solid-state drives (SSDs) are increasingly being used in computers throughout the enterprise. Although they can be higher in cost than traditional hard disks, they make up for this with high performance, reliability, and low power consumption. Because SSDs have no moving parts, they also run quietly and cool. How do they do this? SSDs use flash memory modules rather than platters, and there are no disk heads that need to travel over platters to read data. Instead, data is accessed directly from the flash memory over multiple internal flash buses. Typically, SSDs use NAND flash memory modules that have either multilevel cells (MLCs) storing two bits per cell or single-level cells (SLCs) storing one bit per cell.

In data centers where reducing power and cooling requirements is extremely important, you might want to use SSDs. Indeed, a typical SSD uses around 400 to 700 milliwatts of power and runs cool as opposed to the typical SCSI hard drive, which uses 4 to 7 watts of power and requires cooling. Before you deploy SSDs, however, keep in mind that a SATA SSD is not the same as a SATA hard drive. Most SSDs require specialized hard disk controllers to operate whether they are SATA compliant or not.

SSDs are ideal for high random read, low write workloads. For enterprise use, you should keep in mind that SSDs have duty-cycle and lifespan limitations. Check the warranty and specifications to determine an SSD's specific duty-cycle and lifespan limitations. Duty-cycle limitations, often listed in Total Bytes Written or Bytes Per Day, directly affect how many times the flash memory can be written to. Lifespan limitations directly affect how long the SSD will be viable. Often, SSDs are optimized for durability to extend their lifespan, but doing so might require significant overhead. As an example, one current enterprise SSD had a 7 percent provisioning overhead, meaning 7 percent of the raw drive capacity was reserved for code storage and wear leveling. With a 400 GB SSD, this means that approximately 28 GB of the raw capacity is dedicated to provisioning overhead, leaving 372 GB of raw capacity for data storage.

SATA was designed to replace IDE. SATA drives are increasingly popular as a low-cost alternative to SCSI. SATA II and SATA III, the most common SATA interfaces, are designed to operate at 3 gigabits per second and 6 gigabits per second, respectively. Windows Server 2012 R2 provides improved support for SATA drives by reducing metadata inconsistencies and allowing

SATA drives to cache data more efficiently. Improved disk caching helps protect cached data in the event of an unexpected power loss.

Although Windows Server 2012 R2 can be used with SCSI, EIDE, and SATA hardware devices, your computer must be configured specifically to work with these devices. For example, your computer needs a SCSI controller card to use SCSI devices. Although some older computer system motherboards don't have SATA input ports, you can install a SATA controller card to add support for SATA drives.

Choosing external devices

External hardware devices are devices you connect to your computer. Because you don't have to open your computer's case to connect external devices, you typically don't need to power down or unplug your computer before installing an external device. This makes external devices easier to install and means you can attach most external devices without having to restart your computer.

Most current computers use external devices with USB, FireWire, external SATA (eSATA), or a combination of these interfaces. An example of each interface is shown in Figure 7-1.

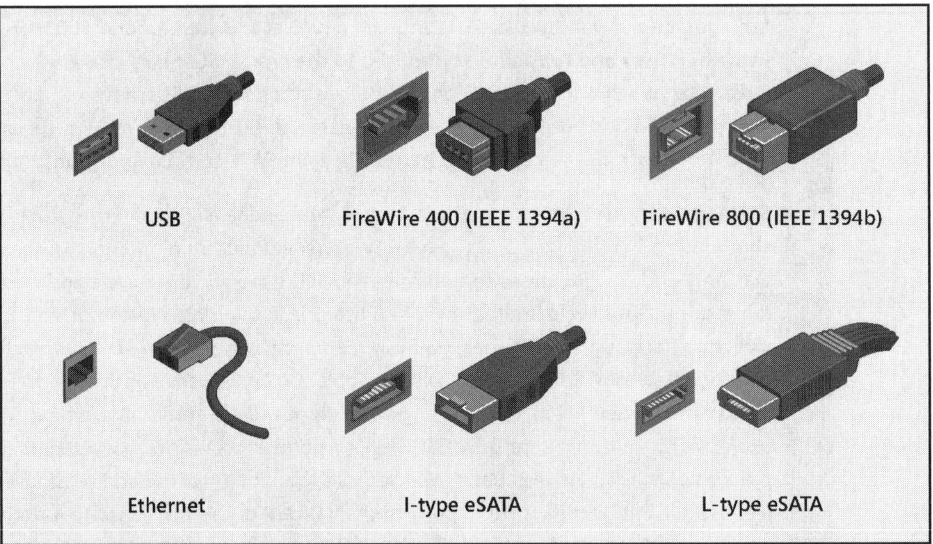

Figure 7-1 These are current interfaces for external devices.

USB 2.0 is the industry standard while the world transitions to USB 3.0. USB 2.0 devices can be rated as either full speed (up to 12 Mbps) or high speed (up to 480 Mbps). High-speed USB 2.0 supports data transfers at a maximum rate of 480 megabits per second, with sustained data transfer rates usually from 10 to 30 megabits per second. The actual sustainable transfer rate depends on many factors, including the type of device, the data you are transferring, and the speed of your computer. Each USB controller on your computer has a fixed amount of bandwidth, which all devices attached to the controller must share. If your computer's USB port is an earlier version, USB 1.0 or USB 1.1, you can use USB 2.0 and USB 3.0 devices, but the transfer rates will be significantly slower. The same is true when using a USB 2.0 device in a USB 3.0 port. Figure 7-2 compares connectors for USB 2.0 and USB 3.0.

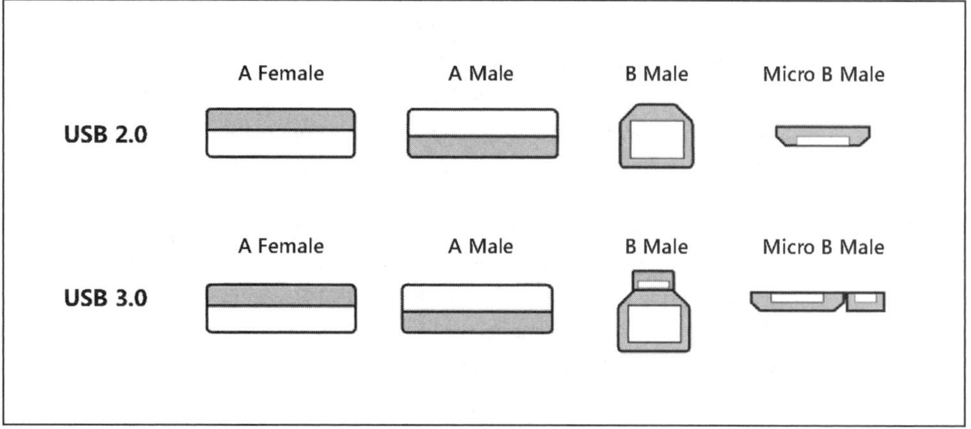

Figure 7-2 Compare USB 2.0 and USB 3.0 connectors.

Inside OUT

Using USB 3.0

USB 3.0 has transfer rates up to 4.8 Gbps, which is 10 times faster than the maximum transfer rate of USB 2.0. To use USB 3.0, a computer must have USB 3.0–compliant ports and buses, and you must connect USB 3.0–compatible devices to computers using USB 3.0–compatible cables. Often, USB 3.0 ports and cables can be easily differentiated from USB 2.0 ports and cables. This is because USB 3.0 ports and cables normally have a blue color coding on the inside.

The blue coding is only one of several physical differences between USB 2.0 and USB 3.0 ports and cables. USB 2.0 cables have four wires within the cable and provide power up to 500 milliamps (mA). USB 3.0 cables have eight wires within the cable and provide power up to 900 mA. Although USB 2.0 ports have four internal connectors, USB 3.0 ports have eight internal connectors.

In addition, although USB 3.0 is capable of transfer rates up to 4.8 Gbps, the sustained data transfer rate is much lower. The bus type also might be a limiting factor because older buses might not be capable of reaching the maximum rate. For example, PCIe 1.0a and ExpressCard 1.0 buses have a maximum transfer rate of 2.5 Gbps.

TROUBLESHOOTING

Connecting USB 3.0 to USB 2.0 and vice versa

USB 3.0 cables and ports have different connectors than USB 2.0 cables and ports do. To operate properly, USB 3.0 devices require USB 3.0 cables. USB 3.0 cables with standard connectors (A-type connectors), like the connector shown in Figure 7-1, can be used with USB 2.0 devices and plugged into USB 2.0 ports, but they are subject to the USB 2.0 transfer rate and power limitations. USB 2.0 devices and cables with standard connectors can be plugged into USB 3.0 ports and will work properly. USB 2.0 devices and cables with other connector types (B-type or micro B-type connectors) will not work properly with USB 3.0 ports. That said, although you might be able to fit a USB 2.0 cable with a B-type connector into a USB 3.0 B port, data will not transfer properly because of the different wiring configuration.

When you have USB devices connected to a monitor, the monitor acts like a USB hub device. As with any USB hub device, all devices attached to the hub share the same bandwidth, and the total available bandwidth is determined by the speed of the USB input to which the hub is connected on your computer. Generally speaking, never connect devices through a server's monitor when end-user performance is a concern.

FireWire, also called IEEE 1394, is a high-performance connection standard for most Windows-based computers. This interface uses a peer-to-peer architecture in which peripherals negotiate bus conflicts to determine which device can best control a data transfer. FireWire has several configurations, including FireWire 400, FireWire 800, and FireWire 1600. FireWire 400 (IEEE 1394a) has maximum sustained transfer rates of up to 400 Mbps. IEEE 1394b allows 400 Mbps (S400), 800 Mbps (S800), and 1600 Mbps (S1600). As with USB devices, if you connect an IEEE 1394b device to an IEEE 1394a port or vice versa, the device operates at the significantly reduced FireWire 400 transfer speed.

eSATA is an ultra-high-performance connection standard, primarily used with high-performance external devices. With external hard drives, eSATA provides a secure, reliable, and ultra-fast connection. eSATA has maximum sustained transfer rates of up to 3 Gbps. Note that there are several types of eSATA connectors and cables and that eSATA and internal SATA cables and connectors cannot be used interchangeably.

Inside OUT

Using FireWire devices

Although Windows Server 2012 R2 can be used with FireWire hardware devices, a computer must be configured specifically to work with these devices. Specifically, a computer needs a FireWire controller card.

When working with FireWire, keep in mind FireWire ports and cables have different shapes and connectors, making it easy to tell the difference between them—if you know what you're looking for. Early FireWire implementations, which I'll call standard FireWire (as opposed to FireWire 400 or FireWire 800), have a different number of pins on their connector cables and a different number of connectors on their ports. Because of this, you can tell standard FireWire and FireWire 400 apart by looking closely at the cables and ports.

If you look closely at standard FireWire cables and ports, you'll see four pins or four connectors. If you look closely at FireWire 400 cables and ports, you'll see six pins or six connectors. Although standard FireWire and FireWire 400 cables have rectangular-shaped connectors with one short, flat end and one rounded end, FireWire 800 cables are square, and one of the long sides has a notch.

When you are purchasing external devices, you might want to get a device with multiple interfaces. A device with multiple interfaces will give you more configuration options.

Installing devices

Every hardware component installed on a system has an associated device driver. Drivers are used to handle the low-level communications tasks between the operating system and hardware components. When you install a hardware component through the operating system, you tell the operating system about the device driver it uses. From then on, the device driver loads automatically and runs as part of the operating system.

Understanding device installation

Unlike early versions of Windows, Windows Server 2012 R2 is very good at detecting devices that were not installed after upgrading or installing the operating system. If a device wasn't installed because Windows Server didn't include the driver, the built-in hardware diagnostics will, in many cases, detect the hardware and then use the automatic update framework to retrieve the required driver the next time Windows Update runs, provided that Windows Update is enabled and you've allowed driver updating and operating system updating.

Windows can also check for device software and device info. Device software, if available from the device manufacturers, typically includes a custom app for working with the device and a device driver. Device info provides additional information about the device and can include the product name, model number, and manufacturer name.

After upgrading or installing the operating system, you should check for driver updates and apply them as appropriate before trying other techniques to install device drivers. Device Installation Settings control whether Windows Server checks for drivers automatically. The settings also control whether Windows Server checks for driver updates, device software, and device info. To access these settings, open the System Properties dialog box, tap or click the Hardware tab, and then tap or click Device Installation Settings. You now have several options:

- **Yes, Do This Automatically (Recommended).** When selected, Windows Server checks for and downloads drivers for new devices and driver updates automatically as part of the Windows Update process. Windows Server also checks for and downloads device software and device info.

- **Always Install The Best Driver Software From Windows Update.** When selected, Windows Server checks for and downloads drivers for new devices and driver updates automatically as part of the Windows Update process. You control whether you want to check for and download device software and device info by either selecting or clearing the Automatically Get The Device App And Info check box.

- **Never Install Driver Software From Windows Update.** When selected, Windows Server does not check for or download drivers for new devices or driver updates automatically as part of the Windows Update process. You control whether you want to check for and download device software and device info by either selecting or clearing the Automatically Get The Device App And Info check box.

Typically, device driver updates are seen as optional updates. The exceptions are for essential drivers, such as those for video, network adapters, and hard disk controllers.

When looking for driver updates, you'll want to view all available updates on a computer, rather than only the important updates, to determine whether device driver updates are available. To install available driver updates, follow these steps:

1. In Control Panel\System And Security, tap or click Windows Update. In Windows Update, tap or click View Available Updates. If the computer has installed the updates it last downloaded, the View Available Updates option isn't available. In this case, you can tap or click Check For Updates to see whether there are new updates for the computer and then view the available updates (if any).

Inside OUT

Controlling how Windows Update works with devices

Although driver updates can be downloaded automatically through Windows Update, they are not installed automatically. The only drivers that are installed automatically are those required for new hardware and newly connected devices. Here, Windows Server checks the driver cache for drivers when you connect the device. If the driver is available in the cache, Windows Server installs the device.

In Group Policy, the Specify Search Order For Device Driver Source Locations policy can override this default behavior. This policy is found under Computer Configuration \Administrative Templates\System\Device Installation. If you set this policy to Always Search Windows Update, the operating system will search Windows Update for drivers rather than the driver cache doing so by default, and this search occurs only once. If the computer isn't connected to the Internet, the search will occur the next time the computer is connected to the Internet. The policy also can be set to search Windows Update only if needed or never to search Windows Update.

In Group Policy, the Turn Off Access To All Windows Update Features policy controls whether Windows Update can be used. This policy is under Computer Configuration \Administrative Templates\System\Internet Communication Management\Internet Communication Settings. If you enable this policy, all Windows Update features are blocked and unavailable to users. Users will also be unable to access the Windows Update website. In early releases of the Windows operating system, other policies could be used to control driver search locations and driver search prompts. However, these policies do not apply to current Windows operating systems.

2. When Windows finishes checking for updates, you might find that both important updates and optional updates are available. If the computer is set to install updates automatically, important updates will be installed as part of automatic maintenance. You can install important updates immediately by clicking the related link and then clicking Install.

3. Most driver updates are listed as optional updates, and optional updates are not installed automatically. If optional updates are available, tap or click the related link and review the available optional updates. Select the check boxes for the optional updates that you want to install and then tap or click Install.

Inside OUT

Using Bluetooth devices

Windows Server supports Bluetooth, Bluetooth LE, and Inter-Integrated Circuit (I2C) transports. Before these devices can be used, they must be discovered and paired with Windows Server. To discover and pair a device with Windows Server, complete the following steps:

1. **In Control Panel, select Add A Device under the Hardware heading to have Windows search for available devices.**
2. **In the Add A Device Wizard, select the device, select Next, and then select Finish. Keep in mind that some devices require you to enable Bluetooth and then attempt to pair on the device.**

You'll know a new device installed because it will be available for you to use. You also can confirm device availability in either Devices And Printers or Device Manager:

- From Control Panel, you can open Devices And Printers by tapping or clicking View Devices And Printers under the Hardware heading.
- From Server Manager, you can open Device Manager by selecting Computer Management on the Tools menu and then selecting Device Manager in the left pane of Computer Management.

Not all devices have a custom driver. For example, with USB devices that do not have a custom driver, you often can use the generic Winusb.sys driver, which is the default USB driver included with Windows Server. When you connect a USB device that doesn't have a custom driver, Windows Server might use the generic Winusb.sys driver automatically. If this driver isn't used automatically, you can manually select the generic Winusb.sys driver when installing the device.

Keep in mind that the generic USB driver isn't for USB devices with their own classifications. Devices with their own classifications have their own generic drivers, which you can install. Devices with their own classifications include the following:

- Audio devices
- Audio/video devices
- Human interface devices (HIDs)
- Image devices
- Printers

- Mass storage devices
- Smart cards
- Wireless host and hub controllers

Human interface devices are interactive input devices that are used to control computers directly, including:

- Controls found on devices such as interactive displays, barcode readers, smartphones, and other consumer electronics
- Front-panel controls such as knobs, switches, buttons, and sliders on devices, such as the volume controls on speakers and headsets
- Keyboards and pointing devices such as standard mouse devices, trackballs, and joysticks
- Sensory devices such as accelerometers and gyroscopes

Human interface devices are a device class over USB. Windows Server supports USB, Bluetooth, Bluetooth LE, and Inter-Integrated Circuit (I2C) as transports for HID and HID clients for mouse and mapper drivers, keyboard and keypad drivers, system control drivers (such as power buttons and laptop lid open/close sensors), consumer device controls, pen devices, touch screens, sensors, and UPS batteries. Windows Server does not support older interactive input devices such as HID mini-drivers.

When a device has a custom driver, Windows Server might automatically detect the new device, but the Driver Software Installation component might run into problems installing the device. If this happens, the installation silently fails. You'll know installation failed because the device will not be available for you to use. In Devices And Printers, you should see warning icons for both the computer and the device. In this case, if you touch or move the mouse pointer over the computer device, you should see error status messages such as the following:

```
Status: Driver is unavailable
```

```
Status: Driver Error
```

When you tap or click the computer device, the details pane should show the Needs Troubleshooting status. After a failed installation, you can attempt to install the device by following these steps:

1. In Devices And Printers, press and hold or right-click the device and then select Properties.
2. In the Properties dialog box, on the Hardware tab, tap or click the Properties button.

3. On the General tab, select Change Settings. On the Driver tab, select Update Driver. This starts the Update Driver Software Wizard.

4. Specify whether you want to install the drivers automatically or manually by selecting the driver from a list or specific location. (See Figure 7-3.)

   NOTE

   Updated drivers can add functionality to a device, improve performance, and resolve device problems. However, you should rarely install the latest drivers on a computer without first testing them in a test environment. Test first, then install.

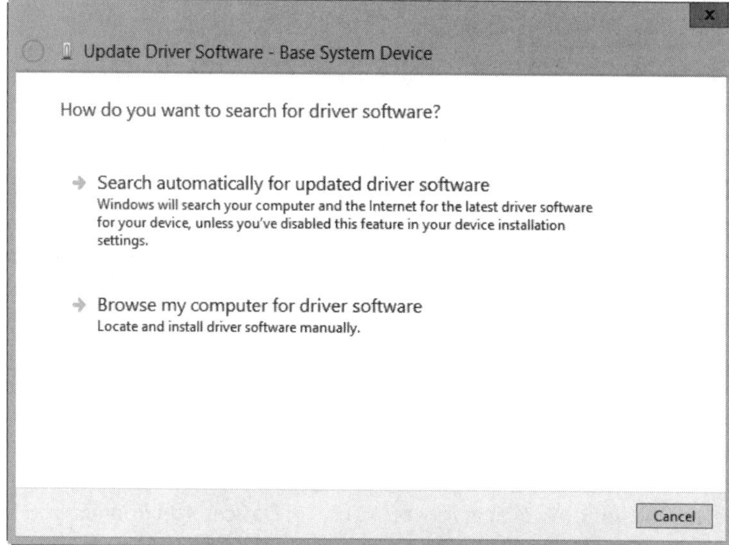

Figure 7-3 Choose to install drivers automatically or manually.

5. If you elect to search automatically for the driver, and Device Installation Settings allow this, Windows Server checks for the device driver using either Windows Update or WSUS. Then, if a driver is available, Windows Server downloads it and installs it automatically. In this case, tap or click Close to complete the process and then skip the remaining steps.

6. If you chose to install the driver manually, you have the opportunity to do one of the following, as shown in Figure 7-4:

   - **Search for the driver.** If you want to search for drivers, tap or click Browse to select a search location. Use the Browse For Folder dialog box to select the start folder for the search and then tap or click OK. Because all subfolders of the selected folder are searched automatically, you can select the drive root path, such as C, to search an entire drive.

- **Choose a driver to install.** If you want to choose the driver to install, tap or click Let Me Pick From A List Of Device Drivers On My Computer. The wizard then displays a list of common hardware types. Select the appropriate hardware type, such as Storage Controllers or Network Adapters, and then tap or click Next. Scroll through the list of manufacturers to find the manufacturer of the device and then choose the appropriate device in the right pane.

NOTE

If the manufacturer or device you want to use isn't listed, insert the media containing the device driver disc or USB flash drive and then tap or click Have Disk. Follow the prompts. Afterward, select the appropriate device.

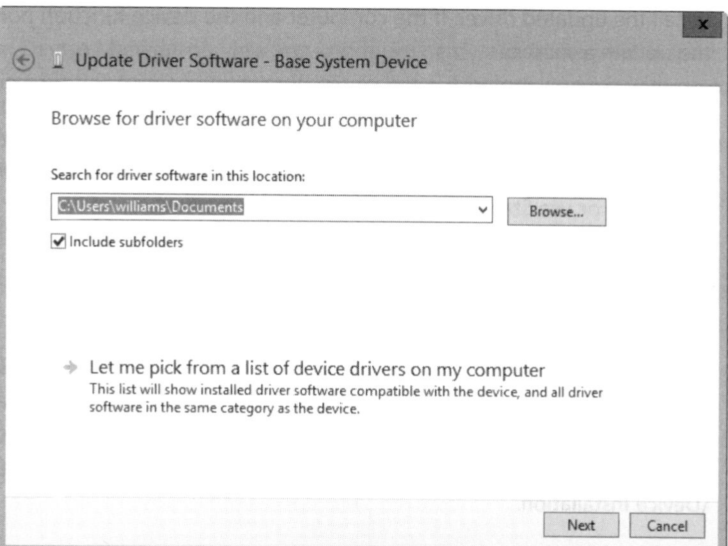

Figure 7-4 Search for or select a driver to install.

7. After selecting a device driver through a search or a manual selection, continue through the installation process by tapping or clicking Next. Tap or click Close when the driver installation is completed. If the wizard can't find an appropriate driver, you need to obtain one and then repeat this procedure. Keep in mind that in some cases you'll need to restart the system to activate the newly installed device driver.

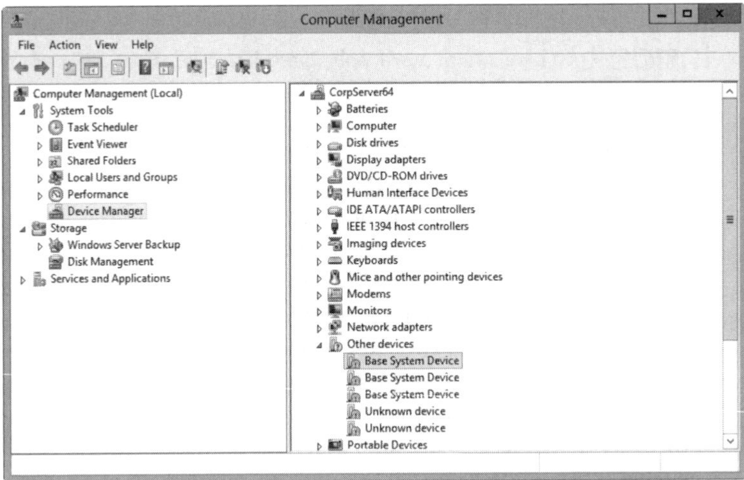

Figure 7-5 Use Device Manager to work with hardware devices.

3. Expand a device type to see a list of the specific instances of that device type.

After you access Device Manager, you can work with any of the installed devices. If you press and hold or right-click a device entry, a shortcut menu is displayed. The available options depend on the device type, but they include the following:

- **Properties.** Displays the Properties dialog box for the device
- **Uninstall.** Uninstalls the device and its drivers
- **Disable.** Disables the device but doesn't uninstall it
- **Enable.** Enables a device if it's disabled
- **Update Driver Software.** Starts the Update Driver Software Wizard, which you can use to update the device driver
- **Scan For Hardware Changes.** Tells Windows Server 2012 R2 to check the hardware configuration and determine whether there are any changes

NOTE

The device list shows warning symbols if there are problems with a device. A yellow warning symbol with an exclamation point indicates a problem with a device. A red X indicates a device that was improperly installed or disabled by the user or the administrator for some reason.

You can use the options on the View menu in Device Manager to change the defaults for which types of devices are displayed and how the devices are listed. The options are as follows:

- **Devices By Type.** Displays devices by the type of device installed, such as disk drive or printer. The connection name is listed below the type. This is the default view.
- **Devices By Connection.** Displays devices by the connection type, such as audio and video codecs.
- **Resources By Type.** Displays the status of allocated resources by the type of device using the resource. Resource types are direct memory access (DMA) channels, input/output (I/O) ports, interrupt requests (IRQs), and memory addresses.
- **Resources By Connection.** Displays the status of all allocated resources by connection type rather than device type.
- **Show Hidden Devices.** Displays non–Plug and Play devices and devices that have been physically removed from the computer but whose drivers haven't been uninstalled.

Inside OUT

View and save device settings for local and remote computers

You can use Computer Management to view and work with settings on remote computers. Press and hold or right-click Computer Management in the console tree and then select Connect To Another Computer on the shortcut menu. In the Select Computer dialog box, choose Another Computer and then type the fully qualified name of the computer you want to work with, such as **entdc01.microsoft.com**, where *entdc01* is the computer name, and *microsoft.com* is the domain name. If you don't know the computer name, tap or click Browse to search for the computer you want to work with.

If you want detailed driver lists for multiple computers, you can get this using the Driverquery command-line utility. Use the */V* parameter to get verbose output about all drivers or the */SI* parameter to display properties only for signed drivers, such as **driverquery /v** or **driverquery /si**. If you want to write the information to a file, use the output redirection symbol (>) followed by the name of the file, such as **driverquery /si > system-devices.txt**.

To list devices on remote computers, use the */S* parameter followed by a computer name or Internet Protocol (IP) address to specify a remote computer to query. You can also specify the Run As permissions by using */U* followed by the user name and */P* followed by the user's password. Here's an example: **driverquery /v /s corpserver01 /u wrstanek /p 49iners**.

Working with device drivers

Each hardware component installed on a computer has an associated device driver. The job of the device driver is to describe how the operating system uses the hardware abstraction layer (HAL) to work with a hardware component. The HAL handles the low-level communication tasks between the operating system and a hardware component. By installing a hardware component through the operating system, you are telling the operating system about the device driver it uses. From then on, the device driver loads automatically and runs as part of the operating system.

Device driver essentials

Windows Server 2012 R2 includes an extensive library of device drivers. In the base installation of the operating system, these drivers are maintained in the file repository of the driver store. Some service packs you install will also include updates to the driver store. You can find drivers in the FileRepository folder under %SystemRoot%\System32\DriverStore. The DriverStore folder also contains subfolders for localized driver information. You'll find a subfolder for each language component configured on the system. For example, for localized U.S. English driver information, you'll find a subfolder called en-US.

Every device driver in the driver store is certified to be fully compatible with Windows Server 2012 R2 and is digitally signed by Microsoft to assure the operating system of its authenticity. When you install a new Plug and Play–compatible device, Windows Server 2012 R2 checks the driver store for a compatible device driver. If one is found, the operating system automatically installs the device.

Every device driver has an associated Setup Information file. This file, which ends with the .inf extension, is a text file containing detailed configuration information about the device being installed. The information file also identifies any source files the driver uses. Source files have the .sys extension. Drivers are also associated with a component manifest (component.man) file. The manifest file is written in Extensible Markup Language (XML), includes details on the driver's digital signature, and might include Plug and Play information the device uses to configure itself automatically.

Every driver installed on a system has a source (.sys) file in the %SystemRoot%\System32\Drivers folder. When you install a new device driver, the driver is written to a subfolder of %SystemRoot%\System32\Drivers, and configuration settings are stored in the registry. The driver's .inf file is used to control the installation and write the registry settings. If the driver doesn't already exist in the driver store, it does not already have an .inf file or other related files on the system. In this case, the driver's .inf file and other related files are written to a subfolder of %SystemRoot%\System32\DriverStore\FileRepository when you install the device.

Understanding and troubleshooting driver signing

Speaking of new device drivers, Microsoft requires you to use signed device drivers. Every device driver in the driver cache is digitally signed, which certifies the driver as having passed extensive testing by the WHQL. A device driver with a digital signature signed by Microsoft should not cause your system to crash or become unstable. The presence of a digital signature signed by Microsoft also ensures that the device driver hasn't been tampered with. If a device driver doesn't have a digital signature signed by Microsoft, it hasn't been approved for use through testing, or its files might have been modified from the original installation by another program. This means that unsigned drivers are much more likely than any other program you've installed to cause the operating system to freeze or the computer to crash.

The assurances you get with digitally signed drivers aren't applicable to unsigned device drivers. With an unsigned driver, there is no guarantee that it has been tested thoroughly, and if the driver is poorly written, it is much more likely to cause the operating system to freeze or the server to crash than any other program you've installed. Because of this, Windows Server will not let you install unsigned drivers.

That said, an invalid or missing digital signature on a driver for an important device could prevent a server from starting. There are several ways you can work around this, allowing you to boot the server and fix the problem. The two key options require you to start the server in safe mode.

If the computer won't start normally, the Recovery screen is displayed during startup. On the Recovery screen, tap or click Troubleshoot. On the Advanced Options screen, tap or click Startup Settings. Next, on the Windows Startup Settings screen, tap or click Restart. When the server restarts, you need to select the safe mode you want to use.

With the standard safe modes, the basic drivers loaded include the mouse, monitor, keyboard, mass storage, and base video. If one of the basic drivers is the source of the problem, though, you won't be able to use one of the standard safe modes. Because of this, select Disable Driver Signature Enforcement as the start mode.

Viewing driver information

To view detailed information about a device, press and hold or right-click the device and select Properties or just double-tap or double-click the related entry in Device Manager. This opens the device's Properties dialog box, as shown in Figure 7-6. Most devices have at least two tabs, either General and Properties or General and Driver.

The most important information on the General tab is the device status. If the device is working properly, this is specifically stated. Otherwise, the error status of the device is shown. If the device is disabled, you have an option to enable the device (as shown in Figure 7-7).

Figure 7-6 Use the device's Properties dialog box to obtain essential information about a device, including whether it is functioning properly.

Figure 7-7 Disabled devices are listed with an error status because they aren't functioning; you can enable them by tapping or clicking Enable Device.

You can temporarily disable a device by selecting Disable on the Driver tab. If you later want to enable the device, tap or click the Enable Device button on the General tab and then, when the Troubleshooting Wizard starts, tap or click Next and then tap or click Finish.

The Driver tab, shown in Figure 7-8, provides basic information about the driver provider, creation date, version, and digital signature. You should be wary of any drivers that list the provider as Unknown or that are listed as Not Digitally Signed. Drivers signed by Microsoft are listed as being signed by Microsoft Windows or Microsoft Windows Hardware Compatibility Publisher.

Figure 7-8 Use the Driver tab to determine the driver provider, creation date, version, and digital signature.

You can view additional information about the driver by tapping or clicking Driver Details. If no driver files are required or none have been loaded for the device, you see a message stating this. Otherwise, you see the names and locations of all associated files, including an icon that indicates the signing status of each individual file. Selecting a file in this list displays details for that file in the lower section of the dialog box, as shown in Figure 7-9.

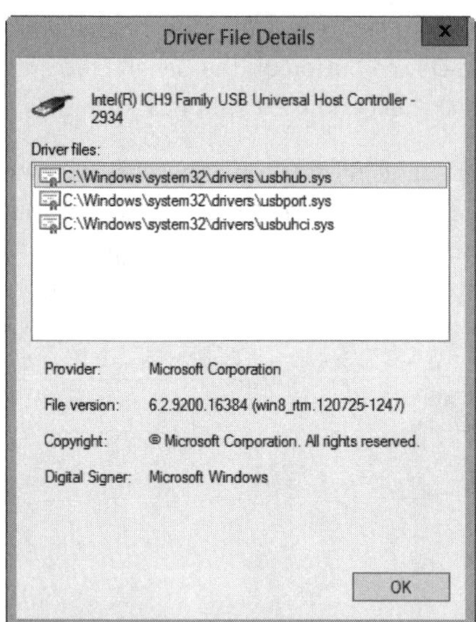

Figure 7-9 The Driver File Details dialog box displays information on the driver file locations, the provider, and the file versions.

Viewing Advanced, Resources, and other settings

Devices often have other tabs, such as Advanced, Resources, and Power Management. Most network adapters have an Advanced tab. As shown in Figure 7-10, these options can control transmission preferences. You should change these options only if you are trying to resolve specific performance or connectivity issues as directed by the device manufacturer or a Microsoft Knowledge Base article. The setting that causes the most problems is Speed & Duplex. Most of the time, you want this set to Auto Detect or Auto Negotiation. Sometimes, however, to correct a specific problem, you must use a preset speed and duplex setting such as 100 Mbps Half Duplex or 1,000 Mbps Full Duplex. You should do this, however, only when this setting is recommended based on your network configuration or the issue you are trying to troubleshoot.

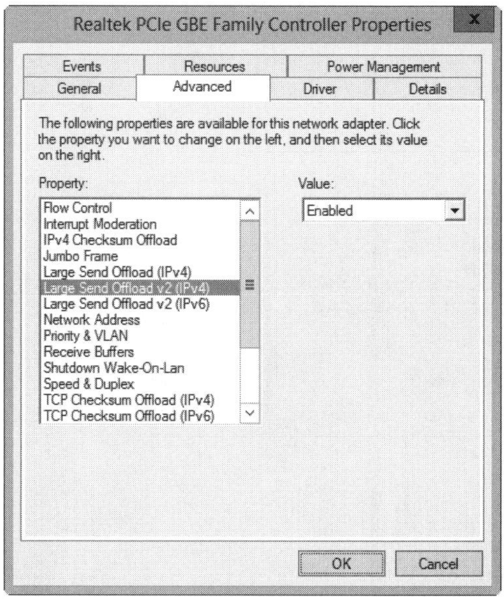

Figure 7-10 You'll find that most network adapters have an Advanced tab for setting transmission preferences.

Any device that uses system resources will have a Resources tab like the one shown in Figure 7-11.

The Resources tab options show the device resources that are currently assigned and their settings. There are four types of device resources:

- **DMA.** The DMA channel the device uses. Values are shown as integers, such as 02.
- **Memory Range.** The range of memory addresses the device uses. Values are shown in hexadecimal format, such as E8206000–E8206FFF.
- **I/O Range.** The range of I/O ports the device uses. Values are shown in hexadecimal format, such as 5400–543F.
- **IRQ Line.** The IRQ line the device uses. Values are shown as integers, such as 10.

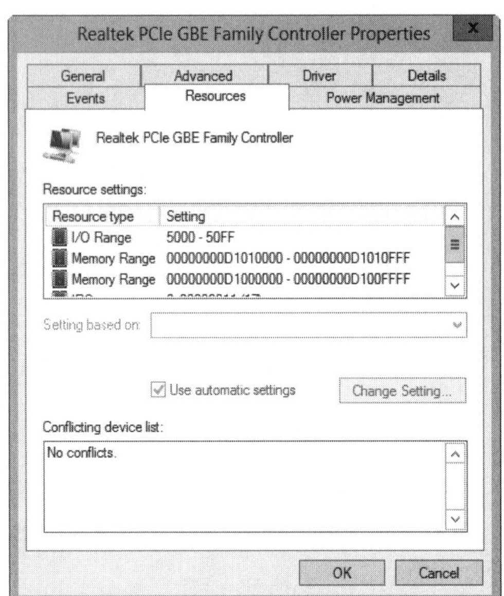

Figure 7-11 Any device that uses system resources has a Resources tab.

Devices can use multiple I/O and memory ranges. For example, the Video Graphics Adapter (VGA) on one of our computers used three I/O ranges and three memory ranges. In addition, multiple PCIe devices can share the same IRQs when using Advanced Configuration and Power Interface (ACPI) BIOS. This is because ACPI BIOS allows IRQ sharing. To learn more about resource sharing and configuration options, see "Resolving resource conflicts" later in this chapter.

Installing and updating device drivers

Device drivers are essential to the proper operation of Windows Server. A faulty device driver can cause many problems on your systems—everything from unexpected restarts to application hangs to blue screens. To make it easier to detect and diagnose problems, you should maintain an inventory of all installed device drivers on systems you manage. Previously, I talked about using the Driverquery command to obtain a list of drivers for computers throughout the network. Ideally, the driver information should be stored on a centralized network share rather than on individual computers, or it could be printed out and placed in a binder where it is easily accessible. You should then periodically check manufacturer websites for known problems with related device drivers and for updated drivers. Windows Update can also help you because driver updates are made available through this service and can be installed automatically.

Although you can be fairly certain drivers obtained through Windows Update are newer than installed versions, this isn't the case for drivers you download yourself, and you should always double-check the driver version information before installation. As discussed previously, the current driver version is displayed in the driver's Properties dialog box, as shown in Figure 7-12. Double-tap or double-click the device in Device Manager to display the driver's Properties dialog box and then select the Driver tab, as shown in Figure 7-12. Be sure to check both the driver date and the driver version.

Figure 7-12 Check the current driver date and version.

Next, check the driver version information for the driver you downloaded. To do this, extract the downloaded driver files to a folder. In the folder, you should find .dll or .sys files. Press and hold or right-click one of these files and choose Properties. Then, in the Properties dialog box, tap or click the Version tab to find the version information.

To continue with the installation of downloaded drivers, check to see whether the driver download includes a Setup program. If it does, run this program so that the proper files are copied to your system. If the drivers aren't installed as part of setup, you can install and update the drivers by using the Update Driver Software Wizard. The wizard can search for updated device drivers in the following locations:

- On the local computer
- On a hardware installation disc
- On the Windows Update site or your organization's Windows Update server

In Group Policy, the main policy that controls access to Windows Update is Turn Off Access To All Windows Update Features. This policy is under Computer Configuration\Administrative Templates\System\Internet Communication Management\Internet Communication Settings. If you enable this policy setting, all Windows Update features are blocked and unavailable to users. Users will also be unable to access the Windows Update website. In early releases of the Windows operating system, other policies could be used to control driver search locations and driver search prompts. However, these policies do not apply to current Windows operating systems.

You can install and update device drivers by following these steps:

1. In Computer Management, select the Device Manager node. You should now see a complete list of devices installed on the system. By default, this list is organized by device type.
2. Press and hold or right-click the device you want to manage and then select Update Driver Software. This starts the Update Driver Software Wizard.
3. You can specify whether you want to install the drivers automatically or manually by selecting the driver from a list or specific location.

   NOTE

   Updated drivers can add functionality to a device, improve performance, and resolve device problems. However, you should rarely install the latest drivers on a user's computer without first testing them in a test environment. Test first, then install.

4. If you elect to install the driver automatically, Windows Server 2012 R2 looks for a more recent version of the device driver and installs the driver if found. If a more recent version of the driver is not found, Windows Server 2012 R2 keeps the current driver. In either case, tap or click Close to complete the process and then skip the remaining steps.
5. If you chose to install the driver manually, you next have the opportunity to do one of the following:
   - **Search for the driver.** If you want to search for drivers, tap or click Browse to select a search location. Use the Browse For Folder dialog box to select the start folder for the search and then tap or click OK. Because all subfolders of the selected folder are searched automatically, you can select the drive root path, such as C, to search an entire drive.
   - **Choose the driver to install.** If you want to choose the driver to install, tap or click Let Me Pick From A List Of Device Drivers On My Computer. The wizard then displays a list of common hardware types. Select the appropriate hardware type,

such as Modems or Network Adapters, and then tap or click Next. Scroll through the list of manufacturers to find the manufacturer of the device and then choose the appropriate device in the right pane.

NOTE

If the manufacturer or device you want to use isn't listed, insert the media containing the device driver or USB flash drive and then tap or click Have Disk. Follow the prompts. Afterward, select the appropriate device.

6. After selecting a device driver through a search or a manual selection, continue through the installation process by tapping or clicking Next. Tap or click Close when the driver installation is completed. If the wizard can't find an appropriate driver, you need to obtain one and then repeat this procedure. Keep in mind that in some cases you'll need to restart the computer to activate the newly installed or updated device driver.

Restricting device installation by using Group Policy

In addition to specifying driver installation and search restrictions, you can use Group Policy settings to allow or prevent installation of devices based on the device type. The related policy settings are found under Computer Configuration\Administrative Templates\System\Device Installation\Device Installation Restrictions and include the following:

- Allow Administrators To Override Device Installation Restriction Policies
- Allow Installation Of Devices Using Drivers That Match These Device Setup Classes
- Prevent Installation Of Drivers That Match These Device Setup Classes
- Allow Installation Of Devices That Match Any Of These Device IDs
- Prevent Installation Of Devices That Match Any Of These Device IDs
- Prevent Installation Of Removable Devices
- Prevent Installation Of Devices Not Described By Other Policy Settings
- Time (In Seconds) To Force Reboot When Required

You can configure these policies by following these steps:

1. Access the policy for the appropriate site, domain, or organizational unit (OU).
2. Expand Computer Configuration, Administrative Templates, System, Device Installation, and Device Installation Restrictions.

3. Double-tap or double-click the appropriate policy to view its Properties dialog box.

4. Set the state of the policy as Not Configured if you don't want the policy to be applied, Enabled if you want the policy to be applied, or Disabled if you want to block the policy from being used (all as permitted by the Group Policy configuration).

5. If you are enabling the policy and it has a Show option, tap or click Show to use the Show Contents dialog box to specify which device IDs should be matched to this policy. Tap or click OK twice.

Device installation restrictions will not take effect until computers are restarted. To force computers to restart when device installation restrictions are changed, you can enable and configure the Time (In Seconds) To Force Reboot When Required policy. For example, you might want to force computers to restart within 60 minutes of the policy change. If so, you'd enter 3600 in the Reboot Timeout (In Seconds) box.

Rolling back drivers

Occasionally, you'll find that an updated driver doesn't work as expected. It could cause problems such as device failure or system instability. Generally, this shouldn't occur when you've installed signed device drivers. However, it can sometimes occur with any device driver—even those published through Windows Update.

If you suspect that an updated driver is causing the system or device problems you are experiencing, you can attempt to recover the system to the previously installed device driver. To do this, follow these steps:

1. If you are having problems starting the system, you need to start the system in safe mode.

2. In Computer Management, select the Device Manager node. You should now see a complete list of devices installed on the system. By default, this list is organized by device type.

3. Press and hold or right-click the device you want to manage and then select Properties. This opens the Properties dialog box for the device.

4. Tap or click the Driver tab and then tap or click Roll Back Driver. When prompted to confirm the action, tap or click Yes.

5. Tap or click Close to close the driver's Properties dialog box.

IMPORTANT

If the driver file hasn't been updated, a backup drive file won't be available; the Roll Back Driver button will be disabled, and you will not be able to tap or click it. In this case, you should check the manufacturer's website for available versions of the driver for the device.

Removing device drivers for removed devices

Windows device drivers for Plug and Play devices are loaded and unloaded dynamically. You can remove the driver for a device only when the device is plugged in. This means the proper way to remove a device from a system is first to uninstall its related device driver and then to remove the device from the system.

One reason for uninstalling a device is to remove a device that you no longer use or need. Start by uninstalling the related device driver. Open Computer Management and then select the Device Manager node. Press and hold or right-click the device you want to remove and then select Uninstall. When prompted, tap or click OK to confirm that you want to remove the driver. Windows Server 2012 R2 then removes the related files and registry settings.

At this point, you can shut down the system and remove the related hardware component if you want to. However, you might first want to check to see how the computer operates without the device in case some unforeseen problem or error occurs. So, rather than removing the device, you want to disable it. Disabling the device prevents Windows from reinstalling the device automatically the next time you restart the system. You disable a device by pressing and holding or right-clicking it in Device Manager and then selecting Disable.

Sometimes when you are troubleshooting and trying to get a device to work properly, you might want to uninstall or unplug the device temporarily. Here, you could disable the device and then monitor the system to see whether problems previously experienced recur, or you could reinstall the device to see whether normal operations are restored. Uninstalling and then reinstalling the device forces Windows to go back to the device's original device and registry settings, which can sometimes recover the device.

After you uninstall a device driver, one way to get Windows Server 2012 R2 to reinstall the device is to restart the computer. You can also try to rescan for devices using Device Manager by selecting the computer node in the main pane and then selecting Scan For Hardware Changes on the Action menu. Either way, the operating system should detect the uninstalled device as new hardware and then automatically reinstall the necessary device driver. If this doesn't happen, you must reinstall the device manually by using the Add Hardware Wizard as discussed in "Adding non–Plug and Play, older hardware" later in this chapter.

Uninstalling, reinstalling, and disabling device drivers

Uninstalling a device driver uninstalls the related device. When a device isn't working properly, sometimes you can completely uninstall the device, restart the system, and then reinstall the device driver to restore normal operations. You can uninstall and then reinstall a device by following these steps:

1. Open Computer Management and then select the Device Manager node. You should now see a complete list of devices installed on the system. By default, this list is organized by device type.

2. Press and hold or right-click the device you want to manage and then select Uninstall. When prompted to confirm the action, tap or click OK.

3. Restart the system. Windows Server 2012 R2 should detect the presence of the device and automatically reinstall the necessary device driver. If the device isn't automatically reinstalled, reinstall it manually as discussed in the "Installing and updating device drivers" section.

To prevent a device from being reinstalled automatically, disable the device instead of uninstalling it. You disable a device by pressing and holding or right-clicking it in Device Manager and then selecting Disable.

Managing hardware

Windows Plug and Play technology does a good job of detecting and automatically configuring new hardware. However, if the hardware doesn't support Plug and Play or it isn't automatically detected, you need to enter information about the new hardware into the Windows Server 2012 R2 system. You do this by using the Add Hardware Wizard to install the hardware device and its related drivers on the system. You can also use this wizard to troubleshoot problems with existing hardware.

Adding non–Plug and Play, older hardware

Although Windows Server 2012 R2 doesn't detect or set up non–Plug and Play devices automatically, it does maintain a driver cache for these devices. You might also be able to use an older driver if a Windows Server 2012 R2 device driver isn't available. In either case, you install the device by using the Add Hardware Wizard. Follow these steps:

1. If the device has installation media or a downloadable Setup program, run it to copy the driver files to your hard disk.

2. Connect the device to the computer. For internal devices, you must shut down the computer, add the device, and then restart the computer.

3. Open Computer Management and then select the Device Manager node.
4. Select the computer node in the main pane and then choose Add Legacy Hardware on the Action menu.
5. In the Add Hardware Wizard, read the introductory message and then tap or click Next.
6. Determine whether you want the wizard to search for new hardware or you want to locate and install the driver manually (as shown in Figure 7-13):
   - If you choose the search option, the wizard searches for and attempts to detect the new hardware automatically. The process can take several minutes to go through all the device types and options. When the search is complete, any new devices found are displayed, and you can select one.
   - If you choose the manual option, or if no new devices are found in the automatic search, you have to select the hardware type yourself. Select the type of hardware, such as Storage Controllers or Network Adapters, and then tap or click Next. Scroll through the list of manufacturers to find the manufacturer of the device and then choose the appropriate device in the right pane.

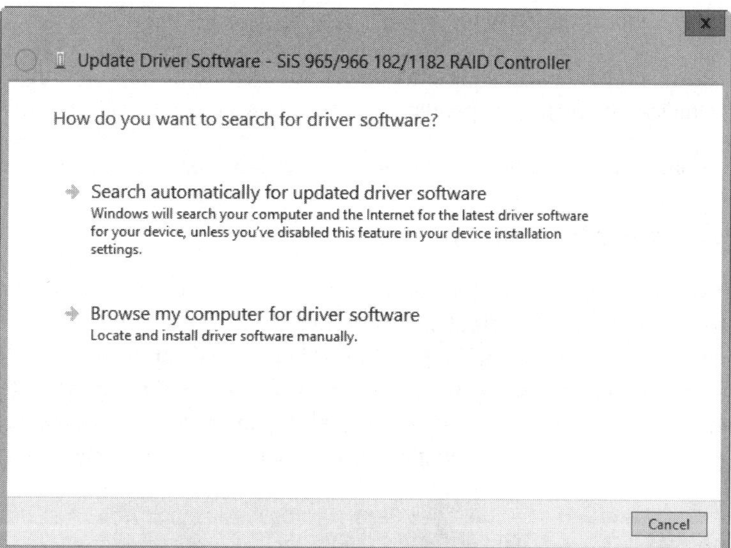

Figure 7-13 Search for or select the new hardware to install.

7. After you complete the selection and installation process, tap or click Next and then tap or click Next again to confirm that you want to install the hardware.

8. After the wizard installs the drivers for the hardware device, tap or click Finish. The new hardware should now be available.

Enabling and disabling hardware

When a device isn't working properly, sometimes you'll want to uninstall or disable it. Uninstalling a device removes the driver association for the device so that it temporarily appears that the device has been removed from the system. The next time you restart the system, Windows Server 2012 R2 might try to reinstall the device. Typically, Windows Server 2012 R2 reinstalls Plug and Play devices automatically, but it does not automatically reinstall non–Plug and Play devices.

Disabling a device turns it off and prevents Windows Server 2012 R2 from using it. Because a disabled device doesn't use system resources, you can be sure that it isn't causing a conflict on the system.

You can uninstall or disable a device by following these steps:

1. Open Computer Management and then select the Device Manager node. You should now see a complete list of devices installed on the system. By default, this list is organized by device type.

2. Press and hold or right-click the device you want to manage and then select Enable, Uninstall, or Disable, depending on what you want to do with the device.

3. If prompted to confirm the action, tap or click Yes or OK as appropriate.

Troubleshooting hardware

Windows Server 2012 R2 built-in hardware diagnostics can detect many types of problems with hardware devices. If a problem is detected, you might see a Problem Reporting balloon telling you there is a problem. Tapping or clicking this balloon opens Action Center. Action Center can also be accessed in Control Panel by tapping or clicking the System And Security link and then selecting Action Center. To open Action Center, tap or click the Action Center icon in the notification area of the taskbar and then select Open Action Center.

Inside OUT

Using Action Center for hardware troubleshooting

Action Center might have a solution for the hardware problem the computer is experiencing. If so, you can apply the solution or get more information about the problem by using the provided options. To check for solutions to known problems, click the Check For Solutions link on the Maintenance panel.

While you are working with Action Center, click the View Reliability History link to open Reliability Monitor to review the computer's reliability history. If hardware devices are causing reliability problems, the problem history will depict this. Select an item in the history to review its details. Additional options are available for saving the reliability history, viewing all problem reports, and checking for solutions to all known problems.

Events related to malfunctioning hardware often will be written to the system logs. You can quickly find events related to a specific device by following these steps:

1. Open Computer Management and then select the Device Manager node.
2. Press and hold or right-click the device that you want to troubleshoot and then select Properties.
3. If there's a problem with a device, there will be an error status and a related error code on the General tab.
4. On the Events tab, you see the most recent events related to the device, as shown in Figure 7-14. Select an event to view its details in the Information panel. Tap or click View All Events to open a custom view for the device in Event Viewer. The custom view will show all available events for the device so you can review them for troubleshooting.

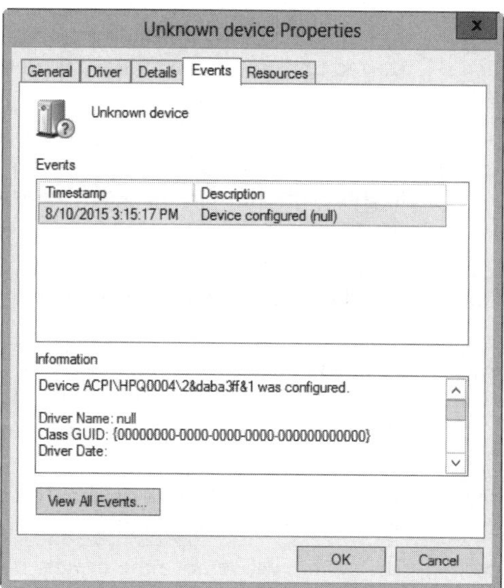

Figure 7-14 Review events to troubleshoot the device.

Whenever a device is installed incorrectly or has another problem, Device Manager displays a warning icon indicating that the device has a problem. If you double-tap or double-click the device, an error code displays on the General tab of the device's Properties dialog box. As Table 7-1 shows, this error code can also be helpful when trying to solve device problems. Most of the correction actions assume that you selected the General tab from the device's Properties dialog box.

Table 7-1 Common device errors and techniques to resolve them

Error Message	Correction Action
This device is not configured correctly. (Code 1)	Obtain a compatible driver for the device and tap or click Update Driver on the Driver tab to start the Update Driver Software Wizard.
The driver for this device might be corrupted, or your system might be running low on memory or other resources. (Code 3)	Tap or click Update Driver on the Driver tab to run the Update Driver Software Wizard. You might see an "Out of Memory" message at startup because of this.
This device cannot start. (Code 10)	Tap or click Update Driver on the Driver tab to run the Update Driver Software Wizard. Don't try to find a driver automatically. Instead, choose the manual install option and select the device driver you want to use.
This device cannot find enough free resources that it can use. (Code 12)	Resources assigned to this device conflict with another device, or the BIOS is incorrectly configured. Check the BIOS and check for resource conflicts on the Resources tab of the device's Properties dialog box.
This device cannot work properly until you restart your computer. (Code 14)	Typically, the driver is installed correctly but will not be started until you restart the computer.
Windows cannot identify all the resources this device uses. (Code 16)	Check whether a signed driver is available for the device. If one is available and you already installed it, you might need to manage the resources for the device. Check the Resources tab of the device's Properties dialog box.
This device is asking for an unknown resource type. (Code 17)	Reinstall or update the driver by using a valid, signed driver.
Reinstall the drivers for this device. (Code 18)	After an upgrade, you might need to log on as an administrator to complete device installation. If this is not the case, tap or click Update Driver on the Driver tab to reinstall the driver.
Your registry might be corrupted. (Code 19)	Remove and reinstall the device. This should clear out incorrect or conflicting registry settings.
Windows is removing this device. (Code 21)	The system will remove the device. The registry might be corrupted. If the device continues to display this message, restart the computer.

Error Message	Correction Action
This device is disabled. (Code 22)	This device has been disabled using Device Manager. To enable it, select Use This Device (Enable) under Device Usage on the General tab of the device's Properties dialog box.
This device is not present, is not working properly, or does not have all its drivers installed. (Code 24)	This might indicate a bad device or bad hardware. This error code can also occur with previous ISA devices; upgrade the driver to resolve the issue.
The drivers for this device are not installed. (Code 28)	Obtain a compatible driver for the device and then tap or click Update Driver to start the Update Driver Software Wizard.
This device is disabled because the firmware of the device did not give it the required resources. (Code 29)	Check the device documentation on how to assign resources. You might need to upgrade the BIOS or enable the device in the system BIOS.
This device is not working properly because Windows cannot load the drivers required for this device. (Code 31)	The device driver might be incompatible with Windows Server. Obtain a compatible driver for the device and tap or click Update Driver to start the Update Driver Software Wizard.
A driver for this device was not required and has been disabled. (Code 32)	A dependent service for this device has been set to Disabled. Check the event logs to determine which services should be enabled and started.
Windows cannot determine which resources are required for this device. (Code 33)	This might indicate a bad device or bad hardware. This error code can also occur with previous ISA devices; upgrade the driver, refer to the device documentation on how to set resource usage, or do both.
Windows cannot determine the settings for this device. (Code 34)	The older device must be manually configured. Verify the device jumpers or BIOS settings and then configure the device resource usage by using the Resources tab of the device's Properties dialog box.
Your computer's system firmware does not include enough information to properly configure and use this device. (Code 35)	This error occurs on multiprocessor systems. Update the BIOS; check for a BIOS option to use MPS 1.1 or MPS 1.4. Usually, you want MPS 1.4.
This device is requesting a Peripheral Component Interconnect (PCI) interrupt but is configured for an ISA interrupt (or vice versa). (Code 36)	ISA interrupts are nonshareable. If a device is in a PCI slot but the slot is configured in BIOS as "reserved for ISA," the error might be displayed. Change the BIOS settings.
Windows cannot initialize the device driver for this hardware. (Code 37)	Run the Update Driver Software Wizard by tapping or clicking Update Driver on the Driver tab.
Windows cannot load the device driver for this hardware because a previous instance of the device driver is still in memory. (Code 38)	A device driver in memory is causing a conflict. Restart the computer.

Error Message	Correction Action
Windows cannot load the device driver for this hardware. The driver might be corrupted or missing. (Code 39)	Check to ensure that the hardware device is properly installed and connected and that it has power. If it is properly installed and connected, look for an updated driver or reinstall the current driver.
Windows cannot access this hardware because its service key information in the registry is missing or recorded incorrectly. (Code 40)	The registry entry for the device driver is invalid. Reinstall the driver.
Windows has stopped this device because it has reported problems. (Code 43)	The device was stopped by the operating system. You might need to uninstall and then reinstall the device. The device might have problems with the no-execute processor feature. In this case, check for a new driver.
An application or service has shut down this hardware device. (Code 44)	The device was stopped by an application or service. Restart the computer. The device might have problems with the no-execute processor feature. In this case, check for a new driver.

Resolving resource conflicts

Anyone who remembers IRQ conflicts will be thankful that current computers support ACPI BIOS. With ACPI BIOS, resources are allocated automatically by the operating system at startup, and multiple devices can share the same IRQ settings. These changes mean IRQ conflicts are largely a thing of the past. However, ACPI depends on Plug and Play, and devices that are not fully compatible can sometimes cause problems, particularly previous ISA devices.

TROUBLESHOOTING

Check the device slot configuration

Some conflicts occur because PCI interrupts are shareable, whereas ISA interrupts are nonshareable. Typically, this is a BIOS problem. If a device is in a PCI slot, but the slot is configured in BIOS as "reserved for ISA," a conflict can occur. You must change the BIOS settings rather than the resource configuration to resolve the problem.

If you suspect a device conflict is causing a problem with the current device, check the Conflicting Device list in the lower portion of the Resources tab. It will either list No Conflicts or the specific source of a known conflict. In Device Manager, you can quickly check resource allocations by choosing Resources By Type or Resources By Connection on the View menu.

In Figure 7-15, both ISA and PCI devices are using IRQ settings. Note that each ISA device has a separate IRQ setting, whereas multiple PCI devices share the same IRQ settings. This is very typical. Note also that the PCI Modem device has a question mark as an icon. This is because the device isn't configured properly, not because there's a conflict. In this example, there are no conflicts.

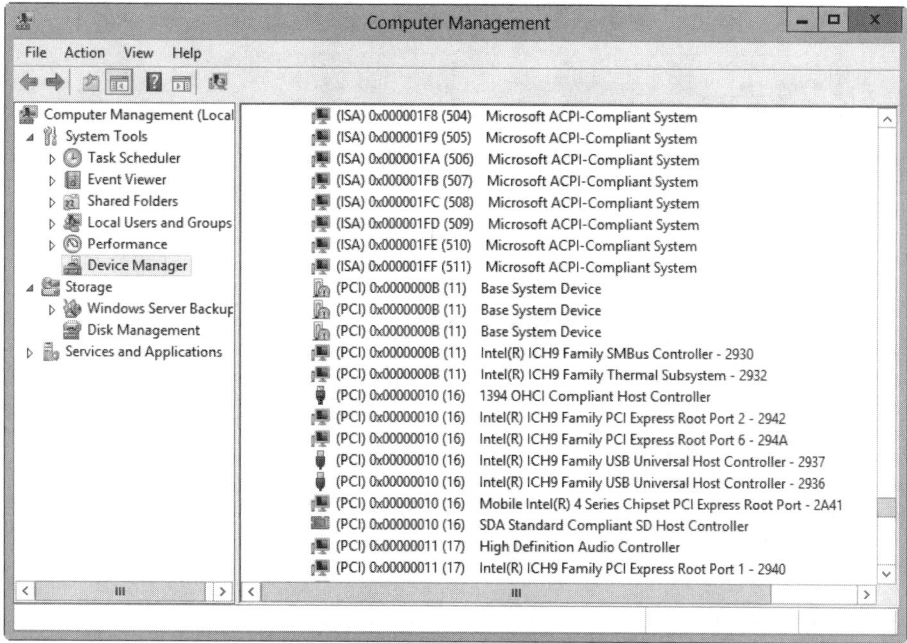

Figure 7-15 View resources by type or resources by connection to check resource settings in Device Manager.

Another way to check for conflicts is to use the System Information utility (Msinfo32.exe). In Server Manager, select System Information on the Tools menu. In System Information, expand Hardware Resources and then select Conflicts/Sharing.

As shown in Figure 7-16, a list of all resources that are in use is displayed. Again, keep in mind that devices can share IRQ settings thanks to ACPI, so what you are looking for are two unrelated devices sharing the same memory addresses or I/O ports, which would cause a conflict. Remember that related devices can share memory addresses and I/O ports. In the example, the PCI Express Root Complex shares the same I/O port as the Direct Memory Access Controller, and the Mobile Express Root Port shares the same memory addresses as the Basic Display Adapter resources. That's okay because this is typical and not causing an issue.

You can try to resolve resource conflicts in several ways. Some devices use jumpers to manage resource settings, and in this case, the operating system cannot control the resource settings. To make changes, you must shut down the computer, remove the device, change the jumper settings, and then replace the device. In some cases, the jumpers are managed through software rather than a physical jumper switch. Here, you would use the device setup or configuration utility to change the resource settings.

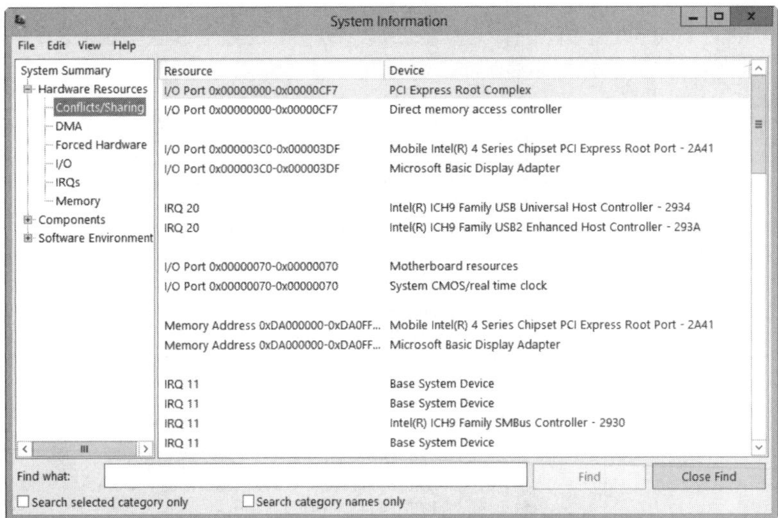

Figure 7-16 Use System Information to check for resource conflicts.

For PCI devices, you can try swapping the cards between PCI slots. This will help if the IRQ or other resource settings are assigned on a per-slot basis, as is the case with some motherboards. You might be able to check the motherboard documentation to see which IRQ interrupts are assigned to which slots. In any case, you need to experiment to see which card configuration works.

For PCI devices, a conflict could also be caused by the device driver and the way it works with ACPI BIOS. You should check to see whether an updated device driver and a BIOS update are available. Installing one or both should resolve the conflict.

As a last resort, you can change the resource settings manually for some devices in Device Manager. On the Resources tab, select the resource type that you want to work with. If you can make a change, you should be able to clear the Use Automatic Settings check box and then see whether any of the alternate configurations in the Setting Based On box resolve the conflict. Keep in mind that you are now manually managing the resource settings. To enable the Windows operating system again to manage the settings automatically, you must select the Use Automatic Settings check box.

CHAPTER 8

Managing the registry

Everyone who accesses a computer, whether in a workgroup or on a domain, at one time or another has accessed the Microsoft Windows registry whether the person realizes it or not. Whenever you log on, your user preferences are read from the registry. Whenever you make changes to the system configuration, install applications or hardware, or make other changes to the working environment, the changes are stored in the registry. Whenever you uninstall hardware, applications, or system components, these changes are also recorded in the registry.

The registry is the central repository for configuration information in Windows. Applications, system components, device drivers, and the operating system kernel all use the registry to store settings and obtain information about user preferences, system hardware configuration, and system defaults. The registry also stores information about security settings, user rights, local accounts, and much more. In domains, Windows does not store information about domain accounts or network objects in the registry; these settings are managed by Active Directory Domain Services (AD DS).

With so much information being read from and written to the registry, it is not only important for administrators to understand its structures and uses; it is essential. You should know the types of data the registry works with, what type of data is stored where, and how to make changes if necessary. This is important because often when you must fine-tune the system configuration or correct errors to stabilize systems, you might be instructed to access the registry and make a particular change. Generally, the instructions assume you know what you're doing. Unfortunately, if you attempt such a change and really don't know what you're doing, you could make it so the system won't boot at all. So, with this in mind, let's look at how the registry works and how you can work with it.

Introducing the registry

The registry is written as a binary database with the information organized in a hierarchy. This hierarchy has a structure much like a file system uses and is an inverted tree with the root at the top of the tree. Any time the Windows operating system must obtain system default values or information about your preferences, it obtains this information from the registry. When you install programs or make changes in Control Panel, these changes usually are written to the registry.

NOTE

I say "usually" because in Windows domains, some configuration information is written to Active Directory. For example, information about user accounts and network objects is stored in Active Directory. In addition, when you promote a member server to a domain controller, key registry settings that apply to the server, such as the default configuration values, are transferred to Active Directory and thereafter managed through Active Directory. If you were later to demote the domain controller, the original registry settings would not be restored either. Instead, the default settings are restored as they would appear on a newly installed server.

The registry's importance is that it stores most of a system's state. If you make preference and settings changes to a system, these changes are stored in the registry. If a system dies and cannot be recovered, you don't have to install a new system and then configure it to look like the old one. You could instead install Microsoft Windows Server 2012 R2 and then restore a backup of the failed system's registry. This restores all the preferences and settings of the failed system on the new system.

Although it's great that the registry can store settings you've made, you might be wondering what else the registry is good for. Well, in addition to storing settings you've made, the registry stores settings that the operating system makes. For example, the operating system kernel stores information needed by device drivers in the registry, including the driver initialization parameters, which enables the device drivers to configure themselves to work with the system's hardware.

Many other system components also use the registry. When you install Windows Server, the setup choices you make are used to build the initial registry database. Setup modifies the registry whenever you add hardware to or remove hardware from a system. Similarly, application setup programs modify the registry to store the application installation settings and determine whether components of the application are already installed. Then, when you run applications, the applications use the registry settings.

Current Windows operating systems don't always store application settings directly in the registry and might, in fact, read some settings from a user's profile. This behavior occurs because of User Account Control (UAC). Of the many features UAC implements, two key features change the way Windows installs and runs applications: application run levels and application virtualization.

To support run levels and virtualization, all applications that run on current Windows operating systems have a security token, which reflects the level of privileges required to run the application. Applications written for Windows Vista and later can have either an *administrator* token or a *standard user* token. Applications with administrator tokens require elevated privileges to run and perform core tasks. After it's started in elevated mode, an application with an administrator token can perform tasks that require administrator privileges and write to system locations of the registry and the file system.

However, applications with standard user tokens do not have elevated privileges to run and perform core tasks. After it's started in standard user mode, an application with a standard user token must request elevated privileges to perform administration tasks. For all other tasks, the application should not run using elevated privileges. Further, the application should write data only to nonsystem locations of the registry and the file system.

Standard user applications run in a special compatibility mode and use file system and registry virtualization to provide virtualized views of resources. When an application attempts to write to a system location, Windows Vista and later give the application a private copy of the file or registry value. Any changes are then written to the private copy, and this private copy, in turn, is stored in the user's profile data. If the application attempts to read or write to this system location again, it is given the private copy from the user's profile to work with. By default, if an error occurs when working with virtualized data, the error notification and logging information show the virtualized location rather than the actual location the application was trying to work with.

Inside OUT

The Transactional Registry

Windows Server 2012 R2 implements transactional technology in the kernel to preserve data integrity and handle error conditions when writing to the NTFS file system and the registry. Applications that are written to take advantage of the Transactional Registry can use transactions to manage registry changes as discrete operations that can be committed if successful or rolled back if unsuccessful. While a transaction is active, registry changes are not visible to users or other applications—it is only when Windows Server 2012 R2 commits the transaction that the changes are applied fully and become visible. Transactions used with the registry can be coordinated with any other transactional resource, such as Microsoft Message Queuing (MSMQ). If the operating system fails during a transaction, work that has started to commit is written to the disk, and incomplete transactional work is rolled back.

The registry provider built into Windows PowerShell is designed to be used with transactions as well. In fact, when you manage the registry using Windows PowerShell, you script your changes within a transaction. Here, you use Start-Transaction to start a transaction before you modify the registry. Next, you make and verify your changes.

Finally, either you finalize your changes by using Stop-Transaction or you roll back your changes by using Undo-Transaction. You can learn more about scripting the registry with Windows PowerShell in *Windows PowerShell 2.0 Administrator's Pocket Consultant* (Microsoft Press, 2009).

Understanding the registry structure

Many administrative tools are little more than friendly user interfaces for managing the registry, especially when it comes to Control Panel. So, rather than having you work directly with a particular area of the registry, Microsoft provides tools you can use to make the necessary changes safely and securely. Use these tools—that's what they are for.

CAUTION

The importance of using the proper tools to make registry changes cannot be overstated. If there's a tool to manage an area of the registry, you should use it. Don't fool around with the registry just because you can. Making improper changes to the registry can cause a system to become unstable, and in some cases, it could even prevent the system from booting.

Inside OUT

Controlling virtualization

In Local Security Policy, Security Options can enable or disable registry virtualization. With Windows Vista and later, User Account Control: Virtualize File And Registry Write Failures To Per-User Locations enables the redirection of legacy application write failures to defined locations in the registry and file system. This feature is designed to allow legacy programs that require administrator privileges to run. When enabled by the default setting, this setting allows the redirection of application write failures to defined user locations for both the file system and the registry. When you disable this setting, applications that write data to protected locations silently fail.

To view or modify this setting in the Local Security Settings console, open the Local Security Policy console, expand the Local Policies node in the left pane, and then select the Security Options node. In the main pane, you should now see a list of policy settings. Scroll down through the list of security settings. Double-tap or double-click User Account Control: Virtualize File And Registry Write Failures To Per-User Locations. On the Local Security Setting tab of the dialog box, you see the current enabled or disabled state of the setting. To change the state of the setting, select Enabled or Disabled as appropriate and then tap or click OK.

As you can see, nearly everything you do with the operating system affects the registry in one way or another. That's why it's so important to understand what the registry is used for, how you can work with it, how you can secure it, and how you can maintain it.

The registry is first a database. Like any other database, it is designed for information storage and retrieval. Any registry value entry can be identified by specifying the path to its location. For example, the path HKEY_LOCAL_MACHINE\SOFTWARE\Microsoft\ServerManager \DoNotOpenServerManagerAtLogon specifies a registry value you can use to enable or disable the automatic display of Server Manager at logon.

Figure 8-1 shows this value in the registry. Because of its hierarchical structure, the registry appears to be organized much like a file system. In fact, its structure is often compared to that of a file system. However, this is a bit misleading because there is no actual folder/file representation on a system's hard disk to match the structure the registry uses. The registry's actual physical structure is separate from the way registry information is represented. Locations in the registry are represented by a logical structure that has little correlation to how value entries are stored.

Windows Server doesn't keep the entire registry in paged pool memory. Instead, 256-kilobyte (KB) views of the registry are mapped into system cache as needed. This is an important change from the original architecture of the registry, which effectively limited the registry to about 80 percent of the total size of paged pool memory. Now registry implementation is limited only by available space in the paging file.

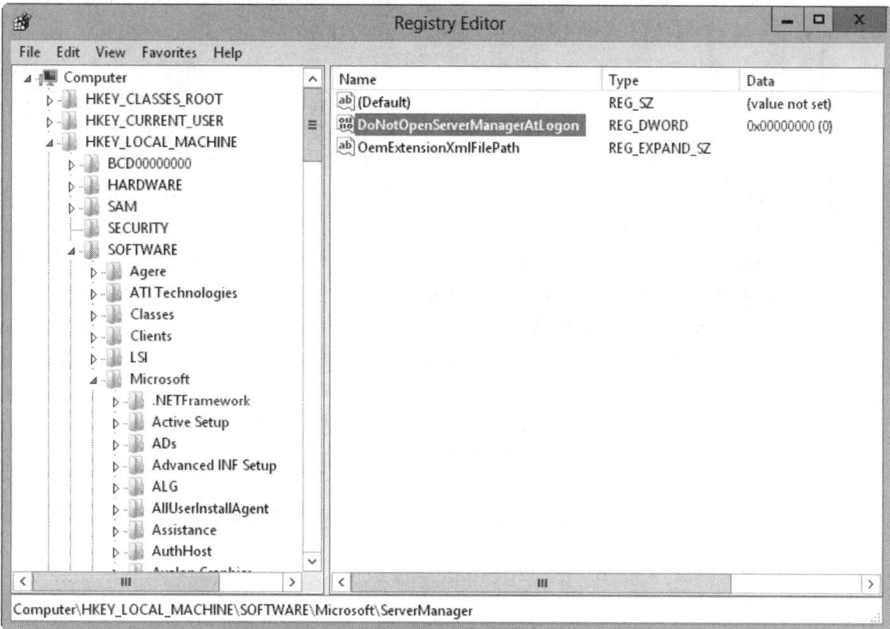

Figure 8-1 Access a value according to its path in the registry.

At startup, 256 KB mapped views of the registry are loaded into system cache so that Windows Server 2012 R2 can quickly retrieve configuration information. Some of the registry's information is created dynamically, based on the system hardware configuration at startup, and doesn't exist until it is created. For the most part, however, the registry is stored in persistent form on disk and read from a set of files called *hives*. Hives are binary files that represent a grouping of keys and values. You find the hive files in the %SystemRoot%\System32\Config directory. Within this directory, you also find .sav and .log files, which serve as backup files for the registry. In Windows Explorer, you might need to enable File Name Extensions in the View pane to see full file names.

Inside OUT

Windows Server manages the registry size and memory use

Early releases of Windows Server stored the entire registry in paged, pooled memory. For 32-bit systems, this limited the registry to approximately 160 megabytes (MBs) because of the layout of the virtual address space in the operating system kernel. Unfortunately, in this configuration as the registry grows in size, it uses a considerable amount of paged, pooled memory and can leave too little memory for other kernel-mode components.

Current releases of Windows Server resolve this problem by changing the way the registry is stored in memory. Here, 256 KB mapped views of the registry are loaded into the system cache as necessary by Cache Manager. The rest of the registry is stored in the paging file on disk. Because the registry is written to system cache, it can exist in system random access memory (RAM) and be paged to and from disk as needed. In previous versions of the Windows operating system, the operating system enabled you to control the maximum amount of memory and disk space the registry could use. With the improved memory management features, the operating system has now taken over control of managing how much memory the registry uses. Most member servers use between 24 and 32 MBs of memory for the registry. Domain controllers or servers that have many configuration components, services, and applications can use considerably more. That said, one of my key domain controllers uses only 28 to 42 MBs of memory for the registry. This represents quite a change from the old architecture, when the in-memory requirements of the registry could be up to 160 MBs.

To read the registry, you need a special editor. The editor provided in Windows Server is Registry Editor. By using Registry Editor, you can navigate the registry's logical structure from the top of the database to the bottom. From the top down, the levels of the database are defined as root keys, subkeys, and value entries.

At the top of the registry hierarchy are the root keys. Each root key contains several subkeys, which contain other subkeys and value entries. The names of value entries must be unique within the associated subkey, and the value entries correspond to specific configuration parameters. The settings of those configuration parameters are the values stored in the value entry. Each value has an associated data type that controls the type of data it can store. For example, some value entries store only binary data; others store only strings of characters. The value's data type controls this.

Inside OUT

Regedit replaces Regedt32

Unlike early versions of the Windows operating system that included two versions of Registry Editor, current releases of Windows Server ship with a single version. This version, Regedit.exe, integrates all the features of both the previous registry editors. From the original Regedit.exe, it gets its core features. From Regedt32.exe, which is no longer available, it gets its security and favorites features. By using the Permissions feature, you can view and manage permissions for registry values. By using the Favorites feature, you can create and use favorites to access stored locations within the registry quickly.

Regedt32 *really* is gone—although I, like many administrators, still refer to it. It is, after all, the editor administrators used because it gave us the ability to manage registry security, and it is the one that was recommended for administrators over Regedit. Because old habits die hard, Windows Server 2012 R2 still has a stub file for Regedt32. However, if you run Regedt32, the operating system, in fact, starts Regedit.

We can now break down the registry path HKEY_LOCAL_MACHINE\SOFTWARE\Microsoft\Windows NT\CurrentVersion\Winlogon\AllowMultipleTSSessions so that it is more meaningful. Here, *HKEY_LOCAL_MACHINE* is the root key. Each entry below the root key until we get to *AllowMultipleTSSessions* represents a subkey level within the registry hierarchy. Finally, *AllowMultipleTSSessions* is the actual value entry.

The registry is very complex, and it is often made more confusing because documentation on the subject uses a variety of terms beyond those already discussed. When reading about the registry in various sources, you might see references to the following:

- **Subtrees.** *Subtree* is the name for the tree of keys and values stemming from a root key down the registry hierarchy. In documentation, you often see root keys referred to as subtrees. What the documentation means when it refers to a subtree is the branch of keys and values contained within a specified root key.

- **Keys.** Technically, root keys are the top of the registry hierarchy, and everything below a root key is either a subkey or a value entry. In practice, subkeys are often referred to as keys. It's just easier to refer to such and such a key—sort of like when we refer to "such and such a folder" rather than saying "subfolder."
- **Values.** A value is the lowest level of the registry hierarchy. For ease of reference, value entries are often simply referred to as values. Technically, however, a value entry comprises three parts: a name, data type, and value. The name identifies the configuration setting. The data type identifies the format for the data. The value is the actual data within the entry.

Now that you know the basics of the registry's structure, let's dig deeper and take a closer look at the root keys, major subkeys, and data types.

Registry root keys

The registry is organized into a hierarchy of keys, subkeys, and value entries. The root keys are at the top of the hierarchy and form the primary branches, or subtrees, of registry information. There are two physical root keys: HKEY_LOCAL_MACHINE and HKEY_USERS. These physical root keys are associated with actual files stored on the disk and are divided into additional logical groupings of registry information. As shown in Table 8-1, the logical groupings are simply subsets of information gathered from HKEY_LOCAL_MACHINE and HKEY_USERS.

Table 8-1 Registry subtrees

Subtree	Description
Physical Subtree	
HKEY_LOCAL_MACHINE (HKLM)	Stores all the settings that pertain to the hardware currently installed on the machine.
HKEY_USERS (HKU)	Stores user profile data for each user who has previously logged on to the computer locally and a default user profile.
Logical Subtree	
HKEY_CLASSES_ROOT (HKCR)	Stores all file associations and object linking and embedding (OLE) class identifiers. This subtree is built from HKEY_LOCAL_MACHINE\SOFTWARE\Classes and HKEY_CURRENT_USER\SOFTWARE\Classes.

HKEY_CURRENT_CONFIG (HKCC)	Stores information about the hardware configuration with which you started the system. This subtree is built from HKEY_LOCAL_MACHINE\SYSTEM \CurrentControlSet\Hardware Profiles\Current, which in turn is a pointer to a numbered subkey that has the current hardware profile.
HKEY_CURRENT_USER (HKCU)	Stores information about the user currently logged on. This key has a pointer to HKEY_USERS \UserSID, where UserSID is the security identifier for the current user and for the default profile discussed previously.

Inside OUT

The registry on 64-bit Windows systems

The registry on 64-bit Windows systems is divided into 32-bit and 64-bit keys. Many keys are created in both 32-bit and 64-bit versions, and although the keys belong to different branches of the registry, they have the same name. On these systems, Registry Editor (Regedit.exe) is designed to work with both 32-bit and 64-bit keys.

Registry keys are either shared or redirected for use under Windows on Windows 64 (WOW64). With shared keys, a physical copy of each key is mapped into each logical view of the registry, and applications make calls into these logical views. With redirected keys, the registry redirector intercepts calls to the redirected keys and maps them to the actual physical location in the registry.

HKEY_LOCAL_MACHINE

HKEY_LOCAL_MACHINE, abbreviated as HKLM, contains all the settings that pertain to the hardware currently installed on a system. It includes settings for memory, device drivers, installed hardware, and startup. Applications are supposed to store settings in HKLM only if the related data pertains to everyone who uses the computer.

As Figure 8-2 shows, HKLM contains the following major subkeys:

- BCD00000000
- HARDWARE
- SAM
- SECURITY

- SOFTWARE
- SYSTEM

These subkeys are discussed in the sections that follow.

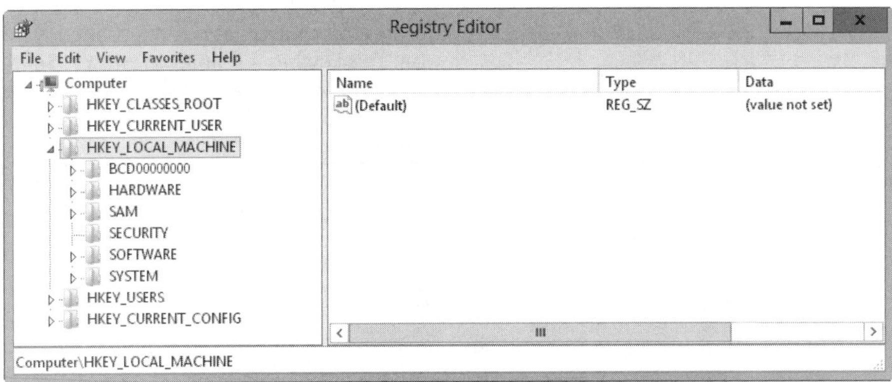

Figure 8-2 Access HKEY_LOCAL_MACHINE in the registry.

HKLM\BCD00000000

The HKLM\BCD00000000 key stores information regarding the configuration and state of the computer's Boot Configuration Data (BCD). BCD provides a firmware-independent approach for managing the boot environment for Windows systems. As discussed in Chapter 3, "Boot configuration," you manage the BCD store by using the BCDEdit tool (and not through the related registry keys).

The BCD architecture has three main components: stores, objects, and elements. A store is a top-level component that establishes the namespace and acts as a container for BCD objects and elements. There are three general types of BCD objects:

- **Application objects.** Describe boot environment objects such as Windows Boot Manager or Windows Boot Loader
- **Inheritable objects.** Act as containers for elements that are shared across multiple object instances
- **Device objects.** Act as containers for elements that describe complex devices such as a RAM disk that was created from a Windows Imaging file

Application objects have an image type and an application type associated with them. The image type specifies how the executable for the application is loaded, such as through the firmware or by a boot application. The application type specifies what the application does, and the standard application types are listed in Table 8-2.

Table 8-2 BCD application types

Application type	Description
Boot sector	A 16-bit, real-mode application for BIOS-based systems, which can be used to restart the boot process and load a non-Windows operating system
Firmware boot manager	Manages the firmware boot for Extensible Firmware Interface (EFI) systems
Ntldr	Loads versions of Windows earlier than Windows Vista on BIOS-based systems.
Windows boot loader	Loads a particular version or configuration of Windows
Windows boot manager	Controls boot of the system; in a multi-boot system, displays a boot selection menu to the user
Windows memory tester	An application for performing memory diagnostics
Windows resume application	Restores Windows to its running state when a computer resumes from hibernation

Each BCD object has a globally unique identifier, or GUID. For example, the GUID of the Windows resume application is 5824ba7d-acee-11e1-ba52-cfa3fef36259. In the registry, the GUID sets the key path, and each object has a description entry and associated elements entries.

HKLM\HARDWARE

HKLM\HARDWARE stores information about the hardware configuration for the computer. This key is re-created by the operating system each time you start Windows Server 2012 R2, and it exists only in memory, not on disk. To build this key, the operating system enumerates every device it can find by scanning the system buses and by searching for specific classes of devices, such as serial ports, keyboards, and pointer devices.

Under HKLM\HARDWARE, you'll find four standard subkeys that are dynamically created at startup and contain the information gathered by the operating system. These subkeys are as follows:

- **ACPI.** Contains information about the Advanced Configuration and Power Interface (ACPI), which is part of the system BIOS that supports Plug and Play and advanced power management. This subkey doesn't exist on non-ACPI-compliant computers.
- **DESCRIPTION.** Contains hardware descriptions, including those for the system's central processor, floating-point processor, and multifunction adapters. For portable computers,

one of the multifunction devices lists information about the docking state. For any computer with multipurpose chip sets, one of the multifunction devices lists information about the controllers for disks, keyboards, parallel ports, serial ports, and pointer devices. There's also a catchall category for other controllers, such as when a computer has a PC Card controller.

- **DEVICEMAP.** Contains information that maps devices to device drivers. You'll find device mappings for keyboards, pointer devices, parallel ports, Small Computer System Interface (SCSI) ports, serial ports, and video devices. Of particular note is that within the VIDEO subkey is a value entry for the VGA-compatible video device installed on the computer. This device is used when the computer must start in VGA display mode.
- **RESOURCEMAP.** Contains mappings for the hardware abstraction layer (HAL), for the Plug and Play Manager, and for available system resources. Of particular note is the Plug and Play Manager. It uses this subkey to record information about devices it knows how to handle.

Additional nonstandard subkeys can exist under HKLM\HARDWARE. The subkeys are specific to the hardware the computer uses.

HKLM\SAM

HKLM\SAM stores the Security Accounts Manager (SAM) database. When you create local users and groups on member servers and workstations, the accounts are stored in HKLM\SAM. This key is also used to store information about built-in user and group accounts and group membership and aliases for accounts.

By default, the information stored in HKLM\SAM is inaccessible through Registry Editor. This is a security feature designed to help protect the security and integrity of the system.

HKLM\SECURITY

HKLM\SECURITY stores security information for the local machine. It contains information about cached logon credentials, policy settings, service-related security settings, and default security values. It also has a copy of HKLM\SAM. As with the HKLM\SAM subkey, this subkey is inaccessible through Registry Editor. This is a security feature designed to help protect the security and integrity of the system.

HKLM\SOFTWARE

HKLM\SOFTWARE stores machine-wide settings for every application and system component installed on the system. This includes setup information, executable paths, default configuration settings, and registration information. Because this subkey resides under HKLM, the information here is applied globally. This is different from the HKCU\SOFTWARE configuration settings, which are applied on a per-user basis.

As Figure 8-3 shows, you'll find many important subkeys within HKLM\SOFTWARE, including the following:

- **Classes.** Contains all file associations and OLE class identifiers. This is also the key from which HKEY_CLASSES_ROOT is built.
- **Clients.** Stores information about protocols and shells used by every client application installed on the system. This includes the calendar, contacts, mail, media, and news clients.
- **Microsoft.** Contains information about every Microsoft application and component installed on the system. This includes their complete configuration settings, defaults, registration information, and much more. You'll find most of the graphical user interface (GUI) preferences under HKLM\SOFTWARE\Microsoft\Windows\CurrentVersion. You'll find the configuration settings for most system components, language packs, hot fixes, and more under HKLM\SOFTWARE\Microsoft\Windows NT\CurrentVersion.
- **ODBC.** Contains information about the Open Database Connectivity (ODBC) configuration on the system. It includes information about all ODBC drives and ODBC file Data Source Names (DSNs).
- **Policies.** Contains information about local policies for applications and components installed on the system.

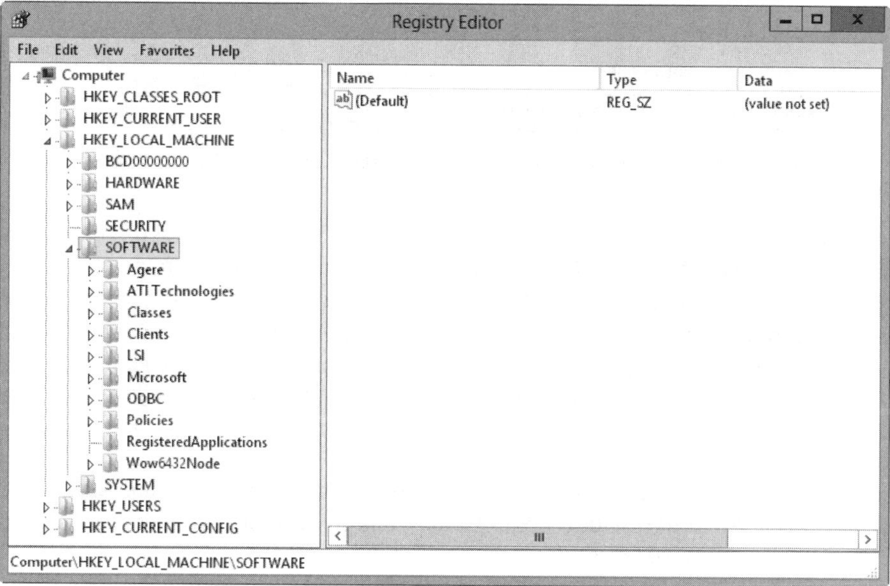

Figure 8-3 Access HKEY_LOCAL_MACHINE\SOFTWARE in the registry.

HKLM\SYSTEM

HKLM\SYSTEM stores information about device drivers, services, startup parameters, and other machine-wide settings. You'll find several important subkeys within HKLM\SYSTEM. One of the most important is HKLM\SYSTEM\CurrentControlSet, as shown in Figure 8-4.

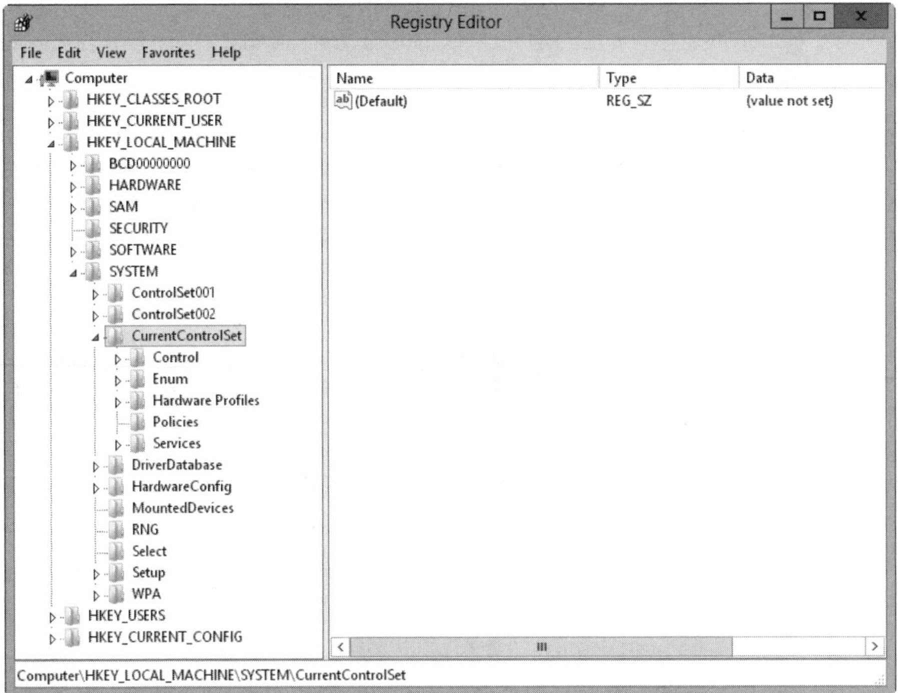

Figure 8-4 Access HKEY_LOCAL_MACHINE\SYSTEM\CurrentControlSet in the registry.

CurrentControlSet contains information about the set of controls and services used for the last successful boot of the system. This subkey always contains information on the set of controls actually in use and represents the most recent successful boot. The operating system writes the control set as the final part of the boot process so that it updates the registry as appropriate to reflect which set of controls and services was last used for a successful boot. This is, in fact, how you can boot a system to the Last Known Good Configuration after it crashes or experiences a Stop error.

HKLM\SYSTEM also contains previously created control sets. These are saved under the subkeys named ControlSet001, ControlSet002, and so forth. Within the control sets, you'll find four important subkeys:

- **Control.** Contains control information about key operating system settings, tools, and subcomponents, including the HAL, keyboard layouts, system devices, interfaces, and device classes. Under BackupRestore, you'll find the saved settings for Backup, which include lists of Automated System Recovery (ASR) keys, files, and registry settings not to restore. Under the SafeBoot subkey, you'll find the control sets used for minimal and network-only boots of the system.

- **Enum.** Contains the complete enumeration of devices found on the computer when the operating system scans the system buses and searches for specific classes of devices. This represents the complete list of devices present during startup of the operating system.

- **Hardware Profiles.** Contains a subkey for each hardware profile available on the system. The first hardware profile, 0000, is an empty profile. The other numbered profiles, beginning with 0001, represent profiles that are available for use on the system. The profile named Current always points to the profile the operating system is currently using.

- **Services.** Contains a subkey for each service installed on the system. These subkeys store the necessary configuration information for their related services, which can include startup parameters and security and performance settings.

Another interesting subkey is HKLM\SYSTEM\MountedDevices. The operating system creates this key and uses it to store the list of mounted and available disk devices. Disk devices are listed according to logical volume configuration and drive-letter designator.

HKEY_USERS

HKEY_USERS, abbreviated as HKU, contains a default user profile and user-profile data for every user who has previously logged on to the computer locally. Each user's profile is owned by that user unless you change permissions or move profiles. Profile settings include the user's desktop configuration, environment variables, folder options, menu options, printers, and network connections.

User profiles are saved in subkeys of HKEY_USERS according to their security identifiers (SIDs). A *SecurityID_Classes* subkey represents file associations that are specific to a particular user. For example, if a user sets Adobe Photoshop as the default program for .jpeg and .jpg files and this is different from the system default, entries within this subkey show this association.

When you use Group Policy, the policy settings are applied to the individual user profiles stored in this key. The default profile specifies how the machine behaves when no one is logged on and is used as the base profile for new users who log on to the computer. For example, if you want to ensure that the computer uses a password-protected screen saver when no one is logged on, you modify the default profile accordingly. The subkey for the default user profile is easy to pick out because it is named HKEY_USERS\.DEFAULT.

NOTE

The profile information stored in HKU is loaded from the profile data stored on disk. The default location for profiles is %SystemDrive%\Users*UserName*, where *UserName* is the user's pre–Windows 2000 logon name.

HKEY_CLASSES_ROOT

HKEY_CLASSES_ROOT, abbreviated as HKCR, stores all file associations that tell the computer which document file types are associated with which applications and which action to take for various tasks—such as open, edit, close, or play—based on a specified document type. For example, if you double-tap or double-click a .doc file, the document typically is opened for editing in Microsoft Word. This file association is added to HKCR when you install Microsoft Office or Word. If Microsoft Office or Word isn't installed, a .doc file is opened instead in WordPad because of a default file association created when the operating system is installed.

HKCR is built from HKEY_LOCAL_MACHINE\SOFTWARE\Classes and HKEY_CURRENT_USER \SOFTWARE\Classes. The former provides computer-specific class registration, and the latter provides user-specific class registration. Because the user-specific class registrations have precedence, this allows for different class registrations for each user of the machine. This is different from previous versions of the Windows operating system, in which the same class registration information was provided for all users of a particular machine.

HKEY_CURRENT_CONFIG

HKEY_CURRENT_CONFIG, abbreviated as HKCC, contains information about the hardware configuration with which you started the system, which is also referred to as the machine's boot configuration. This key contains information about the current device assignments, device drivers, and system services that were present at boot time.

HKCC is built from HKEY_LOCAL_MACHINE \SYSTEM\CurrentControlSet\Hardware Profiles \Current, which in turn is a pointer to a numbered subkey that contains the current hardware profile. If a system has multiple hardware profiles, the key points to a different hardware profile, depending on the boot state or the hardware profile selection made at startup.

HKEY_CURRENT_USER

HKEY_CURRENT_USER, abbreviated as HKCU, contains information about the user currently logged on. This key has a pointer to HKEY_USERS*UserSID*, where *UserSID* is the security identifier for the current user and for the default profile discussed previously. Microsoft requires applications to store user-specific preferences under this key. For example, Microsoft Office settings for individual users are stored under this key. In addition, as discussed previously, HKEY_CURRENT_USER\SOFTWARE\Classes stores the user-specific settings for file associations.

TIP

If you don't want users to be able to set their own file associations, you could change the permissions on HKLM\SOFTWARE\Classes so that users can't alter the global settings you want them to have. For more information about registry permissions, see the "Securing the registry" section later in this chapter.

Registry data: How it is stored and used

Now that you know more about the registry's structure, let's take a look at the actual data within the registry. Understanding how registry data is stored and used is just as important as understanding the registry structure.

Where registry data comes from

As mentioned previously, some registry data is created dynamically during the startup of the operating system, and some is stored on disk so that it can be used each time you boot a computer. The dynamically created data is volatile, meaning that when you shut down the system, it is gone. For example, as part of the startup process, the operating system scans for system devices and uses the results to build the HKEY_LOCAL_MACHINE\HARDWARE subkey. The information stored in this key exists only in memory and isn't stored anywhere on disk.

However, registry data stored on disk is persistent. When you shut down a system, this registry data remains on disk and is available the next time you boot the system. Some of this stored information is very important, especially when it comes to recovering from boot failure. For example, by using the information stored in HKEY_LOCAL_MACHINE\SYSTEM\CurrentControlSet, you can boot by using the Last Known Good Configuration. If the registry data was corrupted, however, this information might not be available, and the only way to recover the system is to try repairing the installation or reinstalling the operating system.

To help safeguard the system and ensure that one section of bad data doesn't cause the whole registry to fail to load, Windows Server 2012 R2 has several built-in redundancies and fail-safe processes. For starters, the registry isn't written to a single file. Instead, it is written to a set of files called hives. There are six main types of hives, each representing a group of keys and values. Most of the hives are written to disk in the %SystemRoot%\System32\Config directory. Within this directory, you'll find these hive files:

- DEFAULT, which corresponds to the HKEY_USERS\.DEFAULT subkey
- DRIVERS, which corresponds to the HKLM\DRIVERS subkey
- SAM, which corresponds to the HKEY_LOCAL_MACHINE\SAM subkey
- SECURITY, which corresponds to the HKEY_LOCAL_MACHINE\SECURITY subkey

- SOFTWARE, which corresponds to the HKEY_LOCAL_MACHINE\SOFTWARE subkey
- SYSTEM, which corresponds to the HKEY_LOCAL_MACHINE\SYSTEM subkey

The remaining hive files are stored in individual user-profile directories with the default name of Ntuser.dat. These files are, in fact, hive files that are loaded into the registry and used to set the pointer for the HKEY_CURRENT_USER root key. When no user is logged on to a system, the user profile for the default user is loaded into the registry. When an actual user logs on, this user's profile is loaded into the registry.

NOTE

The root keys not mentioned are HKEY_CURRENT_CONFIG and HKEY_CLASSES_ROOT. The on-disk data for HKEY_CURRENT_CONFIG comes from the subkey from which it is built: HKEY_LOCAL_MACHINE \SYSTEM\CurrentControlSet\Hardware Profiles \Current. Similarly, the on-disk data for HKEY_CLASSES_ROOT comes from HKEY _LOCAL_MACHINE \SOFTWARE\Classes and HKEY_CURRENT_USER\SOFTWARE\Classes.

Every hive file has associated log files—even Ntuser.dat. Windows Server 2012 R2 uses the log files to help protect the registry during updates. When a hive file is to be changed, the operating system writes the change to a log file and stores this log file on disk. The operating system then uses the change log to write the changes to the actual hive file. If the operating system were to crash while a change is being written to a hive file, the operating system could use the change log later to roll back the change, resetting the hive to its previous configuration.

Inside OUT

How Windows Server 2012 R2 starts over with a clean registry

Ever wonder how Windows Server 2012 R2 can reset the registry to that of a clean install after you demote a domain controller? Examine %SystemRoot%\System32 \Config\RegBack on a domain controller, and you'll see backup files. These files represent the backed-up state of the registry Windows Server creates prior to promoting a member server to a domain controller. By loading these files into the registry and then writing them to disk as the original hive files, a demoted server is returned to its original state.

Types of registry data available

When you work your way down to the lowest level of the registry, you see the actual value entries. Each value entry has a name, data type, and value associated with it. Although value entries have a theoretical size limit of 1,024 KBs, most value entries are less than 1 KB in size. In fact, many value entries contain only a few bits of data. The type of information stored in these bits depends on the data type of the value entry.

The data types defined include the following:

- **REG_BINARY.** Raw binary data without any formatting or parsing. You can view binary data in several forms, including standard binary and hexadecimal. In some cases, if you view the binary data, you see the hexadecimal values and the text characters these values define.
- **REG_DWORD.** A binary data type in which 32-bit integer values are stored as 4-byte-length values in hexadecimal. REG_DWORD is often used to track values that can be incremented, 4-byte status codes, or Boolean flags. With Boolean flags, a value of 0 means the flag is off (false), and a value of 1 means the flag is on (true).
- **REG_LINK.** A Unicode string specifying a symbolic link to another registry value.
- **REG_NONE.** Data without a particular type that is displayed in Registry Editor in hexadecimal format as a binary value.
- **REG_QWORD.** A binary data type in which 64-bit integer values are stored as 8-byte-length values in hexadecimal. REG_QWORD is often used to track large values that can be incremented, 8-byte status codes, or Boolean flags. With Boolean flags, a value of 0 means the flag is off (false), and a value of 1 means the flag is on (true).
- **REG_SZ.** A fixed-length string of Unicode characters. REG_SZ is used to store values that are meant to be read by users and can include names, descriptions, and so on in addition to stored file system paths.
- **REG_EXPAND_SZ.** A variable-length string that can include environment variables that are to be expanded when the data is read by the operating system, its components, or services in addition to installed applications. Environment variables are enclosed in percentage signs (%) to set them off from other values in the string. For example, %SystemDrive% refers to the SystemDrive environment variable. A REG_EXPAND_SZ value that defines a path to use could include this environment variable, such as %SystemDrive%\Program Files\Common Files.
- **REG_MULTI_SZ.** A multiple-parameter string that can be used to store multiple string values in a single entry. Each value is separated by a standard delimiter so that the individual values can be picked out as necessary.
- **REG_RESOURCE_LIST.** A value that stores a series of nested arrays and that was designed to store a resource list for hardware device drivers or a physical device a driver controls. The value is displayed in Registry Editor in hexadecimal format as a binary value.

- **REG_RESOURCE_REQUIREMENTS_LIST.** A value that stores a series of nested arrays and that was designed to store a list of hardware resources for device drivers or a physical device a driver controls. The value is displayed in Registry Editor in hexadecimal format as a binary value.
- **REG_FULL_RESOURCE_DESCRIPTOR.** A value with an encoded resource descriptor such as a list of resources used by a device driver or a hardware component. REG_FULL_RESOURCE_DESCRIPTOR values are associated with hardware components such as a system's central processors, floating-point processors, or multifunction adapters.

The most common data types you'll see in the registry are REG_SZ and REG_DWORD. The vast majority of value entries have these data types. The most important thing to know about these data types is that one is used with strings of characters, and the other is used with binary data that is normally represented in hexadecimal format. And don't worry; if you have to create a value entry—typically, you do so because you are directed to by a Microsoft Knowledge Base article in an attempt to resolve an issue—you are usually told which data type to use. Again, more often than not, this data type is either REG_SZ or REG_DWORD.

Registry administration

Windows Server 2012 R2 provides several tools for working with the registry. The main tool, of course, is Registry Editor, which you start by typing **regedit** or **regedt32** at the command line or in the Run dialog box. Another tool for working with the registry is the REG command. Both tools can be used to view and manage the registry. Keep in mind that although both tools are considered editors, Windows Server 2012 R2 applies any changes you make immediately. Thus, any change you make is applied automatically to the registry without you having to save the change.

CAUTION

As an administrator, you have permission to make changes to most areas of the registry. This allows you to make additions, changes, and deletions as necessary. However, before you do this, you should always make a backup of the system state along with the registry first, as discussed in "Backing up and restoring the registry" later in this chapter. This helps ensure that you can recover the registry in case something goes wrong when you are making your modifications.

Searching the registry

One of the common tasks you'll want to perform in Registry Editor is to search for a particular key. You can search for keys, values, and data entries by using Find on the Edit menu.

Don't let the simplicity of the Find dialog box, shown in Figure 8-5, fool you—there is a bit more to searching the registry than you might think. So, if you want to find what you're looking for, do the following:

- The Find function in Registry Editor searches from the current node forward to the last value in the final root key branch. So, if you want to search the complete registry, you must select the Computer node in the left pane before you select Find on the Edit menu or press Ctrl+F.
- Type the text you want to find in the Find What box. You can search only for standard American Standard Code for Information Interchange (ASCII) text. Therefore, if you're searching for data entries, Registry Editor searches only string values (REG_SZ, REG_EXPAND_SZ, and REG_MULTI_SZ) for the specified text.
- Use the Look At options to control where Registry Editor looks for the text you want to find. You can search on key names, value names, and text within data entries. If you want to match only whole strings instead of searching for text within longer strings, select the Match Whole String Only check box.

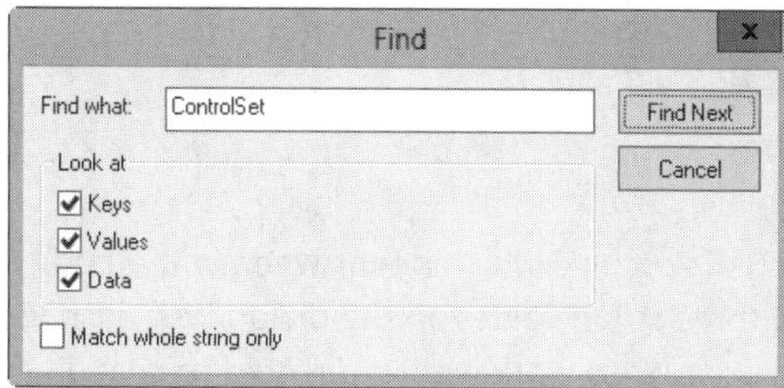

Figure 8-5 Search the registry.

After you make your selections, tap or click Find Next to begin the search. If Registry Editor finds a match before reaching the end of the registry, it selects and displays the matching item. If the match isn't what you're looking for, press F3 to search again from the current position in the registry.

Modifying the registry

When you want to work with keys and values in the registry, you typically are working with subkeys of a particular key. This enables you to add a subkey and define its values and to remove subkeys and their values. You cannot, however, add or remove root keys or insert keys at the root node of the registry. Default security settings within some subkeys might also prohibit you from working with their keys and values. For example, by default you cannot create, modify, or remove keys or values within HKLM\SAM and HKLM\SECURITY.

Modifying values

The most common change you'll make to the registry is to modify an existing value. For example, a Knowledge Base article might recommend changing a value from 0 to 1 to enable a certain feature in Windows Server 2012 R2 or from 1 to 0 to disable it. To change a value, locate the value in Registry Editor and then, in the right pane, double-tap or double-click the value name. This opens an Edit dialog box, the style of which depends on the type of data you are modifying.

The most common values you'll modify are REG_SZ, REG_MULTI_SZ, and REG_DWORD. Figure 8-6 shows the Edit String dialog box, which opens when you modify REG_SZ values. In the dialog box, you typically replace the existing value shown in the Value Data box with the value you need to enter.

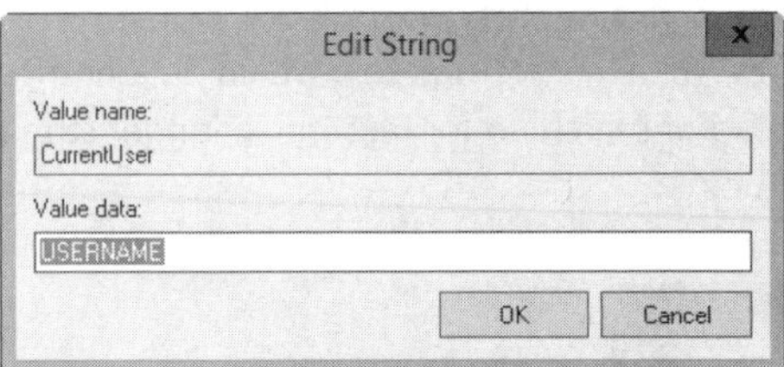

Figure 8-6 Use the Edit String dialog box.

Figure 8-7 shows the Edit Multi-String dialog box, which opens when you modify REG_MULTI_SZ values. In this example, there are three string values. In the dialog box, each value is separated by a new line to make the values easier to work with. If directed to change a value, you typically need to replace an existing value; make sure you don't accidentally modify the entry before or after the entry you are working with. If directed to add a value, you begin typing on a new line following the last value.

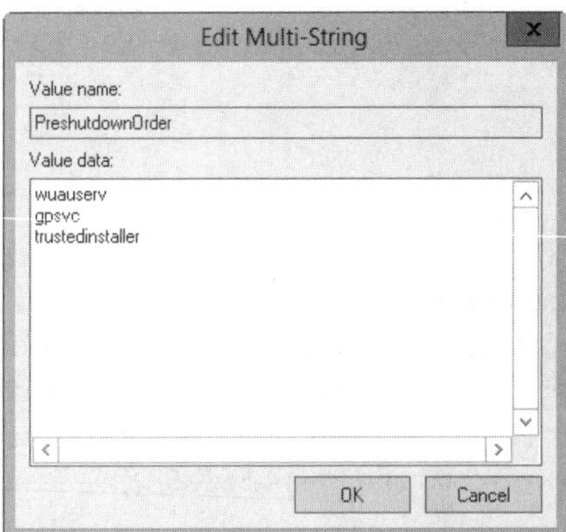

Figure 8-7 Use the Edit Multi-String dialog box.

Figure 8-8 shows the Edit DWORD Value dialog box, which opens when you modify REG_DWORD values. In this example, the value is displayed in hexadecimal format. Typically, you won't need to worry about the data format. You just enter a new value as you've been directed. For example, if the current value entry represents a flag, the data entry of 1 indicates the flag is on (or true). To turn off the flag (switch it to false), you replace the 1 with a 0.

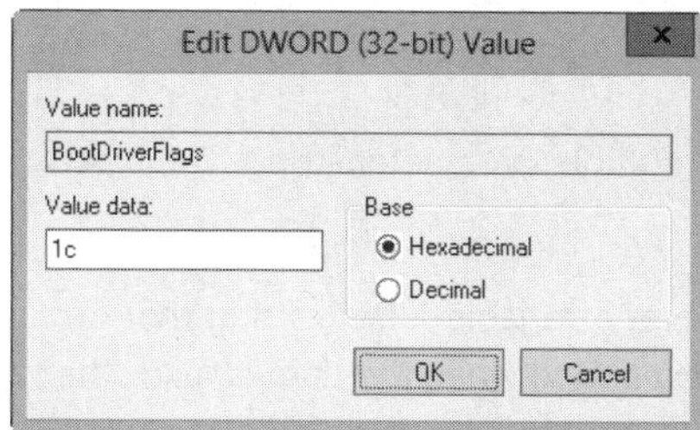

Figure 8-8 Use the Edit DWORD Value dialog box.

> NOTE
>
> **The Windows Clipboard is available when you are working with Registry Editor. This means you can use the Copy, Cut, and Paste commands just as you do with other Windows programs. If a value in a Knowledge Base article is difficult to type, you might want to copy it to the Clipboard and then paste it into the Value Data box of the Edit dialog box.**

Adding keys and values

As noted previously, you can add or remove keys in most areas of the registry. The exceptions pertain to the root node, root keys, and areas of the registry where permissions prohibit modifications.

You add new keys as subkeys of a selected key. Access the key you want to work with and then add the subkey by pressing and holding or right-clicking the key and selecting Edit, New, and then Key. Registry Editor creates a new key and selects its name so that you can set it as appropriate. The default name is New Key #1.

A default value entry is associated with the new key automatically. The data type for this default value is REG_SZ. Just about every key in the registry has a similarly named and typed value entry, so don't delete this value entry. Either set its value by double-tapping or double-clicking it to open the Edit String dialog box or create additional value entries under the selected key.

To create additional value entries under a key, press and hold or right-click the key and then select New followed by one of these menu options:

- **String Value.** Used to enter a fixed-length string of Unicode characters. The type is REG_SZ.

- **Binary Value.** Used to enter raw binary data without any formatting or parsing. The type is REG_BINARY.
- **DWORD (32-bit) Value.** Used to enter binary data type in which 4-byte integer values are stored. The type is REG_DWORD.
- **QWORD (64-bit) Value.** Used to enter binary data type in which 8-byte integer values are stored. The type is REG_QWORD.
- **Multi-String Value.** Used to enter a multiple-parameter string. The type is REG_MULTI_SZ.
- **Expandable String Value.** Used to enter a variable-length string that can include environment variables that are to be expanded when the data is read. The type is REG_EXPAND_SZ.

Creating a new value adds it to the selected key and gives it a default name of New Value #1, New Value #2, and so on. The name of the value is selected for editing so that you can change it immediately. After you change the value name, double-tap or double-click the value name to edit the value data.

Removing keys and values

Removing keys and values from the registry is easy but should never be done without careful forethought to the possible consequences. That said, you delete a key or value by selecting it and then pressing the Delete key. Registry Editor will ask you to confirm the deletion. After you do this, the key or value is permanently removed from the registry. Keep in mind that when you remove a key, Registry Editor removes all subkeys and values associated with the key.

Modifying the registry of a remote machine

You can modify the registry of remote computers without having to log on locally. To do this, select Connect Network Registry on the File menu in Registry Editor and then use the Select Computer dialog box to specify the computer you want to work with. In most cases, all you must do is type the name of the remote computer and then tap or click OK. If prompted, you might need to enter the user name and password of a user account that is authorized to access the remote computer.

After you connect, you get a new icon for the remote computer under your Computer icon in the left pane of Registry Editor. Double-tap or double-click this icon to access the physical root keys on the remote computer (HKEY_LOCAL_MACHINE and HKEY_USERS). The logical root keys aren't available because they are either dynamically created or are simply pointers to subsets of information from within HKEY_LOCAL_MACHINE and HKEY_USERS. You can then edit the computer's registry as necessary. When you are done, you can select Disconnect Network Registry on the File menu and then choose the computer from which you want to disconnect. Registry Editor then closes the registry on the remote computer and breaks the connection.

When working with remote computers, you can also load or unload hives as discussed in "Loading and unloading hive files" later in this chapter. If you're wondering why you would do this, the primary reason is to work with a specific hive, such as the hive that points to Diane Prescott's user profile because she inadvertently changed the display mode to an invalid setting and can no longer access the computer locally. With her user profile data loaded, you could edit the registry to correct the problem and then save the changes so that she can once again log on to the system.

Inside OUT

Managing the registry by using preferences

Rather than managing the registry on individual computers, you can use Group Policy preference items to configure the registry on any computer that processes a particular Group Policy Object (GPO). As when you configure the registry manually, you can use Group Policy preferences to create, modify, and delete registry keys and their values. Group Policy then writes the registry preferences during its normal refresh cycle and, in this way, your registry preferences are deployed automatically. For more information on Group Policy, see Chapter 17, "Managing Group Policy," in *Windows Server 2012 R2 Inside Out: Services, Security, and Infrastructure* (Microsoft Press, in press).

Importing and exporting registry data

Sometimes you might find that it is necessary or useful to copy all or part of the registry to a file. For example, if you've installed a service or component that requires extensive configuration, you might want to use it on another computer without having to go through the whole configuration process again. Instead, you could install the service or component baseline on the new computer, export the application's registry settings from the previous computer, copy them over to the other computer, and then import the registry settings so that the service or component is properly configured. Of course, this technique works only if the complete configuration of the service or component is stored in the registry, but you can probably see how useful being able to import and export registry data can be.

By using Registry Editor, it is easy to import and export registry data. This includes the entire registry, branches of data stemming from a particular root key, and individual subkeys and the values they contain. When you export data, you create a .reg file that contains the designated registry data. This registry file is a script that can then be loaded back into the registry of this or any other computer by importing it.

NOTE

Because the registry script is written as standard text, you can view it and, if necessary, modify it in any standard text editor. Be aware, however, that double-tapping or double-clicking the .reg file starts Registry Editor, which asks you whether you want to import the data into the registry. If you are concerned about this, save the data to a file with the .hiv extension because double-tapping or double-clicking files with this extension won't start Registry Editor. You must manually import files with the .hiv extension (or you could just change the file extension to .reg when it is time to use the data).

To export registry data, press and hold or right-click the branch or key you want to export and then select Export. You can also press and hold or right-click the root node for the computer you are working with, such as Computer for a local computer, to export the entire registry. Either way, you'll see the Export Registry File dialog box as shown in Figure 8-9. Use the Save In selection list to choose a save location for the .reg file and then type a file name. The Export Range panel shows you the selected branch within the registry that will be exported. You can change this as necessary or select All to export the entire registry. Then tap or click Save to create the .reg file.

Figure 8-9 Export registry data to a .reg file so that it can be saved and, if necessary, imported on this or another computer.

Inside OUT

Want to export the entire registry quickly?

You can export the entire registry at the command line by typing **regedit /e SaveFile**, where *SaveFile* is the complete file path to where you want to save the copy of the registry. For example, if you want to save a copy of the registry to C:\Corpsvr06-regdata .reg, you type **regedit /e C:\corpsvr06-regdata.reg**.

You can also extend this technique to determine rapidly the exact registry values the operating system modifies when you make a change to a system or application setting. Start by opening the application of the System utility you want to work with and a command prompt window. Next, export the registry prior to making the change you want to track. Then immediately and without doing anything else, make the change you want to track and export the registry to a different file, using the command-prompt window you opened previously. Finally, use the file comparison tool (fc.exe) to compare the two files. For example, if you saved the original registry to orig.reg and then changed registry to new.reg, you could type the following command at a command prompt to write the changes to a file called changes.txt: **fc /u orig.reg new.reg > changes.txt**. When you examine the changes.txt file in a text editor, you'll see a comparison of the registry files and the exact differences between the files.

CHAPTER 8

Importing registry data adds the contents of the registry script file to the registry of the computer you are working with, either creating new keys and values if they don't already exist or overwriting keys and values if they do exist. You can import registry data in one of two ways. You can double-tap or double-click the .reg file, which starts Registry Editor and asks you whether you want to import the data, or you can select Import on the File menu and then use the Import Registry File dialog box to select and open the registry data file you want to import.

Inside OUT

Using export or import processes to distribute registry changes

The export and import processes provide a convenient way to distribute registry changes to users. You could, for example, export a subkey with an important configuration change and then mail the associated .reg file to users so that they could import it just by double-tapping or double-clicking it. Alternatively, you could copy the .reg file to a network share where users could access and load it. Either way, you have a quick and easy way to distribute registry changes. Officially, however, distributing registry changes in this manner is frowned upon because of the potential security problems associated with doing so. The preferred technique is to distribute registry changes through Group Policy.

Loading and unloading hive files

Just as you sometimes must import or export registry data, you sometimes need to work with individual hive files. The most common reason for doing this, as discussed previously, is when you must modify a user's profile to correct an issue that prevents the user from accessing or using a system. Here, you would load the user's Ntuser.dat file into Registry Editor and then make the necessary changes. Another reason for doing this is to change a particular part of the registry on a remote system. For example, if you need to repair an area of the registry, you could load the related hive file into the registry of another machine and then repair the problem on the remote machine.

Loading and unloading hives affects only HKEY_LOCAL_MACHINE and HKEY_USERS, and you can perform these actions only when you select one of these root keys. Rather than replacing the selected root key, the hive you are loading then becomes a subkey of that root key. HKEY_LOCAL_MACHINE and HKEY_USERS are, of course, used to build all the logical root keys used on a system, so you could work with any area of the registry.

After you select either HKEY_LOCAL_MACHINE or HKEY_USERS in Registry Editor, you can load a hive for the current machine or another machine by selecting Load Hive on the File menu. Registry Editor then prompts you for the location and name of the previously saved hive file. Select the file and then tap or click Open. Afterward, enter a name for the key under which you want the hive to reside while it is loaded into the current system's registry and then tap or click OK.

> NOTE
>
> You can't work with hive files that are already being used by the operating system or another process. You could, however, make a copy of the hive and then work with it. At the command line, type **reg save** followed by the abbreviated name of the root key to save and the file name to use for the hive file. For example, you could type **reg save hkcu c:\curr-hkcu.hiv** to save HKEY_LOCAL_MACHINE to a file called Curr-hkcu.hiv on drive C. Although you can save the logical root keys (HKCC, HKCR, HKCU) in this manner, you can save only subkeys of HKLM and HKU by using this technique.

When you are finished working with a hive, you should unload it to clear it out of memory. Unloading the hive doesn't save the changes you've made—as with any modifications to the registry, your changes are applied automatically without the need to save them. To unload a hive, select it and choose Unload Hive on the File menu. When prompted to confirm, tap or click Yes.

Working with the registry from the command line

If you want to work with the registry from the command line, you can do so using the REG command. REG is run using the permissions of the current user and can be used to access the registry on both local and remote systems. As with Registry Editor, you can work only with HKEY_LOCAL_MACHINE and HKEY_USERS on remote computers. These keys are used, of course, to build all the logical root keys used on a system, so you can work with any area of the registry on a remote computer.

REG has different subcommands for performing various registry tasks. These commands include the following:

- **REG ADD.** Adds a new subkey or value entry to the registry.
- **REG COMPARE.** Compares registry subkeys or value entries.
- **REG COPY.** Copies a registry entry to a specified key path on a local or remote system.
- **REG DELETE.** Deletes a subkey or value entry from the registry.
- **REG EXPORT.** Exports registry data and writes it to a file.

> NOTE
>
> **These files have the same format as files you export from Registry Editor. Typically, however, they are saved with the .hiv extension, so double-tapping or double-clicking files with this extension won't start Registry Editor.**

- **REG FLAGS.** Sets or queries the flags on a registry key. Flags that can be associated with keys include DONT_VIRTUALIZE, DONT_SILENT_FAIL, and RECURSE_FLAG.
- **REG IMPORT.** Imports registry data and either creates new keys and value entries or overwrites existing keys and value entries.
- **REG LOAD.** Loads a registry hive file.
- **REG QUERY.** Lists the value entries under a key and the names of subkeys (if any).
- **REG RESTORE.** Writes saved subkeys and entries back to the registry.
- **REG SAVE.** Saves a copy of specified subkeys and value entries to a file.
- **REG UNLOAD.** Unloads a registry hive file.

You can learn the syntax for using each of these commands by typing **reg** followed by the name of the subcommand you want to learn about and then **/?**. For example, if you want to learn more about REG ADD, you type **reg add /?** at the command line.

Inside OUT

Accessing the registry in Windows PowerShell

Using Windows PowerShell to work with the registry is a bit more complicated. With Windows PowerShell, you work with registry keys in much the same was as you work with files and folders. You access keys and values in a registry location by using Set-Location. Because the HKLM and HKCU root keys are available by default, you can access HKLM by using:

```
set-location hklm:
```

You would then be able to work with registry keys and values in HKLM. For example, to view the available keys, you'd type get-childitem. To work with root keys other than HKLM and HKCU, you must register them as new Windows PowerShell drives. After you do that, you can work with these root keys and set them as locations you want to access. For more information on using Windows PowerShell to work with the registry, see *Windows PowerShell 2.0 Administrator's Pocket Consultant* (Microsoft, 2009).

Backing up and restoring the registry

By now, it should be clear how important the registry is and that it should be protected. I'll go so far as to say that part of every backup and recovery plan should include the registry. Backing up and restoring the registry usually isn't done from within Registry Editor, however. It is handled through the Windows Server Backup utility or through your preferred third-party backup software. Either way, you have an effective means to minimize downtime and ensure that the system can be recovered if the registry becomes corrupted.

You can make a backup of the entire registry very easily at the command line. Just type **regedit /e *SaveFile***, where *SaveFile* is the complete file path to the save location for the registry data. Following this, you could save a copy of the registry to C:\Backups\Regdata.reg by typing **regedit /e c:\backups\regdata.reg**. You would then have a complete backup of the registry.

You can also easily make backups of individual root keys. To do this, you use REG SAVE. Type **reg save** followed by the abbreviated name of the root key you want to save and the file name to use. For example, you could type **reg save hkcu c:\backups\hkcu.hiv** to save HKEY_CURRENT_USER to a file in the C:\Backups directory. Again, although you can save the logical root keys (HKCC, HKCR, HKCU) in this manner, you can save only subkeys of HKLM and HKU by using this technique.

Okay, so now you have your fast and easy backups of registry data. What you do not have, however, is a sure way to recover a system if the registry becomes corrupted and the system cannot be booted. Partly, this is because you have no way to boot the system to get at the registry data.

You create a system state backup to help you recover the registry and get a system to a bootable state. The system state backup includes essential system files needed to recover the local system and registry data. All computers have system state data, which must be backed up in addition to other files to restore a complete working system.

Normally, you back up the system state data when you perform a normal (full) backup of the rest of the data on the system. Thus, if you are performing a full recovery of a server rather than a repair, you use the complete system backup and system state data to recover the server completely.

That said, you can create separate system state backups. The fastest and easiest way to do so is to use Wbadmin, the command-line counterpart to Windows Server Backup. You create a system state backup using Wbadmin by entering the following command at an elevated command prompt:

```
wbadmin start systemstatebackup -backuptarget:StorageDrive
```

Here, *StorageDrive* is the drive letter for the storage location, such as:

```
wbadmin start systemstatebackup -backuptarget:d:
```

Maintaining the registry

The registry is a database, and like any other database, it works best when it is optimized. Optimize the registry by reducing the amount of clutter and information it contains. This means uninstalling unnecessary system components, services, and applications. One way to uninstall components, services, and applications is to use the Uninstall Or Change A Program utility in Control Panel. This utility allows you to remove Windows components and their related services safely in addition to applications installed using the Windows Installer. In Control Panel, tap or click the Uninstall A Program link under the Programs heading to access the Uninstall Or Change A Program utility.

Most applications include uninstall utilities that attempt to remove the application, its data, and its registry settings both safely and effectively. Sometimes, however, applications either do not include an uninstall utility or, for one reason or another, do not fully remove their registry settings. This is where registry maintenance utilities come in handy.

At the Microsoft Download Center on the web, you'll find a download package for the Microsoft Fix It Portable. This download package includes several files and a helper application designed to be installed on removable media so that you can easily use Fix It Portable on any computer that has a problem. Learn more about this program and get the downloadable executable at *http://support.microsoft.com/mats/Program_Install_and_Uninstall/*. At the Microsoft website, instead of choosing Run Now, click the advanced options and then click the download option to save the executable file. After downloading, run the executable file and follow the prompts to create the Fix It Portable folder. Then copy this folder to the computer with a problem and run the Launch Fix It application.

In addition to being able to clear out registry settings for programs you've installed and then uninstalled, you can use this utility to recover the registry to the state it was in prior to a failed or inadvertently terminated application installation. This works as long as the application used the Windows Installer.

NOTE

Fix It Portable replaces the Windows Installer Clean Up Utility and Windows Installer Zapper. The program requires Windows PowerShell and the Microsoft .NET Framework 3.5 to be installed. Fix It Portable uses the Windows Diagnostics and Troubleshooting framework to resolve problems.

Using the Microsoft Fix It Utility

Fix It Portable can remove registry settings for applications that were installed using the Windows Installer. It is most useful for cleaning up registry remnants of applications that were partially uninstalled or for which uninstall failed. It is also useful for cleaning up applications that can't be uninstalled or reinstalled because of partial or damaged settings in the registry. It isn't, however, intended to be used as an uninstaller. Use it when the normal uninstallation process fails.

NOTE

Keep in mind that the profile of the current user is part of the registry. Because of this, Fix It Portable will remove user-specific installation data from this profile. It won't, however, remove this information from other profiles.

To use Microsoft Fix It to uninstall and clean up a program, complete the following steps:

1. If you've already run the installer package for Microsoft Fix It, you can start this utility by running the Launch Fix It executable. The utility can run from removable media.

2. Locate the Fix Problems With Programs That Can't Be Installed Or Uninstalled troubleshooter and then click the related Run Now option.

3. When the troubleshooter starts, select the option that enables you to select the fixes to apply.

4. Next, specify that you are having a problem uninstalling a program. Windows will then diagnose the problem by checking the update information in the registry.

5. Select the program you want to uninstall from a list of installed programs and then click Next.

6. When asked whether you want to uninstall and clean up, click Yes, Try Uninstall. At the end of the uninstall process, you can view and save a troubleshooting report.

Removing registry settings for active installations that have failed

Application installations can fail during installation or after installation. When applications are being installed, an *InProgress* key is created in the registry under the HKLM\SOFTWARE\Microsoft\Windows\CurrentVersion\Installer subkey. If installation fails, the system might not be able to edit or remove this key, which could cause the application's setup program to fail the next time you try to run it. Running the Program Install And Uninstall Troubleshooter for Microsoft Fix It clears out the *InProgress* key, which should enable you to run the application's setup program.

After installation, applications rely on their registry settings to configure themselves properly. If these settings become damaged or the installation becomes damaged, the application won't run. Some programs have a repair utility that can be accessed just by rerunning the installation. During the repair process, the Windows Installer might attempt to write changes to the registry to repair the installation or roll it back to get back to the original state. If this process fails for any reason, the registry can contain unwanted settings for the application. Running the Program Install And Uninstall Troubleshooter for Microsoft Fix It also clears out the rollback data for the active installation. Rollback data is stored in the HKLM\SOFTWARE\Microsoft\Windows\CurrentVersion\Installer\Rollback key.

Any running installation also has rollback data.

Removing partial or damaged settings for individual applications

When an application can't be successfully uninstalled, you can attempt to clean up its settings from the registry by using the Program Install And Uninstall Troubleshooter for Microsoft Fix It. Because the current user's profile is part of the registry, user-specific settings for the application will be removed from this profile.

Securing the registry

The registry is a critical area of the operating system. It has some limited built-in security to reduce the risk of settings being inadvertently changed or deleted. In addition, some areas of the registry are available only to certain users. For example, HKLM\SAM and HKLM\SECURITY are available only to the LocalSystem user. This security, in some cases, might not be enough, however, to prevent unauthorized access to the registry. Because of this, you might want to set tighter access controls than the default permissions, and you can do this from within the registry. You can also control remote access to the registry and configure access auditing.

Preventing access to the registry utilities

One of the best ways to protect the registry from unauthorized access is to prevent user access to the registry in the first place. For a server, this means tightly controlling physical security and allowing only administrators the right to log on locally. For other systems or when it isn't practical to prevent users from logging on locally to a server, you can configure the permissions on Regedit.exe and Reg.exe so that they are more secure. You could also remove Registry Editor and the REG command from a system, but this can introduce other problems and make managing the system more difficult, especially if you also prevent remote access to the registry.

To modify permissions on Registry Editor, access the %SystemRoot% folder, press and hold or right-click Regedit.exe, and then select Properties. In the Regedit Properties dialog box, tap or click the Security tab, as shown in Figure 8-10. Add and remove users and groups as necessary and then set permissions as appropriate. Permissions work the same as with other types of files. You select an object and then allow or deny specific permissions. See Chapter 19, "File security, access controls and auditing," for details.

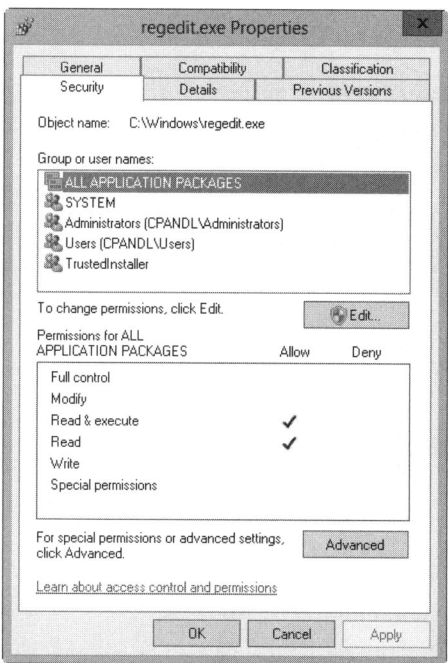

Figure 8-10 Tighten controls on Registry Editor to limit access to it.

To modify permissions on the REG command, access the %SystemRoot%\System32 folder, press and hold or right-click Reg.exe, and then select Properties. In the Reg Properties dialog box, tap or click the Security tab. As Figure 8-11 shows, users and administrators can use this command by default. Add and remove users and groups as necessary and then set permissions as appropriate.

> **NOTE**
>
> **I'm not forgetting about Regedt32. It's only a link to Regedit.exe, so you don't really need to set its access permissions. The permissions on Regedit.exe will apply regardless of whether users attempt to run Regedt32 or Regedit.exe.**

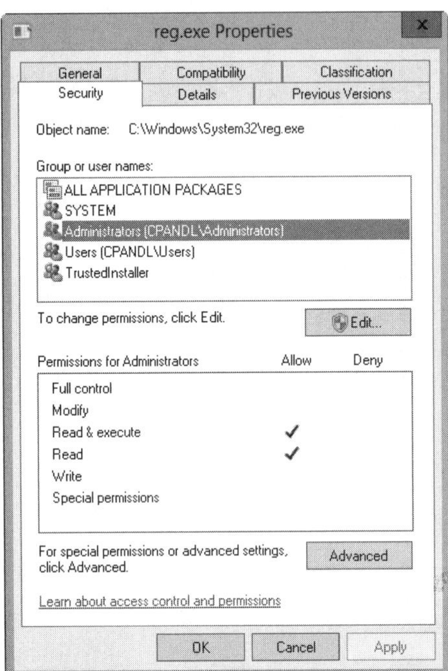

Figure 8-11 Reg.exe is designed to be used by users and administrators and to be run from the command line; its permissions reflect this.

Applying permissions to registry keys

Keys within the registry also have access permissions. Rather than editing these permissions directly, I recommend you use an appropriate security template. Using the right security template locks down access to the registry for you, and you won't have to worry about making inadvertent changes that will prevent systems from booting or applications from running.

That said, in some limited situations, you might want to or have to change permissions on individual keys in the registry. To do this, start Registry Editor and then navigate to the key you want to work with. When you find the key, press and hold or right-click it; select Permissions or select the key and then choose Permissions on the Edit menu. This opens a Permissions For dialog box similar to the one shown in Figure 8-12. Permissions work the same as for files. You can add and remove users and groups as necessary. You can select an object and then allow or deny specific permissions.

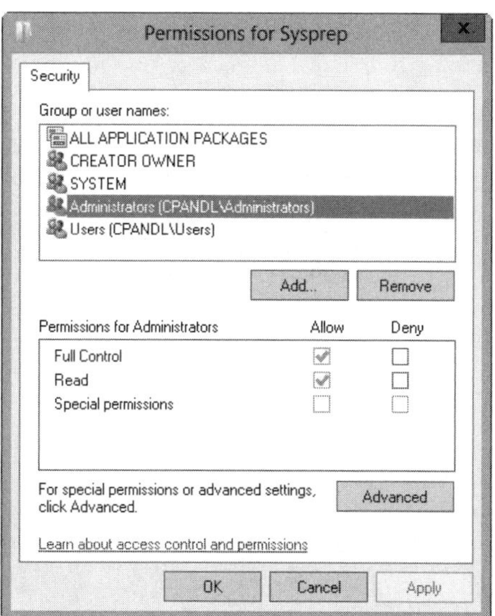

Figure 8-12 Use the Permissions For dialog box to set permissions on specific registry keys.

Many permissions are inherited from higher-level keys and are unavailable. To edit these permissions, you must open the Advanced Security Settings dialog box by tapping or clicking the Advanced button. As Figure 8-13 shows, the Advanced Security Settings For dialog box shows the current owner of the selected key and enables you to reassign ownership. By default, when you reassign ownership, only the selected key is affected, but if you want the change to apply to all subkeys of the currently selected key, choose Replace Owner On Subcontainers And Objects.

CAUTION

Be sure you understand the implications of taking ownership of registry keys. Changing ownership could inadvertently prevent the operating system or other users from running applications, services, or application components.

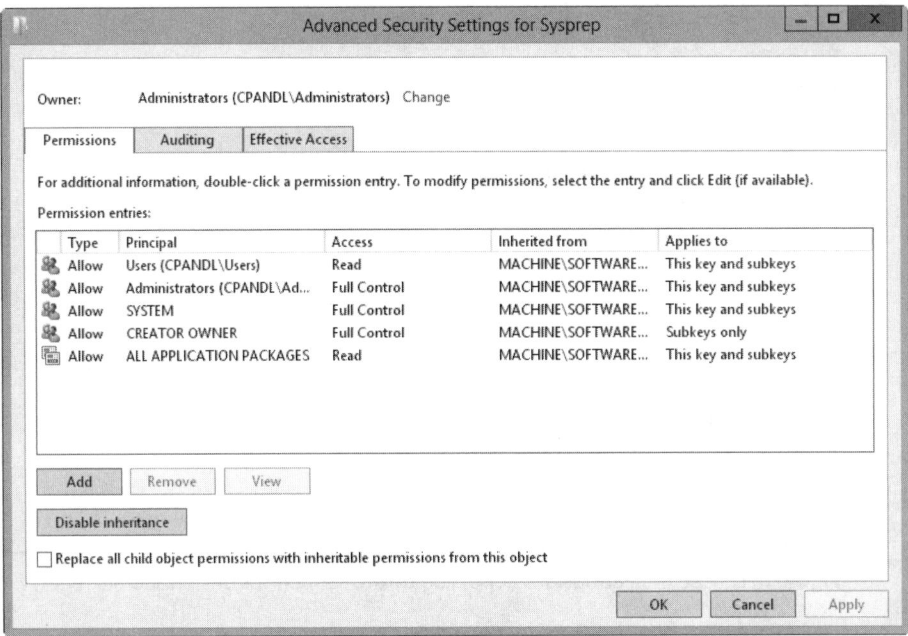

Figure 8-13 Use the Advanced Security Settings For dialog box to change the way permissions are inherited or set and to view auditing settings, ownership, and effective permissions.

The dialog box also has three tabs:

- **Permissions.** The Inherited From column on the Permissions tab shows where the permissions are inherited from. Usually, this is the root key for the key branch you are working with, such as CURRENT_USER. You can use the Add and Edit buttons on the Permissions tab to set access permissions for individual users and groups. Table 8-3 shows the individual permissions you can assign.
- **Auditing.** Enables you to configure auditing for the selected key. The actions you can audit are the same as the permissions listed in Table 8-3. See the "Registry root keys" section earlier in this chapter.
- **Effective Access.** Shows you which permissions would be given to a particular user or group based on the current settings. This is helpful because permission changes you make in the Permissions tab aren't applied until you tap or click OK or Apply.

Table 8-3 Registry permissions and their meanings

Permission	Meaning
Full Control	Allows user or group to perform any of the actions related to any other permission
Query Value	Allows querying the registry for a subkey value
Set Value	Allows creating new values or modifying existing values below the specified key
Create Subkey	Allows creating a new subkey below the specified key
Enumerate Subkeys	Allows getting a list of all subkeys of a particular key
Notify	Allows registering a callback function that is triggered when the selected value changes
Create Link	Allows creating a link to a specified key
Delete	Allows deleting a key or value
Write DAC	Allows writing access controls on the specified key
Write Owner	Allows taking ownership of the specified key
Read Control	Allows reading the discretionary access control list (DACL) for the specified key

Controlling remote registry access

Hackers and unauthorized users can attempt to access a system's registry remotely just as you do. If you want to be sure they are kept out of the registry, you can prevent remote registry access. One way that remote access to a system's registry can be controlled is through the registry key, HKLM\SYSTEM\CurrentControlSet\Control\SecurePipeServers\Winreg. If you want to limit remote access to the registry, you can start by changing the permissions on this key.

If this key exists, the following occurs:

1. Windows Server 2012 R2 uses the permissions on the key to determine who can access the registry remotely, and by default, any authenticated user can do so. In fact, authenticated users have Query Value, Enumerate Subkeys, Notify, and Read Control permissions on this key.

2. Windows Server 2012 R2 then uses the permissions on the keys to determine access to individual keys.

If this key doesn't exist, Windows Server 2012 R2 allows all users to access the registry remotely and uses the permissions on the keys only to determine which keys can be accessed.

Inside OUT

Services might need remote access to the registry

Some services require remote access to the registry to function correctly. These include the Directory Replicator service and the Spooler service. If you restrict remote access to the registry, you must bypass the access restrictions. Either add the account name of the service to the access list on the *Winreg* key or list the keys to which services need access in the *Machine* or *Users* value under the *AllowedPaths* key. Both values are REG_MULTI_SZ strings. Paths entered in the *Machine* value allow machine (LocalSystem) access to the locations listed. Paths entered in the *Users* value allow users access to the locations listed. As long as there are no explicit access restrictions on these keys, remote access is granted. After you make changes, you must restart the computer so that registry access can be reconfigured on startup.

Windows Vista and later Windows versions disable remote access to all registry paths by default. As a result, the only registry paths remotely accessible are those explicitly permitted as part of the default configuration or by an administrator. In Local Security Policy, you can use Security Options to enable or disable remote registry access. With Windows Vista and later Windows versions, the following additional security settings are provided for this purpose:

- Network Access: Remotely Accessible Registry Paths
- Network Access: Remotely Accessible Registry Paths And Subpaths

These security settings determine which registry paths and subpaths can be accessed over the network, regardless of the users or groups listed in the access control list (ACL) of the *Winreg* registry key. A number of default paths are set, and you should not modify these default paths without carefully considering the damage that changing this setting might cause.

You can follow these steps to access and modify these settings in the Local Security Settings console:

1. Open Local Security Policy. If you enabled Show Administrative Tools as a Start setting, you see a related tile on the Start screen. Another way to do this is by pressing the Windows key, typing **secpol.msc** into the Apps Search box, and then pressing Enter.
2. Expand the Local Policies node in the left pane and then select the Security Options node.
3. In the main pane, you should now see a list of policy settings. Scroll down through the list of security settings. As appropriate, double-tap or double-click Network Access:

Remotely Accessible Registry Paths or Network Access: Remotely Accessible Registry Paths And Subpaths.

4. On the Local Policy Setting tab of the Properties dialog box, you see a list of remotely accessible registry paths or a list of remotely accessible registry paths and subpaths, depending on which security setting you are working with. You can now add or remove paths or subpaths as necessary. Note that the default settings are listed on the Explain tab.

NOTE

Windows Server 2012 R2 has an actual service called the Remote Registry service. This service does, in fact, control remote access to the registry. You want to disable this service only if you are trying to protect isolated systems from unauthorized access, such as when the system is in a perimeter network and is accessible from the Internet. If you disable the Remote Registry service before starting the Routing And Remote Access service, you cannot view or change the Routing And Remote Access configuration. Routing And Remote Access reads and writes configuration information to the registry, and any action that requires access to configuration information could cause Routing And Remote Access to stop functioning. To resolve this, stop the Routing And Remote Access service, start the Remote Registry service, and then restart the Routing And Remote Access service.

Auditing registry access

Access to the registry can be audited, as can access to files and other areas of the operating system. Auditing enables you to track which users access the registry and what they're doing. All the permissions listed in Table 8-3 can be audited. However, you usually limit what you audit to only the essentials to reduce the amount of data that is written to the security logs and the resource burden on the affected server.

Before you can enable auditing of the registry, you must enable the auditing function on the system you are working with. You can do this either through the server's local policy or through the appropriate Group Policy Object (GPO). The policy that controls auditing is Computer Configuration\Windows Settings\Security Settings\Local Policies\Audit Policy. For more information on auditing, see Chapter 19.

After auditing is enabled for a system, you can configure how you want auditing to work for the registry. This means configuring auditing for each key you want to track. Thanks to inheritance, this doesn't mean you have to go through every key in the registry and enable auditing for it. Instead, you can select a root key or any subkey to designate the start of the branch for which you want to track access and then ensure that the auditing settings are inherited for all subkeys below it. (This is the default setting.)

Say, for example, you want to audit access to HKLM\SAM and its subkeys. To do this, you follow these steps:

1. After you locate the key in Registry Editor, press and hold or right-click it and select Permissions or select the key and then choose Permissions on the Edit menu. This opens the Permissions For SAM dialog box.
2. In the Permissions For SAM dialog box, tap or click the Advanced button.
3. In the Advanced Security Settings dialog box, tap or click the Auditing tab.
4. Tap or click Add to open the Auditing Entry For SAM dialog box. Click Select A Principal to open the Select User Or Group dialog box.
5. Type the name of a user or a group account. Be sure to reference the user account name rather than the user's full name. Only one name can be entered at a time.
6. Tap or click Check Names. If a single match is found for each entry, the dialog box is automatically updated and the entry is underlined. Otherwise, you'll see an additional dialog box. If no matches are found, you've either entered the name incorrectly or you're working with an incorrect location. Modify the name in the Name Not Found dialog box and try again or tap or click Locations to select a new location. When multiple matches are found, in the Multiple Names Found dialog box, select the name or names you want to use and then tap or click OK.
7. Tap or click OK. The user or group is added as Principal, and the Auditing Entry For dialog box is updated to show this. Only basic permissions are listed by default. Click Show Advanced Permissions to display the special permissions, as shown in Figure 8-14.
8. Use the Applies To list to specify how the auditing entry is to be applied. The options include the following:
   - **This Key Only.** The auditing entries apply only to the currently selected key.
   - **This Key And Subkeys.** The auditing entries apply to this key and any subkeys of this key.
   - **Subkeys Only.** The auditing entries apply to any subkeys of this key but not to the key itself.

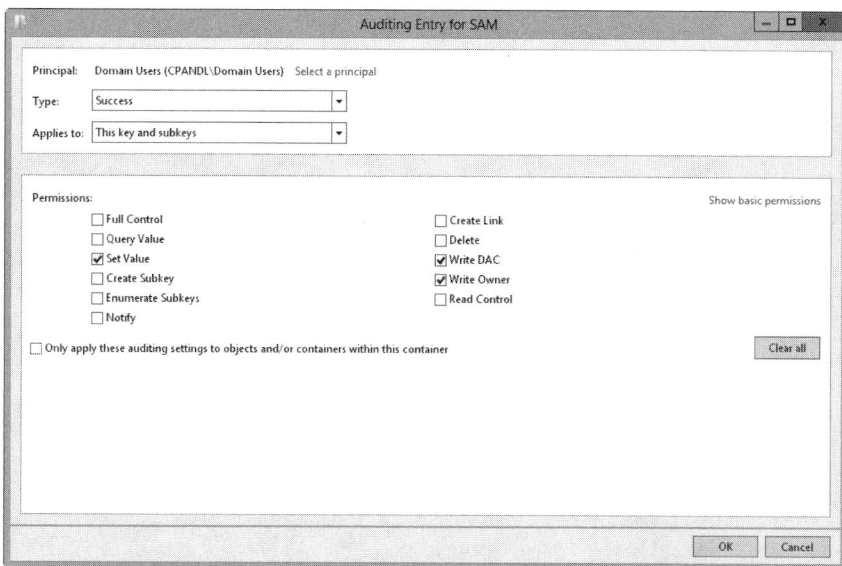

Figure 8-14 Use the Auditing Entry For dialog box to specify the permissions you want to track.

9. Use the Type list to specify whether you are configuring auditing for successful access, failed access, or both and then specify which actions should be audited. The events you can audit are the same as the special permissions listed in Table 8-3.

10. Repeat steps 4 through 9 to configure auditing for other users or groups.

11. The auditing entries are applied to subkeys by default through inheritance. If you want to replace the auditing entries on all child objects of this key with this key's auditing entries, select Replace All Child Object Auditing Entries With Inheritable Auditing Entries From This Object.

12. Tap or click OK twice.

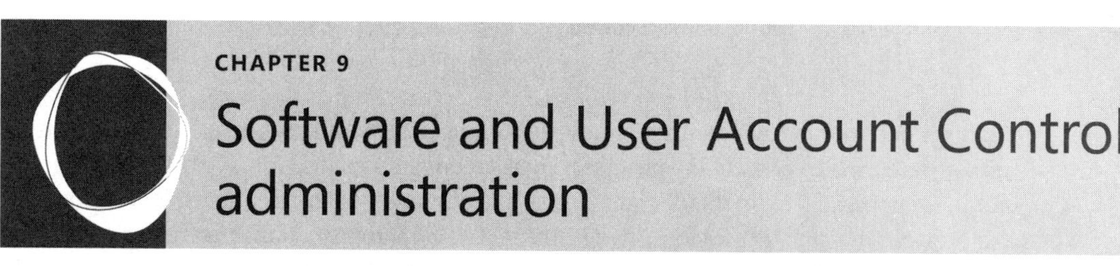

CHAPTER 9

Software and User Account Control administration

The security architecture in Microsoft Windows Server 2012 R2 and Windows 8.1 controls the way accounts are used and applications are installed and run. Windows Server 2012 R2 has two general types of user accounts: standard user accounts and administrator user accounts. Standard users can perform any general computing tasks, such as starting programs, opening documents, and creating folders, and can perform any support tasks that do not affect other users or the security of the computer. Administrators, however, have complete access to the computer and can make changes that affect other users and the security of the computer. Windows 8.1 adds a special type of local account called a *Microsoft account*, which can be thought of as a synchronized local account and is not available on earlier releases of Windows.

Like Windows 8.1, Windows Server 2012 R2 runs programs, some of which are designed specifically for client–server environments in addition to desktop apps. An app is a program in the most general sense. However, apps are fairly new to Windows and have many distinct characteristics, as I discuss in Chapter 7 of my book *Windows 8.1 Administration Pocket Consultant: Essentials & Configuration* (Microsoft Press, 2013). With that in mind, this chapter focuses specifically on software applications that are installed as programs rather than as apps.

Software installation essentials

Software installation, configuration, and maintenance are processes that require elevated privileges. As discussed later in this chapter, under "Mastering User Account Control," elevation is a feature of User Account Control (UAC). Because of User Account Control, the operating system can detect the installation of software. When the operating system detects a software installation–related process, it prompts for permission or consent prior to allowing you to install, configure, or maintain software on your computer. This means you must either install software by using an account with administrator privileges or provide administrator permissions when prompted. It also means administrator privileges are required to perform the following software maintenance tasks:

- Change/Update
- Repair/Reinstall
- Uninstall/Remove

Windows does not include an Add/Remove Programs utility. Instead, it relies completely on the software itself to provide the necessary installation features through a related setup program. As discussed later in this chapter, under "Maintaining application integrity," Windows also provides the architecture for software access tokens and restrictions that require software programs to write to specific system locations. Software applications not specifically designed to support this architecture are considered noncompliant applications. Thus, software is either compliant or noncompliant.

Part of the installation process involves validating your credentials and checking the software's compatibility. Most software applications have a setup program that uses Windows Installer, InstallShield, or Wise Install. The job of the installer program is to track the installation process and make sure the installation completes successfully. If the installation fails, the installer is also responsible for restoring a computer to its original state by reversing all the changes the setup program makes. Although this works great in theory, you can encounter problems, particularly when you are installing noncompliant programs. Noncompliant programs won't have and won't be able to use the features of the latest versions of installer programs, and as a result, they sometimes cannot uninstall a program completely.

Because a partially uninstalled program can spell disaster for a computer, you should protect yourself by backing up a server prior to installing any software. By backing up a server, you can be sure that you can fully recover the server to the state it was in prior to installing the software. This way, if you run into problems, you'll have an effective recovery strategy.

Before installing any software, you should do the following:

- Check to see whether it is compatible. You can determine compatibility in several ways. You can check the software packaging, which should specify whether the program is compatible. Alternatively, you can check the software developer's website for a list of compatible operating systems.
- Check the software developer's website for updates for the program. If available, download the updates prior to installing the software and then install them immediately after completing the software installation. Some software programs have automated update processes that you can use to check for updates after installing the software. In this case, after installation, run the software and then use the built-in update feature to check for updates.

Diagnosing a problem you are having as a compatibility issue isn't always easy. For deeper compatibility issues, you might need to contact the software developer's technical support staff. To avoid known compatibility issues with noncompliant applications, Windows Server includes an automated detection feature known as the Program Compatibility Assistant.

If the Program Compatibility Assistant detects a known compatibility issue when you run a noncompliant application, it notifies you about the problem and provides possible solutions for resolving the problem automatically. You can then allow the Program Compatibility Assistant to reconfigure the application for you. Although the Program Compatibility Assistant is helpful, it can't detect or avoid all compatibility issues. You might have to configure compatibility manually. One way to do this is to press and hold or right-click the software shortcut, select Properties, and then use the options on the Compatibility tab to configure software compatibility options.

> IMPORTANT
>
> **Don't use the Program Compatibility Assistant or similar compatibility features to install older virus detection, backup, or system programs. These programs might attempt to modify your computer's file systems in a way that is incompatible with Windows Server and thus prevent Windows Server from starting.**

Installation using software application media is straightforward. Not all programs have distribution media on a disc or flash drive. If you download a program from the Internet, it'll probably be in a .zip or self-extracting executable file, and you can install the program by following these steps:

1. Start File Explorer. Extract the program's setup files by using one of the following techniques:
   - If the program is distributed in a .zip file, press and hold or right-click the file and select Extract All. This opens the Extract Compressed (Zipped) Folders dialog box. Tap or click Browse, select a destination folder, and then tap or click OK. Tap or click Extract.
   - If the program is distributed in a self-extracting executable file, double-tap or double-click the .exe file to extract the setup files. You'll see one of several types of prompts. If prompted to run the file, tap or click Run. If prompted to extract the program files or select a destination folder, tap or click Browse, select a destination folder, and then tap or click OK. Tap or click Extract or OK as appropriate.
2. In File Explorer, browse the setup folders and find the necessary setup program file. Double-tap or double-click the setup file to start the installation process.
3. When Setup starts, follow the prompts to install the software.

If software installation fails and the software used an installer, follow the prompts to allow the installer to restore your computer to its original state. Otherwise, exit Setup and then try rerunning Setup to complete the installation or uninstall the program. If this doesn't work, you can use the techniques discussed in "Maintaining the registry" in Chapter 8, "Managing the registry," to clean up the installer settings.

Installing software is only one part of software management. Often, after you install software, you need to make configuration changes to your computer or the software itself. You might need to reconfigure, repair, or uninstall the software, or you might need to resolve problems with the way the software starts or runs.

After you install software, you can manage its installation by using the Programs And Features page in Control Panel. Windows Server takes advantage of the features of the installer program used with your software. This means you'll have more configuration options than you otherwise would. For example, previously, most software allowed you to rerun Setup to uninstall the program but didn't necessarily allow you to rerun Setup to change or repair the software. Windows Server provides these features to make it easier to manage your software.

You can use the Programs And Features page to reconfigure, repair, or uninstall software by following these steps:

1. In Control Panel, tap or click Uninstall A Program under Programs.
2. In the Name list, select the program you want to work with and then select one of the following options on the toolbar:
   - **Change.** Modifies the program's configuration
   - **Repair.** Repairs the program's installation
   - **Uninstall.** Uninstalls the program
   - **Uninstall/Change.** Uninstalls or changes a program with an older installer program

You can use Task Manager to work with running programs. To access Task Manager, press and hold or right-click the lower-left corner of the Start screen or the desktop and then tap or click Task Manager. Alternatively, press Ctrl+Alt+Delete and then click Task Manager. If the Summary view is displayed when you open Task Manager, tap or click More Details.

Use the information and options provided on the Processes, Performance, and Details tabs to get more information about running programs. When you select a program or process on the Processes tab, you can terminate the process by tapping or clicking End Task. You learn more about Task Manager in Chapter 10, "Performance monitoring and tuning."

Mastering User Account Control

User Account Control (UAC) seeks to improve usability while enhancing security by controlling how standard user and administrator user accounts are used. User Account Control does this by limiting the scope of administrator-level access privileges and requiring all applications to run in a specific user mode. In this way, UAC prevents users from making inadvertent changes to system settings and locks down the computer to prevent unauthorized applications from installing or performing malicious actions.

Elevation, prompts, and the secure desktop

Current releases of Windows make it easy to determine which tasks standard users can perform and which tasks administrators can perform. You might have noticed the multicolored shield icon next to certain options in windows, wizards, and dialog boxes. This is the Permissions icon. It indicates that the related option requires administrator permissions to run. That doesn't mean you'll see a prompt, though. The way the prompt works depends on the following:

- Whether UAC allows changing Windows settings without prompting
- Whether the computer is a member of a workgroup or a domain
- Whether you are logged on as a standard user or an administrator

NOTE

UAC is disabled in Server Core installations. With other Windows Server installations, the best way to configure the UAC prompt is to use Group Policy settings. In Control Panel, tap or click System And Security. Under the Action Center heading, tap or click Change User Account Control Settings. On the User Account Control Settings page, use the slider to choose when to be notified about changes to the computer.

By default, when you are logged on to a computer as a standard user, you see a User Account Control (UAC) prompt when programs try to make changes to the computer that require administrator permissions and when programs try to change Windows settings. In a workgroup, the prompt shows the accounts of administrators. If you tap or click an account, you must then enter the password for that account and then tap or click Yes.

In a domain, as shown in Figure 9-1, the prompt shows the logon domain and provides user name and password boxes. To proceed, you must enter the name of an administrator account, type the account's password, and then tap or click Yes. The task or application then runs with administrator permissions.

Whether the computer is in a workgroup or domain, the prompt shows the name of the program requesting elevation, the publisher of that program, and the file origin. If you have any question about the authenticity of the request, tap or click Show Details. You then see the program location, which shows the full path to the program's executable. For verified publishers, display their verification certificate by clicking the link provided.

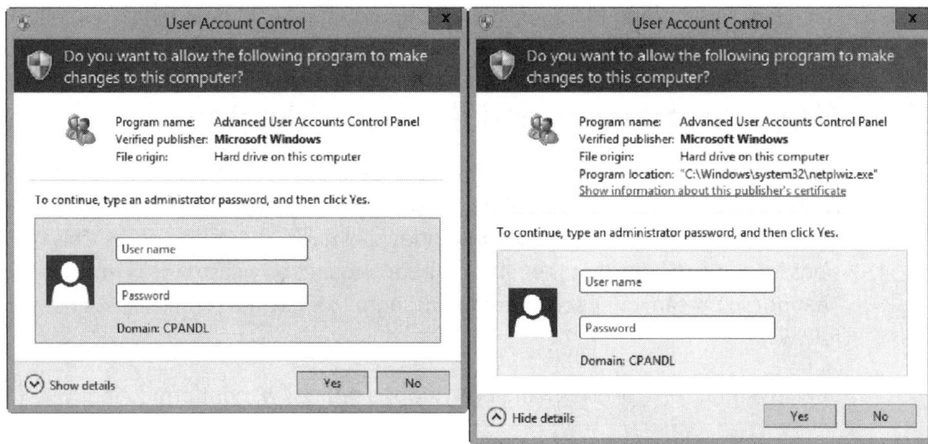

Figure 9-1 User Account Control requires a password to run certain applications when the user is not logged on with an administrator account.

> NOTE
>
> **The first screen capture shows the UAC prompt without details. The second screen capture shows the UAC prompt with details.**

The prompt works differently when you are logged on with an administrator account. Here, it doesn't matter whether the computer is in a workgroup or a domain, and the prompt doesn't require an account selection or a password. Instead, your current credentials are used, and you are simply prompted to confirm that you want to allow the task or program to make changes to the computer. If you click Yes, the task or application then runs with administrator permissions. (See Figure 9-2.)

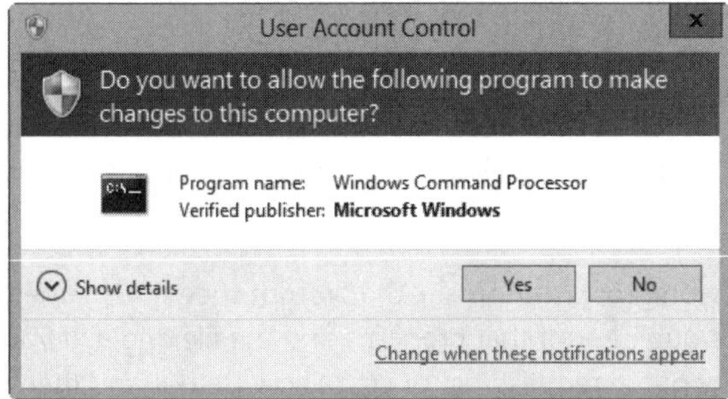

Figure 9-2 User Account Control prompts users when they are already logged on with an administrator account.

The process of getting approval prior to running an application in administrator mode and prior to performing actions that change system-wide settings is known as *elevation*. Elevation enhances security by reducing the exposure and attack surface of the operating system. It does this by providing notification when you are about to perform an action that could affect system settings, such as installing an application, and it eliminates the ability of malicious programs to invoke administrator privileges without your knowledge and consent.

Prior to the elevation and display of the User Account Control (UAC) prompt, Windows Server performs several background tasks. The key task you need to know about is that Windows Server switches to a secure, isolated desktop prior to displaying the prompt. The purpose of switching to the secure desktop is to prevent other processes or applications from providing the required permissions or consent. All other running programs and processes continue to run on the interactive user desktop, and only the prompt itself runs on the secure desktop.

Elevation, prompts, and the secure desktop are aspects of User Account Control that affect you the most. Although they seem restrictive at first, these features prevent users from making inadvertent changes to system settings, and they lock down the computer to prevent unauthorized applications from installing or performing malicious actions.

The key component of UAC that determines whether and how administrators are prompted is Admin Approval Mode. By default, all administrators, except the built-in local administrator account, run in and are subject to Admin Approval Mode. Therefore, all administrators, except the built-in local administrator account, see the elevation prompt whenever they run administrator applications.

Configuring UAC and Admin Approval Mode

In Group Policy under Local Policies\Security Options, five security settings determine how Admin Approval Mode and elevation prompting works. Table 9-1 summarizes these security settings. Remember, Group Policy gives you the flexibility to configure UAC as needed for specific environments. For example, if servers at a remote office are in a separate GPO from workstations at that office, you could configure UAC for servers one way and UAC for workstations another way.

Table 9-1 Security settings related to Admin Approval Mode

Security Setting	Description
User Account Control: Admin Approval Mode For The Built-in Administrator Account	Determines whether users and processes running as the built-in local administrator account are subject to Admin Approval Mode. By default, this feature is disabled, which means the built-in local administrator account is not subject to Admin Approval Mode or to the elevation-prompt behavior stipulated for other administrators in Admin Approval Mode. If you enable this setting, users and processes running as the built-in local administrator will be subject to Admin Approval Mode and subject to the elevation-prompt behavior stipulated for other administrators in Admin Approval Mode.
User Account Control: Behavior Of The Elevation Prompt For Administrators In Admin Approval Mode	Determines whether administrators subject to Admin Approval Mode see an elevation prompt when running administrator applications and determines how the elevation prompt works. By default, administrators are prompted for consent when running administrator applications. You can configure this option so that administrators are prompted for credentials, as is the case with standard users. You can also configure this option so that administrators are not prompted at all—in which case, the administrators will not be able to elevate privileges. This doesn't prevent administrators from pressing and holding or right-clicking an application shortcut and selecting Run As Administrator.
User Account Control: Behavior Of The Elevation Prompt For Standard Users	Determines whether users logged on with a standard user account see an elevation prompt when running administrator applications. By default, users logged on with a standard user account are prompted for the credentials of an administrator when running administrator applications. You can also configure this option so that users are not prompted—in which case, the users will not be able to elevate privileges by supplying administrator credentials. This doesn't prevent users from pressing and holding or right-clicking an application shortcut and selecting Run As Administrator.
User Account Control: Run All Administrators In Admin Approval Mode	Determines whether users logged on with an administrator account are subject to Admin Approval Mode. By default, this feature is enabled, which means administrators are subject to Admin Approval Mode and subject to the elevation-prompt behavior stipulated for administrators in Admin Approval Mode. If you disable this setting, users logged on with an administrator account are not subject to Admin Approval Mode and therefore are not subject to the elevation-prompt behavior stipulated for administrators in Admin Approval Mode.

Security Setting	Description
User Account Control: Switch To The Secure Desktop When Prompting For Elevation	Determines whether Windows Server switches to the secure desktop before prompting for elevation. As the name implies, the secure desktop restricts the programs and processes that have access to the desktop environment. In this way, it reduces the possibility that a malicious program or user could gain access to the process being elevated. By default, this security option is enabled. If you don't want Windows Server to switch to the secure desktop prior to prompting for elevation, you can disable this setting. However, if you do this, you'll make the computer more susceptible to malware and attack.

In a domain environment, you can use Active Directory–based Group Policy to apply the desired security configuration to a particular set of computers. Just configure the desired settings to a Group Policy Object (GPO) that applies to those computers.

For workgroup configurations or for a special case, you can configure these security settings on a per-computer basis, using local security policy. To access local security policy and configure UAC settings, follow these steps:

1. Select Local Security Policy on the Tools menu in Server Manager. This starts the Local Security Policy console.

2. In the console tree, under Security Settings, expand Local Policies and then select Security Options, as shown in Figure 9-3.

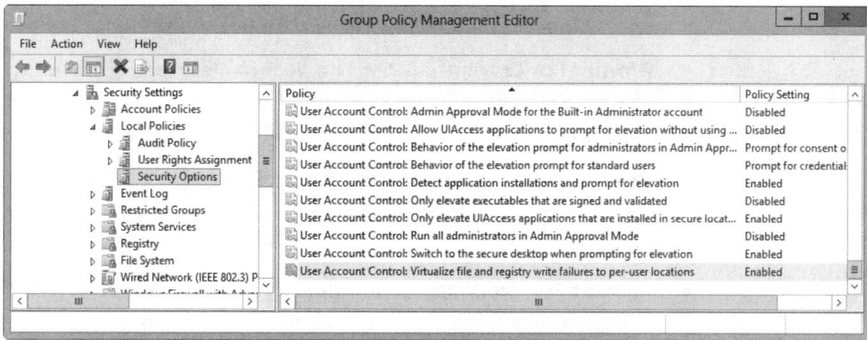

Figure 9-3 Configure UAC options through local security policy.

3. Double-tap or double-click User Account Control: Admin Approval Mode For The Built-in Administrator Account. This opens the related properties dialog box shown in Figure 9-4. Select Enabled to turn on this setting or Disabled to turn off this setting. Tap or click OK.

CHAPTER 9

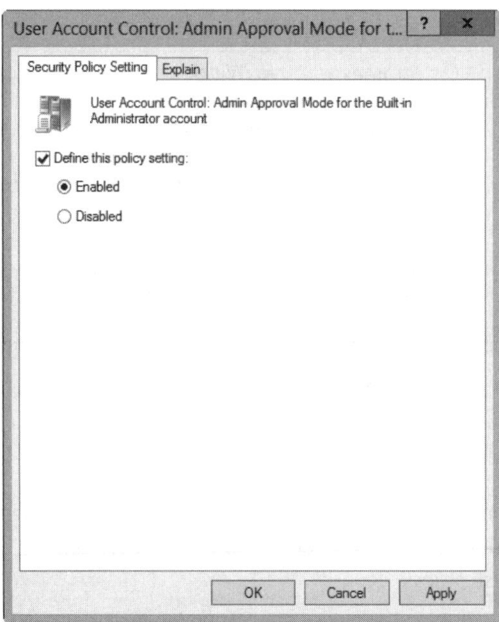

Figure 9-4 Configure Admin Approval Mode For The Built-in Administrator Account.

4. Double-tap or double-click User Account Control: Behavior Of The Elevation Prompt For Administrators In Admin Approval Mode. The available options are used as follows:
   - **Elevate Without Prompting.** Enters Admin Approval Mode and elevates to the user's highest available privileges without prompting for consent or credentials.
   - **Prompt For Credentials On The Secure Desktop.** Switches to the secure desktop and then prompts for credentials before elevating to the user's highest available privileges.
   - **Prompt For Consent On The Secure Desktop.** Switches to the secure desktop and then prompts for consent before elevating to the user's highest available privileges.
   - **Prompt For Credentials.** Prompts for credentials before elevating to the user's highest available privileges but doesn't switch to the secure desktop.
   - **Prompt For Consent.** Prompts for consent before elevating to the user's highest available privileges but doesn't switch to the secure desktop.
   - **Prompt For Consent For Non-Windows Binaries.** When running non-Windows applications that require elevation, prompts for consent on the secure desktop before elevating to the user's highest available privileges. This is the default.

5. Double-tap or double-click User Account Control: Behavior Of The Elevation Prompt For Standard Users. The available options are Automatically Deny Elevation Requests, Prompt For Credentials On The Secure Desktop, and Prompt For Credentials.

   IMPORTANT

   If you deny elevation requests, elevation prompts will not be presented to users. This includes Remote Assistance users who might be trying to assist a user remotely.

6. Double-tap or double-click User Account Control: Run All Administrators In Admin Approval Mode. Select Enabled to turn on this setting or Disabled to turn off this setting. Tap or click OK.

7. Double-tap or double-click User Account Control: Switch To The Secure Desktop When Prompting For Elevation. Select Enabled to turn on this setting or Disabled to turn off this setting. Tap or click OK.

Maintaining application integrity

To help maintain internal consistency and application integrity, Windows Server defines two run levels for applications: standard and administrator. Windows Server determines whether a user needs elevated privileges to run a program by supplying most applications and processes with a security token. If an application has a standard token, or if an application cannot be identified as an administrator application, elevated privileges are not required to run the application, and Windows Server starts it as a standard application by default. If an application has an administrator token, elevated privileges are required to run the application, and Windows Server prompts the user for permission or confirmation prior to running the application.

Application access tokens

Applications are said to be either compliant or noncompliant. Any application written specifically for Windows Server 2008 or later is considered a compliant application. Any application written for an earlier version of Microsoft Windows or not certified as compliant is considered a noncompliant application.

Distinguishing between compliant and noncompliant applications is important because of the architecture changes required to support UAC. Compliant applications use UAC to reduce the attack surface of the operating system. They do this by preventing unauthorized programs from installing or running without the user's consent and by restricting the default privileges granted to applications. This, in turn, makes it harder for malicious programs to take over a computer.

The Application Information service facilitates running interactive applications with an administrator access token. By default, this service is stopped and configured for manual startup. When this service is stopped, you will be unable to start interactive applications with the additional administrator privileges you might require to perform tasks.

Inside OUT

Examining administrator and standard user access tokens

You can see the difference between the administrator user and standard user access tokens by opening two command prompt windows. Run the first command prompt with elevation by tapping or clicking and selecting Run As Administrator. Run the other command prompt as a standard user.

In the administrator command prompt window, type the following:

1. **cd %UserProfile%**
2. **whoami /all > admin.txt**

In the standard command prompt window, type the following:

1. **whoami /all > user.txt**
2. **fc user.txt admin.txt**

The resulting output is a comparison of the differences between your administrator access token and your standard access token. Both access tokens will have the same security identifiers (SIDs), but the elevated administrator access token will have more privileges than the standard user access token.

Applications derive their security context from the current user's access token. By default, the Local Security Authority (LSA) turns all users into standard users even if they are members of the Administrators group. When a member of an administrator group logs on to a computer on which UAC is enabled, the LSA creates two access tokens for two logon sessions: one with administrator rights and one with administrator rights filtered out. The filtered access token is used to start the user's desktop. The other logon session runs as an administrator and is accessed when tasks are elevated. Thus, if an administrator user has consented to the use of her administrator privileges, the unfiltered access token (which contains all the user's privileges) is used to start the application or process rather than the user's standard access token. Also, note that the access tokens contain separate logon IDs because they are related to different logon sessions.

Most applications can run using a standard user access token. Whether applications need to run with standard or administrator privileges depends on the actions the applications perform.

Applications that require administrator privileges, referred to as *administrator applications*, differ in several ways from user applications that require standard user privileges, referred to as *user applications*.

Administrator applications require elevated privileges to run and perform core tasks. When started in elevated mode, an application with a user's administrator access token can perform tasks that require administrator privileges and write to system locations of the registry and the file system.

Standard user applications do not require elevated privileges to run and perform core tasks. When started in standard user mode, an application with a user's standard access token must request elevated privileges to perform administration tasks. For all other tasks, the application should not run using elevated privileges. Further, the application should write data only to nonsystem locations of the registry and the file system.

Inside OUT

Virtualization for noncompliant applications

You configure any applications not specifically written for or certified as compatible as noncompliant applications. Such applications run using a user's standard access token by default. To prevent these applications from making changes to the operating system that could cause problems, they run in a special compatibility mode. In this mode, the operating system uses file system and registry virtualization to provide virtualized views of file and registry locations.

When a noncompliant application attempts to write to a system location, the operating system gives the application a private copy of the file or registry value. Any changes the application makes are then written to the private copy, and this private copy, in turn, is stored in the user's profile data. If the application attempts to read or write to this system location again, the operating system gives it the private copy from the user's profile to work with.

By default, if an error occurs when the application is working with virtualized data, the error notification and logging information show the virtualized location rather than the actual location that the application is trying to work with. This ensures that there is consistency between how virtualization is used and how related errors are reported.

If you are an application developer and are debugging an application, you can use options on Task Manager's Details tab to put an application you are testing in virtualized mode. Press and hold or right-click the application's primary process and then tap or click UAC Virtualization. Repeat this process to exit virtualized mode.

TROUBLESHOOTING

Virtualization exceptions

Some application tasks always require administrative privileges. These tasks cannot be performed with a standard access token. Virtualization is designed for applications that are not UAC-compliant but require a full administrator access token to work properly. Virtualization doesn't apply to applications that are elevated and run with a full administrator access token. Virtualization is not supported for native Windows 64-bit applications and is disabled for applications that have a requested execution-level attribute in their application manifest.

You can verify that an application that won't work properly has a problem running as a standard user just by pressing and holding or right-clicking the application icon and then tapping or clicking Run As Administrator. There's a problem if the application works when running with a full administrator access token but doesn't run when using a standard access token. However, because the application might write to areas of the file system or registry that cause problems with stability or startup, you should test this theory only on nonproduction computers. You can try to resolve the problem by using one of the compatibility databases in the current version of the Microsoft Application Compatibility Toolkit, or you can use the toolkit to create your own compatibility databases.

Application run levels

Because of UAC, the processes related to installing and running applications have also changed. In earlier versions of Windows, the Power Users group gave users specific administrator privileges to perform basic system tasks when installing and running applications. Compliant applications do not require the use of the Power Users group; this group is maintained only for compatibility with older, noncompliant applications.

Windows Server detects application installations and prompts users for elevation to continue the installation by default. Installation packages for Windows Server–compliant applications use application manifests that contain run-level designations to help track required privileges. Application manifests define the application's desired privileges as one of the following:

- **RunAsInvoker.** Runs the application with the same privileges as the user. Any user can run the application. For a standard user or a user who is a member of the Administrators group, the application runs with a standard access token. The application runs with higher privileges only if the parent process from which it is started has an administrator access token. For example, if you start an elevated command prompt window and then start an application from this window, the application runs with an administrator access token.

- **RunAsHighest.** Runs the application with the highest privileges of the user. The application can be run by both administrator users and standard users. The tasks that can be performed by the application depend on the user's privileges. For a standard user, the application runs with a standard access token. For a user who is a member of a group with additional privileges—such as the Backup Operators, Server Operators, or Account Operators groups—the application runs with a partial administrator access token that contains only the privileges the user has been granted. For a user who is a member of the Administrators group, the application runs with a full administrator access token.
- **RunAsAdmin.** Runs the application with administrator privileges. Only administrators can run the application. For a standard user or a user who is a member of a group with additional privileges, the application runs only if the user can be prompted for credentials required to run in elevated mode or if the application is started from within an elevated process, such as from an elevated command prompt window. For a user who is a member of the Administrators group, the application runs with an administrator access token.

Windows Server protects application processes by labeling them with integrity levels ranging from high to low. Applications that modify system data, such as Disk Management, are considered high integrity, whereas those performing tasks that could compromise the operating system, such as Internet Explorer, are considered low integrity. Applications with lower integrity levels cannot modify data in applications with higher integrity levels.

Windows Server identifies the publisher of any application that attempts to run with an administrator's full access token. Then, depending on that publisher, Windows Server marks the application as a compliant application, a publisher verified (signed) application, or a publisher not verified (unsigned) application. When you are installing or running an application, the elevation prompt is designed to help identify the potential security risk of installing or running the application. First, the prompt is color-coded. Second, the elevation prompt displays a unique message depending on the category to which the application belongs.

When working with the elevation prompt, keep the following in mind:

- Red is a strong warning, representing likely danger. If the application is from a blocked publisher or is blocked by Group Policy, the elevation prompt has a red background and displays the message, "The application is blocked from running."
- Yellow is a general warning, indicating potential danger. If the application is unsigned (or is signed but not yet trusted), the elevation prompt has a yellow background and red shield icon and displays the message, "An unidentified program wants access to your computer."

- Blue/green is for administrative elevation. If the application is administrative (such as Server Manager), the elevation prompt has a blue/green background and displays the message, "Windows needs your permission to continue."
- Gray is for general elevation. If the application has been signed by Authenticode and is trusted by the local computer, the elevation prompt has a gray background and displays the message, "A program needs your permission to continue."

Only core Windows processes can access the secure desktop prompt. This serves to secure the elevation process further by preventing spoofing of the elevation prompt. The secure desktop is enabled by default in Group Policy.

Configuring run levels

By default, only applications running with a user's administrator access token run in elevated mode. Sometimes, you want an application running with a user's standard access token to be in elevated mode. For example, you might want to start the command prompt window in elevated mode so that you can perform administrator tasks.

In addition to application manifests discussed previously, Windows Server provides three ways to set the run level for applications. You can choose to perform one of the following:

- **Running an application once as an administrator.** You can run an application once as an administrator by pressing and holding or right-clicking the application's shortcut or menu item and then selecting Run As Administrator, as shown in Figure 9-5. If you are using a standard account and prompting is enabled, you are prompted for consent before the application is started. If you are using a standard account and prompting is disabled, the application will fail to run. If you are using an administrator account and prompting for consent is enabled, you are prompted for consent before the application is started.

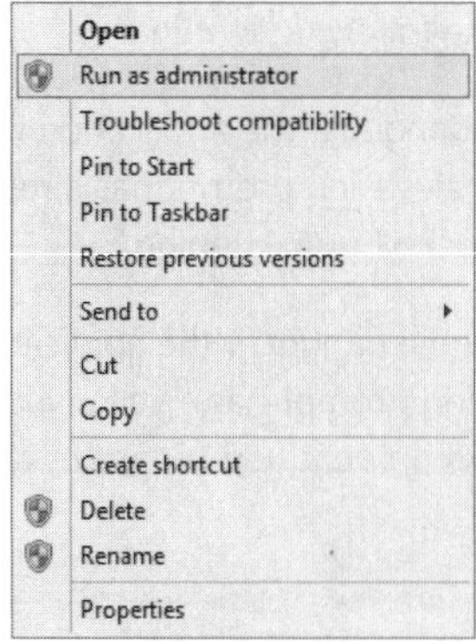

Figure 9-5 Run an application as an administrator from the shortcut menu.

- **Always running an application as an administrator.** Windows Server also enables you to mark an application so that it always runs with administrator privileges. This is useful for resolving compatibility issues with older applications that require administrator privileges. It is also useful for compliant applications that normally run in standard mode but that you use to perform administrative tasks. You cannot mark system applications or processes always to run as an administrator. Only nonsystem applications and processes can be marked that way. You can mark an application always to run as an administrator by pressing and holding or right-clicking the application's shortcut and then selecting Properties. In the Properties dialog box, tap or click the Compatibility tab. Under Privilege Level, select the Run This Program As An Administrator check box, as shown in Figure 9-6, and then tap or click OK.

NOTE

If Run This Program As An Administrator is unavailable, it means that the application is blocked from always running as elevated, the application does not require administrative credentials to run, or you are not logged on as an administrator.

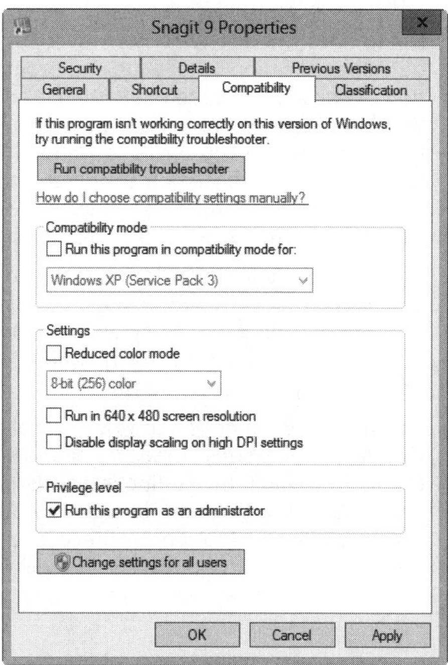

Figure 9-6 The option always to run a program as an administrator is selected.

Controlling application installation and run behavior

In Group Policy under Local Policies\Security Options, six security settings determine how application installation and run behavior work. Table 9-2 summarizes these security settings.

Table 9-2 Security settings related to application installation and run behavior

Security Setting	Description
User Account Control: Allow UIAccess Applications To Prompt For Elevation Without Using The Secure Desktop	Determines whether User Interface Accessibility (UIAccess) applications can bypass the secure desktop to increase usability in certain instances. By default, this setting is disabled. When enabled, UIAccess programs are allowed to respond to elevation prompts on the user's behalf (which increases the risk that the prompt could be manipulated by a malicious program). This setting primarily applies to Remote Assistance scenarios because this is the key UIAccess program in use. To avoid problems, be sure to have users select Allow IT Expert To Respond To User Account Control Prompts when making a remote assistance request.
User Account Control: Detect Application Installations And Prompt For Elevation	Determines whether Windows Server automatically detects application installation and prompts for elevation or consent. Because this setting is enabled by default, Windows Server automatically detects application installations and prompts users for elevation or consent to continue the installation. If you disable this setting, users are not prompted—in which case, the users will not be able to elevate permissions by supplying administrator credentials.
User Account Control: Only Elevate Executables That Are Signed And Validated	Determines whether Windows Server allows the running of only executables that are signed and validated. By default, this setting is disabled. When enabled, Windows enforces the public key certificate change validation of an executable before permitting it to run.
User Account Control: Only Elevate UIAccess Applications That Are Installed In Secure Locations	Determines whether Windows Server validates that UIAccess applications are secure before allowing them to run. By default, this setting is disabled. When enabled, only UIAccess applications in secure locations on the file system are allowed to run. Secure locations are limited to subdirectories of Program Files, including Program Files directories specifically for x86 or x64.

Security Setting	Description
User Account Control: Switch To The Secure Desktop When Prompting For Elevation	Determines whether the elevation request prompt is displayed on the secure desktop to isolate the prompt from all other processes, which enhances security by preventing the password from being read by any other (and possibly malicious) program. By default, this setting is enabled. This means the prompt is displayed on the secure desktop (and requires a response before a user can do anything else). If you disable this setting, the prompt is displayed without switching to the secure desktop (and a user's desktop isn't locked while waiting for a response).
User Account Control: Virtualize File And Registry Write Failures To Per-User Locations	Determines how Windows Server notifies users about application write errors. Because this setting is enabled by default, error notifications and error logging related to virtualized files and registry values show the virtualized location rather than the actual location to which the application was trying to write. If you disable this setting, error notifications and error logging related to virtualized files and registry values show the actual location to which the application was trying to write.

For workgroup configurations or for a special case, you can configure these security settings on a per-computer basis by using local security policy. To access local security policy and configure UAC settings, follow these steps:

1. Select Local Security Policy on the Tools menu in Server Manager. This starts the Local Security Policy console.
2. In the console tree, under Security Settings, expand Local Policies and then select Security Options.
3. Double-tap or double-click the setting you want to work with to open its properties dialog box.
4. All settings related to application installation and run behavior can be defined and then configured. Make any necessary changes and then tap or click OK. Repeat this procedure to modify the related security settings as necessary.

In a domain environment, you can use Active Directory–based Group Policy to apply the desired security configuration to a particular set of computers. Just apply the desired settings to a GPO that applies to those computers.

CHAPTER 10

Performance monitoring and tuning

Performance monitoring and tuning is the process of tracking system performance to establish baselines and identify and resolve problems. When you install a server, you should create a performance baseline to see how the server is performing given its current resources and typical usage. If a server isn't performing as expected, is unresponsive, or is generating errors, you want to investigate. Many tools are designed to help you monitor server performance and troubleshoot performance issues. This chapter discusses the key tools for fine-tuning the system configuration, tracking system health, and troubleshooting the event logs. In the next chapter, you learn more about comprehensive monitoring techniques you can use for establishing performance baselines and pinpointing performance bottlenecks.

Tuning performance, memory usage, and data throughput

Out of the box, Microsoft Windows Server 2012 R2 is optimized for general network environments. The operating system might not, however, be optimized for the way a particular system is being used in your organization. You can often improve Windows operating system and application performance considerably simply by fine-tuning the way a system uses resources.

Tuning Windows operating system performance

You don't want the Windows operating system to tie up too much processing power displaying visual effects when administrators or other users are logged on to a server. So, if you're wondering why all the fancy visuals are turned off in the standard configuration of Windows Server 2012 R2, this is why—the processing power is better used supporting the server's roles and applications than displaying fancy visuals to users who log on.

In most cases, you want to keep the visual effects to the bare minimum, which is what the default configuration after installation does. This ensures that users who log on either locally or remotely won't severely affect the performance of the system just by logging on and displaying menus and dialog boxes. You can check or change the visual effects options by using the Performance Options dialog box. In Control Panel, tap or click System And Security,

System, and then Advanced System Settings. On the Advanced tab in the System Properties dialog box, tap or click the Settings button in the Performance panel to display the Visual Effects tab in the Performance Options dialog box, as shown in Figure 10-1.

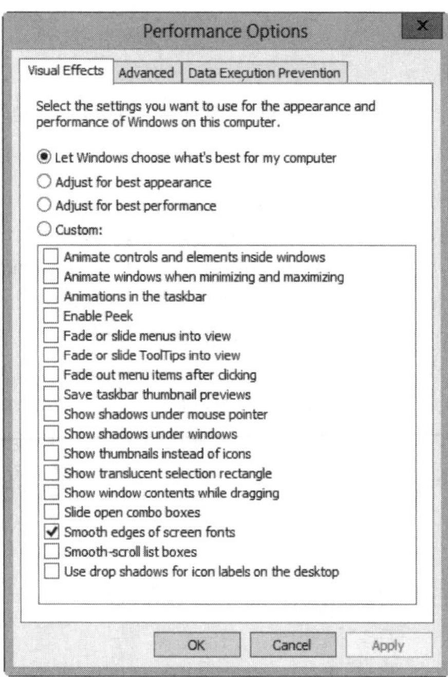

Figure 10-1 Change visual effects options in the Performance Options dialog box.

Tuning processor scheduling

The way the Windows operating system performs for applications and installed services is determined by the processor-scheduling configuration. Processor-scheduling options control how much of processor resources are allocated to applications running on a server, which in turn determines the responsiveness of applications. You can optimize processor scheduling for the following application types:

- **Programs.** When processor scheduling is optimized for programs, the active (foreground) application running on the system gets the best response time and the greatest share of available resources. Generally, you want to use this option only on development servers or when you are using Windows Server 2012 R2 as your desktop operating system.

- **Background services.** When processor scheduling is optimized for background services, all applications receive equal amounts of processor resources, and the active application doesn't get the best response time. Generally, you want to use this option for production servers.

You can check or change processor-scheduling configuration by using the Advanced tab of the Performance Options dialog box. In Control Panel, tap or click System And Security, System, and then Advanced System Settings. On the Advanced tab in the System Properties dialog box, tap or click the Settings button in the Performance panel to open the Performance Options dialog box. Finally, select the Advanced tab, as shown in Figure 10-2, in the Performance Options dialog box.

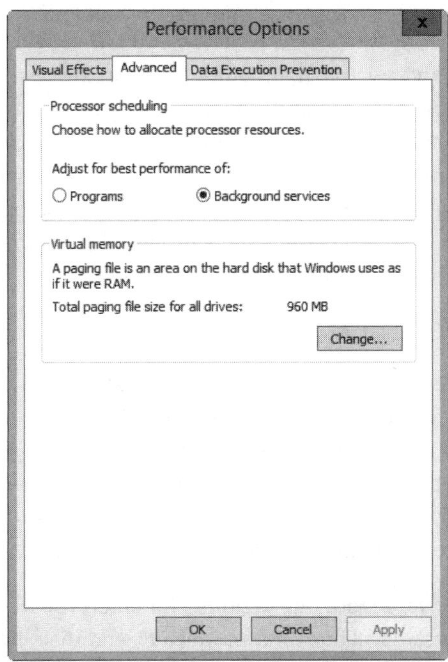

Figure 10-2 Configure processor-scheduling options.

Tuning virtual memory

Windows Server 2012 R2 uses virtual memory to allow a system to page parts of memory to disk. This makes it possible for a system to create a paging file on disk and use more memory space than is physically available. All servers have an initial paging file. It is created automatically on the drive containing the operating system during installation and setup, and it is written as a file named Pagefile.sys.

In some cases, you can improve a server's performance by optimizing the way the paging file is used. You do this by configuring the size of the paging file so that it is optimal given the server's RAM and usage. Although Windows Server 2012 R2 can expand paging files incrementally as needed, you want to size the paging file so that it is as large as it needs to be for typical usage conditions. This helps reduce fragmentation of data within the paging file and keeps the server from having to expand the paging file continually.

You can also fix the paging file size so that the server needn't spend any resources expanding the paging file. This helps ensure that paging files don't become fragmented, which can result in poor system performance. If you want to manage virtual memory manually, you use a fixed virtual memory size in most cases. To do this, set the initial size and the maximum size to the same value. This ensures that the paging file is consistent and can be written to a single contiguous file (if possible, given the amount of space on the volume).

If a server has multiple hard-disk drives and a very large memory configuration, you might consider creating a paging file for multiple physical hard-disk drives on the system. Multiple paging files can improve the performance of virtual memory on symmetric multiprocessing (SMP) machines with eight or more processors and a large amount of RAM. When you use multiple paging files, you create several smaller paging files rather than one big one. For example, if the paging file should be set to 8,192 megabytes (MBs) and the system has two disk drives, you could configure both drives to use a paging file 4,096 MBs in size.

IMPORTANT

If you're trying to decide whether to use a solid-state drive (SSD) rather than a physical hard disk for a paging file, I recommend reading the Inside Out sidebar, "Understanding solid-state drives," in Chapter 7, "Managing and troubleshooting hardware." A solid-state drive isn't necessarily a better (or worse) choice than a physical hard disk for hosting a paging file. Base your choice on the server workload and the solid-state drive's capabilities (specifically, the stated duty cycle and lifespan limitations).

If you decide to use a solid-state drive, choose one designed for enterprise workloads. Enterprise solid-state drives have wear-leveling features, which extend their lifetime and improve overall performance. Whether you choose a solid-state drive with multilevel cells (MLCs) storing two bits per cell or single-level cells (SLCs) storing one bit per cell will be based on your budget and performance targets. Typically, MLC SSDs are cheaper than SLC SSDs but don't last as long.

Inside OUT

Consider the RAID configuration of disks when setting the paging file location

You should always consider the redundant array of independent disks (RAID) configuration of disks when setting the paging file location. RAID configurations can slow down read/write performance for the paging file. By using RAID 1, you typically get better write performance than you do with RAID 5. By using RAID 5, you typically get better read performance than with RAID 1. So, there's a trade-off to be made with either RAID configuration.

In most cases for computers with 8 gigabytes (GBs) or less of RAM, I recommend setting the total paging file size so that it's twice the physical RAM size on the system. For instance, on a computer with 2,048 MBs of RAM, you would ensure that the Total Paging File Size For All Drives setting is at least 4,096 MBs. On systems with more than 8 GBs of RAM, you should follow the hardware manufacturer's guidelines for configuring the paging file. Typically, this means setting the paging file to be the same size as physical memory.

When you're trying to fine-tune the paging file size, look closely at the actual workload of the server in typical and peak conditions. Applications and their processes can reserve large blocks of virtual memory and then commit it as needed. Applications do this to try to ensure that the operating system allocates committed memory contiguously. This reserved virtual memory doesn't count toward the total, combined amount of physical and virtual memory that can be committed at any one time, also referred to as the *commit limit*.

If you want to try to optimize the paging file size, focus on the actual amount of committed physical and virtual memory for all active processes, the *current commit charge*, and compare this to the commit limit. The current commit charge cannot exceed the commit limit. Ideally, you want to size the paging file to accommodate the maximum total commit charge for the applications, services, and processes you want to run simultaneously while still allowing some overhead for unexpected usage peaks beyond this and testing the usage under typical-load and peak-load conditions.

Keep in mind, the commit limit will increase as the commit charge approaches it when a server has a system-managed paging file (until either exhausting its address space or reaching the 64-bit application-accessible address space limit). As the operating system approaches the maximum commit limit that is possible or explicitly configured, performance will degrade. You might see application failures or even a system failure.

Inside OUT

Types of virtual memory

Virtual memory can be divided into several broad types, including reserved, file-mapping view, private, and page file–backed. Reserved virtual memory doesn't count toward the commit limit until it's actually allocated and committed. File-mapping views, which represent files on disk, don't count toward the limit, either, except when an application requests copy-on-write. Private virtual memory counts toward the limit because it's for the garbage-collection heap, native heap, and language allocators. It's called "private" because it can't be shared between processes. Page file–backed virtual memory includes sections of virtual memory that applications use.

Inside OUT

Paging file and address space limits

Windows Server 2012 R2 can have paging files that are up to 16 terabytes (TBs) in size and can support up to 16 paging files, with each on a separate volume. Sixty-four-bit processes use 64-bit pointers and have a theoretical maximum address space of 16 exabytes (2^{64} bytes). Windows Server defines regions in the address space for processes and various resources. The process address space for user-mode applications is 8,192 GBs (8 TBs). Resource address spaces for nonpaged pool, paged pool, and system page table entries are 128 GBs each. The resource address space for the file cache is 1,024 GBs (1 TB).

Following this, you want to set the minimum size of the paging file to the greater of (1) the maximum total commit charge you determined minus the amount of physical RAM on the server or (2) the size needed to accommodate the type of crash dump the server is configured for. Then, set the maximum size of the paging file to accommodate unexpected usage peaks beyond this. Here are some examples:

- If you determine the maximum total commit charge for the expected typical workload to be 5,796 MBs, you could set this as the minimum paging file size and then set the maximum to 8,694 MBs, which is 1.5 times the minimum, or you could just set a fixed paging file size of 8,694 MBs by using this value for the minimum and maximum sizes.
- If you determine the maximum total commit charge for the peak observed workload to be 9,184 MBs, you could set this as the minimum paging file size and then set the

maximum to 11,480 MBs, which is 1.25 times the minimum, or you could just set a fixed paging file size of 11,480 MBs by using this value for the minimum and maximum sizes. You also might want to look at creating multiple paging files. If so, you might want to evaluate the performance of a single paging file compared to multiple, smaller paging files in a test environment before using this approach on production servers.

You can track the total commit charge and commit limit in Task Manager. Open Task Manager by pressing and holding or right-clicking the taskbar and then tapping or clicking Task Manager on the shortcut menu. Alternatively, press Ctrl+Shift+Esc.

When you are working with the expanded view in Task Manager, you'll find details about system resources on the Performance tab. Tap or click Memory in the left pane to see detailed information about memory usage in the main pane, as shown in Figure 10-3. The first value listed under the Committed heading is the current commit charge. The second value is the current commit limit. The total physical memory (RAM) on the server is shown in the upper-right corner of the main pane.

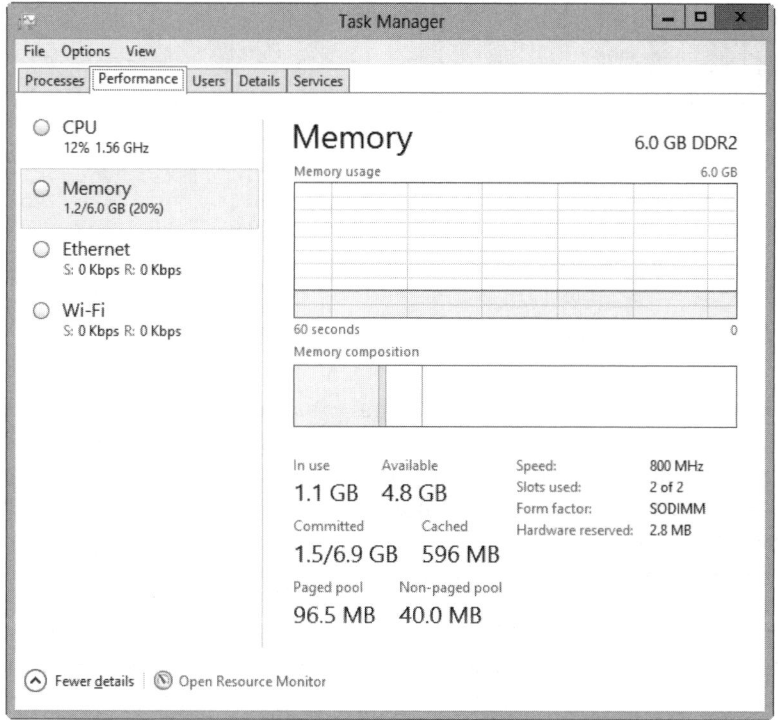

Figure 10-3 View memory usage on the server.

Other important tuning, memory, and data considerations

You can manage the paging file configuration by using the Virtual Memory dialog box, shown in Figure 10-4. To open this dialog box, tap or click the Advanced tab in the System Properties dialog box and then tap or click the Settings button in the Performance panel to display the Performance Options dialog box. Finally, select the Advanced tab in the Performance Options dialog box and then tap or click Change in the Virtual Memory panel. Alternatively, type **SystemPropertiesPerformance** in the Everywhere Search box and then press Enter.

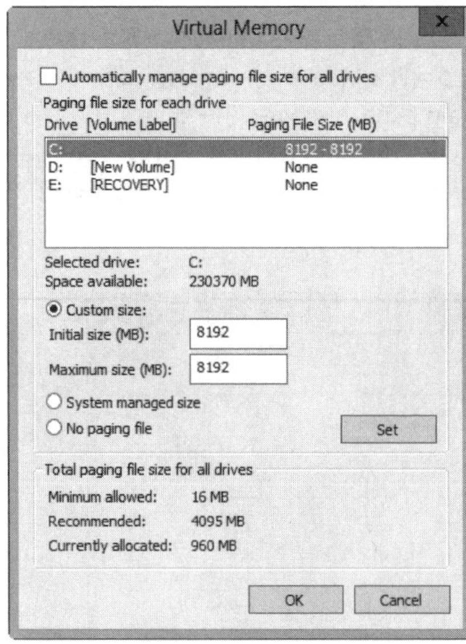

Figure 10-4 Manage the paging file configuration.

Windows Server 2012 R2 automatically manages virtual memory much better than its predecessors do. Typically, Windows Server 2012 R2 allocates virtual memory at least as large as the total physical memory installed on the computer. You control whether Windows automatically manages virtual memory by using the Automatically Manage Paging File Size For All Drives check box. When this check box is selected, Windows automatically manages virtual memory. When this check box is cleared, you can manually manage memory.

The upper section of the Virtual Memory dialog box shows the current paging file location and size. Each volume is listed with information about its associated paging file (if any). When the operating system manages a volume's paging file, the paging file is listed as System Managed. When a volume has a paging file, the initial and maximum size values set for it are shown. If the paging file has a size that can be incremented, the initial and maximum sizes will be different, such as 768–9,216 MB. If the paging file has a fixed size (recommended), the initial and maximum sizes will be the same, such as 8,704–8,704 MB.

By selecting a disk drive in the top portion of the Virtual Memory dialog box, you can configure whether and how the paging file is used. Usually, you want to select Custom Size and then set the Initial Size and Maximum Size options. Tap or click Set to apply the changes before you configure another disk drive. When you are finished configuring paging file usage, tap or click OK. You are then prompted to restart the server for the changes to take effect. Tap or click OK. When you close the System utility, you are prompted to restart the system for the changes to take effect. Tap or click Yes to restart the computer now or tap or click No if you plan to restart the server later.

TROUBLESHOOTING

Be careful when setting or moving the paging file

Some documentation recommends moving the paging file from the system drive to a different drive to improve performance. Don't do this without understanding the implications of doing so. The paging file is also used for debugging purposes when a Stop error occurs. On the system volume, the initial size of the paging file must be as large as the current physical RAM. If it isn't, Windows Server won't be able to write Stop information to the system drive when fatal errors occur. Because of this, my recommendation is to leave the paging file on the system drive.

CAUTION

As you set the paging file for individual drives, pay particular attention to the Total Paging File Size For All Drives information. Generally, you don't want to configure a server so that the Currently Allocated value is 0 MB. This means no paging file is configured, which will make it harder for you to troubleshoot STOP messages because no dump file will be generated. Keep in mind that lack of a paging file won't necessarily affect performance. Enterprise server hardware tends to have a lot of RAM. If the server was sized correctly for its workload and has a lot of RAM, it might rarely page to disk.

Tracking a system's general health

The fastest, easiest way to track a system's general health is to use Task Manager or Resource Monitor. Unlike some of the other performance tools that require some preparation before you can use them, you can start and use these tools without any preparation. This makes them very useful when you want to see what's going on with a system right away.

Monitoring essentials

By using Task Manager, you can track running applications and processes and determine resource usage. This can help you understand how a server is performing and whether there are any problems, such as applications that aren't running or processes that are hogging system resources. You can open Task Manager by pressing Ctrl+Shift+Esc or by typing **taskmgr** in the Everywhere Search box and then pressing Enter.

The first time you open Task Manager, you see the summary view, which shows a quick summary of applications running in the foreground. To get more information about running tasks, tap or click More Details. You then see the expanded view, which has multiple tabs that you can use to get information about all running processes, system performance, connected users, and configured services. When you next open Task Manager, you see the view you used last because the last-used view is displayed initially.

To work with the expanded view in Task Manager, the key issue you must understand is the distinction between an application and a process. Basically, the executable name of an application, such as Taskmgr.exe, is known to the operating system as its image name, and whenever you start an application, the operating system starts one or more processes to support it. As Figure 10-5 shows, Task Manager has five tabs:

- **Processes.** Shows apps, background processes, and Windows processes that were run on the system and displays whether they're running, suspended, or not responding. It also enables you to interact with applications and halt their execution.
- **Performance.** Displays current processor, memory, and network usage. It includes graphs and detailed statistics. Enabled network connections are listed by their display name.
- **Users.** Details the users currently logged on to the system. It includes local users and users connected through Remote Desktop sessions. You can use this tab to disconnect, log off, and send console messages to these users. You also can use it to see the processes users are running.
- **Details.** Lists the image name of the processes running on the system, including those run by the operating system and users. It includes usage statistics for system resources allocated to each process, and you can use it to interact with and stop processes.
- **Services.** Shows the system services configured on the server. It includes their status, such as running or stopped.

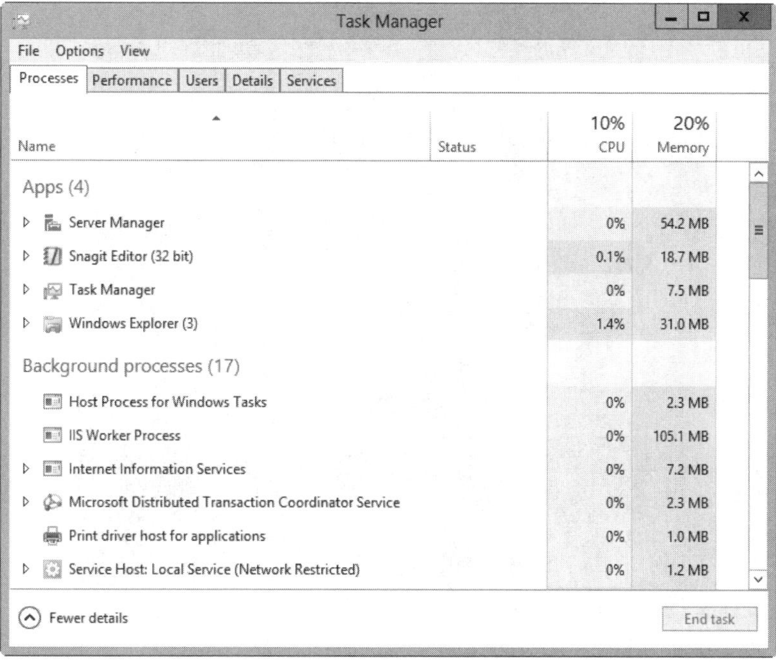

Figure 10-5 Use Task Manager to track resource usage.

CAUTION

Task Manager uses system resources while it's running. Because of this, you should run it only while you are tracking performance.

No single command-line tool performs all the same functions as Task Manager. The closest tools in functionality are the Windows PowerShell cmdlets, get-process and get-service. You obtain detailed information about running processes by using get-process and detailed information about configured services by using get-service.

As Figure 10-6 shows, the standard output of get-process is much more detailed than the default Task Manager view, especially when it comes to current per-process resource usage and activity. To run get-process, access a Windows PowerShell prompt and then type **get-process**.

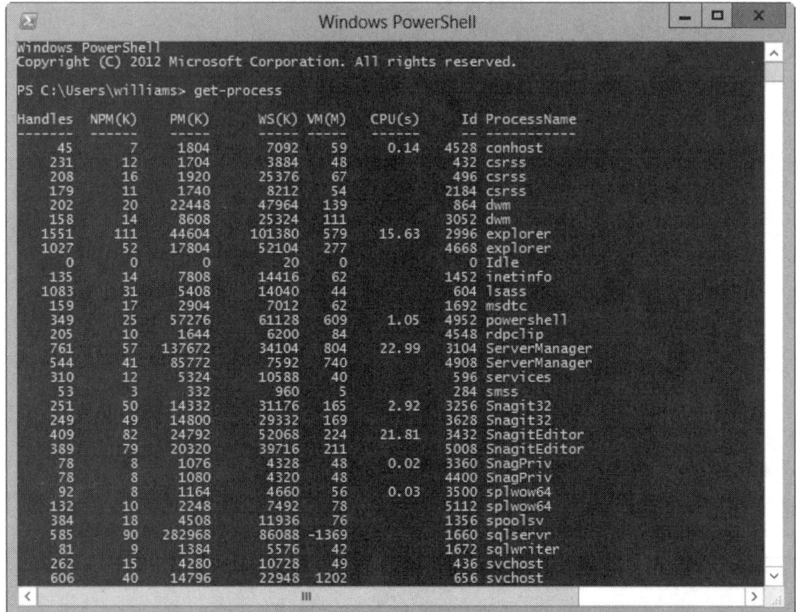

Figure 10-6 Use get-process to track running applications and processes and determine resource usage.

Use get-process to reduce resource usage

Because get-process is text-based rather than a graphical utility, it will, in most cases, use fewer system resources than Task Manager. On systems for which you are very concerned about resource usage and the possibility of bogging down a system by tracking performance information, you might initially want to start tracking performance by using get-process.

As Figure 10-7 shows, the standard output for get-service shows the status of each configured service along with its internal name and display name. To run get-service, access a Windows PowerShell prompt and then type **get-service**.

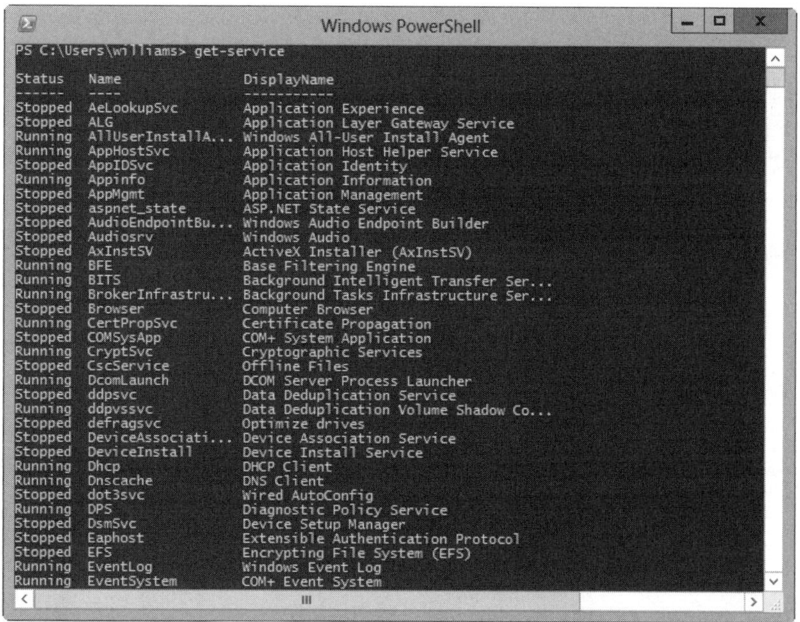

Figure 10-7 Use get-service to track the status of configured services.

The sections that follow discuss how to use these tools to gather information about systems and resolve problems. The focus of the discussion is on Task Manager, get-process, and get-service, which should be your primary tools for tracking a system's general health.

Getting processor and memory usage for troubleshooting

The Performance tab in Task Manager, shown in Figure 10-8, should be the first tab you check if you suspect there is a performance issue with a system. It enables you to determine current processor, memory, and network usage quickly, and it graphs some historical usage statistics based on data collected since you started Task Manager.

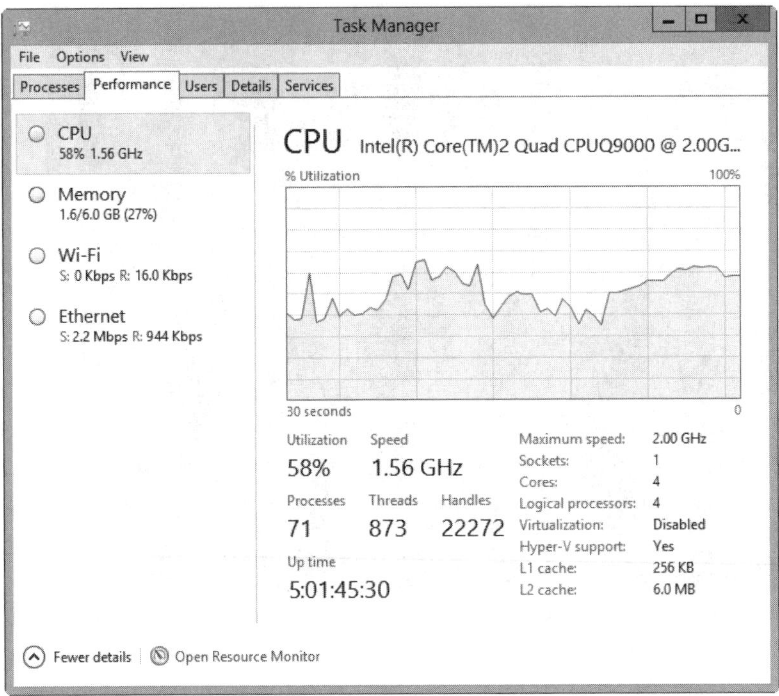

Figure 10-8 The Performance tab provides a summary of current processor, memory, and network usage and some historical usage statistics based on data collected since you started Task Manager.

TROUBLESHOOTING

Using performance views and graphs

When you are troubleshooting performance issues, you'll often want to refer to the graphs or summary details regarding CPU, memory, and network usage. The full view, however, can sometimes get in the way of your work, especially if you have several other windows open. Here, you might want to switch to the summary view of the Performance tab.

To do this, press and hold or right-click in the left pane of the Performance tab and then select Summary View. This reduces the Task Manager window so that it shows only a summary view of the performance statistics. If you also want to see summary graphs, press and hold or right-click the summary view and then select Show Graphs. Now you'll see the summary statistics and the summary graphs. This combined summary view is what I use when I'm monitoring performance issues.

When you are working with the summary view of the Performance tab and want to switch back to the expanded view, just press and hold or right-click the summary view and then select Summary View. This clears the Summary View selection.

NOTE

Another handy view is the graph summary view, which shows only the currently selected graph. When you are working with the expanded view of the Performance tab, you can switch to the graph summary view just by double-tapping or double-clicking the graph in the main pane. While you are working with the graph summary view, you also can switch between graph categories. For example, if you are viewing the CPU graph, you can switch to the memory graph. To do this, press and hold or right-click in the graph summary view, select View, and then choose the type of graph. Switch back to the expanded view at any time by pressing and holding or right-clicking the summary view and then selecting Graph Summary View. This clears the Graph Summary View selection.

Some of the performance data is self-explanatory. When you select CPU in the left pane, the main window shows the CPU usage. The Overall Utilization graph shows the overall percentage of processor resources being used and is the default graph. If a system has multiple discrete sockets containing CPUs, you also see a history graph for each CPU by default. If a system has multiple logical processors, you also can view the workload on each logical processor in separate graphs. To change the graph view, press and hold or right-click in the main pane, select Change Graph To, and then choose a viewing style.

In Figure 10-8, note the additional information about CPU usage. This information, which is shown below the graph, includes the following:

- **Utilization.** Shows the percentage of CPU utilization.
- **Speed.** Shows the (average) current speed of processor.
- **Maximum Speed.** Shows the maximum speed the process is capable of.

NOTE

If a server's processor or processors are throttled—to save power or for some other reason—the (average) current speed and the maximum speed will be different.

- **Sockets.** Shows the number of discrete sockets containing processors.
- **Cores.** Shows the total number of processor cores.

- **Logical Processors.** Shows the total number of active logical processors. If this value is less than the total number of processor cores, some portion of functionality has been disabled.
- **Virtualization.** Shows whether virtualization is enabled or disabled.
- **L1 Cache.** Shows the size of the L1 cache if the computer's processor or processors have L1 cache.
- **L2 Cache.** Shows the size of the L2 cache if the computer's processor or processors have L2 cache.

Also shown are summary statistics for handles, threads, processes, and uptime. The Processes area shows the number of processes in use. Threads shows the number of threads in use. Threads allow concurrent execution of process requests. Handles shows the number of input/output (I/O) file handles in use. Because each handle requires system memory to maintain, this is important to note. Up Time shows the total amount of time the system has been up since it was last started.

In Figure 10-8, you see an example of a system with moderate CPU usage but with very little ongoing paging file or networking activity. A system with CPU usage consistently at these levels might warrant some additional monitoring to determine whether you should add resources to the system. You want to determine whether these are typical usage conditions and whether actual peak usage was significantly higher.

If these are average usage conditions and peak usage was significantly higher, increasing the processor speed or adding processors could improve performance and allow for better handling of peak usage situations. If these statistics represent peak usage conditions and typical usage conditions were much less, the system probably wouldn't need additional resources. In addition, sometimes the CPU usage can be high if the system has too little memory. A quick check of the memory usage of the server (including its current and peak usage) shows, however, that this isn't the case for this particular system.

IMPORTANT

When CPU throttling is being used, don't just look at the percentage of utilization—also look at the current CPU speed. In Figure 10-8, not only is the server only running at 58 percent CPU utilization, the average current CPU speed is 1.56 gigahertz (GHz), which is 36 percent below the server's maximum speed of 2.00 GHz.

Figure 10-9 shows performance data for the same system. In this example, the system has high CPU usage. In many cases, CPU usage is at 99 percent, and the CPU speed is nearly at its maximum. If CPU usage was consistent at this level, I might suspect a runaway process and look for a process that is causing the problem. Here, however, there are times when CPU usage isn't maxed out, and you'd definitely want to take a closer look at what's going on, starting with memory usage.

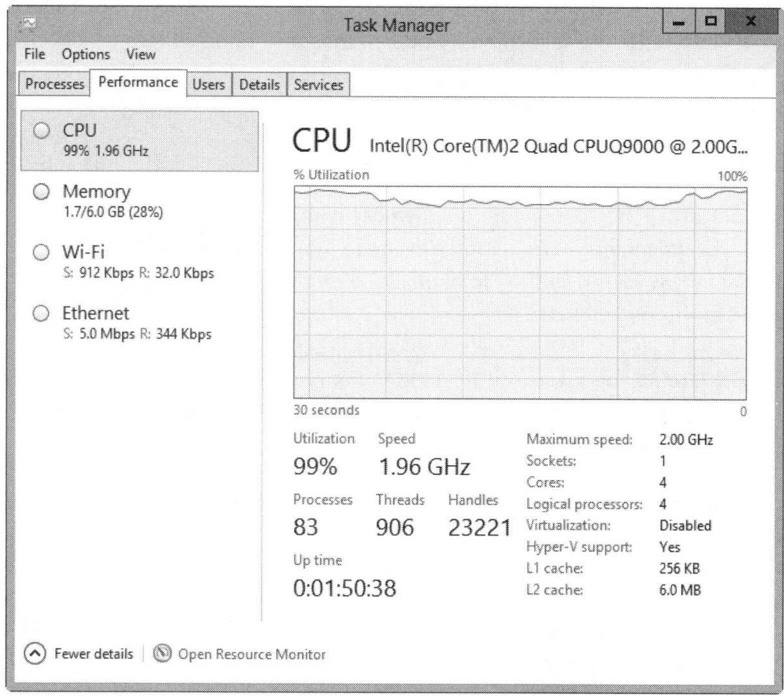

Figure 10-9 Heavy activity on the system is causing CPU usage to soar and, in many cases, to max out.

Figure 10-10 shows the server's memory usage, which is displayed by selecting Memory in the left pane. Note that the total physical memory (RAM) on the server is shown in the upper-right corner of the main pane. Note also the following:

- **Cached.** Shows the physical memory used for system caching. This value represents the total amount of modified memory (needing to be written to disk before being available) and standby memory (containing cached data and code not actively being used).
- **In Use.** Shows the currently allocated physical memory. Use this value to help you determine the current paging file size. The size of the paging file is the difference between the current commit charge and the in-use memory.
- **Available.** Shows the unallocated (available) physical memory. Use this value to help you determine whether the server is running out of available physical memory.

- **Committed.** Shows the current commit charge as the first value and the commit limit as the second value.
- **Memory Composition.** Depicts in-use and available memory graphically, according to its status as in use (allocated), modified (needing to be written to disk before being available), standby (containing cached data and code not actively being used), and free (unallocated).

NOTE

Tap or rest the mouse pointer on a memory-composition item to see a precise numeric value. Keep in mind that the total allocated physical memory is the sum of the in-use and modified values, and the total unallocated physical memory is the sum of the standby and free memory.

- **Paged Pool.** Shows noncritical kernel memory used by the operating system kernel. Noncritical portions of kernel memory can be paged to disk and don't have to reside in physical memory (RAM).
- **Non-paged Pool.** Shows critical kernel memory used by the operating system kernel. Critical portions of kernel memory must operate in physical memory (RAM) and cannot be paged to disk.

When you are reviewing Figure 10-10, one thing to note right away is that the system has quite a bit of available RAM—around 4.4 GBs. In checking the paging, you can see the current commit charge isn't very large either. It is only 2.1 GBs, and the difference between the commit charge and in-use RAM is only 0.6 GBs, meaning only 0.6 GBs is being paged to disk.

Such a large amount of available RAM and such little use of the paging file tells me that processes, disk I/O, or both activities are using up CPU resources. If this level of usage is consistent, you have a problem that needs investigating. Here, increasing the server's RAM or virtual memory will not solve the problem. Instead, you need to start by checking for system processes that have high CPU usage time, which tells you what activities are causing the strain on the server's processors. If the high CPU usage activities are related to installed applications, roles, or role services, you might want to consider adding CPUs to the server. Generally, you add CPUs to a server in matched pairs. In this example, the server has two CPUs, so you want to consider upgrading to four CPUs. You might also consider offloading some of the system's load. For example, you could move one of its roles or applications to a different server.

Another scenario you might encounter is when the server has little available RAM and a large paging file. A small amount of available RAM is a concern, and if this level of usage is consistent, you might consider changing the way applications use RAM, adding RAM, or both. A large amount of virtual memory being used (relative to available physical RAM) is also an area of possible concern that might make you consider adding physical RAM. Although increasing the amount of RAM could offer some relief to the CPU, it might not be enough, so you could consider increasing the processor speed or adding processors. You might also consider offloading some of the system's load. For example, you could move one of its roles or applications to a different server.

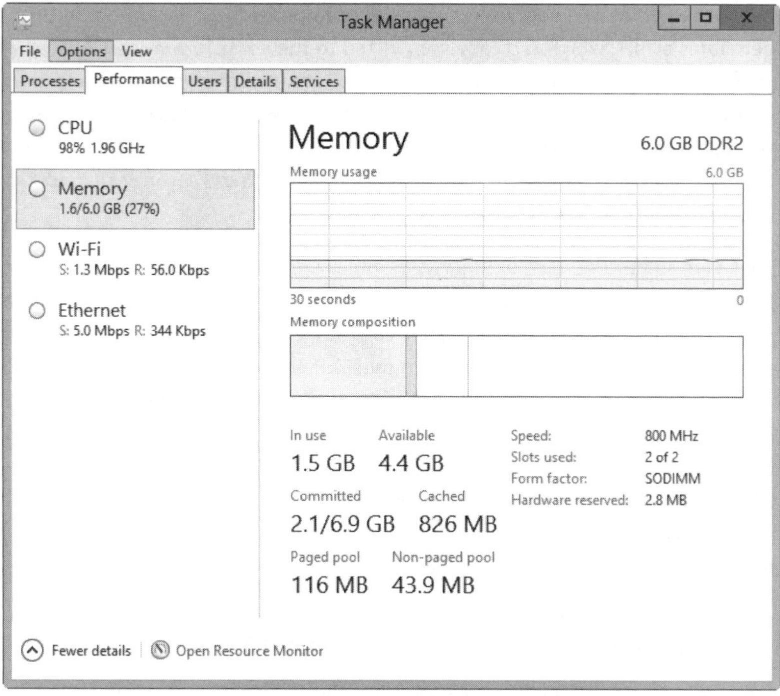

Figure 10-10 Use the Memory graphs to check memory usage and composition.

Inside OUT

Physical configuration of memory

The physical configuration of the memory is shown along with other memory information. This is handy because otherwise you would have to get this information from the System Information utility or elsewhere. Note the speed, slots used, and form factor. Generally, when adding memory to a server, you need to use memory that has the same speed and form factor as existing memory—and as required by the system bus. If you want to add memory and no additional slots are available, you need to replace the existing memory.

TROUBLESHOOTING

Resolving problems with RAM modules

Physical memory is installed on a server by using available memory slots. Typically, memory is installed in matched pairs and according to the number of memory channels. When you boot a server with invalid or improperly configured memory, the server generates errors, which typically are written to the console window. Related events might also be written to the hardware event logs in firmware, the system event logs in the operating system, or both. You can use these error messages and events to help you diagnose and resolve memory problems. For pinpointing physical failures within the memory chips themselves, you can use the Windows Memory Diagnostic Tool (Memdiag.exe).

That said, some problems with RAM modules are less obvious than one might think, and a missing RAM module is one problem you might not recognize immediately. RAM modules don't really go missing. They can, however, be improperly seated (meaning not fully pushed into their slot and connected), incompatible (meaning not the correct speed, form factor, or both), or bad (meaning failed or broken). One quick way to identify this type of problem is to note the total physical memory and the total number of memory slots being used. If either or both don't match up to what you expect, there's a problem—for example, if the server has 16 GBs of RAM and the current total is shown as 8 GBs or if the server has memory in four slots and only three are shown as being used.

Getting information on running applications

The Processes tab in Task Manager, shown in Figure 10-11, lists applications being run by users and the operating system along with status details that show whether the applications are running, suspended, or not responding. If an application has an open file, such as a Microsoft Word document, the name of the file is also shown. By default, applications are grouped into three general categories:

- **Apps.** Programs running in the foreground
- **Background processes.** Programs running in the background
- **Windows processes.** Processes run by the operating system

IMPORTANT

Generally, foreground processes are processes being run by a user logged on to a computer's local console. In contrast, background processes include any processes run by the operating system, local services, network services, and remote users. Thus, if you are trying to track processes for remote users on the Processes tab, you look under the

Background Processes group rather than the Apps group. However, the Users tab provides a better approach for identifying the specific processes local and remote users are running. On this tab, each process a particular user is running is listed under the user's logon name.

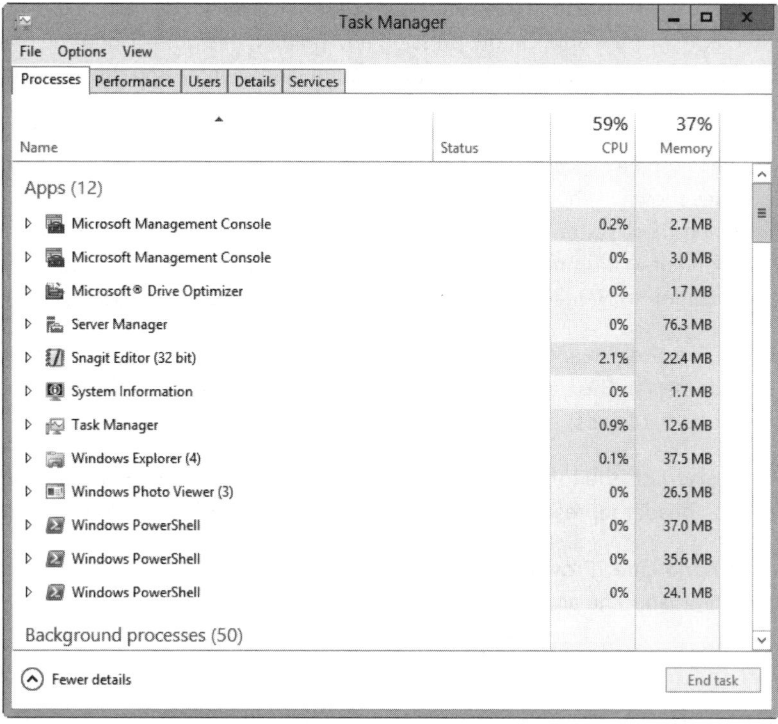

Figure 10-11 The Processes tab in Task Manager tracks applications users are running.

You can use Group By Type on the View menu to control whether grouping is used. If you clear this option, processes are listed alphabetically without grouping by type. If a process has related subprocesses, you can tap or click a process to view the subprocesses.

To work with an application, select it by tapping or clicking it in the task list. You can then press and hold or right-click the application name to select End Task, Create Dump File, Go To Details, Open File Location, Search Online, and Properties. Don't overlook the usefulness of Go To Details when you press and hold or right-click. Use this when you're trying to find the primary process for a particular application because selecting this option highlights the related process on the Details tab. Select Create Dump File to create a dump file for debugging an application. Select Search Online to start a search with your default search provider in your default browser. The search keywords are the image name and descriptive name of the process.

The Status column shows abnormal process statuses, if any. If you see an application with a status of Not Responding, the application might be frozen, and you might want to select it and then tap or click End Task. Keep in mind that the Not Responding message can also be an indicator that an application is busy and should be left alone until it finishes. Generally, when an application is running without errors and might have unsaved data, don't use End Task to stop the application. Instead, try to exit the program gracefully. You can do this by expanding the related entry for the application, pressing and holding or right-clicking the related subprocess, selecting Switch To to switch to the application, and then exiting the application as you normally would.

Other columns on the Processes tab provide additional information about running processes. Use the values shown in the CPU and Memory columns to determine which processes are overconsuming these system resources. You can add other columns by pressing and holding or right-clicking any column header and then selecting options for the additional columns to display. In addition to Name and Status, the available columns are as follows:

- **CPU.** Lists the percentage of CPU utilization for the process (across all physical and logical processors). The bold value in the column header represents the total CPU utilization for the server (across all physical and logical processors).
- **Memory.** Lists the total physical memory reserved for the process. The bold value in the column header represents the total physical memory utilization for the server.
- **Command Line.** Provides the full file path to the executable running the process and any command-line arguments passed in when the process was started.
- **PID.** Provides the numeric identifier for the process.
- **Process Name.** Provides the name of the process or executable running the process.
- **Publisher.** Shows the publisher of the process, such as Microsoft Corporation.
- **Type.** Provides the general process type as app, background process, or Windows process, which is useful if you clear Group By Type on the View menu.

Monitoring and troubleshooting processes

You can view information about processes running on a system by using the Details tab of Task Manager or by running get-process. The Task Manager display differs greatly from the output provided by get-process. The Details tab shows all processes that are running, including those run by the operating system, local services, network services, a user account logged on to the local console, and remote users.

The default view of the Details tab shows each running process by image name and user name. Here, the image name is the name of the executable for the process, and the user name is the name of the user or service running the process.

The CPU column shows the percentage of processor utilization for each process. The Memory column shows the amount of memory the process is currently using. By default, processes are sorted by image name, but you can change this by tapping or clicking any of the available column headers to sort the information based on that column. Tapping or clicking again on the same column reverses the sort order. For example, tap or click User Name to sort the user names alphabetically. Tap or click User Name again to reverse sort the user names.

As you might recall from Figure 10-6, get-process shows much more detailed information for each process. This information is useful for troubleshooting. If you press and hold or right-click any column header and then choose Select Columns, you'll see a dialog box that enables you to add columns to the Details tab. To get the additional information get-process shows, the following columns should be selected:

- PID
- CPU
- CPU Time
- Working Set (Memory)
- Memory (Private Working Set)
- Memory (Shared Working Set)
- Commit Size
- Handles

You will then have a process display like the one shown in Figure 10-12.

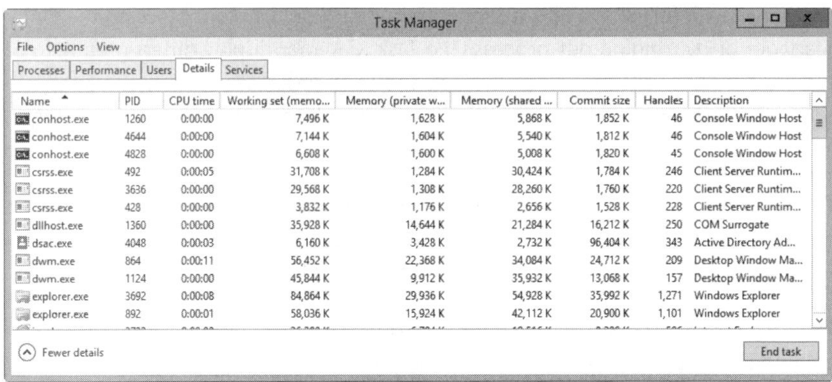

Figure 10-12 The Details tab provides detailed information on running processes according to image name and user name.

TROUBLESHOOTING

Isolate 32-bit or 64-bit processes

Sixty-four-bit Windows operating systems can only run 32-bit or 64-bit processes. If you want to isolate 32-bit or 64-bit processes, add the Platform column to the Details tab. You can then quickly determine whether a process is 32-bit or 64-bit.

For deeper troubleshooting, I recommend adding a few more columns, such as the following:

- Base Priority
- Image Path Name
- Page Faults
- PF Delta
- Threads
- Working Set Delta (Memory)

Okay, so now that you've added all these extra columns of information, you are probably wondering what it all means and why you want to track it. As stated previously, you primarily use this information for troubleshooting. It helps you pinpoint which processes are hogging system resources and the type of resources the resource hogs are using. When you know what's going on with processes, you can modify the system or its applications accordingly to resolve a performance problem.

Table 10-1 summarizes the information provided by these and other process-related statistics. The value in parentheses following the Task Manager column name is the name of the corresponding get-process property (if available). If by monitoring processes you notice what looks like a problem, you probably want to start more detailed monitoring of the system. One tool to consider is System Monitor, which is discussed in Chapter 11, "Comprehensive performance analysis and logging."

NOTE

For formatting purposes, the get-process property names are shown with brackets where necessary. The actual property names do not contain hyphens.

Table 10-1 **Process statistics and how they can be used**

Column Name	Description
Base Priority [BasePriority]	Shows the priority of the process. Priority determines how much of the system resources are allocated to a process. The standard priorities are Low (4), Below Normal (6), Normal (8), Above Normal (10), High (13), and Real-Time (24). Most processes have a Normal priority by default, and the highest priority is given to real-time processes.
Commit Size [VirtualMemorySize]	Shows the amount of virtual memory allocated to and reserved for a process. Virtual memory is memory on disk and is slower to access than pooled memory. By configuring an application to use more physical RAM, you might be able to increase performance. To do this, however, the system must have available RAM. If it doesn't, other processes running on the system might slow down.
CPU [CPU]	Shows the percentage of CPU utilization for the process. The System Idle Process shows what percentage of CPU power is idle. A 99 in the CPU column for the System Idle Process means 99 percent of the system resources currently aren't being used. If the system has low idle time (meaning high CPU usage) during peak or average usage, you might consider upgrading to faster processors or adding processors.
CPU Time [TotalProcessorTime]	Shows the total amount of CPU time used by the process since it was started. Tap or click the column header to see quickly the processes that are using the most CPU time. If a process is using a lot of CPU time, the related application might have a configuration problem. This could also indicate a runaway or nonresponsive process that is unnecessarily tying up the CPU.

Column Name	Description
Handles [HandleCount]	Shows the number of file handles maintained by the process. The number of handles used is an indicator of how dependent the process is on the file system. Some processes have thousands of open file handles. Each file handle requires system memory to maintain.
Image Path Name [Path]	Shows the full path to the executable for the process.
Name [ProcessName]	Shows the name of the process.
NP Pool [NonpagedSystemMemorySize]	Shows the amount of virtual memory for a process that cannot be written to disk. The nonpaged pool is an area of RAM for objects that can't be written to disk. You should note processes that require a high amount of nonpaged pool memory. If there isn't enough free memory on the server, these processes might be the reason for a high level of page faults.
Page Faults	Shows page faults caused by the process. Page faults occur when a process requests a page in memory and the system can't find it at the requested location. If the requested page is elsewhere in memory, the fault is called a soft page fault. If the requested page must be retrieved from disk, the fault is called a hard page fault. Most processors can handle large numbers of soft faults. Hard faults, however, can cause significant delays. If there are a lot of hard faults, you might need to increase the amount of memory or reduce the system cache size.
Paged Pool [PagedSystemMemorySize]	Shows the amount of committed virtual memory for a process that can be written to disk. The paged pool is an area of RAM for objects that can be written to disk when they aren't used. As process activity increases, so does the amount of pool memory the process uses. Most processes have more paged pool than nonpaged pool requirements.
Peak Working Set (Memory) [PeakWorkingSet]	Shows the maximum amount of memory the process used, including both the private working set and the nonprivate working set. If peak memory is exceptionally large, this can indicate a memory leak.
PF Delta	Shows the change in the number of page faults for the process recorded since the last update. As with memory usage, you might see an increase in page faults when a process is active and then a decrease as activity slows.
PID [Id]	Shows the run-time identification number of the process.
Session ID [SessionId]	Shows the identification number user (session) within which the process is running. This corresponds to the ID value listed on the Users tab.

Column Name	Description
Threads [Threads]	Shows the number of threads that the process is using. Most server applications are multithreaded, which allows concurrent execution of process requests. Some applications can dynamically control the number of concurrently executing threads to improve application performance. Too many threads, however, can actually reduce performance because the operating system has to switch thread contexts too frequently.
Working Set (Memory) [WorkingSet]	Shows the amount of memory the process is currently using, including both the private working set and the non-private working set. The private working set is memory the process is using that cannot be shared with other processes. The nonprivate working set is memory the process is using that can be shared with other processes. If memory usage for a process slowly grows over time and doesn't go back to the baseline value, this can indicate a memory leak.
Working Set Delta (Memory)	Shows the change in memory usage for the process recorded since the last update. A constantly changing memory delta can indicate that a process is in use, but it could also indicate a problem. Generally, the memory delta might show increasing memory usage when a process is being used and then show a negative delta (indicated by parentheses in Task Manager) as activity slows.

At a Windows PowerShell prompt, you can get key stats for all processes by following these steps:

1. Run all the processes on the server and store them in the *$a* variable by entering:

   ```
   $a = get-process
   ```

2. Use the *InputObject* parameter to pass the process objects stored in *$a* to get-process and then pass the objects to the format-table cmdlet along with the list of properties you want to see by entering:

   ```
   get-process -inputobject $a | format-table -property ProcessName,
   BasePriority, HandleCount, Id, NonpagedSystemMemorySize,
   PagedSystemMemorySize, PeakPagedMemorySize, PeakVirtualMemorySize,
   PeakWorkingSet, SessionId, Threads, TotalProcessorTime,
   VirtualMemorySize, WorkingSet, CPU, Path
   ```

   NOTE

   The order of the properties in the comma-separated list determines the display order. If you want to change the display order, just move the property to a different position in the list.

When you know the process you want to examine, you don't need to use this multistep procedure. Just enter the name of the process without the .exe or .dll instead of using *–inputobject $a*. In this example, you list details about the Explorer process:

```
get-process explorer | format-list -property ProcessName, BasePriority,
HandleCount, Id, NonpagedSystemMemorySize, PagedSystemMemorySize,
PeakPagedMemorySize, PeakVirtualMemorySize, PeakWorkingSet, SessionId,
Threads, TotalProcessorTime, VirtualMemorySize, WorkingSet, CPU, Path
```

You can enter part of a process name and use an asterisk as a wildcard to match a partial name. In this example, get-process lists any process with a name that starts with *exp*:

```
get-process exp* | format-list -property ProcessName, BasePriority,
HandleCount, Id, NonpagedSystemMemorySize, PagedSystemMemorySize,
PeakPagedMemorySize, PeakVirtualMemorySize, PeakWorkingSet, SessionId,
Threads, TotalProcessorTime, VirtualMemorySize, WorkingSet, CPU, Path
```

Some interesting additional properties you can use with get-process include the following:

- **MinWorkingSet.** The minimum amount of working set memory used by the process
- **Modules.** The executables and dynamically linked libraries used by the process
- **PeakVirtualMemorySize.** The peak amount of virtual memory used by the process
- **PriorityBoostEnabled.** A Boolean value that indicates whether the process's PriorityBoost feature is enabled
- **PriorityClass.** The priority class of the process
- **PrivilegedProcessorTime.** The amount of kernel-mode usage time for the process
- **ProcessorAffinity.** The processor affinity setting for the process
- **Responding.** A Boolean value that indicates whether the process responded when tested
- **StartTime.** The date and time the process was started
- **UserProcessorTime.** The amount of user-mode usage time for the process
- **Description.** A description of the process
- **FileVersion.** The file version of the executable of the process

In Task Manager, you can stop processes that you suspect aren't running properly. To do this, press and hold or right-click the process and choose End Process to stop the process or End Process Tree to stop the process and any other processes it started. To stop a process at a

Windows PowerShell prompt, you can use stop-process. The best way to use stop-process is to identity the process ID of the process that you want to stop rather than a process name. This ensures that you stop only the intended process rather than all instances of processes with a particular process name. By using the *–confirm* parameter, you should also have stop-process prompt you to confirm how you want to proceed. In the following example, you stop the process with the process ID 4524:

```
stop-process -id 4524 -confirm
```

As you are confirming this action and passing through the output, you see a prompt asking you to confirm. You can then:

- Press Y to answer Yes and confirm that you want to perform the action and continue.
- Press A to answer Yes to all prompts and confirm that you want to perform all actions without further prompting.
- Press N to answer No and skip the action and continue to the next action.
- Press L to answer No to all prompts and confirm that you do not want to perform any actions.
- Press S to suspend the pipeline and return to the command prompt. To return to the pipeline later, type **exit**.

Monitoring and troubleshooting services

You can view information about services running on a system by using the Services tab of Task Manager or by running get-service. By default, the Services tab shows all services configured on the system whether they are running, stopped, or in a different state. As shown in Figure 10-13, services are listed by name, process ID (PID), description, status, and group.

Because multiple services typically run under the same process ID, you can quickly sort services by their associated process ID by tapping or clicking the related column heading. You can tap or click the Status column heading to sort services according to their status as Running or Stopped. If you press and hold or right-click a service's listing in Task Manager, you display a shortcut menu that enables you to start a stopped service, stop a started service, or go to the related process on the Details tab.

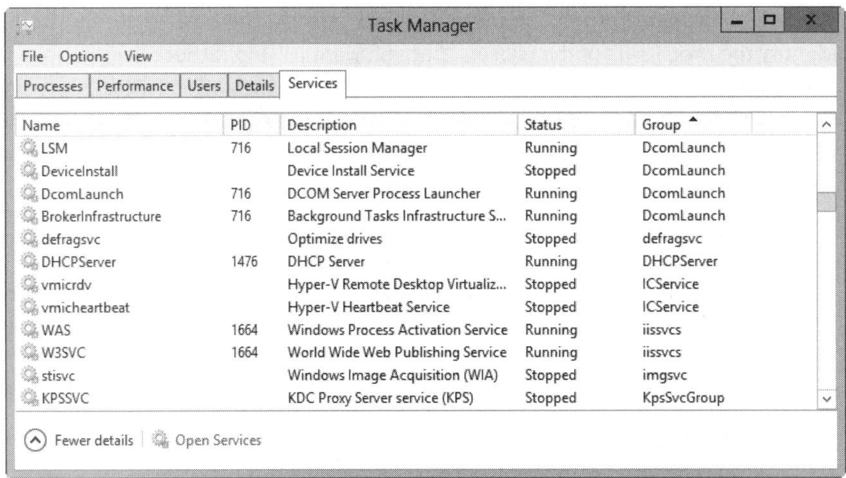

Figure 10-13 The Services tab provides detailed information on configured services.

> NOTE
>
> **You also can work with services by using the Services pane in Server Manager, the Services node in Computer Management, or the Services console.**

The Group column provides additional information about related identities or service host contexts under which a service runs. Services running an identity with a restriction have the restriction appended. For example, a service running under the Local Service identity might be listed as LocalServiceNoNetwork to indicate that the service has no network access, or as LocalSystemNetworkRestricted to indicate that the service has restricted access to the network.

Services that have svchost.exe list their associated context for the *–k* parameter. For example, the RemoteRegistry service runs with the svchost.exe –k regsvc command line, and you see an entry of regsvc in the Group column for this service.

At a Windows PowerShell prompt, you can get the status of configured services just by entering get-service. By default, only the service status, internal name, and display name are shown. Additional properties that you can display include:

- **CanPauseAndContinue.** Indicates whether the service can be paused and resumed
- **CanStop.** Indicates whether you can stop the service
- **DependentServices.** Lists the services that depend on this service
- **ServicesDependedOn.** Lists the services on which this service depends

At a Windows PowerShell prompt, you can get the available details for all services by following these steps:

1. Run all the services on the server and store them in the *$a* variable by entering:

   ```
   $a =  get-service
   ```

2. Use the *–InputObject* parameter to pass the service objects stored in *$a* to get-service and then pass the objects to the format-table cmdlet along with the list of properties you want to see by entering:

   ```
   get-service -inputobject $a | format-table -property Name, DisplayName,
   CanPauseAndContinue, CanStop, DependentServices, ServicesDependedOn, Status
   ```

When you know the service you want to examine, you don't need to use this multistep procedure. Just enter the internal name of the process instead of using *–inputobject $a*. In this example, you list details about the *TermService* process:

```
get-service TermService | format-list -property Name, DisplayName,
CanPauseAndContinue, CanStop, DependentServices, ServicesDependedOn, Status
```

You can enter part of a service name by using an asterisk as a wildcard to match a partial name. In this example, get-service lists any service with a name that starts with *term*:

```
get-service Term* | format-list -property Name, DisplayName,
CanPauseAndContinue, CanStop, DependentServices, ServicesDependedOn, Status
```

To list services by display name, use the *–displayname* parameter and enclose the display name in quotation marks, as shown here:

```
get-service -displayname "Remote Desktop Services" | format-list -property Name,
DisplayName, CanPauseAndContinue, CanStop, DependentServices,
ServicesDependedOn, Status
```

You can use the following cmdlets to manage services:

- **Suspend-Service.** Pauses a service
- **Resume-Service.** Resumes a paused service
- **Start-Service.** Starts a stopped service
- **Stop-Service.** Stops a started service
- **Restart-Service.** Stops and then starts a service

Typically, you use Restart-Service when you suspect a service is having a problem and you want to reset it.

Getting network usage information

On the Performance tab, you can view the current usage of a computer's network connections. When you select the Performance tab, each enabled network connection is listed by name in the left pane along with either a summary view or a summary graph view of current activity. If you select a network connection in the left pane, as shown in Figure 10-14, the main window provides more detailed information about the connection's current usage.

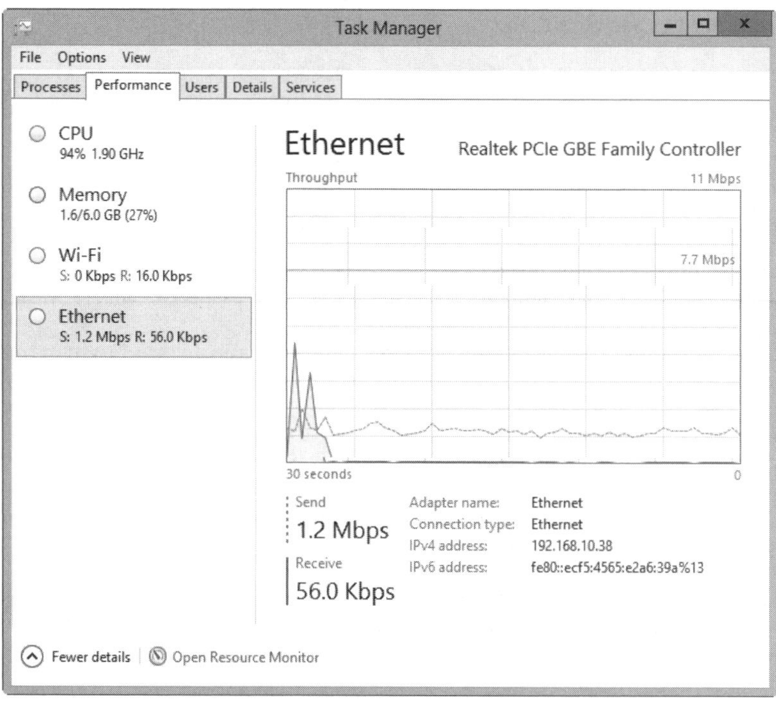

Figure 10-14 Use performance information for network connections to track network activity.

The adapter name is listed above the graph, as is the manufacturer name and model. The graph shows the selected network connection's throughput with send and receive activity plotted separately over time. As the legend below the graph shows, send activity is plotted with a dashed line, and receive activity is plotted with a solid line. Also shown are the current send and receive throughput, scaled according to current activity levels. With this in mind, if there is little current activity, you see activity plotted in Kbps. As activity increases, you might see activity plotted in Mbps or even Gbps.

You can also get more detailed information for a network connection. This information is useful for troubleshooting. If you tap or click the graph and choose View Network Details, you open a dialog box you can use to add columns for summary statistics to the Networking tab. Table 10-2 summarizes the key network statistics available.

Table 10-2 Network statistics and how they can be used

Column Name	Description
Bytes Sent Throughput	Shows the percentage of the current connection bandwidth used by traffic sent from the system.
Bytes Received Throughput	Shows the percentage of the current connection bandwidth used by traffic received by the system.
Bytes Throughput	Shows the percentage of the current connection bandwidth used for all traffic on the network adapter. If this shows 50 percent or more utilization consistently, you'll want to monitor the system more closely and consider adding network adapters.
Bytes Sent	Shows the cumulative total bytes sent on the connection since the system booted.
Bytes Received	Shows the cumulative total bytes received on the connection since the system booted.
Bytes	Shows the cumulative total bytes on the connection since the system booted.
Unicasts	Shows the cumulative number of unicast packets received or sent since the system booted.
Unicasts Sent	Shows the total packets sent by unicast since the system booted.
Unicasts Received	Shows the total packets received by unicast since the system booted.
Nonunicasts	Shows the total number of broadcast packets sent or received since the system booted. Too much broadcast traffic on the network can be an indicator of networking problems. If you see a lot of nonunicast traffic, monitor the amount received during the refresh interval.
Nonunicasts Sent	Shows the total broadcast packets sent since the system booted.
Nonunicasts Received	Shows the total broadcast packets received since the system booted.

Getting information on user and remote user sessions

Members of the Administrators group and any users to whom you specifically grant remote access can connect to systems by using Remote Desktop Services or a Remote Desktop Connection. Both techniques allow users to access systems remotely and use the systems as if they were sitting at the keyboard. In the standard configuration, however, remote access is disabled. You can enable and configure the remote access feature by using Server Manager. In Server Manager, select Local Server in the left pane and then tap or click the Enabled or

Disabled link for Remote Desktop. This opens the System Properties dialog box to the Remote tab, as shown in Figure 10-15.

Figure 10-15 Configure Remote Desktop connections.

In the Remote Desktop panel, select Allow Remote Connections To This Computer. Before you tap or click OK, select the Allow Connections Only From Computers Running Remote Desktop With Network Level Authentication check box if you want to ensure that only more secure connections using Network Level Authentication are permitted. Windows Vista, Windows Server 2008, and later releases of Windows have Network Level Authentication. Most earlier releases of Windows do not.

With Remote Desktop, Windows Server 2012 R2 allows two active console sessions at one time. Console sessions provide full functionality for administration. If you try to log on with a new console session and two others are already logged on to the console, the following happens:

1. You see a prompt stating that too many users are logged on. You can then select a user session to disconnect, or you can tap or click Cancel to exit the session. If you select the Force Disconnect Of This User check box prior to selecting a user, the first user is forcibly disconnected. A user with a Remote Desktop Connection sees a prompt stating, "Your Remote Desktop Services session has ended. A user with a local logon is logged off."

2. If you elect to disconnect a user, that user sees a prompt from Remote Desktop Connection stating that you have requested to disconnect her session. The user has

30 seconds to respond by either tapping or clicking OK to disconnect immediately or tapping or clicking Cancel to deny the request.

3. If 30 seconds elapses without a response, the user is disconnected automatically. A user with a Remote Desktop Connection sees a prompt stating, "Your Remote Desktop Services session has ended. A user with a local logon is logged off."
4. If the user selects Cancel when prompted to disconnect her session, she will see a prompt stating that her request has been denied.

As shown in Figure 10-16, the Users tab lists user connections according to the following factors:

- **User.** The logon name of the user account, such as Wrstanek or Administrator. If you want to see the logon domain and the logon name, select Show Full Account Name on the Options menu.
- **Status.** The status of the connection. This can be either Blank for active connections or Disconnected for connections that have been disconnected.
- **CPU.** Lists the percentage of CPU utilization for the user (across all physical and logical processors). The bold value in the column header represents the total CPU utilization for the server (across all physical and logical processors).
- **Memory.** Lists the total physical memory reserved for the user. The bold value in the column header represents the total physical memory utilization for the server.

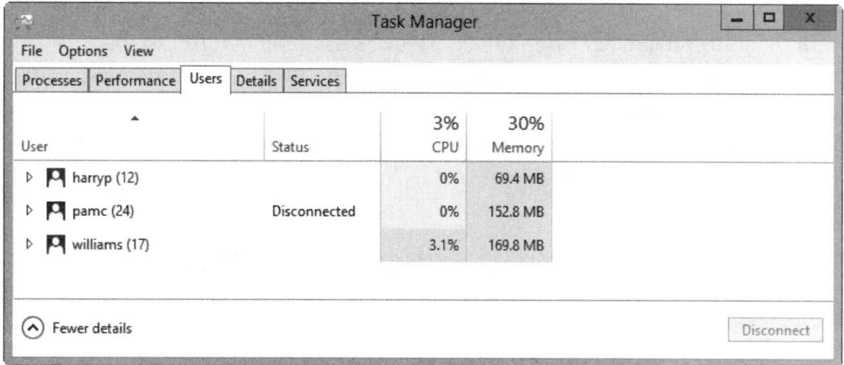

Figure 10-16 Use the Users tab to track and manage user sessions.

CPU and memory utilization details are new for Windows Server 2012 R2 and are helpful for troubleshooting performance issues related to logged-on users. The total utilization value is listed above the column heading, and individual utilization values for each logged-on user are listed below it.

You can add other columns by pressing and holding or right-clicking any column header and then selecting options for the additional columns to display. Other available columns are as follows:

- **ID.** The session ID. All user connections have a unique session ID.
- **Client Name.** The name of the computer from which an active user is connecting. This field is blank for console sessions (and for disconnected sessions).
- **Session.** The type of session. Console is used for users logged on locally. The value is blank for disconnected sessions. Otherwise, this column indicates the connection type and protocol, such as RDP-TCP for a connection using the Remote Desktop Protocol (RDP) with Transmission Control Protocol (TCP) as the transport protocol.

The Users tab can help you determine who is logged on and whether that user's status is active or disconnected. Press and hold or right-click an active session, and you can choose Send Message to send a console message to the user. This message is displayed on the screen of that user's session.

If you must end a user session, you can do this in one of two ways. Pressing and holding or right-clicking the session and choosing Sign Off logs off the user using the normal logoff process. This allows application data and system state information to be saved as it would be during a normal logoff. Pressing and holding or right-clicking the session and choosing Disconnect disconnects a user, but the user's session isn't affected.

You can also connect to or sign off an inactive session. To connect to the session, press and hold or right-click the inactive session and then choose Connect. When prompted, provide the user's password. To log off the user, press and hold or right-click the inactive session and then choose Sign Off. When prompted, confirm that you want to sign out the user, which might cause the user's unsaved data to be lost.

Tracking events and troubleshooting by using Event Viewer

The Windows operating system defines an *event* as any significant occurrence in the operating system or an application that should be recorded for tracking purposes. Informational events can be tracked, as can events that record warnings, errors, and auditing. Critical errors that deserve immediate attention, such as when the server has run out of disk space or memory, are recorded in the logs and displayed on screen.

Understanding the event logs

The Windows service that controls event logging is the Event Log service. When this service is started, events are recorded in one of the available event logs. To work with event logs remotely, remote management and inbound exceptions for Remote Event Log Management must be enabled. For more information, see "Enabling remote management" in Chapter 4, "Managing Windows Server 2012 R2."

Two general types of log files are used:

- **Windows logs.** Logs that the operating system uses to record general system events related to applications, security, setup, and system components
- **Applications and services logs.** Logs that specific applications and services use to record application-specific or service-specific events

Windows logs you see include:

- **Application.** Contains events logged by applications. You find events in this log for Microsoft Exchange Server, SQL Server, Internet Information Services (IIS), and other installed applications. It is also used to record events from printers and, if you configured alert logging, alerts. The default location is %SystemRoot%\System32\Winevt\Logs\Application.Evtx. The default log size is 20,480 KBs.
- **Forwarded Events.** When you configure event forwarding, this log records forwarded events from other servers. The default location is %SystemRoot%\System32\Config\ForwardedEvents.Evtx. The default log size is 20,480 KBs.
- **Security.** Contains events you set for auditing with local or global group policies. Depending on the auditing configuration, you find events for logon, logoff, privilege use, and shutdown in addition to general system events such as the loading of the authentication package by the Local Security Authority (LSA). The default location is %SystemRoot%\System32\Winevt\Logs\Security.Evtx. The default log size is 131,072 KBs on domain controllers and 20,480 KBs on member servers.

  NOTE

  Only administrators are granted access to the Security log by default. If other users need to access the Security log, you must specifically grant them the Manage Auditing And The Security Log user rights. You can learn more about assigning user rights in Chapter 14, "Implementing Active Directory Domain Services," in *Windows Server 2012 R2 Inside Out: Services, Security, & Infrastructure* (Microsoft Press, 2014).

- **Setup.** Records events logged by the operating system or its components during setup and installation. The default location is %SystemRoot%\System32\Winevt\Logs\Setup.Evtx. The default log size is 1028 KBs.
- **System.** Contains events logged by Windows Server and its components. You should routinely check this log for warnings and errors, especially those related to the failure of a service to start at bootup or the improper configuration of a service. The default location is %SystemRoot%\System32\Winevt\Logs\System.Evtx. The default log size is 20,480 KBs.

Applications and services logs you see include:

- **DFS Replication.** Records distributed file system (DFS) replication activities. The default location is %SystemRoot%\System32\Winevt\Logs\Dfs Replication.Evtx. The default log size is 15,168 KBs.
- **Directory Service.** Contains events logged by Active Directory. The primary events relate to the Active Directory database and global catalogs. You find details on database consistency checks, online defragmentation, and updates. The default location is %SystemRoot%\System32\Winevt\Logs\Directory Service.Evtx.
- **DNS Server.** Contains Domain Name System (DNS) queries, responses, and other DNS activities. You might also find details on activities that relate to DNS integration with Active Directory. The default location is %SystemRoot%\System32\Winevt\Logs\DNS Server.Evtx. The default log size is 16,384 KBs.
- **File Replication Service.** Contains events logged by the File Replication Service, a service used to replicate Active Directory changes to other domain controllers. You find details on any important events that took place while a domain controller attempted to update other domain controllers. The default location is %SystemRoot%\System32\Winevt\Logs\File Replication Service.Evtx. The default log size is 20,480 KBs.
- **Hardware Events.** When hardware subsystem event reporting is configured, records hardware events reported to the operating system. The default location is %SystemRoot%\System32\Config\HardwareEvents.Evtx. The default log size is 20,480 KBs.
- **Microsoft\Windows.** Logs that track events related to specific Windows services and features. Logs are organized by component type and event category. Operational logs track events generated by the standard operations of the related component. In some cases, you see supplemental logs for analysis, debugging, and recording administration-related tasks. Most of the related logs have a fixed default log size of 1,028 KBs.

By default, the logs are sized as appropriate for the type of system you are working with and its configuration. In a standard configuration of Windows Server 2012 R2, most logs are sized as listed previously. As shown, most logs have a fairly large maximum size. This includes the DNS Server, System, and Application logs. Because they are less critical, the Directory Service and File Replication Service logs on domain controllers have a maximum size of 1,028 KBs. Because the Security log is so important, it is usually configured with a maximum size of 131,072 KBs on domain controllers and 20,480 KBs on member servers. Primarily, this is to allow the server to record a complete security audit trail when the server is under attack and a large number of security events are generated.

Windows Server 2012 R2 logs are configured to overwrite old events as needed by default. So, when the log reaches its maximum size, the operating system overwrites old events with new events. If desired, you can have Windows automatically archive logs. In this configuration, when the maximum file size is reached, Windows archives the events by saving a copy of the current log in the default directory. Windows then creates a new log for storing current events.

You can also configure logs so that Windows never overwrites events. However, the problem with doing it that way is that when the maximum size is reached, events can't be overwritten, and the system generates an error message telling you that such and such event log is full each time it tries to write an event—and you can quickly get to where dozens of these errors are displayed.

NOTE

You can also control the log configuration through Group Policy. This means changes you make in Group Policy, in turn, could change the maximum log size and which action to take when the maximum log size is reached. For more information about Group Policy, see *Windows Server 2012 R2 Inside Out: Services, Security, & Infrastructure*.

Accessing the event logs and viewing events

You can work with event logs in several ways. When you are working with Server Manager and select the Local Server node, the All Servers node, or a server group node, the right pane will have an Events panel. When you select the server you want to work with in the Servers panel, its events are listed in the Events panel, as shown in Figure 10-17. You can use this panel as follows:

- For a server you are logged on to locally, you can use the Events panel in the Local Server node or the All Servers node to view recent warning and error events in the application and system logs.
- Automatically created server group nodes are organized by server roles, such as Active Directory Domain Services (AD DS) or DNS, and you can view recent error and warning events in logs related to the server role if applicable. Not all roles have associated logs, but some roles, such as AD DS, have multiple associated logs.

- For custom server groups that you or other administrators create, you can use the related Events panel to view recent warning and error events in the application and system logs.

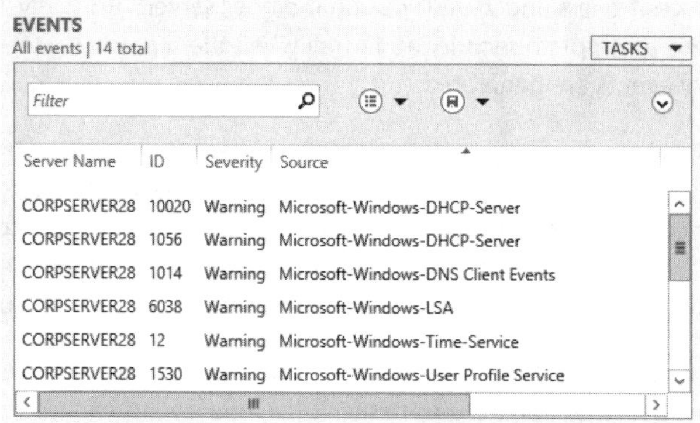

Figure 10-17 Track errors and warnings for servers that have been added for management in Server Manager.

When you want to review all tracked events, you use Event Viewer, shown in Figure 10-18. Event Viewer is available from the Tools menu in Server Manager as a preconfigured console of the same name or as a standard add-in for the Computer Management console. To open Computer Management and access its Event Viewer add-in, select Computer Management from the Tools menu in Server Manager and then select Event Viewer under System Tools.

Event Viewer has custom views and standard views of logs. By using the custom Administrative Events view, you can view all errors and warnings for all logs. By using your own custom views, you can create views to expose particular types and categories of events from any logs you want to track. You can also access event logs directly to view all the events they contain.

You can use the following techniques to work with logs and custom views:

- To view all errors and warnings for all logs, expand Custom Views and then select Administrative Events. In the main pane, you should see a list of all warning and error events for the server.

- To view all errors and warnings for a specific server role, expand Custom Views, expand Server Roles, and then select the role to view. In the main pane, you should see a list of all events for the selected role.

- To view summary information for Windows logs, select the Windows Logs node. You then see a list of available logs by name and type along with the number of events and log size.

- To view summary information for Applications and Services logs, select the Applications And Services Logs node. You then see a list of available logs by name and type along with the number of events and log size.
- To view events in a specific log, expand the Windows Logs node, the Applications And Services Logs node, or both nodes. Select the log you want to view, such as Application or System.

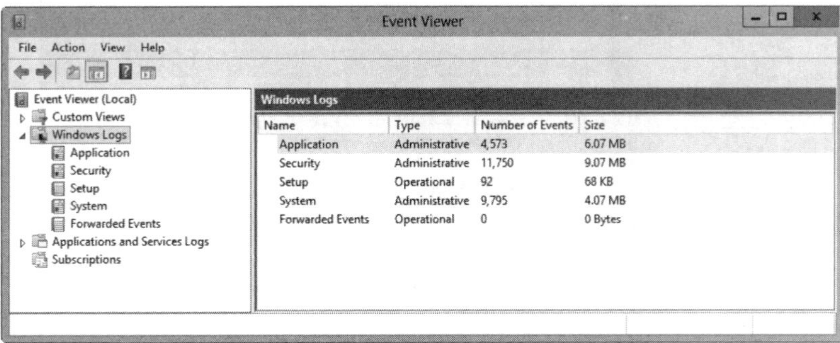

Figure 10-18 The main view in Event Viewer lists the available logs and shows their current size.

As Figure 10-19 shows, individual event entries provide an overview of the event that took place. Each event is recorded according to the date and time the event took place and by the event level. For all the logs except Security, the event levels are classified as Information, Warning, or Error. For the Security log, the event levels are classified as Audit Success or Audit Failure. These event levels have the following meanings:

- **Information.** Generally relates to a successful action such as the success of a service starting up. If you configured Alert logging, the alerts are also recorded with this event type to show they've been triggered.
- **Warning.** Describes events that aren't critical but could be useful in preventing future system problems. Most warnings should be examined to determine whether a preventive measure should be taken.
- **Error.** Indicates a noncritical error or significant problem occurred, such as the failure of a service to start. All errors should be examined to determine what corrective measure should be taken to prevent the error from recurring.
- **Critical.** Indicates a critical error or highly significant problem occurred, such as the Cluster service shutting down because a quorum was lost. All critical errors should be examined to determine what corrective measure should be taken to prevent the critical error from recurring.

- **Audit Success.** Describes an audited security event that completed as requested, such as when a user logs on or logs off successfully.
- **Audit Failure.** Describes an audited security event that didn't complete as requested, such as when a user tries to log on and fails. Audit failure events can be useful in tracking down security issues.

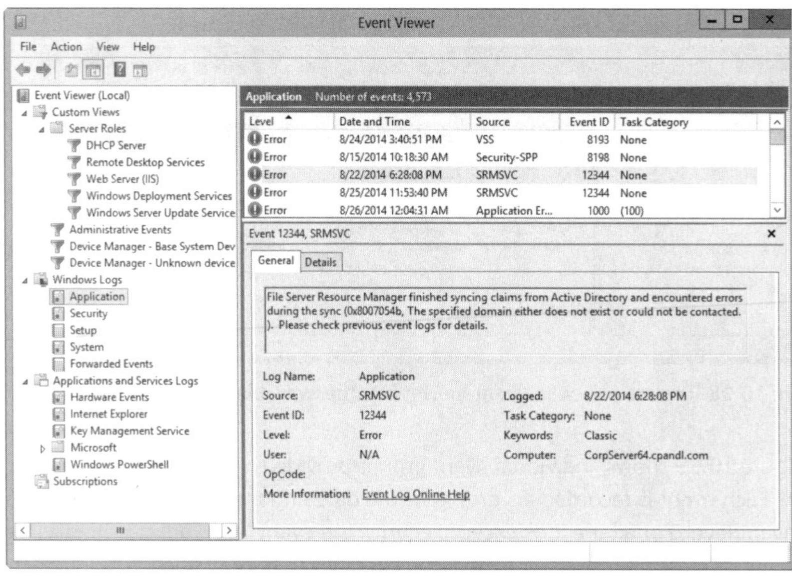

Figure 10-19 Events are logged according to the date and time they occurred and by type.

NOTE

Any attempt by users, services, or applications to perform a task for which they don't have appropriate permissions can be recorded as an audit failure. If someone is trying to break into a system, you might see a large number of audit failure events. If a service or application doesn't have the permissions it needs to perform certain tasks, you might also see a large number of audit failure events.

Other pertinent information recorded with an event includes the event source, event ID, task category, user, and computer. The Source column lists the application, service, or component that logged the event. The Task Category column details the category of the event and is sometimes used to describe the event further. The Event ID column provides an identifier for the specific event that occurred. You can sometimes look up events in the Microsoft Knowledge Base to get more detailed information.

When you select an event, Event Viewer shows additional details in the lower pane, including a general description of the event and other fields of information. The User field shows the name of the user who was logged on when the event occurred (if applicable). If a server process triggered the event, the user name usually is that of the special identity that caused the event. This includes the special identities Anonymous Logon, Local Service, Network Service, and System. Although events can have no user associated with them, they can also be associated with a specific user who was logged on at the time the event occurred.

The Computer field shows the name of the computer that caused the event to occur. Because you are working with a log from a particular computer, this is usually the account name of that computer. However, this is not always the case. Some events can be triggered because of other computers on the network. Some events triggered by the local machine are stored with the computer name as MACHINENAME. For some events, any binary data or error code generated by the event is available on the Details tab.

You can double-tap or double-click any event to open its Properties dialog box. (See Figure 10-20.) The Properties dialog box provides the information that is available in the details pane and a Copy button you can click to copy the event data to the Clipboard. Most of the event descriptions aren't easy to understand, so if you need a little help deciphering the event, tap or click Copy. You can then paste the event description into an email message to another administrator.

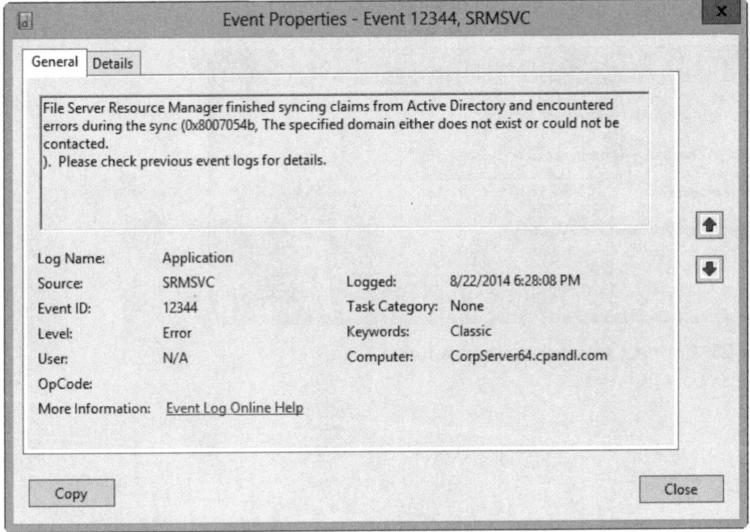

Figure 10-20 Event details include a description of the event and, in some cases, binary data generated by the event.

CHAPTER 10

NOTE

Within every event description is a Help And Support Center link that you can click. This link provides access to the Microsoft website, where you can query for any additional information that might be available on the event.

Viewing event logs on remote systems

You can use Event Viewer to view events on other computers on your network. Start Event Viewer, press and hold or right-click Event Viewer (Local) in the left pane, and then choose Connect To Another Computer. In the Select Computer dialog box, shown in Figure 10-21, type the domain name or Internet Protocol (IP) address of the computer for which you want to view the event log and then tap or click OK. Or you can tap or click Browse to search for the computer you want to use. If you need to specify logon credentials, select the Connect As Another User check box and then tap or click the Set User button. Afterward, type the user name and password to use for logon and then tap or click OK.

NOTE

Keep in mind that you must be logged on as an administrator or be a member of the Administrators group to view events on a remote computer. You must also configure Windows Firewall on the local computer to allow your outbound connection and on the remote computer to allow your inbound connection.

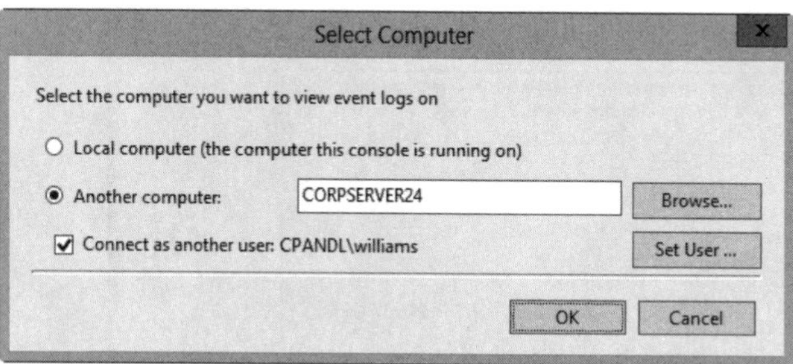

Figure 10-21 Connect to a remote computer.

Inside OUT

Setting a remote computer as the focus for a management tool

By default, Microsoft Management Consoles (MMCs) connect to the local computer. By pressing and holding or right-clicking the console root in either the Computer Management console or the Event Viewer console and selecting Connect To Another Computer, you can use the options provided in the Select Computer dialog box to connect to a remote computer. Server Manager provides a shortcut for remote management. Here, select All Servers in the left pane and then press and hold or right-click the remote server to which you want to connect in the Servers panel. You then see a list of tools you can open and connect automatically to the selected remote computer.

Sorting, finding, and filtering events

Event Viewer provides several ways for you to organize and search for events in the logs. You can sort events based on date or other stored information. You can search a particular event log for specific events and view events one at a time. You can also filter events so that only the specific events you want to see are shown.

Sorting the event logs

By default, logs are sorted so that the newest events are listed first. If you'd rather see the oldest events first, you can do this by tapping or clicking View, pointing to Sort By, and then selecting Date And Time, or you can just tap or click the Date And Time column header. This change must be made for each log in which you want to see the oldest events first.

You can also sort events based on information in other columns. For example, if you wanted to sort the events based on the event level, you would tap or click the Level column header.

Searching the event logs

By using the Find feature, you can search for events within a selected log and view matching events one at a time. Say, for instance, a Microsoft Knowledge Base article says to look for an event with such and such an event source, and you want to search for it quickly. You can use the Find feature to do this.

To search, press and hold or right-click an event log and select Find. In the Find dialog box, type the search text to match and then tap or click Find Next. The first event that matches the search criteria is highlighted in the log. You can double-tap or double-click the event to get more detailed information or tap or click Find Next to find the next match.

Filtering the event logs

The Find option works well if you want to perform quick searches, such as for a single event of a specific type. If you want to perform an extended search, however, such as when you want to review all events of a particular type, there's a better way to do it, and that's to create a filtered view so that only the specific events you want to see are shown.

Windows creates several filtered views of the event logs for you automatically. In Event Viewer, filtered views are listed under the Custom Views node. When you select the Administrative Events node, you see a list of all errors and warnings for all logs. When you expand the Server Roles node and then select a role-specific view, you see a list of all events for the selected role.

You can create and work with filtered views in several ways:

- Create a custom view by filtering the events in a specific log and save this filtered view for later use. Just press and hold or right-click the log and select Create Custom View. This opens the Create Custom View dialog box, as shown in Figure 10-22. Choose the filter options you want to use, as described in Table 10-3, and then tap or click OK. If you are trying to create a filter for more than 10 logs (and really want to do this), tap or click Yes when warned about the possible performance impact. In the Save Filter To Custom View dialog box, type a name and description for the view. Select where to save the custom view. By default, custom views are saved under the Custom view node. You can create a new node by tapping or clicking New Folder, entering the name of the new folder, and then tapping or clicking OK. Tap or click OK to close the Save Filter To Custom View dialog box.

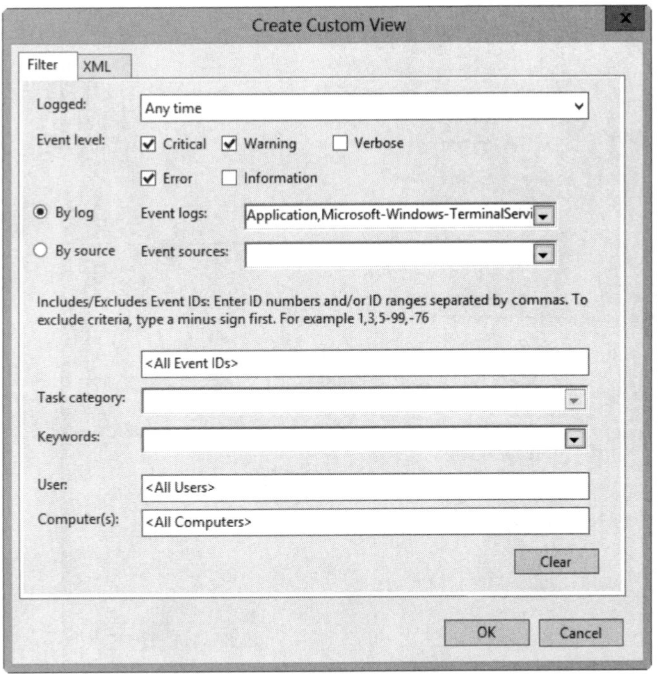

Figure 10-22 Create a custom view for an event log.

- Create a temporary view by filtering the events in a specific log. Just select the log and then press and hold or right-click and select Filter Current Log. This opens the Filter Current Log dialog box, as shown in Figure 10-23. Choose the filter options you want to use, as described in Table 10-3, and then tap or click OK. After you apply the filter, only events with the options you specify are displayed in the selected event log. For the rest of the current Event Viewer session, the filter is applied to the selected log, and you know this because the upper portion of the main pane shows you are working with a filtered log.

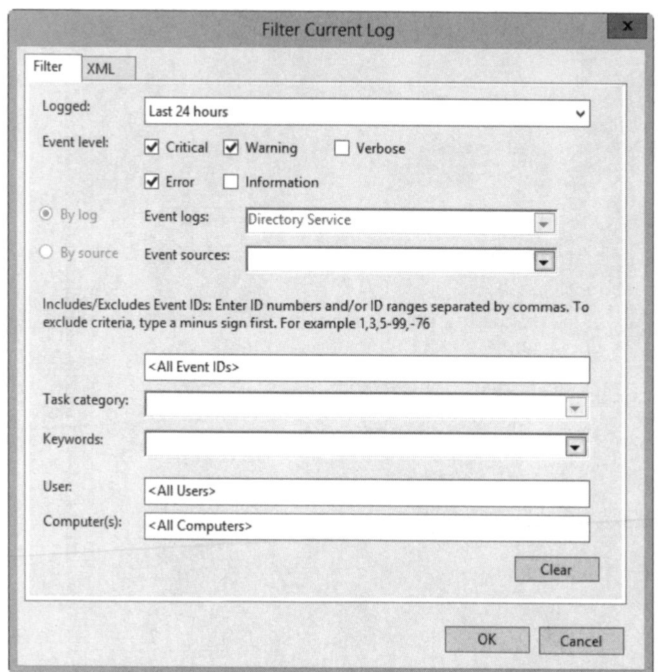

Figure 10-23 Create a temporary view.

Set filter options

You can set as many filter options as you want to narrow the results. Keep in mind, however, that each filter option you apply sets a search criterion that must be matched for an event to be displayed. The options are cumulative, so an event must match all filter options.

Table 10-3 Find and filter options for event logging

Option	Description
Computer	Includes all events associated with a particular computer. Usually, this is the name of the computer whose logs you are working with.
Event ID	Includes or excludes events with the event IDs you specify. Enter ID numbers or ID ranges separated by commas. To exclude an event, enter a minus sign before the event ID.
Event Level	Enables you to include or exclude events by level. The most important event levels are warnings, which indicate that something might pose a future problem and might need to be examined, and errors, which indicate a fatal error or significant problem occurred.

Option	Description
Event Sources	Includes events only from specified sources, such as an application, service, or component that logged the event.
Event Logs	Includes events only from specified logs. When working with a custom log view, the log you press and hold or right-click is selected automatically, and you can't choose additional logs.
Logged	With filters, all events from the first to the last are displayed by default. You can choose to include events from the Last Hour, Last 12 Hours, Last 24 Hours, Last 7 Days, Last 30 Days, or a custom range.
Task Category	Includes events only within a given category. The categories available change based on the event source you choose.
User	Includes events associated with a particular user account that was logged on when the event was triggered. Server processes can log events with the special identities Anonymous Logon, Local Service, Network Service, and System. Not all events have a user associated with them.

You can apply a filter to a custom view as well. To filter a custom view, press and hold or right-click the view and then select Filter Current Custom View. Choose the filter options you want to use and then tap or click OK. For the rest of the current Event Viewer session, the filter is applied to the selected view, and you know this because the upper portion of the main pane shows you are working with a filtered view.

If you later want to clear a filter that is applied to a view or log, press and hold or right-click the log and select Clear Filter. Another option is to save the filtered view as a custom view so that you can access it the next time you open Event Viewer. To do this, press and hold or right-click the filtered log or custom view and select Save Filter To Custom View. Afterward, type a name and description for the view. Select where to save the custom view. By default, custom views are saved under the Custom view node. You can create a new node by tapping or clicking New Folder, entering the name of the new folder, and then tapping or clicking OK. Tap or click OK to close the Save Filter To Custom View dialog box.

Archiving event logs

In most cases, you want to have several months' worth of log data available in case you must go back through the logs to troubleshoot a problem. One way to do this, of course, is to set the log size so that it is large enough to accommodate this. However, this usually isn't practical because individual logs can grow quite large. So, as part of your routine, you might want to archive the log files on critical systems periodically, such as for domain controllers or application servers.

To archive logs automatically, press and hold or right-click the log and select Properties. In the Properties dialog box, select Archive The Log When Full, Do Not Overwrite Events. To create a log archive manually, press and hold or right-click the log in the left pane of Event Viewer and then select Save All Events As. In the Save As dialog box, select a directory and a log file name. Event Log (*.evtx) is the default file type. This saves the file in event log format for access in Event Viewer, but it can be used only when saving logs from the local computer. You can also select .txt to save the log in tab-delimited text format, such as for accessing it in a text editor. For importing the log data into a spreadsheet or database, select .csv to save the log in comma-delimited text format. Select .xml to save the log in Extensible Markup Language (XML) format. After you select a log format, tap or click Save.

Logs saved in Event Log format (.evtx) can be reopened in Event Viewer at any time. To do this, press and hold or right-click the Event Viewer node in the left pane of Event Viewer and choose Open Saved Log. Use the Open Saved Log dialog box to select a directory and a log file. By default, the Event Log Files format is selected in the File Name list. This ensures that logs saved as .evtx, .evt, and .etl are listed. You can also filter the list by selecting a specific file type. When you tap or click Open, Windows opens the Open Saved Log dialog box. Type a name and description for the saved log. Select where to open the log in Event Viewer. By default, saved logs are listed under Saved Logs. You can create a new node by tapping or clicking New Folder, entering the name of the new folder, and then tapping or clicking OK. Tap or click Open to close the Open Saved Log dialog box. Windows loads the saved event log into Event Viewer and adds a related entry to the list of available logs in the left pane, as shown in Figure 10-24.

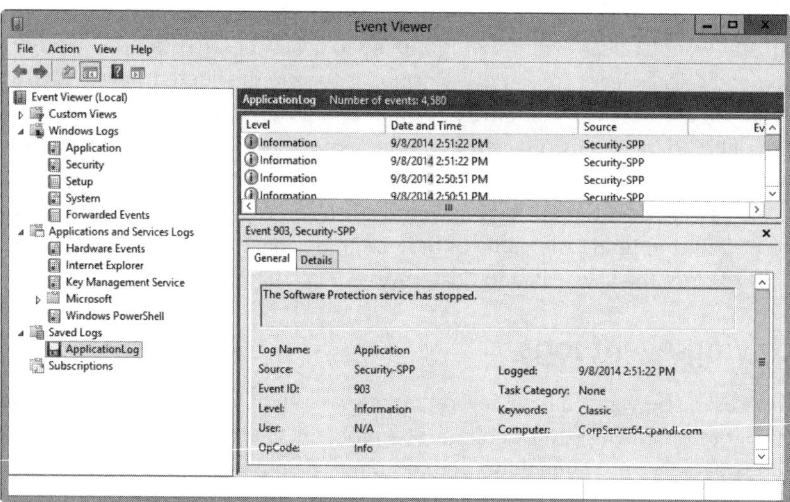

Figure 10-24 Archived logs can be reopened in Event Viewer.

If you later want to remove the saved log from Event Viewer, press and hold or right-click the log and select Delete. When prompted to confirm, tap or click Yes. The saved log file still exists in its original location on the hard disk but no longer is displayed in Event Viewer.

Tracking events using Windows PowerShell

When you are working with a specific system or trying to track down issues, Event Viewer is an excellent tool to use and should be your tool of choice. As you've seen, Event Viewer can also be used to access logs on remote systems. No single command-line tool included with Windows Server 2012 R2 provides the same level of functionality, although the Windows PowerShell cmdlet get-eventlog does come close. You can use get-eventlog to obtain detailed information from the event logs.

Because get-eventlog is a text-based rather than a graphical utility, it will, in most cases, use fewer system resources than Event Viewer. On systems for which you are very concerned about resource usage and the possibility of bogging down a system through your interactive logon, you might initially want to track events by using get-eventlog.

As Figure 10-25 shows, the standard output of get-eventlog provides the essential information about events. To run get-eventlog, access a Windows PowerShell prompt and then type **get-eventlog** followed by the name of the event log you want to examine, such as **application**. If the log name contains spaces, you must enclose the log name in quotation marks, such as **get-eventlog "directory service"**.

```
Windows PowerShell
PS C:\Users\williams> get-eventlog application

   Index Time          EntryType   Source                 InstanceID Message
   ----- ----          ---------   ------                 ---------- -------
    4580 Sep 08 14:51  0           Software Protecti...   1073742727 The Software Protection service has stopped....
    4579 Sep 08 14:51  Information Software Protecti...   1073758208 Successfully scheduled Software Protection serv...
    4578 Sep 08 14:50  0           Software Protecti...   1073742726 The Software Protection service has started....
    4577 Sep 08 14:50  Information Software Protecti...   2147484685 Time-based license remaining validity time 2347...
    4576 Sep 08 14:50  Information Software Protecti...   1073742827 The Software Protection service has completed l...
    4575 Sep 08 14:50  Information Software Protecti...   1073742890 Initialization status for service objects....
    4574 Sep 08 14:50  Information Software Protecti...   1073742724 The Software Protection service is starting....
    4573 Sep 08 14:21  0           Software Protecti...   1073742727 The Software Protection service has stopped....
    4572 Sep 08 14:21  Information Software Protecti...   1073758208 Successfully scheduled Software Protection serv...
    4571 Sep 08 14:20  0           Software Protecti...   1073742726 The Software Protection service has started....
    4570 Sep 08 14:20  Information Software Protecti...   2147484685 Time-based license remaining validity time 2348...
    4569 Sep 08 14:20  Information Software Protecti...   1073742827 The Software Protection service has completed l...
    4568 Sep 08 14:20  Information Software Protecti...   1073742890 Initialization status for service objects....
    4567 Sep 08 14:20  Information Software Protecti...   1073742724 The Software Protection service is starting....
    4566 Sep 08 13:51  0           Software Protecti...   1073742727 The Software Protection service has stopped....
    4565 Sep 08 13:51  Information Software Protecti...   1073758208 Successfully scheduled Software Protection serv...
    4564 Sep 08 13:50  0           Software Protecti...   1073742726 The Software Protection service has started....
    4563 Sep 08 13:50  Information Software Protecti...   2147484685 Time-based license remaining validity time 2348...
    4562 Sep 08 13:50  Information Software Protecti...   1073742827 The Software Protection service has completed l...
    4561 Sep 08 13:50  Information Software Protecti...   1073742890 Initialization status for service objects....
    4560 Sep 08 13:50  Information Software Protecti...   1073742724 The Software Protection service is starting....
    4559 Sep 08 13:34  Information Desktop Window Ma...   1073750833 The Desktop Window Manager has exited with code...
    4558 Sep 08 13:33  Information Desktop Window Ma...   1073750833 The Desktop Window Manager has exited with code...
```

Figure 10-25 Use get-eventlog to work with event logs at the command line.

Any Windows log or Applications And Services log that you can work with in Event Viewer is accessible at the command line. When you follow get-eventlog with the log name, the *–logname* parameter is implied. You can also specify the *–logname* parameter directly, as shown in this example:

```
get-eventlog -logname security
```

By default, get-eventlog returns every event in the specified event log from the newest to the oldest. In most cases, this is simply too much information, and you need to filter the events to get a usable amount of data. One way to filter the event log is to specify that you want to see

CHAPTER 10

details about only the newest events. For example, you might want to see only the 50 or 500 newest events in a log.

By using the *–newest* parameter, you can return only the newest events. The following example lists the 50 newest events in the security log:

```
get-eventlog security -newest 50
```

As shown in Figure 10-25, get-eventlog displays several properties in column format, including Index, TimeGenerated (listed with the column heading Time), Source, InstanceID, EntryType (listed with the column heading Type), and Message. To help make sense of the logs, you might want to group events by type, source, or event ID. When you group events by type, you can more easily separate informational events from critical, warning, and error events. When you group by source, you can more easily track events from specific sources. When you group by event ID, you can more easily correlate the recurrence of specific events.

You can group events by *source*, *eventid*, *entrytype*, and *timegenerated*, using the following technique:

1. Get the events you want to work with and store them in the *$e* variable by entering:

   ```
   $e = get-eventlog -newest 500 -logname application
   ```

2. Use the group-object cmdlet to group the event objects stored in *$e* by a specified property. In this example, you group by *eventid*:

   ```
   $e | group-object -property eventid
   ```

Another way to work with events is to sort them according to a specific property. You can sort by *source*, *eventid*, *entrytype*, or *timegenerated*, using the following technique:

1. Get the events you want to work with and store them in the *$e* variable by entering:

   ```
   $e = get-eventlog -newest 100 -logname application
   ```

2. Use the sort-object cmdlet to sort the event objects stored in *$e* by a specified property. In this example, you sort by *eventtype*:

   ```
   $e | sort-object -property entrytype
   ```

Finally, you might also want to match specific text in a specified property. For example, you might want to return only error events. To do this, you would search the *EntryType* property for occurrences of the word *error*. Here is an example:

1. Get the events you want to work with and store them in the *$e* variable by entering:

   ```
   $e = get-eventlog -newest 500 -logname application
   ```

2. Use the where-object cmdlet to search for specific text in a named property of the event objects stored in *$e*. In this example, you match events with the *error* entry type:

   ```
   $e | where-object {$_.EntryType -match "error"}
   ```

The where-object cmdlet uses a search algorithm that is not case sensitive, meaning you could enter Error, error, or ERROR to match error events. You can also search for warning, critical, and information events. Because where-object considers partial text matches valid, you don't want to enter the full event type. You could also search for *info*, *crit*, or *warn*, as shown here:

```
$e = get-eventlog -newest 500 -logname application
$e | where-object {$_.EntryType -match "warn"}
```

You can also use where-object with other event object properties. The following example searches for event sources containing the text *.NET*:

```
$e = get-eventlog -newest 500 -logname application
$e | where-object {$_.Source -match ".NET"}
```

The following example searches for event ID 1101:

```
$e = get-eventlog -newest 500 -logname application
$e | where-object {$_.Source -match "1101"}
```

Using subscriptions and forwarded events

In an enterprise, you might also want servers to forward specific events to central event-logging servers. To do this, you configure and enable event forwarding on the applicable servers, and then you create subscriptions to the forwarded events on your central event-logging server or servers.

In a domain, you can configure forwarding and collection of forwarded events by following these steps:

1. To configure forwarding, log on to all source computers and type **winrm quickconfig** at an elevated command prompt. This creates a WinRM listener on HTTP://* to accept WS-Man requests to any IP address on the source computer. When prompted to confirm, press **Y**.

2. To configure collection, type **wecutil qc** at an elevated command prompt and then press **Y** when prompted. This starts the Windows Event Collector Service and configures this service to use the delayed-start mode.

3. Add the computer account of the collector computer to the local Administrators group on each of the source computers. In Local Users And Computers, press and hold or right-click Administrators and select Add To Group. In the Properties dialog box, tap or click Add. In the Select Users, Computers, Or Groups dialog box, tap or click Object

Types. In the Object Types dialog box, select Computers and then tap or click OK. In the Select Users, Computers, Or Groups dialog box, type the account name of the collector computer and then tap or click OK twice. Repeat this process as necessary.

You can create a subscription on the central logging server to collect forwarded events by following these steps:

1. Open Event Viewer and connect to the central event-logging server. Afterward, press and hold or right-click the Subscriptions node and select Create Subscription.

2. In the Subscription Properties dialog box, shown in Figure 10-26, type a name for the subscription, such as **All File Servers**. Optionally, enter a description.

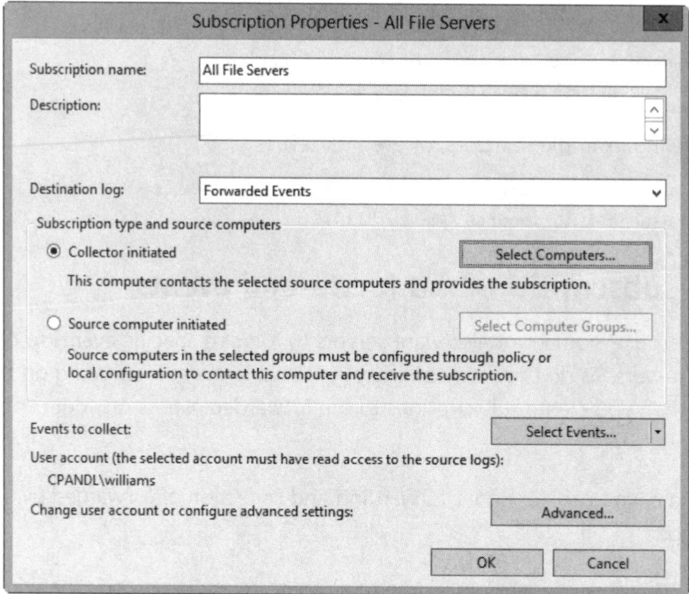

Figure 10-26 Create a subscription to collect forwarded events.

3. The Forwarded Events log is selected as the destination log by default. Generally, this is the log you'll want to use.

4. Collector-initiated event forwarding is the easiest to configure and is the default setting. To specify the computers that forward events to the server, tap or click Select Computers. In the Computers dialog box, tap or click Add Domain Computers. In the Select Computer dialog box, type the account name of a computer that is forwarding events and then tap or click OK twice. Repeat this process as necessary.

5. Tap or click Select Events. In the Query Filter dialog box, select the filter options and logs to use and then tap or click OK.

If you added the computer account of the collector computer to the local Administrators group on each of the source computers, you can use this machine account to collect events. Alternatively, you can use the permissions of a specific user account by doing the following:

1. Tap or click Advanced. In the Advanced Subscription Settings dialog box, select Specific User and then tap or click User And Password, as shown in Figure 10-27.
    a. Use the dialog box provided to enter the credentials for an account that has read access to the source logs on the source computers. Click OK to close the Credentials dialog box.
    b. Optionally, optimize event delivery to minimize bandwidth usage or to minimize latency.
    c. Optionally, set the transfer protocol and port. With HTTP, which is not secure, the default port is 5985. With HTTPS, which is secure, the default port is 5986.
    d. Click OK to close the Advanced Subscription Settings dialog box.

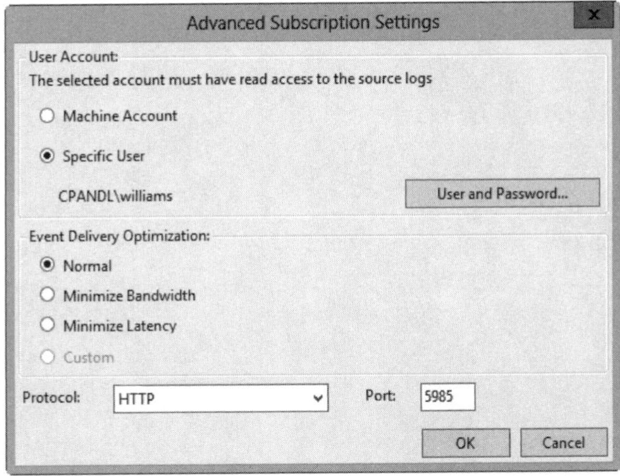

Figure 10-27 Configure a specific user for collection.

    e. Tap or click OK to create the subscription. Now when you access the destination log, you see the forwarded events.

CHAPTER 11

Comprehensive performance analysis and logging

Microsoft Windows Server 2012 R2 provides many tools to help you track performance. In the previous chapter, you looked at tuning performance through configuration settings; using Task Manager to track running processes, users, and network utilization; and using the event logs to track important occurrences the operating system records. Although these tools are excellent and do their jobs well, you might need to dig deeper to establish comprehensive performance baselines, diagnose complex system problems, and optimize system performance.

The key comprehensive monitoring and optimization tools and features available include the following:

- **Performance Monitor.** Can be used to track and display performance information in real time. It gathers information on any performance parameters you configured for monitoring and presents it using a graphical display.
- **Reliability Monitor.** Tracks changes to the system and compares them to changes in system stability, thus giving you a graphical representation of the relationship between changes in the system configuration and changes in system stability.
- **Resource Monitor.** Displays detailed information about resource usage for the server so you can isolate resources that specific processes use.
- **Data Collector Sets and Reports.** Can be considered the logging counterpart to Performance Monitor. By using data collector sets, you can record performance information in real time and store it in a log so that it can be analyzed in a report later.
- **Performance Counter Alerts.** Can be used to notify users when certain events occur or when certain performance thresholds are reached. For example, you could configure a performance alert that lets you know when the C drive is running low on free space or the central processing unit (CPU) is operating at 95 percent or more of capacity.

Before discussing each of these tools in turn, let's look at how you can establish performance baselines.

Establishing performance baselines

Resource Monitor, Reliability Monitor, and Performance Monitor are the tools of choice for monitoring a system's reliability and performance. One of the key reasons for tracking performance information is to establish a baseline for a computer that enables you to compare past performance with current performance. There are several types of baselines you can use, including the following:

- **Postinstallation baselines.** A postinstallation baseline is a performance level that is meant to represent the way a computer performs after installing all the roles, role services, features, and applications that will be used on the system.
- **Typical usage baselines.** A typical usage baseline is a performance level that is meant to represent average usage conditions and serve as a starting point against which you can measure future performance.
- **Test baselines.** A test baseline is a performance level that you use during testing of a system. In the test lab, you might want to simulate peak usage loads and test how the system performs under these conditions.

Although it is important to obtain postinstallation and typical usage baseline values, the more important of the two is the typical usage baseline. This is the baseline you get when you simulate user loads or when users actually start working with a server. Ideally, it represents typical or average loads. After you have a typical usage baseline, you can gather information in the future to try to determine how resource usage has changed and how the computer is performing comparatively.

To be able to establish a baseline, you must collect a representative set of performance statistics. By that, I mean collect the data that you actually need to determine resource usage and performance in future scenarios. If possible, you should also collect several data samples at the same time each day over a period of several days. This gives you a more meaningful data sample.

You must work to keep the baseline in sync with how the server is used. As you install new roles, role services, features, and applications, you must establish new baselines. This ensures that future comparisons with the baseline are accurate and that they use the most current system configuration to determine how resource usage has changed and how the computer is performing comparatively.

Tracking per-process resource usage

As discussed in Chapter 10, "Performance monitoring and tuning," you can use Task Manager to determine the overall utilization of system resources. The Processes and Details tabs in Task Manager provide information about resources being used by running processes. What's missing from Task Manager, however, is the ability to take a deep look at how processes are using resources, and this deep-look capability is exactly what Resource Monitor provides.

You can start Resource Monitor by selecting the related option on the Tools menu in Server Manager. Alternatively, type **Resource Monitor** in the Everywhere Search box and press Enter.

> NOTE
>
> **As with any locally installed administrative tool, Resource Monitor can only be found in an Everywhere Search when you've selected the Show Administrative Tools option. If this option isn't enabled, you can enable it from the Start screen. On Start, press the Windows key+C to display the Charm bar and then select Settings. On the Settings panel, select Tiles and then select Show Administrative Tools.**

When you start Resource Monitor, shown in Figure 11-1, you see that the statistics provided are organized into five general categories:

- Overview
- CPU
- Memory
- Disk
- Network

Each of these categories can be used for comprehensive performance analysis, and in the sections that follow, I show you how.

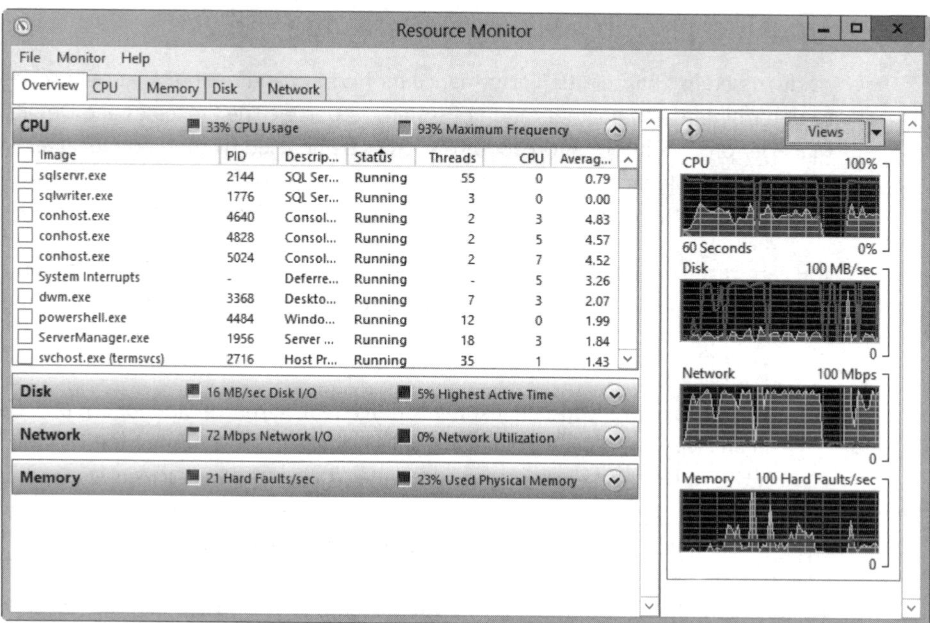

Figure 11-1 Use Resource Monitor to get detailed information about per-process resource utilization.

Getting an overview of resource utilization

The Overview tab in Resource Monitor, shown in Figure 11-2, provides a detailed overview of resource utilization. Top-level utilization statistics are tracked in the graphs and on the panel bars. In accordance with the legend shown on the panel bars, the values are plotted in either green or blue on the corresponding graph. The statistics tracked include the following:

- % CPU usage
- CPU maximum frequency
- Disk I/O bytes per second
- Disk % highest active time
- Network I/O bytes per second
- % Network utilization
- Memory hard faults per second
- % Physical memory used

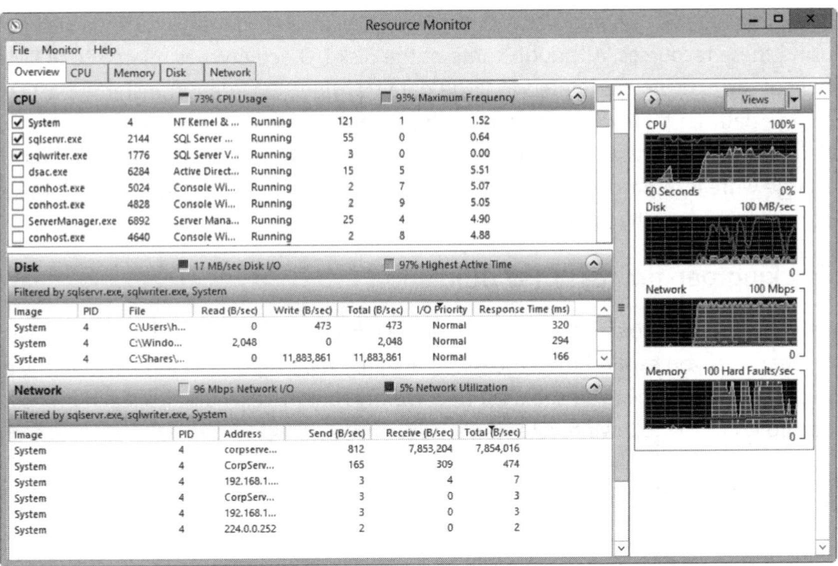

Figure 11-2 The Overview tab in Resource Monitor provides an overview of resource utilization.

At first glance, the information provided seems similar to that available in Task Manager. What's different, however, is that when you select one or more processes on the CPU panel, you see related utilization statistics for the processes on the Disk panel, Network panel, and Memory panel. You also see related activity plotted in orange on the CPU, Disk, Network, and Memory graphs.

NOTE

The CPU, Disk, Network, and Memory panels show a subset of the information available on the related tabs. Your process selections are applied globally so that you can determine exactly how the selected processes are using CPU, disk, network, and memory resources.

In the example, I selected three processes for tracking: sqlservr.exe, System, and sqlwriter.exe. I chose these processes because I already determined in Task Manager that these were some of the most active processes on the server, and I wanted to determine how these processes were affecting the server. I quickly learned that these processes weren't affecting the CPU nearly as much as I thought. Although the processor utilization on the server was performing well at about 70 percent, these processes seemed to be using few actual CPU resources. However, they were high consumers of disk and network resources (and, in fact, accounted for nearly all the disk and network activity).

By examining the disk and network activity, I was able to identify exactly which activities were using these resources. Although some of the disk I/O activity was related to SQL Server, the bulk of the activity was related to large data transfers. One data transfer in particular involved a large data set that was being moved from another file server to the server I was analyzing. You can see this in the three entries under Disk and the first entry under Network. Under Disk, a large write is in progress for the C:\Shares folder. Under Network, a large data set is being received from another server.

Tracking per-process CPU utilization

The CPU tab in Resource Monitor shows the current CPU utilization and the maximum CPU frequency. If you expand the Processes panel (by tapping or clicking the options button), as shown in Figure 11-3, you see a list of currently running executables. Each process is listed according to the following categories:

- **Average CPU.** The average percentage of CPU utilization for the process in the last minute
- **CPU.** The percentage of CPU utilization for the process (across all physical and logical processors)
- **Description.** The name of the process (and sometimes other information as well)
- **Image.** The name of the process or executable running the process
- **PID.** The numeric identifier for the process
- **Status.** The execution status of the process
- **Threads.** The number of threads the process is using

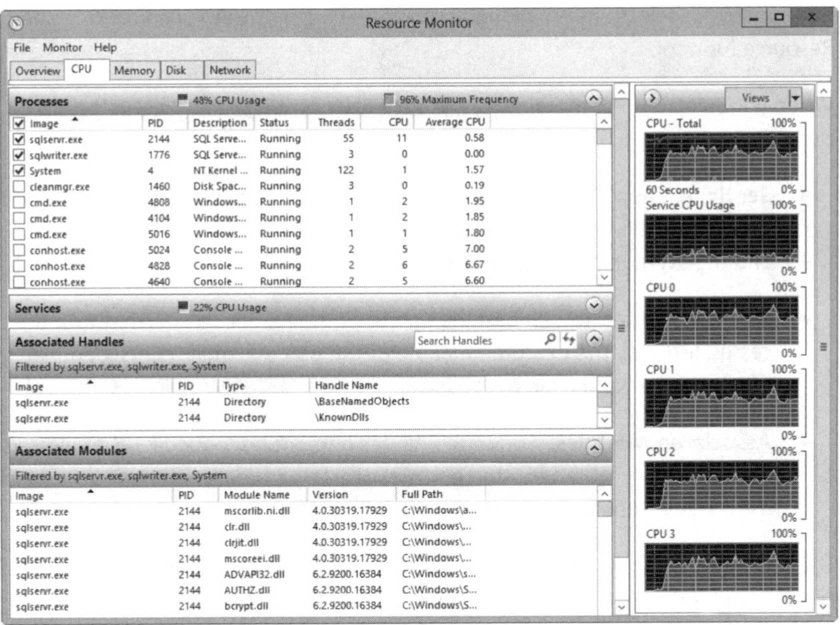

Figure 11-3 The CPU tab in Resource Monitor provides detailed per-process information about CPU utilization.

If you press and hold or right-click any column header and then choose Select Columns, you see a dialog box that enables you to add columns to the CPU panel. The additional columns that are available include the following:

- **Average Cycle.** The average percentage of CPU cycle time for the process (over a 60-second interval).
- **Cycle.** The current percentage of CPU cycle time the process is using.
- **Elevated.** The elevation status of the process. An entry of Yes indicates an elevated process.
- **Operating System Context.** The operating system context in which the process is running, such as Windows Server 2012 R2 or Windows 8.1.
- **Platform.** The platform on which the process is running, either 32-bit or 64-bit.
- **User Name.** The name of the user or service that is running the process.

Select one or more processes on the Processes panel to get more detailed information about how those processes are using CPU resources. As you select processes for tracking, keep in mind that your selections are global. The same selections will appear in the other tabs in Resource Monitor.

When you select one or more processes for tracking, you see additional details on these panels:

- **Services.** Shows the name of the service running a process or processes, along with process identifiers, the status, descriptions of the services, percentage of CPU utilization, and the average percentage of CPU utilization.
- **Associated Handles.** Shows the names of the handles associated with the selected processes, listed by the executable name of the process, the process identifier, the handle type, and the handle file path.
- **Associated Modules.** Shows the names of modules loaded by the selected processes, listed by the executable name of the process, the process identifier, the module name, the module version, and the module file path.

Use this information to help you identify which services are running processes and which handles and modules a process is using. No additional details can be added to the Services, Associated Handles, or Associated Modules panels.

TROUBLESHOOTING

Resolve the CPU performance issue

For troubleshooting performance issues related to a server's processors, you might want to evaluate whether it makes sense to move applications and services from an over-utilized server to another, less-utilized server. You also might want to evaluate whether additional processing power is needed to ensure adequate performance. Faster or additional processors might resolve a performance issue related to high CPU utilization.

Tracking per-process memory utilization

The Memory tab in Resource Monitor shows how processes are using memory, focused primarily on physical memory. As shown in Figure 11-4, the percent utilization of physical memory, the current commit charge, and the hard memory faults are graphed over time. On the Processes panel, individual processes are listed by the following categories:

- **Image.** The name of the process or executable running the process.
- **PID.** The numeric identifier for the process.

- **Hard Faults/Sec.** The average number of hard memory faults per second in the past minute.
- **Commit.** The commit charge for the process, measured in kilobytes (KB). The commit charge represents the amount of virtual memory the operating system reserves for the process.
- **Working Set.** The amount of physical memory the process is currently using.
- **Shareable.** The nonprivate working set for the process, representing the amount of physical memory the process is using that can be shared with other processes.
- **Private.** The private working set for the process, representing the amount of physical memory the process is using that cannot be shared with other processes.

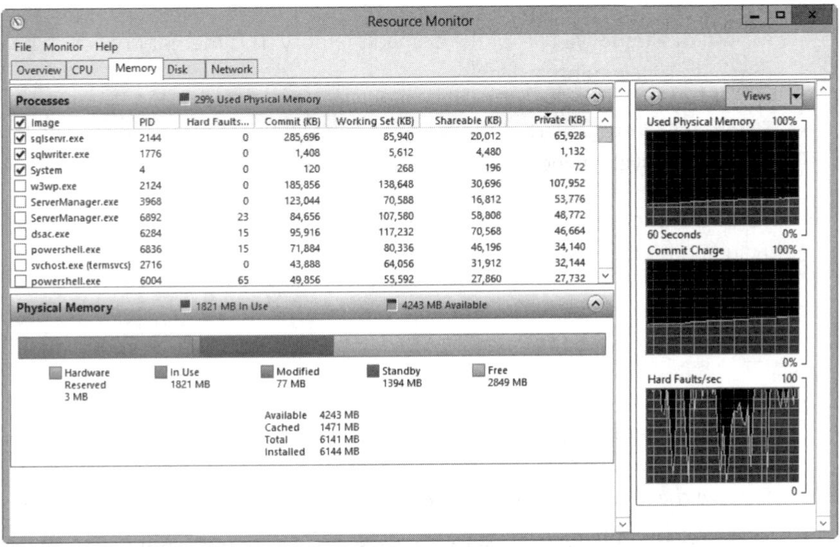

Figure 11-4 The Memory tab in Resource Monitor provides detailed per-process information about CPU utilization.

On the Physical Memory panel, you see a graph showing the composition of in-use and available memory and related usage statistics. Although the details provided are similar to those provided in the Task Manager Performance tab, they are more precise, and you see specific values listed for the following:

- **Available Memory.** The unallocated physical memory (which includes the system's standby memory and free memory).

- **Cached Memory.** Part of the available physical memory. This memory is used for system caching (and includes the system's modified memory and standby memory).
- **Free Memory.** Unallocated memory and part of the available memory. This memory doesn't contain any valuable data and will be used first whenever more memory is needed.
- **Hardware Reserved Memory.** Memory reserved for BIOS and some drivers for other peripherals.
- **In-Use Memory.** Currently allocated physical memory. The size of the paging file is the difference between the current commit charge and the in-use memory.
- **Installed Memory.** The total amount of physical memory installed on the system, including the hardware reserved memory.
- **Modified Memory.** Part of the cached memory. This memory needs to be written to disk before becoming available.
- **Standby Memory.** Part of the cached memory. This memory contains cached data and code not actively being used.
- **Total Memory.** The total amount of physical memory installed on the system, not including hardware reserved memory.

Use this information to help you identify how processes are using memory and whether performance issues are related to memory. No additional details can be added regarding memory usage.

TROUBLESHOOTING

Resolve the memory performance issue

For troubleshooting performance issues related to memory, you might want to evaluate whether it makes sense to move applications and services from a highly utilized server to another, less-utilized server. You also might want to evaluate whether additional physical or virtual memory is needed to ensure adequate performance. Additional memory might resolve a performance issue related to high memory utilization.

Tracking per-process disk utilization

The Disk tab in Resource Monitor shows the number of kilobytes per second being read from or written to disk and the highest percentage usage. As shown in Figure 11-5, processes with disk activity are listed by name, process ID, number of bytes being read per second, number of bytes being written per second, and total read/write bytes per second.

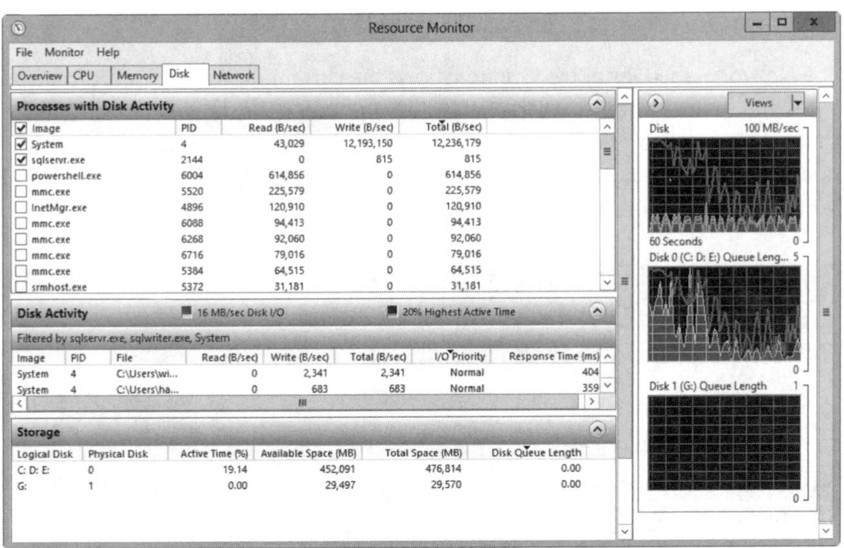

Figure 11-5 The Disk tab in Resource Monitor provides detailed per-process information about CPU utilization.

Select one or more processes on the Processes With Disk Activity panel to get more detailed information about how those processes are using disk resources. As you select processes for tracking, keep in mind that your selections are global. The same selections will appear in the other tabs of Resource Monitor.

When you select one or more processes for tracking, you see additional details on the Disk Activity and Storage panels. To help you quickly identify disk-related performance issues, the Disk Activity panel identifies the files a particular process is reading or writing along with the bytes read per second, bytes written per second, and total read/write bytes per second for each file. Also shown are the I/O priority and the response time.

The Storage panel provides information about the underlying logical and physical disks. The Logical Disk column shows the drive letters of logical disks with I/O activity. The Physical Disk column identifies the specific physical disk where the logical disks were created. If there are performance issues with a server's disks and files are being read from and written to multiple logical disks residing on the same physical disk (or relatively few physical disks as compared to the number of available physical disks), you might be able to improve performance by changing the storage configuration so that I/O activity is spread more evenly across the server's physical disks. You also can try to balance the workload by moving applications and services from an over-utilized server to another, less-utilized server.

Tracking per-process network utilization

The Network tab in Resource Monitor shows the current network bandwidth utilization in kilobytes and the percentage of total bandwidth utilization. As shown in Figure 11-6, processes that are transferring or have transferred data on the network are listed by name, process ID, number of bytes being sent per second, number of bytes received per second, and total bytes sent or received per second.

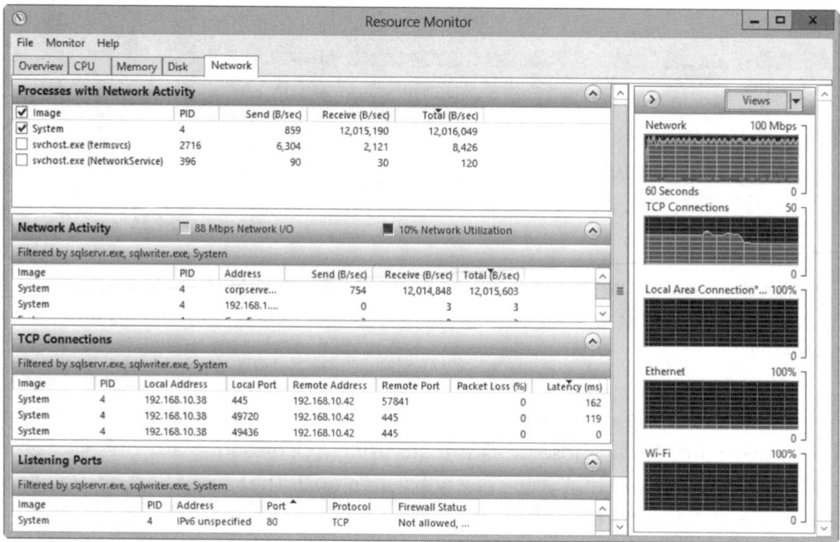

Figure 11-6 The Network tab in Resource Monitor provides detailed per-process information about network utilization.

Select one or more processes on the Processes With Network Activity panel to get more detailed information about how those processes are using network resources. As you select processes for tracking, keep in mind that your selections are global. The same selections will appear on the other tabs of Resource Monitor.

When you select one or more processes for tracking, you see additional details on these panels:

- **Network Activity.** Identifies the name or IP address of the computer to which a process is connected, along with the average number of bytes sent per second in the past minute, the average number of bytes received per second in the past minute, and the total number of bytes transferred per second in the past minute.

- **TCP Connections.** Shows the TCP connections for processes with network activity according to the local addresses, local ports, remote addresses, and remote ports being used. Also shown are the percentage of packets lost during the connection and the roundtrip latency in milliseconds.
- **Listening Ports.** Shows the specific listening ports processes are using with network activity, along with the firewall status.

If there are performance issues with a server's network connections, you might be able to improve performance by installing multiple network adapters in the server and teaming the network cards. You configure network interface card (NIC) teaming by using Server Manager, either through a local logon or using a remote desktop connection. Either way, after you are logged on to the server, you can configure NIC teaming by selecting Local Server in the left pane of Server Manager and then tapping or clicking the link provided for NIC teaming. Next, tap or click Tasks under Teams and then select New Team. Enter a name for the teamed network adapters, such as Team Set 1, select the member adapters, and then tap or click OK.

If you can't add or team network adapters, you can try to reduce the server's network activity by moving applications and services from an over-utilized server to another, less-utilized server.

Tracking the overall reliability of the server

You can use Performance Monitor and Reliability Monitor to track the overall reliability of a server. Performance Monitor graphically displays statistics for the set of performance parameters you selected for display. These performance parameters are referred to as *counters*. When you install additional roles, role services, and features on a system, Performance Monitor might be updated with a set of counters for tracking performance of the related components. You also can update counters when you install additional services and applications.

Performance Monitor, shown in Figure 11-7, creates a graph depicting the counters you're tracking. The update interval for this graph is configurable but is set to one second by default. Tracking information is most valuable when you record performance information in a log file so that it can be played back. When you create alerts, you can notify yourself or others anytime specific performance criteria are met.

You can start Performance Monitor by selecting the related option on the Server Manager Tools menu. Alternatively, type **Performance Monitor** in the Everywhere Search box and press Enter.

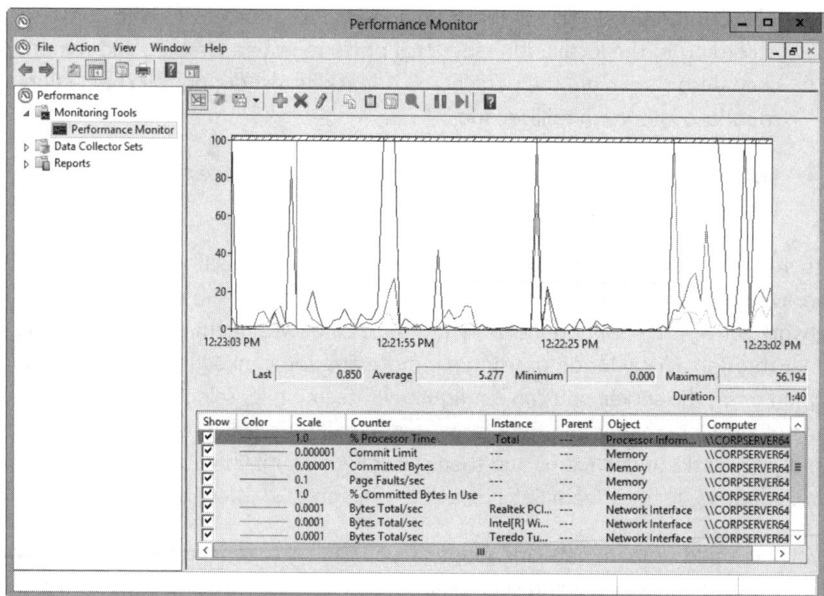

Figure 11-7 Performance Monitor graphically depicts performance.

Reliability Monitor, shown in Figure 11-8, tracks changes to the server and compares them to changes in system stability. In this way, you can see a graphical representation of the relationship between changes in the system configuration and changes in system stability. By recording software installation, software removal, application failure, hardware failure, and Windows failure events, in addition to key events regarding the configuration of the server, you can see a timeline of changes in both the server and its reliability and then use this information to pinpoint changes that are causing problems with stability. For example, if you see a sudden drop in stability, you can tap or click a data point and then expand the related data set, such as Application Failure or Windows Failure, to find the specific event that caused the drop in stability.

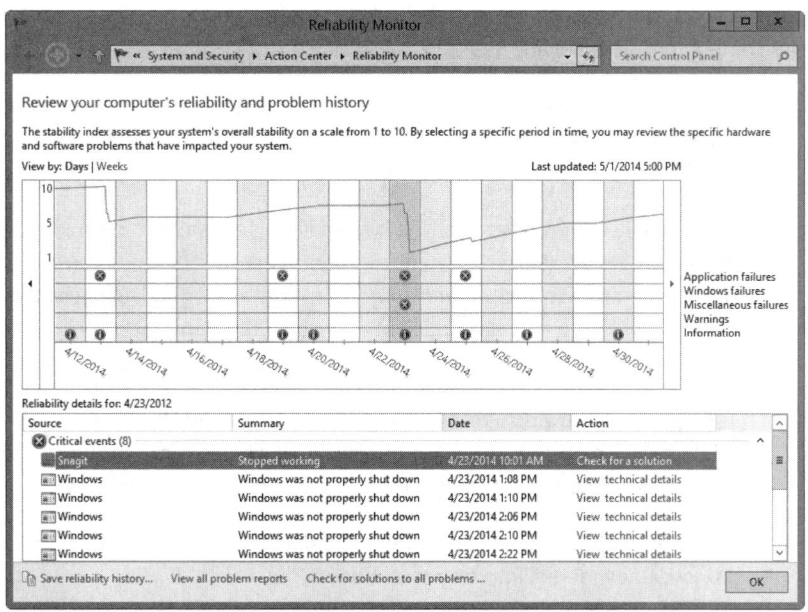

Figure 11-8 Reliability Monitor graphically depicts overall reliability.

> IMPORTANT
>
> **Use Save Reliability History to save complete details about the server's stability for future reference. The information is saved as a Reliability Monitor report and is formatted as XML. Tap or click Save Reliability History and then use the dialog box provided to select a save location and file name for the report. You can view the report in Internet Explorer by double-tapping or double-clicking the file.**

You can access Reliability Monitor from Action Center. On the desktop, tap or click the Action Center icon on the Task bar and then tap or click Open Action Center. In Action Center, expand the Maintenance panel and then tap or click View Reliability History. Alternatively, you can open Reliability Monitor by entering **perfmon /rel** at a command prompt or in the Everywhere Search box.

Although reliability monitoring is enabled by default for Windows clients, it might be disabled for Windows servers. When you open Reliability Monitor on a server where reliability monitoring is disabled, you see that no reliability updates or history details are available. To enable reliability tracking, you must allow the Microsoft Reliability Analysis task, RacTask, to process system reliability data.

RacTask is a scheduled task that runs in the background to collect reliability data. You can find RacTask in the Task Scheduler Library under Microsoft, Windows, RAC. On servers, this task is best used as part of troubleshooting. If RacTask is disabled, you can enable and configure the task by completing the following steps:

1. In Server Manager, on the Tools menu, select Task Scheduler. In the left pane of Task Scheduler, expand Task Scheduler Library\Microsoft\Windows and then select the RAC node.

2. By default, RacTask runs whenever the system is started, daily at approximately 5:00 P.M. (a random delay of up to 15 minutes is added each scheduled run-time) and when Customer Experience Improvement Program events are logged. Because performing reliability analysis and collection daily at around 5:00 P.M. might not be an optimal time, select RacTask in the main pane and then select Properties on the Action menu.

3. In the Properties dialog box, on the Triggers tab, select the One Time trigger and then select Edit. Use the options provided to specify an optimal time to run this task. Select OK twice to close the open dialog boxes.

4. With RacTask still selected in Task Scheduler, select Enable on the Action menu. To run the task once now, select Run on the Action menu.

If you enable the task for troubleshooting, review and modify the default triggers as appropriate for your environment. By default, the task is triggered at startup, once a day at 5:00 P.M., and whenever event 1007 is written to the application log. Event 1007 tracks Customer Experience Improvement Program events, which Microsoft tracks to help improve the overall stability of Windows and Windows Server. Don't enable RacTask without considering the possible performance impact.

Comprehensive performance monitoring

Performance Monitor is a tool designed to track and display performance information in real time. It gathers information on any performance parameters you configured for monitoring and presents it using a graphical display.

Using Performance Monitor

When you are working with Performance Monitor, the main pane graphs any performance items you configured for monitoring, as shown in Figure 11-7. Each performance item you want to monitor is defined by the following three components:

- **Performance objects.** Represent any system component that has a set of measurable properties. A performance object can be a physical part of the operating system such as the memory, the processor, or the paging file; a logical component such as a logical disk or print queue; or a software element such as a process or a thread.

- **Performance object instances.** Represent single occurrences of performance objects. If a particular object has multiple instances, such as when a computer has multiple processors, you can use an object instance to track a specific occurrence of that object. You could also elect to track all instances of an object, such as if you want to monitor all processors on a system.
- **Performance counters.** Represent measurable properties of performance objects. For example, with a processor, you can measure the percentage of processor utilization by using the % Processor Time counter.

In a standard installation of Windows Server 2012 R2, many performance objects are available for monitoring. As you add services, applications, and components, additional performance objects can become available. For example, when you install the Domain Name System (DNS), the DNS object becomes available for monitoring on that computer.

The most common performance objects you want to monitor are summarized in Table 11-1. Like all performance objects, each performance object listed here has a set of counters that can be tracked.

Table 11-1 Commonly tracked performance objects

Performance Object	Description
Cache	Monitors the file system cache, which is an area of physical memory that indicates application I/O activity
Database ==> Instances	Monitors performance for instances of the embedded database management system Windows Server 2012 R2 uses
DFS Replicated Folders	Monitors conflicts, deletions, replication, and other performance factors related to DFS replication folders
DFS Replication Connections	Monitors the data sent and received and other performance statistics for DFS replication connections
DHCPv6 Server	Monitors DHCPv6 message broadcasts and other types of DHCPv6 activities
DirectoryServices	Monitors performance statistics related to Active Directory Domain Services (AD DS)
DNS	Monitors DNS message traffic and other types of DNS activities
IPv4	Monitors IPv4 communications and related activities
IPv6	Monitors IPv6 communications and related activities
LogicalDisk	Monitors the logical volumes on a computer

Performance Object	Description
Memory	Monitors memory performance for system cache (including pooled, paged memory and pooled, nonpaged memory), physical memory, and virtual memory
Network Interface	Monitors the network adapters configured on the computer
Objects	Monitors the number of events, mutexes, processes, sections, semaphores, and threads on the computer
Paging File	Monitors page file current and peak usage
PhysicalDisk	Monitors hard disk read/write activity and data transfers, hard faults, and soft faults
Print Queue	Monitors print jobs, spooling, and print queue activity
Process	Monitors all processes running on a computer
Processor	Monitors processor idle time, idle states, usage, deferred procedure calls, and interrupts
Server	Monitors current server activity and important server usage statistics, including logon errors, access errors, and sessions
Server Work Queues	Monitors server threading and client requests
System	Monitors system-level counters, including processes, threads, context switching of threads, file system control operations, system calls, and system uptime
TCPv4	Monitors TCPv4 communications and related activities
TCPv6	Monitors TCPv6 communications and related activities
Thread	Monitors all running threads and enables you to examine usage statistics for individual threads by process ID
UDPv4	Monitors UDPv4 communications and related activities
UDPv6	Monitors UDPv6 communications and related activities

Selecting performance objects and counters to monitor

The most commonly tracked performance objects are Memory, PhysicalDisk, and Processor. When you first open Performance Monitor, it is configured to graph only the % Processor Time counter. Many other performance counters are available for tracking. To track additional counters, you use the Add Counters dialog box, as shown in Figure 11-9. With the Performance Monitor node selected in the Performance console or Computer Management, you open this dialog box by pressing Ctrl+I or selecting the Add Counters button on the toolbar.

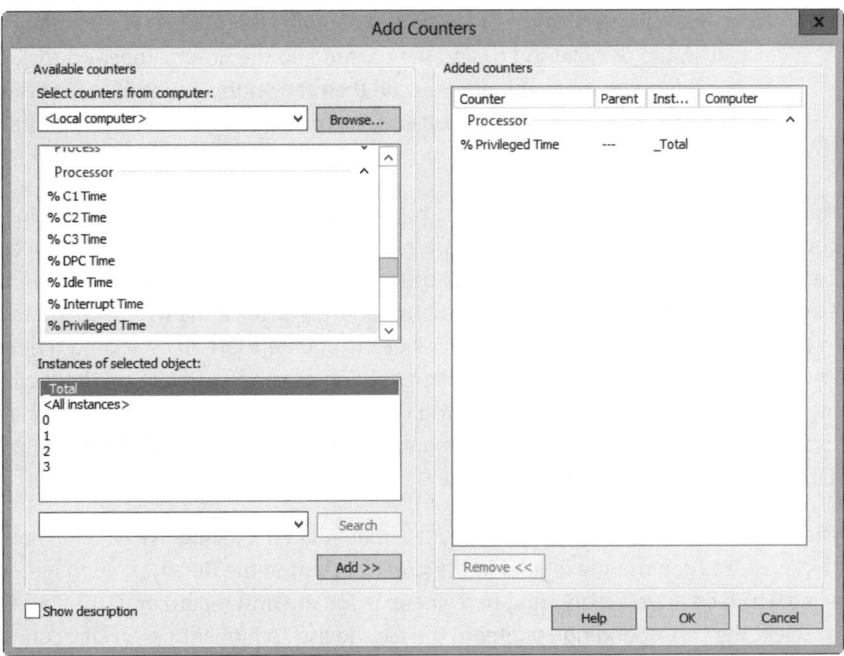

Figure 11-9 Select the objects and the counters that you want to track.

After you open the Add Counters dialog box, you can select objects and counters to track by completing these steps:

1. In the Select Counters From Computer box, enter the Universal Naming Convention (UNC) name of the server you want to work with, such as \\CorpServer62, or choose <Local computer> to work with the local computer. You need to be at least a member of the Performance Monitor Users group in the domain or the local computer to perform remote monitoring.

2. Adding counters to track is easy. Select the type of object you want to work with, such as Memory. When you select an object entry by tapping or clicking it, all related counters are selected. If you expand an object entry, you can see all the related counters and then select individual counters by tapping or clicking them. With a keyboard, use Ctrl+click or Shift+click to select multiple counters.

3. When you select an object or any of its counters, in most cases you see the related instances. Choose _Total to work with a summary view of all counter instances. Choose All Instances to select all counter instances for monitoring or select one or more individual counter instances to monitor.

4. When you select an object or a group of counters for an object in addition to the object instances, tap or click Add to add the counters to the graph. Repeat steps 2 and 3 to add other performance parameters. You can then repeat this process, as necessary, to add counters for other performance objects. Tap or click OK when you're finished adding counters.

As you've seen, it's easy to add counters to track. What isn't so easy is determining which counters you should track. While you are working with the Add Counters dialog box, you can get a detailed explanation of a counter by selecting a counter and then selecting the Show Description check box. If you add too many counters or track the wrong counters, don't worry. In the Performance Monitor view, you can delete counters later by selecting their entries in the lower portion of the details pane and then tapping or clicking Delete on the toolbar or pressing the Delete key on your keyboard. You can also delete all counters being tracked and start over with a clean graph by selecting an entry in the lower portion of the details pane, pressing Ctrl+A, and then pressing the Delete key.

Performance Monitor displays each counter that you are tracking in a different color and line thickness. You can use the legend in the lower portion of the details pane to help you determine which counter is being graphed where. If you are unsure, tap or click a line in the graph to select the corresponding counter in the legend list. To highlight a specific counter so that it is easy to pick out in the graph, select the counter in the legend list and then press Ctrl+H.

Choosing views and controlling the display

Performance Monitor can present counter statistics in several ways. By default, it graphs the statistics. A graph is useful when you are tracking a limited number of counters because you can view historical data for each counter that you are working with. By default, Performance Monitor samples the counters once every second and updates the graph over a 100-second duration. This means that at any given time, up to 100 seconds' worth of data can be on the graph. If you change the sample interval and duration, you can get more information into the chart. For example, if you set the sample interval to once every 10 seconds and the duration to 1000 seconds, you can get up to 1000 seconds' (or about 17 minutes') worth of data on the graph.

You can set the sample interval by using the General tab of the Performance Monitor Properties dialog box, as shown in Figure 11-10. To open this dialog box, press and hold or right-click the Performance Monitor node and select Properties. Set the sample interval and duration by using the Sample Every and Duration text boxes.

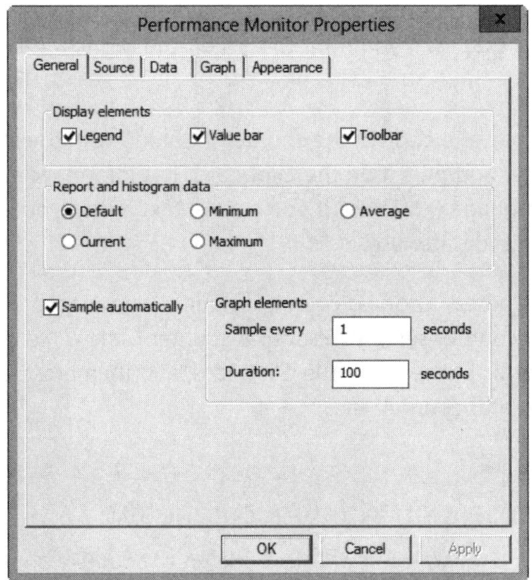

Figure 11-10 Configure the display properties.

The options on the Display Elements panel on the General tab of the Performance Monitor Properties dialog box control the availability of the Legend, Value Bar, and Toolbar. The Legend is displayed at the bottom of the details pane, and it shows the color and line style that are used for each counter. The Value Bar is displayed between the graph and the legend. It shows values related to the counter you selected in the graph or in the legend. The Toolbar is displayed above the graph and provides the basic toolbar functions for working with Performance Monitor. You might find that it is much easier to use the shortcut keys than to tap or click the Toolbar buttons. The Toolbar buttons and their shortcut keys are as follows:

- **View Current Activity.** Ctrl+T; switches the view so that current activity being logged is displayed.
- **View Log Data.** Ctrl+L; switches the view so that data from a performance log can be replayed.
- **Change Graph Type.** Ctrl+G; switches the view to toggle among bar graph, report list, and graph format.
- **Add.** Ctrl+I; opens the Add Counter dialog box, in which you can add counters to track.
- **Delete.** Delete key; removes the counter so that it is no longer tracked.

- **Highlight.** Ctrl+H; highlights the counter by using a white line so that it is easier to see. Highlighting works best with graphs. If you want to turn off the Highlight function, press Ctrl+H again.
- **Copy Properties.** Ctrl+C; creates a copy of the counter list along with the individual configuration of each counter and puts it on the Clipboard. The information is formatted as an Extensible Markup Language (XML) file. If you open a text editor, you could paste in this information and save it for later use.
- **Paste Counter List.** Ctrl+V; pastes a copied counter list into Performance Monitor so that it is used as the current counter set. If you saved a counter list to a file, you just open the file, copy the contents of the file to the Clipboard, and then press Ctrl+V in Performance Monitor to use that counter list.

Save the counter list or use it on different computers

You can use the Copy and Paste commands to track the same set of counters quickly and easily at a later date or to use the set on other computers. Press Ctrl+C to copy the counter list and save it to a file. Then you or someone else can access the counter list when you want to use the same setup again. You could also paste the counter list into an email message so that it can be sent to someone who wants to use the same counter list.

- **Properties** Ctrl+Q; displays the Properties dialog box for a select item.
- **Freeze Display.** Ctrl+F; freezes the display so that Performance Monitor no longer updates the performance information. Press Ctrl+F a second time to resume sampling.
- **Update Data.** Ctrl+U; updates the display by one sampling interval. When you freeze the display, Performance Monitor still gathers performance information; it just doesn't update the display by using the new information. If you want to update the display while it is frozen, use this option.
- **Help.** F1; displays the Performance Monitor Help information.

The Histogram Bar and Report views deserve a bit of additional discussion. In the Histogram Bar view, Performance Monitor represents the performance information by using a bar graph with the last sampling value for each counter displayed on an individual bar within the graph. The sizes of the bars within the graph are adjusted automatically based on the number of performance counters being tracked and can be adjusted to accommodate hundreds of counters. That is, in fact, the biggest advantage of the histogram—it enables you to track a lot of counters more easily. In Figure 11-11, approximately 100 counters are being tracked, and it is easy to pick out which counter is which.

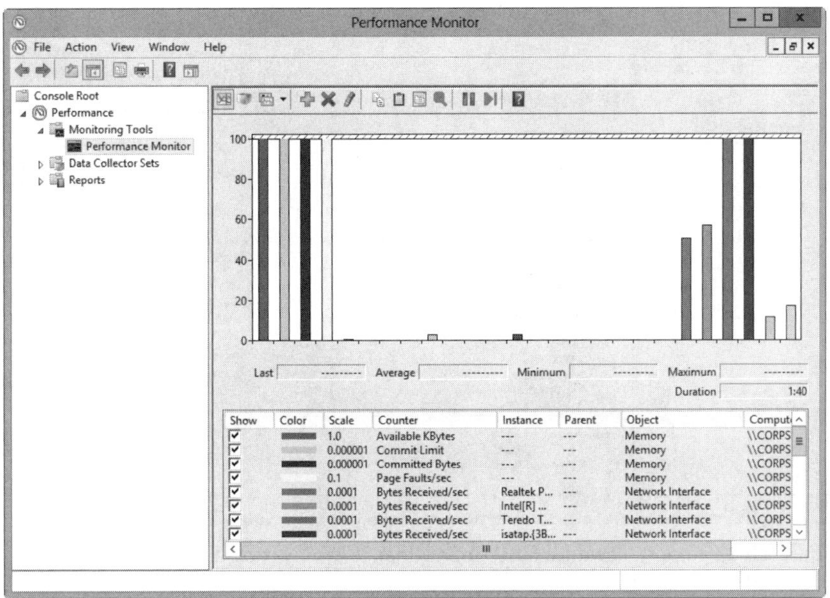

Figure 11-11 The histogram view enables you to track counters easily, using bar graphs.

In the Report view, shown in Figure 11-12, Performance Monitor represents the performance information by using a report list format. In this view, objects and their counters are listed in alphabetical order. Current values are displayed rather than being graphed. If you are trying to determine specific performance values for many counters, this is the best view to use because the actual values are always shown.

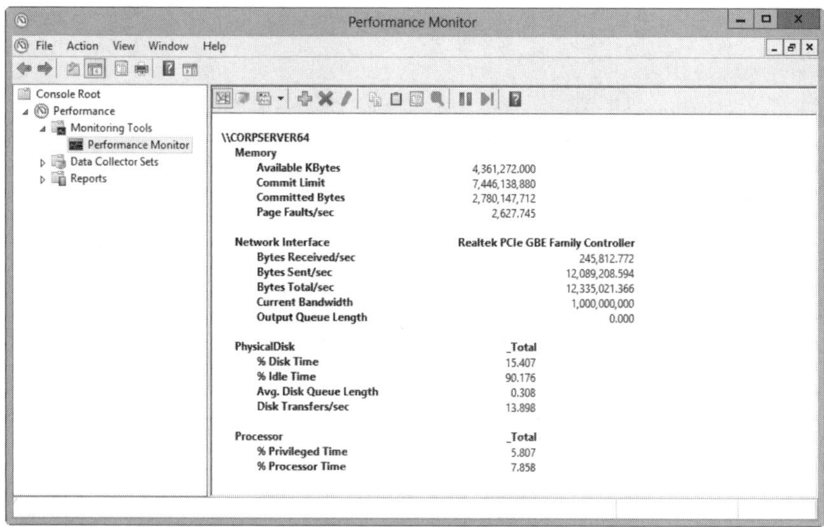

Figure 11-12 Report view gives users performance information as specific values rather than by using graphs or charts.

Monitoring performance remotely

Monitoring performance on the computer for which you are trying to establish a baseline can skew the results. The reason for this is that Performance Monitor uses resources when it is running, particularly when you are graphing performance information, taking frequent samples, or tracking many performance counters. To remove the resource burden (or at least most of it), you should consider monitoring performance remotely. Here, you use one computer to monitor the performance of another computer. Although this does generate some extra network traffic, you get more accurate results for the monitored computer because you're not using its resources for monitoring.

> NOTE
>
> **By default, only administrators can monitor performance remotely. You need to be at least a member of the Performance Monitor Users group in the domain or on the local computer to perform remote monitoring. When you use performance logging, you need to be at least a member of the Performance Log Users group in the domain or on the local computer to work with performance logs on remote computers.**

Configure remote monitoring

You can use any computer running current editions of Windows or Windows Server to perform remote monitoring, and that computer can monitor any other computer running current editions of Windows or Windows Server. The only exceptions are for nonbusiness editions of Windows. The computer you are using for monitoring can even monitor multiple computers.

To begin remote monitoring, select the Performance Monitor node in the Performance Monitor console or in Computer Management. To start with a new counter set and clear out any existing counters, select a counter entry in the lower portion of the details pane, press Ctrl+A, and press the Delete key. Press Ctrl+I to open the Add Counters dialog box. In the Add Counters dialog box, type the UNC name or Internet Protocol (IP) address of the computer you want to monitor remotely in the Select Counters From Computer text box. A UNC computer name or IP address begins with two back slashes (\\). So, for instance, you could type **\\CorpServer03** or **\\192.168.1.56**.

After you type the UNC computer name or IP address, press Tab or tap or click the Performance Object list. When you do this, Performance Monitor attempts to connect to the remote computer and retrieve a list of available performance objects to monitor. You can then choose performance objects and counters to track just as you would for a local computer.

TROUBLESHOOTING

Try the IP address if you can't connect

Performance Monitor should be able to find any computer in any trusted domain of your organization's forest. Sometimes, however, it can't do this and returns an error. If this happens, ensure that you entered the correct computer name. If you did and you still get an error, try entering the UNC path with the computer's IP address. Using an IP address saves Performance Monitor from having to perform a DNS lookup to resolve the computer's name to its IP address.

Compare performance of multiple systems

The Legend area shows the associated UNC computer name or IP address for each performance counter you are tracking. If you want to see how performance compares on different computers, use your monitoring computer to track the same performance counters on these computers. You can then make direct comparisons of how these computers perform relative to each other.

Resolving performance bottlenecks

Generally, a *bottleneck* is any condition that keeps a computer from performing at its best. Bottlenecks can also apply when one resource is preventing another resource from performing optimally. For example, if a system doesn't have enough physical memory, it doesn't matter whether it has a fast processor or a slow processor. The system will still perform poorly because it doesn't have enough available physical memory and must rely heavily on the paging file, reading and writing to disk frequently.

Memory is usually the main bottleneck on both workstations and servers. It is the resource you should examine first to determine why a system isn't performing as expected. But memory isn't the only bottleneck. The processor, disk subsystem, and networking components are also sources of potential performance bottlenecks.

Resolving memory bottlenecks

Windows applications use a lot of memory. If you install a server with the minimum amount of memory required, it won't perform at its optimal level because a server's memory requirements depend on many factors, including the services, components, and applications that are installed on it and the server's configuration.

Computers use both physical and virtual memory. Physical memory is represented by the amount of random access memory (RAM) installed. Virtual memory is memory written to a paging file on disk. Reading from and writing to the paging file involve the disk subsystem, and it is much slower than accessing physical memory. Because of this, you don't want a system to have to use the paging file too frequently.

Before you set out to monitor memory usage, you should check to ensure that the computer has the recommended amount of memory for the operating system and the applications it is running. After you've done this, you can determine how the system is using memory and check for problems. Look closely at the amount of memory available and the amount of virtual memory being used. If the server has very little available memory, you might need to add memory to the system. In general, you want the available memory to be no less than 5 percent of the total physical memory on the server. If the server is using a high ratio of virtual memory to total physical memory on the system, you might need to add physical memory as well.

Look at the way the system is using the paged pool and nonpaged pool memory. The paged pool is an area of system memory for objects that can be written to disk when they aren't used. The nonpaged pool is an area of system memory for objects that can't be written to disk. If the size of the paged pool is large relative to the total amount of physical memory on the system, you might need to add memory to the system. If the size of the nonpaged pool is large relative to the total amount of virtual memory allocated to the server, you might want to increase the virtual memory size.

Look at the way the system is using the paging file. A page fault occurs when a process requests a page in memory and the system can't find it at the requested location. If the requested page is elsewhere in memory, the fault is called a *soft page fault*. If the requested page must be retrieved from the paging file on disk, the fault is called a *hard page fault*. Most processors can handle large numbers of soft faults. Hard faults, however, can cause significant delays. If there are a high number of hard page faults, you might need to increase the amount of memory or reduce the size of the system cache.

Counters you can use to check for memory bottlenecks include the following:

- **Memory\Available Bytes.** Records the number of bytes of physical memory available to processes running on the server. When less than 5 percent of memory is free, the system is low on memory, and performance can suffer. The server might page excessively to disk to try to keep up with resource demands. Memory is critically short if 128 megabytes (MBs) or less of memory is free; in this case, the system might page excessively to disk and try to borrow memory from running processes to keep up with resource demands. If the system is very low on memory, it could also point to a possible memory leak.

- **Memory\Committed Bytes.** Records the number of bytes of committed virtual memory. This represents memory that has been paged to disk and is in use. If a server is using too much virtual memory relative to the total physical memory on the system, you might need to add physical memory.

- **Memory\Commit Limit.** Shows the total available physical and virtual memory. As the number of committed bytes grows, the paging file is allowed to grow up to its maximum size, which can be determined by subtracting the total physical memory on the system from the commit limit. If you set the initial paging file size too small, the system will repeatedly extend the paging file, and this requires system resources. It is better to set the initial paging file size as appropriate for typical usage or just use a fixed paging file size. For a fixed paging file, set the size to at least two times the size of RAM.

- **Memory\Page Faults/Sec.** Records the average number of page faults per second. It includes both hard and soft page faults. Soft faults result in memory lookups. Hard faults require access to disk.

- **Memory\Pages/Sec.** Records the number of memory pages that are read from disk or written to disk to resolve hard page faults. It is the sum of Memory\Pages Input/Sec and Memory\Pages Output/Sec.

- **Memory\Pages Input/Sec.** Records the rate at which pages are read from disk to resolve hard page faults. Hard page faults occur when a requested page isn't in memory and the computer has to go to disk to get it. Too many hard faults can cause significant delays and hurt performance.
- **Memory\Pages Output/Sec.** Records the rate at which pages are written to disk to free up space in physical memory. If the server has to free up memory too often, it indicates that not enough physical memory (RAM) is on the system.
- **Memory\Pool Paged Bytes.** Represents the size in bytes of the paged pool. The paged pool is an area of system memory for objects that can be written to disk when they aren't used. If the size of the paged pool is large relative to the total amount of physical memory on the system, you might need to add memory to the system. If this value slowly increases in size over time, a kernel-mode process might have a memory leak.
- **Memory\Pool Nonpaged Bytes.** Represents the size in bytes of the nonpaged pool. The nonpaged pool is an area of system memory for objects that can't be written to disk. If the size of the nonpaged pool is large relative to the total amount of virtual memory allocated to the server, you might want to increase the virtual memory size. If this value slowly increases in size over time, a kernel-mode process might have a memory leak.
- **Paging File\%Usage.** Records the percentage of the paging file currently in use. If this value approaches 100 percent for all instances, you should consider either increasing the virtual memory size or adding physical memory to the system. This ensures that the server has additional memory if it needs it, such as when the server load grows.
- **Paging File\%Usage Peak.** Records the peak size of the paging file as a percentage of the total paging file size available. A high value can mean that the paging file isn't large enough to handle increased load conditions.
- **Physical Disk\%Disk Time.** Records the percentage of time that the selected disk spent servicing read and write requests. Keep track of this value for the physical disks that have paging files. If you see this value increasing over several monitoring periods, you should monitor paging-file usage more closely and consider adding physical memory to the system.
- **Physical Disk\Avg. Disk Queue Length.** Records the average number of read and write requests that were waiting for the selected disk during the sample interval. Keep track of this value for the physical disks that have paging files. If you see this value increasing over time and the Memory\Page Reads/Sec is also increasing, the system is performing a lot of paging-file reads.

- **Physical Disk\Avg. Disk Sec/Transfer.** Records the length in seconds of the average disk transfer. Track this value for the physical disks that have paging files in conjunction with Memory\Pages/Sec. Memory\Pages/Sec tracks the number of reads and writes for the paging file. If you multiply the Physical Disk\Avg. Disk Sec/Transfer by the Memory\Pages/Sec value, you have an excellent indicator of how much of the disk access time paging is using. Use the result to help you decide whether to move the paging files to faster disks or add physical memory to the system.

Resolving processor bottlenecks

After you've eliminated memory as a potential bottleneck, you should examine the system's processor usage to determine whether there are any potential bottlenecks. Processor bottlenecks can occur if a process's threads need more processing time than is available. This, in turn, causes the processor queue to grow because threads have to wait to get processing time. As a result, the system response suffers, and the system appears sluggish or nonresponsive.

Excess interrupts are another common reason for processor bottlenecks. Each time drivers or disk subsystem components, such as hard disk drives or network components, generate an interrupt, the processor has to stop what it is doing to handle the request because requests from hardware take priority. However, poorly designed drivers and components can generate false interrupts, which tie up the processor for no reason. System boards or components that are failing can generate false interrupts as well.

> TROUBLESHOOTING
>
> ***Rule out processor affinity as an issue on multiprocessor systems***
>
> **On multiprocessor systems, you might need to rule out processor affinity as a cause of a processor bottleneck. By using processor affinity, you can set a program or process to use a specific processor to improve its performance. Assigning processor affinity, however, can block access to the processor for other programs and processes.**

If a system's processors are the performance bottleneck, adding memory, drives, or network connections won't overcome the problem. Instead, you might need to upgrade the processors to faster clock speeds or add processors to increase the server's upper capacity. You could also move processor-intensive applications, such as Microsoft Exchange Server, to another server.

Counters you can use to check for processor bottlenecks include the following:

- **System\Processor Queue Length.** Records the number of threads waiting to be executed. These threads are queued in an area shared by all processors on the system. If this counter has a sustained value of 10 or more threads, you might need to upgrade the processors to faster clock speeds or add processors to increase the server's upper capacity.

- **Processor\%Processor Time.** Records the percentage of time the selected processor is executing a nonidle thread. You should track this counter separately for all processor instances on the server. If the %Processor Time values for all instances are high (above 75 percent) while the network interface and disk input/output (I/O) throughput rates are relatively low, you might need to upgrade the processors to faster clock speeds or add processors to increase the server's upper capacity.
- **Processor\%User Time** Records the percentage of time the selected processor is executing a nonidle thread in User mode. *User mode* is a processing mode for applications and user-level subsystems. A high value for all process instances might indicate that you need to upgrade the processors to faster clock speeds or add processors to increase the server's upper capacity.
- **Processor\%Privileged Time.** Records the percentage of time the selected processor is executing a nonidle thread in Privileged mode. *Privileged mode* is a processing mode for operating system components and services, allowing direct access to hardware and memory. A high value for all processor instances might indicate that you need to upgrade the processors to faster clock speeds or add processors to increase the server's upper capacity.
- **Processor\Interrupts/Sec.** Records the average rate, in incidents per second, that the processor received and serviced hardware interrupts. Compare this value to your baselines. If this value changes substantially (I mean by thousands of interrupts) without a corresponding increase in activity, the system might have a hardware problem. To resolve this problem, you must identify the device or component that is causing the problem. Start with devices that have drivers you've updated recently.

Resolving disk I/O bottlenecks

With the high-speed disks available today, a system's hard disks are rarely the primary reason for a bottleneck. It is more likely that a system is having to do a lot of disk reads and writes because there isn't enough physical memory available, and the system has to page to disk. Because reading from and writing to disk is much slower than reading and writing memory, excessive paging can degrade the server's overall performance. To reduce the amount of disk activity, you want the system to manage memory as efficiently as possible and page to disk only when necessary.

That said, you can do several things with a system's hard disks to improve performance. If the system has faster drives than the ones used for the paging file, you might consider moving the paging file to those disks. If the system has one or more drives that are doing most of the work and other drives that are mostly idle, you might be able to improve performance by balancing the load across the drives more efficiently.

To help you gauge disk I/O activity better, use the following counters:

- **PhysicalDisk\%Disk Time.** Records the percentage of time the physical disk is busy. Track this value for all hard disk drives on the system in conjunction with Processor\%Processor Time and Network Interface Connection\Bytes Total/Sec. If the %Disk Time value is high and the processor and network connection values aren't high, the system's hard disk drives might be creating a bottleneck. You might be able to improve performance by balancing the load across the drives more efficiently or adding drives and configuring the system so that they are used.

    NOTE

    Redundant array of independent disks (RAID) devices can cause the PhysicalDisk\%Disk Time value to exceed 100 percent. For this reason, don't rely on PhysicalDisk\%Disk Time for RAID devices. Instead, use PhysicalDisk\Current Disk Queue Length.

- **PhysicalDisk\Current Disk Queue Length** Records the number of system requests that are waiting for disk access. A high value indicates that the disk waits are affecting system performance. In general, you want to have very few waiting requests.

    NOTE

    Physical disk queue lengths are relative to the number of physical disks on the system and proportional to the length of the queue minus the number of drives. For example, if a system has two drives and there are six waiting requests, that could be considered a proportionally large number of queued requests; but if a system has eight drives and there are 10 waiting requests, that is considered a proportionally small number of queued requests.

- **PhysicalDisk\Avg. Disk Write Queue Length.** Records the number of write requests that are waiting to be processed.
- **PhysicalDisk\Avg. Disk Read Queue Length.** Records the number of read requests that are waiting to be processed.
- **PhysicalDisk\Disk Writes/Sec.** Records the number of disk writes per second. It indicates how much disk I/O activity there is. By tracking the number of writes per second and the size of the write queue, you can determine how write operations are affecting disk performance. If lots of write operations are queuing and you are using RAID 5, it could indicate that you would get better performance by using RAID 1. Remember that by using RAID 5, you typically get better read performance than with RAID 1. So, there's a tradeoff to be made by using either RAID configuration.

- **PhysicalDisk\Disk Reads/Sec.** Records the number of disk reads per second. It indicates how much disk I/O activity there is. By tracking the number of reads per second and the size of the read queue, you can determine how read operations are affecting disk performance. If lots of read operations are queuing and you are using RAID 1, you might get better performance by using RAID 5. Remember that by using RAID 1, you typically get better write performance than with RAID 5. So, as mentioned, there's a tradeoff to be made by using either RAID configuration.

Resolving network bottlenecks

The network that connects your computers is critically important. Its responsiveness, or lack thereof, weighs heavily on the way users perceive the responsiveness of their computers and any computers to which they connect. It doesn't matter how fast their computers are or how fast your servers are. If there's a big delay (and big network delays are measured in tens of milliseconds) between when a request is made and the time it's received, users might think systems are slow or nonresponsive.

Unfortunately, in most cases, the delay (latency) users experience is beyond your control. It's a function of the type of connection the user has and the route the request takes to your server. The total capacity of your server to handle requests and the amount of bandwidth available to your servers are factors you can control, however. Network capacity is a function of the network cards and interfaces configured on the servers. Network bandwidth availability is a function of your organization's network infrastructure and how much traffic is on it when a request is made.

Because modern servers often ship with multiple network cards, be sure to check all enabled network adapters. If a server has multiple adapters, you might want to enable and configure NIC teaming to ensure that the available bandwidth is used optimally. When NIC teaming is being used, you also want to ensure that the configuration is optimized for the way the server is currently being used. In Server Manager, you can configure NIC teaming as a Local Server option, which means you must log on locally to the server you want to configure or access the server through a Remote Desktop Connection.

When hosting virtual machines (VMs) on a hypervisor, such as Hyper-V, NIC teaming is not required. A common hypervisor configuration has trunked network connections that carry multiple virtual LANs (VLANs), or logical networks. Using NIC teaming on a VM running Windows Server 2012 that has a physical uplink through a hypervisor trunked network connection does not provide any load balancing or redundancy capabilities. Physical trunked network connections to a hypervisor are often teamed and connected to a redundant pair of physical switches, providing load balancing and redundancy to all VMs hosted on the hypervisor.

Counters you can use to check network activity and look for bottlenecks include the following:

- **Network Interface\Bytes Total/Sec.** Records the rate at which bytes are sent and received over a network adapter. Track this value separately for each network adapter configured on the system. If the Bytes Total/Sec for a particular adapter is substantially slower than you'd expect, given the speed of the network and the speed of the network card, you might want to check the network card configuration. Check to see whether the link speed is set for half duplex or full duplex. In most cases, you want to use full duplex.
- **Network Interface\Current Bandwidth.** Estimates the current bandwidth for the selected network adapter in bits per second. Track this value separately for each network adapter configured on the system. Most servers use 100 Mbps, 1 Gbps, or 10 Gbps network cards, which can be configured in many ways. Someone might have configured a 1 Gbps card for 100 megabits per second (Mbps). If that is the case, the current bandwidth might be off by a factor of 10.
- **Network Interface\Bytes Received/Sec.** Records the rate at which bytes are received over a network adapter. Track this value separately for each network adapter configured on the system.
- **Network Interface\Bytes Sent/Sec.** Records the rate at which bytes are sent over a network adapter. Track this value separately for each network adapter configured on the system.

TROUBLESHOOTING

Compare network activity to disk time and processor time

Compare these values in conjunction with PhysicalDisk\%Disk Time and Processor\%Processor Time. If the disk time and processor time values are low, but the network values are very high, a capacity problem might exist. Solve the problem by optimizing the network card settings or by adding a network card.

You might be able to improve network performance by installing multiple network adapters and teaming the network cards. You configure NIC teaming by using Server Manager, selecting Local Server in the left pane, and then tapping or clicking the link provided for NIC teaming. You can then create and configure NIC teams.

Inside OUT

NIC teaming

NIC teaming allows multiple network adapters' bandwidth to be aggregated for the purposes of load balancing and failover protection. Windows Server 2012 R2 supports up to 32 network adapters aggregated into a team. In turn, these aggregated adapters then present one or more virtual adapters, referred to as *team network adapters*, to the operating system. Each team network adapter organizes network traffic by virtual LAN (VLAN), enabling applications to connect simultaneously to different VLANs.

When you are configuring NIC teaming, you can tap or click Additional Properties to configure the teaming mode, load-balancing mode, and standby-adapter mode. By default, team network adapters use the switch-independent team mode, which doesn't require the network switch to participate in the teaming; this allows the team network adapters to be connected to different switches. Alternatively, you can configure:

- Static teaming as the teaming mode, which requires you to configure the switch and the server to work with NIC teaming. Here, you typically use a server-class switch and identify which links form the team. Because there is no error detection and correction, you must be certain the network cables are properly connected.
- Link Aggregation Control Protocol (LACP) as the teaming mode, which uses Institute of Electrical and Electronics Engineers (IEEE) 802.1ax LACP to create the NIC team automatically by dynamically identifying links between the server and the switch. Here, you typically use a server-class switch and enable LACP on the appropriate switch ports.

If you have a server-class switch, the switch likely supports IEEE 802.1ax (also referred to as IEEE 802.3ad), and you can gain some additional performance benefits by having the switch participate in the teaming.

For load balancing, the default mode (Address Hash) creates a simple hash for packets and then assigns packets that have a particular hash to one of the available team network adapters. This can help balance the workload across the team network adapters. Alternatively, if a server has virtual machines, you can use the MAC address of each virtual machine to determine how traffic is balanced. Load balancing by MAC address works best when virtual machines have similar workloads. Keep in mind that failover between network adapters in a virtual machine might result in traffic being sent with the MAC address of a different network adapter. If so, to prevent this from being blocked automatically, NIC teaming must be set to allow MAC spoofing or have the *AllowTeaming=On* parameter set, using the Set-VmNetworkAdapter cmdlet in Windows PowerShell.

Finally, the Standby Adapter setting enables you to specify whether all network adapters are active. Typically, for optimal performance, you want all network adapters in a team to be active. However, you can designate one or more network adapters in a team as standby adapters. Exactly as its name suggests, a *standby adapter* is inactive until another active adapter fails and is then activated as part of failover. Keep in mind that, technically, you can place a single network adapter in a team. However, you need two or more network adapters for fault protection through failover.

Performance logging

Windows Server 2012 R2 uses data collector sets and reports. Data collector sets enable you to specify sets of performance objects and counters that you want to track. When you create a data collector set, you can easily start or stop monitoring the performance objects and counters included in the set. In a way, this makes data collector sets similar to the performance logs used in earlier releases of Windows. However, data collector sets are much more sophisticated. You can use them in the following ways:

- Use a single data set to generate multiple performance counter and trace logs.
- Assign access controls to manage who can access collected data.
- Create multiple run schedules and stop conditions for monitoring.
- Use data managers to control the size of collected data and reporting.
- Generate reports based on collected data.

In Performance Monitor, you can review currently configured data collector sets and reports under the Data Collector Sets and Reports nodes, respectively. As shown in Figure 11-13, you find data sets and reports that are user-defined and system-defined. User-defined data sets are created by users for general monitoring and performance tuning. System-defined data sets are created by the operating system to aid in automated diagnostics.

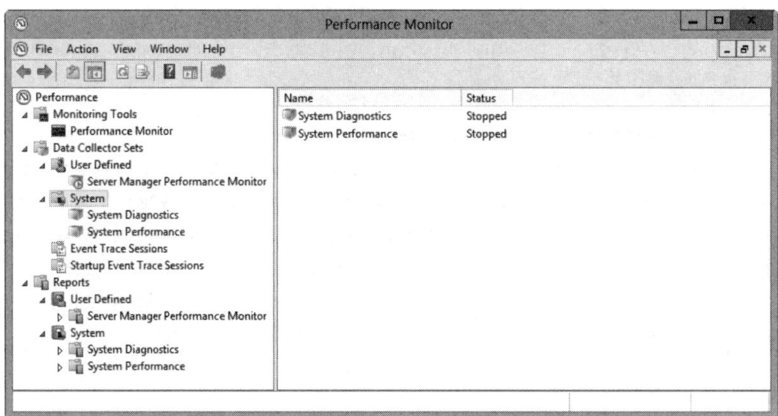

Figure 11-13 Review the available data collector sets and reports.

Creating and managing data collector sets

In Performance Monitor, you can view the currently configured data collector sets by expanding the Data Collector Sets node and then expanding the User Defined and System nodes. When you select a data collector set in the left pane, you see a list of the related data collectors in the main pane listed by name and type.

Data collector set types include the following:

- **Configuration.** The Configuration type is for data collectors that record changes to particular registry paths.
- **Trace.** The Trace type is for data collectors that record performance data whenever related events occur.
- **Performance Counter.** The Performance Counter type is for data collectors that record data on selected counters when a predetermined interval has elapsed.

Windows Server 2012 R2 uses event traces to track a wide variety of performance statistics. You can view running event traces by selecting Event Trace Sessions. You can then stop a data collector running a trace by pressing and holding or right-clicking it and selecting Stop.

Some event traces are configured to start automatically with the operating system. These event traces are called *startup event traces*. You can view the enabled or disabled status of event traces configured to run automatically when you start the computer by selecting Startup Event Trace Sessions. You can start a trace by pressing and holding or right-clicking a startup data collector and selecting Start As Event Trace Session. You can delete a startup data collector by pressing and holding or right-clicking it and then selecting Delete.

You can save a data collector as a template that can be used as the basis of other data collectors by pressing and holding or right-clicking the data collector and selecting Save Template. In the Save As dialog box, select a directory, type a name for the template, and then tap or click Save. The data collector template is saved as an XML file that can be copied to other systems.

You can delete a user-defined data collector by pressing and holding or right-clicking it and then selecting Delete. If a data collector is running, you need to stop collecting data first and then delete the collector. Deleting a collector deletes the related reports as well.

Using data collector templates

Performance Monitor includes several preconfigured templates for gathering general diagnostics information, which can include information about the system configuration and performance:

- **Basic.** Generates a report that includes basic information about the computer, CPU and disk utilization, and active network adapters. After you create a data collector set based on this template, you can add or remove counters and change the scheduling by editing the properties of the data collector set. When you are reviewing the data, be sure to drill down into the details. For example, under disks, examine the *hot files*, which are the files causing the most disk I/O activity. Also, be sure to examine the resource overview closely; it provides a summary analysis of CPU, network, disk, and memory usage. Note that this basic data is included in the reports for the other predefined collector sets. Default run-time: 60 seconds.

- **Active Directory Diagnostics.** Generates a report that provides detailed diagnostics data for Active Directory, which includes registry keys, performance counters, and trace events. On domain controllers, you can use this data to help troubleshoot Active Directory performance issues. Pay particular attention to the Active Directory diagnostics and tuning data provided in the report. For example, with searches, be sure to examine the detailed data provided for unique searches, directory search by object, search status codes, searches with the most CPU utilization, and clients with the most CPU usage. Also, don't overlook the tuning parameters for the registry. Default run-time: 300 seconds.

- **System Performance.** Generates a report that provides detailed performance data regarding local hardware resources, system response times, and processes on the local computer. Use this information to identify the possible causes of performance issues. Note that the system performance data is included in the report for system diagnostics. Default run-time: 60 seconds.

- **System Diagnostics.** Generates a report that provides detailed diagnostics data, which includes the status of local hardware resources, system response times, and processes on the local computer along with system information and configuration data. Suggests ways to maximize performance and streamline system operation. Be sure to examine the entries under basic system checks closely, particularly those for hardware devices and drivers. Default run-time: 60 seconds.

On member servers, system data collector sets are created automatically for system diagnostics and system performance. On domain controllers, a system data collector set for Active Directory diagnostics is also created. If you press and hold or right-click the related entry under Data Collector Sets and then select Start, Performance Monitor generates a report that you can review to evaluate performance and begin diagnostics for troubleshooting.

Although you can't modify the system data collector sets that were created automatically, you can create new collector sets based on the predefined templates and then modify their settings. To do this, follow these steps:

1. In Performance Monitor, under the Data Collector Sets node, press and hold or right-click the User Defined node in the left pane, point to New, and then choose Data Collector Set.

2. In the Create New Data Collector Set Wizard, type a name for the data collector, such as **Custom System Diagnostics**. Create From A Template (Recommended) is selected by default, as shown in Figure 11-14. Tap or click Next.

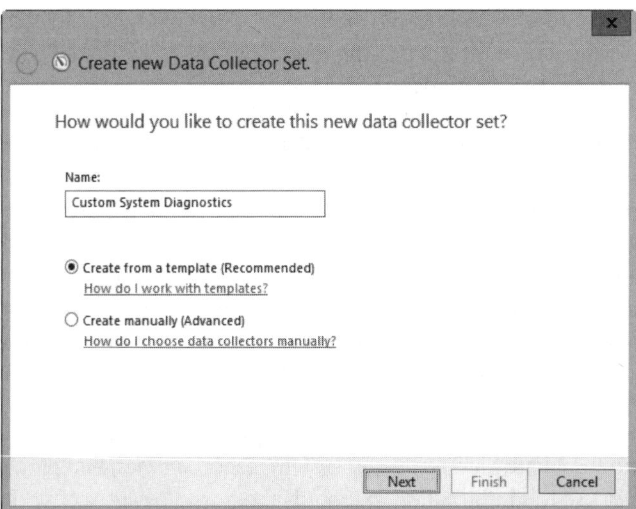

Figure 11-14 Specify the name of the collector set and base the set on a template.

3. On the Which Template Would You Like To Use page, shown in Figure 11-15, select the template to use or click Browse to search for a saved template. When you are ready to continue, tap or click Next.

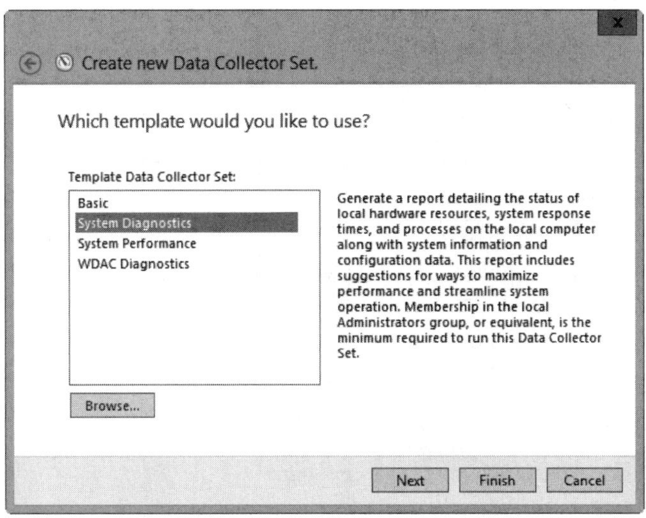

Figure 11-15 Select a predefined template to use or browse for a saved template.

4. On the Where Would You Like The Data To Be Saved page, type the root path to use for logging collected data. Alternatively, tap or click Browse and then use the Browse For Folder dialog box to select the logging directory. Tap or click Next when you are ready to continue.

5. On the Create The Data Collector Set page, the Run As box lists <Default> as the user to indicate that the log will run under the privileges and permissions of the default system account. To run the log with the privileges and permissions of another user, tap or click Change. Type the user name and password for the desired account and then tap or click OK. User names can be entered in DOMAIN\USERNAME format, such as CPANDL\WilliamS for the WilliamS account in the CPANDL domain.

6. Select Open Properties For This Data Collector Set and then tap or click Finish. This saves the data collector set, closes the wizard, and then opens the related Properties dialog box.

7. By default, logging is configured to start manually. To configure a logging schedule, tap or click the Schedule tab and then tap or click Add. You can now set the active range, start time, and run days for data collection. Figure 11-16 shows an example.

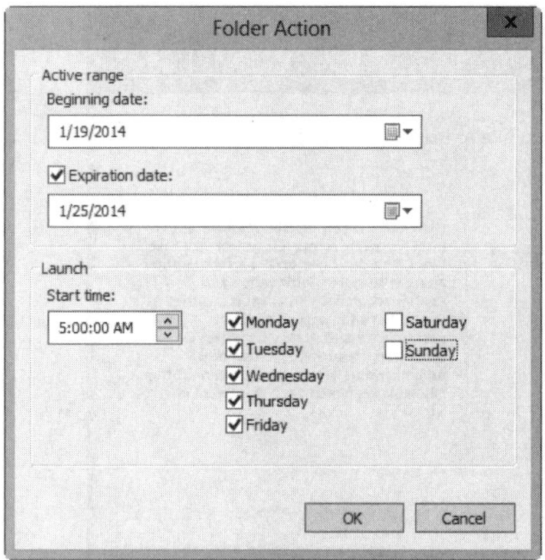

Figure 11-16 Set the logging schedule for the collector set.

8. By default, logging stops only if you set an expiration date as part of the logging schedule. Using the options on the Stop Condition tab, you can configure the log file to stop manually after a specified period of time, such as seven days, or when the log file is full (if you set a maximum size limit).

9. Tap or click OK when you finish setting the logging schedule and stop conditions. You can manage the data collector as explained in "Creating and managing data collector sets" earlier in this chapter. If you want Windows to run a scheduled task when data collection stops, configure the tasks on the Task tab in the Properties dialog box.

Collecting performance counter data

Data collectors can be used to record performance data on the selected counters at a specific sampling interval. For example, you could sample performance data for the CPU every 15 minutes. The default location for logging is %SystemDrive%\PerfLogs\Admin. Log files can grow in size very quickly. If you plan to log data for an extended period, be sure to place the log file on a drive with lots of free space. Remember, the more frequently you update the log file, the greater the drive space and CPU resource usage on the system.

To collect performance counter data, follow these steps:

1. In Performance Monitor, under the Data Collector Sets node, press and hold or right-click the User Defined node in the left pane, point to New, and then choose Data Collector Set.

2. In the Create New Data Collector Set Wizard, shown in Figure 11-17, type a name for the data collector, such as **Memory Monitor** or **Physical Disk Monitor**. Afterward, select Create Manually (Advanced) and then tap or click Next.

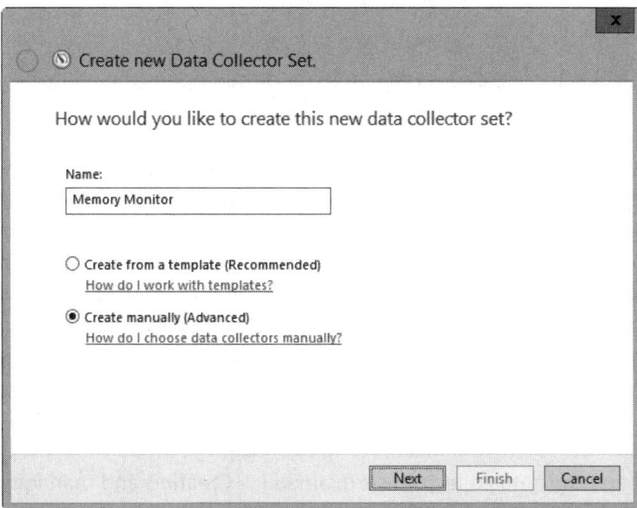

Figure 11-17 Specify the name of the collector set.

3. On the What Type Of Data Do You Want To Include page, Create Data Logs is selected by default. Select the Performance Counter check box and then tap or click Next.

4. On the Which Performance Counters Would You Like To Log page, tap or click Add. This opens the Add Counters dialog box, which you can use as previously discussed to select the performance counters to track. When you are finished selecting counters, tap or click OK.

5. On the Which Performance Counters Would You Like To Log page, type in a sample interval and select a time unit in seconds, minutes, hours, days, or weeks. The sample interval specifies when new data is collected. For example, if you sample every 15 minutes, the data log is updated every 15 minutes. Tap or click Next when you are ready to continue.

6. On the Where Would You Like The Data To Be Saved page, type the root path to use for logging collected data. Alternatively, tap or click Browse and then use the Browse For Folder dialog box to select the logging directory. Tap or click Next when you are ready to continue.

7. On the Create The Data Collector Set page, the Run As box lists <Default> as the user to indicate that the log will run under the privileges and permissions of the default system

account. To run the log with the privileges and permissions of another user, tap or click Change. Type the user name and password for the desired account and then tap or click OK. User names can be entered in DOMAIN\USERNAME format, such as CPANDL\WilliamS for the WilliamS account in the CPANDL domain.

8. Select Open Properties For This Data Collector Set and then tap or click Finish. This saves the data collector set, closes the wizard, and then opens the related Properties dialog box.

9. By default, logging is configured to start manually. To configure a logging schedule, tap or click the Schedule tab and then tap or click Add. You can now set the active range, start time, and run days for data collection.

10. By default, logging stops only if you set an expiration date as part of the logging schedule. By using the options on the Stop Condition tab, you can configure the log file to stop manually after a specified period of time, such as seven days, or when the log file is full (if you set a maximum size limit).

11. Tap or click OK when you finish setting the logging schedule and stop conditions. You can manage the data collector as explained in "Creating and managing data collector sets" earlier in this chapter. If you want Windows to run a scheduled task when data collection stops, configure the tasks on the Task tab in the Properties dialog box.

Collecting performance trace data

You can use data collectors to record performance trace data whenever events related to their source providers occur. A source provider is an application or operating system service that has traceable events.

To collect performance trace data, follow these steps:

1. In Performance Monitor, under the Data Collector Sets node, press and hold or right-click the User-Defined node in the left pane, point to New, and then choose Data Collector Set.

2. In the Create New Data Collector Set Wizard, type a name for the data collector, such as **Disk IO Trace** or **Logon Trace**. Afterward, select Create Manually (Advanced) and then tap or click Next.

3. On the What Type Of Data Do You Want To Include page, Create Data Logs is selected by default. Select the Event Trace Data check box and then tap or click Next.

4. On the Which Event Trace Providers Would You Like To Enable page, tap or click Add.

5. In the Event Trace Providers dialog box, shown in Figure 11-18, select an event trace provider to track, such as Active Directory: NetLogon, and then tap or click OK.

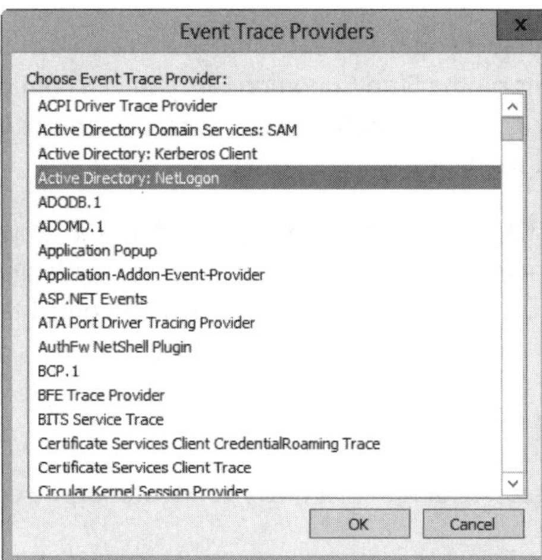

Figure 11-18 Select an event trace provider to track.

6. On the Which Event Trace Providers Would You Like To Enable page, you can configure property values to track. By selecting individual properties in the Properties list and tapping or clicking Edit, you can track particular property values rather than all values for the provider. Repeat this process to select other event trace providers to track. Tap or click Next when you are ready to continue.

7. On the Where Would You Like The Data To Be Saved page, type the root path to use for logging collected data. Alternatively, tap or click Browse and then use the Browse For Folder dialog box to select the logging directory. Tap or click Next when you are ready to continue.

8. On the Create The Data Collector Set page, the Run As box lists <Default> as the user to indicate that the log will run under the privileges and permissions of the default system account. To run the log with the privileges and permissions of another user, tap or click Change. Type the user name and password for the desired account and then tap or click OK. User names can be entered in DOMAIN\USERNAME format, such as CPANDL\WilliamS for the WilliamS account in the CPANDL domain.

9. Select Open Properties For This Data Collector Set, and then tap or click Finish. This saves the data collector set, closes the wizard, and then opens the related Properties dialog box.

10. By default, logging is configured to start manually. To configure a logging schedule, tap or click the Schedule tab and then tap or click Add. You can now set the active range, start time, and run days for data collection.

11. By default, logging stops only if you set an expiration date as part of the logging schedule. Using the options on the Stop Condition tab, you can configure the log file to stop manually after a specified period of time, such as seven days, or when the log file is full (if you set a maximum size limit).

12. Tap or click OK when you finish setting the logging schedule and stop conditions. You can manage the data collector as explained in "Creating and managing data collector sets" earlier in this chapter. If you want Windows to run a scheduled task when data collection stops, configure the tasks on the Task tab in the Properties dialog box.

Collecting configuration data

You can use data collectors to record changes in registry configuration. To collect configuration data, follow these steps:

1. In Performance Monitor, under the Data Collector Sets node, press and hold or right-click the User-Defined node in the left pane, point to New, and then choose Data Collector Set.

2. In the Create New Data Collector Set Wizard, type a name for the data collector, such as **System Registry Info** or **Current User Registry Info**. Afterward, select Create Manually (Advanced) and then tap or click Next.

3. On the What Type Of Data Do You Want To Include page, Create Data Logs is selected by default. Select the System Configuration Information check box and then tap or click Next.

4. On the Which Registry Keys Would You Like To Record page, tap or click Add. Type the registry path to track. Repeat this process to add other registry paths to track. Tap or click Next when you are ready to continue.

5. On the Where Would You Like The Data To Be Saved page, type the root path to use for logging collected data. Alternatively, tap or click Browse and then use the Browse For Folder dialog box to select the logging directory. Tap or click Next when you are ready to continue.

6. On the Create The Data Collector Set page, the Run As box lists <Default> as the user to indicate that the log will run under the privileges and permissions of the default system account. To run the log with the privileges and permissions of another user, tap or click Change. Type the user name and password for the desired account and then tap or

click OK. User names can be entered in DOMAIN\USERNAME format, such as CPANDL\WilliamS for the WilliamS account in the CPANDL domain.

7. Select Open Properties For This Data Collector Set and then tap or click Finish. This saves the data collector set, closes the wizard, and then opens the related Properties dialog box.

8. By default, logging is configured to start manually. To configure a logging schedule, tap or click the Schedule tab and then tap or click Add. You can now set the active range, start time, and run days for data collection.

9. By default, logging stops only if you set an expiration date as part of the logging schedule. By using the options on the Stop Condition tab, you can configure the log file to stop manually after a specified period of time, such as seven days, or when the log file is full (if you set a maximum size limit).

10. Tap or click OK when you finish setting the logging schedule and stop conditions. You can manage the data collector as explained in "Creating and managing data collector sets" earlier in this chapter. If you want Windows to run a scheduled task when data collection stops, configure the tasks on the Task tab in the Properties dialog box.

Viewing data collector reports

When you're troubleshooting problems, you'll often want to log performance data over an extended period of time and then review the data to analyze the results. For each data collector that has been or is currently active, you'll find related data collector reports. As with data collector sets themselves, data collector reports are usually organized into two general categories: user-defined and system-defined.

To view data collector reports in Performance Monitor, expand the Reports node and then expand the individual report node for the data collector you want to analyze. Under the data collector's report node, you find individual reports for each logging session, as shown in Figure 11-19. A logging session begins when logging starts and ends when logging is stopped.

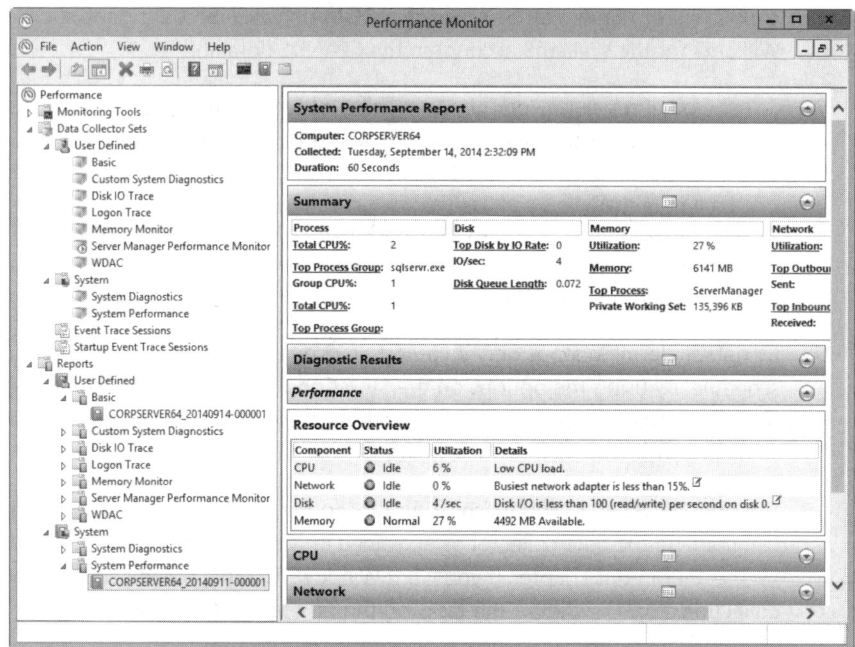

Figure 11-19 Access a report to view the collected data.

The most recent log is the one with the highest log number. To view a log and analyze its related data graphically, double-tap or double-click it. Keep in mind that if a data collector is actively logging, you won't be able to view the most recent log. You can stop collecting data by pressing and holding or right-clicking a data collector set and selecting Stop. Collected data is shown by default in a graph view from the start of data collection to the end of data collection. Only counters that you selected for logging will be available. If a report doesn't have a counter that you want to work with, you need to modify the data collector properties, restart the logging process, and then check the logs again.

NOTE

Open the most recent report for a data collector set directly by pressing and holding or right-clicking a data collector set and then selecting Latest Report. This shortcut works only if reports are available.

Save a data collector set as a template that can be used on the current server and other servers by pressing and holding or right-clicking a data collector set and then selecting Save Template. Next, in the Save As dialog box, select a save location, type a name for the template, and then tap or click Save.

You can modify the report details by using the following techniques:

1. In Performance Monitor, press and hold or right-click the Performance Monitor node and then select Properties. In the Performance Monitor Properties dialog box, tap or click the Source tab.
2. Specify data sources to analyze. Under Data Source, select Log Files and then tap or click Add to open the Select Log File dialog box. You can now select an additional log file to analyze.
3. Specify the time window that you want to analyze. Tap or click Time Range and then drag the Total Range bar to specify the appropriate starting and ending times. Drag the left edge to the right to move up the start time. Drag the right edge to the left to move down the end time.
4. Tap or click the Data tab. You can now select counters to view. Select a counter and then tap or click Remove to remove it from the graph view. Tap or click Add to open the Add Counters dialog box, which you can use to select the counters that you want to analyze.
5. Tap or click OK. In the monitor pane, tap or click the Change Graph Type button to select the type of graphing.

Inside OUT

Use the Data Manager to automate report cleanup

Use the Data Manager to determine how much data can be generated and stored for each user-defined data collector set. To open the Data Manager, press and hold or right-click a user-defined data set and then select Data Manager.

Settings on the Data Manager tab enable you to ensure that a minimum amount of free space is available before generating reports, control the maximum number of subfolders that can be created during report generation, configure whether the oldest or largest existing data set is cleaned up either before or after a report is generated, and much more.

Settings on the Actions tab enable you to specify cleanup actions. For example, reports based on the predefined templates are cleaned up in several ways by default. After one day, a .cab file is created containing the report data, and then the report data itself is deleted. After eight weeks, the .cab file is deleted. After 24 weeks, any remaining data is deleted, including the report itself.

Configuring performance counter alerts

You can configure alerts to notify you when certain events occur or when certain performance thresholds are reached. You can send these alerts as network messages and as events that are logged in the application event log. You can also configure alerts to start applications and performance logs.

To configure an alert, follow these steps:

1. In Performance Monitor, under the Data Collector Sets node, press and hold or right-click the User-Defined node in the left pane, point to New, and then choose Data Collector Set.

2. In the Create New Data Collector Set Wizard, type a name for the data collector, such as **Memory Alert** or **Full Disk Alert**. Afterward, select Create Manually (Advanced) and then tap or click Next.

3. On the What Type Of Data Do You Want To Include page, select Performance Counter Alert and then tap or click Next.

4. On the Which Performance Counters Would You Like To Monitor page, shown in Figure 11-20, tap or click Add to open the Add Counters dialog box. This dialog box is identical to the Add Counters dialog box discussed previously. Use the Add Counters dialog box to add counters that trigger the alert. Tap or click OK when you're finished.

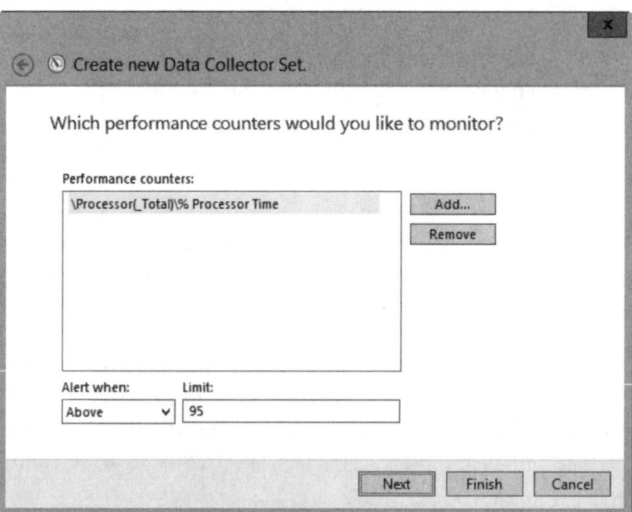

Figure 11-20 Select the performance counters for the alerts.

5. In the Performance Counters panel, select the first counter and then use the Alert When text box to set the occasion when an alert for this counter is triggered. Alerts can be triggered when the counter is above or below a specific value. Select Above or Below and then set the trigger value. The unit of measurement is whatever makes sense for the currently selected counter or counters. For example, to alert if processor time is over 95 percent, you select Above and then type **95**. Repeat this process to configure other counters you've selected and then tap or click Next.

6. On the Create The Data Collector Set page, the Run As box lists <Default> as the user to indicate that the log will run under the privileges and permissions of the default system account. To run the log with the privileges and permissions of another user, tap or click Change. Type the user name and password for the desired account and then tap or click OK. User names can be entered in DOMAIN\USERNAME format, such as CPANDL\WilliamS for the WilliamS account in the CPANDL domain.

7. Select Open Properties For This Data Collector Set and then tap or click Finish. This saves the data collector set, closes the wizard, and then opens the related Properties dialog box.

8. By default, logging is configured to start manually. To configure a logging schedule, tap or click the Schedule tab and then tap or click Add. You can now set the active range, start time, and run days for data collection.

9. By default, logging stops only if you set an expiration date as part of the logging schedule. Using the options on the Stop Condition tab, you can configure the log file to stop manually after a specified period of time, such as seven days, or when the log file is full (if you set a maximum size limit).

10. Tap or click OK when you finish setting the logging schedule and stop conditions. You can manage the data collector as explained in "Creating and managing data collector sets" earlier in this chapter. If you want Windows to run a scheduled task when data collection stops, configure the tasks on the Task tab in the Properties dialog box.

Monitoring performance from the command line

Windows Server 2012 R2 includes a command-line utility called Typeperf for writing performance data to the command line. You can use it to monitor the performance of both local and remote computers. The available parameters for Typeperf are summarized in Table 11-2.

Table 11-2 Parameters for Typeperf

Parameter	Description
–cf <filename>	Specifies a file containing a list of performance counters to monitor.
–config <filename>	Specifies the settings file containing command options.
–f <CSV|TSV|BIN|SQL>	Sets the output file format. The default is .csv for comma-separated values.
–o <filename>	Sets the path of an output file or SQL database.
–q [object]	Lists installed counters for the specified object.
–qx [object]	Lists installed counters with instances.
–s <ComputerName>	Sets the server to monitor if no server is specified in the counter path.
–sc <samples>	Sets the number of samples to collect.
–si <[[hh:]mm:]ss>	Sets the time between samples. The default is 1 second.
–y	Answers Yes to all questions without prompting.

It looks complicated, I know, but Typeperf is fairly easy to use after you get started. In fact, all you really need to provide to get basic monitoring information is the path to the performance counter you want to track. The performance counter path has the following syntax:

```
\\ComputerName\ObjectName\ObjectCounter
```

Here, the path starts with the UNC computer name or IP address of the local or remote computer you are working with and includes the object name and the object counter to use. If you want to track System\Processor Queue Length on CORPSVR02, you type

```
typeperf "\\corpsvr02\System\Processor Queue Length"
```

> NOTE
>
> **You might have noticed that I enclosed the counter path in double quotation marks. Although this is good form for all counter paths, it is required in this example because the counter path includes spaces.**

You can also easily track all counters for an object by using an asterisk (*) as the counter name, such as in the following:

```
typeperf "\\corpsvr02\Memory\*"
```

Here, you track all counters for the *Memory* object.

A slight problem is introduced for objects that have multiple instances. For these objects, such as the *Processor* object, you must specify the object instance you want to work with. The syntax for this is as follows:

```
\\ComputerName\ObjectName(ObjectInstance)\ObjectCounter
```

Here, you follow the object name with the object instance in parentheses. To work with all instances of an object that has multiple instances, you use _Total as the instance name. To work with a specific instance of an object, use its instance identifier. For example, if you want to examine the Processor\%Processor Time counter, you must use either the following to work with all processor instances:

```
typeperf "\\corpsvr02\Processor(_Total)\%Processor Time"
```

or the code shown next to work with a specific processor instance:

```
typeperf "\\corpsvr02\Processor(0)\%Processor Time"
```

In this case, that is the first processor on the system.

By default, Typeperf writes its output to the command line in a comma-delimited list. You can redirect the output to a file by using the *–o* parameter and set the output format by using the *–f* parameter. The output format indicators are CSV for a comma-delimited text file, TSV for a tab-delimited text file, BIN for a binary file, and SQL for a SQL binary file. Consider the following example:

```
typeperf "\\corpsvr02\Memory\*" -o perf.bin -f bin
```

Here, you track all counters for the *Memory* object and write the output to a binary file called Perf.bin in the current directory.

If you need help determining the available counters, type **typeperf –q** followed by the object name for which you want to view counters, such as in the following:

```
typeperf -q Memory
```

If an object has multiple instances, you can list the installed counters with instances by using the *–qx* parameter, such as in the following:

```
typeperf -qx PhysicalDisk
```

You can use this counter information as input to Typeperf as well. Add the *–o* parameter and write the output to a text file, such as in the following:

```
typeperf -qx PhysicalDisk -o perf.txt
```

Then, edit the text file so that only the counters you want to track are included. You can then use the file to determine which performance counters are tracked by specifying the *–cf* parameter followed by the file path to this counter file. Consider the following example:

```
typeperf -cf perf.txt -o c:\perflogs\perf.bin -f bin
```

Here, Typeperf reads the list of counters to track from Perf.txt and then writes the performance data in binary format to a file in the C:\PerfLogs directory.

The one problem with Typeperf is that it will sample data once every second until you tell it to stop by pressing Ctrl+C. This is fine when you are working at the command line and monitoring the output. It doesn't work so well, however, if you have other things to do—and most administrators do. To control the sampling interval and set how long to sample, you can use the *–si* and *–sc* parameters, respectively. For example, if you want Typeperf to sample every 60 seconds and stop logging after 120 samples, you could type this:

```
typeperf -cf perf.txt -o C:\perf\logs\perf.bin -f bin -si 60 -sc 120
```

Inside OUT

Use Windows PowerShell for performance monitoring

Windows PowerShell includes several cmdlets for performance monitoring. The one you'll use the most is Get-Counter. You use Get-Counter to get objects representing real-time performance counter data. The paths you work with when specifying counters are similar to those used with Typeperf. For example, you track all counters for the *Memory* object on CorpSvr35 by entering the following command:

```
get-counter "\\corpsvr35\Memory\*"
```

If you want to examine the Processor\%Processor Time counter, you either work with all processor instances:

```
get-counter "\\corpsvr35\Processor(_Total)\%Processor Time"
```

or with a specific processor instance:

```
get-counter "\\corpsvr35\Processor(0)\%Processor Time"
```

Need to know which counters are available for an object? Just type **get-counter -listset** followed by the object name, such as:

```
get-counter -listset Memory
```

Here, you list all the counters for the *Memory* object.

Analyzing trace logs at the command line

You can examine trace log data by using the Tracerpt command-line utility. Tracerpt processes trace logs, and you can use it to generate trace analysis reports and dump files for the events generated. Commonly used parameters for Tracerpt are summarized in Table 11-3.

Table 11-3 Parameters for Tracerpt

Parameter	Description
–o [*filename*]	Sets the text output file to which the parsed data should be written. The default is Dumpfile.xml.
–summary [*filename*]	Sets the name of the text file to which a summary report of the data should be written. The default is Summary.txt.
–report [*filename*]	Sets the name of the text file to which a detailed report of the data should be written. The default is Workload.xml.
–rt <*session_name* [*session_name* ...]>	Sets the real-time event trace session data source to use instead of a converted log file.
–config <*filename*>	Specifies a settings file containing command options.
–y	Answers Yes to all questions without prompting.
-of <CSV|EVTX|XML>	Sets the dump file format.
-f <XML|HTML>	Sets the report file format.
–export <*filename*>	Sets the name of the event schema export file. The default is schema.man.

The most basic way to use Tracerpt is to specify the name of the trace log to use. By default, 1trace logs are written to C:\PerfLogs. So, if a log in this directory was named SysP_000002.etl, you could analyze it by typing the following:

```
tracerpt C:\Perflogs\SysP_000002.etl
```

Here, four files are created in the current directory. The parsed output is written to Dumpfile.xml, a summary report is written to Summary.txt, a detailed report is written to Workload.xml, and an event schema report file is written to schema.man.

You could also specify the exact files to use for output as shown in the following example:

```
tracerpt C:\Perflogs\ SysP_000002.etl -o c:\sysp.csv
 -summary c:\sysp-summary.txt -report sysp-report-.txt
```

CHAPTER 11

CHAPTER 12

Storage management essentials

Data is stored throughout the enterprise on a variety of systems and storage devices, the most common of which are hard disk drives but also can include storage-management devices and removable media devices. Managing and maintaining the myriad systems and storage devices are the responsibilities of administrators. If a storage device fails, runs out of space, or encounters other problems, serious negative consequences can result. Servers could crash, applications could stop working, and users could lose data, all of which affects the productivity of users and the organization's bottom line. You can help prevent such problems and losses by implementing sound storage-management procedures that enable you to evaluate your current and future storage needs and help you meet current and future performance, capacity, and availability requirements. You then must configure storage appropriately for the requirements you've defined.

Essential storage technologies

One of the few constants in Microsoft Windows operating system administration is that data storage needs are ever increasing. It seems that only a few years ago a 2-terabyte (TB) hard disk was huge and something primarily reserved for Windows servers rather than Windows workstations. Now Windows workstations ship with large hard disks as standard equipment, and some even ship with striped drives that allow workstations to have spanned drives that have multi-terabyte volumes—and all of that data must be backed up and stored somewhere other than on the workstations to protect it. This has meant that back-end storage solutions have had to scale dramatically as well. Server solutions that were once used for enterprise-wide implementations are now being used increasingly at the departmental level, and the underlying architecture for the related storage solutions has had to change dramatically to keep up.

> **Inside OUT**
>
> ***Storage technologies are in transition***
>
> Storage technologies are in transition from traditional approaches to standards-based approaches. As a result, several popular tools and favored features are being phased out. Officially, a tool or feature that is being phased out is referred to as *deprecated*. When Microsoft deprecates a tool or feature, that means it might not be in future releases of the operating system. Rather than not cover popular tools and features, I've chosen to discuss what is actually available in the operating system right now. That means I discuss both favored standbys and new options.
>
> Like other Windows operating systems before them, Windows 8.1 and Windows Server 2012 R2 will have long product life cycles. For most people deploying these operating systems today, what's in the box right now is what matters most, not what might or might not be in the box in a future release. My recommendation is to continue to use your favorite tools and features for servers you've already deployed and then transitioned to Windows Server 2012 R2. Before you deploy new servers on new hardware, however, you should review the available storage options and then make informed decisions about the tools and features to use on those new servers.

Using internal and external storage devices

To help meet the increasing demand for data storage and changing requirements, organizations are deploying servers with a mix of internal and external storage. In internal-storage configurations, drives are connected inside the server chassis to a local disk controller and are said to be directly attached. You'll sometimes see an internal storage device referred to as *direct-attached storage (DAS)*.

In external-storage configurations, servers connect to external, separately managed collections of storage devices that are either network-attached or part of a storage area network. Although the terms *network-attached storage* (*NAS*) and *storage-area network* (*SAN*) are sometimes used as if they are one and the same, the technologies differ in how servers communicate with the external drives.

NAS devices are connected through a regular Transmission Control Protocol/Internet Protocol (TCP/IP) network. All server-storage communications go across the organization's local area network (LAN), as shown in Figure 12-1, and typically use file-based protocols for communications, which can include Server Message Block (SMB), distributed file system (DFS), and Network File System (NFS). This means the available bandwidth on the network can be shared by clients, servers, and NAS devices. For best performance, the network should be running at 1 gigabit per second (Gbps) or higher. Networks operating at slower speeds can experience a serious decrease in performance as clients, services, and storage devices try to communicate using the limited bandwidth.

Inside OUT

Working with NFS

You add support for NFS by adding the Server For NFS role to a file server. Windows Server 2012 R2 supports NFS 3 and NFS 4.1. NFS 3 brings with it support for continuous availability. NFS 4.1 adds supports for stateful connections with improved security and lower bandwidth usage. Support for NFS 3 and NFS 4.1 also enables you to deploy and run VMware ESXi reliably on virtual machines from file-based storage access over NFS. You also can deploy Server For NFS reliably in a clustered configuration.

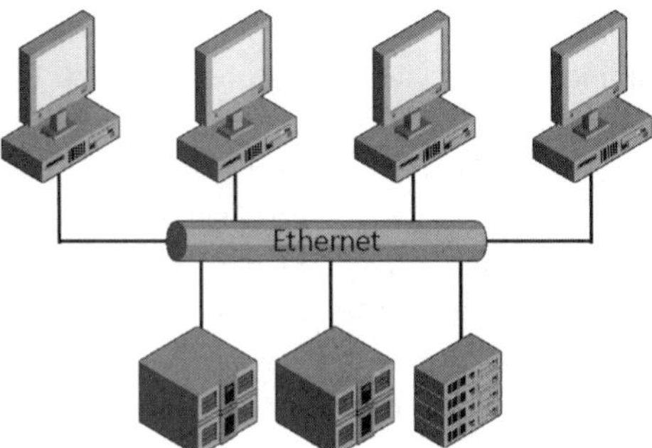

Figure 12-1 In a NAS, server-storage communications are on the LAN.

A SAN typically is physically separate from the LAN and is independently managed. As shown in Figure 12-2, this isolates the server-to-storage communications so that traffic doesn't affect communications between clients and servers. Several SAN technologies are implemented, including Fibre Channel Protocol (FCP), a more traditional SAN technology that delivers high reliability and performance, and Internet SCSI (iSCSI), which delivers good reliability and performance at a lower cost than Fibre Channel. As the name implies, iSCSI uses TCP/IP networking technologies on the SAN so that servers can communicate with storage devices by using IP. The SAN is still isolated from the organization's LAN.

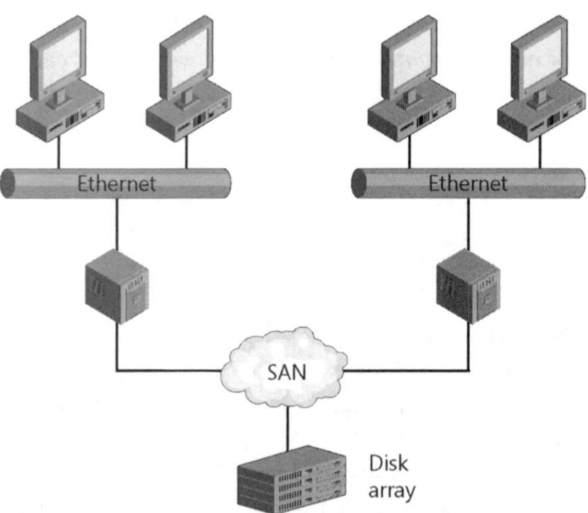

Figure 12-2 In a SAN, server-storage communications don't affect communications between clients and servers.

You should be aware that iSCSI uses traditional IP facilities to transfer data over LANs, wide area networks (WANs), or the Internet. Here, iSCSI clients (initiators) send Small Computer System Interface (SCSI) commands to targeted iSCSI storage devices (targets) on remote servers. iSCSI consolidates storage and allows hosts—which can include web, application, and database servers—to access the storage as if it were locally attached. Initiators can locate storage resources by using Internet Storage Name Service (iSNS). iSNS isn't required for communications, but it does provide management services similar to those for Fibre Channel networks. iSNS emulates the fabric services of Fibre Channel and can manage both Fibre Channel and iSCSI devices.

Although Fibre Channel requires special cabling, iSCSI uses standard Ethernet cabling and technically can operate over the same network as standard IP traffic. However, if iSCSI isn't operated on a dedicated network or subnet, performance can be severely degraded.

With TCP/IP, TCP is the transport protocol for IP networks. With Fibre Channel, FCP is a transport protocol used to transport SCSI commands over the Fibre Channel network. Fibre Channel networks can use a variety of topologies, including the following:

- Point-to-point (FC-PTP), where two devices are connected directly
- Arbitrated loop (FC-AL), where all devices are in a ring, similar to token ring networking
- Switched fabric (FC-SW), where all devices or device rings are connected to switches, similar to Ethernet

The standard model for Fibre Channel has five layers:

- FC0, the physical layer, which includes cables and connectors
- FC1, the data-link layer
- FC2, the network layer
- FC3, the common services layer
- FC4, the protocol-mapping layer

Windows Server 2012 R2 includes support for Fibre Channel over Ethernet (FCoE), a technology that allows IP network and SAN data traffic to be consolidated on a single network. FCoE encapsulates Fibre Channel frames over Ethernet and supports 10 Gbps and higher networks. With FCoE, the FC0 and FC1 layers of the Fibre Channel model are replaced with Ethernet, and FCoE operates in the FC2, or network, layer. This is different from iSCSI, which runs on top of TCP and IP. In addition, although iSCSI is routable across IP networks, FCoE isn't routable in the IP layer and won't work across routed IP networks.

You should also note that although Fibre Channel has priority-based flow controls, these controls aren't part of standard Ethernet. As a result, both FCoE and iSCSI needed enhancements to support priority-based flow controls and prevent the frame loss that might occur otherwise. These enhancements, provided in the Data Center Bridging suite of Institute of Electrical and Electronics Engineers (IEEE) standards, include the encapsulation of native frames, extensions to Ethernet to prevent frame loss, and mapping between ports/IDs and Ethernet media access control (MAC) addresses.

Several competing network protocols are available to provide fabric functionality to Fibre Channel devices over an IP network and to make the technology work over long distances. One is called Internet Fibre Channel Protocol (iFCP). iFCP uses gateways and routing to enable connectivity and TCP for error detection and correction and for congestion control. A similar technology, called Fibre Channel over IP (FCIP), also is available. FCIP uses storage tunneling, by which Fibre Channel frames are encapsulated and then forwarded over an IP network, using TCP.

Storage-management features and tools

Windows Server 2012 R2 includes many features for working with SANs and handling storage management in general. Volume Shadow Copy Service (VSS) enables administrators to create point-in-time copies of volumes and individual files called *snapshots*. This makes it possible to back up these items while files are open and applications are running and to restore them to a specific point in time. You can use VSS also to create point-in-time copies of documents on shared folders. These copies are called *shadow copies*.

NOTE

Users can recover their own files when VSS is enabled. After you configure shadow copy, point-in-time backups of documents contained in the designated shared folders are created automatically, and users can quickly recover files that have been deleted or unintentionally altered as long as the Shadow Copy Client has been installed on their computer.

The basic VSS functionality is built into the file and storage services and accessed through the File Server VSS provider. You can extend the basic functions in several ways. One of these ways is to add the File Server VSS Agent Service. You use this role service to create consistent snapshots of server application data such as virtual machine files from Hyper-V. You install the agent service on a file server when you want to back up applications that are storing data files on the file server. Here, you are backing up application data stored on file shares, which is different from user data stored on file shares (which is managed using the standard File Server VSS provider).

Windows Server 2012 R2 also includes storage providers. Storage providers make it possible for storage devices from multiple vendors to interoperate. To do this, Microsoft provides Storage Management application programming interfaces (APIs) that management tools and storage hardware can use, allowing for a unified interface for managing storage devices from multiple vendors and making it easier for administrators to manage a mixed-storage environment. Standard storage providers are built into the file and storage services.

Windows Server 2012 R2 also supports the Storage Management Initiative (SMI-S) standard and storage providers that comply with this standard. Add this support by adding the Windows Standards-Based Storage Management feature. This feature enables the discovery, management, and monitoring of storage devices, using management tools that support the SMI-S standard. It does this by installing related Windows Management Instrumentation (WMI) classes and cmdlets.

When your file servers are using iSCSI, Fibre Channel, or both storage device types, you might also want to install Multipath I/O, iSNS Server service, and Data Center Bridging—all of which are installable features.

Multipath I/O supports SAN connectivity by establishing multiple sessions or connections to storage devices. Using Multipath I/O, you can configure as many as 32 physical paths to external storage devices that can be used simultaneously and load balanced if necessary. The purpose of having multiple paths is to have redundancy and possibly increased throughput. If you also have multiple host bus adapters, you improve the chances of recovery from a path failure. However, if a path failure occurs, there might be a short period of time when the drives on the SAN aren't accessible. Microsoft Multipath I/O (MPIO) supports iSCSI, Fibre Channel, and Serial Attached SCSI (SAS).

iSNS Server service helps iSNS clients discover iSCSI storage devices on an Ethernet network and automates the management and configuration of iSCSI and Fibre Channel storage devices (as long as Fibre Channel devices use iFCP gateways). Data Center Bridging helps manage bandwidth allocation for offloaded storage traffic on converged network adapters, which is useful with iSCSI and FCoE.

Other file and storage features you might want to install on file servers include the following:

- **Enhanced Storage.** Supports additional functions made available by devices that support hardware encryption and enhanced storage. Enhanced storage devices support IEEE standard 1667 to provide enhanced security, which can include authentication at the hardware level of the storage device.
- **Windows Search Service.** Allows for faster file searches for resources on the server from clients that are compatible with this service. Keep in mind, however, that this feature is designed primarily for desktop and small office implementations (and not for large enterprises).
- **Windows Server Backup.** The standard backup utility included with Windows Server 2012 R2.

Server Manager is your primary tool for managing storage. Windows Server 2012 R2 also has several command-line tools for managing local storage and storage-replication services. These tools include the following:

- **DiskPart.** Used to manage basic and dynamic disks and the partitions and volumes on those disks. It is the command-line counterpart to the Disk Management tool and includes features not found in the graphical user interface (GUI) tool, such as the capability to extend partitions on basic disks.

  NOTE

  DiskPart cannot be used to manage Storage Spaces. Windows 8.1 and Windows Server 2012 R2 might be the last versions of Windows to support Disk Management, DiskPart, and DiskRaid. The Virtual Disk Service (VDS) COM interface is being superseded by the Storage Management API. You can continue to use Disk Management and DiskPart to manage basic and dynamic disks.

- **Dfsdiag.** Used to perform troubleshooting and diagnostics for DFS.
- **Dfsradmin.** Used to manage and monitor DFS replication throughout the enterprise. You also use this tool for troubleshooting and diagnosing problems. This tool replaces Health_Chk and the other tools it worked with.

- **Dfsutil.** Used to configure DFS, back up and restore DFS directory trees (namespaces), copy directory trees, and troubleshoot DFS.
- **Fsutil.** Used to get detailed drive information and perform advanced file system maintenance. You can manage sparse files and reparse points, disk quotas, and other advanced features of NTFS.
- **Mountvol.** Used to manage volume automounting. By using volume mount points, administrators can mount volumes to empty NTFS folders, giving the volumes a drive path rather than a drive letter. This means it is easier to mount and unmount volumes, particularly with SANs.
- **Vssadmin.** Used to view and manage the Volume Shadow Copy Service (VSS) and its configuration.

Many Windows PowerShell cmdlets are available for managing storage as well. These cmdlets are module-specific and correspond to the storage component you want to manage. Available modules include the following:

- **BitsTransfer.** Used to manage the Background Intelligent Transfer Service (BITS).
- **BranchCache.** Used to configure and check the status of Windows BranchCache.
- **DFSN.** Used to manage DFS namespaces.
- **FileServerResourceManager.** Used to manage File Server Resource Manager.
- **iSCSI.** Used to manage iSCSI connections, sessions, targets, and ports.
- **IscsiTarget.** Used to mount and manage iSCSI virtual disks.
- **SmbShare.** Used to configure and check the status of standard file sharing.
- **Storage.** Used to manage disks, partitions, and volumes in addition to storage pools and Storage Spaces. It cannot be used to manage dynamic disks.

You learn more about the technologies behind these modules later in this chapter. The easiest way to learn more about these Windows PowerShell modules is to examine how their associated cmdlets work. You list the cmdlets associated with a module by using:

```
get-command -module ModuleName
```

Here, *ModuleName* is the name of the module you want to examine, such as the following:

```
get-command -module iscsi
```

After you list the cmdlets associated with an imported module, you can get more information about a particular cmdlet by using:

```
get-help CmdletName -detailed
```

Here, *CmdletName* is the name of the cmdlet to examine in detail, such as the following:

```
get-help connect-iscsitarget -detailed
```

Storage-management role services

You use File And Storage Services to configure your file servers. Several file and storage services are installed by default with any installation of Windows Server 2012 R2. These include File Server, which you use to manage file shares that users can access over the network, and Storage Services, which you use to manage various types of storage, including storage pools and Storage Spaces. Storage pools group disks so that you can create virtual disks from the available capacity. Each virtual disk you create is a storage space. You learn how to work with storage pools and Storage Spaces in Chapter 17, "Managing storage spaces."

Windows Server 2012 R2 also supports thin provisioning of Storage Spaces. With *thin provisioning*, you can create large virtual disks without having the actual space available. This enables you to provision storage to meet future needs and grow storage as needed. You also can reclaim storage that is no longer needed by trimming storage. To see how thin provisioning works, consider the following scenarios:

- Your file server is connected to a storage array with 2 TBs of actual storage but with the capability to grow to 10 TBs as needed (by installing additional hard disks). When you set up storage, you provision it as if additional storage were already available. One way to do this is to create a storage pool that has a total size of 10 TBs and then create five thin disks with 2 TBs of storage each.

- Your eight file servers are connected to a SAN with 10 TBs of actual storage but with the capability to grow to 80 TBs as needed (by installing additional hard disks). When you set up storage, you provision it as if additional storage were already available. One way to do this is to create a storage pool on each file server that has a total size of 10 TBs. Next, within each storage pool, you create five thin disks with 2 TBs of storage each.

With thin-disk provisioning, volumes use space from the storage pool as needed, up to the volume size. Here, the actual storage utilization for a volume is based on the total size of the data stored on the volume. If a volume doesn't grow, the storage space is never allocated and isn't wasted.

Contrast this with fixed-disk provisioning, by which a volume has a fixed size and uses space from the storage pool equal to its volume size. Here, the storage utilization for a volume is fixed and based on the total size of the volume itself. Because the storage is pre-allocated with a fixed size, any unused space isn't available for other volumes.

You can enhance file storage in many ways by using the additional role services that are available for File And Storage Services. One of the first role services you might consider using is BranchCache For Network Files. You add the BranchCache For Network Files role service to enable enhanced support for Windows BranchCache on your file servers and to optimize data transfer over the WAN for caching.

Windows BranchCache is a file-caching feature that works in conjunction with BITS. By enabling branch caching in Group Policy, you enable computers to retrieve documents and other types of files from a local cache rather than retrieving files from servers over the network. This improves response times and reduces transfer times.

Branch caching can be used in either a distributed cache mode or a hosted cache mode. With the distributed cache mode, desktop computers running compatible versions of Windows host and send distributed file caches, and caching servers running at remote offices are not needed. With the hosted cache mode, compatible file servers at remote offices host local file caches and send them to clients. Generally, whether distributed or hosted, the caches at one office location are separate from caches at other office locations. That said, the Active Directory configuration and the way Group Policy is applied ultimately determine whether computers are considered part of one office location or another.

Branch caching is designed as a WAN solution. It optimizes bandwidth usage for files transferred with either SMB or Hypertext Transfer Protocol (HTTP). Your content servers can be located anywhere on your network and in public or private cloud data centers. You enable branch caching on web servers and BITS-based application servers by adding the BranchCache feature. If you are deploying hosted cache servers, you add the BranchCache feature to these servers as well. You don't install this feature on your file servers, however. Instead, you add the BranchCache For Network Files role service.

Inside OUT

Enhancing BranchCache

BranchCache For Network Files can take advantage of data deduplication techniques to optimize data transfers. Because of this, it is recommended that you also install the Data Deduplication role service on your file servers, but don't do this without a firm understanding of what data deduplication is and how it works. If you have multiple file servers, you might also want to enable hash publication per share to improve performance. For file servers that aren't domain members, you enable hash publication in local policy. For file servers that are domain members, you typically want to isolate your BranchCache-enabled file servers in their own organizational units (OUs) and then enable hash publication in the appropriate GPO (Group Policy Object) or GPOs that are applied to these OUs. Either way, the Hash Publication For BranchCache policy is what you want to work with. This policy is found under Computer Configuration \Administrative Templates\Network\Lanman Server.

The Data Deduplication service can be installed with or without the BranchCache For Network Files role service. Data Deduplication uses subfile, variable-size chunking and compression to achieve higher storage efficiency. The service does this by segmenting files into 32 KB to 128 KB chunks, identifying duplicate chunks, and replacing the duplicates with references to a single copy. Because optimized files are stored as reparse points, files on the volume are no longer stored as data streams. Instead, they are replaced with stubs that point to data blocks within a common chunk store.

Previously, I mentioned the File Server VSS Agent Service, which you install on file servers when you want to ensure that you can make consistent backups of server application data using VSS-aware backup applications. When working with iSCSI, you also must install the iSCSI target VSS hardware provider on the initiator server you use to perform backups of iSCSI virtual disks. This ensures that the snapshots are application-consistent and can be restored at the logical unit number (LUN) level. If you don't use the iSCSI target VSS hardware provider on the initiator, server backups might not be consistent, and you might not be able to recover your iSCSI virtual disks completely. On management computers running storage-management applications, you must install the iSCSI target Virtual Disk Service (VDS) hardware provider. The iSCSI target VSS hardware provider and the iSCSI target VDS hardware provider are part of the iSCSI Target Storage Provider role service.

Another role service you might want to use with iSCSI is the iSCSI Target Server service. This role service turns any computer running Windows Server into a network-accessible block storage device. You can use this continuously available block storage to support network/diskless boot, shared storage on non-Windows iSCSI initiators, and development environments where you need to test applications prior to deploying them to SAN storage. Because the service uses standard Ethernet for its transport, no additional hardware is needed.

Although SMB is the default file-sharing protocol, other file-sharing solutions are available, including Network File System (NFS) and DFS. To enable NFS on your file servers, you add the Server For NFS service. This service provides a file-sharing solution for enterprises with mixed Windows and UNIX environments. When you install Server For NFS, users can transfer files between Windows Server and UNIX operating systems by using the NFS protocol. DFS, however, isn't an interoperability solution. Instead, DFS is a robust, enterprise solution for file sharing that you can use to create a single directory tree that includes multiple file servers and their file shares.

The DFS tree can contain more than 5,000 shared folders in a domain environment (or 50,000 shared folders on a standalone server), located on different servers, enabling users to find files or folders easily that are distributed across the enterprise. DFS directory trees can also be published in Active Directory Domain Services so that they are easy to search.

DFS has two key components:

- **DFS Namespaces.** You can use DFS Namespaces to group shared folders located on different servers into one or more logically structured namespaces. Each namespace appears as a single shared folder with a series of subfolders. However, the underlying structure of the namespace can come from shared folders on multiple servers at different sites.
- **DFS Replication.** You can use DFS Replication to synchronize folders on multiple servers across local or wide area network connections by using a multimaster replication engine. The replication engine uses the Remote Differential Compression (RDC) protocol to synchronize only the portions of files that have changed since the last replication.

You can use DFS Replication with DFS Namespaces or by itself. When a domain is running in a Windows 2008 domain functional level or higher, domain controllers use DFS Replication to replicate the SYSVOL directory.

DFS supports multiple roots and closest-site selection

Windows Server 2012 R2 supports multiple DFS roots and closest-site selection. The capability to host multiple DFS roots enables you to consolidate and reduce the number of servers needed to maintain DFS. By using closest-site selection, DFS uses Active Directory site metrics to route a client to the closest available DFS server.

File Server Resource Manager (FSRM) installs a suite of tools that administrators can use to manage data stored on servers better. Using FSRM, you can do the following:

- **Define file-screening policies.** You use file-screening policies to block unauthorized, potentially malicious types of content. You can configure active screening, which does not allow users to save unauthorized files, or passive screening, which allows users to save unauthorized files but monitors or warns about usage (or you can configure both).
- **Configure Resource Manager disk quotas.** By using Resource Manager disk quotas, you can manage disk space usage by folder and by volume. You can configure quotas with a specific limit as a hard limit (meaning a limit can't be exceeded) or a soft limit (meaning a limit can be exceeded).
- **Generate storage reports.** You can generate storage reports as part of disk-quota and file-screening management. Storage reports identify file usage by owner, type, and other parameters. They also help identify users and applications that violate screening policies.

You learn more about FRSM in Chapter 20, "Managing file screening and storage reporting."

Inside OUT

Windows Storage Server 2012 R2

Windows Storage Server 2012 R2 is a platform for NAS appliances. Several editions are available, including a rather limited Workgroup edition and a full-featured Standard edition. If you purchase a NAS that uses Windows Storage Server 2012 R2 Workgroup or Standard, you can manage it using many of the techniques I discuss in this book. In fact, you'll be able to manage storage provisioning, pooling, virtual disks, volumes, and much more by using Server Manager and Windows PowerShell if you want to.

You'll also be able to open the storage-provisioning wizards I discuss directly within the original equipment manufacturer (OEM) appliance. Also supported are central access policies, NIC teaming, DFS Namespaces, DFS Replication, Server For NFS, iSCSI targets, FSRM, folder redirection, offline files, offloaded data transfers, and the Resilient File System (ReFS).

Booting from SANs and using SANs with clusters

Windows Server 2012 R2 supports booting from a SAN, having multiple clusters attached to the same SAN, and having a mix of clusters and standalone servers attached to the same SAN. To boot from a SAN, the external storage devices and the host bus adapters of each server must be configured appropriately to allow booting from the SAN.

When multiple servers must boot from the same external storage device, you must either configure the SAN in a switched environment or attach it from each host to one of the storage subsystem's Fibre Channel ports. A switched or direct-to-port environment allows the servers to be separate from one another, which is essential for booting from a SAN.

Fibre Channel Arbitrated Loop isn't allowed

The use of a Fibre Channel Arbitrated Loop (FC-AL) configuration is not supported because hubs typically don't allow the servers on the SAN to be isolated properly from one another—and the same is true when you have multiple clusters attached to the same SAN or a mix of clusters and standalone servers attached to the same SAN.

Each server on the SAN must have exclusive access to the logical disk from which it is booting, and no other server on the SAN should be able to detect or access that logical disk. For multiple-cluster installations, the SAN must be configured so that a set of cluster disks is accessible by only one cluster and is completely hidden from the rest of the clusters. By default, Windows Server 2012 R2 will attach and mount every logical disk that it detects when the host bus adapter driver loads, and if multiple servers mount the same disk, the file system can be damaged.

To prevent file system damage, the SAN must be configured so that only one server can access a particular logical disk at a time. You can configure disks for exclusive access by using a type of LUN management such as LUN masking, LUN zoning, or a preferred combination of these techniques. You can use the File And Storage Services node in the Server Manager console to manage Fibre Channel and iSCSI SANs that support Storage Management APIs and have a configured storage provider.

TROUBLESHOOTING

Detecting SAN configuration problems

On an improperly configured SAN, multiple hosts can access the same logical disks. This isn't what you want to happen, but it does happen, and you might be able to detect this configuration problem when you are working with the logical disks. Try using File Explorer from multiple hosts to access the logical disks on the SAN. If you try to access a logical disk and receive an Access Denied, Device Not Ready, or similar error message, this can indicate that another server has access to the logical disk you are attempting to use. You might see another indicator of an improperly configured SAN when you add or configure logical disks. If you notice that multiple servers report that they've found new hardware when adding or configuring logical disks, there is a

configuration problem with the SAN. If there is a configuration problem with clusters, you can see the following error events in the System logs:

- Warning event ID 11 with event source %HBADriverName%, "The driver detected a controller error on Device\Storport*N*."
- Warning event ID 50 with event source Disk, "The system was attempting to transfer file data from buffers to \Device\HarddiskVolume*N*. The write operation failed, and only some of the data may have been written to the file."
- Warning event ID 51 with event source FTDISK, "An error was detected on device during a paging operation."
- Warning event ID 9 with event source %HBADriverName%, "Lost Delayed Write Data: The device, \Device\Storport*N*, did not respond within the timeout period."
- Warning event ID 26 with event source Application Popup, "Windows—Delayed Write Failed: Windows was unable to save all the data for the file \Device\HarddiskVolume*N*\MFT$. The data has been lost. This error may be caused by a failure of your computer hardware or network connection. Please try to save this file elsewhere."

Working with SMB 3.0

Server Message Block (SMB) is the standard technology used for file sharing. SMB 3.0 was released with Windows 8 and Windows Server 2012 and has been revised as SMB 3.02 with Windows 8.1 and Windows Server 2012 R2. Earlier releases of Windows support different versions of SMB. Windows 7 and Windows Server 2008 R2 support SMB 2.1. Windows Vista and Windows Server 2008 support SMB 2.0.

SMB 2.1 was an incremental improvement over SMB 2.0, which brought several important changes for file sharing, including support for BranchCache and large maximum transmission units (MTUs). SMB 3.0 has the following important improvements:

- **SMB Direct.** Provides support for network adapters that have Remote Direct Memory Access (RDMA) capability, allowing fast, offloaded data transfers and helping achieve high speeds and low latency while using few CPU resources. Previously, this capability was one of the key advantages of Fibre Channel block storage.
- **SMB encryption.** Provides secure data transfer by encrypting data automatically and without having to deploy Internet Protocol security (IPsec) or another encryption solution. SMB encryption can be enabled for an entire server (meaning for all its file shares) or for individual file shares as needed.

- **SMB Multichannel.** Allows servers to use multiple connections and network interfaces simultaneously, increasing fault tolerance and throughput. Configure network interface card (NIC) teaming to take advantage of this feature.
- **SMB scale-out.** Allows clustered file servers in an active-active configuration to aggregate bandwidth across the cluster. This provides simultaneous access to data files through all nodes in the cluster and enables administrators to load balance across cluster nodes simply by moving file server clients.
- **SMB signing.** Introduces AES-CCM and AES-CMAC for signing. Typically, signing with Advanced Encryption Standard (AES) is dramatically faster than signing with HMAC-SHA256 (which SMB 2/SMB 2.1 used).
- **SMB Transparent Failover.** Enables administrators to perform maintenance on nodes in a clustered file server without affecting applications storing data on the server's file shares. If a failure occurs, SMB clients transparently reconnect to another cluster node. This provides the benefits of a multicontroller storage array without having to purchase one.

NOTE

You not only can use the SMB Direct, SMB Multichannel, and SMB scale-out features to implement manageable, scalable active-active file shares, you also can use these features to share an existing Fibre Channel SAN's storage over SMB 3.0. This gives you a gateway to a SAN and extends your storage options.

Keep in mind that SMB is a client/server technology. For backward compatibility, newer clients continue to support older versions of the technology. While establishing a connection to a file share, an SMB client negotiates the SMB version to use for that connection based on the highest commonly supported SMB version. This process is referred to as *dialect negotiation*.

During dialect negotiation, the version downgrade is automatic, such that an SMB 3.0 client connecting to an SMB 2.1 server will use SMB 2.1 for that connection. Because earlier versions of SMB are less secure, forcing a client to downgrade the version used is one way someone might try to gain unauthorized access.

SMB 3.0 includes a security feature that attempts to detect forced downgrade attempts. If such an attempt is detected, the connection is disconnected, and Event ID 1005 is logged in the Microsoft-Windows-SmbServer/Operational log. This security feature works only when a client tries to force a downgrade from SMB 3.0 to SMB 2.0/SMB 2.1. It doesn't work if a client attempts to downgrade to SMB 1.0. For this reason, Microsoft recommends disabling support for SMB 1.0, which is only used by early Windows operating systems.

SMB 3.02 adds several improvements over SMB 3.0, including the following:

- Performance enhancements for SMB Direct
- Support for multiple SMB instances on scale-out file servers
- Automatic rebalancing of client connections to scale-out file servers

Inside OUT

Checking for and disabling SMB 1.0

Before you disable SMB 1.0, you should determine whether any clients are using SMB 1.0. Windows 2000, Windows XP, and Windows Server 2003 use SMB 1.0. Computer browser functionality also relies on SMB 1.0. To determine whether any SMB clients are currently using SMB 1.0, you can run the following command on each file server:

```
Get-SmbSession | Select ClientUserName,ClientComputerName,Dialect |
Where-Object {$_.Dialect -lt 2.00}
```

Keep in mind that this command must be run with elevated privileges and returns information only about active connections to SMB shares. You can disable SMB 1.0 support by removing the SMB 1.0/CIFS File Sharing Support feature from your file servers. You also can disable SMB 1.0 support by running the following command at an elevated Windows PowerShell prompt on each file server:

```
Uninstall-WindowsFeature fs-smb1
```

To finalize the removal process, you need to restart the server. You can easily run this command on multiple file servers. One technique is to invoke a remote command, as shown in this example:

```
Invoke-Command -ComputerName fileserver12, fileserver23, fileserver45
-ScriptBlock {Uninstall-WindowsFeature fs-smb1}
```

Here, you run the code block on FileServer12, FileServer23, and FileServer45. You must restart the servers to complete the removal process.

If you want to ensure that SMB encryption is used whenever possible, you can enable SMB encryption on either a per-server or per–file share basis. To enable encryption for an entire server and all its SMB file shares, run the following command at an elevated Windows PowerShell prompt on the server:

```
Set-SmbServerConfiguration -EncryptData $true
```

To enable encryption for a specific file share rather than an entire server, run the following command at an elevated Windows PowerShell prompt on the server:

```
Set-SmbShare –Name ShareName -EncryptData $true
```

Here, *ShareName* is the name of the share for which encryption should be used when possible, such as the following:

```
Set-SmbShare –Name CorpData -EncryptData $true
```

You also can turn on encryption when you create a share as well. To do this, run the following command at an elevated Windows PowerShell prompt on the server:

```
New-SmbShare –Name ShareName -Path PathName –EncryptData $true
```

Here, *ShareName* is the name of the share for which encryption should be used when possible, and *PathName* is the path to an existing folder to share, such as the following:

```
New-SmbShare –Name CorpData -Path D:\Data –EncryptData $true
```

When you want to enable encryption support on multiple file servers, you can invoke remote commands. Consider the following example:

```
$servers = get-content c:\files\server-list.txt
Invoke-command -computername $servers -scriptblock {Set-SmbServerConfiguration
-EnableSMB1Protocol $false}
```

Here, C:\Files\Server-list.txt is the path to a text file containing a list of the file servers to configure. In this file, each file server should be listed on a separate line, as shown here:

```
FileServer12
FileServer23
FileServer45
```

The command will then be invoked on each of the file servers.

Installing and configuring file services

File servers are central repositories for an organization's data. As you seek to manage and distribute the data stored on your organization's file servers, you might find that you need to optimize file and storage services. Although basic file and storage services are installed by default on servers running Windows Server 2012 R2, you must specifically configure other services and features as they're needed. Use the Add Roles And Features Wizard in Server Manager to add the appropriate role services and features and then use the related management tools to configure the role services and features as needed.

Configuring the File And Storage Services role

You can add role services and features to a file server by following these steps:

1. In Server Manager, tap or click Manage and then tap or click Add Roles And Features or select Add Roles And Features in the Quick Start pane. This starts the Add Roles And Features Wizard. If the wizard displays the Before You Begin page, read the Welcome text and then tap or click Next.

   NOTE

   Beginning with Windows Server 2012, binary source files for roles, role services, and features can be removed to enhance security. If the binaries for the tools you want to use have been removed, you need to install the tools by specifying a source. For more information about role and feature binaries, see Chapter 6, "Configuring roles, role services, and features."

2. On the Select Installation Type page, Role-Based Or Feature-Based Installation is selected by default. Tap or click Next.
3. On the Select Destination Server page, you can choose to install roles and features on running servers or virtual hard disks. After you make your selection, do one of the following and then tap or click Next:
   a. Select the server that you want to configure. Keep in mind that only servers running Windows Server 2012 R2 and that have been added for management in Server Manager are listed.
   b. Select the server host to use and then type the UNC path to the offline virtual hard disk (VHD) file on that server, as shown in Figure 12-3. Keep in mind that Windows Server 2012 R2 must already be installed on the VHD. Alternatively, tap or click Browse and then use the Browse For Virtual Hard Disks dialog box to locate the offline VHD.

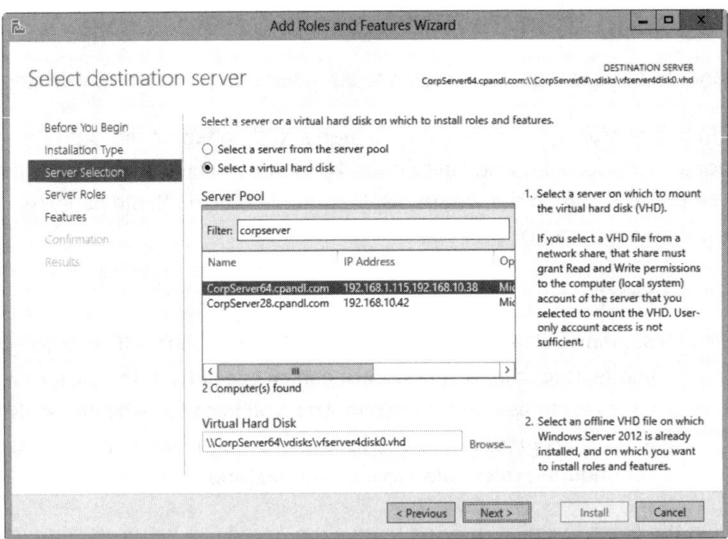

Figure 12-3 If you are adding roles and features to a VHD, specify the UNC path to the VHD.

4. On the Select Server Roles page, select File And Storage Services. Expand the related node and select the additional role services to install, as shown in Figure 12-4. If additional features are required to install a role, you see an additional dialog box. Tap or click Add Features to close the dialog box and add the required features to the server installation. When you are ready to continue, tap or click Next.

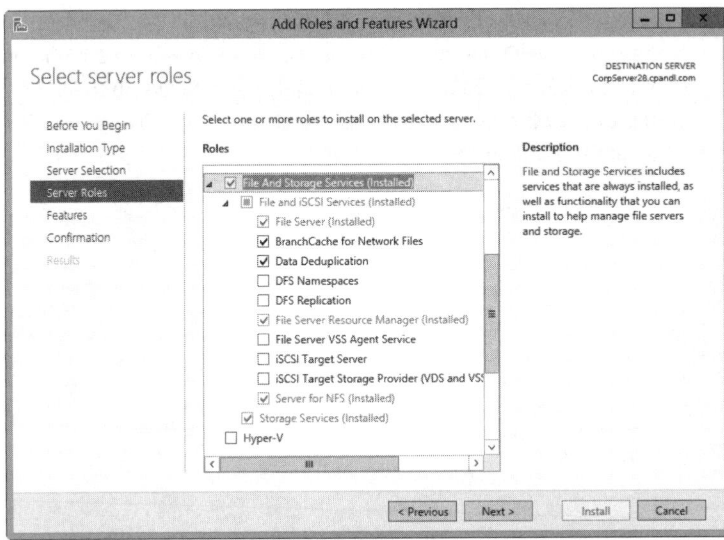

Figure 12-4 Select the appropriate role services for the file server.

5. On the Select Features page, shown in Figure 12-5, select any features you want to install. If additional features are required to install a feature you selected, you see an additional dialog box. Tap or click Add Features to close the dialog box and add the required features to the server installation. When you are ready to continue, tap or click Next.

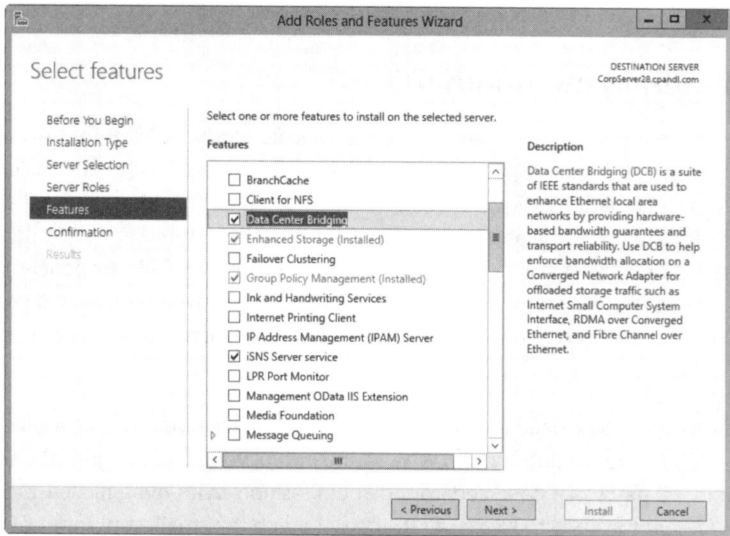

Figure 12-5 Select the additional features for the file server.

6. On the Confirm Installation Selections page, tap or click the Export Configuration Settings link to generate an installation report that can be displayed in Internet Explorer.

7. If the server on which you want to install roles or features doesn't have all the required binary source files, the server gets the files through Windows Update by default or from a location specified in Group Policy. You also can specify an alternate path for the required source files. To do this, click the Specify An Alternate Source Path link, type that alternate path in the box provided, and then tap or click OK. For network shares, enter the UNC path to the share, such as \\CorpServer14\WinServer2012\. For mounted Windows images, enter the Windows Imaging (WIM) path prefixed with WIM and including the index of the image to use, such as WIM:\\CorpServer14\WinServer2012\install.wim:4.

8. After you review the installation options and save them as necessary, tap or click Install to begin the installation process. The Installation Progress page tracks the progress of the installation. If you close the wizard, tap or click the Notifications icon in Server Manager and then tap or click the link provided to reopen the wizard.

9. When Setup finishes installing the server with the roles and features you selected, the Installation Progress page is updated to reflect this. Review the installation details to ensure that all phases of the installation were completed successfully. Note any additional actions that might be required to complete the installation, such as restarting the server or performing additional installation tasks. If any portion of the installation failed, note the reason for the failure. Review the Server Manager entries for installation problems and take corrective actions as appropriate.

Configuring multipath I/O

Hardware vendors typically supply a Device Specific Module (DSM) for SAN hardware and software for configuring multipath I/O. That said, the Multipath I/O feature includes the Microsoft DSM and some basic configuration options. The Microsoft DSM supports the Active/Active controller model and the asymmetric logical unit access controller model. It also implements path selection policies failover, failback, and load balancing. Failover policies enable you to configure a secondary path that should be used if a preferred path fails. If you want the preferred path to be used automatically when it becomes operational again, you can configure a failback policy.

Several types of load-balancing policies are available, including round-robin, dynamic least queue depth, and weighted path. With round-robin, you can configure the DSM to use all available I/O paths in a balanced, round-robin fashion. With dynamic least queue depth, you can configure the DSM to route I/O to the path with the smallest number of outstanding requests. With weighted path, you assign each path a weight to indicate its relative priority with regard to a particular application, and the DSM selects the path with the least weight among the available paths.

Devices that support the Active/Active controller model are referred to as *Active/Active devices* and, by default, are configured to use round-robin. Generally, devices that support the asymmetric logical unit access (ALUA) controller model comply with the SCSI Primary Commands-3 (SPC-3) standard or later and, by default, are configured to use failover.

You manage the multipath I/O (MPIO) configuration using the MPIO Properties dialog box, the Mpclaim command-line tool, or the cmdlets of the MPIO module in Windows PowerShell. After you install the Multipath I/O feature by using the Add Roles And Features Wizard, these tools are available on the server. You open the MPIO Properties dialog box, shown in Figure 12-6, by selecting MPIO on the Tools menu in Server Manager.

> NOTE
>
> **You can get a list of the available cmdlets for working with MPIO by typing get-command -module mpio at a Windows PowerShell prompt.**

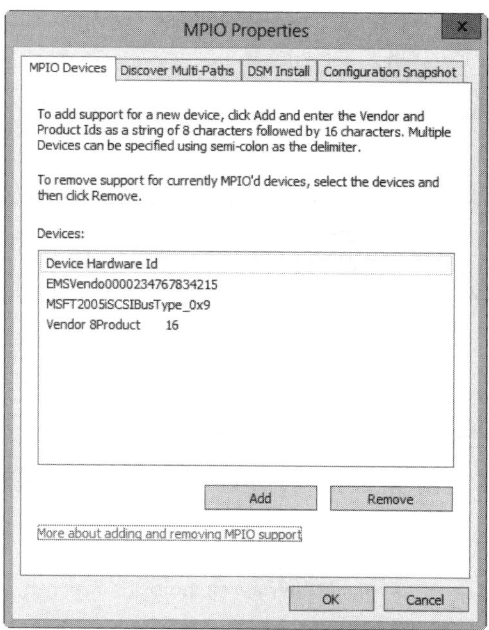

Figure 12-6 Manage the multipath I/O configuration.

After you enable MPIO, you might also want to do the following:

- Enable automatic claiming of iSCSI devices for MPIO.
- Set the default load-balancing policy.
- Set the Windows disk timeout.

For MPIO to manage a device, you must first add the hardware ID for the device to MPIO. You can add devices either manually or automatically.

Automatic claiming of iSCSI devices allows MPIO to configure available iSCSI devices with multiple paths automatically. Enable this feature by entering the following at an elevated Windows PowerShell prompt:

```
Enable-MSDSMAutomaticClaim -BusType iSCSI
```

Load balancing and fault tolerance are core features of MPIO. You set the default load-balancing policy by using Get-MSDSMGlobalDefaultLoadBalancePolicy. The default policies available are:

- Failover only, which allows one active path, with all other paths designated as standby paths for failover. Use the *FOO* value.

- Round-robin, which sets all available paths to be load-balanced using a round-robin technique. Use the *RR* value.
- Least queue path, which load-balances by sending I/O to the path with the fewest I/O requests. Use the *LQD* value.
- Least blocks, which load-balances by sending I/O to the path with the smallest number of data blocks currently being processed. Use the *LB* value.

Set the default load-balancing policy by entering the following command at an elevated Windows PowerShell prompt:

```
Get-MSDSMGlobalDefaultLoadBalancePolicy -Policy PolicyValue
```

Here, *PolicyValue* is one of the accepted policy values—*FOO*, *RR*, *LQD*, *LB*, or *NONE*.

You set the timeout value for new disks by using Set-MPIOSetting. The basic syntax is:

```
Set-MPIOSetting -NewDiskTimeout NumSeconds
```

Here, *NumSeconds* is the number of seconds to wait before reaching the timeout.

Set-MPIOSetting accepts other parameters as well:

- **–PathVerifyEnabled.** When set to *–PathVerifyEnabled $true*, path verification by MPIO is enabled on all paths according to *–PathVerificationPeriod*. By default, this feature is disabled.
- **–PathVerificationPeriod.** When *–PathVerifyEnabled* is set to *$true*, this parameter sets the interval for path verification. For example, use *–PathVerificationPeriod* to verify MPIO on all paths every 60 seconds. The default value is every 30 seconds.
- **–PDORemovePeriod.** Controls the amount of time (in seconds) that a multipath pseudo-LUN will remain in system memory even after losing all paths to the device. When the removal period is exceeded, all pending I/O operations are stopped and set as failed, and the failure is passed on to applications. The default value is 20 seconds.
- **–RetryCount.** Controls the number of times a failed I/O is retried. The default value is *3*.
- **–RetryInterval.** Sets the number of seconds to wait before retrying a failed I/O. The default is 1 second.

Before you change MPIO settings, you should determine what the current settings are. You can do this by entering Get-MPIOSetting at the Windows PowerShell prompt.

Adding and removing multipath hardware devices

You manually add devices to MPIO by using the MPIO Properties dialog box, which is opened by selecting MPIO on the Tools menu in Server Manager. To configure a device manually to use multipath I/O, follow these steps:

1. Open the MPIO Properties dialog box. On the MPIO Devices tab, you see a list of currently configured multipath devices. If the device you want to work with is not listed, tap or click Add.

2. In the Add MPIO Support dialog box, type the vendor ID as an eight-character string followed by the product ID for the device as a 16-character string. Tap or click OK.

3. You are prompted to restart the server to complete the operation. Tap or click Yes to restart the server.

At an elevated command prompt, you also can use Mpclaim to configure devices to use multipath I/O as well. The basic syntax for installing a device follows:

```
Mpclaim -r -i [-a | -c | -d DeviceId]
```

The *–r* parameter indicates that you want to restart the server to allow the device installation to be completed. Although you can suppress the restart by using the *–n* parameter instead of *–r*, the device will not be installed and available for use until you restart the server. Use the *–a* parameter to configure multipath I/O support for all compatible devices. Use the *–c* parameter to configure multipath I/O support for all SPC-3–compliant devices. Use the *–d* parameter followed by a device's hardware ID to install a specific hardware device. The hardware ID of a device includes the vendor ID as an eight-character string followed by the product ID for the device as a 16-character string. In the following example, you install a device with EMSVendo0000234767834215 as the hardware ID:

```
Mpclaim -r -i -d EMSVendo0000234767834215
```

Alternatively, you can use Get-MSDSMSupportedHw to list available devices by their hardware ID and New-MSDSMSupportedHw to add a device to MPIO.

By using the MPIO Properties dialog box, you can remove a device from MPIO by following these steps:

1. Open the MPIO Properties dialog box. The MPIO Devices tab shows a list of currently configured multipath devices.

2. Select the device that should no longer use multiple path IO and then tap or click Remove.

3. You are prompted to restart the server to complete the operation. Tap or click Yes to restart the server.

At an elevated command prompt, you can use Mpclaim to uninstall multipath I/O for a device as well. The basic syntax for installing a device follows:

```
Mpclaim -r -u [-a | -c | -d DeviceId]
```

Except for the *–u* parameter for uninstalling a device, the other parameters are the same as when you are installing MPIO for a device. The following example uninstalls the previously installed device:

```
Mpclaim -r -u -d EMSVendo0000234767834215
```

Alternatively, you can use Get-MSDSMSupportedHw to list available devices by their hardware ID and Remove-MSDSMSupportedHw to remove a device from MPIO.

Managing and maintaining MPIO

The MPIO Properties dialog box has several other tabs that you can use for general management of MPIO:

- **Discover Multi-Paths.** When you select the Discover Multi-Paths tab, Windows runs a discovery algorithm to examine added device instances and determine whether multiple instances represent the same LUN through different paths. Available multipath devices are then listed by their hardware ID. The hardware ID combines a vendor's name and a product string that matches a device ID that is maintained by MPIO. Tap or click Add to add hardware IDs for Fibre Channel devices that use Microsoft DSM.
- **DSM Install.** Use the options on this tab to install DSMs provided by independent hardware vendors (IHVs). Keep in mind that many SPC-3–compliant storage arrays can use the Microsoft DSM, and you might not need to install an IHV DSM.
- **Configure Snapshot.** Use the options on this tab to save the current MPIO configuration to a log file. Because the log includes details about the DSM, paths, and path states, you can use this information for troubleshooting.

Inside OUT

Discover iSCSI and SAS devices

On the Discover Multi-Paths tab, you also can discover iSCSI devices and SAS devices and add MPIO support for the discovered devices automatically. To discover iSCSI devices, select the Add Support For iSCSI Devices check box. To discover SAS devices, select the Add Support For SAS Devices check box. Adding support for iSCSI, SAS, or both allows the Microsoft Device Specific Module (MSDSM) to claim all iSCSI, SAS, or both devices for MPIO.

You configure the load-balancing policy for LUNs by using their disk properties. In Computer Management, select Disk Management and then press and hold or right-click the disk you want to work with. In the Properties dialog box, click the MPIO tab. Use the Select MPIO Policy list to choose the load-balancing policy for the selected disk. If you use Failover Only as the load-balancing policy, you can configure a preferred path to the storage. This path is used for automatic failback.

Meeting performance, capacity, and availability requirements

Whether you are working with internal or external disks, you should follow the same basic principles to help ensure that the chosen storage solutions meet your performance, capacity, and availability requirements. Storage performance is primarily a factor of the disk's access time (how long it takes to register a request and scan the disk), seek time (how long it takes to find the requested data), and transfer rate (how long it takes to read and write data). Storage capacity relates to how much information you can store on a volume or logical disk.

Although early NTFS implementations limited the maximum volume size and file size to 32 GBs, later implementations extended these limits. This means you can have a maximum NTFS volume size of 256 TBs minus 64 KBs when you are using 64 KB clusters, and 16 TBs minus 4 KBs when you are using 4 KB clusters. The maximum file size on an NTFS volume is 16 TBs minus 64 KBs. Further, a maximum of 4,294,967,294 files can be created on each volume, and a single server can manage hundreds of volumes (theoretically, around 2,000).

Storage availability relates to fault tolerance. You ensure availability for essential applications and services by using availability technologies. If a server has a problem or if a particular application or service fails, you have a way to continue operations by failing over to another server. In addition to clusters, you can help ensure availability by saving redundant copies of data, keeping spare parts, and, if possible, making standby servers available. At the disk and data levels, availability is enhanced by using redundant array of independent disks (RAID) technologies. RAID enables you to combine disks and improve fault tolerance.

RAID can be implemented in hardware or software. When hardware RAID controllers are installed on servers, the internal controller can be used to implement RAID on the server's internal disks. When a server is allocated storage from a storage array, one or more logical unit numbers, or LUNs, are assigned. Each LUN is a virtual disk. Typically, hardware RAID configured within the storage array is used to spread the LUN across multiple physical disks (also called *spindles*).

Windows Server 2012 R2 supports several software RAID options, including traditional software-based RAID and Storage Spaces. Traditional software RAID is the software-based RAID technology built into the operating system and available in earlier releases of Windows. Storage Spaces provide resilient storage using new technologies and are preferred over traditional software RAID. However, each of these software-implemented RAID levels requires processing power and memory resources to maintain. By using hardware RAID, you use separate hardware controllers (RAID controllers) to maintain the disk arrays. Although this requires the purchase of additional hardware, it takes the burden off the server and can improve performance. Why? In a hardware-implemented RAID system, a server's processing power and memory aren't used to maintain the disk arrays. Instead, the hardware RAID controller (which is installed internally or in a storage array) handles all the necessary processing tasks.

The RAID levels available with a hardware implementation depend on the hardware controller /storage array and the vendor's implementation of RAID technologies. Some hardware RAID configurations include RAID 0 (disk striping), RAID 1 (disk mirroring), RAID 0+1 (disk striping with mirroring), RAID 5 (disk striping with parity), and RAID 5+1 (disk striping with parity plus mirroring). Table 12-1 provides a summary of these RAID technologies. The table entries are organized by listing the highest RAID level to the lowest.

Table 12-1 Hardware RAID configurations for clusters

RAID Level	RAID Type	RAID Description	Advantages and Disadvantages
5+1	Disk striping with parity plus mirroring	Uses at least six volumes, with each one on a separate drive. Each volume is configured identically as a mirrored striped set with parity error checking.	Provides a high level of fault tolerance but has a lot of overhead.
5	Disk striping with parity	Uses at least three volumes, with each one on a separate drive. Each volume is configured as a striped set with parity error checking. In the case of failure, data can be recovered.	Provides fault tolerance with less overhead than mirroring. It has better read performance than disk mirroring.

RAID Level	RAID Type	RAID Description	Advantages and Disadvantages
1	Disk mirroring	Uses two volumes on two drives. The drives are configured identically, and data is written to both drives. If one drive fails, no data is lost because the other drive contains the data. This approach does not include disk striping.	Provides redundancy with better write performance than disk striping with parity.
0+1	Disk striping with mirroring	Uses two or more volumes, with each one on a separate drive. The volumes are striped and mirrored. Data is written sequentially to drives that are identically configured.	Provides redundancy with good read and write performance.
0	Disk striping	Uses two or more volumes, with each one on a separate drive. Volumes are configured as a striped set. Data is broken into blocks, called stripes, and then written sequentially to all drives in the striped set.	Provides speed and performance without data protection.

Configuring Hyper-V

The Microsoft virtualization technology is Hyper-V. Hyper-V is a virtual machine technology that enables multiple guest operating systems to run concurrently on one computer and provide separate applications and services to client computers. When you deploy Hyper-V, the Windows hypervisor acts as the virtual machine engine, providing the necessary layer of software for installing guest operating systems.

Understanding Hyper-V

Hyper-V can be installed only on computers with 64-bit processors that implement hardware-assisted virtualization and hardware-enforced data execution protection. Specifically, you must enable virtualization support in firmware and either Intel XD bit (execute disable bit) or AMD NX bit (no execute bit) as appropriate.

Virtualization can offer performance improvements, reduce the number of servers, and reduce the total cost of ownership (TCO). Although you can use both Windows 8.1 and Windows Server 2012 R2 to deploy virtualized computers, Hyper-V for Windows Server is very different from Client Hyper-V for Windows 8.1. The focus in this section is on Hyper-V for Windows Server 2012 R2.

Windows Server 2012 R2 supports AMD Virtualization (AMD-V) and Intel Virtualization Technology (Intel VT). AMD-V is included in second-generation and later AMD Opteron processors and other AMD processors. Third-generation AMD Opteron processors feature Rapid Virtualization Indexing (RVI) to accelerate the performance of virtualized applications. Intel VT is included in most current Intel Xeon processors in addition to Intel vPro and some other Intel processors. Keep in mind that older processors with virtualization might have different features from newer processors, and these differences can present special challenges when you are migrating from one hardware platform to another.

IMPORTANT

Windows Server 2012 R2 also supports second-level address translation (SLAT) as implemented by Intel and AMD processors. SLAT adds a second level of paging below the architectural paging tables in the server's processors. This improves performance by providing an indirection layer from virtual machine memory access to physical memory access. On Intel-based processors, this feature is called *extended page tables (EPTs)*, and on AMD-based processors, this feature is called *nested page tables (NPTs)*.

TROUBLESHOOTING

Hyper-V compatibility issues

Just as different processors have different sets of supported virtualization features, Windows itself has different implementations of Hyper-V. Because of this, the Hyper-V management tools in Windows Server 2012 R2 can be used to manage only the current version of Hyper-V. The tools cannot be used to manage earlier versions of Hyper-V.

Windows Server 2012 R2 supports many virtualization features, including live migration and dynamic virtual machine storage. You can use live migration to move running virtual machines transparently either from one node of a cluster to another or from one nonclustered server to another. You also can perform multiple live migrations simultaneously. With dynamic virtual machine storage, you can add or remove virtual hard disks and physical disks while a virtual machine is running. You also can move the virtual disks of running virtual machines from one storage location to another without downtime.

Virtual machines also can be stored on SMB 3.0 file shares. Typically, you use this feature by creating the virtual machine and a virtual hard disk on the SMB 3.0 file share. Initially, the virtual machine will think it is using local storage. You then change the storage type by migrating the virtual machine storage from a local configuration to a file-share configuration. Hyper-V also supports connections to Fibre Channel storage, using virtual Fibre Channel.

Installing Hyper-V

Virtual machines require virtual networks to communicate with other computers. When you install Hyper-V, you can create one virtual network for each adapter available. After installing Hyper-V, you can create and manage virtual networks by using Virtual Network Manager. Microsoft recommends reserving one network adapter for remote access to the server. You do this by not designating the adapter for use with a virtual network.

You can install Hyper-V on a server with a virtualization-enabled processor by completing these steps:

1. In Server Manager, tap or click Manage and then tap or click Add Roles And Features. If the wizard displays the Before You Begin page, read the Welcome text and then tap or click Next.
2. On the Select Installation Type page, Role-Based Or Feature-Based Installation is selected by default. Tap or click Next.
3. On the Select Destination Server page, select the server on which you want to install Hyper-V and then tap or click Next. Keep in mind that only servers running Windows Server 2012 R2 and that have been added for management in Server Manager are listed.
4. On the Select Server Roles page, select Hyper-V as the role to install. If additional features are required to install a role, you see an additional dialog box. Tap or click Add Features to close the dialog box and add the required features to the server installation. When you are ready to continue, tap or click Next three times, skipping the Features page and the Hyper-V page.
5. On the Create Virtual Switches page, shown in Figure 12-7, select a network adapter on which to create a virtual switch. A virtual switch is needed so that virtual machines can communicate with other computers. The virtual switch enables virtual machines to connect to the physical network. When you are ready to continue, tap or click Next.

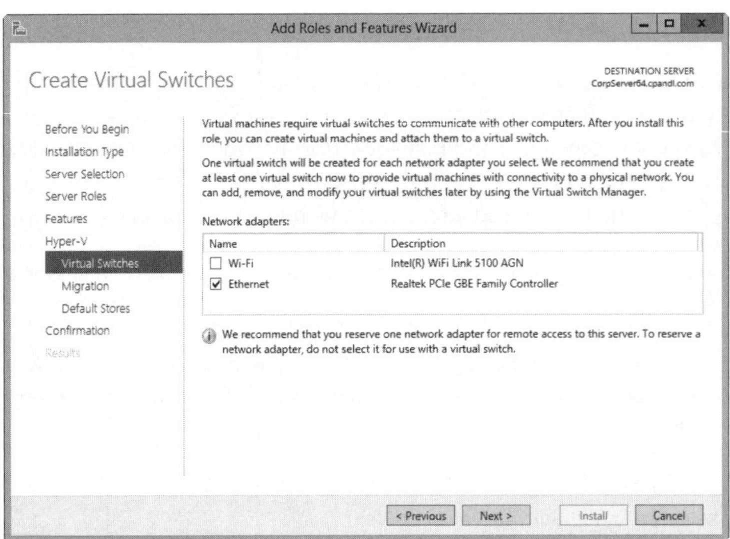

Figure 12-7 Select the network adapter to use as a virtual switch.

6. On the Virtual Machine Migration page, you can enable live migrations of virtual machines on this server by selecting the check box provided. You don't have to enable this feature now; instead, you can enable this feature later by modifying the Hyper-V settings. However, if you enable live migrations, you also must choose the Credential Security Support Provider (CredSSP) protocol or Kerberos for authentication. Kerberos is the most secure, but you also must configure constrained delegation. CredSSP is less secure but doesn't require you to configure constrained delegation. When you are ready to continue, tap or click Next.

7. On the Default Stores page, you can accept the current default locations for virtual hard disk files and virtual machine configuration files or enter new default locations. Regardless of your choices, you can modify the defaults later, using the Hyper-V settings. When you are ready to continue, tap or click Next.

8. On the Confirm Installation Selections page, tap or click the Export Configuration Settings link to generate an installation report that can be displayed in Internet Explorer. If the server on which you want to install Hyper-V doesn't have all the required binary source files, the server gets the files from Windows Update by default or from a location specified in Group Policy. You also can specify an alternate path for the required source files. To do this, click the Specify An Alternate Source Path link, type the alternate path in the box provided, and then tap or click OK.

9. Because a restart is required to complete the installation of Hyper-V, you might want to select the Restart The Destination Server check box. Tap or click Install to begin the installation process. The Installation Progress page tracks the progress of the installation. If you close the wizard, tap or click the Notifications icon in Server Manager and then tap or click the link provided to reopen the wizard.

10. When Setup finishes installing Hyper-V, the Installation Progress page is updated to reflect this. Review the installation details to ensure that all phases of the installation were completed successfully. If you didn't restart the server, a restart will be pending and required to complete the installation.

Creating virtual machines

Installing Hyper-V on a server establishes the server as a virtualization server. Each virtual machine you install on the server must be assigned resources to use and then be configured. The number of virtual machines you can run on any individual server depends on the server's hardware configuration and workload. During setup, you specify the amount of memory available to a virtual machine. Although you can change that memory allocation, the amount of memory actively allocated to a virtual machine cannot be used in other ways.

You create and manage virtual machines by using Hyper-V Manager, shown in Figure 12-8. Start Hyper-V Manager by selecting Hyper-V Manager on the Tools menu in Server Manager.

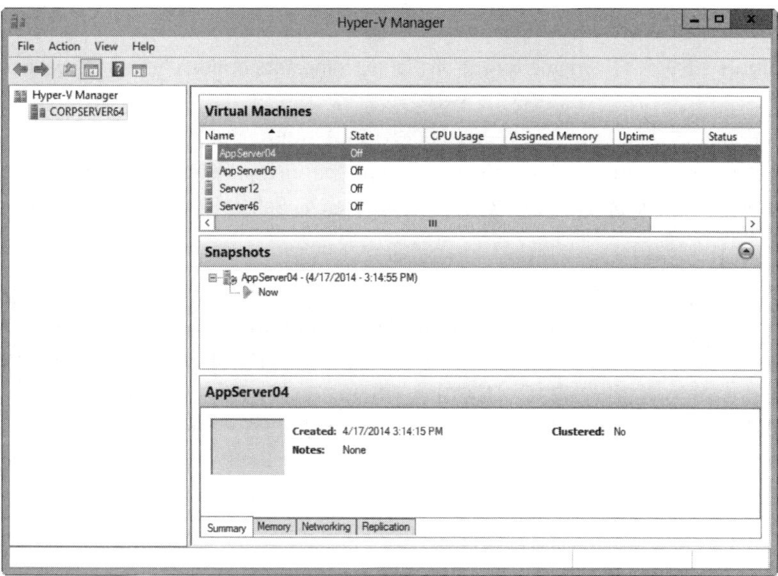

Figure 12-8 Use Hyper-V Manager to install and manage virtual machines.

To install and configure a virtual machine, complete the following steps:

1. In Hyper-V Manager, press and hold or right-click the server node in the left pane, point to New, and then select Virtual Machine. This starts the New Virtual Machine Wizard.
2. Tap or click Next to display the Specify Name And Location page, shown in Figure 12-9. In the Name text box, enter a name for the virtual machine, such as AppServer02.

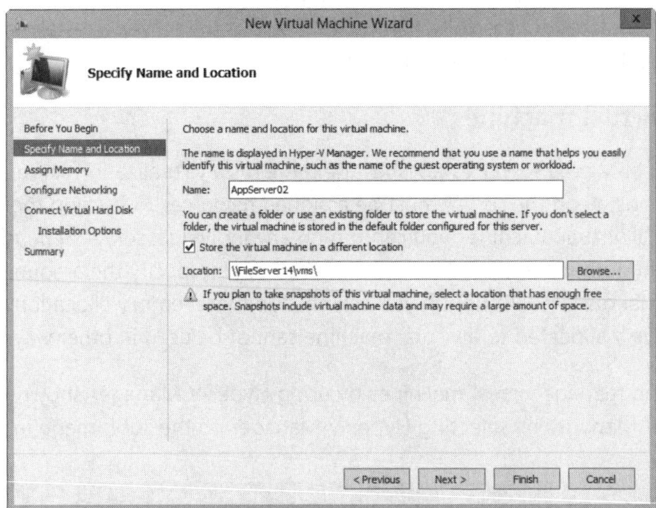

Figure 12-9 Set the name for the virtual machine and, optionally, its storage location.

3. By default, the virtual machine data is stored in the default location for the server. To select a different location, select the Store The Virtual Machine In A Different Location check box, tap or click Browse, and then use the Select Folder dialog box to select a save location.
4. Tap or click Next. On the Specify Generation page, specify whether you want to create a Generation 1 or Generation 2 virtual machine. Use Generation 1 if you plan to deploy non-Windows operating systems and versions of Windows prior to Windows 8 or Windows Server 2012. Use Generation 2 if you plan to deploy Windows Server 2012, Windows Server 2012 R2, 64-bit versions of Windows 8, or 64-bit versions of Windows 8.1.

NOTE

Generation 1 provides the same support as previous versions of Hyper-V. Generation 2 supports secure boot, boot from a SCSI virtual hard disk, boot from a SCSI virtual DVD, PXE boot by using a standard network adapter, and Unified Extensible Firmware Interface (UEFI) firmware.

5. Tap or click Next. On the Assign Memory page, specify the amount of memory to allocate to the virtual machine. In most cases, you should reserve at least the minimum amount of memory recommended for the operating system you plan to install. You might also want to enable dynamic memory allocation.

6. Tap or click Next. On the Configure Networking page, use the Connection list to select a network adapter to use. Each new virtual machine includes a network adapter, and you can configure the adapter to use an available virtual switch for communicating with other computers.

7. Tap or click Next. On the Connect Virtual Hard Disk page, use the options provided to name and set the location of a virtual hard disk for the virtual machine. Each virtual machine requires a virtual hard disk so that you can install an operating system and required applications.

8. Tap or click Next. On the Installation Options page, select Install An Operating System From A Boot CD/DVD-ROM. If you have physical distribution media, insert the distribution media and then specify the CD/DVD drive to use. If you want to install from an .iso image, select Image File, tap or click Browse, and then use the Open dialog box to select the image file to use.

9. Tap or click Next and then tap or click Finish.

10. In Hyper-V Manager, press and hold or right-click the name of the virtual machine and then tap or click Connect.

11. In the Virtual Machine Connection window, tap or click Start. After the virtual machine is initialized, the operating system installation should start automatically. Continue with the operating system installation as you normally would.

When the installation is complete, log on to the virtual machine and configure it as you would any other server. From then on, you manage the virtual machine much as you would any other computer except that you can externally control its state, available resources, and hardware devices by using Hyper-V Manager. In addition, when it comes to backups, several approaches are available:

- Back up the host server and all virtual machine data.
- Back up the host server and only the configuration data for virtual machines.
- Log on to virtual machines and perform normal backups as you would with any other server.
- Use Hyper-V manager to create point-in-time snapshots of virtual machines.

Ideally, you should use a combination of these approaches to ensure that your host server and virtual machines are protected. In some cases, you might want to back up the host server and configuration data and then log on to each virtual machine and use normal backups. Other times, you might want to back up the host machine and all virtual machine data. You will likely want to supplement your backup strategy by creating point-in-time snapshots of virtual machines.

CHAPTER 13

Configuring disks and storage

One of your most important tasks as a Windows Server administrator is configuring and maintaining storage. Increasingly, servers use both physical drives installed internally and virtual disks from attached storage. Whether you work with virtual disks from attached storage or physical disks installed within servers, you must configure the disks for use by choosing a disk partition style and a disk storage type to use. After you configure drives, you prepare them to store data by partitioning them and creating file systems.

Windows Server supports two techniques for partitioning disks: traditional and standards-based. In this chapter, after discussing disk partition styles and disk storage types, I examine traditional techniques for creating volume sets and arrays. Subsequent chapters look at important disk management topics, including drive encryption, file system management, file sharing, and file security. I look at standards-based techniques for creating and managing volumes in Chapter 17, "Managing Storage Spaces."

Configuring storage

When you install disks, you must configure them for use by choosing a disk partition style and a disk storage type to use. After you configure drives, you prepare them to store data by partitioning them and creating file systems in the partitions. *Partitions* are sections of physical drives that function as if they are separate units. This enables you to configure multiple logical disk units even if a system has only one physical drive and to apportion disks appropriately to meet the needs of your organization.

Using the Disk Management tools

When you want to manage basic or dynamic disks, one of the tools you can use is Disk Management, which is shown in Figure 13-1. Disk Management also is a snap-in included in Computer Management and can be added to any custom Microsoft Management Console (MMC) you create.

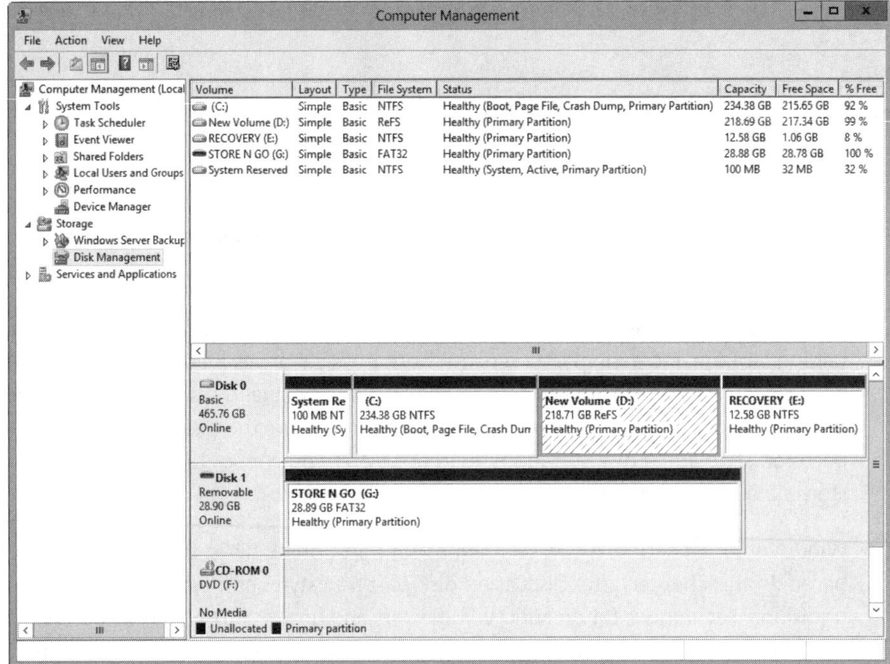

Figure 13-1 Disk Management is the primary tool for managing storage.

IMPORTANT

Although Disk Management is a trusty favorite for working with disks, it might not be available in future releases of Windows and cannot be used to manage Storage Spaces. Dynamic disks also are being phased out in favor of Storage Spaces and might not be available in future versions of Windows.

Disk Management makes it easy to work with any available internal and external drives on both local and remote systems. When you start Computer Management by tapping or clicking the related option on the Tools menu in Server Manager, you're automatically connected to the local computer on which you're running Computer Management. In Computer Management, expand Storage and then select Disk Management. You can now manage the drives on the local system.

To work with a remote system, press and hold or right-click the Computer Management entry in the left pane and select Connect To Another Computer on the shortcut menu. This opens the Select Computer dialog box (shown in Figure 13-2). Type the domain name or IP address of the system whose drives you want to view and then tap or click OK.

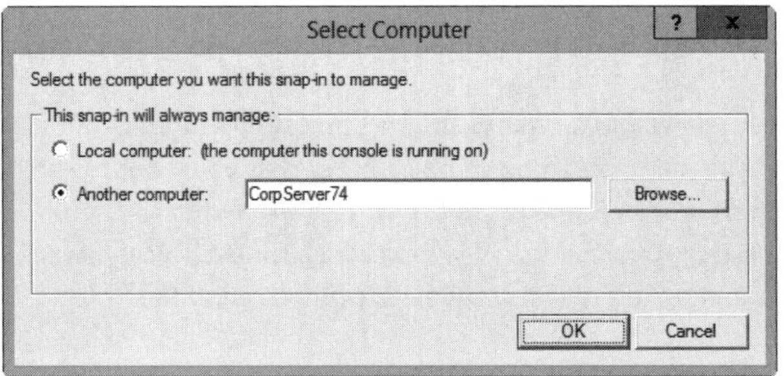

Figure 13-2 Select the remote system to manage with Computer Management.

IMPORTANT

Server Manager also provides a shortcut for remote management. Select All Servers in the left pane, press and hold or right-click the remote server to which you want to connect in the Servers panel, and then select Computer Management. This opens Computer Management and connects to the remote server automatically. Keep in mind that the remote management of computers is a feature that must be enabled. As discussed in Chapter 4, "Managing Windows Server 2012 R2," you need to enable inbound rules on the Windows Firewall for each management area you want to work with.

Disk Management has three views:

- **Disk List.** Shows a list of physical disks on, or attached to, the selected system. It includes details on type, capacity, unallocated space, and status. It is the only disk view that shows the device type, such as Small Computer System Interface (SCSI) or Integrated Device Electronics (IDE), and the partition style, such as master boot record (MBR) or GUID partition table (GPT).
- **Graphical View.** Displays summary information for disks graphically according to disk capacity and the size of disk regions. By default, disk and disk-region capacity are shown on a logarithmic scale, meaning the disks and disk regions are displayed proportionally.
- **Volume List.** Shows all volumes on the selected computer (including hard-disk partitions and logical drives). It includes details on volume layout, type, file system, status, capacity, and free space. It also shows whether the volume has fault tolerance and the related disk usage overhead. The fault-tolerance information is for software redundant array of independent disks (RAID) only.

Change the scaling options to get different disk views

You can also specify that you want all disks to be the same size regardless of capacity (which is useful if you have many disk regions on disks) or that you want to use a linear scale in which disk regions are sized relative to the largest disk (which is useful if you want to get perspective on capacity). To change the size settings for Graphical View, tap or click View and then Settings. In the Settings dialog box, click the Scaling tab.

Volume List and Graphical View are the default views. In Figure 13-1, the Volume List view is in the top-right corner, and the Graphical View is in the bottom-right corner. To change the top view, select View, choose Top, and then select the view you want to use. To change the bottom view, select View, choose Bottom, and then select the view you want to use.

The command-line counterpart to Disk Management is the DiskPart utility. You can use DiskPart to perform all Disk Management tasks. DiskPart is a text-mode command interpreter that you invoke so that you can manage disks, partitions, and volumes. As such, DiskPart has a separate command prompt and its own internal commands. Although earlier releases of DiskPart did not allow you to format partitions, logical drives, and volumes, the version that ships with Windows Server 2012 R2 enables you to do this using the internal format command.

You invoke the DiskPart interpreter by typing **diskpart** at the command prompt. DiskPart is designed to work with physical hard disks installed on a computer, which can be internal, external, or a mix of both. Although it will list other types of disks—such as CD/DVD drives, removable media, and universal serial bus (USB)–connected flash random access memory (RAM) devices—and enable you to perform some minimal tasks, such as assigning a drive letter, these devices are not supported.

After you invoke DiskPart, you can list available disks, partitions, and volumes by using the following list commands:

- **List Disk.** Lists all internal and external hard disks on the computer
- **List Volume.** Lists all volumes on the computer (including hard-disk partitions and logical drives)
- **List Partition.** Lists partitions, but only on the disk you selected

Then you must give focus to the disk, partition, or volume you want to work with by selecting it. Giving a disk, partition, or volume focus ensures that any commands you type act only on that disk, partition, or volume. To select a disk, type **select disk *N***, where *N* is the number of the disk you want to work with. To select a volume, type **select volume *N***, where *N* is the number of the volume you want to work with. To select a partition, first select its related disk by typing **select disk *N*** and then select the partition you want to work with by typing **select partition *N***.

If you use the list commands again after selecting a disk, partition, or volume, you see an asterisk (*) next to the item with focus. When you are finished working with DiskPart, type **exit** at the DiskPart prompt to return to the standard command prompt.

Listing 13-1 shows a sample DiskPart session. As you can see, when you first invoke DiskPart, it shows the operating system and DiskPart version you are using and the name of the computer you are working with. When you list available disks, the output shows you the disk number, status, size, and free space. It also shows the disk-partition style and type. If there's an asterisk in the Dyn column, the disk is a dynamic disk. Otherwise, it is a basic disk. If there's an asterisk in the Gpt column, the disk uses the GPT partition style. Otherwise, it is an MBR disk. You'll find more information on partition styles in "Using the MBR and GPT partition styles" later in this chapter.

Listing 13-1 Using DiskPart: An example

```
C:\> diskpart

   Microsoft DiskPart version 6.3.9600
   Copyright (C) 1999-2013 Microsoft Corporation.
   On computer: CORPSVR02

   DISKPART> list disk

   Disk ###    Status        Size      Free     Dyn   Gpt
   --------    ----------   -------   ------    ---   ---
     Disk 0    Online       465 GB      0 B      *     *
     Disk 1    Online       292 GB     27 GB
     Disk 2    Online       378 GB     90 GB

   DISKPART> list volume

     Volume ###   Ltr   Label        Fs    Type        Size      Status    Info
     ----------   ---   ---------   ----- -------     -------   ------    ------
     Volume 0      F    HRM_SSS_X64  UDF   DVD-ROM     3525 MB   Healthy
     Volume 1           System Rese  NTFS  Partition   100 MB    Healthy   System
     Volume 2      C                 NTFS  Partition   234 GB    Healthy   Boot
     Volume 3      D    New Volume   REFS  Partition   218 GB    Healthy
     Volume 4      E    Recovery     NTFS  Partition    12 GB    Healthy
     Volume 5      G    Store n Go   FAT32 Removable    28 GB    Healthy

   DISKPART> select disk 0

   Disk 0 is now the selected disk.
```

```
DISKPART> list partition

  Partition ###  Type              Size     Offset
  -------------  ----------------  -------  -------
  Partition 1    Primary            100 MB  1024 KB
  Partition 2    Primary            234 GB   101 MB
  Partition 3    Primary            218 GB   234 GB
  Partition 4    Primary             12 GB   453 GB

DISKPART> select partition 2

Partition 2 is now the selected partition.

DISKPART> list partition

  Partition ###  Type              Size     Offset
  -------------  ----------------  -------  -------
  Partition 1    Primary            100 MB  1024 KB
* Partition 2    Primary            234 GB   101 MB
  Partition 3    Primary            218 GB   234 GB
  Partition 4    Primary             12 GB   453 GB

DISKPART> exit

Leaving DiskPart...

C:\>
```

Adding new disks

Windows Server 2012 R2 supports both Standard Format and Advanced Format hard drives. Standard Format drives have 512 bytes per physical sector and are also referred to as *512b drives*. Advanced Format drives have 4,096 bytes per physical sector and are referred to as *512e drives*. 512e represents a significant shift for the hard-drive industry, and it allows for large, multi-terabyte drives.

When working with physical disks, keep in mind that disks perform physical media updates in the granularity of their physical sector size. 512b disks work with data 512 bytes at a time; 512e disks work with data 4,096 bytes at a time. Having a larger physical sector size is what enables drive capacities to jump well beyond previous physical capacity limits.

Inside OUT

Deploying 512e disks

512e disks might require some architecture changes in your applications. For best performance, applications must be updated to read and write data properly in this new level of granularity (4,096 bytes). Otherwise, when there is only a 513-byte write, 512e hard disks must perform additional work to complete the sector write.

Wondering how to determine whether a disk is 512b or 512e? Use Fsutil to determine bytes per physical sector by typing the following at an elevated prompt:

```
Fsutil fsinfo ntfsinfo DriveDesignator
```

Here, *DriveDesignator* is the designator of the drive to check, such as:

```
Fsutil fsinfo ntfsinfo c:
```

You can list detailed sector information, as shown in the following example for the C: drive:

```
Fsutil fsinfo sectorinfo c:
```

Thanks to hot-swapping and Plug and Play technologies, the process of adding new internal disks is much easier than in the past. If a computer supports hot swapping of disks, you can install new internal disks without having to shut down the computer. Just insert the hard disk drives you want to use. If the computer doesn't support hot swapping, you need to shut down the computer, insert the drives, and restart the computer.

Either way, after you insert the drives you want to use, log on and access Disk Management in the Computer Management tool or in Server Manager. If the new drives have already been initialized, meaning they have disk signatures, they should be brought online automatically when you select Rescan Disks from the Action menu. If you are working with new drives that haven't been initialized, meaning they lack a disk signature, when you choose to initialize the new disk, Windows Server 2012 R2 opens the Initialize Disk dialog box. In the Initialize Disk dialog box, select either the MBR or GPT partitioning style. When you tap or click OK, Windows writes a disk signature to the disks and initializes the disks with the basic disk type.

If you don't want to use the Initialize Disk dialog box, you can close it and use Disk Management instead to view and work with the disk. In the Disk List view, the disk is marked with a red downward-pointing arrow icon, the disk's type is listed as Unknown, and the disk's status is listed as Not Initialized. You can then press and hold or right-click the disk's icon and select Online. Press and hold or right-click the disk's icon again and select Initialize Disk. You can then initialize the disk. In the Initialize Disk dialog box, select either the MBR or GPT partitioning style. Tap or click OK so that Windows can write a disk signature and initialize the disk with the basic disk type.

At an elevated, administrator Windows PowerShell prompt, you can use Get-Disk to list available disks and Initialize-Disk to initialize new disks.

Inside OUT

Windows Server 2012 R2 can use disk write caching

As discussed previously, storage performance is primarily a factor of a disk's access time (how long it takes to register a request and scan the disk), seek time (how long it takes to find the requested data), and transfer rate (how long it takes to read and write data). By enabling disk write caching, you can reduce the number of times the operating system accesses the disk by caching disk writes and then performing several writes at once. In this way, disk performance is primarily influenced by seek time and transfer rate.

The drawback of disk write caching is that in the event of a power or system failure, the cached writes might not be written to disk, and this can result in data loss. Windows Server 2012 R2 allows you to enable or disable disk write caching on a per-disk basis. Keep in mind that some server applications require disk write caching to be enabled or disabled, and if these applications use a particular set of disks, these disks must use the required setting for disk write caching.

To configure disk write caching, start Computer Management, expand the System Tools node, and select Device Manager. In the details pane, expand Disk Drives, press and hold or right-click the disk drive you want to work with, and then select Properties. In the Device Properties dialog box, click the Policies tab. Select or clear Enable Write Caching On The Disk as appropriate. If the drive has a separate power supply that allows it to flush its buffer in case of power failure, also select Turn Off Windows Write-Cache Buffer Flushing On The Device. Tap or click OK.

Using the MBR and GPT partition styles

The term *partition style* refers to the method that Windows Server uses to organize partitions on a disk. Two partition styles are available: MBR and GPT. GPT is becoming the primary disk type for Windows Server and is supported by all current editions of Windows and Windows Server.

GPT is recommended for disks larger than 2 terabytes (TBs) on x86 and x64 systems or any disks used on Itanium-based computers. The key difference between the GPT partition style and the MBR partition style has to do with how partition data is stored.

> NOTE
>
> **For this discussion, I focus on the basic storage type and won't get into the details of the dynamic storage type. That's covered in the next section. Note also that for virtual machines and Hyper-V specifically, you should use GPT only for data disks and not for boot disks. The reason for this is that Hyper-V emulates a basic input/output system (BIOS) firmware environment and won't recognize the Extensible Firmware Interface (EFI).**

Working with MBR disks

MBR uses a partition table that describes where the partitions are located on the disk. The first sector on a hard disk contains the MBR and a master boot code that's used to boot the system. The MBR resides outside of partitioned space.

> NOTE
>
> **It's easy to confuse *master boot record* with *boot sector*. These are different structures on the hard drive. The master boot record contains the disk signature and partition table and is the first sector of the hard drive. A boot sector contains the BIOS parameter block and marks the first sector of the file system.**

MBR disks support a maximum volume size of up to 4 TBs unless they're dynamic disks and use RAID. Two special types of partitions are associated with them. The first partition type, called a *primary partition*, is used with drive sections that you want to access directly for file storage. You make a primary partition accessible to users by creating a file system on it and assigning it a drive letter or mount point. The second partition type, called an *extended partition*, is used when you want to divide a section of a disk into one or more logical units called *logical drives*. Here, you create the extended partition first and then create the logical drives within it. You then create a file system on each logical drive and assign a drive letter or mount point.

Each MBR drive can have up to four primary partitions or three primary partitions and one extended partition. It is the extended partition that enables you to divide a drive into more than four parts.

> NOTE
>
> **These rules apply to MBR disks that use the basic storage type. There's also a storage type called *dynamic*. I discuss basic and dynamic storage types in "Working with basic and dynamic disks" later in this chapter.**

Working with GPT disks

GPT disks don't have a single MBR. With GPT disks, critical partition data is stored in the individual partitions, and there are redundant primary and backup partition tables. Further, checksum fields are maintained to allow for error correction and to improve partition structure integrity.

Inside OUT

GPT headers and error checking

GPT disks use a primary and a backup partition table. Each partition table has a header that defines the range of logical block addresses on the disk that partition entries can use. The GPT header also defines its location on the disk, its globally unique identifier (GUID), and a 32-bit cyclic redundancy check (CRC32) checksum that verifies the integrity of the GPT header. The primary GPT header is created directly after the protected boot sector on the disk. The backup GPT header is located in the last sector on the disk.

Firmware acts as the interface between a computer's hardware and its operating system. Although most computers use the BIOS as their firmware, the EFI also is available. Generally, only systems that use EFI can boot directly to a GPT disk, but all current Windows and Windows Server operating systems can use GPT disks for data.

A computer's firmware verifies the integrity of the GPT headers by using the CRC32 checksum. The checksum is a calculated value that determines whether there are errors in a GPT header. If the primary GPT header is damaged, firmware checks the backup header. If the backup header's checksum is valid, the backup GPT header is used to restore the primary GPT header. The process of restoring the GPT header works much the same way if it is determined that the backup header is damaged—only in reverse. If both the primary and backup GPT headers are damaged, the Windows operating system won't be able to access the disk.

GPT disks support raw partitions of up to 18 exabytes (EBs) in size and up to 128 partitions per disk. EFI-based computers using GPT disks for boot have two required partitions and one or more optional original equipment manufacturer (OEM) or data partitions. The required partitions are the EFI system partition (ESP) and the Microsoft Reserved (MSR) partition. Although the optional partitions that you see depend on the system configuration, the optional partition type you see the most is the primary partition. Primary partitions are used to store user data on GPT disks. With Windows Server 2012 R2, a typical new disk has the GPT partition style with a recovery partition and an EFI system partition.

Keep in mind that additional GPT disks (data disks) do not require an ESP. Further, a basic GPT disk might not contain primary partitions. For example, when you install a new disk and configure it as a GPT disk, the Windows operating system automatically creates the ESP and MSR partitions, but it does not create primary partitions.

Although GPT offers a significant improvement over MBR, it does have limitations. You cannot use GPT with removable disks, disks that are directly attached using USB or FireWire interfaces, or disks attached to shared storage devices on server clusters.

CAUTION

To make changes to GPT disks, you should use only Disk Management or DiskPart. If you are working in the EFI firmware environment, you'll find a version of DiskPart available as well—DiskPart.efi.

Understanding legacy and protective MBRs

Most workstations and servers ship with Unified Extensible Firmware Interface (UEFI). Although UEFI is replacing BIOS and EFI as the top-level firmware interface, it doesn't replace all the functionality in either BIOS or EFI and typically is wrapped around BIOS or EFI.

With respect to UEFI, GPT is the preferred partitioning scheme, and a protective MBR can be located on any disk that uses the GPT disk layout. A legacy MBR and a protective MBR differ in many important ways. A legacy MBR is located at the first logical block on a disk that is not using the GPT disk layout. The first 512 bytes on an MBR disk have the following layout:

- The MBR begins with a 424-byte boot code, which is used to select an MBR partition record and load the first logical block of that partition. The boot code on the MBR is not executed by UEFI.
- The boot code is followed by a 4-byte unique MBR disk signature, which the operating system can use to identify the disk and distinguish it from other disks on the system. The unique signature is written by the operating system and is not used by UEFI.
- A 2-byte separator follows the disk signature. At byte offset 446, there is an array of four MBR partition records; each record is 16 bytes in length. Block 510 contains 0x55, and block 511 contains 0xAA. Block 512 is reserved.

Each of the four partition records defines the first and last logical blocks that a particular partition uses on a disk. The partition records have the following layout:

- The MBR partition record begins with a 1-byte boot indicator. For example, a value of 0x80 identifies a bootable legacy partition. Any other value indicates that this is not a bootable legacy partition. UEFI doesn't use this value.

- The boot indicator is followed by a 3-byte address identifying the start of the partition. At byte offset 4, a 1-byte value indicates the operating system type, which is followed by a 3-byte value that identifies the end of the partition. UEFI doesn't use these values.
- At byte offset 8, a 4-byte value indicates the first logical block of the partition, and a 4-byte value follows, indicating size of the partition in units of logical blocks. UEFI uses both of these values.

If an MBR partition has an operating system type value of 0xEF, firmware must add the UEFI system partition GUID to the handle for the MBR partition. This enables boot applications, operating system loaders, drivers, and other lower-level tools to locate the UEFI system partition, which must physically reside on the disk.

A protective MBR can be located at the first logical block on a disk that is using the GPT disk layout. The protective MBR precedes the GUID Partition Table Header and is used to maintain compatibility with tools that do not understand GPT partition structures.

The purpose of the protective MBR is to protect the GPT partitions from boot applications, operating system loaders, drivers, and other lower-level tools that don't understand the GPT partitioning scheme. The protective MBR does this by defining a fake partition covering the entire disk.

When a disk has a protective MBR, the first 512 bytes on the disk have the following layout:

- The protective MBR begins with a 424-byte boot code, which UEFI doesn't execute.
- The boot code is followed by a 4-byte disk signature, which is set to zero and isn't used by UEFI.
- A 2-byte separator follows the disk signature. This separator is set to zero and isn't used by UEFI.
- At byte offset 446, there is an array of four MBR partition records; each record is 16 bytes in length. Only the first partition record—the protective partition record—is used. The other partition records are set to zero.
- Block 510 contains 0x55, and block 511 contains 0xAA. Block 512 is reserved.

The protective partition record reserves the entire space on the disk after the first 512 bytes for the GPT disk layout. The protective partition record has the following layout:

- The protective partition record begins with a 1-byte boot indicator that is set to 0x00, which indicates a nonbootable partition. The boot indicator is followed by a 3-byte address identifying the start of the partition at 0x000200, which is the first usable block on the disk.

- At byte offset 4, a 1-byte value is set to 0xEE to indicate the operating system type as GPT Protective. This is followed by a 3-byte value that identifies the last usable block on the disk, which is the end of the partition (or 0xFFFFFF if it is not possible to represent this value).
- At byte offset 8, a 4-byte value is set to 0x00000001, which identifies the logical block address of the GPT partition header. This is followed by a 4-byte value indicating the size of the disk minus one block (or 0xFFFFFFFF if the size of the disk is too large to be represented).

Using and converting MBR and GPT disks

Tasks for using MBR and GPT disks are similar but not necessarily identical. Partitions and volumes on MBR and GPT disks can be formatted by using FAT, FAT32, exFAT, NTFS, and ReFS. When you create partitions or volumes in Disk Management, you have the opportunity to format the disk and assign it a drive letter or mount point as part of the volume creation process. Although Disk Management enables you to format the partitions and volumes on MBR disks by using FAT, FAT32, exFAT, NTFS, and ReFS, you can format partitions and volumes on GPT disks by using FAT, FAT32, NTFS, and ReFS. Further, keep in mind that you can use Windows Server Backup to back up MBR and GPT disks and their volumes whether they are formatted with FAT, FAT32, exFAT, NTFS, or ReFS.

You can change partition table styles from MBR to GPT or from GPT to MBR. Changing partition table styles can be useful when you want to move disks between computers or you receive new disks that are formatted for the wrong partition table style. You can convert partition table styles only on empty disks, however. This means the disks must be either new or newly formatted. You could, of course, empty a disk by removing its partitions or volumes.

You can use both Disk Management and DiskPart to change the partition table style. To use Disk Management to change the partition style of an empty disk, start Computer Management from the Administrative Tools menu or by typing **compmgmt.msc** at the command line, expand the Storage node, and then select Disk Management. All available disks are displayed. Press and hold or right-click the disk to convert in the Graphical View and then tap or click Convert To GPT Disk or Convert To MBR Disk as appropriate.

To use DiskPart to change the partition style of an empty disk, invoke DiskPart by typing **diskpart** and then selecting the disk you want to convert. For example, if you want to convert disk 3, type **select disk 3**. After you select the disk, you can convert it from MBR to GPT by typing **convert gpt**. To convert a disk from GPT to MBR, type **convert mbr**.

Using the disk storage types

The term *storage type* refers to the method that Windows Server uses to structure disks and their contents. Windows Server offers several storage types, including basic disk, dynamic disk, removable disk, and virtual disk. The storage type you use doesn't depend on the processor architecture—it can depend, however, on whether you are working with fixed or nonfixed disks. When you are working with fixed disks, you can use basic, dynamic, or both storage types on any edition of Windows Server, and you can create virtual disks. When you are working with nonfixed disks, the disk has the removable storage type automatically, but generally, you cannot create a virtual disk.

Working with basic and dynamic disks

Basic disks use the same disk structure as early versions of the Windows operating system. When using basic disks, you are limited to creating four primary partitions per disk or three primary partitions and one extended partition. Within an extended partition, you can create one or more logical drives. For ease of reference, primary partitions and logical drives on basic disks are known as *basic volumes*. Dynamic disks were introduced with early Windows operating systems as a way to improve disk support by requiring fewer restarts after disk configuration changes, improve support for combining disks, and enhance fault tolerance using RAID configurations. All volumes on dynamic disks are known as *dynamic volumes*.

Windows Server 2012 R2 systems can use both basic and dynamic disks. You cannot, however, mix disk types when working with volume sets. Note also that although you can continue to use dynamic disks with Windows 8.1 and Windows Server 2012 R2, dynamic disks are being phased out in favor of Storage Spaces. If you want to mirror the volume that hosts the operating system, you might want to use dynamic disks because this is one of the best approaches. Otherwise, Microsoft recommends using Storage Spaces instead of dynamic disks.

All disks, regardless of whether they are basic or dynamic, have five special types of drive sections:

- **Active.** The active partition or volume is the drive section for system cache and startup. Some devices with removable storage might be listed as having an active partition (although they don't actually have the active partition).
- **Boot.** The boot partition or volume contains the operating system and its support files. The system and boot partition or volume can be the same.
- **Crash dump.** The crash dump is the partition to which the computer attempts to write dump files in the event of a system crash. By default, dump files are written to the %SystemRoot% folder, but they can be located on any desired partition or volume.
- **Page file.** A page file partition or volume contains a paging file that the operating system uses. Because a computer can page memory to multiple disks, according to the way virtual memory is configured, a computer can have multiple page file partitions or volumes.

- **System.** The system partition or volume contains the hardware-specific files needed to load the operating system. The system partition or volume can't be part of a striped or spanned volume.

The volume types are set when you install the operating system. You can mark a partition as active to ensure that it is the one from which the computer starts. You can do this only for partitions on basic disks. You can't mark an existing dynamic volume as the active volume, but you can convert a basic disk containing the active partition to a dynamic disk. After the update is complete, the partition becomes a simple volume that's active.

Using and converting basic and dynamic disks

You can't use dynamic disks on portable computers. When you are working with desktop computers and servers, you only can use dynamic disks with drives connected to internal controllers (as well as some eSATA controllers). Although you can't use dynamic disks with portable or removable drives on these computers, you can connect such a drive to an internal controller or a recognized eSATA controller and then use Disk Management to import the drive.

Basic disks and dynamic disks are managed in different ways. For basic disks, you use primary and extended partitions. Extended partitions can contain logical drives. Dynamic disks enable you to combine disks to create spanned volumes, to mirror disks to create mirrored volumes, and to stripe disks by using RAID 0 to create striped volumes. You can also create RAID-5 volumes for high reliability on dynamic disks.

You can change storage types from basic to dynamic and from dynamic to basic. When you convert a basic disk to a dynamic disk, existing partitions are changed to volumes of the appropriate type automatically, and existing data is not lost. Converting a dynamic disk to a basic disk isn't so easy and can't be done without taking some drastic measures. You must delete the volumes on the dynamic disk before you can change the disk back to a basic disk. Deleting the volumes destroys all the information they contain, and the only way to get it back is to restore the data from backup.

You should consider a number of things when you want to change the storage type from basic to dynamic. To be converted successfully, an MBR disk must have 1 megabyte (MB) of free space at the end of the disk. This space is used for the dynamic disk database, which tracks volume information. Without this free space at the end of the disk, the conversion will fail. Because both Disk Management and DiskPart reserve this space automatically, you need to be concerned about whether this space is available only if you used third-party disk management utilities. However, if the disk was formatted using another version of the Windows operating system, this space might not be available either.

A GPT disk must have contiguous, recognized data partitions to be converted successfully. If the GPT disk contains partitions that the Windows operating system doesn't recognize, such as those created by another operating system, you won't be able to convert a basic disk to a dynamic disk. When you convert a GPT disk, the Windows operating system creates LDM Metadata and LDM Data partitions as discussed in "LDM metadata and LDM data partitions" later in this chapter. GPT disks that are dynamic store the dynamic disk database in the LDM partitions instead of out at the end of the drive as on an MBR disk.

You can't convert a disk if the system or boot partition uses software RAID. You must stop using the software RAID before you convert the disk.

Both Disk Management and DiskPart can be used to change the storage type.

Using Disk Management to convert a basic disk to a dynamic disk To use Disk Management to convert a basic disk to a dynamic disk, start Computer Management from the Administrative Tools menu or by typing **compmgmt.msc** at the command line, expand the Storage node, and then select Disk Management. In Disk Management, press and hold or right-click a basic disk that you want to convert, either in Disk List view or in the left pane of Graphical View, and select Convert To Dynamic Disk.

In the Convert To Dynamic Disk dialog box (shown in Figure 13-3), select the disks you want to convert. If you're converting a RAID volume, be sure to select all the basic disks in the set because they must be converted together. Tap or click OK when you're ready to continue.

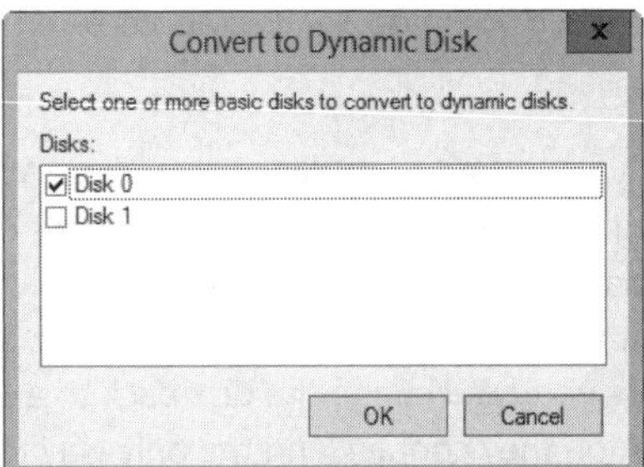

Figure 13-3 Select the disks to convert.

Next, as shown in Figure 13-4, the Disks To Convert dialog box shows the disks you're converting along with details of the disk contents. To see the drive letters and mount points that are associated with a disk, select the disk in the Disks list and then tap or click Details. If a disk cannot be converted for some reason, the Will Convert column will show No, and the Disk Contents column will provide a reason. You must correct whatever problem is noted before you can convert the disk.

When you're ready to start the conversion, tap or click Convert. Disk Management then warns you that after you finish the conversion, you won't be able to boot previous versions of the Windows operating system from volumes on the selected disks. Tap or click Yes to continue. If a selected drive contains the boot partition, system partition, or a partition in use, you see another warning, telling you that the computer will need to be rebooted to complete the conversion process.

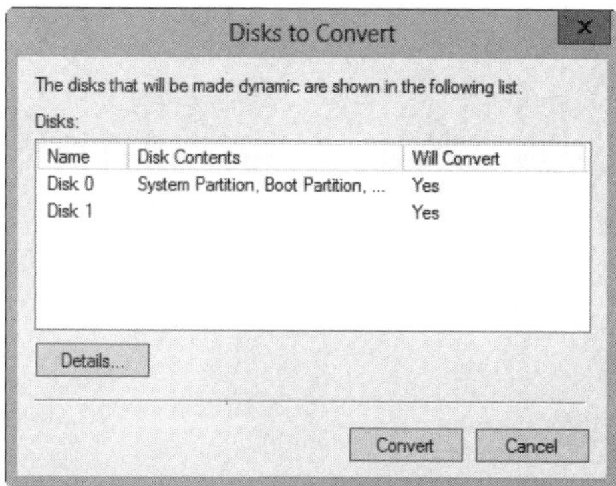

Figure 13-4 Confirm that the disk can be converted.

Using DiskPart to convert a basic disk to a dynamic disk To use DiskPart to convert a basic disk to a dynamic disk, invoke DiskPart by typing **diskpart** and then select the disk you want to convert. For example, if you want to convert disk 2, type **select disk 2**. After the disk is selected, you can convert it from basic to dynamic by typing **convert dynamic**.

Using Disk Management to change a dynamic disk back to a basic disk To use Disk Management to change a dynamic disk back to a basic disk, you must first delete all dynamic volumes on the disk. Then press and hold or right-click the disk and select Convert To Basic Disk. This changes the dynamic disk to a basic disk, and you can then create new partitions and logical drives on the disk.

Using DiskPart to convert a dynamic disk to a basic disk To use DiskPart to convert a dynamic disk to a basic disk, invoke DiskPart by typing **diskpart** and then select the disk you want to convert. For example, if you want to convert disk 2, type **select disk 2**. If there are any existing volumes on the disk, you must delete them. You can do this by typing **clean**. However, be sure to move any data the disk contains to another disk prior to deleting the disk volumes.

After you delete all the volumes on the disk, you can convert the disk from dynamic to basic by typing **convert basic**. This changes the dynamic disk to a basic disk, and you can then create new partitions and logical drives on the disk.

Creating and managing virtual hard disks for Hyper-V

You can use Disk Management to create, attach, and detach virtual hard disks. To create a virtual hard disk, choose Create VHD from the Action menu. In the Create And Attach Virtual Hard Disk dialog box, shown in Figure 13-5, tap or click Browse. Use the Browse Virtual Disk

Files dialog box to select where you want to create the .vhd file for the virtual hard disk. Type a name for the virtual hard disk and then tap or click Save.

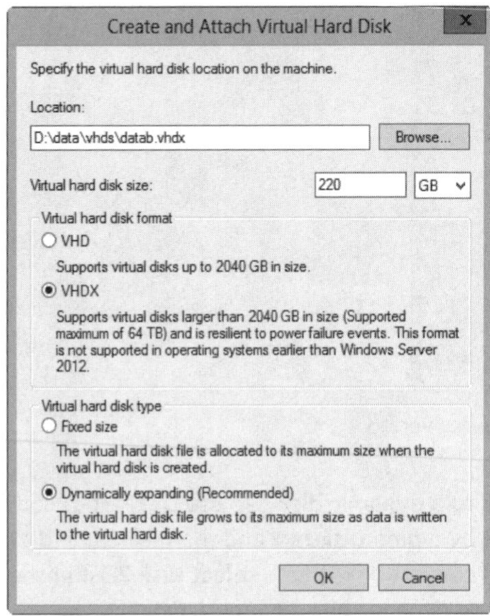

Figure 13-5 Specify the location, format, and type for the virtual hard disk.

In the Virtual Hard Disk Size field, enter the size of the disk in MB, GB, or TB. Keep in mind that disk sizes aren't necessarily fixed.

Next, choose a virtual hard disk format. Two virtual hard disk formats are available:

- Standard virtual disks with the .vhd extension, which are backward compatible with earlier releases of Windows Server and support a maximum disk size of 2,040 GBs.
- Enhanced virtual disks with the .vhdx extension, which are compatible only with Windows Server 2012 R2 and support enhanced features, including a maximum size of 64 TBs and improved handling of power failures.

Use the Virtual Hard Disk Type options to specify whether the size of the VHD dynamically expands to its fixed maximum size as data is saved to it or uses a fixed amount of space regardless of the amount of data stored on it. When you tap or click OK, Disk Management creates the virtual hard disk.

The VHD is attached automatically and added as a new disk. To initialize the disk for use, press and hold or right-click the disk entry in Graphical View and then tap or click Initialize Disk. In the Initialize Disk dialog box, shown in Figure 13-6, the disk is selected for initialization. Specify the disk type as MBR or GPT and then tap or click OK.

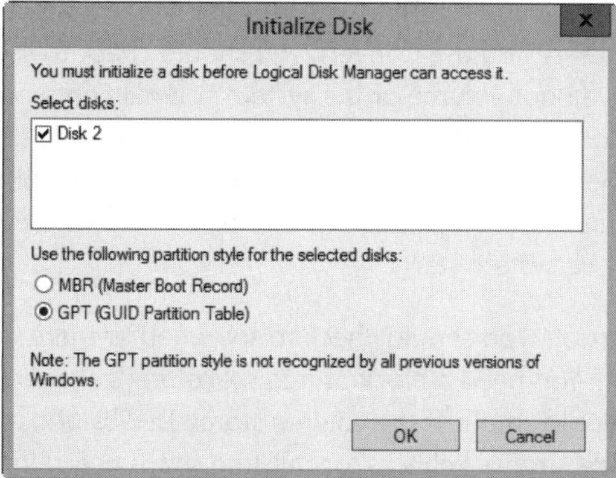

Figure 13-6 Specify the disk to initialize and set its partition style.

After initializing the disk, press and hold or right-click the unpartitioned space on the disk and create a volume of the appropriate type. After you create the volume, the VHD is available for use.

After you create, attach, initialize, and format a VHD, you can work with a virtual disk in much the same way as you work with other disks. You can write data to and read data from a VHD. You can boot the computer from a VHD. You can take a VHD offline or put a VHD online by pressing and holding or right-clicking the disk entry in Graphical View and selecting Offline or Online, respectively. If you no longer want to use a VHD, you can detach it by pressing and holding or right-clicking the disk entry in Graphical View, selecting Detach VHD, and then tapping or clicking OK in the Detach Virtual Hard Disk dialog box.

You also can use VHDs created with other programs. If you created a VHD using another program or have a detached VHD you want to attach, you can work with the VHD by completing the following steps:

1. In Disk Management, tap or click Attach VHD on the Action menu.
2. In the Attach Virtual Hard Disk dialog box, tap or click Browse. Use the Browse Virtual Disk Files dialog box to select the .vhd or .vhdx file for the virtual hard disk and then tap or click Open.
3. If you want to attach the VHD in read-only mode, select Read-Only. Otherwise, the VHD will open in read-write mode. Tap or click OK to attach the VHD.

Converting FAT or FAT32 to NTFS

On both MBR and GPT disks, you can convert FAT or FAT32 partitions, logical drives, and volumes to NTFS by using the Convert command. This preserves the file and directory structure without the need to reformat. Before you use Convert, you should check to see whether the volume is being used as the active boot volume or is a system volume containing the operating system. If it is a system volume, Convert must have exclusive access to the volume before it can begin the conversion. Because exclusive access to boot or system volumes can be obtained only during startup, you see a prompt asking whether you want to schedule the drive to be converted the next time the system starts.

As part of the preparation for conversion, you should check to see whether there's enough free space to perform the conversion. You need a block of free space that's about 25 percent of the total space the volume uses. For example, if the volume stores 12 GBs of data, you should have about 3 GBs of free space. Convert checks for this free space before running, and if there isn't enough, it won't convert the volume.

> CAUTION
>
> **Conversion is one-way only. You can convert only from FAT or FAT32 to NTFS. You can't convert from NTFS to FAT or from NTFS to FAT32 without deleting the volume and re-creating it using FAT or FAT32. You can't convert exFAT or ReFS volumes to NTFS.**

You run Convert at the command line. Its syntax is as follows:

```
convert volume /FS:NTFS
```

Here, *volume* is the drive letter followed by a colon, drive path, or volume name. So, for instance, if you want to convert the E drive to NTFS, type **convert e: /fs:ntfs**. This starts Convert. As shown in the following example, Convert checks the current file system type and then prompts you to enter the existing volume label for the drive:

```
The type of the file system is FAT32.
Enter current volume label for drive E:
```

As long as you enter the correct volume label, Convert continues as shown in the following example:

```
Volume CORPDATA created 4/10/2014 12:53 PM
Volume Serial Number is AA6B-CEDE
Windows is verifying files and folders...
File and folder verification is complete.
Windows has checked the file system and found no problems.
   91,827,680 KB total disk space.
   91,827,672 KB are available.
```

```
   8,192 bytes in each allocation unit.
   11,478,460 total allocation units on disk.
   11,478,459 allocation units available on disk.

Determining disk space required for file system conversion...
Total disk space:              91927860 KB
Free space on volume:          91929680 KB
Space required for conversion:        12080460 KB
Converting file system
Conversion complete
```

Here, Convert examines the file and folder structure and then determines how much disk space is needed for the conversion. If there is enough free space, Convert performs the conversion. Otherwise, it exits with an error, stating there isn't enough free space to complete the conversion.

Several additional parameters are available, including */v*, which tells Convert to display detailed information during the conversion, and */x*, which tells Convert to force the partition or volume to dismount before the conversion if necessary. You can't dismount a boot or system drive—these drives can be converted only when the system is restarted.

On converted boot and system volumes, Convert applies the same default security as that applied during Windows setup. On other volumes, Convert sets security so that the Users group has access but doesn't give access to the special Everyone group. If you don't want security to be set, you can use the */Nosecurity* parameter. This parameter tells Convert to remove all security attributes and make all files and directories on the disk accessible to the Everyone group. In addition, you can use the */Cvtarea* parameter to set the name of a contiguous file in the root directory to be a placeholder for NTFS system files.

Working with removable disks

Removable is the standard disk type associated with removable storage devices. Working with removable disks is similar to working with fixed disks. Removable storage devices can be formatted by using exFAT, FAT16, FAT32, or NTFS. All current versions of the Windows operating system also support exFAT with removable storage devices.

The exFAT file system is the next-generation file system in the FAT (FAT12/16, FAT32) family. exFAT is essentially FAT64. Although it retains the ease-of-use advantages of FAT32, exFAT overcomes the FAT32 4 GB file size limit and the FAT32 32 GB partition size limit on Windows systems. exFAT also supports allocation unit sizes of up to 32,768 KBs. exFAT is designed so that it can be used with and easily moved between any compliant operating system or device.

> NOTE
>
> **Windows Vista and later support hot-pluggable media that use NTFS volumes. This feature enables you to format USB flash devices and similar media with NTFS.**

Removable disks support network file and folder sharing. You configure sharing on removable disks in the same way you configure standard file sharing. You can assign share permissions, configure caching options for offline file use, and limit the number of simultaneous users. You can share an entire removable disk or share individual folders stored on the removable disk. You can also create multiple share instances.

Removable disks differ from standard NTFS sharing in that there isn't an extensive underlying security architecture. With exFAT, FAT, or FAT32, the stored folders and files have only basic attributes, including read-only and hidden attribute flags that you can set and basic permissions for read and read/write access for specific users.

Managing MBR disk partitions on basic disks

A disk using the MBR partition style can have up to four primary partitions and up to one extended partition. This enables you to configure MBR disks in one of two ways: using one to four primary partitions or using one to three primary partitions and one extended partition. After you partition a disk, you format the partitions to assign drive letters or mount points.

> **Inside OUT**
>
> ***Drive letter assignment is initiated during installation***
>
> The drive letters that are available depend on how a system is configured. The initial drive letters a computer uses are assigned during the installation of the operating system. Setup does this by scanning all fixed hard disks as they are enumerated.
>
> For MBR disks, Setup assigns a drive letter to the first primary partition, starting with C. Setup then scans for floppy disks and, if any are installed, assigns drive letters, starting with A. Afterward, Setup scans CD/DVD-ROM drives and assigns the next available letter, starting with D. Finally, Setup scans all fixed hard disks and assigns drive letters to all remaining primary partitions.
>
> With GPT disks, Setup assigns drive letters to all primary partitions on the GPT disk, starting with C. Setup then scans for floppy drives and, if any are installed, assigns the next available drive letter, starting with A. Finally, Setup scans CD/DVD-ROM drives and assigns the next available letter, starting with D.

Creating partitions and simple volumes

The Disk Management user interface has one set of dialog boxes and wizards for both partitions and volumes. The first three volumes on a basic drive are created automatically as primary partitions. If you try to create a fourth volume on a basic drive, the remaining free space on the drive is converted automatically to an extended partition with a logical drive of the size you designate by using the new volume feature it created in the extended partition. Any subsequent volumes are created in the extended partitions and logical drives automatically.

In Disk Management, you create partitions, logical drives, and simple volumes by following these steps:

1. In the Graphical View of Disk Management, press and hold or right-click an unallocated or free area on the disk and then choose New Simple Volume. This starts the New Simple Volume Wizard. Read the Welcome page and then tap or click Next.
2. On the Specify Volume Size page, as shown in Figure 13-7, use the Simple Volume Size In MB field to specify how much of the available disk space you want to use for the volume. Keep the following in mind before you set the size and tap or click Next:
   - You can size a primary partition to fill an entire disk, or you can size it as appropriate for the system you're configuring. Keep in mind that the file system types available when you are formatting the volume depend on the size of the volume you are creating.
   - You can size extended partitions to fill any available unallocated space on a disk. Because an extended partition can contain multiple logical drives, each with its own file system, consider carefully how you might want to size logical drives before creating the extended partition. In addition, if a drive already has an extended partition or is removable, you won't be able to create an extended partition.

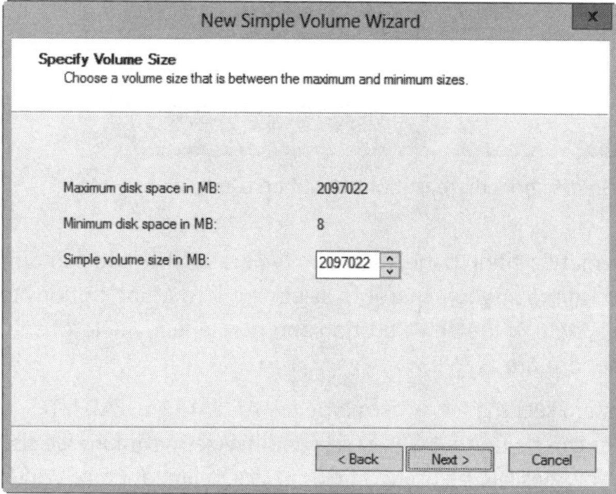

Figure 13-7 Size the partition appropriately.

3. If you are creating a primary partition, use the Assign Drive Letter Or Path page, as shown in Figure 13-8, to assign a drive letter or path. You can do one of the following and then click Next:
   - Assign a drive letter by choosing Assign The Following Drive Letter and then selecting an available drive letter in the selection list provided. Generally, the drive letters E through Z are available for use. (Drive letters A and B are used with floppy drives, drive letter C is for the primary partition, and drive letter D is for the computer's CD/DVD-ROM drive.)
   - Mount a path by choosing Mount In The Following Empty NTFS Folder and then typing the path to an existing folder. You can also tap or click Browse to search for or create a folder.
   - Choose Do Not Assign A Drive Letter Or Drive Path if you want to create the partition without assigning a drive letter or path.

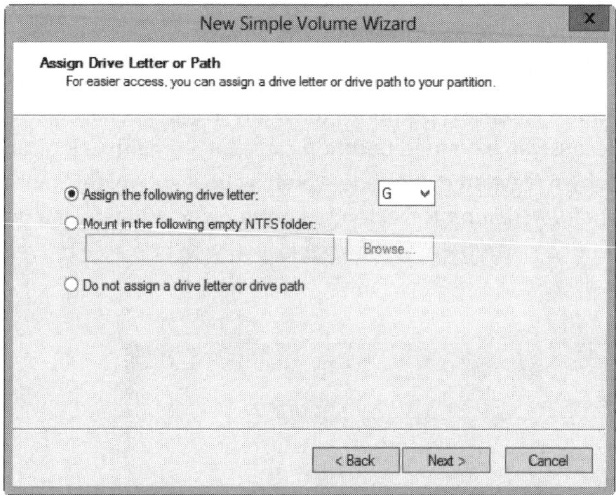

Figure 13-8 Specify how the partition should be used.

4. Using the Format Partition page, as shown in Figure 13-9, you can opt not to format the partition at this time or you can opt to select the formatting options to use. Formatting creates a file system in the new partition and permanently deletes any existing data. The formatting options are as follows:
   - File System sets the file system type as FAT, FAT32, exFAT, NTFS, or ReFS. FAT volumes can be up to 4 GBs in size and have a maximum file size limit of 2 GBs. FAT32 volumes can be up to 32 GBs in size (a limitation of Windows Server) and have a maximum file size of 4 GBs. exFAT volumes can be up to 256 TBs in size.

With ReFS and NTFS, files and volumes can be up to 2 TBs in size on MBR disks and up to 18 EBs in size on GPT disks.

Choose the partition format with care

If you don't know which file system to use, it is best in most cases to use NTFS. Only NTFS volumes can also use advanced file access permissions, compression, encryption, disk quotas, shadow copies, remote storage, and sparse files. There are exceptions, of course. If you want to be able to boot multiple operating systems, you might want to use FAT or FAT32. When a boot partition is formatted by using FAT, you can boot to just about any operating system. When a boot partition is formatted by using FAT32, you can boot to any version of the Windows operating system. Further, because FAT32 doesn't have the journaling overhead of NTFS, it is more efficient at handling large files that change frequently—particularly, files that have small, incremental changes, such as log files. This means, in some cases, that FAT32 will read and write files faster than NTFS. However, if you use FAT32, you won't be able to use any of the advanced file system features of Windows Server 2012 R2. When resilience is important, don't overlook ReFS, a new file system for Windows Server 2012 R2 that I discuss in Chapter 15, "File system essentials."

- Allocation Unit Size sets the cluster size for the file system. This is the basic unit in which disk space is allocated, and by default, it is based on the size of the volume. Note that ReFS volumes have a fixed allocation unit size.

Choosing an allocation unit size

In most cases, the default size is the best option to use, but you can override this feature by setting a different value. If you use lots of small files, you might want to use a smaller cluster size, such as 512 or 1,024 bytes. With these settings, small files use less disk space. Although sizes of up to 256 KBs are allowed, you will not be able to use compression on NTFS if you use a size larger than 4 KBs.

- Volume Label sets a text label for the partition that is used as its volume name. If you must change a partition's volume label, you can do this from the command line by using the Label command or from File Explorer by pressing and holding or right-clicking the volume, selecting Properties, and then typing a new label on the General tab.
- Perform A Quick Format specifies that you want to format the partition without checking for errors. Although you can use this option to save you a few minutes,

it's better to check for errors because this enables Disk Management to mark bad sectors on the disk and lock them out.

- Enable File And Folder Compression turns on compression so that files and folders on this partition are compressed automatically. Compression is available only for NTFS. For more information about using compression, see "Using file-based compression" in Chapter 15.

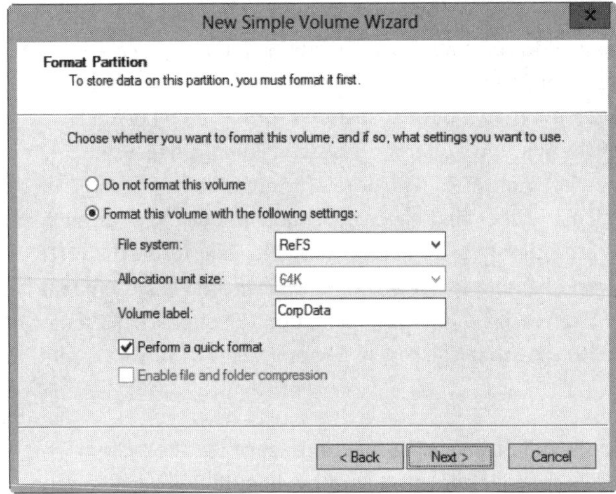

Figure 13-9 Format the partition now or opt to format the partition later.

5. Tap or click Next. The final page shows you the options you selected. If the options are correct, tap or click Finish. The wizard then creates the partition and configures it.

Formatting a partition, logical drive, or volume

Before you can use a primary partition, logical drive, or volume, you must format it. Formatting creates the file structures necessary to work with files and folders. If you want to clean out a partition, logical drive, or volume and remove all existing data, you can use formatting to do this as well.

You need not format if you want to convert to NTFS

Although you can use formatting to change the type of file system, you don't have to do this to change from FAT or FAT32 to NTFS. Instead, to convert to NTFS, you can use the Convert command, which preserves any existing data. For more information about Convert, see "Converting FAT or FAT32 to NTFS" earlier in this chapter.

CAUTION

A partition with unformatted space on a disk is listed with RAW as the file system type. A formatted partition is listed with its appropriate file system type, such as NTFS. If you reformat a formatted partition, you will destroy all data in the partition.

To format a primary partition, logical drive, or volume, follow these steps:

1. In Disk Management, press and hold or right-click the primary partition, logical drive, or volume you want to format and then choose Format. This opens the Format dialog box, as shown in Figure 13-10.

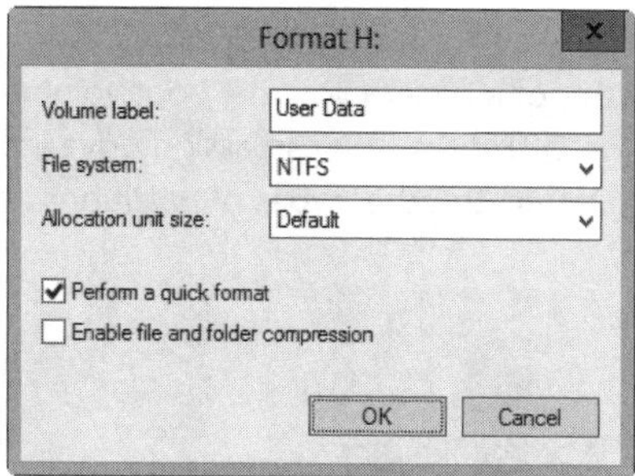

Figure 13-10 Set the formatting options and then tap or click OK.

2. In the Volume Label box, type a descriptive label for the primary partition, logical drive, or volume. In most cases, you want to use a label that helps you and other administrators determine what type of data is stored in the partition or on the logical drive.

3. Select the file system type. The available types depend on the size of the volume you are formatting. Keep in mind that only NTFS enables you to use the advanced file system features of Windows Server 2012 R2, including advanced file access permissions, compression, encryption, disk quotas, shadow copies, remote storage, and sparse files.

4. Use the Allocation Unit Size field to specify the basic unit in which disk space should be allocated. In most cases, the default size is the best option to use. Note that ReFS volumes have a fixed allocation unit size.

5. Select the Perform A Quick Format check box if you want to format the partition without checking for errors. Although this option can save you a few minutes, Disk Management won't mark bad sectors on the disk or lock them out, and this can lead to problems with data integrity later on.

6. If you want files and folders to be compressed automatically, select the Enable File And Folder Compression check box. Compression is available only for NTFS. To learn more about compression, see "Using file-based compression" in Chapter 15.

7. Tap or click OK to begin formatting using the specified options. When prompted to confirm, tap or click OK again.

Configuring drive letters

Each primary partition, logical drive, or volume on a disk can have one drive letter and one or more drive paths associated with it. You can assign, change, or remove driver letters and mount points at any time without having to restart the computer. Windows Server 2012 R2 also allows you to change the drive letter associated with CD/DVD-ROM drives. You cannot, however, change or remove the drive letter of a system volume, boot volume, or any volume that contains a paging file. In addition, on GPT disks, you can assign drive letters only to primary partitions. You cannot assign drive letters to other types of partitions on GPT disks.

Inside OUT

Changing the drive letter of a system or boot volume

If you installed the operating system on a drive with an odd drive letter, such as F or H, it would seem that you are stuck with it, which might not be best if you really want the operating system to be on a different drive letter, such as C. Although you can use Disk Management to change the drive letter of a system volume, a boot volume, and volumes that contain paging files, you shouldn't change these volumes without determining what impact this change has on the operating system and installed applications. Installed applications that rely on drive letters might not run correctly.

To add, change, or remove a drive letter, press and hold or right-click the primary partition, logical drive, or volume in Disk Management and choose Change Drive Letter And Paths. This opens the dialog box shown in Figure 13-11.

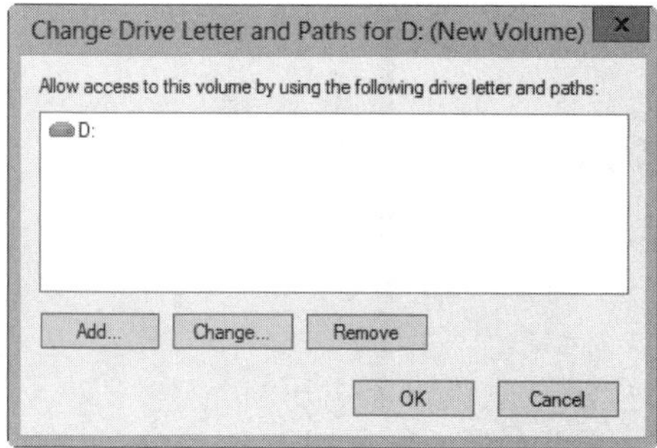

Figure 13-11 Configure the drive letter used for the partition, drive, or volume.

Any current drive letter and mount points associated with the selected drive are displayed. You have the following options:

- **Add a drive letter.** If the primary partition, logical drive, or volume doesn't yet have a drive-letter assignment, you can add one by tapping or clicking Add. In the Add Drive Letter Or Path dialog box that opens, select the drive letter to use from the drop-down list and then tap or click OK.
- **Change an existing drive letter.** If you want to change the drive letter, tap or click Change, select the drive letter to use from the drop-down list, and then tap or click OK. Confirm the action when prompted by tapping or clicking Yes.
- **Remove a drive letter.** If you want to remove the drive letter, tap or click Remove and then confirm the action when prompted by tapping or clicking Yes.

NOTE

When you change or remove a drive letter, the volume or partition will no longer be accessible using the old drive letter, and this can cause programs using the volume not to work properly, or it can cause the programs to stop running.

After you make a change, the new drive letter or mount point assignment is made automatically as long as the volume or partition is not in use. If the partition or volume is in use, Windows Server 2012 R2 displays the warning shown in Figure 13-12.

This prompt tells you the drive is in use and the new drive letter won't be assigned until you restart the computer. At this point, you can tap or click No to cancel the change or tap or click Yes to accept the change and continue. If you cancel the change, the new drive letter is not assigned. If you accept the change and continue, the old drive letter remains available for use by users and programs until you restart the computer. When you restart the computer, the new drive letter is applied.

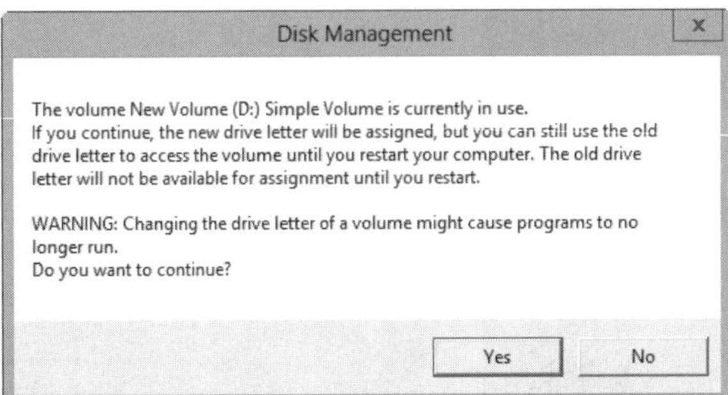

Figure 13-12 New drive letters are not assigned to in-use drives until you restart the computer.

Configuring mount points

Any volume or partition can be mounted to an empty NTFS folder as long as the folder is on a fixed disk drive rather than a removable media drive. A volume or partition mounted in such a way is called a *mount point*. Each volume or partition can have multiple mount points associated with it. For example, you could mount a volume to the root folder of the C drive as both C:\EngData and C:\DevData, giving the appearance that these are separate folders.

The real value of mount points, however, lies in how they give you the capability to create the appearance of a single file system from multiple hard disk drives without having to use spanned volumes. Consider the following scenario: A department file server has four data drives—drive 1, drive 2, drive 3, and drive 4. Rather than mount the drives as D, E, F, and G, you decide it would be easier for users to work with the drives if they were all mounted as folders of the system drive, which is C:\Data. You mount drive 1 to C:\Data\UserData, drive 2 to C:\Data\CorpData, drive 3 to C:\Data\Projects, and drive 4 to C:\Data\History. If you then shared the C:\Data folder, users could access all the drives by using a single share.

> NOTE
>
> **Wondering why I mounted the drives under C:\Data rather than C:\, as is recommended in some documentation? The primary reason I did this is to help safeguard system security. I didn't want users to have access to other directories, which include the operating system directories, on the C drive.**

To add or remove a mount point, press and hold or right-click the volume or partition in Disk Management and choose Change Drive Letter And Paths. This opens the Change Drive Letter And Paths For dialog box (as shown in Figure 13-13), which shows any current mount point and mount points associated with the selected drive.

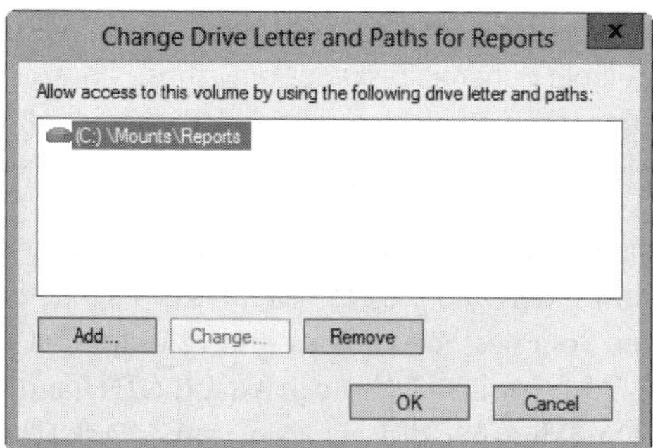

Figure 13-13 Add or remove a mount point.

You now have the following options:

- **Add a mount point.** Tap or click Add. In the Add Drive Letter Or Path dialog box, select Mount In The Following Empty NTFS Folder, as shown in Figure 13-14. Type the path to an existing folder or tap or click Browse to search for or create a folder. Tap or click OK to mount the volume or partition.

  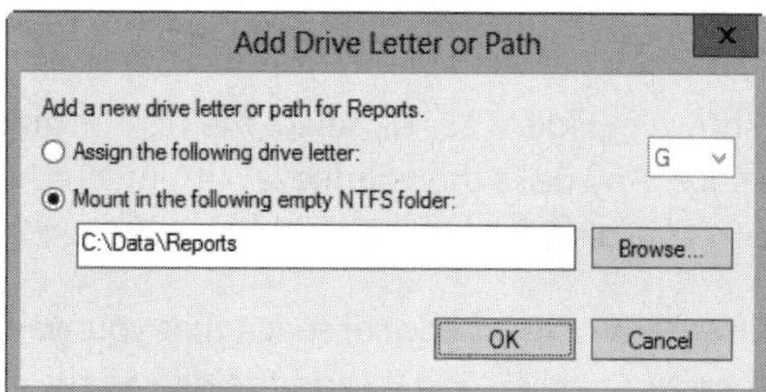

  Figure 13-14 Select the path for the new mount point.

- **Remove a mount point.** If you want to remove a mount point, select the mount point and then tap or click Remove. When prompted to confirm the action, tap or click Yes.

  NOTE

  You can't change a mount point assignment after making it. However, you can just remove the mount point you want to change and then add a new mount point so that the volume or partition is mounted as appropriate.

Extending partitions

You can extend volumes on both basic and dynamic disks by using either Disk Management or DiskPart. This is handy if you create a partition that's too small and you want to extend it so that you have more space for programs and data. In extending a volume, you convert areas of unallocated space and add them to the existing volume. For spanned volumes on dynamic disks, the space can come from any available dynamic disk, not only those on which the volume was originally created. Thus, you can combine areas of free space on multiple dynamic disks and use those areas to increase the size of an existing volume.

Before you try to extend a volume, be aware of several limitations. First, you can extend simple and spanned volumes only if they are formatted and the file system is NTFS (and in some instances, ReFS). You can't extend striped volumes. You can't extend volumes that aren't formatted or that are formatted with FAT, FAT32, or exFAT. You can extend NTFS (and in some instances, ReFS) volumes on both basic and dynamic disks by using either Disk Management or DiskPart.

By using Disk Management, you can extend a simple or spanned volume by following these steps:

1. Open Disk Management. Press and hold or right-click the volume that you want to extend and then select Extend Volume. This option is available only if the volume meets the previously discussed criteria and free space is available on one or more of the system's dynamic disks.
2. In the Extend Volume Wizard, read the introductory message and then tap or click Next.
3. On the Select Disks page, shown in Figure 13-15, select the disk or disks from which you want to allocate free space. Any disks the volume is currently using are selected automatically. By default, all remaining free space on those disks is selected for use.
4. With dynamic disks, you can specify the additional space that you want to use on other disks. Select the disk and then tap or click Add to add the disk to the Selected list box. In the Selected list box, select each disk that you want to use and, in the Select The Amount Of Space In MB list box, specify the amount of unallocated space to use on the selected disk.
5. Tap or click Next, confirm your options, and then tap or click Finish.

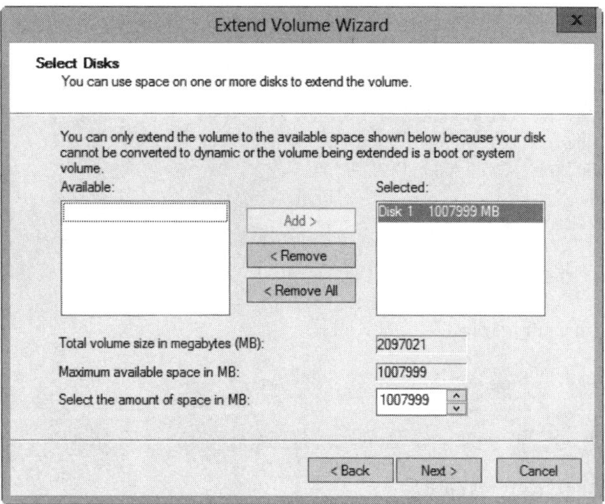

Figure 13-15 Specify the amount of space to add to the volume.

By using DiskPart, you can extend partitions by using the command line. To extend a partition, invoke DiskPart by typing **diskpart** at the command prompt. List the disks on the computer by typing **list disk**. After you check the free space of each disk, select the disk by typing **select disk *N***, where *N* is the disk you want to work with. Next, list the partitions on the selected disk by typing **list partition**. Select the last partition in the list by typing **select partition *N***, where *N* is the partition you want to work with.

Now that you've selected a partition, you can extend it. To extend the partition to the end of the disk, type **extend**. To extend the partition by a set amount, type **extend size=*N***, where *N* is the amount of space to add in megabytes. For example, if you want to add 90 GBs to the partition, type **extend size=90000**.

Listing 13-2 shows an actual DiskPart session in which a disk is extended. You can use this as an example to help you understand the process of extending disks. Here, disk 2 has 119 GBs of free space, and its primary partition is extended so that it fills the disk.

Listing 13-2 Extending disks

```
C:\> diskpart

     Microsoft DiskPart version 6.3.9600
     Copyright (C) 1999-2013 Microsoft Corporation.
     On computer: CORPSVR02
```

```
DISKPART> list disk

  Disk ###  Status    Size     Free    Dyn    Gpt
  --------  --------  -----    -----   ---    ---
  Disk 0    Online    1560 GB 504 GB     *      *
  Disk 1    Online    1290 GB   0 B
  Disk 2    Online    370 GB  119 GB

DISKPART> select disk 2

Disk 2 is now the selected disk.

DISKPART> list partition

  Partition ###  Type      Size     Offset
  -------------  --------- -------  -------
  Partition 1    Primary   370 GB    32 KB

DISKPART> select partition 1

Partition 1 is now the selected partition.

DISKPART> extend

DiskPart successfully extended the partition.

DISKPART> exit

Leaving DiskPart...

C:\>
```

To extend a partition on a dynamic disk to free space on another disk, you use the following syntax:

```
extend size=X disk=Y
```

Here, size=*X* sets the amount of space to use in megabytes, and disk=*Y* sets the number of the disk from which to allocate the space. Following this, you could allocate 50 GBs of free space from disk 0 to the selected disk in the previous example (disk 2) by using the following command:

```
extend size=50000 disk=0
```

Shrinking partitions

You can shrink volumes on both basic and dynamic disks by using either Disk Management or DiskPart. This is handy if you create a partition that's too large and you want to shrink it so that you have more space for other partitions. In shrinking a volume, you convert areas of allocated but unused space to free space by removing them from an existing volume.

As with extending volumes, several limitations apply to shrinking volumes. First, you can shrink simple and spanned volumes only if they are formatted and the file system is NTFS. You can't shrink striped volumes. You can't shrink volumes that are formatted with FAT, FAT32, exFAT, or ReFS. However, you can shrink volumes that have not been formatted. If a volume is heavily fragmented, you might have to defragment the volume to free up additional space before shrinking.

By using Disk Management, you can shrink a simple or spanned volume by following these steps:

1. Open Disk Management. Press and hold or right-click the volume that you want to shrink and then select Shrink Volume. This option is available only if the volume meets the previously discussed criteria.

2. In the field provided in the Shrink dialog box shown in Figure 13-16, enter the amount of space to shrink. The Shrink dialog box provides the following information:

   - **Total Size Before Shrink In MB.** Lists the total capacity of the volume in megabytes. This is the formatted size of the volume.
   - **Size Of Available Shrink Space In MB.** Lists the maximum amount by which the volume can be shrunk. This doesn't represent the total amount of free space on the volume; rather, it represents the amount of space that can be removed, not including any data reserved for the master file table, volume snapshots, page files, and temporary files.
   - **Enter The Amount Of Space To Shrink In MB.** Lists the total amount of space that will be removed from the volume. The initial value defaults to the maximum amount of space that can be removed from the volume. For optimal drive performance, you want to ensure that the drive has at least 10 percent of free space after the shrink operation.
   - **Total Size After Shrink In MB.** Lists what the total capacity of the volume in megabytes will be after the shrink. This is the new formatted size of the volume.

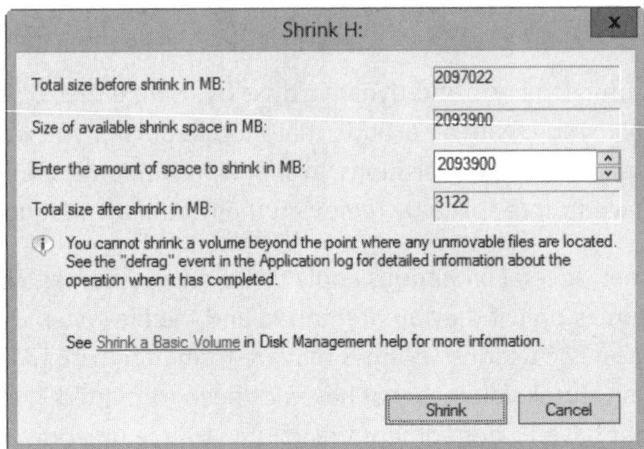

Figure 13-16 Specify the amount of space to shrink from the volume.

3. Tap or click Shrink to shrink the volume.

By using DiskPart, you can shrink partitions by using the command line. To shrink an NTFS-formatted partition, invoke DiskPart by typing **diskpart** at the command prompt. List the disks on the computer by typing **list disk**. After you check the free space of each disk, select the disk by typing **select disk *N***, where *N* is the disk you want to work with. Next, list the partitions on the selected disk by typing **list partition**. Select the last partition in the list by typing **select partition *N***, where *N* is the partition you want to work with.

Now that you've selected a partition, you can shrink it. To determine the maximum amount of space by which you can shrink the disk, type **shrink querymax**. To shrink the partition by the maximum amount, type **shrink**. To shrink the partition by a set amount, type **shrink desired=*N***, where *N* is the amount of space to remove in megabytes. For example, if you want to remove 225 GBs from the partition, type **shrink desired=225000**.

Listing 13-3 shows an actual DiskPart session in which you shrink a disk. You can use this as an example to help you understand the process of shrinking disks. Here, you determine that 40 GBs of space are available for shrinking on the selected partition and then you shrink the partition by 32 GBs.

Listing 13-3 Shrinking disks

```
C:\> diskpart

   Microsoft DiskPart version 6.3.9600
   Copyright (C) 1999-2013 Microsoft Corporation.
     On computer: CORPSVR02

     DISKPART> list disk
```

```
  Disk ###  Status    Size     Free    Dyn    Gpt
  --------  --------  -----  -----   ---    ---
  Disk 0    Online    1560 GB 504 GB   *      *
  Disk 1    Online    1290 GB   0 B
  Disk 2    Online    489 GB    0 B

DISKPART> select disk 2

Disk 2 is now the selected disk.

DISKPART> list partition

  Partition ###   Type       Size     Offset
  -------------   --------- -------  -------
  Partition 1     Primary   489 GB    32 KB

DISKPART> select partition 1

Partition 1 is now the selected partition.

DISKPART> shrink querymax

The maximum number of reclaimable bytes is: 40 GB

DISKPART> shrink desired=32000

DiskPart successfully shrunk the partition by: 32000 MB

DISKPART> exit

Leaving DiskPart...

C:\>
```

Deleting a partition, logical drive, or volume

Deleting a partition, logical drive, or volume removes the associated file system and all associated data. When you delete a logical drive, the logical drive is removed from the associated extended partition, and its space is marked as free. When you delete a partition or volume, the entire partition or volume is deleted, and its space is marked as Unallocated. If you want to delete an extended partition that contains logical drives, however, you must delete the logical drives before trying to delete the extended partition.

In Disk Management, you can delete a partition, logical drive, or volume by pressing and holding or right-clicking it and then choosing Delete Partition, Delete Logical Drive, or Delete Volume, as appropriate. When prompted to confirm the action, tap or click Yes.

Managing GPT disk partitions on basic disks

GPT disks can have the following types of partitions:

- ESP
- MSR partition
- Primary partition
- Logical Disk Manager (LDM) Metadata partition
- LDM Data partition
- OEM or Unknown partition

Each of these partition types is used and managed in different ways.

ESP

EFI-based computers must have one GPT disk that contains an ESP. This partition is similar to the system volume on a computer with an MBR boot disk in that it contains the files that are required to start the operating system. Windows Server 2012 R2 creates the ESP during setup and formats it by using FAT. Normally, the partition is sized so that it is at least 100 MBs in size or 1 percent of the disk, up to a maximum size of 1,000 MBs.

The ESP is shown in Disk Management but isn't assigned a drive letter or mount point. All Disk Management commands associated with the ESP are disabled, however, and you cannot store data on it, assign a drive letter to it, or delete it by using Disk Management or DiskPart. The ESP has several directories that contain the operating system boot loader, such as Ia64ldr.efi, and other files that are necessary to start the operating system in addition to utilities such as Diskpart.efi and Nvrboot.efi. Other directories are created as necessary by the operating system.

The only way to access these directories is to use the EFI firmware's Boot Manager or the MountVol command. If you access the ESP, don't make changes, additions, or deletions unless you've been specifically directed to by a Microsoft Knowledge Base article or other official documentation by an OEM vendor. Any changes you make could prevent the system from starting.

> **Inside OUT**
>
> *You can create an ESP if necessary—but do so only if directed to*
>
> Although the ESP is normally created for you automatically when you install Windows Server 2012 R2, there are some limited instances when you might be directed to create an ESP after installing an additional GPT disk on a server, such as when you want to use the new disk as a boot device rather than the existing boot device. You can create the necessary ESP by using DiskPart. Select the disk you want to work with and then type **create partition efi size=N**, where *N* is at least 100 MBs or 1 percent of the disk, up to a maximum size of 1000 MBs. After you create the partition, follow the vendor-directed or Microsoft-directed guidelines for preparing the partition for use. Never create an ESP unless you are directed to do so, however. One instance in which you must create an ESP is when you want to establish and boot to mirrored GPT disks. Here, you must prepare the second disk of the mirror so that it can be booted, and you do this by creating the necessary ESP and MSR partitions.

MSR partitions

EFI-based computers that use GPT for boot must have an MSR partition on every GPT disk. The MSR partition contains additional space the operating system might need to perform disk operations. For example, when you convert a basic GPT disk to a dynamic GPT disk, the Windows operating system uses 1 MB of the MSR partition space to create the LDM Metadata partition, which is required for the conversion.

The MSR partition is not shown in Disk Management and does not receive a drive letter or mount point. The Windows operating system creates the MSR partition automatically. For the boot disk, it is created along with the ESP when you install the operating system. An MSR partition is also created automatically when a disk is converted from MBR to GPT and any time you access a GPT disk that doesn't already have an MSR partition in Disk Management or DiskPart.

If a GPT disk contains an ESP as the first partition on the disk, the MSR partition is usually the second partition on the disk. If a GPT disk does not contain an ESP, the MSR partition is typically the first partition on the disk. However, if a disk already has a primary partition at the beginning of the disk, the MSR partition is placed at the end of the disk.

The MSR partition is sized according to the size of the associated disk. For disks up to 16 GBs in size, it normally is 32 MBs in size. For all other disks, it normally is 128 MBs in size.

Inside OUT

You can create an MSR partition if necessary—but do so only if directed to

The MSR partition normally is created for you automatically when you install Windows Server 2012 R2. It can also be created automatically when you access a secondary GPT disk that doesn't already have an MSR partition in Disk Management or DiskPart. You shouldn't attempt to create an MSR partition unless you are directed to by vendor-specific or Microsoft-specific documentation. In this case, you can use DiskPart to create the partition. Select the disk you want to work with and then type create partition msr size=N, where *N* is 32 for disks up to 16 GBs in size and 128 for all other disks.

Primary partitions

You create primary partitions on basic disks to store data. GPT disks support up to 128 partitions, which can be a mix of required and optional partitions. Every primary partition you create appears in the GUID partition entry array within the GPT header. If you convert a basic disk that contains primary partitions to a dynamic disk, the primary partitions become simple volumes, and information about them is then stored in the dynamic disk database and not in the GUID partition entry array.

To create a primary partition, complete the following steps:

1. In Disk Management Graphical View, press and hold or right-click an area marked Unallocated on a basic disk and then choose New Simple Volume. This starts the New Simple Volume Wizard. Tap or click Next.
2. The partition is created as a primary partition automatically. Use the Assign Drive Letter Or Path page to assign a drive letter or path. You can also choose Do Not Assign A Drive Letter Or Drive Path if you want to create the partition without assigning a drive letter or path. Tap or click Next.
3. Use the Format Partition page to set the formatting options. If you opt not to format the partition at this time, you can format the partition later as discussed in "Formatting a partition, logical drive, or volume" earlier in this chapter.
4. Tap or click Next. The final page shows you the options you've selected. If the options are correct, tap or click Finish. The wizard then creates the partition and configures it.

LDM Metadata and LDM Data partitions

Windows Server 2012 R2 creates LDM Metadata and LDM Data partitions when you convert a basic GPT disk to a dynamic GPT disk. The LDM Metadata partition is 1 MB in size and is used to store the partitioning information needed for the conversion. The LDM Data partition is the partition in which the actual dynamic volumes are created.

The LDM Data partition represents sections of unallocated space on the converted disk and sections that had basic partitions that are now dynamic volumes. For example, if a disk had a primary boot partition that spanned the whole disk, the converted disk will have a single LDM Data partition. If a disk had a boot partition and other primary partitions, it will have two LDM Data partitions after the conversion: one for the boot volume and one for the rest of the partitions. Although the LDM Metadata and LDM Data partitions are not shown in Disk Management and do not receive drive letters or mount points, you can use this space by creating primary partitions as discussed in the previous section.

OEM or unknown partitions

GPT disks can have partitions that are specific to OEM implementations, and your vendor documentation should describe what they are used for. The Windows operating system might display these partitions in Disk Management as Healthy (Unknown Partition). You cannot, however, manipulate these partitions in Disk Management or DiskPart. In addition, if an unknown partition lies between two known partitions on a GPT disk, you typically can't convert the disk from the basic disk type to the dynamic disk type.

Managing volumes on dynamic disks

Any disk using the MBR or GPT partition style can be configured as a dynamic disk. Unlike basic disks, which have basic volumes that can be created as primary partitions, extended partitions, and logical drives, dynamic disks have dynamic volumes that can be created as the following types:

- **Simple volumes.** A simple volume is a volume that's on a single drive and has the same purpose as a primary partition.
- **Spanned volumes.** A spanned volume is a volume that spans multiple drives.
- **Striped volumes.** A striped volume is a volume that uses RAID 0 to combine multiple disks into a striped set.
- **Mirrored volumes.** A mirrored volume is a volume that uses RAID 1 to mirror a primary disk onto a secondary disk that is available for disaster recovery.

- **RAID-5 volumes.** A RAID-5 volume is a volume that uses RAID 5 to create a fault-tolerant striped set on three or more disks.

Techniques for creating and managing these volume types are discussed in the sections that follow. Keep in mind that the RAID technology built into the operating system is software-based and is being phased out. Standards-based storage also has software RAID options, and they're preferred for new server deployments. See Chapter 17 for complete details on Storage Spaces.

Creating a simple or spanned volume

You create simple and spanned volumes in much the same way. The differences between these volume types are subtle:

- A simple volume uses free space from a single disk to create a volume. Windows can write to the selected disk until there is no more free space available within the volume.
- A spanned volume is used to combine the disk space on multiple disks to create the appearance of a single volume. Windows always writes to the first disk in the spanned set first, and then, when this disk fills, Windows writes to the second disk, and so on.

If you later need more space, you can extend a simple or spanned volume type by using Disk Management. Here, you select an area of free space on any available disk and add it to the volume. When you extend a simple volume onto other disks, it becomes a spanned volume. Any volume that you want to extend should be formatted by using NTFS or ReFS because only NTFS and ReFS volumes can be extended.

Simple and spanned volumes aren't fault tolerant. If you create a volume that spans disks and one of those disks fails, you won't be able to access the volume. Any data on the volume will be lost. You must restore the data from backup after you replace the failed drive and re-create the volume.

To create a simple or spanned volume, complete the following steps:

1. In Disk Management Graphical View, press and hold or right-click an area marked Unallocated on a dynamic disk and then choose New Simple Volume or New Spanned Volume as appropriate. Read the Welcome page and then tap or click Next.
2. If you select New Spanned Volume, you next see the Select Disks page shown in Figure 13-17. Use this page to select disks that should be part of the volume and to size the volume segments on the designated disks. Select one or more disks from the list of disks that are available and have unallocated space. Tap or click Add to add the disk or disks to the Selected list box. Next, select each of the disks in turn and then specify the

amount of space you want to use on the selected disk. Tap or click Next when you are ready to continue.

NOTE

If you started with a dynamic disk, the disk wizard shows both basic and dynamic disks with available disk space. If you add space from a basic disk that is not a system or boot volume, the wizard will attempt to convert the disk to a dynamic disk before creating the volume set. Before tapping or clicking Yes to continue, make sure you really want to do this because this can affect how the operating system uses the disk.

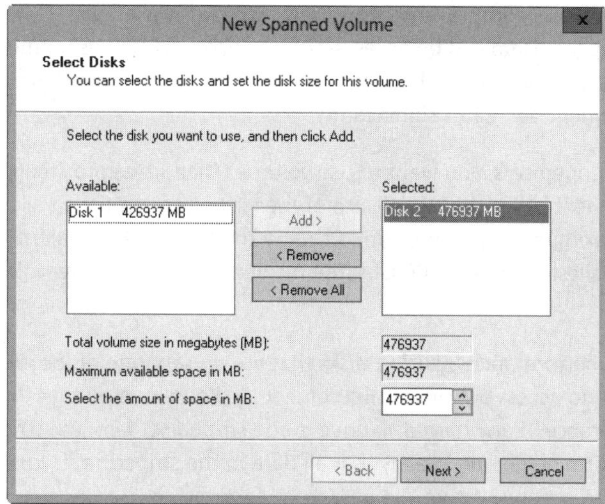

Figure 13-17 Select the disks that should be part of the volume and then specify how much space to use on each disk.

3. Use the Assign Drive Letter Or Path page to assign a drive letter or path. You can also choose Do Not Assign A Drive Letter Or Drive Path if you want to create the partition without assigning a drive letter or path. Tap or click Next.
4. Use the Format Volume page to set the formatting options. Simple and spanned volumes can be formatted by using FAT, FAT32, NTFS, or ReFS. With spanned volumes, you also can format by using exFAT. If you think you might need to extend the volume at a later date, you might want to use NTFS because NTFS can be easily extended. If you opt not to format the partition at this time, you can format the partition later as discussed in "Formatting a partition, logical drive, or volume" earlier in this chapter.
5. Tap or click Next. The final page shows you the options you selected. If the options are correct, tap or click Finish. The wizard then creates the volume and configures it.

Configuring RAID 0: Striping

RAID level 0 is disk striping. With disk striping, two or more volumes—each on a separate drive—are configured as a striped set. Unlike spanning, Windows breaks the data to be written into blocks called *stripes* and then writes the stripes sequentially to all disks in the set. So, if there are three disks in the set, Windows writes part of the data to the first disk, part of the data to the second disk, and part of the data to the third disk; this process of alternating among the disks is called *striping*.

Although the boot and system volumes shouldn't be part of a striped set, you can place volumes for a striped set on up to 32 drives, but in most circumstances, sets with 2 to 5 volumes offer the best performance improvements. When 3 to 32 drives are used, the major advantage of disk striping is speed. Data can be accessed on multiple disks by using multiple drive heads, which improves performance considerably. When you try to use more than 32 drives, the performance improvement decreases significantly.

When you create striped sets, you want to use volumes that are approximately the same size. Disk Management bases the overall size of the striped set on the smallest volume size. Specifically, the maximum size of the striped set is a multiple of the smallest volume size. For example, if the smallest volume is 100 GBs, the maximum size for a three-disk striped set is 300 GBs.

You can maximize performance by using disks that are on separate disk controllers. This enables the system to access the drives simultaneously. Keep in mind that this configuration offers no fault tolerance. If any hard disk drive in the striped set fails, the striped set can no longer be used, which essentially means that all data in the striped set is lost. You need to re-create the striped set and restore the data from backups.

You can create a striped set by following these steps:

1. In the Disk Management Graphical View, press and hold or right-click an area marked Unallocated on a dynamic disk and then choose New Striped Volume. This starts the New Striped Volume Wizard. Read the Welcome page and then tap or click Next.
2. Create the volume as described in "Creating a simple or spanned volume" earlier in this chapter. The key difference is that you need at least two dynamic disks to create a striped volume.

After you create a striped volume, you can use the volume just like any other volume. You can't extend a striped set after it's created. Therefore, you should carefully consider the setup before you implement it.

Recovering a failed simple, spanned, or striped disk

Simple disks are the easiest to troubleshoot and recover because only one disk is involved. Spanned or striped disks, however, have multiple disks, and the failure of any one disk makes the entire volume unusable. The drive status might show as Missing, Failed, Online (Errors), Offline, or Unreadable.

The Missing (and sometimes Offline) status usually happens if drives have been disconnected or powered off. If the drives are part of an external storage device, check the storage device to ensure that it is connected properly and has power. Reconnecting the storage device or turning on the power should make the drives accessible. You then must start Disk Management and rescan the disks by selecting Rescan Disks from the Action menu. When Disk Management finishes, press and hold or right-click the drive that was missing and then choose Reactivate.

The Failed, Online (Errors), and Unreadable statuses indicate input/output (I/O) problems with the drive. As before, try rescanning the drive and then try to reactivate it. If the drive doesn't come back to the Healthy state, you might need to replace it.

Moving dynamic disks

One of the advantages that dynamic disks have over basic disks is that you can easily move them from one computer to another. For example, if, after setting up a server, you decide that you don't really need its two additional hard disk drives, you could move them to another server where they could be used better. Before you move disks, you should access Disk Management on the server where the dynamic disks are currently installed and check their status. The status should be Healthy. If it isn't, you should fix any problems before moving the disks.

Moving system disks requires additional planning

Before you move a system disk from one computer to another, you must ensure that the computers have identically configured disk subsystems. If they don't, the Plug and Play ID on the system disk from the original computer won't match what the new computer is expecting. As a result, the new computer won't be able to load the right drivers, and boot will fail.

You cannot move drives with BitLocker Drive Encryption by using this technique. BitLocker Drive Encryption wraps drives in a protected seal so that any offline tampering is detected and results in making the disk unavailable until an administrator unlocks it. Before you can move a BitLocker-encrypted drive, you must remove BitLocker Drive Encryption.

Next, check to see whether any dynamic disks that you want to move are part of a spanned, extended, mirrored, striped, or RAID-5 set. If they are, you should make a note of which disks are part of which set and plan to move all disks in a set together. If you are moving only part of a disk set, you should be aware of the consequences. For spanned, extended, or striped volumes, moving only part of the set makes the related volumes unusable on the current computer and on the computer to which you are planning to move the disks. If you plan to move only one disk of a mirrored volume, you should break the mirror before you move it. This ensures that you can keep using the disks on both computers. For RAID-5 volumes, you should move all the disks in the set if possible. If you move only part of the RAID-5 set, you might find that you can't use the set on either computer.

To move the disks, open Computer Management and then, in the left pane, select Device Manager. In the Device List, expand Disk Drives. This shows a list of all the physical disk drives on the computer. Press and hold or right-click each disk that you want to move and then select Uninstall. If you are unsure which disks to uninstall, press and hold or right-click each disk and select Properties. In the Properties dialog box, click the Volumes tab and then choose Populate. This shows you the volumes on the selected disk. In Computer Management, select Disk Management. Press and hold or right-click each disk that you want to move and then select Remove Disk.

After you perform these procedures, you can move the dynamic disks. If the disks are hot swappable and this feature is supported on both computers, remove the disks from the original computer and then install them on the destination computer. Otherwise, turn off both computers, remove the drives from the original computer, and then install them on the destination computer. When you're finished, restart the computers. On the destination computer, access Disk Management and then select Rescan Disks on the Action menu. When Disk Management finishes scanning the disks, press and hold or right-click any disk marked Foreign and tap or click Import. You should now be able to access the disks and their volumes on the destination computer.

NOTE

When you move dynamic disks, the volumes on those disks should retain the drive letters they had on the previous computer. If a drive letter is already used on the destination computer, a volume receives the next available drive letter. If a dynamic volume previously did not have a drive letter, it does not receive a drive letter when moved to another computer. In addition, if auto-mounting is disabled, the volumes aren't automatically mounted, so you must manually mount volumes and assign drive letters.

Configuring RAID 1: Disk mirroring

For RAID 1, disk mirroring, you configure two volumes on two drives identically. Data is written to both drives. If one drive fails, no data is lost because the other drive contains the data. After you repair or replace the failed drive, you can restore full mirroring so that the volume is once again fault tolerant.

By using disk mirroring, you gain the advantage of redundancy. Because disk mirroring doesn't write parity information, mirrored volumes can usually offer better write performance than disk striping with parity. The key drawback, however, is that disk mirroring has a 50 percent overhead, meaning it effectively cuts the amount of storage space in half. For example, to mirror a 750 GB drive, you need another 750 GB drive. That means you use 1,500 GBs of space to store 750 GBs of information.

As with disk striping, you'll often want the mirrored disks to be on separate disk controllers. This provides redundancy for the disk controllers. If one of the disk controllers fails, the disk on the other controller is still available. When you use two disk controllers to duplicate data, you're using a technique known as *disk duplexing* rather than disk mirroring—but why mince words?

You can create a mirrored set either by using two new disks or by adding a mirror to an existing volume. As with other RAID techniques, mirroring is transparent to users. Users see the mirrored set as a single volume that they can access and use like any other drive.

Creating a mirrored set by using two new disks

To create a mirrored set by using two new disks, start Disk Management. In Graphical View, press and hold or right-click an area marked Unallocated on a dynamic disk and then choose New Mirrored Volume. This starts the New Mirrored Volume Wizard. Tap or click Next. Create the volume as described in "Creating a simple or spanned volume" earlier in this chapter. The key difference is that you must create two identically sized volumes, and these volumes must be on separate dynamic drives. The volumes can be formatted by using NTFS or ReFS. You won't be able to continue past the Selected Disks page until you select the two disks that you want to work with.

When you tap or click Finish, you return to the main Disk Management window, and Disk Management creates the mirrored set. During the creation of the mirror, you see a status of Resynching. This tells you that Disk Management is creating the mirror. When this process finishes, you'll have two identical volumes. Both volumes will show the same drive letter in Disk Management, but the separation of volumes is transparent to users. Users see the mirror set as a single volume. The volume status should be listed as Healthy. This is the normal status for volumes. If the status changes, you might need to repair or resync the mirrored set, as discussed in "Resolving problems with mirrored sets" later in this chapter.

Adding a mirror to an existing volume

You can also use an existing volume to create a mirrored set. For this to work, the volume you want to mirror must be a simple volume and you must have an area of unallocated space on a second dynamic drive with an equal or larger amount of space than the existing volume. When you add a mirror onto this unallocated space, Disk Management creates a volume that is the same size and file system type as the simple volume you are mirroring. It then copies the data from the simple volume to the new volume by using a process called *resynching*.

To add a mirror to an existing volume, start Disk Management. In Graphical View, press and hold or right-click the simple volume you want to mirror and then select Add Mirror. This opens the Add Mirror dialog box. Use the Disks list to select a location for the mirror and then tap or click Add Mirror. Windows Server 2012 R2 begins the mirror creation process, and you see a status of Resynching on both volumes.

When the resynching is complete, you have two identical copies of the original volume. Although both volumes show the same drive letter in Disk Management, the separation of volumes is transparent to users. Users see the mirror set as a single volume.

Mirroring boot and system volumes

Disk mirroring is often used to mirror boot and system volumes. Mirroring these volumes ensures that you can boot the server in case of a single drive failure.

Mirroring boot and system volumes on MBR disks

When you want to mirror boot or system volumes on MBR disks, the process is straightforward. You start with two disks, which I'll call Disk 0 and Disk 1, where Disk 0 has the system files and Disk 1 is a new disk. The system disk is typically a basic disk that must be upgraded to a dynamic disk before you can mirror it—mirroring is possible only on dynamic disks.

To begin, upgrade Disk 0 to a dynamic disk and then upgrade Disk 1 as discussed in "Using and converting basic and dynamic disks" earlier in this chapter. In Disk Management, press and hold or right-click the boot or system volume that you want to mirror and then select Add Mirror. This opens the Add Mirror dialog box. Select the disk onto which you want to add the mirror (Disk 1 in the example) and then tap or click Add Mirror. Windows Server 2012 R2 begins the mirror creation process, and you see a status of Resynching on both volumes. When the resynching is complete, the status should change to Healthy.

During the creation of the mirror, the operating system should add an entry to the system's Boot Manager that enables you to boot to the secondary mirror. Resolving a primary mirror failure is much easier with this entry in the Boot Manager file than without it because all you need to do is select the entry to boot to the secondary mirror. If you mirror the boot volume and a secondary mirror entry is not created for you, you could modify the boot entries in the Boot Manager to create one by using the BCD Editor (bcdedit.exe).

If a system fails to boot to the primary system volume, restart the system and select Boot Mirror - Secondary Plex for the operating system you want to start. The system should start up normally. After you successfully boot the system to the secondary drive, you can schedule the maintenance necessary to rebuild the mirror if desired.

Mirroring boot and system volumes on GPT disks

Mirroring boot and system volumes on GPT disks isn't the same as for MBR disks. Primarily, this is because GPT disks used to boot the operating system have an ESP and an MSR partition that must be created on the disk in a certain order. Thus, to mirror boot and system volumes on GPT disks, you must create the necessary partitions on the second disk of the mirrored set and tell the operating system that these partitions can be used for booting.

> NOTE
>
> **As stated previously, not all computers are capable of booting to GPT disks. Only EFI-based computers can boot to GPT disks.**

To get started, you need two disks that use the GPT partition style and the basic storage type. One of the disks should already be designated as the boot volume. I'll refer to this volume as Disk 0. The other disk should be identical in size or larger than the boot volume. I'll refer to this volume as Disk 1. Disk 1 should be a clean disk, meaning it can't already have partitions on it; so, if necessary, copy any data on the disk to another disk or make a backup of the data and then delete any existing partitions. You can use DiskPart to do this by completing the following steps:

1. At the command prompt, invoke DiskPart by typing **diskpart**. List the disks available on the system by typing **list disk**.

2. Select the disk you'll use as the secondary boot disk. Following the example, this is Disk 1, so you type **select disk 1**.

3. List the partitions on this disk by typing **list partition**.

4. If there are any existing partitions, select and delete each partition in turn. For example, if the disk has Partition 1, you type **select partition 1** and then type **delete partition override**. The *Override* parameter ensures that you can delete nonuser partitions.

After you make sure the second disk doesn't contain any partitions, list the available disks again by typing **list disk** and then select the disk you'll use as the current boot disk. Following the example, this is Disk 0, so you type **select disk 0**. List the partitions on this disk by typing **list partition**. The output you see will be similar to the following:

```
Partition ###   Type             Size        Offset
-------------   ---------------------   -------
Partition 1     System           316 MB      32 KB
Partition 2     Primary          9992 MB     312 MB
Partition 3     Reserved         32 MB       9 GB
```

The output shows you which partitions are being used as the ESP and MSR partitions. The ESP is listed with the partition type System. The MSR partition is listed with the partition type Reserved. Note the size of each partition. Here, System is 316 MBs, and Reserved is 32 MBs.

You now must create the ESP and MSR partitions on the second disk by completing the following steps:

1. In DiskPart, select this disk to give it focus. Following the example, you type **select disk 1**.
2. Afterward, you create the ESP first by typing **create partition efi size=*N***, where *N* is the size previously noted, such as **size=316**.

   NOTE

   The target disk must still be basic at this point. If you already converted the disk to dynamic, steps 2 and 3 will result in errors.

3. Create the MSR partition by typing **create partition msr size=*N***, where *N* is the size previously noted, such as **size=32**.
4. If you type **list partition**, you should see that both partitions have been created and are sized appropriately, like as follows:

```
Partition ###     Type              Size        Offset
-------------     -----------------------       -------
Partition 1       System            316 MB      32 KB
Partition 2       Reserved          32 MB       316 MB
```

Next, you must prepare the ESP for use by assigning it a drive letter, formatting it, and copying over the necessary startup files from the current boot volume. To do this, follow these steps:

1. In DiskPart, select the partition by typing **select partition 1**.
2. Assign a drive letter by typing **assign letter=*X***, where *X* is the drive letter, such as **letter=H**.
3. Format the ESP as FAT. Following the example, you type **format /fs=fat quick**.
4. After formatting is complete, select the current boot volume. Following the example, you type **select disk 0**.
5. Type **select partition 1** to select the ESP on the current boot volume.
6. Assign this partition a drive letter by typing **assign letter=*X***, where *X* is the drive letter to assign, such as **letter=I**.

7. Exit DiskPart by typing **exit**.
8. Use the XCOPY command to copy all the files from the ESP on the current boot volume to the ESP on the second disk. Following the example, you type **xcopy i:*.* h: /s /h**. The */s* and */h* parameters ensure that hidden system files are copied.

You now must convert both drives to the dynamic storage type. Start with the second disk and then convert the current boot disk. Follow these steps:

1. Invoke DiskPart by typing **diskpart**.
2. Select the disk you are going to use as the secondary boot disk. Following the example, this is Disk 1, so you type **select disk 1**.
3. Convert the disk by typing **convert dynamic**.
4. Select the current boot disk. Following the example, this is Disk 0, so you type **select disk 0**.
5. Convert the disk by typing **convert dynamic**.
6. Exit DiskPart by typing **exit**.
7. You must shut down and restart the computer to complete the conversion process for the current boot disk. In some cases, this process takes several reboots to complete.

   NOTE

   You don't have to delete the drive letters assigned in the previous procedure. These drive letters will not be reassigned after the restart.

When the conversion process is complete, log on to the system and then follow these steps to mirror the boot drive:

1. Invoke DiskPart by typing **diskpart**.
2. Select the current boot disk. Following the example, this is Disk 0, so you type **select disk 0**.
3. Add the disk to use as the second drive to this volume to create the mirrored set. Following the example, you type **add disk=1**.

   DiskPart then begins the mirror creation process by synchronizing the data on both volumes.

During the creation of the mirror, the operating system should add an entry to the system's Boot Manager that allows you to boot to the secondary mirror. Resolving a primary mirror failure is much easier with this entry in the Boot Manager file than without it because all you need to do is select the entry to boot to the secondary mirror. If you mirror the boot volume and a secondary mirror entry is not created for you, you could modify the boot entries in the Boot Manager to create one by using the BCD Editor (bcdedit.exe).

If a system fails to boot to the primary system volume, restart the system and select Boot Mirror - Secondary Plex for the operating system you want to start. The system should start up normally. After you successfully boot the system to the secondary drive, you can schedule the maintenance necessary to rebuild the mirror if desired.

Now if you shut down the system and restart it, you should be able to boot successfully to either the primary or the secondary boot disk.

Configuring RAID 5: Disk striping with parity

RAID 5, disk striping with parity, offers fault tolerance with less overhead and better read performance than disk mirroring. To configure RAID 5, you use three or more volumes, each on a separate drive, as a striped set, similar to RAID 0. Unlike RAID 0, however, RAID 5 adds parity error checking to ensure that the failure of a single drive won't bring down the entire drive set. In the event of a single drive failure, the set continues to function with disk operations directed at the remaining disks in the set. The parity information can also be used to recover the data by using a process called *regeneration*.

RAID 5 works like this: Each time the operating system writes to a RAID-5 volume, the data is written across all the disks in the set. Parity information for the data, used for error checking and correction, is written to disk as well, but it's always written on a separate disk from the one used to write the data. For example, if you are using a three-volume RAID-5 set and save a file, the individual data bytes of the file are written to each of the disks in the set. Parity information is written as well but not to the same disk as one of the individual data bytes. Thus, a disk in the set could have a chunk of the data or the corresponding parity information, but not both. This, in turn, means that the loss of one disk from the set doesn't cause the entire set to fail.

Like any type of RAID, RAID 5 has its drawbacks. First, if multiple drives in the set fail, the entire set will fail and you won't be able to regenerate the set from the parity information. Why? If multiple drives fail, there won't be enough parity information to use to recover the set. Second, having to generate and write parity information every time data is written to disk slows down the write process (and, in the case of software RAID, reduces processing power). To compensate for the performance hit, hardware RAID controllers have their own processors that handle the necessary processing—and this is why hardware RAID is preferred over software RAID.

Okay, so RAID 5 gives you fault tolerance at some cost to performance. It does, however, have less overhead than RAID 1. By using RAID 1, you have 50 percent overhead, which effectively cuts the amount of storage space in half. By using RAID 5, the overhead depends on the number of disks in the RAID set. With three disks, the overhead is about one-third. If you have three 750 GB drives using RAID 5, you use 2250 GBs of space to store about 1,500 GBs of information. If you have additional disks, the overhead is reduced incrementally but not significantly.

To create a RAID-5 set, start Disk Management. In Graphical View, press and hold or right-click an area marked Unallocated on a dynamic disk and then choose New RAID-5 Volume. This starts the New RAID-5 Volume Wizard. Tap or click Next. Create the volume as described in "Creating a simple or spanned volume" earlier in this chapter. The key difference is that you must select free space on three or more dynamic drives.

When you tap or click Finish, you return to the main Disk Management window and Disk Management creates the RAID-5 set. During the creation of the set, you see a status of Resynching. This tells you that Disk Management is creating the RAID-5 set. When this process finishes, you have three or more identical volumes, all of which show the same drive letter in Disk Management. Users, however, see the RAID-5 set as a single volume. The volume status should be listed as Healthy. This is the normal status for volumes. If the status changes, you might need to repair or regenerate the RAID-5 set as discussed in "Resolving problems with RAID-5 sets" later in this chapter.

Breaking or removing a mirrored set

Windows Server 2012 R2 provides two ways to stop mirroring. You can break a mirrored set, which creates two separate but identical volumes, or you can remove a mirror, which deletes all the data on the removed mirror.

To break a mirrored set, follow these steps:

1. In Disk Management, press and hold or right-click one of the volumes in the mirrored set and then choose Break Mirrored Volume.
2. Confirm that you want to break the mirrored set by tapping or clicking Yes. If the volume is currently in use, you see another warning dialog box. Confirm that it's okay to continue by tapping or clicking Yes.

   Windows Server 2012 R2 then breaks the mirrored set, creating two independent volumes.

To remove a mirror, follow these steps:

1. In Disk Management, press and hold or right-click one of the volumes in the mirrored set and then choose Remove Mirror. This opens the Remove Mirror dialog box.

2. In the Remove Mirror dialog box, select the disk from which to remove the mirror. If the mirror contains a boot or system volume, you should remove the mirror from the secondary drive rather than from the primary. For example, if Drive 0 and Drive 1 are mirrored, remove Drive 1 rather than Drive 0.
3. Confirm the action when prompted. All data on the removed mirror is deleted.

Resolving problems with mirrored sets

Occasionally, data on mirrored volumes can get out of sync. Typically, this happens if one of the drives in the set goes offline or experiences temporary I/O problems and, as a result, data can be written only to the drive that's online. To reestablish mirroring, you must bring both drives online and then resynchronize the mirror, but you must rebuild the set using a disk with the same partition style—either MBR or GPT. The corrective action you take depends on the drive status.

> NOTE
>
> **When mirroring boot volumes, Windows requires you to use the same partition style. With data volumes, you can mirror between MBR and GPT.**

The Missing or Offline status usually happens if drives have been disconnected or powered off. If the drives are part of an external storage device, check the storage device to ensure that it is connected properly and has power. Reconnecting the storage device or turning on the power should make the drives accessible. You then must start Disk Management and rescan the missing drive by selecting Rescan Disks on the Action menu. When Disk Management finishes, press and hold or right-click the drive and choose Reactivate Volume. The drive status should change to Regenerating and then to Healthy. If the volume doesn't return to the Healthy status, press and hold or right-click the volume and then choose Resynchronize Mirror.

A status of Failed, Online (Errors), or Unreadable indicates I/O problems with the drive. As before, try rescanning the drive and then try to reactivate the drive. The drive status should change to Regenerating and then to Healthy. If the volume doesn't return to the Healthy status, press and hold or right-click the volume and then choose Resynchronize Mirror.

If these actions don't work, you must remove the failed mirror, replace the bad drive, and then rebuild the mirror. To do this, follow these steps:

1. Press and hold or right-click the failed volume and then select Remove Mirror.
2. You now must mirror the volume on an Unallocated area of free space on a different disk. If you don't have free space, you must create space by shrinking a volume, deleting other volumes, or replacing the failed drive.

3. When you are ready to continue, press and hold or right-click the remaining volume in the original mirror and then select Add Mirror. This opens the Add Mirror dialog box.

4. Use the Disks list to select a location for the mirror and then tap or click Add Mirror. Windows Server 2012 R2 begins the mirror creation process, and you see a status of Resynching on both volumes.

Repairing a mirrored system volume

When you mirror a system volume, an entry that enables you to boot to the secondary mirror is added to the system's boot configuration data, so if a system fails to boot to the primary system volume, restart the system and select Boot Mirror - Secondary Plex for the operating system you want to start. The system should start up normally. After you successfully boot the system to the secondary drive, you can schedule the maintenance necessary to rebuild the mirror if desired.

Rebuilding mirrored system volumes on MBR disks

To rebuild the mirror, you must complete the following steps:

1. Shut down the system and replace the failed drive. Restart the system, using the secondary drive.

2. In Disk Management, press and hold or right-click the remaining volume in the mirrored set and choose Break Mirrored Volume. Tap or click Yes at the prompts to confirm the action.

3. Press and hold or right-click the volume again and choose Add Mirror. Use the Add Mirror dialog box to select the second disk to use for the mirror and then tap or click Add Mirror.

If you want the primary mirror to be on the drive you added or replaced, perform these additional steps:

1. Use Disk Management to break the mirrored set again.

2. Make sure that the primary drive in the original mirror set has the drive letter that was previously assigned to the complete mirror. If it doesn't, assign the appropriate drive letter.

3. Press and hold or right-click the original system volume, select Add Mirror, and then re-create the mirror.

Rebuilding mirrored system volumes on GPT disks

For GPT disks, rebuilding mirrored system volumes is a bit different. To rebuild the mirror, shut down the system and replace the failed drive and then restart the system, using the secondary drive. In Disk Management, press and hold or right-click the remaining volume in the mirrored set and choose Break Mirrored Volume. Tap or click Yes at the prompts to confirm the action. After this, you can use the secondary boot disk as your primary boot disk and follow the procedures outlined in "Mirroring boot and system volumes on MBR disks" earlier in this chapter to re-enable mirroring properly, using the secondary disk as the primary.

Resolving problems with RAID-5 sets

Most problems with RAID-5 sets have to do with the intermittent or permanent failure of a drive. If one of the drives in the set goes offline or experiences temporary I/O problems, parity data cannot be properly written to the set and, as a result, the set's status shows as Failed Redundancy and the failed volume's status changes to Missing, Offline, or Online (Errors).

You must bring all drives in the RAID-5 set online. If the status of the problem volume is Missing or Offline, make sure that the drive has power and is connected properly. You then must start Disk Management and rescan the missing drive by choosing Rescan Disks from the Action menu. When Disk Management finishes, press and hold or right-click the drive and choose Reactivate. The drive status should change to Regenerating and then to Healthy. If the volume doesn't return to the Healthy status, press and hold or right-click the volume and then tap or click Regenerate Parity.

A status of Failed, Online (Errors), or Unreadable indicates I/O problems with the drive. As before, try rescanning the drive and then try to reactivate the drive. The drive status should change to Regenerating and then to Healthy. If the volume doesn't return to the Healthy status, press and hold or right-click the volume and then tap or click Regenerate Parity.

If one of the drives still won't come back online, you must repair the failed region of the RAID-5 set. Press and hold or right-click the failed volume and then select Remove Volume. You now must press and hold or right-click an unallocated space on a separate dynamic disk with the same partition style—either MBR or GPT—and choose Repair Volume. This space must be at least as large as the region to repair, and it can't be on a drive the RAID-5 set is already using. If you don't have enough space, Repair Volume is unavailable and you must free space by shrinking a volume, deleting other volumes, or replacing the failed drive.

CHAPTER 14

TPM and BitLocker Drive Encryption

Many of the security features built into the Microsoft Windows operating system are designed to protect a computer from attacks by individuals accessing the computer over the network or from the Internet. But what about when individuals have direct physical access to a computer? Then, many of Windows security safeguards don't apply. For example, if someone can boot a computer—even if it is to another operating system that person has installed—he or she could gain access to any data stored on the computer, perhaps even your organization's most sensitive data. To protect a computer from individuals who have direct access to it, current Windows and Windows Server operating systems include the Trusted Platform Module Services architecture and BitLocker Drive Encryption. Together, these features help protect a computer from many types of attacks by individuals who have direct access to it.

Working with trusted platforms

Current Windows and Windows Server operating systems include the Encrypting File System (EFS) for encrypting files and folders. Using EFS, users can protect sensitive data so that it can be accessed only by using their public key certificate. Encryption certificates are stored as part of the data in a user's profile. As long as users have access to their profiles and the encryption keys they contain, they can access their encrypted files.

Although EFS offers excellent protection for your data, it doesn't necessarily safeguard the computer from attack by someone who has direct physical access. When a user loses a computer, a computer has been stolen, or the attacker is logging on to a computer, EFS might not protect the data because the attacker might be able to gain access to the computer before it boots. He could then access the computer from another operating system and change the computer's configuration. He might then be able to hack into a logon account on the original operating system so that he can log on as the user or configure the computer so that he can log on as a local administrator. If he can do this without having to reset the password of the user or the administrator who encrypted the files, the attacker could eventually gain full access to a computer and its encrypted data.

To seal a computer from physical attack and wrap it in an additional layer of protection, current Windows and Windows Server operating systems include the Trusted Platform Module (TPM) Services architecture. TPM Services protect a computer by using a dedicated hardware component called a TPM, a microchip that is usually installed on the motherboard of a computer where it communicates with the rest of the system using a hardware bus. Computers can use a TPM to provide enhanced protection for data, to ensure early validation of the boot file's integrity, and to guarantee that a disk has not been tampered with while the operating system was offline.

A TPM can create cryptographic keys and encrypt them so that they can be decrypted only by the TPM. This process, referred to as *wrapping* or *binding*, protects the key from disclosure. A TPM has a master wrapping key called the Storage Root Key (SRK); it's stored within the TPM itself to ensure that the private portion of the key is secure.

Computers that have a TPM can create a key that has been not only wrapped but also sealed. The process of sealing the key ensures that the key is tied to specific platform measurements and can be unwrapped only when those platform measurements have the same values they had when the key was created. This is what gives TPM-equipped computers increased resistance to attack.

Because TPM stores private portions of key pairs separately from memory controlled by the operating system, keys can be sealed to the TPM to provide absolute assurances about the state of a system and its trustworthiness. TPM keys are unsealed only when the integrity of the system is intact. Further, because the TPM uses its own internal firmware and logical circuits for processing instructions, it does not rely on the operating system and is not subject to external software vulnerabilities.

The TPM can also be used to seal and unseal data that is generated outside the TPM, and this is where the true power of the TPM lies. In current Windows and Windows Server operating systems, the feature that accesses the TPM and uses it to seal a computer is called BitLocker Drive Encryption. Although BitLocker Drive Encryption can be used in both TPM and non-TPM configurations, the most secure method is to use TPM.

When you use BitLocker Drive Encryption and a TPM to seal the boot manager and boot files of a computer, the boot manager and boot files can be unsealed only if they are unchanged since they were last sealed. This means you can use the TPM to validate a computer's boot files in the pre-operating system environment. When you seal a hard disk by using a TPM, the hard disk can be unsealed only if the data on the disk is unchanged since it was last sealed. This guarantees that a disk has not been tampered with while the operating system was offline.

When you use BitLocker Drive Encryption and do not use a TPM to seal the boot manager and boot files of a computer, the TPM cannot be used to validate a computer's boot files in the pre-operating system environment. This means there is no way to guarantee the integrity of the boot manager and boot files of a computer.

Managing TPM

A computer must be equipped with a compatible TPM and compatible firmware to take advantage of the TPM. Current Windows and Windows Server operating systems support TPM version 1.2 and require Trusted Computing Group (TCG)–compliant firmware. Firmware that is TCG-compliant supports the Static Root of Trust Measurement as defined by the Trusted Computing Group. In some configurations of TPM and BitLocker Drive Encryption, you also need to make sure the firmware supports reading USB flash drives at startup.

Understanding TPM states and tools

The TPM Services architecture provides the basic features required to configure and deploy TPM-equipped computers. This architecture can be extended with a feature called BitLocker Drive Encryption, which is discussed in "Introducing BitLocker Drive Encryption" later in this chapter.

Before you can use TPM, you must turn the TPM on in firmware and initialize the TPM for first use in software. As part of the initialization process, you set the owner password on the TPM. After it is enabled, you can manage the TPM configuration.

In some cases, computers that have a TPM might ship with it turned off. If so, you must turn the TPM on in firmware. With one of my computers, I needed to do the following:

1. Start the computer and then press F2 during startup to access the firmware. In the firmware, I opened the Advanced screen and then the Peripheral Configuration screen.
2. On the Peripheral Configuration screen, Trusted Platform Module was listed as an option. After scrolling down to highlight this option, I pressed Enter to display an options menu. From the menu, I chose Enable and then pressed Enter.
3. To save the changes to the setting and exit the firmware, I pressed F10. When prompted to confirm that I wanted to exit, I pressed Y, and the computer then rebooted.

Next, you need to initialize and prepare the TPM for first use in software. As part of this process, you take ownership of the TPM, which sets the owner password on the TPM. After the TPM is enabled, you can manage its configuration. Several tools for working with the TPM are available:

- **Trusted Platform Module Management.** An MMC console for configuring and managing the TPM. You can access this tool by typing **tpm.msc** in the Apps Search box and then pressing Enter.

- **Manage The TPM Security Hardware.** A wizard for creating the required TPM owner password. You can access this tool by typing **tpminit** in the Apps Search box and then pressing Enter.

When you are working with Trusted Platform Module Management, you can determine the exact state of the TPM. If you try to start Trusted Platform Module Management without turning the TPM on, you see an error like the one shown in Figure 14-1.

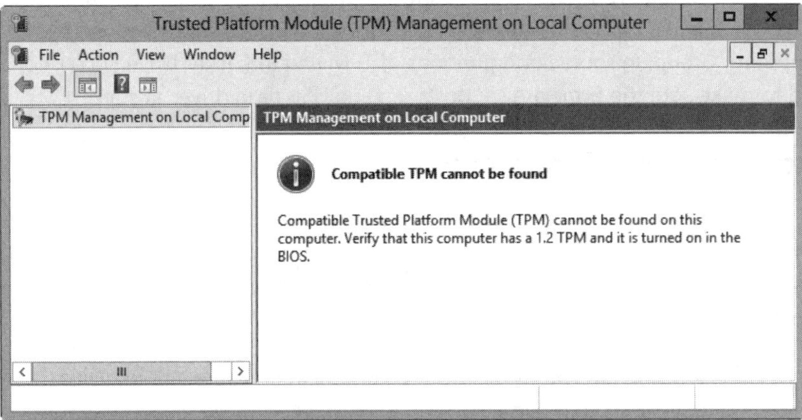

Figure 14-1 An error occurs when you start Trusted Platform Module Management without turning the TPM on.

Similarly, if you try to run Manage The TPM Security Hardware without turning the TPM on, you see an error like the one shown in Figure 14-2.

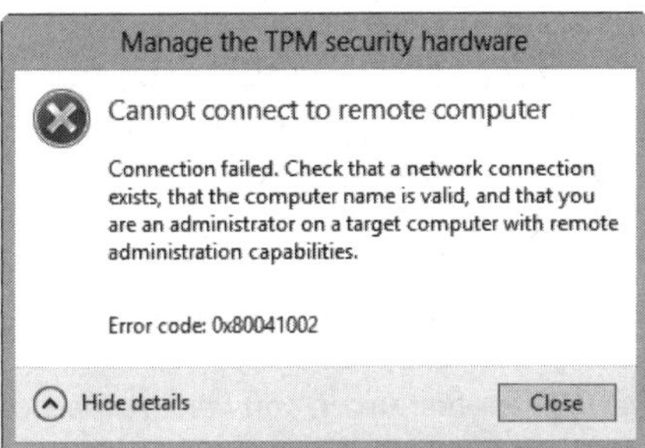

Figure 14-2 An error occurs when you try to run the Manage The TPM Security Hardware Wizard without turning the TPM on.

IMPORTANT

To perform TPM management tasks on a local computer, you must be a member of the local computer's Administrators group or be logged on as the local computer administrator. In addition, access to the Trusted Platform Module Management console can be restricted in Group Policy. If you are unable to open the console, check whether a Group Policy Object (GPO) being processed includes Management Console restrictions. Related policies are found in the Administrative Templates for User Configuration under Windows Components\Microsoft Management Console.

Only when you've turned on the TPM in firmware can you access and work with the TPM tools. When you are working with the Trusted Platform Module Management console, shown in Figure 14-3, you should note the TPM status and the TPM manufacturer information. The TPM status indicates the state of the TPM. The TPM manufacturer information shows whether the TPM supports specification version 1.2 or 2.0. Support for TPM version 1.2 or later is required.

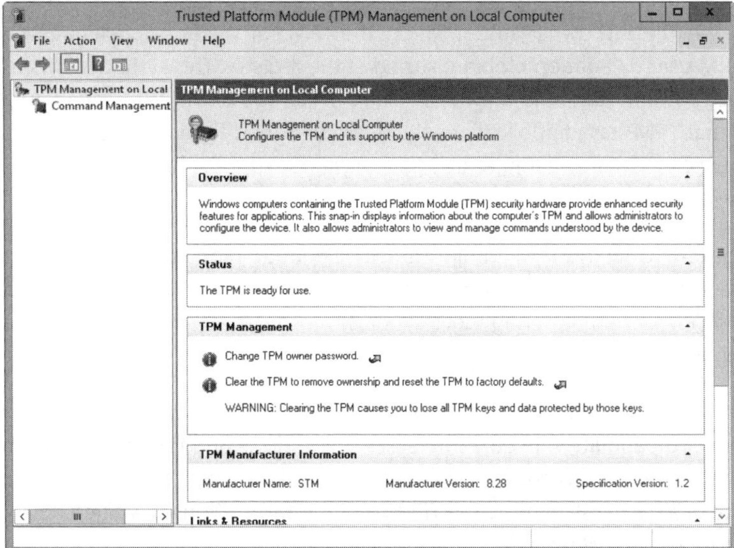

Figure 14-3 Use the Trusted Platform Module Management console to initialize and manage the TPM.

Although earlier releases of Windows showed the exact TPM state as listed in Table 14-1, Windows 8.1 and Windows Server 2012 R2 normally show a status of either "The TPM is ready for use" or "The TPM is not ready for use." If the TPM is ready for use, the TPM is on, and ownership has been taken.

Table 14-1 TPM status indicators and their meaning

Status Indicator	Meaning
The TPM is on, and ownership has not been taken.	The TPM is turned on in firmware, but it hasn't been initialized yet.
The TPM is on, and ownership has been taken.	The TPM is turned on in firmware, and it has been initialized.
The TPM is off, and ownership has not been taken.	The TPM is turned off in software, and it hasn't been initialized yet.

Managing TPM owner authorization information

Windows 8.1 and Windows Server 2012 R2 include fundamental changes in the way the TPM is used. One of these changes is the ability to set the level of authorization information stored in the registry as any of the following:

- **Full.** The full TPM owner authorization, the TPM administrative delegation blob, and the TPM user delegation blob are stored in the registry. This setting allows a TPM to be used without requiring remote or external storage of the TPM owner authorization. Note that TPM-based applications that were designed for earlier versions of Windows or that rely on TPM anti-hammering logic might not support full TPM owner authorization in the registry.
- **Delegated.** Only the TPM administrative delegation blob and the TPM user delegation blob are stored in the registry. This level is appropriate for TPM-based applications that rely on TPM anti-hammering logic. When you use this setting, Microsoft recommends storing the TPM owner authorization remotely or externally.
- **None.** No TPM owner authorization information is stored in the registry. Use this setting for compatibility with earlier releases of Windows and for applications that require external or remote storage of the TPM owner authorization. When you use this setting, remote or external storage of the TPM owner authorization is required, just as it was in earlier releases of Windows.

You set the level of authorization information stored in the registry by using the Configure The Level Of TPM Owner Authorization Information Available To The Operating System policy. You can find this policy in the Administrative Templates policies for Computer Configuration under System\Trusted Platform Module Services. Keep in mind that if you change the policy setting from Full to Delegated or vice versa, the full TPM owner authorization value is regenerated, and any copies of the original TPM value become invalid. Note also that when this policy is set to Delegated or None, you are prompted for the TPM owner password before you can perform most TPM administration tasks. Figure 14-4 shows an example.

Figure 14-4 Supply the TPM owner password if prompted for one.

With earlier releases of Windows, Microsoft recommended remotely storing the TPM owner authorization in Active Directory for domain-joined computers, which could be accomplished by enabling the Turn On TPM Backup To Active Directory Domain Services policy, extending the schema for the directory, and setting the appropriate access controls.

Enabling backup to Active Directory changes the default way TPM owner information is stored. Specifically, when Turn On TPM Backup To Active Directory Domain Services is enabled and Configure The Level Of TPM Owner Authorization Information Available To The Operating System is disabled or not configured, only the TPM administrative delegation blob and the TPM user delegation blob are stored in the registry. Here, to store the full TPM owner information, you must use the Enabled setting of Full (or disable the Active Directory backup of the TPM owner authorization).

You find the following related policies under System\Trusted Platform Module Services:

- Ignore The Default List Of Blocked TPM Commands
- Ignore The Local List Of Blocked TPM Commands
- Standard User Lockout Duration
- Standard User Individual Lockout Threshold
- Standard User Total Lockout Threshold
- Configure the List of Blocked TPM Commands

CHAPTER 14

These policies control the way command block lists are used and when lockout is triggered after multiple failed authorization attempts. An administrator can fully reset all lockout-related parameters in the Trusted Platform Module Management console. On the Action menu, tap or click Reset TPM Lockout. When the full TPM owner authorization is stored in the registry, you don't need to provide the TPM owner password. Otherwise, follow the prompts to provide the owner password or select the file containing the TPM owner password.

Preparing and initializing a TPM for first use

Initializing a TPM prepares it for use on a computer so that you can use the TPM to secure volumes on the computer's hard drives. The initialization process involves turning on the TPM and then setting ownership of it. By setting ownership, you are assigning a password that helps ensure that only the authorized TPM owner can access and manage the TPM. The full TPM owner authorization and password are stored in the registry. In an Active Directory domain, you can configure Group Policy to save TPM passwords.

To initialize the TPM and create the owner password, complete the following steps:

1. Open the Trusted Platform Module Management console. On the Action menu, choose Prepare The TPM to start the Manage The TPM Security Hardware Wizard (tpminit). If a TPM was previously initialized and then cleared, you are prompted to restart the computer and follow on-screen instructions during startup to reset the TPM in firmware.

   Here, when I clicked Restart, I needed to enter firmware by pressing F2 during startup. I then needed to disable TPM, save the changes, and exit firmware. This triggered an automatic reset. After this, I needed to enter firmware by pressing F2 so I could enable the TPM, save changes, and then exit firmware. This triggered another automatic reset. When the operating system loaded, I logged on and then needed to restart the Manage The TPM Security Hardware Wizard.

   > NOTE
   >
   > **You must have administrator privileges to manage the TPM configuration. In addition, if the Manage The TPM Security Hardware Wizard detects firmware that does not meet Windows requirements or if no TPM is found, you will not be able to continue and should ensure that the TPM has been turned on in firmware. Otherwise, you see the Create The TPM Owner Password page.**

2. When the wizard finishes its initial tasks, you see a prompt similar to the one shown in Figure 14-5. Tap or click Restart to restart the computer.

Figure 14-5 Restart the computer after the TPM is initialized.

Typically, hardware designed for Windows 8.1 and Windows Server 2012 R2 can automatically complete the initialization process. On other hardware, you need physical access to the computer to respond to the manufacturer's firmware confirmation prompt. Figure 14-6 shows an example.

3. You must press F10 to enable and activate the TPM and allow a user to take ownership of the TPM.

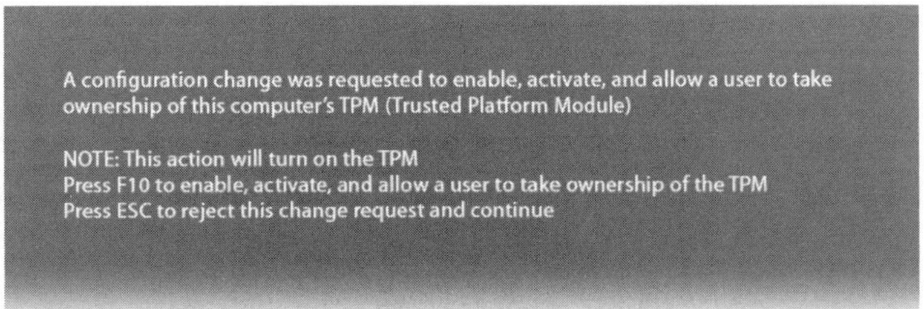

Figure 14-6 Confirm that you want to enable and activate the TPM and allow a user to take ownership of it.

When Windows starts and you log on, the Manage The TPM Security Hardware Wizard continues running. Windows takes ownership of the TPM. Setting ownership on the TPM prepares it for use with the operating system. After ownership is set, TPM is ready for use and you see confirmation of this, as shown in Figure 14-7.

4. Before tapping or clicking Close, save the TPM owner password. Tap or click Remember My TPM Owner Password. In the Save As dialog box, select a location to save the password backup file and then tap or click Save. By default, the password backup file is saved as *ComputerName*.tpm.

   In the TPM Management console, the status should be listed as "The TPM is ready for use."

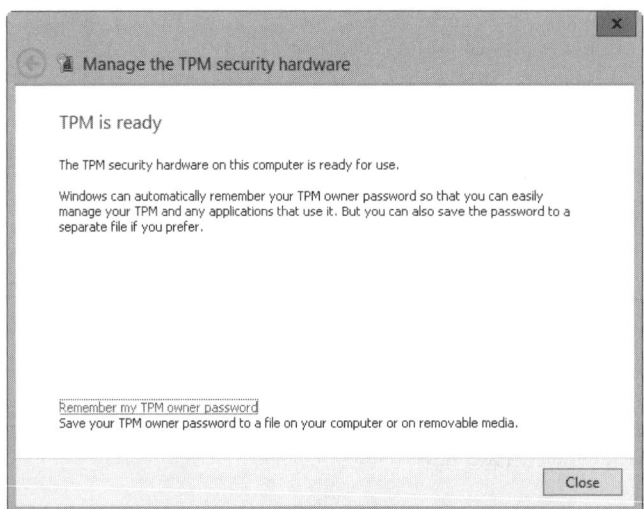

Figure 14-7 With ownership set, the TPM is ready for use.

Inside OUT

Backing up the TPM owner password

Typically, you want to save the TPM owner password to removable media, such as a USB flash drive, and store it in a secure location. In a domain in which the Turn On TPM Backup To Active Directory Domain Services policy is applied, you won't have the option to save the TPM password. Here, the password is saved to Active Directory automatically.

The password backup file is an unencrypted XML file that can be opened in any text editor to confirm the name of the computer the password belongs to. In the following example, the password was created for CorpServer15:

```
<?xml version="1.0" encoding="UTF-8"?>
<tpmOwnerData version="1.0" softwareAuthor="Microsoft Windows
[Version 6.3.9600]" creationDate="2015-02-12T12:23:32-07:32"
creationUser="CORPSERVER15\Administrator" machineName="CORPSERVER15">
      <tpmInfo manufacturerId="1335342671"/>
      <ownerAuth>cEBACDgNV8Z2EBJbERTSD87KICB=
</ownerAuth>
</tpmOwnerData>
```


Turning an initialized TPM on or off

Computers that have a TPM might ship with the TPM turned on. If you decide not to use it, you should take ownership of the TPM and then turn it off. This ensures that the operating system owns the TPM but the TPM is in an inactive state. If you want to reconfigure or recycle a computer, you should clear the TPM. Clearing the TPM invalidates any stored keys, and data encrypted by these keys can no longer be accessed.

You must have administrator privileges to manage the TPM state. Turn the TPM off by opening the Trusted Platform Module Management console and then tapping or clicking Turn TPM Off on the Action menu.

When the full TPM owner authorization is stored in the registry, you don't need to provide the TPM owner password. Otherwise, follow the prompts to provide the owner password or select the file containing the TPM owner password.

After you follow the previous procedure to turn off the TPM in software, you can turn it on in software at any time by following the steps in the "Preparing and initializing a TPM for first use" section earlier in this chapter.

Clearing the TPM

Clearing the TPM erases information stored on the TPM and cancels the related ownership of the TPM. You should clear the TPM when a TPM-equipped computer is to be recycled. Clearing the TPM invalidates any stored keys, and data encrypted by these keys can no longer be accessed.

After clearing the TPM, you should take ownership of it. This writes new information to the TPM. You might then want to turn off the TPM so that it isn't available for use.

You must have administrator privileges to clear the TPM. Clear the TPM, take ownership, and then turn off the TPM by completing the following steps:

1. Start the Trusted Platform Module Management console. On the Action menu, tap or click Clear TPM. This starts the Manage The TPM Security Hardware Wizard.

   IMPORTANT

   When you clear the TPM, the TPM is reset to factory defaults. Because of this, you lose all keys and the data protected by those keys. When the full TPM owner authorization is stored in the registry, you do not need the TPM owner password to clear the TPM.

2. Read the warning on the Clear The TPM Security Hardware page, shown in Figure 14-8, and then tap or click Restart. Tap or click Cancel to exit without clearing the TPM.

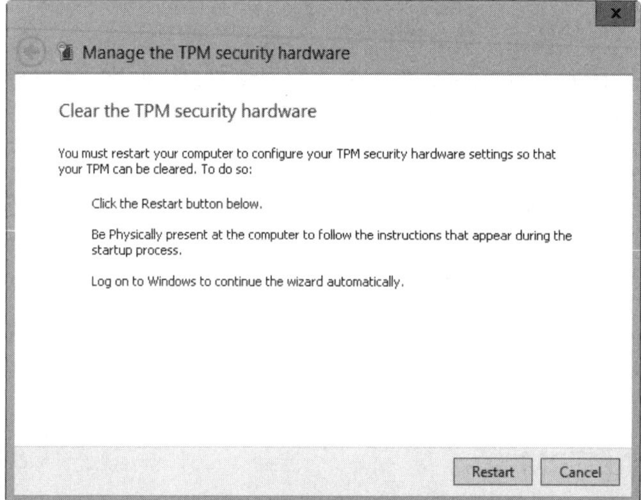

Figure 14-8 Confirm that you want to clear the TPM by tapping or clicking Restart.

Typically, hardware designed for Windows 8.1 and Windows Server 2012 R2 can automatically complete the re-initialization process. On other hardware, you need physical access to the computer to respond to the manufacturer's firmware confirmation prompt. Figure 14-9 shows an example.

3. Here, you must press F12 to clear, enable, and activate the TPM or press Esc to cancel and continue loading the operating system.

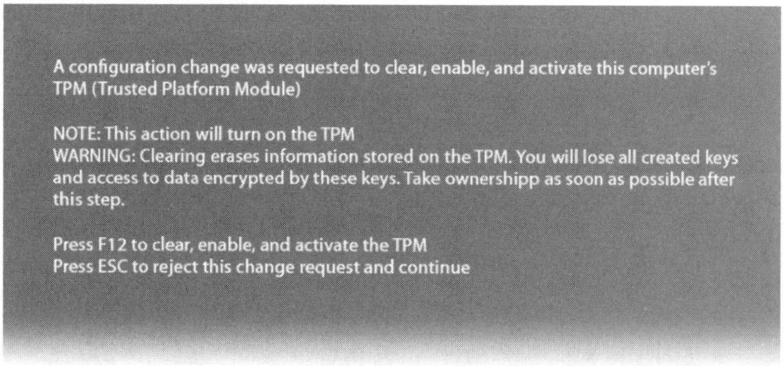

A configuration change was requested to clear, enable, and activate this computer's TPM (Trusted Platform Module)

NOTE: This action will turn on the TPM
WARNING: Clearing erases information stored on the TPM. You will lose all created keys and access to data encrypted by these keys. Take ownershipp as soon as possible after this step.

Press F12 to clear, enable, and activate the TPM
Press ESC to reject this change request and continue

Figure 14-9 Confirm the configuration change when prompted.

When Windows starts and you log on, the Manage The TPM Security Hardware Wizard continues running. Windows takes ownership of the TPM. Setting ownership on the TPM prepares it for use with the operating system. After ownership is set, the status should be listed as "The TPM is ready for use."

Changing the TPM owner password

You can change the TPM owner password at any time. Generally, you do this if you suspect that the TPM owner password has been compromised. Your company's security policy also might require TPM owner password changes in certain situations.

You must have administrator privileges to change the TPM owner password. To change the TPM owner password, complete the following steps:

1. Start the Trusted Platform Module Management console. On the Action menu, tap or click Change Owner Password. This starts the Manage The TPM Security Hardware Wizard.

2. When the full TPM owner authorization is stored in the registry, you don't need to provide the TPM owner password. Otherwise, follow the prompts to provide the owner password or select the file containing the TPM owner password.

3. On the Create The TPM Owner Password page, shown in Figure 14-10, you can elect to create the password automatically or manually:

   - If you want the wizard to create the password for you, select Automatically Create The Password (Recommended). The new TPM owner password is displayed. Tap or click Change Password.

- If you want to create the password, select Manually Create The Password. Type and confirm a password of at least eight characters and then tap or click Change Password.

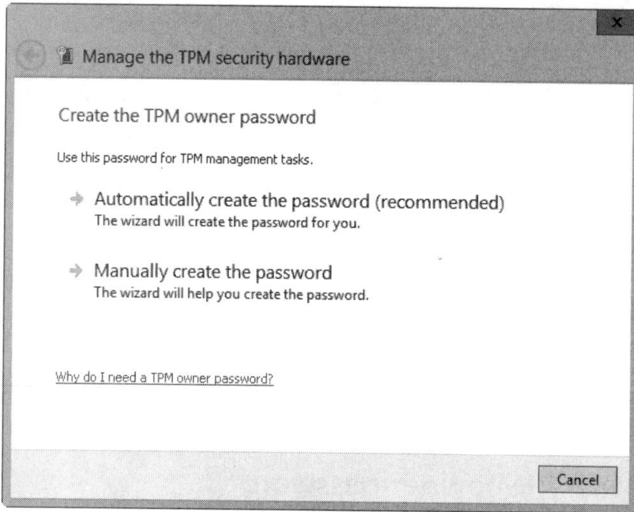

Figure 14-10 Create a new password.

4. Before tapping or clicking Close, you might want to save the TPM owner password. Tap or click Remember My TPM Owner Password. In the Save As dialog box, select a location to save the password backup file and then tap or click Save.

Introducing BitLocker Drive Encryption

BitLocker Drive Encryption is designed to protect the data on lost, stolen, or inappropriately decommissioned computers. Without BitLocker Drive Encryption, a user with direct physical access to a computer has many ways to gain full control and then access the computer's data whether that data was encrypted with EFS or not. For example, a user could use a boot disk to boot the computer and reset the administrator password. A user could also install and then boot to a different operating system and then use this operating system to unlock the other installation.

Inside OUT

Understanding BitLocker To Go

Although BitLocker Drive Encryption and BitLocker To Go are often referred to simply as *BitLocker*, they are separate but similar features. BitLocker Drive Encryption is designed to protect the data on the internal hard drives and is a volume-level encryption technology. BitLocker To Go is designed to protect the data on removable data drives, such as external hard drives and USB flash drives, and is a virtual-volume encryption technology. Standard BitLocker encrypts by wrapping the entire volume or only the used portion of the volume in protected encryption. BitLocker To Go, however, creates a virtual volume on a USB flash drive. This virtual volume is encrypted by using an encryption key stored on the USB flash drive.

BitLocker essentials

BitLocker Drive Encryption prevents all access to a computer's drives except by authorized personnel by wrapping entire drives or only the used portions of volumes in tamper-proof encryption. If a user tries to access a BitLocker-encrypted drive, the encryption prevents the user from viewing or manipulating the data in any way. This dramatically reduces the risk of an unauthorized person gaining access to confidential data by using offline attacks.

CAUTION

BitLocker Drive Encryption reduces disk throughput. Because of this, you might want to use this technology on an enterprise server only if the server is not in a physically secure location and requires additional protection.

BitLocker Drive Encryption can use a TPM to validate the integrity of a computer's boot manager and boot files at startup and to guarantee that a computer's hard disk has not been tampered with while the operating system was offline. BitLocker Drive Encryption also stores measurements of core operating system files in the TPM.

Every time the computer is started, Windows validates the boot files, the operating system files, and any encrypted volumes to ensure that they have not been modified while the computer is offline. If the files have been modified, Windows alerts the user and refuses to release the key required to access Windows. The computer then goes into Recovery mode, prompting the user to provide a recovery key before allowing access to the boot volume. Recovery mode is also used if a BitLocker-encrypted disk drive is transferred to another system.

BitLocker Drive Encryption can be used in both TPM and non-TPM computers. If a computer has a TPM, BitLocker Drive Encryption uses the TPM to provide enhanced protection for your data and to ensure early boot file integrity. These features together help prevent unauthorized viewing and accessing of data by encrypting the entire Windows volume and by safeguarding the boot files from tampering. If a computer doesn't have a TPM or its TPM isn't compatible with Windows, BitLocker Drive Encryption can be used to encrypt entire volumes and, in this way, protect the volumes from being tampered with. This configuration, however, doesn't allow the added security of early boot file integrity validation.

BitLocker modes

On computers with a compatible TPM that is initialized, BitLocker Drive Encryption typically uses one of the following TPM modes:

- **TPM-Only.** In this mode, only the TPM is used for validation. When the computer boots, the TPM validates the boot files, the operating system files, and any encrypted volumes. Because the user doesn't need to provide an additional startup key, this mode is transparent to the user and the user logon experience is unchanged. However, if the TPM is missing or the integrity of files or volumes has changed, BitLocker enters Recovery mode and requires a recovery key or password to regain access to the boot volume.

- **TPM and PIN.** In this mode, both the TPM and a user-entered numeric key are used for validation. When the computer boots, the TPM validates the boot files, the operating system files, and any encrypted volumes. The user must enter a PIN when prompted to continue startup. If the user doesn't have the PIN or is unable to provide the correct PIN, BitLocker enters Recovery mode instead of booting to the operating system. As before, BitLocker also enters Recovery mode if the TPM is missing or the integrity of boot files or encrypted volumes has changed.

- **TPM and Startup Key.** In this mode, both the TPM and a startup key are used for validation. When the computer boots, the TPM validates the boot files, the operating system files, and any encrypted volumes. The user must have a USB flash drive with a startup key to log on to the computer. If the user doesn't have the startup key or is unable to provide the correct startup key, BitLocker enters Recovery mode. As before, BitLocker also enters Recovery mode if the TPM is missing or the integrity of boot files or encrypted volumes has changed.

- **TPM and Smart Card Certificate.** In this mode, both the TPM and a smart card certificate are used for validation. When the computer boots, the TPM validates the boot files, the operating system files, and any encrypted volumes. The user must have a smart card with a valid certificate to log on to the computer. If the user doesn't have a smart card with a valid certificate and can't provide one, BitLocker enters Recovery mode. As before, BitLocker also enters Recovery mode if the TPM is missing or the integrity of boot files or encrypted volumes has changed.

Inside OUT

Using the TPM when three-factor authentication is required

A less commonly used TPM mode requires a TPM, PIN, and startup key. Use this mode when the highest security is required or when your organization requires three-factor authentication. This mode can be configured only by using the Manage-bde command-line utility. Here, when the computer boots, the TPM validates the boot files, the operating system files, and any encrypted volumes. The user must insert the startup key prior to startup and then enter a PIN when prompted to continue startup. If the user doesn't have the startup key, PIN, or both, BitLocker enters Recovery mode instead of booting to the operating system. As before, BitLocker also enters Recovery mode if the TPM is missing or the integrity of boot files or encrypted volumes has changed.

When working with BitLocker Drive Encryption and a TPM, don't overlook the importance of Network Unlock. The Network Unlock feature allows the system volume on a computer with a TPM to be automatically unlocked on startup as long as the computer is joined and connected to a domain. When the computer is not joined and connected to a domain, other means of validation can be used, such as a startup PIN.

On computers without a TPM or on computers that have incompatible TPMs, the operating system can be configured to use an unlock password for the system drive. To configure this, you must enable the Configure Use Of Passwords For Operating System Drives policy in the Administrative Templates policies for Computer Configuration under Windows Components \BitLocker Drive Encryption\Operating System Drives. As with logon passwords, the unlock password can be configured with minimum length and complexity requirements. The default minimum password length is eight characters, meaning the password must be at least eight characters long. Complexity requirements can be any of the following:

- Always validated, using the Require Password Complexity setting
- Not validated, using the Do Not Allow Password Complexity setting
- Validated if possible, using the Allow Password Complexity setting

The unlock password is validated when you enable BitLocker Drive Encryption and set the password and whenever a user changes the password. With required complexity, you can only set a password (and enable encryption) when the computer can connect to a domain controller and validate the complexity of the password. With allowed complexity, the computer attempts to validate the complexity of the password when you set it but will allow you to continue and enable encryption if no domain controllers are available.

On computers without a TPM or on computers that have incompatible TPMs, BitLocker Drive Encryption also can use:

- **Startup Key Only mode.** This mode requires a USB flash drive containing a startup key. The user inserts the USB flash drive in the computer before turning it on. The key stored on the flash drive unlocks the computer.
- **Smart Card Certificate Only mode.** This mode requires a smart card with a valid certificate. The user validates the smart card certificate after turning on the computer. The certificate unlocks the computer.

IMPORTANT

Standard users can reset the BitLocker PIN and password on operating system drives, fixed data drives, and removable data drives. This is an important change for Windows 8, Windows Server 2012, and later versions of Windows. If you don't want standard users to be able to perform these tasks, enable the Disallow Standard Users From Changing The PIN Or Password policy. This Computer Configuration policy is found under Windows Components\BitLocker Drive Encryption\Operating System Drives.

BitLocker changes

BitLocker Drive Encryption has changed substantially since it was first implemented on Windows Vista and Windows Server 2008. With subsequent releases of Windows, you can:

- Allow a data-recovery agent to be used with BitLocker Drive Encryption. This option is configured through Group Policy. The data-recovery agent allows an encrypted volume to be unlocked and recovered by using a recovery agent's personal certificate or a 48-digit recovery password. You can optionally save the recovery information in Active Directory. In the Administrative Templates policies for Computer Configuration, there are separate policies for operating-system volumes, other fixed drives, and removable drives.
- Deny write access to removable data drives not protected with BitLocker. This option is configured through Group Policy. If you enable this option, users have read-only access to unencrypted removable data drives and read/write access to encrypted removable data drives.
- Encrypt file allocation table (FAT) volumes and NTFS and Resilient File System (ReFS) volumes. When you encrypt FAT volumes, you can specify whether encrypted volumes can be unlocked and viewed on computers running Windows Vista or later. This option is configured through Group Policy and is enabled when you turn on BitLocker. In the Administrative Templates policies for Computer Configuration under Windows

Components\BitLocker Drive Encryption, separate policies for earlier versions of Windows allow FAT-formatted fixed drives and FAT-formatted removable drives to be unlocked and viewed.

In a domain, domain administrators are the default data-recovery agents. A homegroup or workgroup has no default data-recovery agent, but you can designate one. Any user you want to designate as a data-recovery agent needs a personal encryption certificate. You can generate a certificate by using the Cipher utility and then using the certificate to assign the data-recovery agent in Local Security Policy under Public Key Policies\BitLocker Drive Encryption.

Although earlier implementations of BitLocker Drive Encryption supported Advanced Encryption Standard (AES) encryption with a diffuser, Windows 8.1 and Windows Server 2012 R2 move away from this approach to support standard AES with 128-bit encryption by default. Furthermore, if you enable the Choose Drive Encryption Method And Cipher Strength policy, you can set the AES cipher strength to 256-bit encryption. Keep in mind that the cipher strength must be set prior to turning on BitLocker Drive Encryption. Changing the cipher strength has no effect if a drive is already encrypted or encryption is in progress.

Using hardware encryption, secure boot, and Network Unlock

BitLocker Drive Encryption has additional enhancements for Windows 8.1 and Windows Server 2012 R2. You can manage most of these enhancements by using the Administrative Templates policies for Computer Configuration under Windows Components\BitLocker Drive Encryption.

Hardware-encrypted drives

Windows 8.1 and Windows Server 2012 R2 add support for disk drives with hardware encryption (referred to as *encrypted hard drives*). Encryption in hardware is faster and moves the processing burden from the computer's processor to the hardware processor on the hard disk. By default, if a computer has hardware encryption, Windows 8.1 uses it with BitLocker. To use encrypted hard drives with Windows Server 2012 R2, you must add the Enhanced Storage feature.

When the operating system initializes an encrypted hard drive, it activates a security mode that allows the drive controller to generate a media key for every volume created on the encrypted hard drive. This media key set is used to encrypt every byte of data written to the drive and decrypt every byte of data read from the drive. The key set consists of the following:

- **A data-encryption key.** This key encrypts all data on the drive. The key is stored in an encrypted format in a random location on the drive.

- **An authentication key.** This key unlocks data on the drive. A hash of the authentication key is stored on the drive and decrypts the data-encryption key.

An encrypted drive is locked and inaccessible when it is in a powered-off state. When the drive is powered on (as part of the computer startup), the drive remains locked until the authentication key decrypts the data-encryption key. All data read from or written to the drive passes through the encryption engine. If the data-encryption key needs to be changed or erased, the drive doesn't need to be re-encrypted. Instead, the encryption engine creates a new authentication key and then re-encrypts the data-encryption key. Afterward, the data-encryption key can be unlocked with the new authentication key, and data can be read from and written to the drive as before.

Before you enable hardware encryption, consider some important caveats. With data drives, the drive must be in an uninitialized state and in a security-inactive state. With system drives, the drive must be in an uninitialized state and in a security-inactive state, and the computer must always boot natively from Unified Extensible Firmware Interface (UEFI). Further, neither data drives nor system drives can be attached to RAID controllers. Although future updates or service packs could change or remove these restrictions, these are the restrictions as of the time I write this.

IMPORTANT

System drives must boot natively from UEFI 2.3.1 or later and have a defined EFI_STORAGE_SECURITY_COMMAND_PROTOCOL. System drives must also have the Compatibility Support Module (CSM) disabled in UEFI.

Like Windows Server 2012, Windows Server 2012 R2 is designed to be run on computers with UEFI. As discussed in Chapter 3, in the "Boot environment essentials" section, UEFI doesn't replace all the functionality in either basic input/output system (BIOS) or Extensible Firmware Interface (EFI) and can, in fact, be wrapped around BIOS or EFI. When a computer has UEFI and is running Windows 8.1, UEFI is the first link in the chain of trust for secure boot. UEFI 2.3.1 and later can run internal integrity checks that verify the firmware's digital signature before running it. If the firmware's digital signature has been modified or replaced (for example, by a firmware rootkit), the firmware will not load.

With Secure Boot, firmware also verifies the digital signature on the Windows bootloader as part of initialization. If a rootkit is installed and the Windows bootloader has been modified, the computer will be prevented from starting. After Secure Boot, the bootloader verifies the digital signature of the operating system kernel as part of Trusted Boot. Also as part of Trusted Boot, the kernel in turn verifies all remaining boot components, including boot drivers and startup files. Finally, Measured Boot also allows third-party software running on a remote server to verify the security of every startup component.

Optimizing encryption

In Group Policy, you can precisely control whether to permit software-based encryption when hardware encryption is not available and whether to restrict encryption to those algorithms and cipher strengths supported by hardware. To do this, use Group Policy to enable hardware-based encryption for system drives, data drives, or both.

You can enable hardware-based encryption for data drives by using the Configure Use Of Hardware-Based Encryption For Fixed Data Drives policy, shown in Figure 14-11. When the policy is enabled, you must specifically allow software-based encryption when hardware-based encryption isn't available. You can also restrict the encryption algorithms used to a specific subset. Keep in mind that the encryption algorithm is set when a drive is partitioned and that the Choose Drive Encryption Method And Cipher Strength policy doesn't apply to hardware-based encryption.

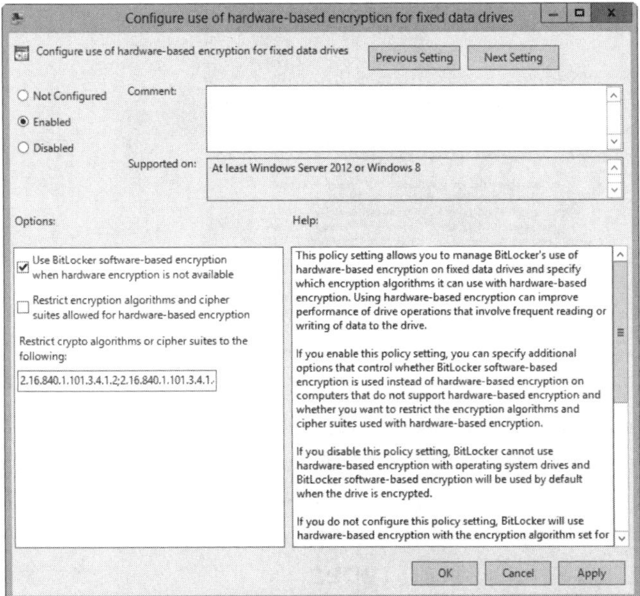

Figure 14-11 Enable and configure the use of hardware-based encryption for fixed data drives.

You can enable hardware-based encryption for system drives by using the Configure Use Of Hardware-Based Encryption For Operating System Drives policy, shown in Figure 14-12. As with data drives, when the policy is enabled, you must keep in mind the following:

- You must specifically allow software-based encryption when hardware-based encryption isn't available.

- You can restrict the encryption algorithms used to a specific subset.
- The Choose Drive Encryption Method And Cipher Strength policy doesn't apply to hardware-based encryption.

Finally, as necessary, use the Configure Use Of Hardware-Based Encryption For Removable Data Drives policy to control whether software-based encryption is permitted when hardware encryption is not available and whether to restrict encryption to those algorithms and cipher strengths the hardware supports.

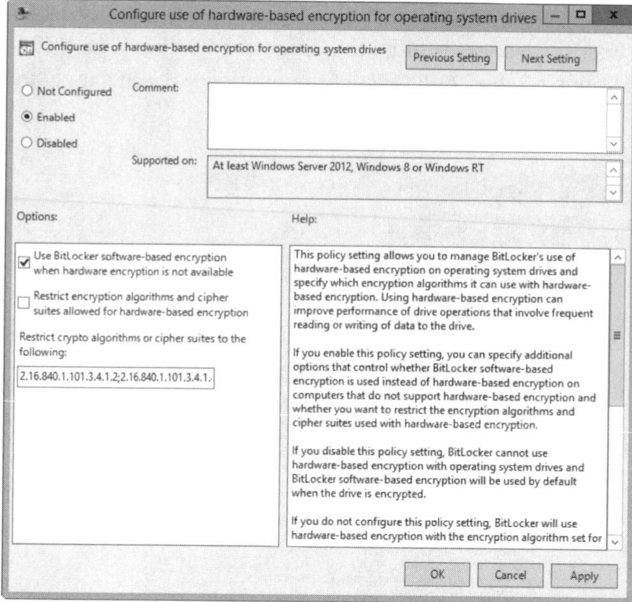

Figure 14-12 Enable and configure the use of hardware-based encryption for operating system drives.

Setting permitted encryption types

Windows Server enables users to encrypt full volumes or used space only. Encrypting full volumes takes longer, but it is more secure because the entire volume is protected. Encrypting used space protects only the portion of the drive used to store data. By default, either option can be used. To allow only one type or the other, you can enable and configure the related Enforce Drive Encryption Type policy for BitLocker. There are separate Enforce Drive Encryption Type policies for the operating system, fixed data, and removable data drives. Figure 14-13 shows the policy for operating system drives. Here, after you select Enabled to enable the policy, you set the encryption type to either Full Encryption or Used Space Only Encryption.

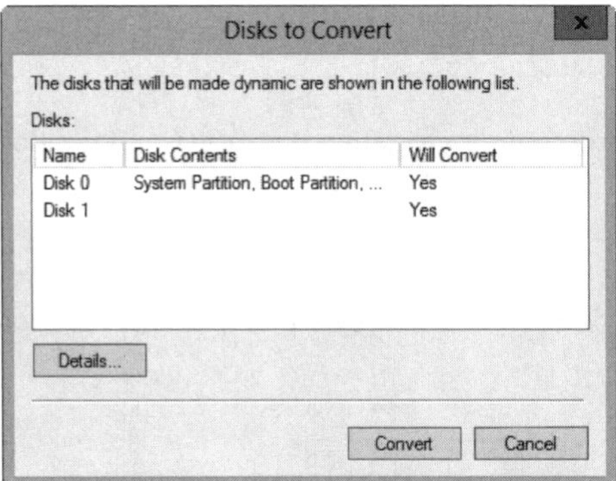

Figure 14-13 Restrict the encryption type if desired.

> IMPORTANT
>
> **In high-security environments, you will want to encrypt entire volumes. At the time of this writing, and unless fixed with a future update or service pack, deleted files appear as free space when you encrypt used space only. As a result, until the files are wiped or overwritten, information in the files could be recovered with certain tools.**

Preparing BitLocker for startup authentication and secure boot

Windows allows you to pre-provision BitLocker so that you can turn on encryption prior to installation. Windows also can be configured to do the following:

- Require additional authentication at startup. If you enable and configure the related policy, Require Additional Authentication At Startup, user input is required, even if the platform lacks a preboot input capability. To allow a USB keyboard to be used on such a platform in the preboot environment, you should set the Enable Use Of BitLocker Authentication Requiring Preboot Keyboard Input On Slates policy to Enabled.
- Allow secure boot for integrity validation. Secure boot is used by default to verify boot configuration data (BCD) settings according to the TPM validation profile settings (also referred to as Secure Boot policy). When you use secure boot, the settings of the Use Enhanced Boot Configuration Data Validation Profile policy are ignored (unless you specifically disable secure boot support by setting Allow Secure Boot For Integrity Validation to Disabled).

You set TPM validation profile settings by platform. For BIOS-based firmware, you use the Configure TPM Platform Validation Profile For BIOS-Based Firmware Configurations policy. For UEFI-based firmware, you use the Configure TPM Platform Validation Profile For Native UEFI

Firmware Configurations policy. When you enable these policies, you specify exactly which platform configuration registers to validate during boot.

For BIOS-based firmware, Microsoft recommends validating Platform Configuration Registers (PCRs) 0, 2, 4, 8, 9, 10, and 11. For UEFI firmware, Microsoft recommends validating PCRs 0, 2, 4, 7, and 11. In both instances, PCR 11 validation is required for BitLocker protection to be enforced. PCR 7 validation is required to support secure boot with UEFI (and you need to enable this by selecting the related option). Figure 14-14 shows an example platform validation profile configuration.

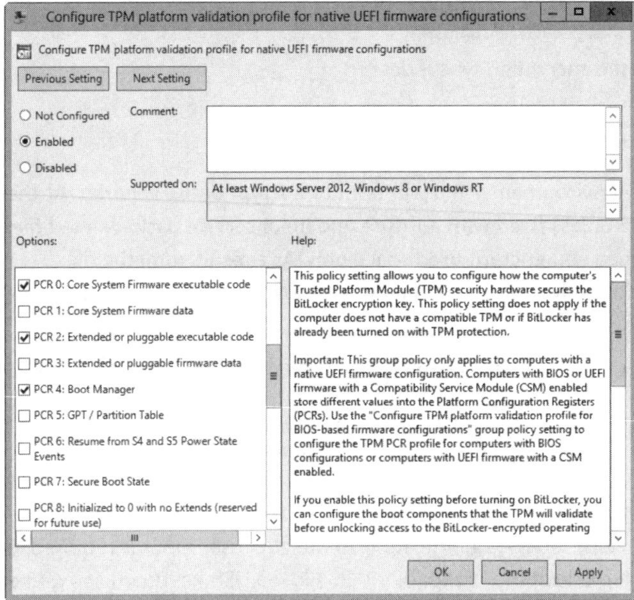

Figure 14-14 Specify the PCRs to validate.

Using Network Unlock

When you protect a computer with BitLocker, you can require additional authentication at startup. Normally, this means a user is required to have a startup key on a USB flash drive, a startup PIN, or both. The Network Unlock feature provides this additional layer of protection without requiring the startup key, startup PIN, or both by automatically unlocking the operating system drive when a computer is started. It does this as long as the following conditions are met:

- The BitLocker-protected computer has an enabled TPM.
- The computer is on a trusted, wired network.

- The computer is joined to and connected to a domain.
- A Network Unlock server with an appropriate Network Unlock certificate is available.

Because the computer must be joined to and connected to the domain for Network Unlock to work, user authentication is still required when a computer is not connected to the domain. When connected to the domain, the client computer (whether it's a Windows desktop or a Windows server) connects to a Network Unlock server to unlock the system drive. You allow Network Unlock to be used by enabling the Allow Network Unlock At Startup policy, as shown in Figure 14-15.

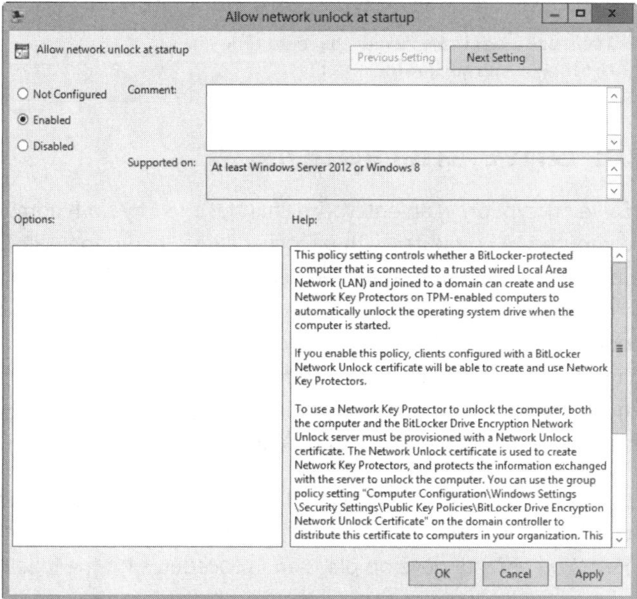

Figure 14-15 Enable Network Unlock at startup if desired.

Typically, the Network Unlock server is a domain controller configured to use and distribute Network Unlock certificates to clients. The Network Unlock certificates, in turn, are used to create the Network Unlock keys.

You can configure a domain controller to distribute this certificate to clients. To do this, create an X.509 certificate for the server—for example, by using Certmsg.mc and then using the BitLocker Driver Encryption Network Unlock Certificate setting to add this certificate to a GPO applied to the domain controller. You can find this Computer Configuration setting under Windows Settings\Security Settings\Public Key Policies.

Provisioning BitLocker prior to deployment

Windows allows you to provision BitLocker during operating system deployment. You can do this from the Windows Pre-Installation Environment (WinPE). It's important to point out that Windows PowerShell includes a Deployment Image Servicing and Management (DISM) module that you can import. Because this module doesn't support wildcards when searching for feature names, you can use the Get-WindowsOptionalFeatures cmdlet to list feature names, as shown in this example:


```
get-windowsoptionalfeature -online | ft
```

To install BitLocker and related management tools completely, use the following command:

```
enable-windowsoptionalfeature -online -featurename bitlocker,
bitlocker-utilities, bitlocker-networkunlock -all
```

Deploying BitLocker Drive Encryption

Deploying BitLocker Drive Encryption in an enterprise changes the way both administrators and users work with computers. A computer with BitLocker Drive Encryption normally requires user intervention to boot to the operating system—a user must enter a PIN, insert a USB flash drive containing a startup key, or use a smart card with a valid certificate. Because of this, after you deploy BitLocker Drive Encryption, you can no longer be sure that you can perform remote administration that requires a computer to be restarted without having physical access to the computer—someone must be available to type in the required PIN, insert the USB flash drive with the startup key, or use a smart card with a valid certificate.

To work around this issue, you can configure Network Unlock on your trusted, wired networks. Before you use BitLocker Drive Encryption, you should perform a thorough evaluation of your organization's computers. You need to develop plans and procedures for the following:

- Evaluating the various BitLocker authentication methods and applying them as appropriate
- Determining whether computers support TPM and, thus, whether you must use TPM or non-TPM BitLocker configurations
- Storing, using, and periodically changing encryption keys, recovery passwords, and other validators used with BitLocker

You also need to develop procedures for the following activities:

- Working with BitLocker-encrypted drives
- Supporting BitLocker-encrypted drives
- Recovering computers with BitLocker-encrypted drives

When developing these procedures, you need to take into account the way BitLocker encryption works and the requirements to have PINs, startup keys, and recovery keys available whenever you work with BitLocker-encrypted computers. After you evaluate your organization's computers and develop basic plans and procedures, you need to develop a configuration plan for implementing BitLocker Drive Encryption.

TROUBLESHOOTING

Several versions of BitLocker

Several implementations of BitLocker Drive Encryption are available: the original as released with Windows Vista, an update for Windows 7 and Windows Server 2008, and an update for Windows 8 and Windows Server 2012. Although computers running Windows 8, Windows Server 2012, and later releases of Windows can work with any of the available versions, earlier versions of Windows can't necessarily work with the latest version of BitLocker. With this in mind, you might need to configure Group Policy to allow access from earlier versions of Windows.

BitLocker Drive Encryption requires a specific disk configuration. To turn on BitLocker Drive Encryption on the drive containing the Windows operating system, the drive must have at least two partitions:

- The first partition is for BitLocker Drive Encryption. This partition, designated as the active partition, holds the files required to start the operating system and is not encrypted.
- The second is the primary partition for the operating system and your data. This partition is encrypted when you turn on BitLocker.

With implementations of BitLocker prior to Windows 7 and Windows Server 2008, you need to create the partitions in a certain way to ensure compatibility. This is no longer the case. When you install Windows 7 and later or Windows Server 2008 and later, an additional partition is created automatically during setup. By default, the Windows Recovery Environment (Windows RE) uses this additional partition. However, if you enable BitLocker on the system volume, Windows usually moves Windows RE to the system volume and then uses the additional partition for BitLocker.

Using BitLocker on a hard disk is easy. On a computer with a compatible TPM, you must create or make available a BitLocker Drive Encryption partition on your hard drive and then initialize the TPM as discussed under "Preparing and initializing a TPM for first use" earlier in this chapter. On a computer without a compatible TPM, you only need to create or make available a BitLocker Drive Encryption partition on your hard drive.

You can use local Group Policy and Active Directory–based Group Policy to help manage and maintain TPM and BitLocker configurations. Group Policy settings for TPM Services are found in Administrative Templates policies for Computer Configuration under System\Trusted Platform Module Services. Group Policy settings for BitLocker are found in Administrative Templates policies for Computer Configuration under Windows Components\BitLocker Drive Encryption. There are separate subfolders for fixed data drives, operating system drives, and removable data drives.

Policies you might want to configure include the following:

- Trusted Platform Module Services policies
  - Configure The Level Of TPM Owner Authorization Information Available To The Operating System
  - Configure The List Of Blocked TPM Commands
  - Ignore The Default List Of Blocked TPM Commands
  - Ignore The Local List Of Blocked TPM Commands
  - Standard User Individual Lockout Threshold
  - Standard User Lockout Duration
  - Standard User Total Lockout Threshold
  - Turn On TPM Backup To Active Directory Domain Services
- BitLocker Drive Encryption policies
  - Choose Default Folder For Recovery Password
  - Choose Drive Encryption Method And Cipher Strength
  - Prevent Memory Overwrite On Restart
  - Provide The Unique Identifiers For Your Organization
  - Validate Smart Card Certificate Usage Rule Compliance
- Fixed Data Drives policies
  - Allow Access To BitLocker-Protected Fixed Data Drives From Earlier Versions Of Windows
  - Choose How BitLocker-Protected Fixed Drives Can Be Recovered

- Configure Use Of Hardware-Based Encryption For Fixed Data Drives
- Configure Use Of Passwords For Fixed Data Drives
- Configure Use Of Smart Cards On Fixed Data Drives
- Deny Write Access To Fixed Drives Not Protected By BitLocker
- Enforce Drive Encryption Type On Fixed Data Drives

- Operating System Drives policies
  - Allow Enhanced PINs For Startup
  - Allow Network Unlock At Startup
  - Allow Secure Boot For Integrity Validation
  - Choose How BitLocker-Protected Operating System Drives Can Be Recovered
  - Configure Minimum PIN Length For Startup
  - Configure TPM Platform Validation Profile For BIOS-Based Firmware Configurations
  - Configure TPM Platform Validation Profile For Native UEFI Firmware Configurations
  - Configure TPM Platform Validation Profile (Windows Vista, Windows 7, Windows Server 2008, Windows Server 2008 R2)
  - Configure Use Of Hardware-Based Encryption For Operating System Drives
  - Configure Use Of Passwords For Operating System Drives
  - Disallow Standard Users From Changing The PIN Or Password
  - Enable User Of BitLocker Authentication Requiring Preboot Keyboard Input On Slates
  - Enforce Drive Encryption Type On Operating System Drives
  - Require Additional Authentication At Startup
  - Reset Platform Validation Data After BitLocker Recovery
  - Use Enhanced Boot Configuration Data Validation Profile

- Removable Data Drives policies
  - Allow Access To BitLocker-Protected Removable Data Drives From Earlier Versions Of Windows
  - Choose How BitLocker-Protected Removable Drives Can Be Recovered
  - Configure Use Of Hardware-Based Encryption For Removable Data Drives
  - Configure Use Of Passwords For Removable Data Drives

- Configure Use Of Smart Cards On Removable Data Drives
- Control Use Of BitLocker On Removable Drives
- Deny Write Access To Removable Drives Not Protected By BitLocker
- Enforce Drive Encryption Type On Removable Data Drives

Active Directory includes TPM and BitLocker recovery extensions for *Computer* objects. For a TPM, the extensions define a single property of the *Computer* object, called *ms-TPM-OwnerInformation*. When the TPM is initialized or when the owner password is changed, the hash of the TPM owner password can be stored as a value of the *ms-TPM-OwnerInformation* attribute on the related *Computer* object. For BitLocker, these extensions define *Recovery* objects as child objects of *Computer* objects and are used to store recovery passwords and associate them with specific BitLocker-encrypted volumes.

By default, Windows stores the full TPM owner authorization, the TPM administrative delegation blob, and the TPM user delegation in the registry. Because of this change, you no longer have to save this information separately to Active Directory for backup and recovery purposes. For more information, see the "Managing TPM owner authorization information" section earlier in this chapter.

Generally, you want to ensure that BitLocker recovery information is always available if it's needed. You can configure Group Policy to save recovery information in Active Directory by using the following techniques:

- With Choose How BitLocker-Protected Fixed Drives Can Be Recovered, enable the policy, accept the default options to allow data-recovery agents, and then save the recovery information in Active Directory.

- With Choose How BitLocker-Protected Operating System Drives Can Be Recovered, enable the policy, accept the default options to allow data-recovery agents, and then save the recovery information in Active Directory.

- With Choose How BitLocker-Protected Removable Drives Can Be Recovered, enable the policy, accept the default options to allow data-recovery agents, and then save the recovery information in Active Directory.

> **Inside OUT**
>
> ***Ensuring FIPS compliance***
>
> For Federal Information Processing Standards (FIPS) compliance, you cannot create or save a BitLocker recovery password. Instead, you need to configure Windows to create recovery keys. The FIPS setting is located in the Security Policy Editor at Local Policies \Security Options\System Cryptography.
>
> Use FIPS-compliant algorithms for encryption, hashing, and signing. To do this, enable System Cryptography: Use FIPS Compliant Algorithms For Encryption, Hashing, And Signing in Local Group Policy or Active Directory Group Policy as appropriate. With this setting enabled, users can save only a recovery key to a USB flash drive. Users cannot save a recovery password to Active Directory Domain Services (AD DS), local folders, or network folders, and they cannot use the BitLocker Drive Encryption Wizard or other methods to create a recovery password. Because recovery passwords cannot be saved to AD DS when FIPS is enabled, Windows displays an error if Group Policy requires AD DS backup.

Setting up and managing BitLocker Drive Encryption

You can configure and enable BitLocker Drive Encryption on both system volumes and data volumes. When you encrypt system volumes, you must unlock the computer at startup, typically by using a TPM and Network Unlock when connected to the domain as well as a TPM, a startup key, a startup PIN, or any required or optional combination of these. To enforce the strictest and highest security possible, use all three authentication methods.

In the current implementation of BitLocker, you do not have to encrypt a computer's system volume prior to encrypting a computer's data volumes. When you use encrypted data volumes, the operating system mounts BitLocker data volumes as it would any other volume, but it requires either a password or a smart card with a valid certificate to unlock the drive.

The encryption key for a protected data volume is created and stored independently from the system volume and all other protected data volumes. To allow the operating system to mount encrypted volumes, the key chain protecting the data volume is stored in an encrypted state on the operating-system volume. If the operating system enters Recovery mode, the data volumes are not unlocked until the operating system is out of Recovery mode.

Setting up BitLocker Drive Encryption is a multistep process that involves the following:

1. Partitioning a computer's hard disks appropriately and installing the operating system (if you are configuring a new computer). Windows Setup partitions the drives for you automatically. However, the volume where BitLocker data is stored must always be the active, system volume.
2. Initializing and configuring a computer's TPM (if applicable).
3. Turning on the BitLocker Drive Encryption feature (as necessary).
4. Checking firmware to ensure that the computer is set to start first from the disk containing the active, system partition and the boot partition, not from USB or CD/DVD drives (which is applicable only when you encrypt system volumes).
5. Turning on and configuring BitLocker Drive Encryption.

After you turn on and configure BitLocker encryption, you can use several techniques to maintain the environment and perform recovery. When you are using a Microsoft account on a non-domain-joined computer, you have an additional save option. You can save the recovery key to the Windows Live SkyDrive. The user's SkyDrive account then contains a BitLocker folder with a separate file for each saved recovery key.

Configuring and enabling BitLocker Drive Encryption

As discussed previously, BitLocker Drive Encryption can be used in a TPM or non-TPM configuration. Both configurations require some preliminary work before you can turn on and configure BitLocker Drive Encryption.

With Windows Vista, Windows 7, Windows 8, and later editions designed for business, BitLocker Drive Encryption and BitLocker Network Unlock should be installed by default.

With Windows Server 2008 and later, you can install BitLocker Drive Encryption, BitLocker Network Unlock, or both as features by using the Add Roles And Features Wizard. Alternatively, on a server, you can install BitLocker Drive Encryption by entering the following command at an elevated Windows PowerShell prompt:

```
add-windowsfeature -name bitlocker, bitlocker-networkunlock -includemanagementtools
```

With either approach, you need to restart the computer to complete the installation process.

After you install BitLocker, you can determine the readiness status of a computer by accessing the BitLocker Drive Encryption console. In Control Panel, tap or click System And Security and then tap or click BitLocker Drive Encryption. If the system isn't properly configured yet, you see an error message either when you open BitLocker Drive Encryption or when you try to encrypt a drive.

If you see this message on a computer with a compatible TPM, refer to "Understanding TPM states and tools" earlier in this chapter to learn more about TPM states and enabling TPM in firmware. If you see this message on a computer with an incompatible TPM or no TPM, you need to change the computer's Group Policy settings so that you can turn on BitLocker Drive Encryption without a TPM.

You can configure policy settings for BitLocker encryption in Local Group Policy or in Active Directory Group Policy. For local policy, you apply the desired settings to the computer's Local Group Policy Object. For domain policy, you apply the desired settings to a Group Policy Object processed by the computer. While you are working with domain policy, you can also specify requirements for computers with a TPM.

To configure the way BitLocker can be used with or without a TPM, follow these steps:

1. Open the appropriate Group Policy Object for editing in the Group Policy Management Editor.
2. Double-tap or double-click the Require Additional Authentication At Startup setting in the Administrative Templates for Computer Configuration under Windows Components \BitLocker Drive Encryption folder\Operating System Drives.
3. In the Require Additional Authentication At Startup dialog box, shown in Figure 14-16, define the policy setting by selecting Enabled. Note that there are several versions of this policy and they are operating-system specific. Configure the version or versions of this policy that are appropriate for your working environment and the computers to which the policy will be applied. The options for each related policy are slightly different because the supported TPM features are slightly different for each operating system.

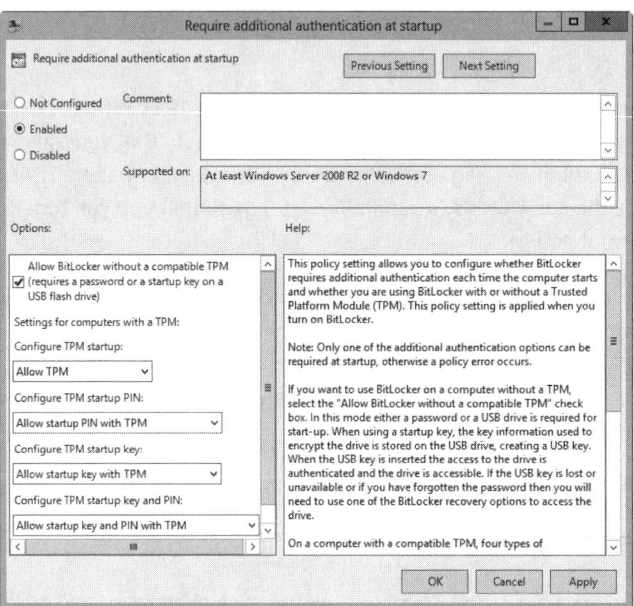

Figure 14-16 Choose the advanced startup options.

4. Do one of the following:
   - If you want to allow BitLocker to be used without a compatible TPM, select the Allow BitLocker Without A Compatible TPM check box. This changes the policy setting so that you can use BitLocker encryption with a startup key on a computer without a TPM.
   - If you want to require BitLocker to be used with a TPM, clear the Allow BitLocker Without A Compatible TPM check box. This changes the policy setting so that you can use BitLocker encryption on a computer with a TPM by using a startup PIN, a startup key, or both.
5. For computers with compatible TPMs, several authentication methods can be used at startup to provide added protection for encrypted data. These authentication methods can be not allowed, allowed, or required. The methods available depend on the specific operating-system version of the policy you are working with.
6. Tap or click OK to save your settings. This policy is enforced the next time Group Policy is applied.
7. Close the Group Policy Object Editor. To force Group Policy to apply immediately to this computer, tap or click Start, type **gpupdate.exe /force** in the Search box, and then press Enter.

Computers that have a startup key or a startup PIN also have a recovery password or certificate. The recovery password or certificate is required in the following circumstances:

- Changes are made to the system startup information.
- The encrypted drive must be moved to another computer.
- The user is unable to provide the appropriate startup key or PIN.

The recovery password or certificate should be managed and stored separately from the startup key or startup PIN. Although users are given the startup key or startup PIN, administrators should be the only ones with the recovery password or certificate. As the administrator, you need the recovery password or certificate to unlock the encrypted data on the volume if BitLocker enters a locked state. Generally, unless you use a common data-recovery agent, the recovery password or certificate is unique to this particular BitLocker encryption. You cannot use it to recover encrypted data from any other BitLocker-encrypted volume—even from other BitLocker-encrypted volumes on the same computer. To increase security, you should store startup keys and recovery data apart from the computer.

When you install BitLocker Drive Encryption and configure policy (if necessary), the BitLocker Drive Encryption console becomes available in Control Panel. When you are configuring BitLocker encryption, the configuration options you have depend on whether the computer has a TPM and on how you configured Group Policy.

Determining whether a computer has BitLocker-encrypted volumes

You can determine whether a computer has BitLocker-encrypted volumes by using Disk Management. In Disk Management, any such encrypted volume is listed as BitLocker Encrypted, as shown in Figure 14-17.

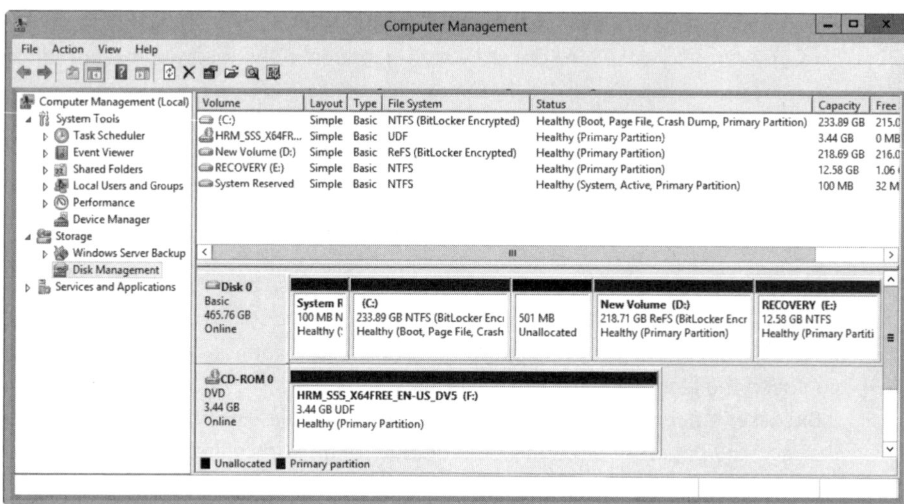

Figure 14-17 Use Disk Management to check for BitLocker-encrypted volumes.

Enabling BitLocker on fixed data drives

Encrypting a fixed data drive protects the data stored on the drive. Any drive formatted with FAT, FAT32, exFAT, NTFS, or ReFS can be encrypted with BitLocker. The length of time it takes to encrypt a drive depends on the amount of data to encrypt, the processing power of the computer, and the level of activity on the computer.

Before you enable BitLocker, you should configure the appropriate Fixed Data Drive policies and settings in Group Policy and then either wait for Group Policy to be refreshed or refresh Group Policy manually. If you don't do this and you enable BitLocker, you might need to turn off BitLocker and then turn it back on because certain state and management flags are set when you turn on BitLocker.

If you dual-boot a computer or move drives between computers, you can use the Allow Access To BitLocker-Protected Fixed Data Drives From Earlier Versions Of Windows setting in Group Policy to ensure that you have access to the volume on other operating systems and computers. Unlocked drives are read-only. To ensure that you can recover an encrypted volume, you should allow data-recovery agents and store recovery information in Active Directory.

You can enable BitLocker encryption on a fixed data drive by following these steps:

1. Open the BitLocker Drive Encryption console. In Control Panel, tap or click System And Security and then tap or click BitLocker Drive Encryption.
2. In the BitLocker Drive Encryption console, available drives are listed by category. Under the Fixed Data Drives heading, tap or click Turn On BitLocker for the fixed data drive you

want to encrypt. BitLocker verifies that your computer meets its requirements and then initializes the drive. If BitLocker is already enabled on the drive, you have management options instead.

3. On the Choose How You Want To Unlock This Drive page, shown in Figure 14-18, choose one or more of the following options and then tap or click Next:
   - **Use A Password To Unlock The Drive.** Select this option if you want the user to be prompted for a password to unlock the drive. Passwords allow a drive to be unlocked in any location and to be shared with other people.
   - **Use My Smart Card To Unlock The Drive.** Select this option if you want the user to use a smart card and enter the smart card PIN to unlock the drive. Because this feature requires a smart card reader, it is normally used to unlock a drive in the workplace and not for drives that might be used outside the workplace.

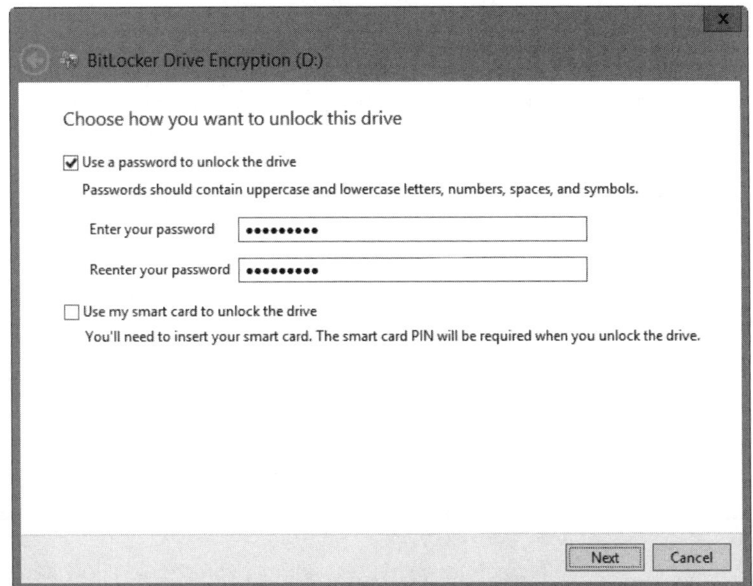

Figure 14-18 Choose an option for unlocking a drive.

> IMPORTANT
>
> **When you tap or click Next, the wizard generates a recovery key. You can use the key to unlock the drive if BitLocker detects a condition that prevents it from unlocking the drive during boot. Note that you should save the key on removable media or on a network share. You can't store the key on the encrypted volume or the root directory of a fixed drive.**

4. On the How Do You Want To Back Up Your Recovery Key? page, choose a save location for the recovery key—preferably, a USB flash drive or other removable media.
5. You can now optionally save the recovery key to another folder, print the recovery key, or both. For each option, tap or click the option and then follow the wizard's steps to set the location for saving or printing the recovery key. When you finish, tap or click Next.
6. If it is allowed in Group Policy, you can elect to encrypt used disk space only or the entire drive and then tap or click Next. Encrypting the used disk space only is faster than encrypting an entire volume. It is also the recommended option for newer computers and drives (except in high-security environments).
7. On the Are You Ready To Encrypt This Drive? page, tap or click Start Encrypting. How long the encryption process takes depends on the amount of data being encrypted and other factors.
8. Because the encryption process can be paused and resumed, you can shut down the computer before the drive is completely encrypted and the encryption of the drive will resume when you restart the computer. The encryption state is maintained in the event of a power loss as well.

Enabling BitLocker on removable data drives

Encrypting removable data drives protects the data stored on the volume. Any removable data drive formatted with FAT, FAT32, exFAT, NTFS, or ReFS can be encrypted with BitLocker. The length of time it takes to encrypt a drive depends on the size of the drive, the processing power of the computer, and the level of activity on the computer.

Before you enable BitLocker, you should configure the appropriate Removable Data Drives policies and settings in Group Policy and then wait for Group Policy to be refreshed. If you don't do this and you enable BitLocker, you might need to turn off BitLocker and then turn it back on because certain state and management flags are set when you turn on BitLocker.

To be sure that you can recover an encrypted volume, you should allow data-recovery agents and store recovery information in Active Directory. If you use a flash drive with earlier versions of Windows, you can use the Allow Access To BitLocker-Protected Removable Data Drives From Earlier Versions Of Windows policy to ensure that you have access to the removable data drive on other operating systems and computers. Unlocked drives are read-only.

You can enable BitLocker encryption on a removable data drive by following these steps:

1. After you connect the removable data drive, open the BitLocker Drive Encryption console. In Control Panel, tap or click System And Security and then tap or click BitLocker Drive Encryption.

2. In the BitLocker Drive Encryption console, available drives are listed by category. Under the Removable Data Drives heading, tap or click Turn On BitLocker for the removable data drive you want to encrypt. BitLocker verifies that your computer meets its requirements and then initializes the drive. If BitLocker is already enabled on the drive, you have management options instead.
3. On the Choose How You Want To Unlock This Drive page, choose one or more of the following options and then tap or click Next:
   - **Use A Password To Unlock The Drive.** Select this option if you want the user to be prompted for a password to unlock the drive. Passwords allow a drive to be unlocked in any location and to be shared with other people.
   - **Use My Smart Card To Unlock The Drive.** Select this option if you want the user to use a smart card and enter the smart card PIN to unlock the drive. Because this feature requires a smart card reader, it is normally used to unlock a drive in the workplace and not for drives that might be used outside the workplace.
4. On the How Do You Want To Back Up Your Recovery Key? page, tap or click Save The Recovery Key To A File.
5. In the Save BitLocker Recovery Key As dialog box, choose a save location and then tap or click Save.
6. You can now print the recovery key if you want to. When you finish, tap or click Next.
7. If it is allowed in Group Policy, you can elect to encrypt used disk space only or the entire drive and then tap or click Next. Encrypting the used disk space only is faster than encrypting an entire volume. It is also the recommended option for newer computers and drives (except in high-security environments).
8. On the Are You Ready To Encrypt This Drive? page, tap or click Start Encrypting. Be sure to pause encryption before removing the drive and then resume the process to complete the encryption. Do not otherwise remove the USB flash drive until the encryption process is complete. How long the encryption process takes depends on the amount of data to encrypt and other factors.

The encryption process does the following:

- It adds an Autorun.inf file, the BitLocker To Go reader, and a Read Me.txt file to the removable data drive.
- It creates a virtual volume with the encrypted contents of the drive.

- It encrypts the virtual volume to protect it. Removable data drive encryption takes approximately 6 to 10 minutes per gigabyte to complete. The encryption process can be paused and resumed as long as you don't remove the drive.

When you connect an encrypted drive, Windows displays a notification on the secure desktop, as shown in Figure 14-19. If the notification disappears before you can tap or click it, just remove and then reinsert the encrypted drive.

Figure 14-19 Tap or click the notification.

Then unlock the encrypted drive by completing the following steps:

1. Tap or click the notification to open the BitLocker dialog box. This dialog box also is displayed on the secure desktop.

2. When you are prompted, enter the password. Optionally, tap or click More Options to expand the dialog box so that you select Automatically Unlock On This Computer to save the password in an encrypted file on the computer's system volume. Finally, tap or click Unlock to unlock the drive so that you can use it.

3. If you forget or lose the password for the drive but have the recovery key, tap or click More Options and then tap or click Enter Recovery Key. Enter the 48-digit recovery key and then tap or click Unlock. This key is stored in the XML-formatted recovery key file as plain text.

Enabling BitLocker on operating-system volumes

Before you can encrypt a system volume, you must remove all bootable media from a computer's CD/DVD drives and from all USB flash drives. You can then enable BitLocker encryption on the system volume by completing the following steps:

1. Open the BitLocker Drive Encryption console. In Control Panel, tap or click System And Security and then tap or click BitLocker Drive Encryption.

2. In the BitLocker Drive Encryption console, available drives are listed by category. Under the Operating System Drives heading, tap or click Turn On BitLocker for the

operating-system drive you want to encrypt. BitLocker verifies that your computer meets its requirements and then initializes the drive. If BitLocker is already enabled on the drive, you have management options instead.

> **NOTE**
>
> **As part of the setup, Windows prepares the required BitLocker partition if necessary. If Windows RE is in this partition, Windows moves Windows RE to the system volume and then uses this additional partition for BitLocker.**
>
> **Note also that if the computer doesn't have a TPM, the Allow BitLocker Without A Compatible TPM option must be enabled for operating-system volumes in the Require Additional Authentication At Startup policy.**

3. As Figure 14-20 shows, you can now configure BitLocker startup preferences. Continue as discussed in the separate procedures that follow. If the computer doesn't have a TPM, your options will be different. You can create a password to unlock the drive, or you can insert a USB flash drive and store the startup key on the flash drive.

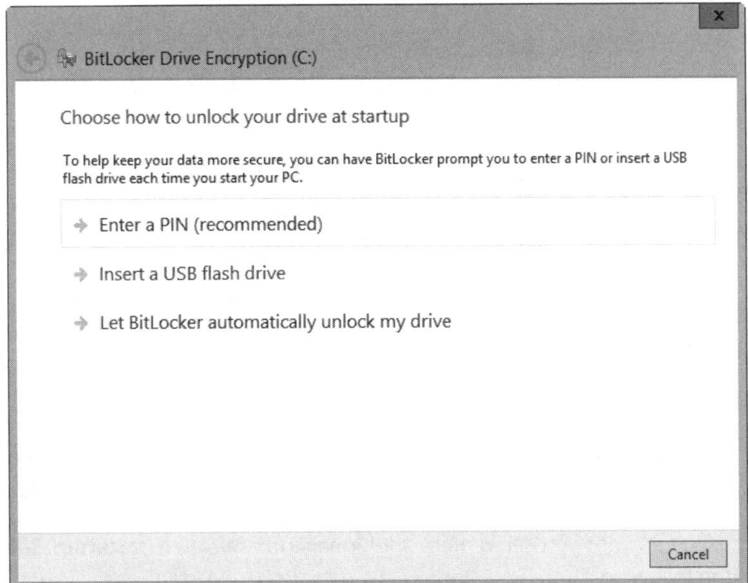

Figure 14-20 Configure BitLocker startup preferences.

When a computer has a TPM, you can use BitLocker to provide basic integrity checks of the volume without requiring any additional keys. In this configuration, BitLocker protects the system volume by encrypting it. This configuration does the following:

- Grants access to the volume to users who can log on to the operating system
- Prevents those who have physical access to the computer from booting to an alternative operating system to gain access to the data on the volume
- Allows the computer to be used with or without a TPM for additional boot security
- Does not require a password or a smart card with a PIN

To use BitLocker without any additional keys, follow these steps:

1. On the Choose How To Unlock Your Drive At Startup page, tap or click Let BitLocker Automatically Unlock My Drive.
2. On the How Do You Want To Back Up Your Recovery Key page, tap or click Save To A File.
3. In the Save BitLocker Recovery Key As dialog box, choose the location of your USB flash drive or an appropriate network share and then tap or click Save. Do not use a USB flash drive that is BitLocker-encrypted.
4. You can now optionally save the recovery key to another location, print the recovery key, or both. Tap or click an option and then follow the wizard's steps to set the location for saving or printing the recovery key. When you finish, tap or click Next.
5. If it is allowed in Group Policy, you can elect to encrypt used disk space only or the entire drive and then tap or click Next. Encrypting the used disk space only is faster than encrypting an entire volume. It is also the recommended option for newer computers and drives (except in high-security environments).
6. On the Encrypt The Drive page, tap or click Start Encrypting. How long the encryption process takes depends on the amount of data to encrypt and other factors.

To enhance security, you can require additional authentication at startup. This configuration does the following:

- Grants access to the volume only to users who can provide a valid key
- Prevents those who have physical access to the computer from booting to an alternative operating system to gain access to the data on the volume
- Allows the computer to be used with or without a TPM for additional boot security

- Requires a password or a smart card with a PIN
- Optionally, uses Network Unlock to unlock the volume when the computer is joined to and connected to the domain

A startup key is different from a recovery key. If you create a startup key, this key is required to start the computer. The recovery key is required to unlock the computer if BitLocker enters Recovery mode, which might happen if BitLocker suspects the computer has been tampered with while the computer was offline.

You can enable BitLocker encryption for use with a startup key by following these steps:

1. Insert a USB flash drive in the computer (if one is not already there). Do not use a USB flash drive that is BitLocker-encrypted.
2. On the Choose How To Unlock Your Drive At Startup page, tap or click Insert A USB Flash Drive.
3. On the Back Up Your Startup Key page, tap or click the USB flash drive and then tap or click Save. Next, you need to save the recovery key. Because you should not store the recovery key and the startup key on the same medium, remove the USB flash drive and insert a second USB flash drive.
4. On the How Do You Want To Back Up Your Recovery Key page, tap or click Save To A File. In the Save BitLocker Recovery Key As dialog box, choose the location of your USB flash drive and then tap or click Save. Do not remove the USB flash drive with the recovery key.
5. You can now optionally save the recovery key to a network folder, print the recovery key, or both. Tap or click an option and then follow the wizard's steps to set the location for saving or printing the recovery key. When you finish, tap or click Next.
6. If it is allowed in Group Policy, you can elect to encrypt used disk space only or the entire drive and then tap or click Next. Encrypting the used disk space only is faster than encrypting an entire volume. It is also the recommended option for newer computers and drives (except in high-security environments).
7. On the Encrypt The Volume page, confirm that Run BitLocker System Check is selected and then tap or click Continue. Confirm that you want to restart the computer by tapping or clicking Restart Now.

The computer restarts, and BitLocker ensures that the computer is BitLocker-compatible and ready for encryption. If the computer is not ready for encryption, you see an error and need to resolve the error status before you can complete this procedure. If the computer is ready for encryption, the Encryption In Progress status bar appears. You can monitor the status of the disk-volume encryption by pointing to the BitLocker Drive Encryption icon in the notification area. By double-tapping or double-clicking this icon, you can open the Encrypting dialog box and either monitor the encryption process more closely or pause the encryption process. Volume encryption takes approximately one minute per gigabyte to complete.

By completing this procedure, you encrypt the operating-system volume and create a recovery key unique to that volume. The next time you turn on your computer, either the USB flash drive with the startup key must be plugged into a USB port on the computer or the computer must be connected to the domain network and using Network Unlock. If the USB flash drive is required for startup and you do not have the USB flash drive containing your startup key, you need to use Recovery mode and supply the recovery key to gain access to the data.

You can enable BitLocker encryption for use with a startup PIN by following these steps:

1. On the Choose How To Unlock Your Drive At Startup page, select Enter A PIN.
2. On the Enter A PIN page, type and confirm the PIN. The PIN can be any number you choose and must be 4 to 20 digits in length. The PIN is stored on the computer.
3. Insert the USB flash drive on which you want to save the recovery key and then tap or click Set PIN. Do not use a USB flash drive that is BitLocker-encrypted.

   Continue with steps 4 through 7 in the previous procedure.

When the encryption process is complete, you have encrypted the entire volume and created a recovery key unique to this volume. If you created a PIN or a startup key, you are required to use the PIN or startup key to start the computer (or the computer must be connected to the domain network and using Network Unlock). Otherwise, you will see no change to the computer unless the TPM changes, the TPM cannot be accessed, or someone tries to modify the disk while the operating system is offline. In these cases, the computer enters Recovery mode, and you need to enter the recovery key to unlock the computer.

Managing and troubleshooting BitLocker

You can determine whether a system volume, data volume, or inserted removable drive uses BitLocker by tapping or clicking System And Security in Control Panel and then double-tapping or double-clicking BitLocker Drive Encryption. You see the status of BitLocker on each volume, as shown in Figure 14-21.

The BitLocker Drive Encryption service must be started for BitLocker to work properly. Normally, this service is configured for manual startup and runs under the LocalSystem account.

To use smart cards with BitLocker, the Smart Card service must be started. Normally, this service is configured for manual startup and runs under the LocalService account.

After you create a startup key or PIN and a recovery key for a computer, you can create duplicates of the startup key, startup PIN, or recovery key as necessary for backup or replacement purposes, using the options on the BitLocker Drive Encryption page in Control Panel.

With fixed data drives and operating-system drives, another way to access this page is to press and hold or right-click the volume in File Explorer and then tap or click Manage BitLocker. If BitLocker is turned off, Turn On BitLocker appears instead.

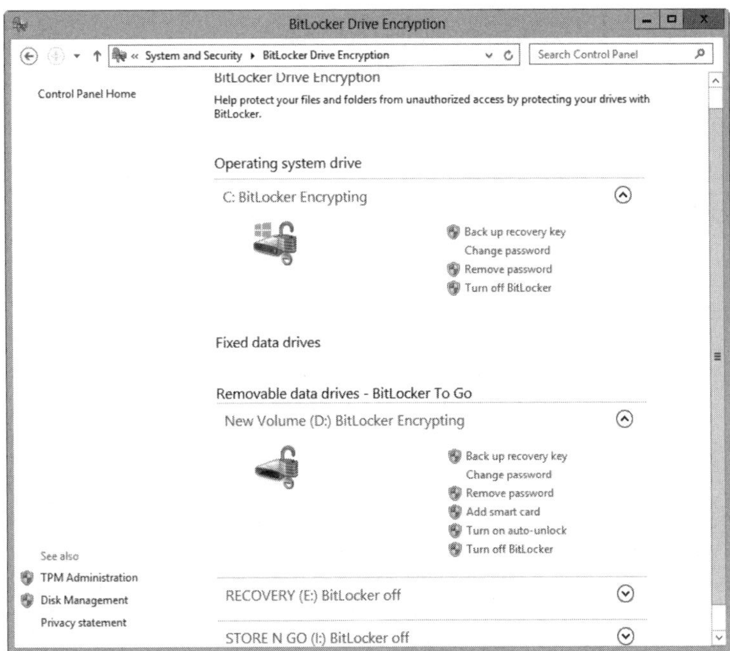

Figure 14-21 Review the current status of BitLocker for each volume.

The management options provided depend on the type of volume you are working with and the encryption settings you choose. The available options include the following:

- **Back Up Recovery Key.** Allows you to save or print the recovery key. Tap or click this option and then follow the prompts.
- **Change Password.** Allows you to change the encryption password. Tap or click this option, enter the old password, and then type and confirm the new password. Tap or click Change Password.
- **Remove Password.** Tap or click this option to remove the encryption password requirement for unlocking the drive. You can do this only if another unlocking method is configured first.

- **Add Smart Card.** Allows you to add a smart card for unlocking the drive. Tap or click this option and then follow the prompts.
- **Remove Smart Card.** Tap or click this option to remove the smart card requirement for unlocking the drive.
- **Change Smart Card.** Allows you to change the smart card used to unlock the drive. Tap or click this option and then follow the prompts.
- **Turn On Auto-Unlock.** Tap or click this option to turn on automatic unlocking of the drive.
- **Turn Off Auto-Unlock.** Tap or click this option to turn off automatic unlocking of the drive.
- **Turn Off BitLocker.** Tap or click this option to turn off BitLocker and decrypt the drive.

Inside OUT

Managing BitLocker in large enterprises

Large enterprises might want to use Microsoft BitLocker Administration and Monitoring (MBAM) to simplify BitLocker provisioning and deployment and to improve compliance and reporting on BitLocker. MBAM is included in Microsoft Desktop Optimization Pack (MDOP) 2013 R2 and is recommended for deployments of Windows 8, Windows Server 2012, and later releases of both. MBAM has client components and a multi-tiered server architecture. The MBAM client must be installed on clients throughout the enterprise. The server architecture uses web portals, web services, SQL databases, and SQL Server Reporting Services.

MBAM 2.0 supports a standalone deployment model and a System Center–integrated model. The key difference between the models is how compliance data and reports are collected and stored. The System Center–integrated model moves compliance data and reporting to System Center Configuration Manager rather than to a standalone website.

When deployed, the administration and monitoring server hosts the HelpDesk Portal and the Self-Service Portal. Administrators can use the HelpDesk Portal to view reports and audit activities and to access recovery data. End users can log on to the Self-Service Portal to look up their own recovery keys without requiring help desk support.

Recovering data protected by BitLocker Drive Encryption

If you configure BitLocker Drive Encryption and the computer enters Recovery mode, you need to unlock the computer. To unlock the computer by using a recovery key stored on a USB flash drive, follow these steps:

1. Turn on the computer. If the computer is locked, the computer opens the BitLocker Drive Encryption Recovery console.
2. When you are prompted, insert the USB flash drive that contains the recovery key and then press Enter.

   The computer unlocks and reboots automatically. You do not need to enter the recovery key manually.

If you saved the recovery key file in a folder on another computer or on removable media, you can use another computer to open and validate the recovery key file. To locate the correct file, find Password ID on the recovery console displayed on the locked computer and write down this number. The file containing the recovery key uses this Password ID as the file name. Open the file and locate the recovery key.

To unlock the computer by typing the recovery key, follow these steps:

1. Turn on the computer. If the computer is locked, the computer opens the BitLocker Drive Encryption Recovery console.
2. Type the recovery key and then press Enter. The computer unlocks and reboots automatically.

A computer can become locked if a user tries to enter the recovery key but is repeatedly unsuccessful. In the recovery console, you can press Esc twice to exit the recovery prompt and turn off the computer. A computer might also become locked if an error related to the TPM occurs or boot data is modified. In this case, the computer halts very early in the boot process, before the operating system starts. At this point, the locked computer might not be able to accept standard keyboard numbers. If that is the case, you must use the function keys to enter the recovery password. Here, the function keys F1–F9 represent the digits 1 through 9, and the F10 function key represents 0.

Disabling or turning off BitLocker Drive Encryption

When you need to make changes to the TPM or make other changes to the system, you might first need to turn off BitLocker encryption temporarily on the system volume. You cannot turn off BitLocker encryption temporarily on data volumes; you can only decrypt data volumes.

To turn off BitLocker encryption temporarily on the system volume, follow these steps:

1. In Control Panel, tap or click System And Security and then double-tap or double-click BitLocker Drive Encryption.
2. For the system volume, tap or click Turn Off BitLocker Drive Encryption.
3. In the What Level Of Decryption Do You Want? dialog box, tap or click Disable BitLocker Drive Encryption.

   By completing this procedure, you temporarily disable BitLocker on the operating-system volume.

To turn off BitLocker Drive Encryption and decrypt a data volume, follow these steps:

1. In Control Panel, tap or click System And Security and then double-tap or double-click BitLocker Drive Encryption.
2. For the appropriate volume, tap or click Turn Off BitLocker Drive Encryption.
3. In the What Level Of Decryption Do You Want? dialog box, tap or click Decrypt The Volume.

To turn off BitLocker Drive Encryption and decrypt a USB flash drive, follow these steps:

1. In Control Panel, tap or click System And Security and then double-tap or double-click BitLocker Drive Encryption.
2. For the appropriate volume, tap or click Turn Off BitLocker Drive Encryption.
3. In the What Level Of Decryption Do You Want? dialog box, tap or click Decrypt The Volume.

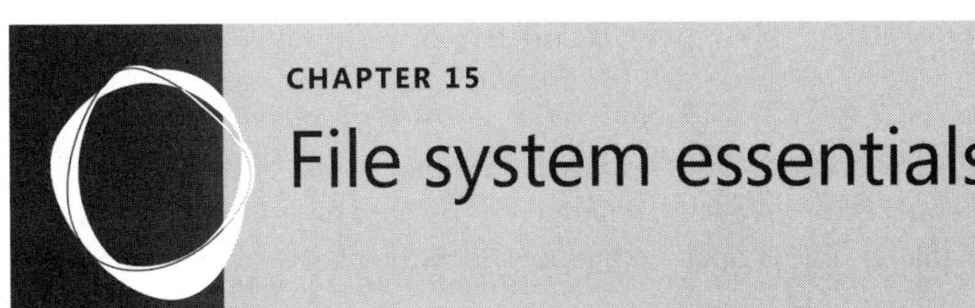

CHAPTER 15

File system essentials

Chapter 12, "Storage management essentials," discussed storage management, which primarily focuses on storage technologies and techniques for configuring storage. As discussed in that chapter, disks can be apportioned in many ways but ultimately must be formatted with a particular file system. The file system provides the environment for working with files and folders. Windows Server 2012 R2 provides FAT and NTFS as the basic file-system types. These file systems and their various extensions, which include the Resilient File System (ReFS), are discussed in this chapter.

Understanding the disk and file-system structure

The basic unit of storage is a *disk*. Regardless of the partition style or disk type, Windows Server 2012 R2 reads data from disks and writes data to disks by using the disk input/output (I/O) subsystem. The I/O subsystem understands the physical and logical structures of disks, which enables it to perform read and write operations. The basic physical structure of a hard disk drive (HDD) includes the following items:

- Platters
- Cylinders
- Tracks
- Clusters
- Sectors

Each hard disk drive has one or more *platters*. Platters are the physical media from which data is read and to which data is written. The disk head travels in a circular path over the platter. This circular path is called a *track*. Tracks are magnetically encoded when you format a disk. Tracks that reside in the same location on each platter form a *cylinder*. For example, if a hard disk drive has four platters, Cylinder 1 consists of Track 1 from all four platters.

Tracks are divided into *sectors*. Sectors represent a subsection within a track and consist of individual bytes. The number of sectors in a track depends on the hard disk drive type and the location of the track on the platter. Tracks closer to the outside of the platter can have more sectors than tracks near the center of the platter.

In contrast, solid-state drives (SSDs) have no moving parts because solid-state drives use flash memory modules rather than platters, and no disk heads need to travel over platters to read data. With solid-state drives, data is accessed directly from the flash memory over multiple internal flash buses. Typically, solid-state drives use NAND flash memory modules that have either multilevel cells (MLCs) storing two bits per cell or single-level cells (SLCs) storing one bit per cell.

Although solid-state drives that use multilevel cells might be cheaper than those with single-level cells, solid-state drives with single-level cells typically provide better reliability and performance. That said, the endurance of both types of solid-states drives isn't as robust as hard disk drives but is improving thanks to wear-leveling algorithms and other techniques that distribute writes more evenly across memory modules, provide enhanced error correction, and might also compress data.

As with hard disks, solid-state drives rely on I/O subsystems that understand their physical and logical structure to perform read and write operations. Overall performance of solid-state drives depends on their controllers, firmware, and caching. Typically, solid-state drives are much faster than hard drives, especially for small block I/O with less than 32-kilobyte (KB) reads.

Inside OUT

When using SSDs makes sense

As solid-state drive capacities improve and prices come down, using solid-state drives in the enterprise makes more and more sense. Many solid-state-drive solutions are available for enterprise servers and enterprise workstations, including those with their own data protection similar to redundant array of independent disks (RAID) systems. Applications that require high performance for reads and have heavy read access can benefit from using solid-state drives. For example, you might want to use enterprise SSDs with applications for media streaming, web accelerators, video on demand, and frequently accessed data-storage warehouses. Solid-state drives might also make sense in storage-tiering scenarios. For example, you could use Tier 1 storage with solid-state drives for hot data and Tier 2 storage with capacity-optimized drives for cool data.

Solid-state hybrid drives bridge the gap between hard disk drives and solid-state drives. A typical hybrid drive combines a small solid-state drive with a large hard disk drive. The flash memory is used for critical operations, such as boot and initial application load, and the hard disk drive is used for all other operations. Special algorithms can be used to capture boot files and place them on the flash to ensure that the hybrid drive always boots from flash memory rather than from the spinning disk. Other algorithms also can be used to move applications and data that are initially loaded or frequently used with the system into the flash memory. The result is a drive that has some of the speed benefits of solid-state drives with a cost that is closer to that of a traditional hard disk drive.

Inside OUT

When using hybrid drives makes sense

Hybrid drives are ideal when you want to reduce boot and initial application load times but don't want to equip your enterprise workstations with more-expensive solid-state drives. As such, you could use the hybrid drives as system boot drives and not necessarily as data drives. Keep in mind that it can take several boots for a hybrid drive to normalize the startup process and achieve the best efficiencies. The same is true for normalizing the startup of frequently used applications.

When you format a disk with a file system, the file system structures the disk using *clusters*, which are logical groupings of sectors. Both FAT and NTFS use the fixed sector size of the underlying disk (which can be either 512 bytes per physical sector with 512b disks or 4,096 bytes per physical sector with 512e disks) but allow the cluster size to be variable. For example, the cluster size might be 4,096 bytes, and if there are 512 bytes per sector, each cluster consists of eight sectors. ReFS is an exception. In current implementations, as of this writing, ReFS has a fixed cluster size of 64 KBs.

Table 15-1 provides a summary of the default cluster sizes for FAT, FAT32, exFAT, NTFS, and ReFS. You can specify the cluster size when you create a file system on a disk, or you can accept the default cluster size setting. Either way, the cluster sizes available depend on the type of file system you are using.

Four FAT file systems

There are four FAT file systems Windows platforms use: FAT12, FAT16, FAT32, and exFAT (FAT64). The difference among them is the number of bits used for entries in their file allocation tables—namely, 12, 16, 32, or 64 bits. From a user's perspective, the main difference among these file systems is the theoretical maximum volume size, which is 16 megabytes (MBs) for a FAT12 volume, 4 gigabytes (GBs) for FAT16, 2 terabytes (TBs) for FAT32, and 256 TBs for FAT64. When the term *FAT* is used without an appended number, it always refers to FAT16.

Table 15-1 Default cluster sizes for Windows Server

Volume Size	Cluster Size				
	FAT16	FAT32	exFAT	NTFS	ReFS
7 MBs to 16 MBs	512 bytes	N/A	4 KBs	512 bytes	N/A
17 MBs to 32 MBs	512 bytes	N/A	4 KBs	512 bytes	N/A
33 MBs to 64 MBs	1 KB	512 bytes	4 KBs	512 bytes	N/A
65 MBs to 128 MBs	2 KBs	1 KB	4 KBs	512 bytes	N/A
129 MBs to 256 MBs	4 KBs	2 KBs	4 KBs	512 bytes	N/A
257 MBs to 512 MBs	8 KBs	4 KBs	32 KBs	512 bytes	N/A
513 MBs to 1024 MBs	16 KBs	4 KBs	32 KBs	1 KB	64 KBs
1025 MBs to 2 GBs	32 KBs	4 KBs	32 KBs	4 KBs	64 KBs
2 GBs to 4 GBs	64 KBs	4 KBs	32 KBs	4 KBs	64 KBs
4 GBs to 8 GBs	N/A	4 KBs	32 KBs	4 KBs	64 KBs
8 GBs to 16 GBs	N/A	8 KBs	32 KBs	4 KBs	64 KBs
16 GBs to 32 GBs	N/A	16 KBs	32 KBs	4 KBs	64 KBs
32 GBs to 2 TBs	N/A	*	128 KBs	4 KBs	64 KBs
2 TBs to 16 TBs	N/A	*	128 KBs	4 KBs	64 KBs
16 TBs to 32 TBs	N/A	*	128 KBs	8 KBs	64 KBs
32 TBs to 64 TBs	N/A	*	128 KBs	16 KBs	64 KBs
64 TBs to 128 TBs	N/A	*	128 KBs	32 KBs	64 KBs
128 TBs to 256 TBs	N/A	*	128 KBs	64 KBs	64 KBs

The important thing to know about clusters is that they are the smallest unit in which disk space is allocated. Each cluster can hold one file at most. So, if you create a 1 KB file and the cluster size is 4 KBs, 3 KBs of empty space in the cluster won't be available to other files. That's just the way it is. If a single cluster isn't big enough to hold an entire file, the remaining file data will go into the next available cluster and then the next until the file is completely stored.

Although the disk I/O subsystem manages the physical structure of disks, Windows Server 2012 R2 manages the logical disk structure at the file-system level. The logical structure of a disk relates to the basic or dynamic volumes you create on a disk and the file systems with which those volumes are formatted. You can format both basic volumes and dynamic volumes by using FAT or NTFS. As discussed in the next section, each file system type has a different structure, and there are advantages and disadvantages of each.

Using FAT

FAT volumes use an allocation table to store information about disk space allocation. FAT can be used with both fixed disks and removable media. For both fixed disks and removable media, FAT is available in 16-bit and 32-bit versions, which are referred to as FAT16 and FAT32. For removable media, you can also use extended FAT (exFAT). The advantage of using exFAT with removable media instead of FAT is that exFAT can be used with any operating system or device that supports this file-system type.

File allocation table structure

Disks formatted using FAT are organized as shown in Figure 15-1. They have a boot sector that stores information about the disk type, starting and ending sectors, the active partition, and a bootstrap program that executes at startup and boots the operating system. This is followed by a reserve area that can be one or more sectors in length.

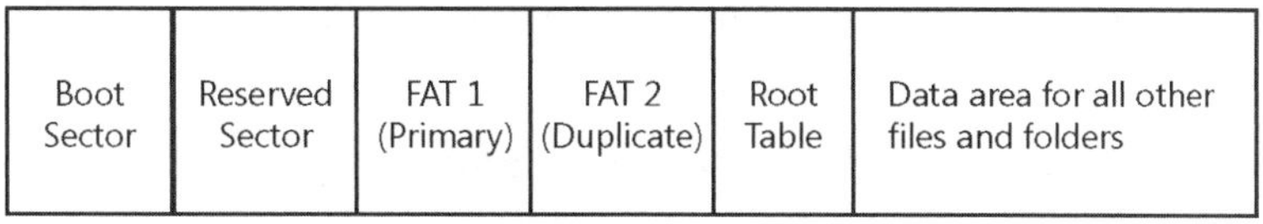

Boot Sector	Reserved Sector	FAT 1 (Primary)	FAT 2 (Duplicate)	Root Table	Data area for all other files and folders

Figure 15-1 Here is an overview of the FAT16 volume structure.

The reserve area is followed by the primary file allocation table, which provides a reference table for the clusters on the volume. Each reference in the table relates to a specific cluster and defines the cluster's status as follows:

- Available (unused)
- In use (meaning a file is using it)
- Bad (meaning it is marked as bad and won't be written to)
- Reserved (meaning it is reserved for the operating system)

If a cluster is in use, the cluster entry identifies the number of the next cluster in the file or indicates that it is the last cluster of a file—in which case, the end of the file has been reached.

FAT volumes also have the following features:

- Duplicate file allocation table, which provides a backup of the primary file allocation table and can be used to restore the file system if the primary file allocation table becomes corrupted

- Root directory table, which defines the starting cluster of each file in the root directory of the file system
- Data area, which stores the actual data for user files and folders

When an application attempts to read a file, the operating system looks up the starting cluster of the file in the file allocation table and then uses the file allocation table to find and read all the clusters in the file.

FAT features

Although FAT supports basic file and folder operations, its features are rather limited. By using FAT, you have the following capabilities:

- You can use Windows file sharing, and the share permissions you assign completely control remote access to files.
- You can use long file names, meaning file and folder names containing up to 255 characters.
- You can use FAT with floppy disks and removable disks.
- You can use Unicode characters in file and folder names.
- You can use uppercase and lowercase letters in file and folder names.

However, FAT has the following disadvantages:

- You can't control local access to files and folders by using Microsoft Windows file and folder access permissions.
- You can't use any advanced file-system features of NTFS, including compression, encryption, disk quotas, and remote storage.

In addition, although FAT16 and FAT32 support small cluster sizes, exFAT does not. Table 15-2 provides a summary of FAT16, FAT32, and exFAT.

> NOTE
>
> **Although Windows Server 2012 R2 can read to or write from FAT32 volumes as large as 2 TBs, the operating system can only format FAT32 volumes up to 32 GBs in size.**

Table 15-2 Comparison of FAT16, FAT32, and exFAT features

Feature	FAT16	FAT32	exFAT
File allocation table size	16-bit	32-bit	64-bit
Minimum volume size	See the following Inside Out tip	33 MBs	33 MBs
Maximum volume size	4 GBs; best at 2 GBs or less	2 TBs; limited in Windows Server to 32 GBs	256 TBs
Maximum file size	2 GBs	4 GBs	Same as volume size
Supports small cluster size	Yes	Yes	No
Supports NTFS features	No	No	No
Use on fixed disks	Yes	Yes	Yes
Use on removable disks	Yes	Yes	Yes
Supports network file sharing	Yes	Yes	Yes
Supports customized disk and folder views	Yes	Yes	Yes

Inside OUT

FAT on very small media

Note that FAT volumes are structured differently, depending on the volume size. When you format a volume that is less than 32,680 sectors (16 MBs), the format program uses 12 bits for FAT12. This means less space is reserved for each entry in the table and more space is made available for data. This technique is meant to be used with very small media, such as floppy disks.

By default, Windows Server sets the size of clusters and the number of sectors per cluster based on the size of the volume. Disk geometry also is a factor in determining cluster size because the number of clusters on the volume must fit into the number of bits the file system uses. The actual amount of data you can store on a single FAT volume is a factor of the maximum cluster size and the maximum number of clusters you can use per volume. This can be written out as a formula:

```
ClusterSize × MaximumNumberOfClusters = MaximumVolumeSize
```

FAT16 supports a maximum of 65,526 clusters and a maximum cluster size of 64 KBs. This is where the limitation of 4 GBs for volume size comes from. With disks less than 32 MBs but more than 16 MBs in size, the cluster size is 512 bytes and there is one sector per cluster with

512b disks. This changes as the volume size increases, up to the largest cluster size of 64 KBs with 128 sectors per cluster on 2 GB to 4 GB volumes.

FAT32 volumes using 512-byte sectors on 512b disks can be up to 2 TBs in size and can use clusters of up to 64 KBs. To control the maximum number of clusters allowed, the Windows operating system reserves the upper 4 bits, however, limiting FAT32 to a maximum 28 bits' worth of clusters. With a maximum recommended cluster size of 32 KBs (instead of the maximum allowable 64 KBs), this means a FAT32 volume on the Windows operating system can be up to 32 GBs in size. Because the smallest cluster size allowed for FAT32 volumes is 512 bytes, the smallest FAT32 volume you can create is 33 MBs.

FAT32 volumes of any size can be mounted

Windows Server 2012 R2 does support mounting FAT32 volumes of up to the theoretical limit of 2 TBs. This enables you to mount volumes larger than 32 GBs that were created on other operating systems or by using third-party utilities.

Inside OUT

Getting volume format and feature information

A quick way to check the file system type and available features of a volume is to type **fsutil fsinfo volumeinfo** *DriveDesignator* at the command prompt, where *DriveDesignator* is the drive letter of the volume followed by a colon, such as C:. For a FAT or FAT32 volume, you see output similar to the following:

```
Volume Name : LogData
Volume Serial Number : 0x70692a2e
Max Component Length : 255
File System Name : FAT32
Preserves Case of filenames
Supports Unicode in filenames
```

Using NTFS

NTFS is an extensible and recoverable file system that offers many advantages over FAT, FAT32, and exFAT. Because it is extensible, the file system can be extended over time with various revisions. As you'll learn shortly, the version of NTFS that ships with Windows Server 2008 and Windows Server 2008 R2 was extended with new features, as was the version of NTFS that ships with Windows Server 2012, but all are designated as having the same internal version as the revision of the NTFS version that shipped with Microsoft Windows Server 2003. Because it is recoverable, volumes formatted with NTFS can be reconstructed if they contain structure errors. Typically, restructuring NTFS volumes is a task performed at startup.

NTFS structure

NTFS volumes have a very different structure and feature set from FAT volumes. The first area of the volume is the boot sector, which is located at sector 0 on the volume. The boot sector stores information about the disk layout, and a bootstrap program executes at startup and boots the operating system. A backup boot sector is placed at the end of the volume for redundancy and fault tolerance.

Instead of a file allocation table, NTFS uses a relational database to store information about files. This database is called the master file table (MFT). It stores a file record of each file and folder on the volume, pertinent volume information, and details on the MFT itself. The first 15 records in the MFT store NTFS metadata as summarized in Table 15-3.

Table 15-3 NTFS metadata

MFT Record	Record Type	File Name	Description
0	MFT	$Mft	Stores the base file record of each file and folder on the volume. As the number of files and folders grows, additional records are used as necessary.
1	MFT mirror	$MftMirr	Stores a partial duplicate of the MFT used for failure recovery. It's also referred to as MFT2.
2	Log file	$LogFile	Stores a persistent history of all changes made to files on the volume, which can be used to recover files.
3	Volume	$Volume	Stores volume attributes, including the volume serial number, version, and number of sectors.
4	Attribute definitions	$AttrDef	Stores a table of attribute names, numbers, and descriptions.
5	Root file name index	$	Stores the details on the volume's root directory.
6	Cluster bitmap	$Bitmap	Stores a table that details the clusters in use.
7	Boot sector	$Boot	Stores the bootstrap program on bootable volumes. Also includes the locations of the MFT and MFT mirror.
8	Bad cluster file	$BadClus	Stores a table mapping bad clusters.
9	Security file	$Secure	Stores the unique security descriptor for all files and folders on the volume.

MFT Record	Record Type	File Name	Description
10	Upcase table	$Upcase	Stores a table used to convert lowercase to matching uppercase Unicode characters.
11	NTFS extension file	$Extend	Stores information on enabled file-system extensions.
12–15	To be determined	To be determined	Reserved records for future use.

The MFT mirror stores a partial duplicate of the MFT that can be used to recover the MFT. If any of the records in the primary mirror become corrupted or are otherwise unreadable and there's a duplicate record in the MFT mirror, NTFS uses the data in the MFT mirror and, if possible, uses this data to recover the records in the primary MFT. It is also important to note that the NTFS version that shipped with Windows Server 2003 and later (NTFS 5.1) has a slightly different metadata mapping from the version that originally shipped with Windows 2000 (NTFS 5.0). In NTFS 5.1, the $LogFile and $Bitmap metadata files are located in a different position on disk than they were originally. This gives a performance advantage of 5 to 8 percent to disks that are formatted under NTFS 5.1 and comes close to approximating the performance of FAT.

NOTE

For NTFS, you typically refer to major version numbers rather than the major version and the revision number. Technically, however, Shadow Copy is a feature of NTFS 5.1 or later. With NTFS 5.1, you gain some additional enhancements, primarily the ability to use shadow copies.

The rest of the records in the MFT store file and folder information. Each of these regular entries includes the file or folder name, security descriptor, and other attributes, including file data or pointers to file data. The MFT record size is set when a volume is formatted and can be 1,024 bytes, 2,048 bytes, or 4,096 bytes, depending on the volume size. If a file is very small, all its contents might be able to fit in the data field of its record in the MFT. When all of a file's attributes, including its data, can be stored in the MFT record, the attributes are called *resident attributes*. Figure 15-2 shows an example of a small file with resident attributes.

If a file is larger than a single record, it has what are called *nonresident attributes*. Here, the file has a base record in the MFT that details where to find the file data. NTFS creates additional areas called *runs* on the disk to store the additional file data. The size of data runs depends on the cluster size of the volume. If the cluster size is 2 KBs or less, data runs are 2 KBs. If the cluster size is larger than 2 KBs, data runs are 4 KBs.

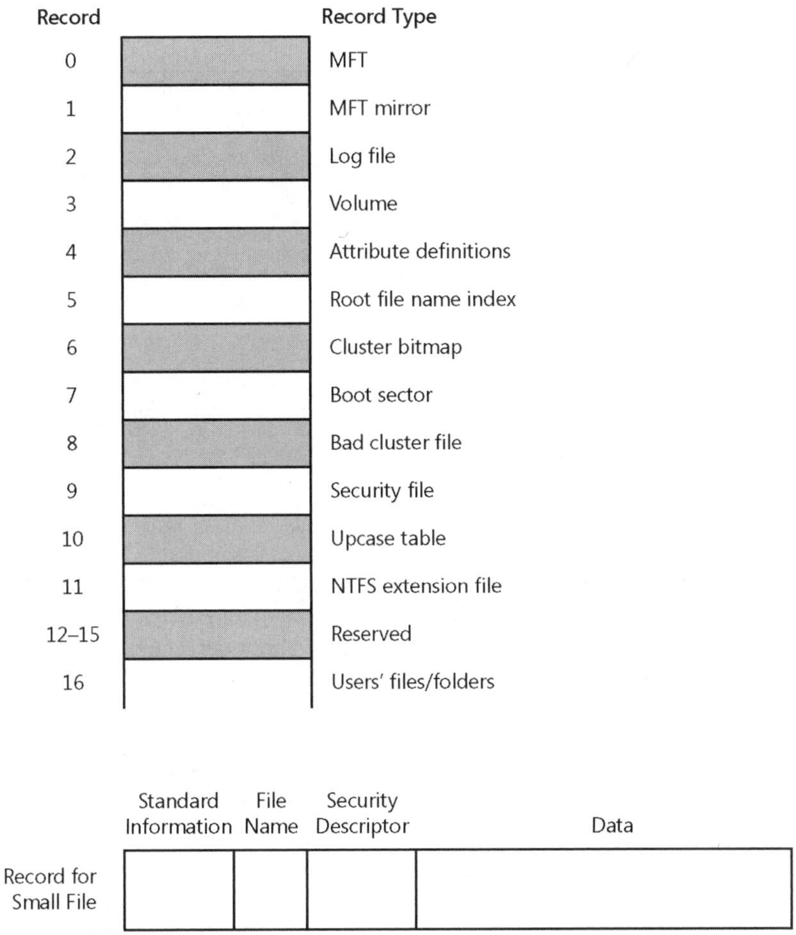

Record	Record Type
0	MFT
1	MFT mirror
2	Log file
3	Volume
4	Attribute definitions
5	Root file name index
6	Cluster bitmap
7	Boot sector
8	Bad cluster file
9	Security file
10	Upcase table
11	NTFS extension file
12–15	Reserved
16	Users' files/folders

	Standard Information	File Name	Security Descriptor	Data
Record for Small File				

Figure 15-2 This figure is a graphical depiction of the MFT and its records.

As Figure 15-3 shows, clusters belonging to the file are referenced in the MFT, using virtual cluster numbers (VCNs). VCNs are numbered sequentially, starting with VCN 0. The Data field in the file's MFT record maps the VCNs to a starting logical cluster number (LCN) on the disk and details the number of clusters to read for that VCN. When these mappings use up all the available space in a record, additional MFT records are created to store the additional mappings.

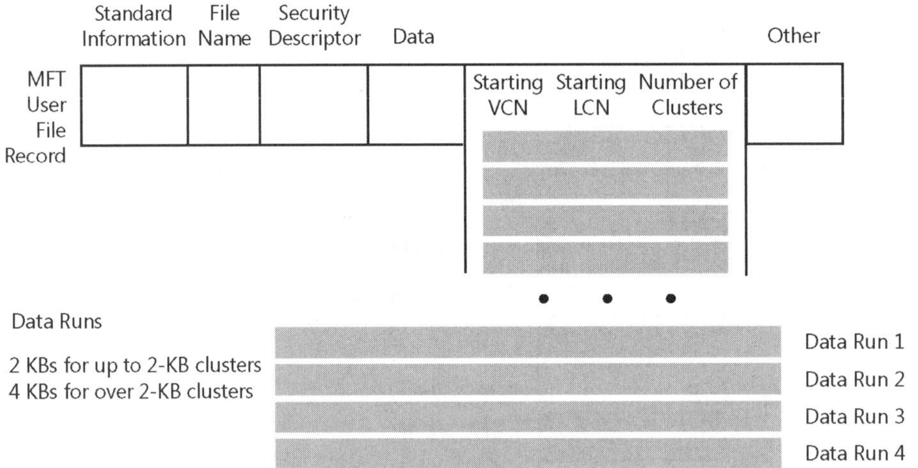

Figure 15-3 This figure shows a graphical depiction of a user file record with data runs.

In addition to the MFT, NTFS reserves a contiguous range of space past the end of the MFT called the *MFT zone*. By default, the MFT zone is approximately 12.5 percent of the total volume space. The MFT zone enables the MFT to grow without becoming fragmented. Typically, the MFT zone shrinks as the MFT grows.

The MFT zone is not used to store user data unless the remainder of the volume becomes full. Fragmentation can and still does occur, however. On volumes with lots of small files, the MFT can use up the MFT zone, and as additional files are added, the MFT has to grow into unreserved areas of the volume. On volumes with just a few large files, the unreserved space on a volume can be used up before the MFT, and in this case, the files start using the MFT zone space.

Inside OUT

The MFT zone can be optimized

By default, the MFT is optimized for environments that have a mix of large and small files. This setting works well if the average file size is 8 KBs or larger. It doesn't work so well if a volume has many very small files, such as when the average size of files is less than 2 KBs or between 2 KBs and 7 KBs. Here, you might want to configure the volume so that it has a larger MFT zone than normal to help prevent the MFT from becoming fragmented. The MFT zone size is set as eighths of the disk.

> You can determine the current MFT zone setting by typing the following command at the command prompt: **fsutil behavior query mftzone**. If this command returns "mft-zone=0," the MFT zone is using the default setting. The default setting, 0, specifies that the MFT zone should use one-eighth (12.5 percent) of the total volume space. This is the same as a setting of 1. You can also use a setting of 2, 3, or 4 to set the MFT zone to use two-eighths (25 percent), three-eighths (37.5 percent), or four-eighths (50 percent) of the total volume space.
>
> You can configure the MFT zone by typing **fsutil behavior set mftzone Value**, where *Value* is the relative size setting to use, such as 2.

NTFS features

Several versions of NTFS are available. NTFS 5.1 is the version of NTFS that was first included in Windows XP and Windows Server 2003. NTFS 5.1 with Local File System (LFS) 2.0 was first included with Windows 8 and Windows Server 2012.

You have the following capabilities when you use NTFS 5.0:

- Advanced file and folder access permissions
- Data streams and change journals
- Encrypting File System (EFS)
- File sharing and full-control remote access to files and folders
- Long file names, meaning file and folder names can contain up to 255 characters
- Reparse points, remote storage, and shadow copies
- Sparse files, disk quotas, and object identifiers
- Unicode characters in file and folder names
- Uppercase and lowercase letters in file and folder names

NTFS 5.1 provides some additional enhancements, primarily the ability to use shadow copies. In similar fashion, NTFS 5.1 with Local File System (LFS) 2.0 also provides some additional enhancements, primarily related to self-healing technology used with Check Disk (Chkdsk.exe) and the update sequence number (USN) change journal. Specifically, NTFS and ReFS use version 2.0 change-journal records by default, which contain 64-bit identifiers. ReFS also implements version 3.0 records, which contain 128-bit identifiers.

Windows Server automatically sets the size of clusters and the number of sectors per cluster based on the size of the volume. Cluster sizes range from 512 bytes to 64 KBs. As with FAT, NTFS has the following characteristics:

- Disk geometry also is a factor in determining cluster size because the number of clusters on the volume must fit into the number of bits the file system uses.
- The actual amount of data you can store on a single NTFS volume is a factor of the maximum cluster size and the maximum number of clusters you can use per volume.

Thus, although volumes have a specific maximum size, the cluster size used on a volume can be a limiting factor. For example, a dynamic volume with a 4 KB cluster size can have dynamic volumes up to 16 TBs, which is different from the maximum allowed dynamic volume size on NTFS.

Analyzing the NTFS structure

If you want to examine the structure of a volume formatted using NTFS, you can use the FSUtil FSinfo command to do this. Type **fsutil fsinfo ntfsinfo *DriveDesignator*** at the command prompt, where *DriveDesignator* is the drive letter of the volume followed by a colon. For example, if you want to obtain information on the C drive, you type

```
fsutil fsinfo ntfsinfo c:
```

The output would be similar to the following:

```
NTFS Volume Serial Number :       0xbcf4c873f4c82125
NTFS Version   :                  3.1
LFS Version    :                  2.0
Number Sectors :                  0x000000001d3c57ff
Total Clusters :                  0x0000000003a78aff
Free Clusters  :                  0x00000000035e477d
Total Reserved :                  0x000000000001e2b0
Bytes Per Sector  :               512
Bytes Per Physical Sector :       512
Bytes Per Cluster :               4096
Bytes Per FileRecord Segment    : 1024
Clusters Per FileRecord Segment : 0
Mft Valid Data Length :           0x0000000004e00000
Mft Start Lcn  :                  0x00000000000c0000
Mft2 Start Lcn :                  0x0000000000000002
Mft Zone Start :                  0x00000000000c4e00
Mft Zone End   :                  0x00000000000cc820
Resource Manager Identifier :     CBDD98AD-E33F-11E1-95F2-C407271F80D4
```

As Table 15-4 shows, FSUtil FSinfo provides detailed information on the NTFS volume structure, including space usage and configuration.

Table 15-4 Details from FSUtil FSinfo

Field	Description
NTFS Volume Serial Number	The unique serial number of the selected NTFS volume.
NTFS Version	The internal NTFS version. Here, 3.1 refers to NTFS 5.1.
Number Sectors	The total number of sectors on the volume in hexadecimal.
Total Clusters	The total number of clusters on the volume in hexadecimal.
Free Clusters	The number of unused clusters on the volume in hexadecimal.
Total Reserved	The total number of clusters reserved for NTFS metadata.
Bytes Per Sector	The number of bytes per sector.
Bytes Per Cluster	The number of bytes per cluster.
Bytes Per FileRecord Segment	The size of MFT file records.
Clusters Per FileRecord Segment	The number of clusters per file record segment, which is valid only if the file record size is as large as or larger than the volume cluster size.
Mft Valid Data Length	The current size of the MFT.
Mft Start Lcn	The location of the first LCN on the disk the MFT uses.
Mft2 Start Lcn	The location of the first LCN on the disk the MFT mirror uses.
Mft Zone Start	The cluster number that marks the start of the region on the disk the MFT reserves.
Mft Zone End	The cluster number that marks the end of the region on the disk the MFT reserves.

Using FSUtil, you can also obtain detailed statistics on NTFS metadata and user file usage since a system was started. To view this information, type **fsutil fsinfo statistics *DriveDesignator*** at the command prompt, where *DriveDesignator* is the drive letter of the volume followed by a colon. For example, if you want to obtain information on the C drive, you type:

```
fsutil fsinfo statistics c:
```

The output is shown in two sections. The first section of the statistics details user file and disk activity and the overall usage of NTFS metadata. As shown in this example, the output shows the number of reads and writes and the number of bytes read or written:

```
File System Type :      NTFS
UserFileReads :         31441
UserFileReadBytes :     857374720
UserDiskReads :         31584
```

CHAPTER 15

```
UserFileWrites :        6302
UserFileWriteBytes :    197198336
UserDiskWrites :        6505
MetaDataReads :         3168
MetaDataReadBytes :     21770240
MetaDataDiskReads :     4165
MetaDataWrites :        3883
MetaDataWriteBytes :    16805888
MetaDataDiskWrites :    4644
```

The second section of the statistics details usage of individual NTFS metadata files. As shown in this example, the output details the number of reads and writes and the number of bytes read or written for each NTFS metadata file:

```
MftReads :              2962
MftReadBytes :          12132352
MftWrites :             2460
MftWriteBytes :         10465280
Mft2Writes :            0
Mft2WriteBytes :        0
RootIndexReads :        0
RootIndexReadBytes :    0
RootIndexWrites :       0
RootIndexWriteBytes :   0
BitmapReads :           8
BitmapReadBytes :       8388608
BitmapWrites :          847
BitmapWriteBytes :      3796992
MftBitmapReads :        1
MftBitmapReadBytes :    65536
MftBitmapWrites :       107
MftBitmapWriteBytes :   442368
UserIndexReads :        1086
UserIndexReadBytes :    4448256
UserIndexWrites :       711
UserIndexWriteBytes :   3153920
LogFileReads :          8
LogFileReadBytes :      32768
LogFileWrites :         5895
LogFileWriteBytes :     36777984
LogFileFull :           0
```

Advanced NTFS features

NTFS has many advanced features that administrators should know about and understand. These features include the following:

- Hard links
- Data streams

- Change journals
- Object identifiers
- Reparse points
- Sparse files
- Transactions

Each of these features is discussed in the sections that follow.

Hard links

Every file created on a volume has a hard link. The hard link is the directory entry for the file, and it is what enables the operating system to find files within folders. On NTFS volumes, files can have multiple hard links. This allows a single file to appear in the same directory with multiple names or to appear in multiple directories with the same name or different names. As with file copies, applications can open a file by using any of the hard links you've created and can modify the file. If you use another hard link to open the file in another application, the application can detect the changes.

Wondering why you'd want to use hard links? Hard links are useful when you want the same file to appear in several locations. For example, you might want a document to appear in a folder of a network share that is available to all users but have an application that requires the document to be in another directory so that it can be read and processed on a daily basis. Rather than moving the file to the application directory and giving every user in the company access to this protected directory, you decide to create a hard link to the document so that it can be accessed separately by both users and the application.

Regardless of how many hard links a file has, the related directory entries all point to the single file that exists in one location on the volume—and this is how hard links differ from copies. With a copy of a file, the file data exists in multiple locations. With a hard link, the file appears in multiple locations but exists in only one location. Thus, if you modify a file by using one of its hard links and save the file, and then someone opens the file using a different hard link, the changes are shown.

> NOTE
>
> **Hard links have advantages and disadvantages. Hard links are not meant for environments in which multiple users can modify a file simultaneously. If Sandra opens a file using one hard link and is working on the file at the same time Bob is working on the file, there can be problems if they both try to save changes. Although this is a disadvantage of hard links, the big advantage of hard links shouldn't be overlooked: if a file has multiple hard links, the file will not be deleted from the volume until all hard links**

are deleted. This means that if someone accidentally were to delete a file that had multiple hard links, the file wouldn't actually be deleted. Instead, only the affected hard link would be deleted. Any other hard links and the file itself would remain.

Because there is only one physical copy of a file with multiple hard links, the hard links do not have separate security descriptors. Only the source file has security descriptors. Thus, if you were to change the access permissions of a file by using any of its hard links, you would actually change the security of the source file and all hard links that point to this file would have these security settings.

You can create hard links by using the FSUtil Hardlink command. Use the following syntax:

```
fsutil hardlink create NewFilePath CurrentFilePath
```

Here, *NewFilePath* is the file path for the hard link you want to create, and *CurrentFilePath* is the name of the existing file to which you are linking. For example, if the file ChangeLog.doc is found in the file path C:\CorpDocs and you want to create a new hard link to this file with the file path C:\UserData\Logs\CurrentLog.doc, you would type

```
fsutil hardlink create C:\UserData\Logs\CurrentLog.doc C:\CorpDocs\ChangeLog.doc
```

Hard links can be created only on NTFS volumes, and you cannot create a hard link on one volume that refers to another volume. Following this logic, you couldn't create a hard link to the D drive for a file created on the C drive.

Data streams

Every file created on a volume has a data stream associated with it. A data stream is a sequence of bytes that contains the contents of the file. The main data stream for a file is unnamed and is visible to all file systems. On NTFS volumes, files can also have named data streams associated with them. Named data streams contain additional information about a file, such as custom properties or summary details. This enables you to associate additional information with a file but still manage the file as a single unit.

After you create a named data stream and associate it with a file, any applications that know how to work with named data streams can access the streams by their names and read the additional details. Many applications support named data streams, including Microsoft Office, Adobe Acrobat, and other productivity applications. This is how you can set summary properties for a Microsoft Word document—such as Title, Subject, and Author—and save that information with the file.

In fact, if you press and hold or right-click any file on an NTFS volume, select Properties, and then tap or click the Details tab, you can see information that is associated with the file using a data stream, as shown in Figure 15-4.

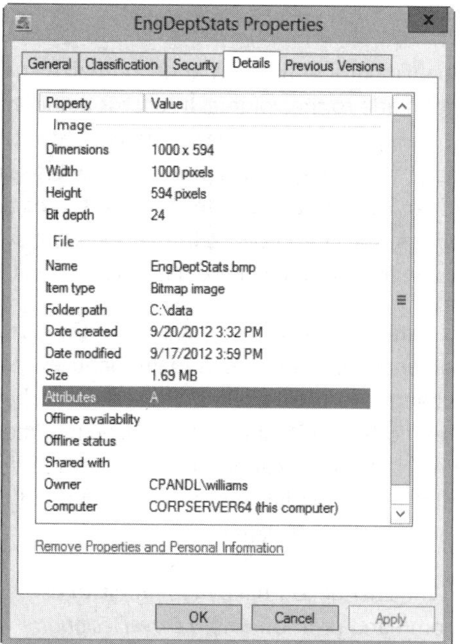

Figure 15-4 Information entered on the Details tab is saved to a named data stream.

Generally speaking, the named data streams associated with a file are used to set the names of its property tabs and to populate the fields of those tabs. This is how other tabs can be associated with some document types and how the Windows operating system can store a thumbnail image within an NTFS file containing an image.

The most important thing to know about streams is that they aren't supported on FAT. If you move or copy a file containing named streams to a FAT volume, you might see the warning prompt labeled "Confirm Stream Loss" telling you additional information is associated with the file and asking you to confirm that it's okay that the file is saved without this information. If you tap or click Yes, only the contents of the file are copied or moved to the FAT volume—and not the contents of the associated data streams. If you tap or click No, the copy or save operation is canceled.

In a file's Properties dialog box on the Details tab, you also have the option of removing properties and personal information associated with a file. You do this by tapping or clicking the Remove Properties And Personal Information link and then selecting a Remove Properties method. Windows accomplishes this task by removing the values from the related data streams associated with the file.

Change journals

An NTFS volume can use an update sequence number (USN) change journal. A change journal provides a complete log of all changes made to the volume. It records additions, deletions, and modifications regardless of who made them or how the additions, deletions, and modifications occurred. As with system logs, the change log is persistent, so it isn't reset if you shut down and restart the operating system. The operating system writes records to the NTFS change log when an NTFS checkpoint occurs. The checkpoint tells the operating system to write changes that would enable NTFS to recover from failure to a particular point in time.

The change journal is enabled when you install certain services, including distributed file system (DFS). Domain controllers and any other computer in the domain that uses these services rely heavily on the change journal. The change journal enables these services to be very efficient at determining when files, folders, and other NTFS objects have been modified. Rather than checking time stamps and registering for file notifications, these services perform direct lookups in the change journal to determine all the modifications made to a set of files. Not only is this faster, it also uses system resources more efficiently.

You can gather summary statistics about the change journal by typing **fsutil usn queryjournal *DriveDesignator*** at the command prompt, where *DriveDesignator* is the drive letter of the volume followed by a colon. For example, if you want to obtain change journal statistics on the C drive, you type:

```
fsutil usn queryjournal c:
```

The output is similar to the following:

```
Usn Journal ID    : 0x01cd77459da4462a
First Usn         : 0x0000000000000000
Next Usn          : 0x0000000002573bf8
Lowest Valid Usn : 0x0000000000000000
Max Usn           : 0x7fffffffffff0000
Maximum Size      : 0x0000000020000000
Allocation Delta : 0x0000000000400000
Minimum record version supported : 2
Maximum record version supported : 2
```

The details show the following information:

- **Usn Journal ID.** The unique identifier of the current change journal. A journal is assigned an identifier on creation and can be stamped with a new ID. NTFS and ReFS use this identifier for an integrity check.
- **First Usn.** The number of the first record that can be read from the journal.
- **Next Usn.** The number of the next record to be written to the journal.

- **Lowest Valid Usn.** The first record that was written into this journal instance. If a journal has a *First Usn* value lower than the *Lowest Valid Usn*, the journal has been stamped with a new identifier since the last USN was written (and this could indicate a discontinuity where changes to some or all files or directories on the volume might have occurred but are not recorded in the change journal).
- **Max Usn.** The highest USN that can be assigned.
- **Maximum Size.** The maximum size in bytes that the change journal can use. On NTFS, if the change journal exceeds this value, older entries are overwritten by truncating the journal at the next NTFS checkpoint.
- **Allocation Delta.** On NTFS, the size in bytes of disk memory that is added to the end and removed from the beginning of the change journal when it becomes full. This is not used with ReFS.
- **Minimum Record Version Supported.** The minimum supported version of USN records, as supported by the file system.
- **Maximum Record Version Supported.** The maximum supported version of USN records, as supported by the file system.

Individual records written to the change journal look like this:

```
File Ref#        :                          0x18e90000000018e9
ParentFile Ref#  :                          0x17c00000000017c0
Usn              :                          0x0000000000000000
SecurityId       :                          0x00000119
Reason           :                          0x00000000
Name (024)       :                          ocmanage.dll
```

The most important information here is the name of the affected file and the security identifier of the object that made the change. You can get the most recent change journal entry for a file by typing **fsutil usn readdata *FilePath***, where *FilePath* is the name of the file for which you want to retrieve change information. For example, if you want to obtain the most recent change journal information on a file with the path C:\DomainComputers.txt, you type:

```
fsutil usn readdata c:\domaincomputers.txt
```

The output is similar to the following:

```
Major Version     :                         0x2
Minor Version     :                         0x0
FileRef#          :                         0x000800000001c306
Parent FileRef#   :                         0x0005000000000005
Usn               :                         0x00000000237cf7f0
Time Stamp        :                         0x0000000000000000
Reason            :                         0x0
```

```
Source Info       :                    0x0
Security Id       :                    0x45e
File Attributes   :                    0x20
File Name Length  :                    0x26
File Name Offset  :                    0x3c
FileName          :                    domaincomputers.txt
```

This data shows the file's reference number in the root file index and that of its parent. It also shows the current USN associated with the file and the file attributes flag. The File Name Length element shows the total length in characters of the file's long and short file names together. This particular file has a file name length of 38 (0×26). That's because the file name has more than eight characters followed by a dot and a three-letter extension. This means the file is represented by NTFS, using long and short file names. The long file name is domain-computers.txt. This is followed by an offset pointer that indicates where the short file name, domain~1.txt, can be looked up, which is where the total file name length of 38 characters comes from.

NOTE

You can examine a file's short file name by typing dir /x *FilePath* at the command prompt, where *FilePath* is the path to the file you want to examine, such as: dir /x c:\domaincomputers.txt.

IMPORTANT

Version 2 records will have a 64-bit FileReferenceNumber and a 64-bit ParentFileReferenceNumber. Version 3 records will have a 128-bit FileReferenceNumber and a 128-bit ParentFileReferenceNumber.

Object identifiers

Another feature of NTFS is the ability to use object identifiers. Object identifiers are 16 bytes in length and are unique on a per-volume basis. Any file that has an object identifier also has the following:

- Birth volume identifier (BirthVolumeID), which is the object identifier for the volume in which the file was originally created
- Birth object identifier (BirthObjectID), which is the object identifier assigned to the file when it was created
- Domain identifier (DomainID), which is the object identifier for the domain in which the file was created

These values are also 16 bytes in length. If a file is moved within a volume or moved to a new volume, it is assigned a new object identifier, but information about the original object identifier assigned when the object was created can be retained by using the birth object identifier.

Several system services use object identifiers to identify files uniquely and identify the volumes with which they are associated. The Distributed Link Tracking (DLT) Client service uses object identifiers to track linked files that are moved within an NTFS volume, to another NTFS volume on the same computer, or to an NTFS volume on another computer.

Any file the DLT Client service uses has an object identifier field set containing values for the object ID, birth volume ID, birth object ID, and domain ID. The actual field set looks like this:

```
Object ID :                 52eac013e3d34445334345453533ab3d
BirthVolume ID :            a23bc3243a5a3452d32424332c32343d
BirthObject ID :            52eac013e3d34445334345453533ab3d
Domain ID :                 00000000000000000000000000000000
```

Here, the file has a specific object ID, birth volume ID, and birth object ID. The domain ID isn't assigned, however, because this is not currently used. You can tell that the the DLT Client service uses the file because the birth volume ID and birth object ID have been assigned and these identifiers are used only by this service. Because the birth volume ID and birth object ID remain the same even if a file is moved, the DLT Client service uses these identifiers to find files no matter where they have been moved.

If you are trying to determine whether the DLT Client service uses a file, you could use the FSUtil ObjectID command to see whether the file has an object identifier field set. Type **fsutil objectid query *FilePath*** at the command prompt, where *FilePath* is the path to the file or folder you want to examine. If the file has an object identifier field set, it is displayed. If a file doesn't have an object identifier field set, an error message appears, stating, "The specified file has no object ID."

Reparse points

On NTFS volumes, a file or folder can contain a reparse point. Reparse points are file system objects with special attribute tags that are used to extend the functionality in the I/O subsystem. When a program sets a reparse point, it stores an attribute tag and a data segment. The attribute tag identifies the purpose of the reparse point and details how the reparse point is to be used. The data segment provides any additional data needed during reparsing.

Reparse points are used for directory junction points and volume mount points. Directory junctions enable you to create a single local namespace by using local folders, local volumes, and network shares. Mount points enable you to mount a local volume to an empty NTFS folder. Both directory junction points and volume mount points use reparse points to mark NTFS folders with surrogate names.

When a file or folder containing a reparse point used for a directory junction point or a volume mount point is read, the reparse point causes the path to be reparsed and a surrogate name to be substituted for the original name. For example, if you were to create a mount point with the file path C:\Data that is used to mount a hard disk drive, the reparse point is triggered whenever the file system opens C:\Data and points the file system to the volume you mounted in that folder. The actual attribute tag and data for the reparse point would look similar to the following:

```
Reparse Tag Value :  0xa0000003
Tag value : Microsoft
Tag value : Name Surrogate
Tag value : Mount Point
Substitute Name offset :   0
Substitute Name length :   98
Print Name offset :  100
Print Name Length :  0
Substitute Name :  \??\Volume{3796c3c1-5106-11d7-911c-806d6172696f}\

Reparse Data Length : 0x0000006e
Reparse Data :
0000 : 00 00 62 00 64 00 00 00  5c 00 3f 00 3f 00 5c 00  ..b.d...\.?.?.\.
0010 : 56 00 6f 00 6c 00 75 00  6d 00 65 00 7b 00 33 00  V.o.l.u.m.e.{.3.
0020 : 37 00 39 00 36 00 63 00  33 00 63 00 31 00 2d 00  7.9.6.c.3.c.1.-.
0030 : 35 00 31 00 30 00 36 00  2d 00 31 00 31 00 64 00  5.1.0.6.-.1.1.d.
0040 : 37 00 2d 00 39 00 31 00  31 00 63 00 2d 00 38 00  7.-.9.1.1.c.-.8.
0050 : 30 00 36 00 64 00 36 00  31 00 37 00 32 00 36 00  0.6.d.6.1.7.2.6.
0060 : 39 00 36 00 66 00 7d 00  5c 00 00 00 00 00        9.6.f.}.\.....
```

The reparse attribute tag is defined by the first series of values, which identifies the reparse point as a Microsoft Name Surrogate Mount Point and specifies the surrogate name to be substituted for the original name. The reparse data follows the attribute tag values and, in this case, provides the fully expressed surrogate name.

Examine reparse points

By using the FSUtil ReparsePoint command, you can examine reparse information associated with a file or folder. Type fsutil reparsepoint query *FilePath* at the command prompt, where *FilePath* is the path to the file or folder you want to examine.

Reparse points are also used by file-system filter drivers to mark files so that they are used with that driver. When NTFS opens a file associated with a file-system filter driver, it locates the driver and uses the filter to process the file as directed by the reparse information. Reparse points are used in this way to implement Remote Storage, which is discussed in the next section.

Sparse files

Often, scientific or other data collected through sampling is stored in large files that are primarily empty except for sparsely populated sections that contain the actual data. For example, a broad-spectrum signal recorded digitally from space might have only several minutes of audio for each hour of actual recording. In this case, a multiple-gigabyte audio file such as the one depicted in Figure 15-5 might have only a few gigabytes of meaningful information. Because there are large sections of empty space and limited areas of meaningful data, the file is said to be sparsely populated and can be referred to as a *sparse file*.

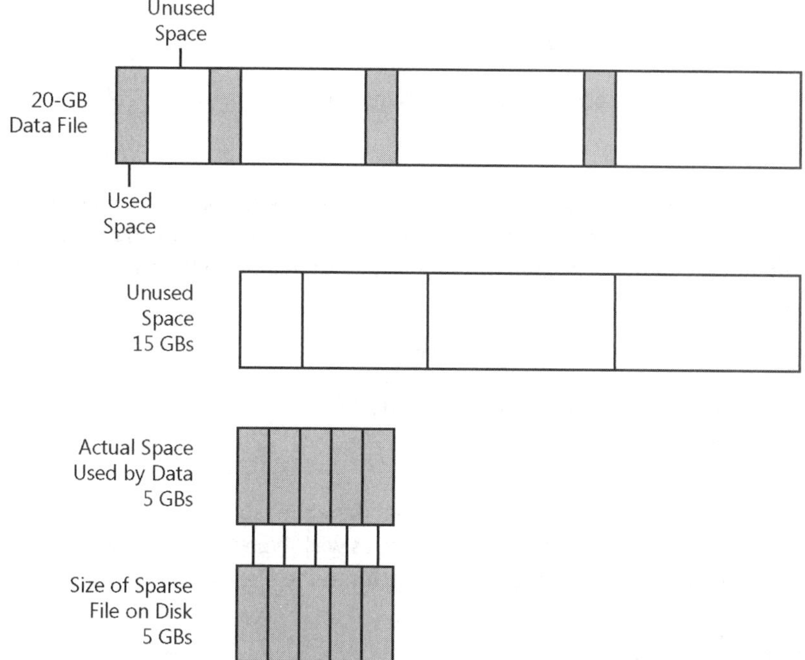

Figure 15-5 This figure shows sparse file usage.

Stored normally, the file would use 20 GBs of space on the volume. If you mark the file as sparse, however, NTFS allocates space only for actual data and marks empty space as unallocated. In other words, any meaningful or nonzero data is marked as allocated and written to disk, and any data composed of zeros is marked as unallocated and is not explicitly written to disk. In this example, this means the file uses only 5 GBs of space, which is marked as allocated, and has unallocated space of 15 GBs.

For unallocated space, NTFS records only information about how much unallocated space there is, and when you try to read data in this space, it returns zeros. This enables NTFS to store the file in the smallest amount of disk space possible while still being able to reconstruct the file's allocated and unallocated space.

In theory, all this works great, but it is up to the actual program working with the sparse file to determine which data is meaningful and which isn't. Programs do this by explicitly specifying the data for which space should be allocated. In Windows Server 2012 R2, several services use sparse files. One of these is the Indexing Service, which stores its catalogs as sparse files.

Using the FSUtil Sparse command, you can easily determine whether a file has the sparse attribute set. Type **fsutil sparse queryflag *FilePath*** at the command prompt, where *FilePath* is the path to the file you want to examine, such as:

```
fsutil sparse queryflag c:\data\catalog.wci\00010002.ci
```

If the file has the sparse attribute, this command returns:

```
This file is set as sparse
```


You can examine sparse files to determine where the byte ranges that contain meaningful (nonzero) data are located by using FSUtil Sparse as well. Type **fsutil sparse queryrange *FilePath*** at the command prompt, where *FilePath* is the path to the file you want to examine, such as:

```
fsutil sparse queryrange c:\data\catalog.wci\00010002.ci
```

The output is the byte ranges of meaningful data within the file, such as:

```
sparse range [0] [28672]
```

In this particular case, the output specifies that there's meaningful data from the start of the file to byte 28672. You can mark files as sparse as well. Type **fsutil sparse setflag *FilePath*** at the command prompt, where *FilePath* is the path to the file you want to mark as sparse.

Transactional NTFS

Windows Server 2012 R2 supports transactional NTFS and Self-Healing NTFS. Transactional NTFS allows file operations on an NTFS volume to be performed transactionally. This means programs can use a transaction to group sets of file and registry operations so that all of them succeed or none of them succeed. While a transaction is active, changes are not visible outside the transaction. Changes are committed and written fully to disk only when a transaction is completed successfully. If a transaction fails or is incomplete, the program rolls back the transactional work to restore the file system to the state it was in prior to the transaction.

Transactions that span multiple volumes are coordinated by the Kernel Transaction Manager (KTM). The KTM supports the independent recovery of volumes if a transaction fails. The local resource manager for a volume maintains a separate transaction log and is responsible for maintaining threads for transactions separate from threads that perform the file work.

By using the FSUtil Transaction command, you can easily determine transactional information. You can list currently running transactions by typing **fsutil transaction list** at the command prompt. You can display transactional information for a specific file by typing **fsutil transaction fileinfo *FilePath*** at the command prompt, where *FilePath* is the path to the file you want to examine, such as:

```
fsutil transaction fileinfo c:\journal\ls-dts.mdb
```

Traditionally, you had to use the Check Disk tool to fix errors and inconsistencies in NTFS volumes on a disk. Because this process can disrupt the availability of Windows systems, Windows Server 2012 R2 uses Self-Healing NTFS to protect file systems without having to use separate maintenance tools to fix problems. Because much of the self-healing process is enabled and performed automatically, you might need to perform volume maintenance manually only when the operating system notifies you that a problem cannot be corrected automatically. If such an error occurs, Windows Server 2012 R2 notifies you about the problem and provides possible solutions.

That said, with Windows 8.1 and Windows Server 2012 R2, self-healing has been enhanced and extended to work better with Check Disk. These improvements enable you to use Check Disk to correct many types of inconsistencies and errors on live (online) volumes, whereas Check Disk previously could perform these types of corrections only with offline volumes.

By using Self-Healing NTFS, the file system is always available and does not need to be corrected offline (in most cases). Self-Healing NTFS does the following:

- Attempts to preserve as much data as possible if corruption occurs, and reduces failed file-system mounting that previously could occur if a volume was known to have errors or inconsistencies. Self-Healing NTFS can repair a volume immediately so that it can be mounted.
- Reports changes made to the volume during repair through existing Chkdsk.exe mechanisms, directory notifications, and USN journal entries. This feature also enables authorized users and administrators to monitor repair operations through status messages.
- Can recover a volume if the boot sector is readable but does not identify an NTFS volume. In this case, you must run an offline tool that repairs the boot sector and then allow Self-Healing NTFS to initiate recovery.

Although Self-Healing NTFS can correct many types of inconsistencies and errors automatically, some issues can be resolved only by running Check Disk (Chkdsk.exe) and allowing Check Disk to work with NTFS to resolve the problems, as discussed earlier in this chapter under "NTFS features."

Inside OUT

Understanding journaling and torn writes

NTFS relies on a journal of transactions to ensure consistency. NTFS updates metadata in place on the disk and uses a journal to track changes, which allows rollback to occur on errors and during recovery. Maintaining metadata in place offers advantages for read performance but can cause writes that are randomized. Updates to a disk can corrupt previously written metadata if power is lost at the time of the write. This is also known as a *torn write*.

Using ReFS

Resilient File System (ReFS), the next-generation file system available with Windows Server 2012 R2, is built on the foundation of NTFS and designed specifically for storage technologies. As such, many of its best features are available only when the file system is used with the new storage technology from Microsoft called Storage Spaces. Although ReFS is not available for Windows desktop operating systems at the time of this writing, Windows desktop operating systems can access data stored on ReFS volumes just as they do data shared from NTFS volumes.

ReFS features

As Table 15-5 shows, ReFS maintains compatibility with key aspects of NTFS, particularly when it comes to security features such as access permissions and share permissions. However, ReFS diverges when it comes to extended features, including support for compression, encryption, and disk quotas. Furthermore, you cannot boot from ReFS or use ReFS with removable media.

Table 15-5 Comparing NTFS and ReFS

Feature	NTFS	ReFS
Preserves and enforces access control lists (ACLs)	Yes	Yes
Preserves the case of file names	Yes	Yes
Supports ACLs	Yes	Yes
Supports BitLocker encryption	Yes	Yes
Supports booting from the file system	Yes	No
Supports case-sensitive file names	Yes	Yes
Supports disk quotas	Yes	No

Feature	NTFS	ReFS
Supports Encrypted File System	Yes	No
Supports extended attributes	Yes	No
Supports file-based compression	Yes	No
Supports hard links	Yes	No
Supports named streams	Yes	No
Supports object identifiers	Yes	No
Supports opening by FileID	Yes	Yes
Supports removable media	Yes	No
Supports reparse points	Yes	Yes
Supports shadow copies	Yes	Yes
Supports short names	Yes	No
Supports sparse files	Yes	Yes
Supports Unicode in file names	Yes	Yes
Supports user data transactions	Yes	No
Supports USN journal	Yes	Yes
Supports volume snapshots	Yes	Yes

Not only are the transactional and self-healing features of NTFS important components of ReFS, but ReFS extends these features in several ways to allow for the automatic verification and online correction of data. ReFS avoids the possibility of torn writes by not writing metadata in place and optimizes for extreme scale by using scalable structures. To provide full end-to-end resilience, ReFS integrates fully with Storage Spaces. This integration does the following:

- Allows for large volume, file, and directory sizes
- Provides data striping for performance and redundancy for fault tolerance
- Provides disk scrubbing and salvage to provide online protection against latent disk errors
- Ensures metadata integrity with checksums
- Provides pooling and virtualizing storage with load balancing and sharing across servers
- Provides optional user data integrity by using integrity streams
- Uses copy on write for improved disk update performance

ReFS reuses the code that implements the file-system semantics of NTFS to ensure compatibility with existing file-system application programming interfaces (APIs). This ensures that the core of the file-system interface is the same and that file operations—including read, write, open, change notification, and close—work in exactly the same way. When working with ReFS, Windows maintains the in-memory file and volume state, enforces security, and maintains memory caching and the synchronization of file data in exactly the same way as with NTFS.

ReFS structures

Where NTFS and ReFS differ greatly is in the on-disk store engine underneath the file-system interface. The on-disk store engine is what implements the on-disk structures such as the MFT. As discussed earlier in the chapter, the MFT represents files and directories by storing a file record of each file and folder on the volume along with pertinent volume information and details on the MFT itself.

The on-disk store engine for NTFS is NTFS.SYS. The on-disk store engine for ReFS is REFS.SYS. REFS.SYS was designed specifically for ReFS.

ReFS uses B+ tree structures to represent all information on the disk. B+ trees scale well from very small, compact structures to very large, multilevel structures, and using B+ trees simplifies the architecture and reduces the size of the code base.

The on-disk store engine uses enumerable tables with sets of key-value pairs. Access into most tables is provided by a unique object identifier, which is stored in a special object table that forms the base of the B+ tree.

The object table at the base of the B+ tree contains a disk offset and checksum for each unique object ID. This makes the object table the root of all structures within the file system. The entries in the object table refer to directories and global system metadata.

As shown in Figure 15-6, directories are represented as tables rooted within the object table. Each directory has an object identifier that acts as a key in the object table, and it has a corresponding value that provides a disk offset for where the table is found on the volume along with a checksum. The directory table contains rows that identify the files in the directory by file name and metadata. File metadata, in turn, identifies file attributes and their actual values. Among these values is a table of offset mappings to file extents. This table contains rows identifying file extents, paired with values that provide the disk offset location for each file extent and an optional checksum. Each file extent contains a section of the data for the parent file.

Inside OUT

Metadata checksums in ReFS

To ensure data integrity, checksums are used with all ReFS metadata. The checksum is stored at the level of a B+ tree page and stored independently of the page itself. Storing the checksum in this way ensures that just about every form of disk corruption can be detected. In addition, by using optional integrity streams, checksums can be added to ensure the integrity of file contents. When integrity streams are enabled, ReFS uses an allocate-on-write approach by which file changes are always written to a location different from the original one. Allocate-on-write ensures that preexisting data is not lost due to a new write. The checksum is updated with the data write to ensure that a consistently verifiable version of a file is always available and that errors and disk corruption can be detected. Because integrity streams reallocate blocks every time file content is changed, they're not appropriate for some applications, such as database systems. Why? Some applications maintain their own checksums of file content and can independently verify and correct data by using the APIs available for Storage Spaces.

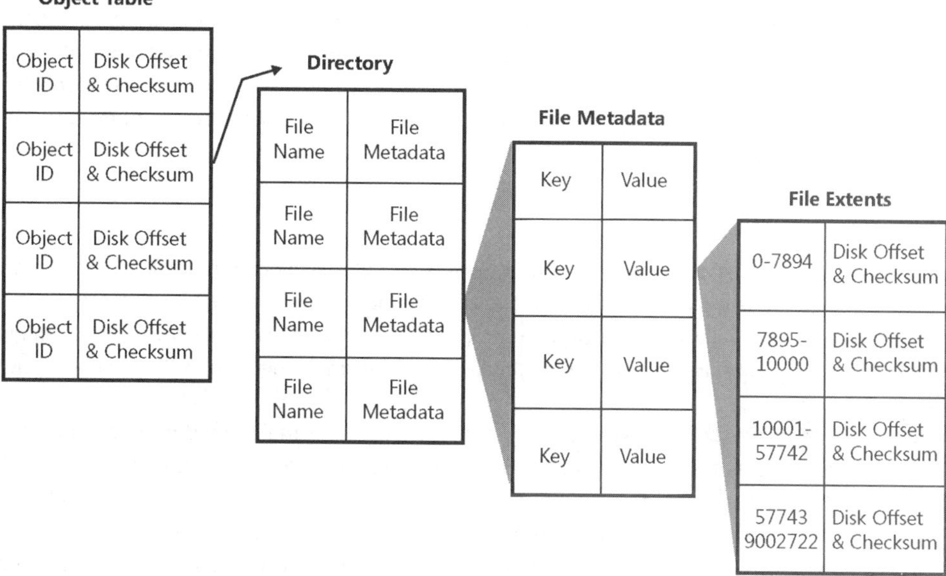

Figure 15-6 This figure shows file structures in ReFS.

Put another way, directories are represented as tables in the file structure. Files are embedded within rows of a directory table and are themselves tables containing rows of file metadata.

The file metadata also represented as a table has a row for each file attribute paired with the related value. Within the file metadata is an embedded table containing rows that identify file extents and provide offset locations to the extents on the volume along with optional checksums.

Other global structures are represented within the file system as tables as well. As an example, ACLs are represented as tables rooted within the object table.

ReFS advantages

ReFS supports file sizes up to 264 – 1 bytes, 264 files in a directory, 264 directories on a volume, and volume sizes up to 278 bytes using 16 KB cluster sizes (in contrast, Windows stack addressing allows 264 bytes). Because B+ trees scale with extreme efficiency, ReFS volumes can perform well whether they contain very large directories, very large files, or both. Disk space allocation is managed using a hierarchical allocator. This allocator represents free space as tables of free-space ranges. Each table has a different level of granularity so that large free-space ranges can be allocated as easily as medium or small free-space ranges, and all are relative to the volume size and available free space.

> NOTE
>
> **ReFS supports large numbers of files and directories by using 128-bit file identifiers. ReFS returns a 128-bit file identifier associated with an opened handle along with the 64-bit volume identifier. For backward compatibility, a 64-bit file identifier can be obtained from the API, but applications making incorrect calls into this API might crash.**

> IMPORTANT
>
> **ReFS uses hierarchical allocators to find optimal allocation quickly. Having a hierarchical allocation system allows related metadata blocks to be placed closer to one another naturally. By consulting the proper layer of the allocator hierarchy, ReFS can quickly determine the best possible placement for small, medium, or large allocations.**

One of the disadvantages of NTFS is that metadata is maintained in place, and this can result in writes that are randomized and in torn writes. ReFS improves reliability and eliminates torn writes by using an allocate-on-write approach. Here, rather than updating metadata in place, the file system writes it to a different location. This technique sometimes is also referred to as *shadow paging*. The transaction architecture, derived from NTFS, is built on top of the allocate-on-write framework to provide failure recovery.

ReFS allocates metadata by using B+ tree structures that allow for fewer, larger reads and writes. It does this by combining related data, such as stream allocations, file attributes, file names, and directory pages. The approach offers read/write efficiencies whether hard disk drives or solid-state drives are used.

ReFS and Storage Spaces were designed to work together. Using mirroring or disk striping with parity, Storage Spaces can safeguard data against disk failures by maintaining copies of data on multiple disks. Whether you are using NTFS or ReFS, these multiple copies of data enable Storage Spaces to correct read failures by reading alternate copies of data, to correct write failures by reallocating data transparently, and to correct complete media loss on read/write. Storage Spaces gains efficiencies with ReFS when it comes to detecting data corruption and lost and misdirected writes. Here, ReFS can detect metadata corruption and lost and misdirected writes by using its checksums and then interface with Storage Spaces to read all the available copies of metadata and choose the correct one by validating the checksum. Next, ReFS instructs Storage Spaces to fix the bad metadata by using the good copies of the metadata. The error detection and correction happens transparently. When integrity streams are enabled for files, this automatic error detection and correction process is applied to each individual extent of a file as well.

IMPORTANT

There is a small CPU overhead for computing checksums and a small additional overhead for storing updated checksums with new data. That said, ReFS uses checksums to detect data corruption and log related events that can help you identify the corruption. Redundant Storage Spaces can correct corruption ReFS detects by using good copies of data to repair bad copies of data.

ReFS integrity streams, data scrubbing, and salvage

ReFS supports two types of data streams: conventional streams and integrity streams. Conventional streams behave identically to NTFS streams but might have metadata associated with them that is integrity protected. Integrity streams are streams that are integrity protected, meaning data is checksummed and updates to data are handled using copy-on-write.

With ReFS, keep in mind that integrity is an attribute that can be applied to files and directories. When a file or directory has the (FILE_ATTRIBUTE_INTEGRITY_STREAM) integrity attribute, it uses integrity streams to protect against data corruption. Only Storage Spaces with redundancy has integrity streams enabled by default.

The integrity attribute is inheritable. When you enable the integrity attribute on a directory, the attribute is inherited by all files and directories created in the directory. Because of this, if you enable the integrity attribute on the root directory of a volume, you can ensure that every file and directory on the volume uses integrity streams by default.

You can enable integrity streams on the root directory of a volume when you format it. Use the following command syntax:

```
format /fs:refs /i:enable Volume
```

Here, *Volume* is the drive designator for the volume to format, such as:

```
format /fs:refs /i:enable m:
```

For empty files, the integrity attribute can be set and unset. For nonempty files, the integrity attribute can be removed only by moving the file to a file system that doesn't support integrity, such as NTFS.

ReFS safeguards against data loss as a result of parts of a volume becoming corrupted over time by periodically scrubbing all metadata and integrity stream data. Data is scrubbed by reading all the redundant copies and validating their corrections by using checksums. If checksums do not match, bad copies are repaired using good copies. Typically, this automatic process occurs only with Storage Spaces that have redundancy enabled.

If metadata or data corruption cannot be automatically repaired, ReFS performs a salvage operation to remove the corrupt metadata or data from the namespace. The salvage operation ensures that irreparable corruption cannot adversely affect sound data. For example, the file system cannot open or delete a corrupt file or directory. By removing the corrupt file or directory, ReFS ensures that an administrator can recover the file or directory from backup or have an application re-create it. When ReFS is running on top of redundant Storage Spaces with integrity streams, an automatic error-detection and correction process, applied to each extent of a file, can recover file and directory data.

Inside OUT

ReFS and Storage Spaces

Note that when ReFS is running on top of Storage Spaces, Storage Spaces corrects bad sectors the disk subsystem detects. When ReFS is running on top of redundant Storage Spaces, ReFS detects other types of data corruption and Storage Spaces corrects them. With parity spaces, parity recomputes original data. With mirrored spaces, the mirror is used to recover the data. The entire process, from marking bad sectors (which are not used again) to allocating new blocks and copying the reconstructed data to these new blocks, happens transparently and automatically.

ReFS can heal B+ trees by using its data-scrubbing processes. Here, it scavenges for bad elements in the B+ trees. ReFS also stores a copy of the boot block that can help a system recover from a corrupt boot block.

Integrity can be enabled when the system is not running on Storage Spaces. When integrity is enabled and ReFS detects a checksum mismatch, ReFS logs an event and fails the read operation by default. If you don't want the read operation to fail, you can configure ReFS to continue with the read operation. A related event will be logged regardless.

Using file-based compression

You can use file-based compression to reduce the number of bits and bytes in files so that they use less space on a disk. The Windows operating system supports two types of compression: NTFS compression, which is a built-in feature of NTFS, and compressed (zipped) folders, which is an additional feature of Windows available on any type of volume. ReFS does not support NTFS compression.

NTFS compression

Windows allows you to enable compression when you format a volume by using NTFS. When a drive is compressed, all files and folders stored on the drive are automatically compressed when they are created. This compression is transparent to users, who can open and work with compressed files and folders just as they do regular files and folders. Behind the scenes, Windows expands the file or folder when it is opened and compresses it again when it is closed. Although this can decrease a computer's performance, it saves space on the disk because compressed files and folders use less space.

You can turn on compression after formatting volumes as well or, if desired, turn on compression only for specific files and folders. After you compress a folder, any new files added or copied to the folder are compressed automatically. If you move a compressed file to a folder on the same volume, it remains compressed. If you move a compressed file to a folder on a different volume, it inherits the compression attribute of the folder.

Moving uncompressed files to compressed folders affects their compression attribute as well. If you move an uncompressed file from a different drive to a compressed drive or folder, the file is compressed. However, if you move an uncompressed file to a compressed folder on the same NTFS drive, the file isn't compressed. Finally, if you move a compressed file to a FAT16, FAT32, exFAT, or ReFS volume, the file is uncompressed because NTFS compression is not supported.

To compress or expand a drive, follow these steps:

1. Press and hold or right-click the drive that you want to compress or expand in File Explorer or in the Disk Management Volume List view and then select Properties. This opens the disk's Properties dialog box, as shown in Figure 15-7.

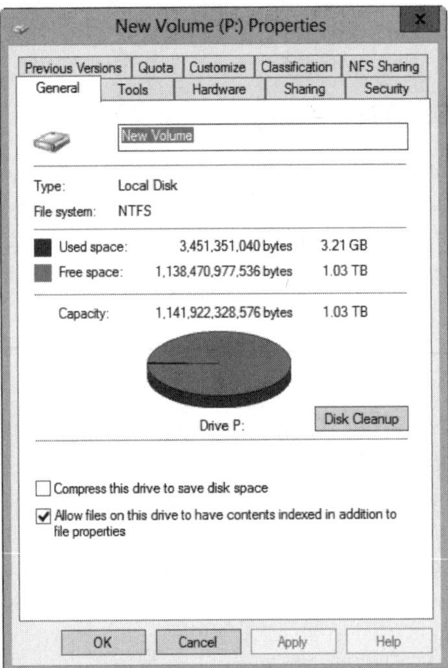

Figure 15-7 You can compress entire volumes or perform selective compression for specific files and folders.

2. Select or clear the Compress This Drive To Save Disk Space check box as appropriate. When you tap or click OK, the Confirm Attribute Changes dialog box shown in Figure 15-8 opens.

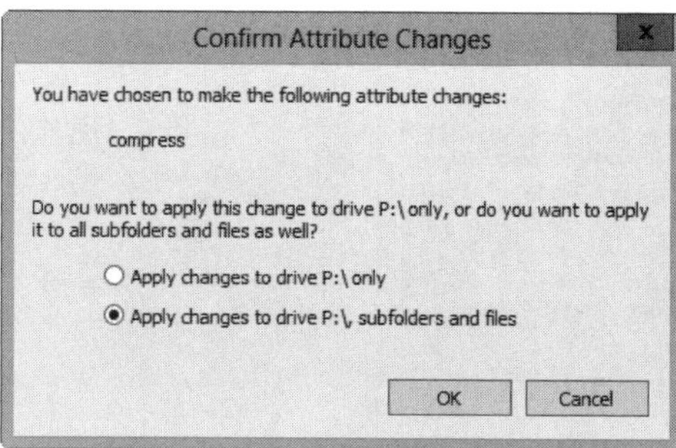

Figure 15-8 Choose a compression option.

3. If you want to apply changes only to the root folder of the disk, select Apply Changes To Drive *X* Only. Otherwise, accept the default, which compresses the entire contents of the disk. Tap or click OK.

   ## CAUTION!

   Although Windows Server 2012 R2 allows you to compress system volumes, this is not recommended because the operating system needs to expand and compress system files each time they are opened, which can seriously affect server performance. In addition, you can't use compression and encryption together. You can use one feature or the other, but not both.

You can selectively compress and expand files and folders as well. The advantage here is that this affects only part of a disk, such as a folder and its subfolders, rather than the entire disk. To compress or expand a file or folder, follow these steps:

1. In File Explorer, press and hold or right-click the file or folder you want to compress or expand and then select Properties.
2. On the General tab of the related Properties dialog box, tap or click Advanced. This opens the Advanced Attributes dialog box shown in Figure 15-9. Select or clear the Compress Contents To Save Disk Space check box as appropriate. Tap or click OK twice.

Figure 15-9 Use the Advanced Attributes dialog box to compress or expand the file or folder.

3. If you are changing the compression attributes of a folder with subfolders, the Confirm Attribute Changes dialog box opens. If you want to apply the changes only to the files in the folder and not to files in subfolders of the folder, select Apply Changes To *X* Only. Otherwise, accept the default, which applies the changes to the files in the folder and its subfolders. Tap or click OK.

Windows Server 2012 R2 also provides command-line utilities for compressing and expanding your data. The compression utility is called Compact (Compact.exe). The expansion utility is called Expand (Expand.exe).

You can use Compact to determine quickly whether files in a directory are compressed. At the command line, change to the directory you want to examine and type **compact** without any additional parameters. If you want to check the directory and all subdirectories, type **compact /s**. The output lists the compression status and compression ratio on every file, and the final summary details tell you exactly how many files and directories were examined and found to be compressed, such as:

```
Of 15435 files within 822 directories
0 are compressed and 15435 are no compressed.
2,411,539,448 total bytes of data are stored in 2,411,539,448 bytes.
The compression ratio is 1.0 to 1.
```

Compressed (zipped) folders

Compressed (zipped) folders are another option for compressing files and folders. When you compress data by using this technique, you use zip compression technology to reduce the number of bits and bytes in files and folders so that they use less space on a disk. Compressed (zipped) folders are identified with a zipper on the folder icon and are saved with the .zip file extension.

Compressed (zipped) folders have several advantages over NTFS compression. Because zip technology is an extension of the operating system rather than of the file system, compressed (zipped) folders can be used on any type of volume. Zipped folders can be password protected to safeguard their contents and can be sent by email. They can also be transferred using File Transfer Protocol (FTP), Hypertext Transfer Protocol (HTTP), or other protocols. An added benefit of zipped folders is that some programs can be run directly from compressed folders without having to be expanded. You can also open files directly from zipped folders.

You can create a zipped folder by selecting a file, folder, or group of files and folders in File Explorer, pressing and holding or right-clicking it, pointing to Send To, and tapping or clicking Compressed (Zipped) Folder. The zipped folder is named automatically by using the file name of the last item selected and adding the .zip extension. If you double-tap or double-click a zipped folder in File Explorer, you can access and work with its contents. As shown in Figure 15-10, the zipped folder's contents are listed according to file name, type, and date. The file information also shows the packed file size, original file size, and compression ratio. Double-tapping or double-clicking a program in a zipped folder runs it (as long as it doesn't require access to other files). Double-tapping or double-clicking a file in a zipped folder opens it for viewing or editing.

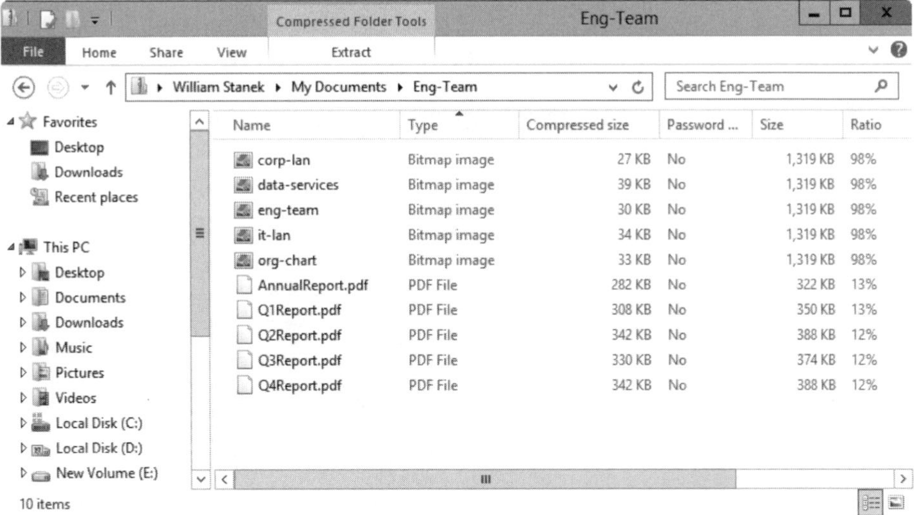

Figure 15-10 Compressed (zipped) folders can be accessed and used like other folders.

While you're working with a zipped folder, you can perform tasks similar to those you can do with regular folders. You can do the following:

- Add other files, programs, or folders to the zipped folder by dragging them to it.
- Copy a file in the zipped folder and paste it into a different folder.
- Remove a file from the zipped folder by using the Cut command so that you can paste it into a different folder.
- Delete a file or folder by selecting it and tapping or clicking Delete.

You can also perform additional tasks that are unique to zipped folders. Press and hold or right-click and then choose Extract All to start the Extraction Wizard, which you can use to extract all the files in the zipped folder and copy them to a new location.

CHAPTER 16

Maintaining and optimizing storage

Windows Server 2012 R2 has many features that reduce the amount of manual maintenance you must perform on disk drives, including NTFS disk quotas, automated disk maintenance, and automated disk optimization. The key to success with these features is a strong understanding of how the features work and how they can be optimized to meet the needs of your organization.

Managing NTFS disk quotas

Even with the large disk drives available today, you'll often find that hard disk space is at a premium, and this is where disk quotas come in handy. Disk quotas are a built-in feature of NTFS that help you manage and limit disk-space usage.

How quota management works

By using disk quotas, you can monitor and control the amount of disk space people who access folders and disks can use. Without quota management, it is hard to monitor the amount of space used by individual users and even harder to control the total amount of space they can use. I refer to monitoring and controlling separately because there's a very important difference between monitoring disk-space usage and controlling it—and the disk quota system enables you to perform these tasks separately or together. You can, in fact, do the following:

- Configure the disk quota system to monitor disk-space usage only, enabling administrators to check disk-space usage manually
- Configure the disk quota system to monitor disk-space usage and generate warnings when users exceed predefined usage levels
- Configure the disk quota system to monitor disk-space usage, generate warnings when users exceed predefined usage levels, and enforce the limits by denying disk space to users who exceed the quota limit

Your organization's culture will probably play a major role in the disk quota technique you use. In some organizations, the culture is such that it is acceptable to monitor space usage and periodically notify users that they are over recommended limits, but it wouldn't be well received if administrators enforced controls that limited disk-space usage to specific amounts. In other organizations, especially larger organizations in which there might be hundreds or thousands of employees on the network, it can make sense to have some controls in place and users might be more understanding of specific controls. Controls at some point become a matter of necessity to help ensure that the administrative staff can keep up with the disk-space needs of the organization.

Disk quotas are configured on a per-volume basis. When you enable disk quotas, all users who store data on a volume are affected by the quota. You can set exceptions for individual users that either set new limits or remove the limits altogether. As users create files and folders on a volume, an ownership flag is applied that says that this particular user owns the file or folder. Thus, if a user creates a file or folder on a volume that the user owns, the file or folder and the space used count toward the user's quota limit. However, because each volume is managed separately, there is no way to set a specific limit for all volumes on a server or across the enterprise.

> NOTE
>
> **For NTFS compressed files and sparse files, the space usage reported can reflect the total space of files rather than the actual space the files use. This happens because the quota system reads the total space the file uses rather than its reduced file size.**

Ownership of files and folders can change in several scenarios. If a user creates a copy of a file someone else owns, the copy is owned by the user who created it because a file is created when the copy is made. File and folder ownership can also change when files are restored from backup. This can happen if you restore the files to a volume other than the one on which the files were created and copy the files over to the original volume. Here, during the copy operation, the administrator becomes the owner of the files. A workaround for this is to restore files and folders to a different location on the same volume and then move the files and folders rather than copying them. When you move files and folders from one location to another on the same volume, the original ownership information is retained.

Administrators can be designated as the owner of files in other ways as well, such as when they install the operating system or application software. To ensure that administrators can always install programs, restore data, and perform other administrative tasks, members of the Administrators group don't have a quota limit as a general rule. This is true even when you enforce disk quotas for all users. In fact, for the Administrators group, the only type of quota you can set is a warning level that warns administrators when they've used more than a set amount of space on a volume. When you think about it, this makes a lot of sense—you don't want to get into a situation in which administrators can't recover the system because of space limitations.

That said, you can apply quotas to individual users—even those who are members of the Administrators group. You do this by creating a separate quota entry for each user. The only account that cannot be restricted in this way is the built-in Administrator account. If you try to set a limit on the Administrator account, the limit is not applied.

Finally, note that all space used on a volume counts toward the disk quota—even space used in the Recycle Bin. Thus, if a user who is over the limit deletes files to get under the limit, the disk quota might still give warnings or, if quotas are enforced, the user still might not be able to write files to the volume. To resolve this issue, the user would need to delete files and then empty the Recycle Bin.

Configuring disk quotas

By default, disk quotas are disabled. If you want to use disk quotas, you must enable quota management for each volume on which you want to use disk quotas. You can enable disk quotas on any NTFS volume that has a drive letter or a mount point. Before you configure disk quotas, think carefully about the limit and warning levels. Set values that make the most sense given the number of users who store data on the volume and the size of the volume. For optimal performance of the volume, you won't want all or nearly all of the disk space to be allocated. For optimal user happiness, you want to ensure that the warning and limit levels are adequate so that the average user can store the necessary data to perform job duties. Quota limits and warning levels aren't "one size fits all" solutions either. Engineers and graphic designers can have very different space needs from a typical user. In the best situations, you configure network shares so that different groups of users have access to different volumes, and these volumes are sized to meet the typical requirements of a particular group.

In some organizations, I've seen administrators set very low quota limits and warning levels on data shares. The idea behind this was that the administrators wanted users to save most of their data on their workstations and put only files that needed to be shared on the data shares. I discourage this approach for two reasons. First, low quota limits and warning levels frustrate users—you don't want frustrated users; you want happy users. Second, you should be encouraging users to store more of their important files on central file servers, not fewer. Central file servers should be part of regular enterprise-wide backup routines, and backing up data safeguards it from loss. In addition, with the Volume Shadow Copy Service, shadow copies of files on shared folders can be created automatically, enabling users to perform point-in-time file recovery without needing help from administrators.

> NOTE
>
> **If you used the DirQuota command-line utility previously for managing disk quotas, note that this tool has been deprecated in Windows Server 2012 R2 and is subject to removal in subsequent releases of the operating system.**

To enable disk quotas on an NTFS volume, follow these steps:

1. In Computer Management, expand Storage and then select Disk Management. In the details pane, press and hold or right-click the volume on which you want to enable quotas and then select Properties.
2. In the Quota Settings dialog box, select the Enable Quota Management check box, as shown in Figure 16-1.

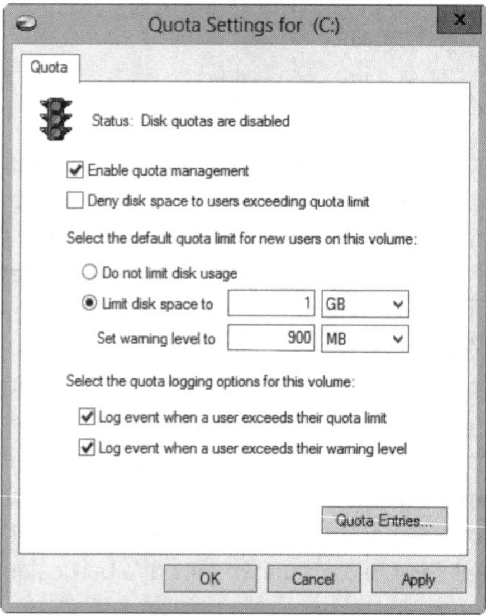

Figure 16-1 Enable quota management on the volume and then configure the disk quota settings.

3. Define a default disk quota limit for all users by choosing Limit Disk Space To and then using the fields provided to set a limit in KB, MB, GB, TB, PB, or EB. Afterward, use the Set Warning Level To field to set the default warning limit. In most cases, you want the disk quota warning limit to be 90 to 95 percent of the disk quota limit. This should create good separation between when warnings occur and when the limit is reached.
4. To prevent users from going over the disk quota limit, select the Deny Disk Space To Users Exceeding Quota Limit check box. This sets a physical limitation for users that prevents them from writing to the volume after the limit is reached.
5. NTFS sends warnings to users when they reach a warning level or limit. To ensure that you have a record of these warnings, you can configure quota-logging options. Select the Log Event check boxes as appropriate.

6. Tap or click OK. If the quota system isn't currently enabled, you see a prompt asking you to enable the quota system. Tap or click OK to allow Windows Server 2012 R2 to rescan the volume and update the disk usage statistics. Keep in mind that actions might be taken against users who exceed the current limit or warning levels. These can include preventing additional writing to the volume, notifying users the next time they try to access the volume on which they've exceeded a warning level or have reached a limit, and logging applicable events in the Application log.

Customizing quota entries for individual users

After you enable disk quotas, the configuration is set for and applies to all users who store data on the volume. The only exception, as noted previously, is for members of the Administrators group. The default disk quotas don't apply to these users. If you want to set a specific quota limit or warning level for a member of the Administrators group, you can do this by creating a custom quota entry for that particular user account. You can also create custom quota entries for users who have special requirements or special limitations.

To view and work with quota entries, access Disk Management, press and hold or right-click the volume on which you enabled quotas, and then select Properties. In the Properties dialog box for the disk, tap or click the Quota tab and then tap or click Quota Entries. You then see a list of quota entries for everyone who has ever stored data on the volume, as shown in Figure 16-2. The entries show the following information:

- **Status.** The status of the disk entries. Normal status is OK. If a user has reached a warning level, the status is Warning. If a user is at or above the quota limit, the status is Above Limit.
- **Name.** The display name of the user account.
- **Logon Name.** The logon name and domain (if applicable).
- **Amount Used.** The amount of disk space used by the user.
- **Quota Limit.** The quota limit set for the user.
- **Warning Level.** The warning level set for the user.
- **Percent Used.** The percentage of disk space used toward the limit.

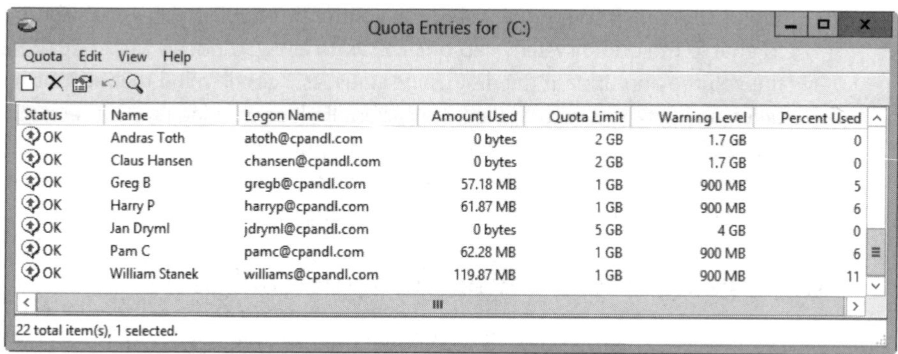

Figure 16-2 Any existing quota entries are shown.

Quota entries get on the list in one of two ways: either automatically if a user has ever stored data on the volume or by an administrator creating a custom entry for a user. You can customize any of these entries—even the ones automatically created—by double-tapping or double-clicking them, which opens the Quota Settings dialog box shown in Figure 16-3, and selecting the appropriate options to either remove the disk quota limits or set new ones.

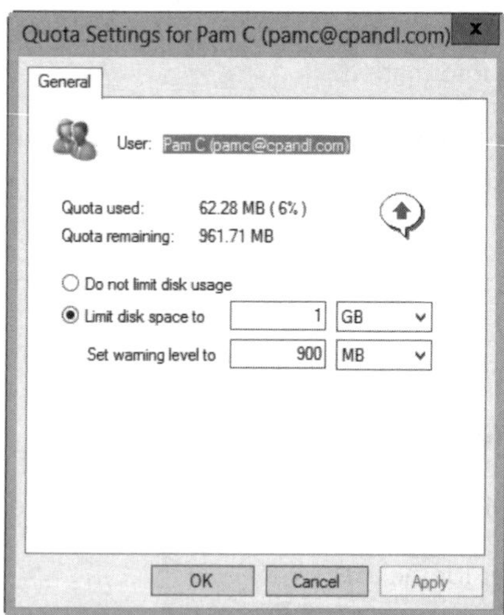

Figure 16-3 You can customize quota entries for individual users as necessary.

NOTE

You can't create quota entries for groups. The only group entry that is allowed is the one for the Administrators account, which is created automatically.

If a user doesn't have an entry in the Quota Entries dialog box, it means that user has not yet saved files to the volume. You can still create a custom entry for the user if you want. To do this, choose Quota, New Quota Entry. This opens the Select Users dialog box shown in Figure 16-4. Use this dialog box to find the user account you want to work with. Type the name of the user account or part of the name and tap or click Check Names. If multiple names match the value you entered, you see a list of names and can choose the one you want to use. Otherwise, the name is filled in for you, and you can tap or click OK to open the Add New Quota Entry dialog box, which has the same options as the Quota Settings dialog box shown in Figure 16-3.

Use locations to access user accounts from other domains

By default, the Select Users dialog box is set to work with users from your logon domain. If you want to add a user account from another domain, tap or click Locations to open the Locations dialog box. Select either the entire directory or the specific domain in which the account is located and tap or click OK.

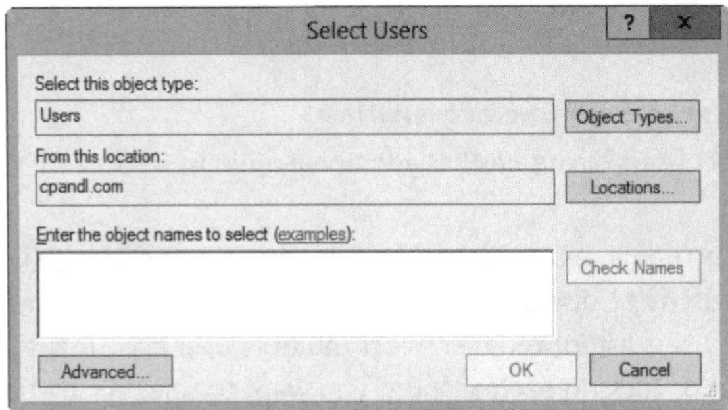

Figure 16-4 Type the name of the user account or part of the name and tap or click Check Names.

In the Quota Entries dialog box, you can use a couple of tricks to add or manage multiple quota entries at once. If you want to add identical quota entries for multiple users, you can do this by choosing Quota, New Quota Entry. This opens the Select Users dialog box. Tap or click Advanced to open the advanced Select Users dialog box, as shown in Figure 16-5.

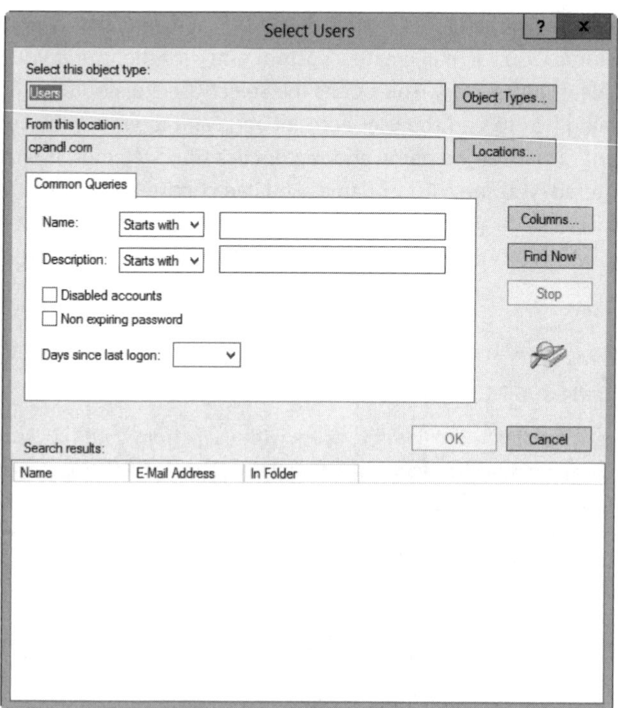

Figure 16-5 The advanced Select Users dialog box has additional options.

You can now search for users by name and description or by tapping or clicking Find Now without entering any search criteria to display a list of available users from the current location. You can select any of the users listed. You can select multiple user accounts by holding down the Ctrl key and tapping or clicking each account you want to select or by holding down the Shift key, selecting the first account name, and then tapping or clicking the last account name to choose a range of accounts. Tap or click OK twice and then use the Add New Quota Entry dialog box to configure the quota options for all the selected users.

To manage multiple quota entries simultaneously, open the Quota Entries dialog box and then select the entries by holding down the Ctrl key and tapping or clicking each entry you want to select or by holding down the Shift key, selecting the first entry, and then tapping or clicking the last entry to choose a range of entries. Afterward, press and hold or right-click one of the selected entries and then choose Properties. You can then configure quota options for all the selected entries at once.

Managing disk quotas after configuration

Users are notified that they have reached a warning level or quota limit when they access the volume on which you configured disk quotas. As an administrator, you want to check for quota violations periodically, and there are several ways you can do this. One way is to access Disk Management, press and hold or right-click the volume that you want to check, and then select Properties. In the Properties dialog box for the disk, tap or click the Quota tab and then tap or click the Quota Entries button. You can then check the current disk usage of users and see whether there are any quota violations. You can also copy selected entries to the Clipboard by pressing Ctrl+C and then pasting them into other applications, such as Microsoft Excel, by using Ctrl+V to help you create reports or lists of disk-space usage.

You can check quota entries from the command line as well. Type **fsutil quota query *DriveDesignator*** at the command prompt, where *DriveDesignator* is the drive letter of the volume followed by a colon, such as D:. If disk quotas are enabled on the volume, you then get a summary of the disk quota settings on the volume, as follows:

```
FileSystemControlFlags          =      0x00000031
   Quotas are tracked and enforced on this volume
   Logging enable for quota limits and threshold
   The quota values are up to date

Default Quota Threshold         =      0x0000000038400000
Default Quota Limit             =      0x0000000040000000

SID Name                        =      CPANDL\edwardh (User)
Change time                     =      Saturday, April 26, 2014
Quota Used                      =      528164252
Quota Threshold                 =      943718400
Quota Limit                     =      1073741824

SID Name                        =      CPANDL\mollyp (User)
Change time                     =      Monday, April 28, 2014
Quota Used                      =      627384965
Quota Threshold                 =      943718400
Quota Limit                     =      1073741824
```

In this example, disk quotas are tracked and enforced on the volume, logging is enabled for both quota limits, and the warning levels and the disk quota values are current. In addition, the default warning limit (listed as the quota threshold) is set to 900 MBs (0 × 038400000 bytes) and the default quota limit is set to 1 GB (0 × 040000000 bytes).

CHAPTER 16

The disk quota summary is followed by the individual disk quota entries for each user who has stored data on the volume or has a custom entry regardless of whether the user has ever written data to the volume. The entries show the following information:

- **SID Name.** The logon name and domain of user accounts or the name of a built-in or well-known group that has a quota entry
- **Change Time.** The last time the quota entry was changed or updated
- **Quota Used.** The amount of space used in bytes
- **Quota Threshold.** The current warning level set for the user in bytes
- **Quota Limit.** The current quota limit set for the user in bytes

When you configure disk quotas, you also have the option to log two types of events in the system logs: one for when a user exceeds the quota limit and another for when a user exceeds the warning level. By default, quota violations are written to the system log once an hour, so if you check the logs periodically, you can see events related to any users who have disk quota violations. It's much easier to check for quota violations from the command line, however. Just type **fsutil quota violations** at the command prompt, and the FSUtil Quota command checks the system and application event logs for quota violations.

NOTE

Wondering why FSUtil Quota Violations checks the system and application logs? Well, in some cases, quota violations for programs running under user accounts are logged in the application log rather than in the system log. To ensure that all quota violations are detected, FSUtil Quota Violations checks both logs.

If no quota violations are found, the output is similar to the following:

```
Searching in System Event Log...
Searching in Application Event Log...
No quota violations detected
```

If there are quota violations, the output shows the event information related to each violation. In the following example, a user reached the warning level (listed as the quota threshold):

```
Searching in System Event Log...
**** A user hit their quota threshold ! ****
   Event ID : 0x40040024
   EventType : Information
   Event Category : 2
   Source : Ntfs
   User: CPANDL\harryt (User)
   Data: D:
Searching in Application Event Log...
```

As you can see, the output shows you the event ID, type, category, and source. It also shows the user who violated the disk quota settings and the volume on which the violation occurred.

Inside OUT

You can change the notification interval for quota violations

As mentioned previously, quota violations are written to the event logs once an hour by default. You can check or change this behavior by using the FSUtil Behavior command. Keep in mind, however, that any changes you make apply to all volumes on the system that use disk quotas. To check the notification interval, type **fsutil behavior query quotanotify**. If the notification interval has been set by you or another administrator, the notification interval is shown in seconds. To set the notification interval, type **fsutil behavior set quotanotify *Interval***, where *Interval* is the notification interval you want to set expressed as the number of seconds. For example, if you want to receive less-frequent notifications, you might want to set the notification interval to 7,200 seconds (2 hours), and you would do this by typing **fsutil behavior set quotanotify 7200**.

Exporting and importing quota entries

If you want to use the same quotas on more than one NTFS volume, you can do this by exporting the quota entries from one volume and importing them on another volume. When you import quota entries, if there isn't a quota entry for the user already, a quota entry will be created. If a user already has a quota entry on the volume, you are asked whether you want to overwrite it.

To export and import quota entries, access Disk Management, press and hold or right-click the volume on which you want to enable quotas, and then select Properties. In the Properties dialog box for the disk, tap or click the Quota tab and then tap or click the Quota Entries button. You then see the Quota Entries dialog box. Select Export from the Quota menu. This opens the Export Quota Settings dialog box.

Choose the location for the file containing the quota settings and then set a name for the file by using the File Name field. Afterward, tap or click Save.

Next, open the Quota Entries dialog box for the drive on which you want to import settings. Select Import on the Quota menu. Then, in the Import Quota Settings dialog box, select the quota settings file that you saved previously. Tap or click Open.

If prompted about whether you want to overwrite an existing entry, tap or click Yes to replace an existing entry or tap or click No to keep the existing entry. Select Do This For All Quota Entries prior to tapping or clicking Yes or No to use the same option for all existing entries.

Automated disk maintenance

Windows Server 2012 R2 performs periodic maintenance daily. Automated maintenance is built on the Windows Diagnostics framework. Windows Server 2012 R2 performs periodic routine maintenance daily at 2:00 A.M. By default, as long as the operating system is idle, this maintenance is performed in the background. If the computer isn't idle, maintenance starts the next time the operating system is idle. Because maintenance runs only when the operating system is idle, maintenance is allowed to run in the background for up to three days. This allows Windows to complete complex maintenance tasks automatically.

Maintenance tasks include software updates, security scanning, system diagnostics, Check Disk activity, and disk optimization. Although maintenance now runs whether a computer is running on AC power or battery power, the Check Disk and disk optimization tasks only run when the computer is running on AC power.

File data is stored in clusters, and the Windows operating system uses a file table to determine where a file begins and on which clusters it is stored. With FAT, the file-allocation table defines the starting cluster of each file in the file system and has pointers to each cluster a file uses. With NTFS, a master file table (MFT) is used. If a file's data can't fit within a single record in this table, clusters belonging to the file are referenced using virtual cluster numbers (VCNs) that map to starting logical cluster numbers (LCNs) on the disk. If a file's pointer or mapping is lost, you might not be able to access the file. Errors can also occur for pointers or mappings that relate to the file tables themselves and to the pointers or mappings for folders.

Preventing disk-integrity problems

FAT tries to prevent disk-integrity problems by maintaining a duplicate file allocation table that can be used to recover the primary file allocation table if it becomes corrupted. Beyond this, FAT doesn't do much to ensure disk integrity. NTFS, however, has several mechanisms for preventing and correcting disk-integrity problems automatically. NTFS stores a partial duplicate of the MFT, which can be used for failure recovery. NTFS also stores a persistent history of all changes made to files on the volume in a log file, and the log file can be used to recover NTFS metadata files, regular data files, and folders. What these file-structure recovery mechanisms all have in common is that they are automatic and you, as an administrator, don't need to do anything to ensure that these disk housekeeping tasks are performed. These mechanisms aren't perfect, however, and errors can occur.

The most common errors relate to the following areas:

- Internal errors in a file's structure
- Free space being marked as allocated
- Allocated space being marked as free

- Partially or improperly written security descriptors
- Unreadable disk sectors not marked as bad

Windows Server 2012 R2 proactively scans volumes for these types of errors as part of automated maintenance. Windows does this using Check Disk. Although automated maintenance triggers the disk scan, the process of calling and managing Check Disk is handled by a separate task. In Task Scheduler, you find the ProactiveScan task in the scheduler library under Microsoft\Windows\Chkdsk, and you can get detailed run information on the task's History tab.

Inside OUT

How automated maintenance works

On servers running Windows Server 2012 R2, automated maintenance runs daily at 2:00 A.M. You can manage the maintenance schedule in Action Center. One way to open Action Center is to type **action center** in the Settings Search box and then press Enter.

In Action Center, expand the Maintenance panel to view related details and options, including the last run-time. In Task Scheduler, the following tasks are triggered by automated maintenance:

- **Microsoft\Windows\Application Experience.** Collects and uploads Application Telemetry information if opted in to the Microsoft Customer Experience Improvement Program (CEIP)
- **Microsoft\Windows\ChkDsk.** Performs a proactive scan of disks
- **Microsoft\Windows\Defrag.** Performs a scan and fragmentation analysis of disks
- **Microsoft\Windows\Device Setup.** Performs metadata refresh of devices
- **Microsoft\Windows\PI.** Updates secure boot variables
- **Microsoft\Windows\Power Efficiency Diagnostics.** Analyzes power usage
- **Microsoft\Windows\Registry.** Performs a backup of the registry
- **Microsoft\Windows\Servicing.** Cleans up components
- **Microsoft\Windows\Shell.** Keeps the search index up to date
- **Microsoft\Windows\Time Synchronization.** Maintains date and time synchronization
- **Microsoft\Windows\Windows Error Reporting.** Processes queued error reports

> Although automated maintenance is scheduled to run daily at 2:00 A.M., maintenance runs only when the operating system is idle. Because of that, you might find that the maintenance ran at a different time. If automated maintenance hasn't run for a while, you can tap or click Start Maintenance to start the automated maintenance manually (with the same requirements regarding being idle). You can change the daily run-time for automated maintenance by tapping or clicking Change Maintenance Settings, selecting a new run hour, such as 12:00 A.M., and then tapping or clicking OK.

Check Disk works on FAT, FAT32, and NTFS volumes and primarily looks for inconsistencies in the file system and its related metadata. It locates errors by comparing the volume bitmap to the disk sectors assigned to files. For files, Check Disk looks at structural integrity, but it won't check for or attempt to repair corrupted data within files that appear to be structurally intact.

However, the way Check Disk performs scan, analysis, and repair has changed. With Windows Server 2012 R2, Check Disk performs either enhanced scan and repair automatically or the scan and repair available with earlier releases of Windows. Whether an enhanced scan and repair or a standard scan and repair is used depends on the type of volume:

- When you use Check Disk with NTFS volumes, Check Disk performs the enhanced online scan and analysis. This means the scan and analysis process typically does not require taking the volume offline or prevent the volume from being used until a repair is required.
- When you use Check Disk with FAT, FAT32, or exFAT, Windows Server 2012 R2 uses the standard scan and repair process. This means the scan and repair process typically requires taking an active volume offline, which prevents the volume from being used.

Because the enhanced approach is new, that's what I'll focus on. When you use Check Disk with NTFS volumes, Check Disk performs an online scan and analysis of the volumes. Check Disk writes information about any detected corruptions in the $corrupt system file. When the scan and analysis process is complete, Check Disk can repair detected corruptions by taking the volume offline temporarily and fixing them.

Storing the corruption information and then repairing the volume while it is dismounted enables Windows to repair volumes rapidly. It also enables users to keep using the disk while a scan is being performed. Typically, offline repair takes only a few seconds, compared to what would have been hours for very large volumes using the standard scan and repair technique.

Keep in mind that unmounting a volume for repair invalidates all open file handles. With the boot/system volume, the repairs are performed the next time you start the computer. As with other volumes, Check Disk uses the detected corruptions, already stored in the $corrupt system file, to repair the boot/system volume rapidly during startup.

Because ReFS is self-correcting, Check Disk isn't needed on ReFS volumes (and won't run on ReFS volumes either). However, it's important to point out that ReFS as originally released did not efficiently correct corruption on parity spaces. With Windows Server 2012 R2, this deficiency has been corrected. ReFS automatically corrects corruption on parity spaces when integrity streams are enabled to detect corrupt data. When corruption is detected, ReFS examines the data copies that the parity spaces contain and then uses the correct version of the data to correct the problem. Because ReFS now supports concurrent I/O requests to the same file, the performance of integrity streams also has been improved.

Running Check Disk interactively

You can run Check Disk interactively as well. With NTFS volumes, one way to do this is to use Server Manager. In Server Manager, select the File And Storage Services node and then select the related Volumes subnode. As shown in Figure 16-6, you then see the available volumes for each server added for management. Next, press and hold or right-click a volume and then select Scan File System For Errors. In the Scan File System For Errors dialog box, tap or click Scan Now. Server Manager displays the percentage of scanning completed. If errors are found, you're notified and can press and hold or right-click the volume and then select Repair File System Errors to resolve them. As discussed earlier, the way the repair process works depends on whether you are working with a boot/system volume or a nonsystem volume.

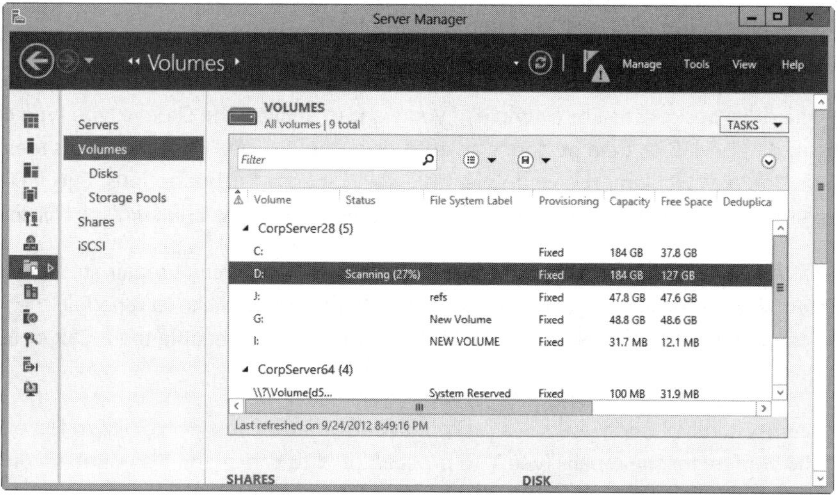

Figure 16-6 Scan a volume for errors in Server Manager.

Another way to check NTFS volumes is to start Check Disk by using either File Explorer or Disk Management. Press and hold or right-click the volume and choose Properties. On the Tools tab of the Properties dialog box, tap or click Check to open the Error Checking dialog box. When you tap or click Scan Drive, the Error Checking dialog box displays the approximate scan and analysis time remaining, as shown in Figure 16-7. If errors are found, you're notified with additional options for repairing them.

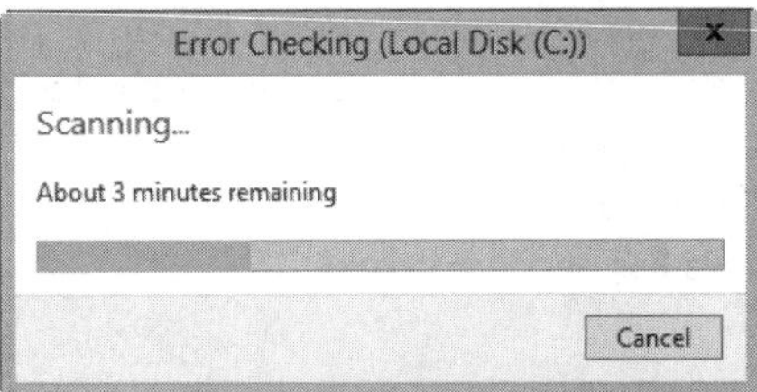

Figure 16-7 Check a disk for errors.

With FAT, FAT32, and exFAT volumes, Windows uses the standard Check Disk, which might require offline scan and repair. Start Check Disk by using either File Explorer or Disk Management. Press and hold or right-click the volume and choose Properties. On the Tools tab of the Properties dialog box, tap or click Check to open the Error Checking dialog box. When you tap or click Scan And Repair Drive, Check Disk begins scanning the volume.

Check Disk can also be run at the command line by using ChkDsk (Chkdsk.exe). The key advantage of using the command-line version is that you get a detailed report of the analysis and repair operations as detailed in "Analyzing FAT volumes by using ChkDsk" and "Analyzing NTFS volumes by using ChkDsk" later in this chapter.

You can run ChkDsk in analysis mode at the command line by typing **chkdsk /scan** followed by the drive designator. For example, if you want to analyze the D drive, you type **chkdsk /scan d:**. Check Disk then performs an analysis of the disk and returns a status message regarding any problems it encounters. Unless you specify further options, Check Disk won't repair problems, however. To repair errors on drive D, you type **chkdsk /spotfix d:**.

Because fixing the volume requires exclusive access to it, you can't repair an active volume. For system volumes, you see a prompt asking whether you would like to schedule the volume for the repair the next time the computer is started. Type **Y** to schedule the repair or **N** to cancel the repair.

For nonsystem volumes, you see a prompt asking whether you would like to force a dismount of the volume for the repair. Type **Y** to proceed or **N** to cancel the dismount. If you cancel the dismount, the prompt asks whether you would like to schedule the repair the next time the computer is started. Here, type **Y** to schedule the repair or **N** to cancel the repair.

You can't run Check Disk with both the */scan* and */spotfix* options. The reason for this is that the scan and repair tasks are now independent of each other.

The complete syntax for ChkDsk is as follows:

```
CHKDSK [volume[[path]filename]] [/F] [/V] [/R] [/X] [/I] [/C] [/B]
  [/L[:size]] [/scan] [/forceofflinefix] [/perf] [/spotfix]
  [/sdcleanup] [/offlinescanandfix]
```

Table 16-1 summarizes the available options and parameters and their uses.

Table 16-1 Command-line parameters for ChkDsk

Option/Parameter	Description
Volume	Sets the volume to work with.
[path]/Filename	On FAT/FAT32, specifies files to check for fragmentation.
Standard Check Disk Options	
/B	Tells ChkDsk to reevaluate any clusters marked as bad on the volume. (/R is implied when you use this parameter.)
/C	On NTFS only, tells ChkDsk not to check for cycles within the folder structure. A cycle is a very rarely occurring type of error in which a directory contains a pointer to itself, causing an infinite loop.
/F	Tells ChkDsk to analyze the disk and fix any errors noted.
/I	On NTFS only, tells ChkDsk to perform a minimum check of indexes.
/L[:Size]	On NTFS only, changes the transaction log file size. The default size is 4096 KBs, which is sufficient most of the time.
/R	Tells ChkDsk to analyze the disk, fix any errors noted, and check for bad sectors. Any bad sectors found are marked as bad. (/F is implied when you use this parameter.)
/V	On FAT/FAT32, lists the full path of every file on the volume. On NTFS, displays cleanup messages related to fixing file-system errors or other discrepancies.
/X	Forces the volume to dismount if necessary. All open file handles to the volume would then be invalid. (/F is implied when you use this parameter.)
Enhanced Check Disk Options	
/forceofflinefix	Bypasses all online repair and queues errors for offline repair. It must be used with /scan.
/offlinescanandfix	Performs an offline scan and fix of the volume.
/perf	Performs the scan as fast as possible by using more system resources.
/scan	Performs an online scan of the volume (the default). Errors detected during the scan are added to the $corrupt system file.
/sdcleanup	Cleans up unneeded security descriptor data. It implies /F (with standard scan and repair).
/spotfix	Allows certain types of errors to be repaired online (the default).

Analyzing FAT volumes by using ChkDsk

When you run ChkDsk, you can get an analysis report. For FAT volumes, a disk analysis report looks like this:

```
The type of the file system is FAT32.
Volume NEW VOLUME created 9/24/2014 9:10 PM
Volume Serial Number is AAAD-2188
Windows is verifying files and folders...
File and folder verification is complete.

Windows has scanned the file system and found no problems.
No further action is required.
    5,107,712 KB total disk space.
           64 KB in 16 hidden files.
          168 KB in 42 folders.
    1,026,340 KB in 145 files.
    4,081,136 KB are available.

        4,096 bytes in each allocation unit.
    1,276,928 total allocation units on disk.
    1,020,284 allocation units available on disk.
```

Here, ChkDsk examines each record in the file allocation table for consistency. It lists all the file and folder records in use and determines the starting cluster for each, using the file allocation table. It checks each file and notes any discrepancies in the output. Any clusters that were marked as in use by files or folders but weren't actually in use are noted, and during repair, the clusters can be marked as available. Other discrepancies noted in the output can be fixed during repair as well.

Analyzing NTFS volumes by using ChkDsk

Disk analysis for NTFS volumes is performed in three stages, and ChkDsk reports its progress during each stage as shown in this sample report:

```
The type of the file system is NTFS.

Stage 1: Examining basic file system structure ...

Stage 2: Examining file name linkage ...

Stage 3: Examining security descriptors ...

Windows has scanned the file system and found no problems.
No further action is required.
```

During the first stage of analysis, ChkDsk verifies file structures. This means ChkDsk examines each file's record in the MFT for consistency. It examines all the file records in use and determines which clusters the file records are stored in, and then it compares this with the volume's cluster bitmap stored in the $Bitmap metadata file. Any discrepancies are tracked. For example, any clusters that were marked as in use by files but weren't actually in use are tracked, and during repair, the clusters can be marked as available.

During the second stage of analysis, ChkDsk verifies directory structure by examining file-name linking, starting with the volume's root directory index, which is stored in the $Metadata file. ChkDsk examines index records, making sure that each index record corresponds to an actual directory on the disk and that each file that is supposed to be in a directory is in the directory. It also checks whether there are files that have an MFT record but don't actually exist in any directory, and during repair, these lost files can be recovered.

During the third stage of the analysis, ChkDsk verifies the consistency of security descriptors for each file and directory object on the volume by using the $Secure metadata file. It does this by validating that the security descriptors work. It doesn't actually check whether the users or groups assigned in the security descriptors exist.

Repairing volumes and marking bad sectors by using ChkDsk

Running ChkDsk with the */scan* option performs an analysis of the volume only. If problems are found, ChkDsk repairs them only if you run ChkDsk again, this time using */spotfix*.

That said, you can scan a volume and force offline repair by using */scan* and */forceofflinefix*, as shown in this example:

```
chkdsk /scan /forceofflinefix
```

You can use */perf* with */scan* to perform a scan faster. The */perf* option allocates more system resources to the scan, which could possibly affect server performance but allows a scan to be completed more quickly.

Standard repair options remain available as well, but they might require offline scan and offline repair in some instances. You can use the */X* parameter to force a volume to dismount if necessary or the */R* parameter to locate bad sectors; each implies the */F* parameter. If you use the */R* parameter, ChkDsk performs an additional step in the analysis and repair that involves checking each sector on the disk to make sure it can be read from and written to correctly. If it finds a bad sector, ChkDsk marks it so that data won't be written to that sector. If the sector was part of a cluster that was in use, ChkDsk moves the good data in that cluster to a new cluster.

The data in the bad sector can be recovered only if there's redundant data from which to copy it. The bad sector won't be used again, so at least it won't cause problems in the future. Checking each sector on a disk is a time-intensive process—and one that you won't perform often. More typically, you'll use **ChkDsk /F** to check for and repair common errors.

NOTE

With standard scan and repair, you can force ChkDsk to reevaluate clusters it has marked as bad by using the */B* parameter. This parameter implies the */R* parameter. Here, ChkDsk again attempts to determine whether it can read from and write to the cluster correctly. If the cluster can be read from and written to correctly, ChkDsk marks the cluster as good so that the disk subsystem can use it.

Automated optimization of disks

As files are created, modified, and moved, fragmentation can occur both within the volume's allocation table and on the volume itself. This happens because files are written to clusters on disk as they are used. The file system uses the first clusters available when writing new data, so as you modify files, different parts of files can end up in different areas of the disk. If you delete a file, an area of the disk is made available, but it might not be big enough to store the next file that is created and, as a result, part of a new file might be written to this newly freed area and part of it might be written somewhere else on the disk.

Although the file system doesn't care whether the file data is on contiguous clusters or spread out across the disk, the fact that data is in different areas of the disk can slow down read/write operations. This means it will take longer than usual to open and save files. It also makes recovering files more difficult in case of serious disk error. Windows Server 2012 R2 provides the Optimize Drives utility, a tool for defragmenting volumes. Unlike Check Disk, which cannot check and repair the operating system volume while it is in use, Optimize Drives can, in most cases, perform online defragmentation of any volume, including the operating system volume.

Preventing fragmentation of disks

Windows Server 2012 R2 analyzes fragmentation and optimizes volumes as part of automated maintenance. Windows does this by using the Optimize Drives utility. Although automated maintenance triggers the disk analysis, the process of calling and managing Optimize Drives is handled by a separate task. In Task Scheduler, you find the ScheduledDefrag task in the scheduler library under Microsoft\Windows\Defrag, and you can get detailed run information on the task's History tab.

Automatic analysis and optimization of disks can occur while the disks are online so long as the computer is on AC power and the operating system is running but otherwise idle. By default, disk optimization is a weekly task rather than a daily task—and there's a good reason for this. Normally, you need to optimize a server's disks only periodically, and optimization once a week is sufficient in most cases. That said, the more frequently data is updated on drives, the more often disks should be optimized.

Windows automatically performs cyclic pickup defragmentation. With this feature, when a scheduled defragmentation pass is stopped and rerun, the computer automatically picks up the next unfinished volume in line to be defragmented. Although nonsystem disks can be rapidly analyzed and optimized, it can take significantly longer to optimize system disks online.

You can control the approximate start time for the analysis and optimization of disks by changing the automated maintenance start time. Windows Server also notifies you if three consecutive runs are missed. All internal drives and certain external drives are optimized automatically as part of the regular schedule, as are new drives you connect to the server.

With manual optimization, Optimize Drives performs an online analysis of volumes and then reports the percentage of fragmentation. If defragmentation is needed, you can then elect to perform online defragmentation. System and boot volumes can be defragmented online as well, and Optimize Drives can be used with FAT, FAT32, exFAT, NTFS, and ReFS volumes.

You can configure and manage automated defragmentation by following these steps:

1. In Computer Management, select the Storage node and then the Disk Management node. Press and hold or right-click a drive and then tap or click Properties.
2. On the Tools tab, tap or click Optimize. In the Optimize Drives dialog box, shown in Figure 16-8, note the last run-time and status of each volume. The status shows the percentage of fragmentation. A volume that needs optimization is listed as Needs Optimization. Otherwise, the volume status is listed as OK.

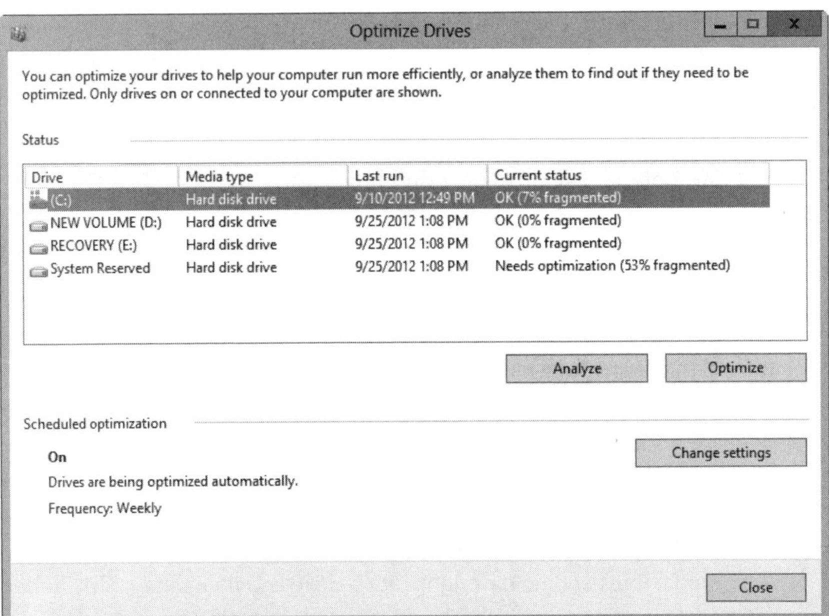

Figure 16-8 Review the status of each volume.

3. Under Scheduled Optimization, note the scheduled optimization settings, which indicate whether automated optimization is enabled and provide the run frequency. If you want to change how optimization works, tap or click Change Settings. This opens the dialog box shown in Figure 16-9. To cancel automated defragmentation, clear the Run On A Schedule check box. To enable automated defragmentation, select Run On A Schedule.

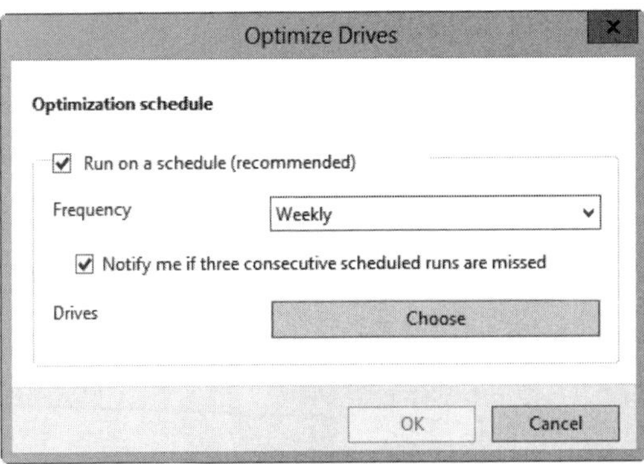

Figure 16-9 Set the schedule for automated optimization of volumes.

4. The default run frequency is set as shown. In the Frequency list, you can choose Daily, Weekly, or Monthly as the run schedule. If you don't want to be notified about missed runs, clear the Notify Me check box.

5. If you want to manage which disks are defragmented, tap or click Choose and then select the volumes to defragment. By default, all disks installed within or connected to the computer are defragmented, and any new disks are defragmented automatically as well. Select the check boxes for disks that should be defragmented automatically and clear the check boxes for disks that should not be defragmented automatically. Tap or click OK to save your settings.

6. Tap or click OK and then tap or click Close.

Fixing fragmentation by using Optimize Drives

By using Optimize Drives, you can check for and correct volume fragmentation problems on FAT, FAT32, and NTFS volumes. The areas checked for fragmentation include the volume, files, folders, page file (if one exists on the volume), and the MFT. You also can defragment volumes with cluster sizes greater than 4 KBs.

You can run the graphical version of Optimize Drives by using either File Explorer or Computer Management. In File Explorer, press and hold or right-click the volume and choose Properties. On the Tools tab of the Properties dialog box, tap or click Optimize to open the Optimize Drives dialog box. In Computer Management, select the Storage node and then the Disk Management node. Press and hold or right-click a drive and then select Properties. On the Tools tab, tap or click Optimize.

In the Optimize Drives dialog box, select a disk and then tap or click Analyze. Optimize Drives then analyzes the disk to determine whether it needs to be defragmented. If so, it recommends that you defragment at this point. If a disk needs to be defragmented, select the disk and then tap or click Optimize. Depending on the size of the disk, defragmentation can take several hours. You can tap or click Stop at any time to stop defragmentation.

NOTE

Optimize Drives needs 10 to 15 percent free space to defragment a disk completely. Optimize Drives uses this space as a sorting area for file fragments. If a volume has less free space, Optimize Drives will only partially defragment it. By default, Optimize Drives performs partial defragmentation by attempting to consolidate only fragments smaller than 64 MBs.

Optimize Drives can also be run at the command line by using Defrag (Defrag.exe). You can run Optimize Drives in analysis mode at the command line by typing **defrag /a** followed by the drive designator. For example, if you want to analyze the fragmentation of the D drive, you type **defrag /a d:**. To analyze and then defragment a volume if defragmentation is necessary, type **defrag** followed by the drive designator, such as **defrag d:**. No parameters are necessary (because the */d* parameter is implied, which performs a traditional defrag).

You defrag multiple drives by providing the designator of each drive you want to defrag, such as:

```
defrag /a c: d: g:
```

This specifies that you want to defrag the C, D, and G drives. By default, Defrag runs with low priority and defrags each volume in turn. Here, that would mean the utility would defrag the C drive, then the D drive, and finally the G drive.

Defrag has several syntaxes. The syntax for analyzing volumes without defragmentation is:

```
defrag volume(s) /a [/h] [/m] | [/u] [/v]
```

Here, when you use */h*, */m*, or both, you cannot use */u*, */v*, or both. The */h* parameter enables you to run the defrag with normal priority, which gives the defrag task the same priority as most other processes and should speed up the defrag. The */m* parameter enables Windows to defrag multiple volumes at the same time, in parallel rather than in a series. The */u* parameter displays the defrag progress, and the */v* parameter displays verbose output, which includes fragmentation statistics. Following this, you could defrag the C, D, and G drives in parallel at normal priority by typing:

```
defrag c: d: g: /a /h /m
```

Analyze (*/a*) is one of several independent tasks that you can perform. Other independent tasks you can perform include traditional defrag (*/d*), optimization (*/o*), and free-space consolidation (*/x*). The syntax for all three variations is the same except for the primary task being performed. As an example, if defrag specifies that drives need to be optimized to reduce fragmentation, you use */o* to do this. The syntax for optimizing fragmented drives is:

```
defrag volume(s) /o [/h] [/m] | [/u] [/v]
```

The optimization process focuses on reduced file fragmentation. Over time, free space on a drive also can become fragmented. You can use the */x* parameter to consolidate the free-space fragments, and the syntax is:

```
defrag volume(s) /x [/h] [/m] | [/u] [/v]
```

> NOTE
>
> **Thinly provisioned virtual disks (Storage Spaces, dynamic virtual hard disks [VHDs], storage area network [SAN] virtual disks) are the only types of disks whose free space is consolidated when optimized.**

Rather than trying to remember all these syntaxes separately, I recommend focusing on the primary tasks you can perform: analysis (*/a*), traditional defrag (*/d*), optimization (*/o*), and free-space consolidation (*/x*). Then consider the additional options you might want to use, including either higher priority (*/h*) and multitasking (*/m*) or progress updates (*/u*) and verbose output (*/v*).

Inside OUT

Optimizing virtual disks

You optimize the internal structures of virtual disks by using the standard optimization tasks, including analysis (*/a*), traditional defrag (*/d*), optimization (*/o*), and free-space consolidation (*/x*). That doesn't necessarily optimize the external structures from which virtual disks are constructed, however, and fragmentation in these external structures can affect virtual disk performance as much as fragmentation of internal structures.

The external structures from which virtual disks are constructed are referred to as *slabs*. A slab is simply an allocation unit or, put another way, a contiguous block of allocated space on the underlying physical disk. The performance of a virtual disk can be affected when there are too many small slabs, too many slabs spread out across the underlying physical disk, or both. You can attempt to consolidate slabs by using the */k* parameter. The syntax is:

```
defrag volume(s) /k [/h] [/m] | [/u] [/v]
```

When you use the */k* parameter, the */l* parameter is implied. The */l* parameter generates trim and unmap hints for sectors that were previously allocated to the virtual disk but the virtual disk no longer uses. The underlying physical disk uses the trim and unmap hints to recover unused space.

You can retrim a virtual disk without performing a slab consolidation. The syntax is:

```
defrag volume(s) /l [/h] [/m] | [/u] [/v]
```

That said, when you optimize standard virtual disks (.vhd), Defrag performs slab consolidation automatically as well but won't retrim automatically. When you optimize differential virtual disks or thinly provisioned virtual disks (Storage Spaces, dynamic VHDs, SAN virtual disks), Defrag doesn't perform slab consolidation automatically but does retrim automatically.

Table 16-2 summarizes available Defrag options and parameters and their uses. Note the */C* and */E* parameters. You use the */C* parameter when you want to defrag all available volumes (and don't want to specify the volumes individually by drive designator). You use the

/E parameter when you want to defrag all available volumes except those specified after the */E* parameter. For example, if you wanted to defrag all available volumes except the D and G drives, you enter:

```
defrag /d /e d: g:
```

Table 16-2 Command-line parameters for Defrag

Option/Parameter	Description
Volume(s)	Sets the volume or volumes to work with.
/A	Performs an analysis only of the specified volume or volumes.
/C	Used instead of a drive letter; tells Defrag to optimize all disks.
/D	Performs an analysis of the specified volume or volumes, followed by optimization if required.
/E	Tells Defrag to optimize all disks except those specified after the parameter.
/G	Optimizes storage tiers on the specified volumes.
/H	Runs Defrag with higher priority, meaning normal priority instead of low priority.
/K	Performs slab consolidation and retrim of virtual disks. This applies to virtual disks only.
/L	Performs retrim of virtual disks. This applies to virtual disks only.
/M	Multitasks the optimization by running Defrag in parallel on each volume specified.
/O	Performs optimization of the specified volume or volumes if fragmented.
/T	Tracks in-progress tasks on the specified volume or volumes.
/U	Provides progress updates on the screen.
/V	Displays verbose output containing fragmentation statistics.
/X	Performs free-space consolidation on the specified volume or volumes.

Understanding the fragmentation analysis

You can perform fragmentation analysis at the command line by using the */a* and */v* parameters. The command-line report shows the summary of fragmentation. The summary looks like this:

```
Invoking analysis on (C:)...

Post Defragmentation Report:

        Volume Information:
```

```
            Volume size                  = 183.99 GB
            Cluster size                 = 4 KB
            Used space                   = 146.14 GB
            Free space                   = 37.85 GB

    Fragmentation:
            Total fragmented space       = 7%
            Average fragments per file   = 1.09

            Movable files and folders    = 716750
            Unmovable files and folders  = 20

    Files:
            Fragmented files             = 8265
            Total file fragments         = 61643

    Folders:
            Total folders                = 32654
            Fragmented folders           = 2274
            Total folder fragments       = 9690

    Free space:
            Free space count             = 2470
            Average free space size      = 15.64 MB
            Largest free space size      = 7.24 GB

    Master File Table (MFT):
            MFT size                     = 921.25 MB
            MFT record count             = 943359
            MFT usage                    = 100%
            Total MFT fragments          = 7

    Note: File fragments larger than 64MB are not included in the
fragmentation statistics.

    You do not need to defragment this volume.
```

The summary of the volume's configuration and space usage reports on the following areas:

- **Overall fragmentation.** Gives an overview of fragmentation showing the percentage of used space that is fragmented, the average number of fragments per file, the total number of files on the volume that are movable, and the total number of unmovable files. Ideally, you want the percentage of fragmentation to be 10 percent or less and the number of fragments per file to be as close to 1.00 as possible.

- **File fragmentation.** Gives an overview of file-level fragmentation showing how many files are fragmented and the total number of excess fragments.

CHAPTER 16

- **Folder fragmentation.** Gives an overview of folder-level fragmentation showing the total number of folders on the volume, how many folders are fragmented, and the total number of excess fragments.
- **Free space fragmentation.** Gives an overview of fragmentation on a volume's unused space showing how much free space is available on the volume, the number of extents on which free space is located, the average amount of free space per extent, and the largest free-space extent.
- **Master file table (MFT) fragmentation.** For NTFS volumes only, gives an overview of fragmentation in the MFT showing the current size of the MFT, the number of records it contains, the percentage of the MFT in use, and the total number of fragments in the MFT. In this example, the MFT has some fragmentation, but the real concern is that it is at 100 percent of its maximum size. Because of this, the MFT could become more fragmented over time—there is still 37.85 GBs of free space on the volume, and if it needs to grow, it will grow into the free space.

If you run Defrag again, using */o*, Optimize Drives sets about cleaning up the drive to give optimal space usage. This won't clear up all fragmentation, but it will help so that disk space is used more efficiently. On a volume like the one shown with very little fragmentation, you won't really see performance improvements after defragmentation. However, if the fragmentation percentage were higher, performance improvements could be considerable.

With virtual disks, slab consolidation and retrim are used to optimize external structures. You can perform these tasks at the command line by using the */k* and */v* parameters. The command-line report shows the summary of optimization. The summary looks like this:

```
Invoking slab consolidation on New Volume (I:)...

        Retrim:  100% complete.

        Slab consolidation: 100% complete.


The operation completed successfully.

Post Defragmentation Report:

        Volume Information:
                Volume size                 = 126.99 GB
                Cluster size                = 4 KB
                Used space                  = 102.06 GB
                Free space                  = 24.93 GB

        Allocation Units:
                Slab count                  = 4063
                Slab size                   = 32 MB
```

CHAPTER 16

```
        Slab alignment              = 31.00 MB
        In-use slabs                = 3266

Slab Consolidation:
        Space efficiency            = 92%
        Potential purgable slabs    = 48
        Slabs pinned unmovable      = 704
        Successfully purged slabs   = 36
        Recovered space             = 1152 MB

Retrim:
        Backed allocations          = 68
        Allocations trimmed         = 18
        Total space trimmed         = 539.82 MB
```

The summary reports on the following areas:

- **Volume Information.** Gives an overview of the volume showing its maximum volume size, cluster size, used space, and free space. Because you are optimizing external structures, free space in the volume doesn't affect whether you can consolidate slabs and retrim.

- **Allocation Units.** Gives an overview of the volume's allocation units showing the total number of slabs allocated to the volume, the size of the slabs, the slab alignment offset, and the number of in-use slabs. The difference between the total slab count and the in-use slab count represents the number of available slabs.

- **Slab Consolidation.** Gives an overview of the slab consolidation showing how efficiently space is being used, the potentially purgable slabs remaining, the number of unmovable slabs, the number of successfully purged slabs, and the total space recovered. Ideally, after consolidating slabs, a high level of space efficiency and relatively few potentially purgable slabs will remain.

- **Retrim.** Gives an overview of the underlying physical disk space recovered by trimming sectors that were previously allocated to the virtual disk but the virtual disk no longer uses. It shows the number of allocations trimmed and the total space recovered.

CHAPTER 17

Managing storage spaces

When you are working with File And Storage Services, you can group available physical disks into storage pools so that you can create virtual disks from available capacity. Each virtual disk you create is a storage space. Storage Spaces are made available through the Storage Services role service, which is automatically installed on every server running Windows Server 2012 R2. Servers also can use data deduplication to find and remove duplication within data, which can help optimize utilization of storage.

Understanding storage spaces

Storage management abstracts storage volumes from the underlying physical layout, resulting in what can be considered a three-layered architecture. In Layer 1, the layout of the physical disks is controlled by the storage subsystem with hardware-based redundant array of independent disks (RAID) controlled by the storage subsystem to ensure that data is redundant and recoverable in case of failure. In Layer 2, virtual disks created by the storage arrays are made available for allocation and servers can apply software-level RAID or other redundancy approaches to help protect against failure at the operating-system level. In Layer 3, the server creates volumes on the virtual disks and these volumes provide the usable file systems for file and data storage.

Put another way, storage-management hardware handles the architecture particulars for data redundancy and the portions of disks that are presented as usable disks. This means the layout of the physical disks is controlled by the storage subsystem instead of by the operating system. With the physical layout of disks (spindles) abstracted, a "disk" can be a logical reference to a portion of a storage subsystem (a virtual disk) or an actual physical disk. This means a disk simply becomes a unit of storage, and volumes can be created to allocate space within disks for file systems.

Windows Server 2012 R2 takes typical storage management a few steps further, enabling you to pool available space on disks so that units of storage (virtual disks) can be allocated from this pool on an as-needed basis. These units of storage, in turn, are apportioned with volumes to allocate space and create usable file systems. This pooled storage is referred to as *storage pools*, and the virtual disks created within a pool are referred to as *storage spaces*. Given a set of disks from the storage subsystem, you can create a single storage pool by allocating all the disks to the pool or multiple storage pools by allocating disks separately to each pool.

In Windows Server 2012 R2, the primary storage-management functions are enabled by the Storage Services role service, which is part of the File And Storage Services role. The core components of the Storage Services role service, which is installed by default on all servers, are what enable you to manage storage spaces and work with storage pools. They include the following:

- Extensions for Server Manager that enable you to manage storage
- Windows Storage Management APIs for Windows PowerShell and Windows Management Instrumentation (WMI)
- Storage Management Provider (SMP) interfaces for Storage Spaces
- Pass-through application programming interface (API) for extensibility, based on WMI

Together, these features enable you to use Server Manager and other compatible management applications, such as System Center 2012 Virtual Machine Manager with Service Pack 1 or later, to connect to and manage Serial Attached SCSI (SAS), USB, and Serial ATA (SATA) disks. These features also enable Server Manager and other compatible management applications to connect to and manage storage arrays and their RAID controllers by using vendor-provided WMI-based provider transports, protocols, or both.

To add support for standards-based storage management, add the Windows Standards-Based Storage Management feature to your file servers. This adds components and updates for working with standards-based volumes as implemented in the Storage Management Initiative Specification (SMI-S). Server Manager and other compatible management applications can then connect to and manage storage arrays and their RAID controllers by using vendor-provided SMI-S providers.

Seamless integration of storage-management applications with devices ensures flexibility and uniform management for the following:

- Discovery and replication
- Thin provisioning
- Snapshot management
- Masking and unmasking
- Enumerating host bus adapter (HBA) ports
- Creating pools, virtual disks, and volumes

You can extend these storage-management capabilities in several ways. Cmdlets for Windows PowerShell enable scriptable management. Add the Data Deduplication role service if you want to enable data deduplication. Add the iSCSI Target Server and iSCSI Target Storage Provider role services if you want the server to host iSCSI virtual disks. Add the Data Center Bridging feature if you want to enforce bandwidth allocation for offloaded storage traffic.

NOTE

Virtual disks created as part of a storage pool are separate and distinct from iSCSI virtual disks. iSCSI virtual disks can be created on a server by using Storage Spaces; they cannot, however, be used in a storage space.

Using and configuring offloaded transfers

Windows Offloaded Data Transfer (ODX), included in Windows Server 2012 R2, allows direct data transfer within or between data-storage devices. Bypassing host computers and transferring data within or between storage arrays ensures maximum efficiency. It not only maximizes array throughput, it also reduces resource usage on the host computers.

IMPORTANT

For an offloaded transfer within an array, the array's copy manager must support ODX. For transfers between arrays, the copy managers for both storage arrays must support cross-storage ODX and be from the same vendor. Storage arrays must be connected using Internet Small Computer System Interface (iSCSI), Fibre Channel, Fibre Channel over Ethernet (FCoE), or SAS. As you set out to use ODX, you should also note the default inactive timer value, the maximum token capacity, and the optimal transfer size of the copy managers that storage arrays use. The default inactive timer value specifies how long the copy manager waits to invalidate the idle token after the timer expiration. The maximum token capacity determines how many offloaded transfers can run simultaneously. The optimal transfer size tells Windows how to send Read/Write commands that are optimally sized for the storage arrays.

With traditional data transfers, data to be transferred is read from the storage through the source server and transferred over the network to the destination server before being written back to the storage through the destination server. This is very inefficient whether servers share storage or use storage from different storage arrays. ODX eliminates this inefficiency.

To see how ODX works at a high level, consider the following scenarios:

- FileServer1 and FileServer2 are running Windows Server 2008 R2, and they are connected to the same storage array from which the servers get their logical unit numbers (LUNs) for storage. You want to move a 2 TB data share from FileServer1 to FileServer2 and initiate the move on FileServer1, which handles the file transfer. Both FileServer1 and FileServer2 use system resources to manage the transfer, which takes several hours and uses a fair amount of CPU and memory resources.

- FileServer1 and FileServer2 are running Windows Server 2012, and they are connected to the same storage array from which the servers get their LUNs for storage. You want to move a 2 TB data share from FileServer1 to FileServer2 and initiate the move on FileServer1. FileServer1 offloads the data transfer to the storage array. Because you are moving data within the same array, the transfer is accomplished rapidly. Because the transfer is offloaded to the array, few CPU or memory resources are used on either FileServer1 or FileServer2.
- FileServer1 and FileServer2 are running Windows Server 2012 R2, and they are connected to different storage arrays from which the servers get their LUNs for storage. You want to move a 2 TB data share from FileServer1 to FileServer2 and initiate the move on FileServer1. FileServer1 offloads the data transfer to its storage array, Array A, which handles the transfer to Array B. Because you are moving data between arrays, the transfer takes longer than moving data within an array. Because the transfer is offloaded, few CPU or memory resources are used on either FileServer1 or FileServer2.

Okay, so that's the top-level view of ODX. To dig deeper into how ODX actually works, let's look at how tokens are used and how you can verify offloaded transfers.

Understanding how offloaded transfers work

When an offloaded transfer is initiated, Windows uses tokens as point-in-time representations of the data being transferred. Instead of routing data through the host, the token is copied between the source server and the destination server. The source server then delivers the token to the source storage array, which performs the actual copy or move while providing status updates regarding the transfer. Step by step, the process looks like this:

1. An application, user, or the operating system itself copies or moves data stored on an array. This initiates a transfer, which the operating system sees as a transfer request.
2. The operating system translates this transfer request into an offloaded transfer and receives a token representing the data.
3. After the token is copied between the source server and the destination server, the source server delivers the token to the source storage array.
4. The source storage array performs the actual copy or move while providing status updates regarding the transfer.

5. With multipath I/O (MPIO), path failover is handled automatically. Here, Windows retries the offloaded transfer. If the retry also fails, Windows can initiate a cluster failover if the server is part of a cluster.
6. With clustering, cluster failover is handled automatically as well. Here, if the transfer was initiated by a cluster-aware application, the application can resume the offloaded transfer after failover.
7. If the transfer can't be resumed or restarted after MPIO path or cluster failover, Windows issues a LUN reset to the storage array. This ends the transfer and all related operations. Windows then returns an I/O failure.

Verifying support for offloaded transfers

With ODX, data transfers are offloaded when you copy or move data stored on an array, whether you use graphical tools, such as File Explorer, or command-line tools, such as XCOPY. You can verify ODX support by examining the file system filter drivers that are attached to volumes. For each filter driver, query the registry to determine whether the filter driver has opted in to ODX support.

List the filter system drivers for a particular volume by entering the following at an elevated Windows PowerShell prompt:

```
fltmc instances -v Volume
```

Here, *Volume* is the drive designator of the volume to examine, such as:

```
fltmc instances -v i:
```

Each filter is listed by name and should have a *SprtFtrs* value. If the supported features value is 3, the filter driver supports ODX. If this value is not 3, the filter driver doesn't support ODX and you need to obtain a different driver from the vendor.

If the *SprtFtrs* value isn't as expected, you also can go into the registry to confirm support. At an elevated Windows PowerShell prompt, enter:

```
get-itemproperty hklm:\system\currentcontrolset\services\filtername
-name "SupportedFeatures"
```

Here, *FilterName* is the name of the filter, as listed by Fltmc. Again, if the supported features value is 3, the filter driver supports ODX. If this value is not 3, the filter driver doesn't support ODX, and you need to obtain a different driver from the vendor.

You can enable ODX support by entering the following at an elevated Windows PowerShell prompt:

```
set-itemproperty hklm:\system\currentcontrolset\control\filesystem
-name "FilterSupportedFeaturesMode" -value 0
```

Disable ODX support by entering the following:

```
set-itemproperty hklm:\system\currentcontrolset\control\filesystem
-name "FilterSupportedFeaturesMode" -value 1
```

Working with available storage

Server Manager is the tool of choice for working with Storage Spaces. In Server Manager, you select the File And Storage Services node to view and work with your storage volumes.

Storage Management Essentials

As Figure 17-1 shows, the File And Storage Services node has multiple subnodes. The Volumes subnode lists allocated storage on each server according to how volumes are provisioned and how much free space each volume has. Volumes are listed regardless of whether the underlying disks are physical or virtual.

Press and hold or right-click a volume to display management options, including the following:

- **Configure Data Deduplication.** Allows you to enable and configure data deduplication for NTFS volumes. If the feature is enabled, you can use this option to disable data deduplication as well.
- **Delete Volume.** Allows you to delete the volume. The space that was used is then marked as unallocated on the related disk.
- **Extend Volume.** Allows you to extend the volume to unallocated space of the related disk.
- **Format.** Allows you to create a new file system on the volume that overwrites the existing volume.
- **Manage Drive Letter And Access Paths.** Allows you to change the drive letter or access path associated with the volume.
- **New iSCSI Virtual Disk.** Allows you to create a new iSCSI virtual disk that is stored on the volume.

- **New Share.** Allows you to create new Server Message Block (SMB) or Network File System (NFS) shares on the volume.
- **Properties.** Displays information about the volume type, file system, health, capacity, used space, and free space. You also can use this option to set the volume label.rft.
- **Repair File System Errors.** Allows you to repair errors detected during an online scan of the file system.
- **Scan File System For Errors.** Allows you to perform an online scan of the file system. Although Windows attempts to repair any errors that are found, some errors can be corrected only by using a repair procedure.

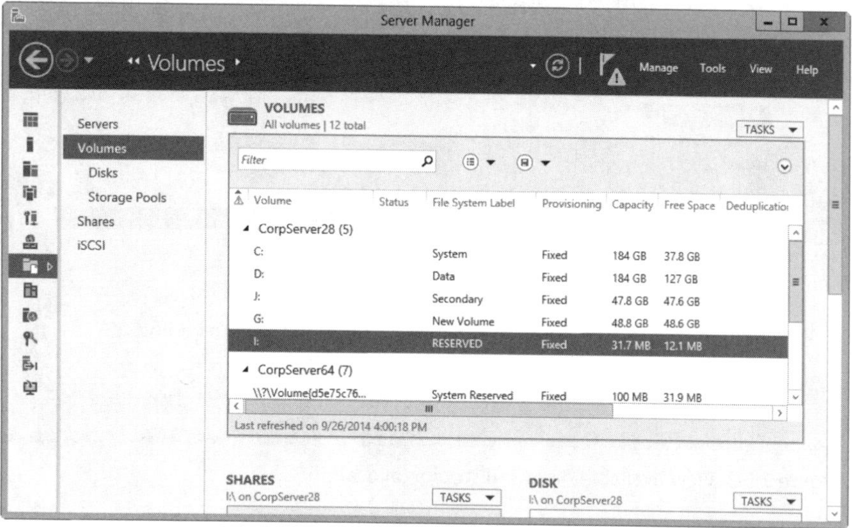

Figure 17-1 View available storage volumes.

The Disks subnode, shown in Figure 17-2, lists the disks available to each server according to total capacity, unallocated space, partition style, subsystem, and bus type. Server Manager attempts to differentiate between physical disks and virtual disks by showing the virtual disk label (if one was provided) and the originating storage subsystem. Press and hold or right-click a disk to display management options, including the following:

- **Bring Online.** Enables you to make an offline disk available for use
- **Take Offline.** Enables you to take a disk offline so that it can no longer be used

- **Reset Disk.** Enables you to reset the disk completely, which deletes all volumes on the disk and removes all available data on the disk
- **New Volume.** Enables you to create a new volume on the disk

NOTE

The Disks subnode does not list physical disks that have the dynamic disk type. If you want to use a disk with Storage Pools, the disk should either be raw (previously unused) or have the basic disk type.

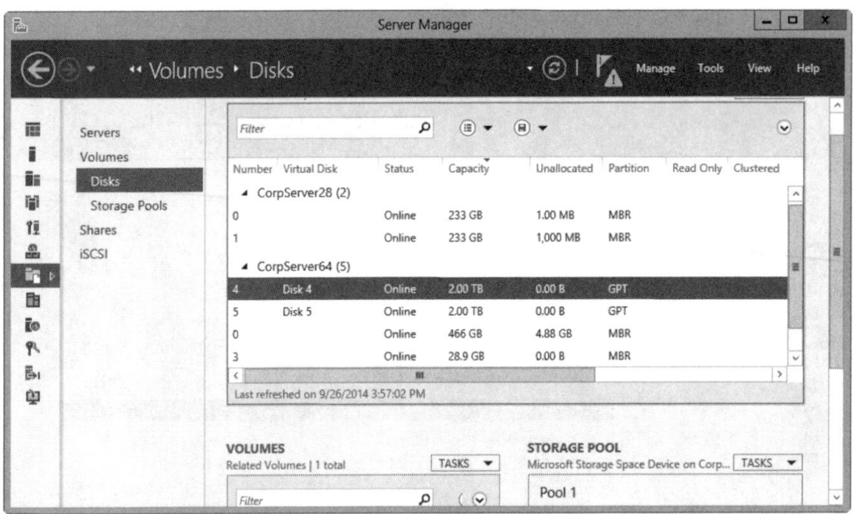

Figure 17-2 View available disks and storage allocation.

The version of Storage Spaces that ships with Windows Server 2012 R2 is different from the version that ships with Windows Server 2012. If you have any questions about which version of Storage Spaces is being used, press and hold or right-click the storage pool you want to examine and then select Properties. In the Properties dialog box, select Details in the left pane and then choose Version on the Property selection list.

Storage pool details also provide details about capacity, status, logical sector size, physical sector size, provisioned space size, thin provisioning alert threshold, and total used space. By default, Storage Space alerts you when storage is approaching capacity and when a storage space reaches 70 percent of the total provisioned size. When you get such an alert, you should consider allocating additional storage.

You can upgrade the version of Storage Spaces a storage pool uses by pressing and holding or right-clicking a storage pool and then selecting Upgrade Storage Pool Version. In addition to correcting issues that can result in error and warning states when creating and managing Storage Spaces, the Windows Server 2012 R2 version of Storage Spaces has many improvements.

Windows Server 2012 R2 supports storage spaces that have dual parity and parity and dual parity spaces on failover clusters. With dual parity, storage spaces are protected against two simultaneous drive failures. Windows Server 2012 R2 also supports the following:

- Automatic rebuild
- Storage tiers
- Write-back caching

With automatic rebuild, Windows Server can automatically rebuild storage spaces from storage pool free space instead of having to use hot spares to recover from drive failures. Here, instead of writing a copy of data that was on a failed disk to a hot spare, the parity or mirrored data is copied to multiple drives in the pool to achieve the previous level of resiliency automatically. As a result, you don't need to allocate hot spares in storage pools specifically, provided that a sufficient number of drives is assigned to the pool to allow for automatic resiliency recovery.

With storage tiers, Windows Server can automatically move frequently used files from slower physical disks to faster solid state drive (SSD) storage. This feature is applicable only when a storage space has a combination of SSD storage and hard disk drive (HDD) storage. In addition, the storage type must be set as fixed, the volumes created on virtual disks must be the same size as the virtual disk, and enough free space must be available to accommodate the preference. For fine-grained management, use the Set-FileStorageTier cmdlet to assign files to standard physical drive storage or faster SSD storage.

When a storage pool uses SSD storage, Windows Server can use write-back caching. Write-back cache buffers small random writes to SSD storage before later writing the data to HDD storage. Buffering writes in this way helps protect against data loss in the event of power failures. For write-back cache to work properly, storage spaces with simple volumes must have at least one SSD, storage spaces with two-way mirroring or single parity must have at least two SSDs, and storage spaces with three-way mirroring or dual parity must have at least three SSDs. When these requirements are met, the volumes automatically use a 1 GB write-back cache by default. You can designate SSDs that should be used for write-back caching by setting the usage as Journal (the default in this configuration). If not enough SSDs are configured for journaling, the write-back cache size is set to 0 (meaning write-back caching will not be used). The only exception is for parity spaces, which then have the write-back cache size set to 32 MB.

If you have any question about the size of the write-back cache, complete the following steps to check the cache size:

1. Press and hold or right-click the virtual disk you want to examine and then select Properties.
2. In the Properties dialog box, select Details in the left pane and then choose WriteCacheSize in the Property selection list.

You also can use this technique to check allocated size, status, provisioned size, provision type, redundancy type, and more.

Creating storage pools and allocating space

Storage Spaces uses physical disks exclusively for data storage. When you add a formatted drive to a storage pool, Windows permanently deletes all the files on that drive.

Storage layers that abstract the physical disk are not compatible with Storage Spaces. These include VHDs, pass-through disks on a virtual machine, and storage subsystems that layer RAID on top of the physical disks. Although Storage Spaces supports SAS, SATA, and USB, Storage Spaces doesn't currently support iSCSI or Fibre Channel controllers. If RAID adapters are used, the adapters must be in non-RAID mode with RAID functionality disabled and must not abstract the physical disks, cache data, or obscure any attached devices.

In Server Manager, you can work with storage pools and allocate space by selecting the File And Storage Services node and then selecting the related Storage Pools subnode. The Storage Pools subnode, shown in Figure 17-3, lists the available storage pools, the virtual disks created within storage pools, and the available physical disks. Keep in mind that what's presented as physical disks might actually be LUNs (virtual disks) from a storage subsystem.

NOTE

The Storage Pools subnode does not list physical disks that have the dynamic disk type. If you want to use a disk with Storage Pools, the disk should either be raw (previously unused) or have the basic disk type. Note also that when you use a disk with Storage Spaces, the disk has a new disk type that is neither the basic disk type nor the dynamic disk type.

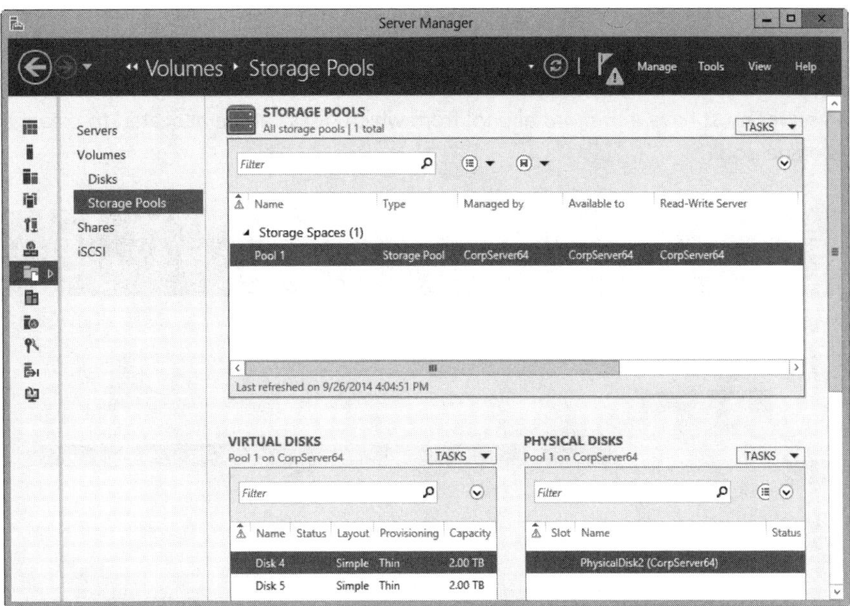

Figure 17-3 View available storage pools.

Working with storage pools is a multistep process:

1. You create storage pools to pool available space on one or more disks.
2. You allocate space from this pool to create one or more virtual disks.
3. You create one or more volumes on each virtual disk to allocate storage for file systems.

The sections that follow examine procedures related to each of these steps.

Creating storage spaces

You can use storage pools to pool available space on disks so that units of storage (virtual disks) can be allocated from this pool. To create a storage pool, you must have at least one unused disk and a storage subsystem to manage it. This storage subsystem can be the one included with the Storage Spaces feature or a subsystem associated with attached storage.

When a computer has hard drives in addition to the hard drive on which Windows is installed, you can allocate one or more of the additional drives to a storage pool. However, keep in mind that if you use a formatted drive with a storage pool, Windows permanently deletes all the files on that drive. In addition, it's important to point out that physical disks with the master boot record (MBR) partition style are converted automatically to the GUID partition table (GPT) partition style when you add them to a storage pool and create volumes on them.

As shown in Figure 17-4, each server that has disks that are unallocated but available to be assigned to a storage pool is listed as having a *primordial pool*. A primordial pool is simply a group of disks managed by and available to a specific server through a storage subsystem. A server must have a primordial pool from which disks can be allocated to create a new storage pool.

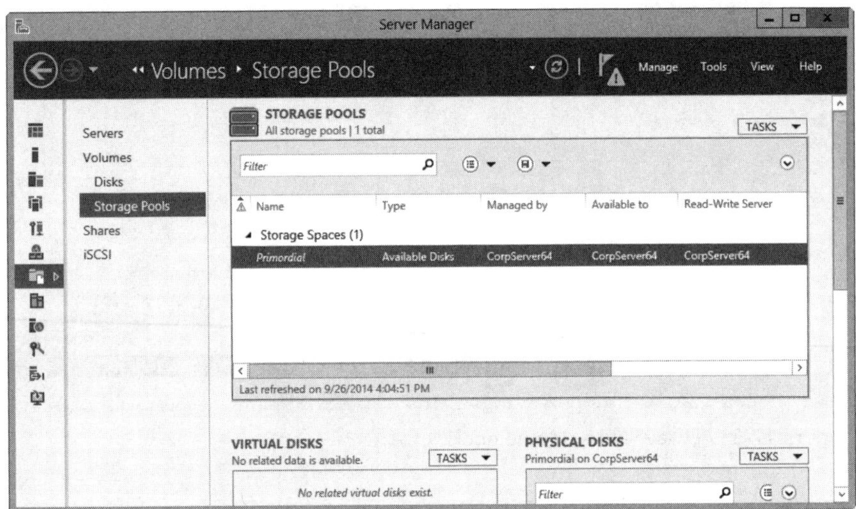

Figure 17-4 Primordial pools represent unallocated but available disks.

Each physical disk allocated to the pool can be handled in one of three ways:

- As a data store that is available for use
- As a data store that can be manually allocated for use
- As a hot spare in case a disk in the pool fails or is removed from the subsystem

If a server has a primordial pool, you can create a storage pool from its unallocated but available disks by completing the following steps:

1. With the Storage Pools subnode selected in Server Manager, tap or click Tasks on the Storage Pools panel and then tap or click New Storage Pool. This starts the New Storage Pool Wizard. If the wizard displays the Before You Begin page, read the Welcome text and then tap or click Next.
2. On the Specify A Storage Pool Name And Subsystem page, shown in Figure 17-5, type a name and description for the storage pool. Select the primordial pool for the server you want to associate the pool with and allocate storage for. For example, if you are

configuring storage for CorpServer64, select the primordial pool that is available to CorpServer64. Tap or click Next.

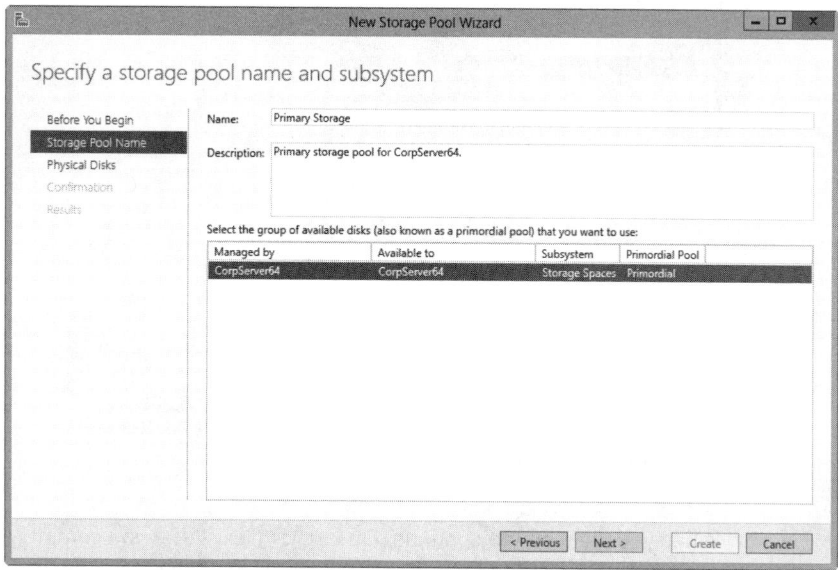

Figure 17-5 Select a primordial pool available to the server.

3. On the Select Physical Disks For The Storage Pool page, shown in Figure 17-6, select the unused physical disks that should be part of the storage pool and then specify the type of allocation for each disk. A storage pool must have two or more disks to use the mirroring and parity features available to protect data in case of error or failure. When setting the Allocation value, choose Automatic to allocate the disk to the pool and make it available for use or Hot Spare to allocate the disk to the pool as a spare disk that is made available for use if another disk in the pool fails or is removed from the subsystem.

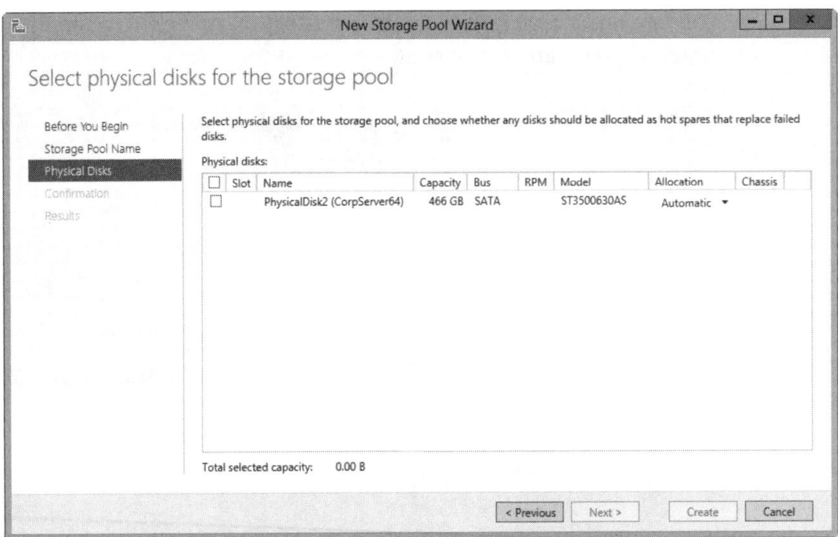

Figure 17-6 Specify the disks for the storage pool.

4. When you are ready to continue, tap or click Next. After you confirm your selections, tap or click Create. The wizard tracks the progress of the pool creation. When the wizard finishes creating the pool, the View Results page is updated to reflect this. Review the details to ensure that all phases were completed successfully and then tap or click Close.

If any portion of the configuration failed, note the reason for the failure and take corrective actions as appropriate before repeating this procedure.

If one of the physical disks is currently formatted with a volume, you get the following error: "Could not create storage pool. One of the physical disks specified is not supported by this operation."

This error occurs because physical disks that you want to add to a storage pool cannot contain existing volumes. To resolve the problem, you must repeat the procedure and select a different physical disk or remove any existing volumes on the physical disk, repeat the procedure, and then select the disk again. Keep in mind that deleting a volume permanently erases all data it contains.

If one of the physical disks is unavailable after being selected, you see the "Could not create storage pool. One or more parameter values passed to the method were invalid." error.This error occurs because a physical disk that was available when you started the New Storage Pool Wizard has become unavailable or is offline. To resolve the problem, you need to (a) repeat the procedure and select a different physical disk or (b) bring the physical disk online or otherwise make it available for use, repeat the procedure, and then select the disk again.

External storage can become unavailable for a variety of reasons. For example, an externally connected cable might have been disconnected or a LUN previously allocated to the server might have been reallocated by a storage administrator.

Creating a virtual disk in a storage space

After you create a storage pool, you can allocate space from the pool to virtual disks that are available to your servers. Each physical disk allocated to the pool can be handled in one of three ways:

- As a data store that is available for use
- As a data store that can be manually allocated for use
- As a hot spare in case a disk in the pool fails or is removed from the subsystem

You can create several types of volumes on virtual disks, including the following:

- **Simple volumes.** Creates a simple volume by writing one copy of your data to one or more drives. With simple volumes, there is no redundancy and no associated overhead. As an example, you can create a single volume that spans two 2 TB drives, making 4 TB of storage available. However, because there is no resiliency, a failure of any drive in a simple volume causes the entire volume to fail.
- **Two-way mirrors.** Creates a mirrored set by writing two copies of a computer's data, helping protect against a single drive failure. Two-way mirrors require at least two drives. With two-way mirrors, there is a one-half (50 percent) overhead for redundancy with two drives. As an example, you could allocate two 2 TB drives as a two-way mirror, giving you 2 TB of mirrored storage.
- **Parity volumes.** Creates a volume that uses disk striping with parity, helping provide fault tolerance with less overhead than mirroring. Parity volumes require at least three drives. With parity volumes, there is a one-third (33.33 percent) overhead for redundancy with three drives. As an example, you could allocate three 2 TB drives as a parity volume, giving you 4 TB of protected storage.
- **Dual parity volumes.** Creates a volume that uses disk striping with two sets of parity data, helping protect against two simultaneous drive failures while requiring less overhead than three-way mirroring. Dual parity volumes require at least seven drives.
- **Three-way mirrors.** Creates a mirrored set by writing three copies of a computer's data and by using disk striping with mirroring, helping protect against two simultaneous drive failures. Although three-way mirrors do not have a penalty for read operations, they do have a performance penalty for write operations because of the overhead associated with having to write data to three disks. This overhead can be mitigated by using

multiple drive controllers. Ideally, you want to ensure that at least three drive controllers are used. Three-way mirrors require at least five drives.

Windows Server 2012 and Windows Server 2012 R2 are the first versions of Windows Server to support dual parity volumes and three-way mirrors. Although dual parity does not have a penalty for read operations, it does have a performance penalty for write operations because of the overhead associated with calculating and writing dual parity values. With standard dual parity volumes, the usable capacity of dual parity volumes is calculated as the sum of the number of volumes minus two times the size of the smallest volume in the array, or (N – 2) * MinimumVolumeSize. For example, with 7 volumes and the smallest volume size of 1 TB, the usable capacity typically is 5 TB [calculated as (7 – 2) * 1 TB = 5 TB].

Logically, it would seem that you need at least six drives to have three mirrored copies of data. However, mathematically, you need only five volumes to create a three-way mirror. Why? If you want three copies of your data, you need at least 15 logical units of storage to create those three copies. Divide 15 by 3 to come up with the number of disks required, and the answer is that you need five disks. Thus, Storage Spaces uses one-third of each disk to store original data and two-thirds of each disk to store copies of data. Following this, a three-way mirror with five volumes has a two-thirds (66.66 percent) overhead for redundancy. Put another way, you could allocate five 3 TB drives as a three-way mirror, giving you 5 TB of mirrored storage (and 10 TB of overhead).

With single parity volumes, data is written out horizontally with parity calculated for each row of data. Dual parity differs from single parity in that row data is stored not only horizontally but also diagonally. If a single disk fails or a read error from a bad bit or block error occurs, the data is re-created by using only the horizontal row parity data (just as in single parity volumes). In the case of a multiple drive issue, the horizontal and diagonal row data are used for recovery.

Consider the following simplified example as a way to understand better how dual parity typically works:

Each horizontal row of data has a parity value, the sum of which is stored on the parity disk for that row (and calculated by using an exclusive OR). Each horizontal parity stripe misses one and only one disk. If the parity value is 2, 3, 1, and 4 on disks 0, 1, 2, and 3 respectively, the parity sum stored on disk 4 (the parity disk for this row) is 10 (2 + 3 + 1 + 4 = 10). If disk 0 were to have a problem, the parity value for the row on this disk could be restored by subtracting the remaining horizontal values from the horizontal parity sum (10 – 3 – 1 – 4 = 2).

The second set of parity data is written diagonally (meaning in different data rows on different disks). Each diagonal row of data has a diagonal parity value, the sum of which is stored on the diagonal parity disk for that row (and calculated by using an exclusive

OR). Each diagonal parity stripe misses two disks: one disk in which the diagonal parity sum is stored and one disk that is omitted from the diagonal parity striping. In addition, the diagonal parity sum includes a data row from the horizontal row parity as part of its diagonal parity sum.

If the diagonal parity value is 1, 4, 3, and 7 on disks 1, 2, 3, and 4 respectively (with four associated horizontal rows), the diagonal parity sum stored on disk 5 (the diagonal parity disk for this row) is 15 (1 + 4 + 3 + 7 = 15), and the omitted disk is disk 0. If disk 2 and disk 4 were to have a problem, the diagonal parity value for the row can be used to restore both of the lost values. The missing diagonal value is restored first by subtracting the remaining diagonal values from the diagonal parity sum. The missing horizontal value is restored next by subtracting the remaining horizontal values for the subject row from the horizontal parity sum for that row.

NOTE

It's important to point out that dual parity as implemented in Storage Spaces uses seven disks, and the previous example was simplified. Although parity striping with seven disks works differently than discussed in the example, the basic approach uses horizontal and vertical stripes.

When a storage pool has a single disk, your only option for allocating space on that disk is to create virtual disks with a simple layout. A simple layout does not protect against disk failure. If a storage pool has multiple disks, you use mirroring or parity to protect data in case of error or failure.

With a mirror layout, data is duplicated on disks by using a mirroring technique similar to what I discussed previously in this chapter. However, the mirroring technique is more sophisticated in that data is mirrored onto two or three disks at a time. Like standard mirroring, this approach has its advantages and disadvantages. Here, if a storage space has two or three disks, you are fully protected against a single disk failure and, if a storage space has five or more disks, you are fully protected against two simultaneous disk failures. The disadvantage is that mirroring reduces capacity by up to 50 percent. For example, if you mirror two 2 TB disks, the usable space is 2 TBs.

With a parity layout, data and parity information are striped across physical disks by using a striping-with-parity technique similar to what I discussed previously in this chapter. Like standard striping with parity, this approach has its advantages and disadvantages. You need at least three disks to protect yourself fully against a single disk failure. You lose some capacity to the striping but not as much as with mirroring. For example, if you enable parity on three 2 TB disks, the usable space is 4 TBs.

You can create a virtual disk in a storage pool by completing the following steps:

1. With the Storage Pools subnode selected in Server Manager, tap or click Tasks on the Virtual Disks panel and then tap or click New Virtual Disk to start the New Virtual Disk Wizard. If the wizard displays the Before You Begin page, read the Welcome text and then select Next.
2. On the Select The Storage Pool page, select the storage pool for the server you want to associate the virtual disk with and allocate storage from. Each available storage pool is listed according to the server it is managed by and available to. Make sure the pool has enough free space to create the virtual disk. Tap or click Next.
3. On the Specify The Virtual Disk Name page, type a name and description for the virtual disk. If you are using a combination of SSD storage and HDD storage, use the check box provided to specify whether you want to create storage tiers. With storage tiers, the most frequently accessed files are automatically moved from slower HDD storage to faster SSD storage. This option is not applicable when the server has only HDD or SSD storage. To continue, select Next.
4. On the Select The Storage Layout page, select the storage layout as appropriate for your reliability and redundancy requirements. The simple layout is the only option for storage pools that contain a single disk. If the underlying storage pool has multiple disks, you can choose a simple layout, mirror layout, or parity layout, as shown in Figure 17-7. Tap or click Next.

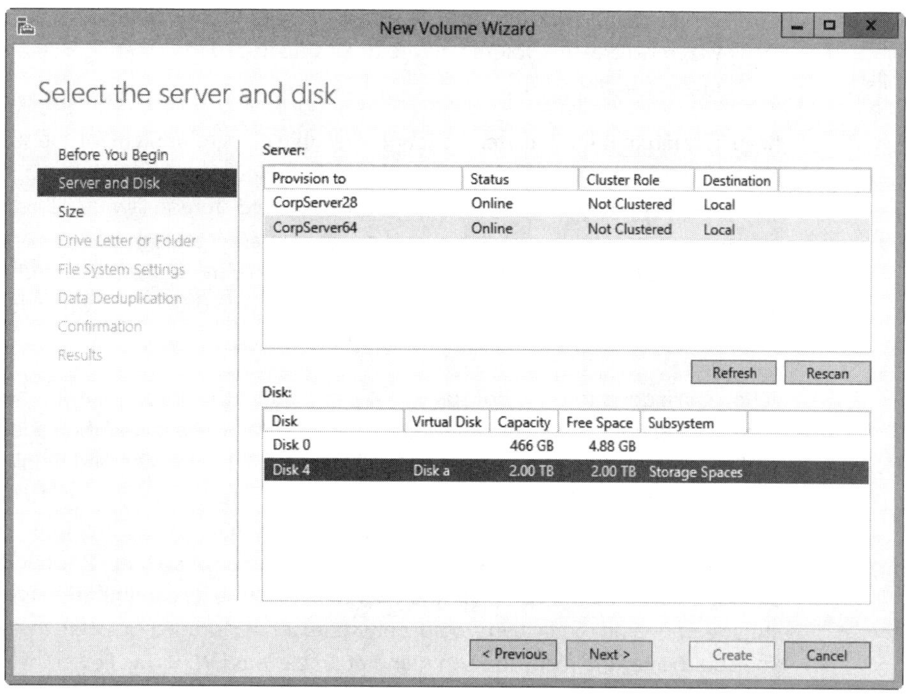

5. On the Specify The Provisioning Type page, select the provisioning type. Storage can be provisioned on a thin disk or a fixed disk. With thin-disk provisioning, the volume uses space from the storage pool as needed, up to the volume size. With fixed provisioning, the volume has a fixed size and uses space from the storage pool equal to the volume size. Tap or click Next.

6. On the Specify The Size Of The Virtual Disk page, use the options provided to set the size of the virtual disk. By selecting Maximum Size, you ensure that the disk is created and sized within the available space. For example, if you are trying to create a 2 TB fixed disk with a simple layout and only 1 TB of space is available, a 1 TB fixed disk will be created. Keep in mind that if a disk is mirrored or striped, it will use more free space than you specify.

7. When you are ready to continue, tap or click Next. After you confirm your selections, tap or click Create. The wizard tracks the progress of the disk creation. When the wizard finishes creating the disk, the View Results page is updated to reflect this. Review the details to ensure that all phases were completed successfully. If any portion of the configuration failed, note the reason for the failure and take corrective actions as appropriate before repeating this procedure.

8. When you tap or click Close, the New Volume Wizard should start automatically. Use the wizard to create a volume on the disk as discussed in "Creating a standard volume" later in this chapter.

Keep in mind that if there aren't enough available disks to implement the storage layout you choose when creating a virtual disk, you get the following error: "The storage pool does not contain enough physical disks to support the selected storage layout." Here, select a different layout or repeat this procedure and select a different storage pool to work with initially. Keep in mind that the storage pool might have one or more disks allocated as hot spares. Hot spares are made available automatically to recover from disk failure when you use mirroring or parity volumes—and cannot otherwise be used.

To force Windows to use a hot spare, you can remove the hot spare from the storage pool by pressing and holding or right-clicking it and selecting Remove and then adding the drive back to the storage pool as an automatically allocated disk by pressing and holding or right-clicking the storage pool and selecting Add Physical Drive. Unfortunately, doing so might cause a storage pool created with a hot spare to report that it is in an Unhealthy state. If you subsequently try to add the drive again in any capacity, you get an error stating, "Error adding task: The storage pool could not complete the operation because its configuration is read-only." The storage pool is not, in fact, in a read-only state. If the storage pool were in a read-only state, you could enter the following command at an elevated Windows PowerShell prompt to clear this state:

```
Get-Storagepool "PoolName" | Set-Storagepool -IsReadonly $false
```

However, entering this command likely will not resolve the problem. To clear this error, I needed to reset Storage Spaces and the related subsystem. You might find it easier just to restart the server. After you reset or restart the server, the storage pool transitions from an error state (where a red circle with an x is showing) to a warning state (where a yellow triangle with an ! is showing). You can then remove the physical disk from the storage pool by pressing and holding or right-clicking it and selecting Remove. Afterward, you can add the physical disk as an automatically allocated disk by pressing and holding or right-clicking the storage pool and selecting Add Physical Drive.

Creating a standard volume

Standard volumes can be created on any physical or virtual disk available. You use the same technique regardless of how the disk is presented to the server. This enables you to create standard volumes on a server's internal disks, on virtual disks in a storage subsystem available to a server, and on virtual iSCSI disks available to a server. If you add the data deduplication feature to a server, you can enable data deduplication for standard volumes created for that server.

You can create a standard volume by completing the following steps:

1. Start the New Volume Wizard. If you just created a storage space, the New Volume Wizard might start automatically. Otherwise, on the Disks subnode, all available disks are listed on the Disks panel. Select the disk you want to work with and then, under Tasks, select New Volume. Similarly, on the Storage Pools subnode, all available virtual disks are listed on the Virtual Disks panel. Select the disk you want to work with and then, under Tasks, select New Volume.

2. On the Select The Server And Disk page, shown in Figure 17-8, select the server for which you are provisioning storage, select the disk where the volume should be created, and then tap or click Next. If you just created a storage space and the New Volume Wizard started automatically, the related server and disk are selected automatically and you just need to tap or click Next.

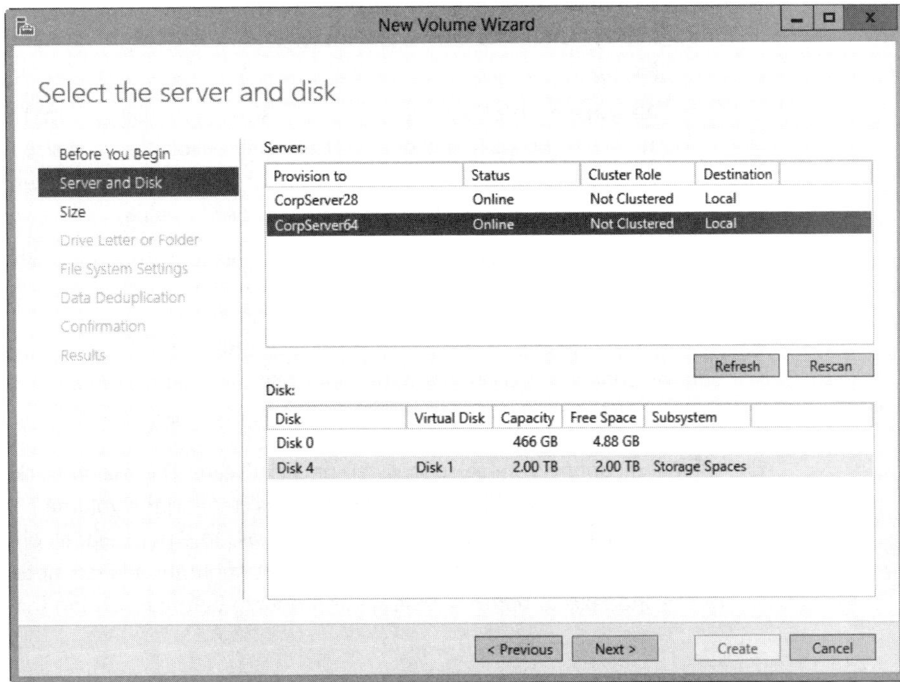

Figure 17-8 Select the server and disk on which the volume should be created.

3. On the Specify The Size Of The Volume page, use the options provided to set the volume size. By default, the volume size is set to the maximum available on the related disk. Tap or click Next.

CHAPTER 17

4. On the Assign To A Drive Letter Or Folder page, specify whether you want to assign a drive letter or path to the volume and then tap or click Next. You use these options as follows:
   - **Drive Letter.** To assign a drive letter, choose this option and then select an available drive letter from the list provided.
   - **The Following Folder.** To assign a drive path, choose this option and then type the path to an existing folder on an NTFS drive or tap or click Browse to search for or create a folder.
   - **Don't Assign To A Drive Letter Or Drive Path.** To create the volume without assigning a drive letter or path, choose this option. You can assign a drive letter or path later if necessary.
5. On the Select File System Settings page, specify how the volume should be formatted, using the following options:
   - **File System.** Sets the file system type, such as NTFS or Resilient File System (ReFS).
   - **Allocation Unit Size.** Sets the cluster size for the file system. This is the basic unit in which disk space is allocated. The default allocation unit size is based on the volume's size and is set dynamically prior to formatting. To override this feature, you can set the allocation unit size to a specific value.
   - **Volume Label.** Sets a text label for the partition. This label is the partition's volume name.
6. If you elected to create an NTFS volume and added data deduplication to the server, you can enable and configure data deduplication, as discussed in "Deduplicating volumes" later in this chapter. When you are ready to continue, tap or click Next.
7. After you confirm your selections, tap or click Create. The wizard tracks the progress of the volume creation. When the wizard finishes creating the volume, the View Results page is updated to reflect this. Review the details to ensure that all phases were completed successfully. If any portion of the configuration failed, note the reason for the failure and take corrective actions as appropriate before repeating this procedure.

Inside OUT

Control timestamp update records to improve performance

In the Registry under HKLM\SYSTEM\CurrentControlSet\Control\FileSystem, the *NtfsDisableLastAccessUpdate* and *RefsDisableLastAccessUpdate* values control whether NTFS and ReFS update the last-access timestamp on each directory when it lists directories on a volume. If you notice that a busy server with a large number of directories isn't very responsive when you list directories, this could be because the file system log buffer in physical memory is filling with timestamp update records. To prevent this, you can set the value to 1. When the value is set to 1, the file system does not update the last-access timestamp, and it does not record timestamp updates in the file system log. Otherwise, when the value is set to 0 (the default), the file system updates the last-access timestamp on each directory it detects, and it records each time change in the file system log.

Diagnosing and resolving problems with storage spaces

Typical problems creating storage spaces and allocating storage were discussed previously. You also might find that a physical disk that should be available for use isn't available. To add a physical disk that has been detected but isn't listed as available, complete the following steps:

1. With the Storage Pools node selected in Server Manager, select Tasks on the Physical Disks panel and then select Add Physical Disk.
2. In the Add Physical Disk dialog box, select the physical disk and then tap or click OK.

Alternatively, if the storage system has not detected the physical disk, select Tasks on the Storage Pools panel and then select Rescan Storage.

Other problems you might experience with storage spaces relate to drive failures and a loss of resiliency. When a storage space uses two-way mirroring, three-way mirroring, parity, or dual parity, you can recover resiliency by reconnecting a disconnected drive or replacing a failed drive. When a storage space uses a simple volume and drives were disconnected, you can recover the volume by reconnecting the drives.

Windows Server restores redundancy by copying data as necessary to the new disk. During this process, the status of the storage space normally is listed as Repairing. You also see a value depicting how much of the repair task is completed. When this value reaches 100 percent, the repair is complete.

When storage spaces use external drives, a missing drive might be a common problem you encounter. In this case, users can continue to work and redundancy will be restored when you reconnect the drive. However, if a drive fails, you need to complete the following steps to restore redundancy:

1. Physically remove the failed drive. If the drive is connected internally, shut down and unplug the computer before you remove the drive; otherwise, just disconnect an externally connected drive.

2. Physically add or connect a replacement drive.

3. On the Storage Spaces panel, press and hold or right-click the storage space you want to configure and then select Add Physical Drive.

4. In the Add Physical Disk dialog box, select the drive that should be allocated to the storage pool.

5. When you tap or click OK, Windows Server prepares the drive and allocates it to the storage pool.

6. At this point, the failed drive should be listed as Retired. Remove the failed drive from the storage space by selecting the related Remove Disk option and then confirm that you want to remove the drive by selecting Yes when prompted.

Selecting the notification icon for Action Center displays the related notifications. If there is a problem with storage spaces, Action Center updates the related notification panel in the desktop notification area with a message stating, "Check Storage Spaces for issues." To open Server Manager, select the notification icon and then select the link provided. In Server Manager, select the File And Storage Services node and then select Storage Pools to get the relevant error and warning icons.

To view errors and warnings for storage pools, press and hold or right-click the storage pool with the error or warning icon and then select Properties. In the Properties dialog box, select Health in the left pane to display the health status and operational status in the main pane. For example, you might find that the health status is listed as Warning and the operation status is listed as Degraded. Degraded is a status you get when there is a loss of redundancy.

To view errors and warnings for virtual disks and their associated physical disks, press and hold or right-click the virtual disk with the error or warning icon and then select Properties. In the Properties dialog box, select Health in the left pane to display the health status and operational status in the main pane. Note the storage layout and the physical disks in use as well. If there is a problem with a physical disk, such as a loss of communication, this status appears. You get a Loss Of Communication status when a physical disk is missing, failed, or disconnected.

Configuring data deduplication

Windows Server 2012 R2 can use data deduplication to find and remove duplication within data while ensuring its integrity and fidelity. When a volume is deduplicated, the data it contains is transformed, and the result includes the following:

- Optimized files
- Unoptimized files
- A chunk store
- Additional free space

Understanding data deduplication

File optimization is a key part of data deduplication. Optimization involves the following:

- Segmenting files into 32 KB to 128 KB chunks
- Identifying duplicate chunks
- Replacing the duplicates with references to a single copy
- Compressing chunks
- Organizing chunks into special container files
- Placing organized chunks in the chunk store

The organized chunks are placed in special container files within the chunk store, which is in the System Volume Information folder. Optimized files on the volume are no longer stored as independent streams. Instead, they are replaced with stubs that point to data blocks within a common chunk store. Because duplicate blocks of data are stored only once within the chunk store, optimized files are transparently assembled during file access, ensuring that users and applications see the correct blocks without any impact or apparent change in behavior.

> IMPORTANT
>
> **A deduplicated volume might contain unoptimized files as well. Files can be omitted from the deduplication process for a variety of reasons. Files smaller than 32 KBs are not deduplicated. Neither are system-state files, encrypted files, or files with extended attributes.**

The integrity of deduplicated data is maintained by using checksum validation on data and metadata. As a further safeguard against corruption, Windows maintains redundant copies of all metadata and the most frequently referenced data. With these safeguards included, the result of optimization is up to 2:1 storage savings for standard data and up to 20:1 storage savings for VHD data.

Data deduplication is for primary data volumes and not for boot, system, or other specialized types of volumes. Ideally, you use data deduplication for primary data volumes that have the following:

- File shares for user documents, with space savings of 30–50 percent on average
- Software deployment shares, with space savings of 70–80 percent on average
- VHD file storage, with space savings of 80–95 percent on average
- Mixed use storage, with space savings of 50–60 percent on average

As part of deduplication, the chunk store is optimized periodically. The default optimization occurs in the background. In addition to periodic optimization, Windows performs garbage collection and data scrubbing periodically. By default, garbage collection and data scrubbing occur weekly at a specified time. Use the Get-DedupSchedule cmdlet to determine the specific times.

> **Inside OUT**
>
> ***Evaluate space savings from deduplication***
>
> **You can use the Deduplication Evaluation tool (DDPEval.exe) to determine the expected space savings from deduplication. Run DDPEval.exe at a command-line, using the following syntax:**
>
> ```
> ddpeval VolumeOrPath
> ```
>
> **Here, *VolumeOrPath* is the drive designator of the volume to evaluate, such as D:; a local file path, such as D:\Data; or a UNC path to a shared folder, such as \\Server15\CorpData.**

Selecting data for deduplication

Data chunks in the chunk store are compressed for most file types by default. File types that aren't compressed in the chunk store include those that are already compressed and those that chunk compression might adversely affect, such as audio and video files. There might be file types that you don't want deduplicated, and you can specify these file types as exclusions. To exclude specific types of files, you need to specify that they shouldn't be included.

Files that are exclusively open for write operations, updated frequently, or heavily accessed aren't good candidates for deduplication because the frequent updates and high access levels cancel the optimization gains. Therefore, use deduplication on volumes with files that aren't constantly being updated or accessed. You'll have better results with these less-utilized volumes.

File age policies can be used to control when files are deduplicated, and this will help reduce early or frequent deduplication of files that are modified regularly. That said, you can configure deduplication to process files that are 0 days old. Deduplication will continue, but it still won't optimize files that are heavily accessed or exclusively open for write operations. Files must be closed when optimization tasks run.

You can enable deduplication on empty volumes and volumes that already contain data. Windows Server 2012 R2 deduplicates data on a single volume at a rate of approximately 10 MBs to 40 MBs per second, depending on server activity levels and capacity, which is approximately 50 GBs to 200 GBs per hour. To ensure that the server doesn't run out of resources, the operating system pauses deduplication if available CPU and memory resources run low.

NOTE

Before you begin deduplication, you should ensure that a volume has ample free space. I recommend having free space of at least 2 to 5 percent of total capacity. For optimal operation, I recommend that volumes continue to have free space of 2 to 5 percent of total capacity as well.

Interoperability with data deduplication

Deduplication works with BranchCache, distributed file system (DFS) replication, and failover clusters, but it doesn't work with hard quotas on volume root folders. In Windows Server 2012 R2, BranchCache and deduplication are designed to work together. Deduplicated files are indexed and hashed, so requests for data can be quickly computed and deduplicated data can be transferred more quickly over the network.

Similarly, with DFS replication, there are performance gains and benefits from interoperability. When files are optimized or unoptimized, replication isn't triggered because the files themselves do not change. Although DFS continues to use Remote Differential Compression (RDC) rather than the chunks in the chunk store for network transfer optimization, files on the DFS replica also can be optimized by using deduplication as long as the replica is running Windows Server 2012 R2.

With failover clusters, each node that accesses deduplicated volumes must have the feature enabled. If so, deduplicated volumes failover gracefully like any other volume. In addition, when a cluster is formed, deduplication schedules are put into the schedule for the cluster. As a result, if a deduplicated volume fails over to another node, the scheduled deduplication task runs as expected at the next scheduled run-time.

When you are using File Server Resource Manager (FRSM) quotas, you can't create hard quotas on the root folder of a volume that is deduplicated. If a volume has a hard quota on its root folder, the actual free space and the quota-restricted space won't match, which might cause deduplication optimization jobs to fail. You can, however, create soft quotas on the root folder of a volume. With soft quotas, FSRM uses the logical size of files for enforcing quotas. As a result, quota usage and any quota thresholds are based on the original size of files rather than on the optimized size.

NOTE

Windows Storage Server supports Single Instance Storage (SIS), which is a deduplication technology. As you might expect, you can't use SIS with data deduplication. Because of this, prior to migrating Windows Storage Server to Windows Server 2012 R2, you should remove SIS by using either SISAdmin.exe within Storage Server or by moving the data to a volume that is not using SIS.

When backing up deduplicated volumes, keep in mind that the technology is supported by block-based backup applications, such as Windows Server Backup. These applications should be able to back up deduplicated data and maintain the optimization in the backup media.

However, file-based backup operations might not support deduplication. As a result, file-based backup operations, such as XCOPY, typically copy files in their original form. Files are transparently assembled in memory during the backup copy operation. Because the deduplication is not retained, the backup target must be large enough to hold the full, original size of the entire data set.

Deduplicating volumes

Before you enable data deduplication on volumes, you should consider the types of files that you don't want compressed as part of data deduplication. Typically, this includes file types that are already compressed. Because data deduplication can be applied using background optimization, throughput optimization, or both, you should consider how and when you want servers to deduplicate volumes.

Servers perform background optimization when they're otherwise idle. Background optimization runs at low priority and is paused whenever the server isn't idle. This pause and resume behavior continues until volumes are fully optimized.

Servers perform throughput optimization according to a specific schedule, such as every day at 1:45 A.M. for 6 hours. Throughput optimization runs at normal priority and uses system resources to maximize the optimization process. When started, optimization continues until it completes or reaches the specified duration value.

IMPORTANT

When you are configuring deduplication settings, be sure to note the difference between per-volume settings and per-server settings. For each volume, you can enable or disable deduplication. You also can set the file age policy and the file extensions to exclude. For each server, you can enable or disable background optimization and throughput optimization. The schedule set for throughput optimization is per-server as well.

You can enable and configure data deduplication as part of the volume-creation process by completing the following steps:

1. On the Enable Data Deduplication page in the New Volume Wizard, use the selection list provided to enable data deduplication, as shown in Figure 17-9. If you are configuring this option on a file server or other standard server, select General Purpose File Server. Otherwise, choose Virtual Desktop Infrastructure (VDI) Server.

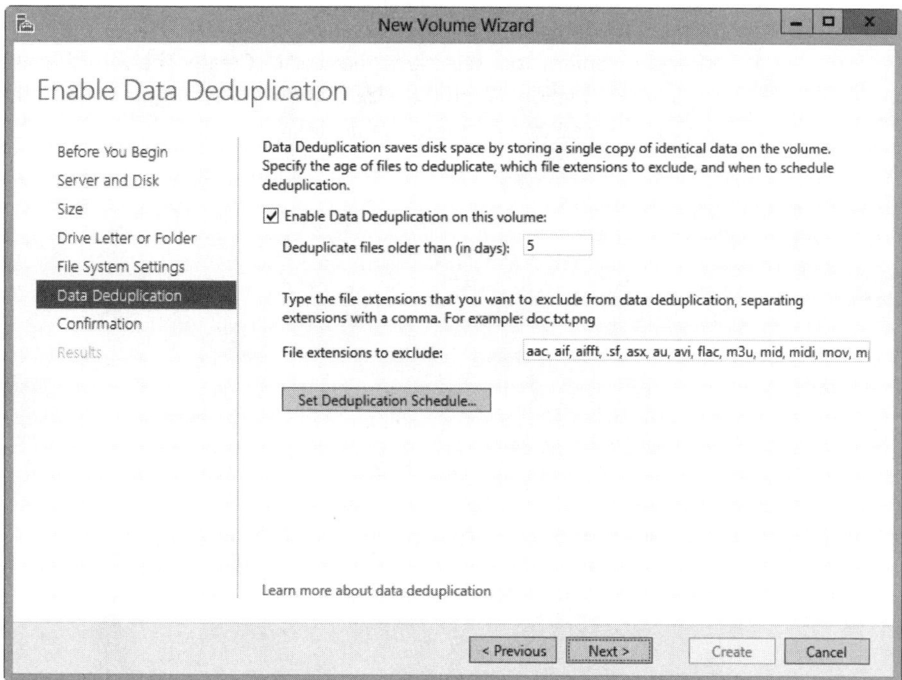

Figure 17-9 Enable deduplication on the volume.

NOTE

The options shown in Figure 17-9 are per-volume.

2. File age policies control when files are deduplicated. In the Deduplicate Files Older Than box, configure deduplication to process files that are a specific number of days old, such as 5 or 10. If you enter 0, files are available for deduplication immediately but must be closed when optimization tasks run.

3. If you want to exclude specific types of files, enter the extensions of those files, separated by a comma.

4. Tap or click Set Deduplication Schedule to open the Deduplication Schedule dialog box shown in Figure 17-10. When you enable deduplication, background optimization is enabled by default. In addition to or instead of background optimization, you also can enable and configure throughput optimization.

   Throughput optimization follows a primary schedule by default, such as every day of the week at 1:45 A.M. for 6 hours. You can add a secondary schedule to help ensure that volumes are fully deduplicated as appropriate. For example, you might want to allow deduplication on Monday through Friday at 1:00 A.M. for 3 hours and deduplication on Saturday and Sunday for 6 hours.

5. Tap or click OK and then tap or click Next.

6. After you confirm your selections, tap or click Create. The wizard tracks the progress of the volume creation. When the wizard finishes creating the volume, the View Results page is updated to reflect this. Tap or click Close.

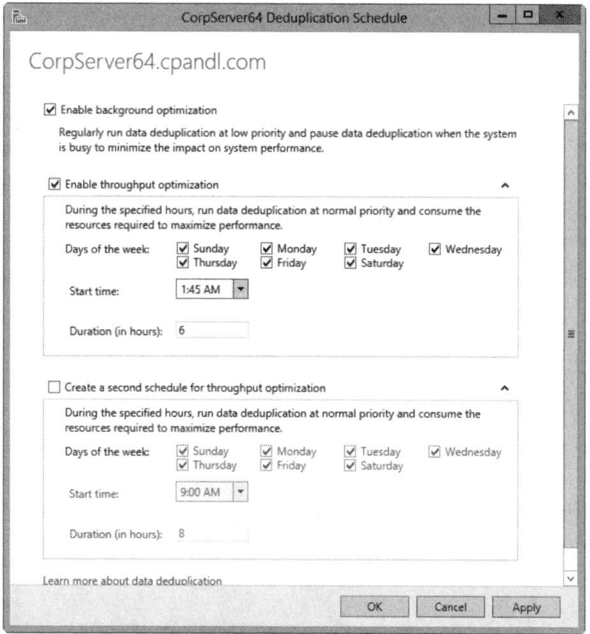

Figure 17-10 Set the deduplication type and schedule.

NOTE

The options shown in Figure 17-10 are per-server.

You don't have to enable deduplication when you create volumes. You can enable and manage data deduplication at any time. With the Volumes subnode selected in Server Manager, press and hold or right-click the volume that you want to manage and then select Configure Data Deduplication. As Figure 17-11 shows, the available configuration options are nearly identical to those discussed previously. The exception is that you now can specify folders to exclude. When you exclude a folder, all contents of the folder are excluded from deduplication, including both files and subfolders and their contents. Specify a folder to exclude by tapping or clicking Add, using the dialog box provided to choose a folder to exclude, and then tapping or clicking Select Folder.

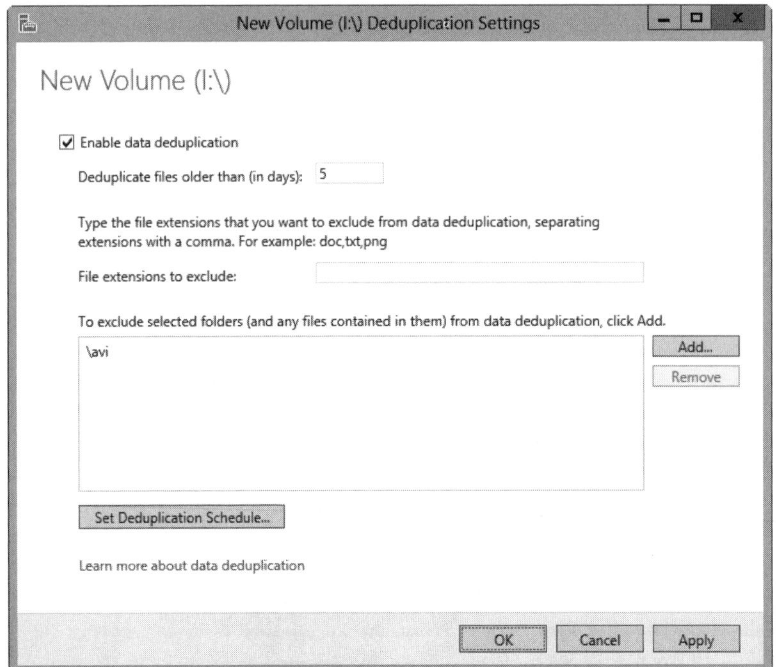

Figure 17-11 Configure deduplication settings for the volume.

Monitoring deduplication

When you add the Data Deduplication role service to a server, related Windows PowerShell cmdlets are installed as well. You can use these cmdlets, as mentioned previously, to track the status of deduplication, determine space savings on volumes, and more. You need to use an elevated Windows PowerShell prompt.

Use Get-DedupStatus to display the status of deduplication for each enabled volume. In the following example, you check deduplication on FileServer28 and FileServer32:

```
Invoke-command -computername fileserver28, fileserver32
-scriptblock {Get-DedupStatus}
```

As shown here, the output shows how much free space is available, how much space was saved using deduplication, the number of optimized files, and the number of in-policy files:

```
FreeSpace   SavedSpace   OptimizedFiles   InPolicyFiles   Volume   PSComputerName
--------    ----------   --------------   -------------   ------   FileServer28
325.55 GB   402.22 GB    32581            32588           I: -     FileServer28
98.82 GB    118.75 GB    29812            28714           K: -     FileServer32
```

You can get more detailed information by formatting the output as a list, as shown here:

```
Get-DedupStatus | fl
```

The information provided for each volume is then much more detailed, as shown in this example for the I volume:

```
Volume                             : I:
VolumeId                           : \\?\Volume{}\
Capacity                           : 466 GB
FreeSpace                          : 325.55 GB
UsedSpace                          : 220.62 GB
UnoptimizedSize                    : 722.68 GB
SavedSpace                         : 502.22 GB
SavingsRate                        : 73 %
OptimizedFilesCount                : 32581
OptimizedFilesSize                 : 685.32 GB
OptimizedFilesSavingsRate          : 78 %
InPolicyFilesCount                 : 32588
InPolicyFilesSize                  : 699.87 GB
LastOptimizationTime               : 9/26/2014 5:32:31 AM
LastOptimizationResult             : 0x00000000
LastOptimizationResultMessage      : The operation completed successfully.
LastGarbageCollectionTime          : 9/26/2014 5:33:01 PM
LastGarbageCollectionResult        : 0x00000000
LastGarbageCollectionResultMessage : The operation completed successfully.
LastScrubbingTime                  : 9/26/2014 6:33:01 AM
LastScrubbingResult                : 0x00000000
LastScrubbingResultMessage         : The operation completed successfully.
```

Use Get-DedupVolume to examine volume-level deduplication. In the following example, you check volume-level deduplication on FileServer28 and FileServer32:

```
Invoke-command -computername fileserver28, fileserver32
-scriptblock {Get-DedupVolume}
```

As shown here, the output shows the status of deduplication on volumes, how much space was saved using deduplication, and the savings rate:

```
Enabled     SavedSpace        SavingsRate       Volume     PSComputer
-------     ----------        -----------       ------
True        502.22 GB         73 %              I:         FileServer28
True        118.75 GB         58 %              K:         FileServer32
```

You can get more detailed information by formatting the output as a list, as shown here:

```
Get-DedupVolume | fl
```

The information provided for volume-level deduplication is then much more detailed, as shown in this example for the I volume:

```
Volume                        : I:
VolumeId                      : \\?\Volume{}\
Enabled                       : True
DataAccessEnabled             : True
Capacity                      : 466 GB
FreeSpace                     : 325.55 GB
UsedSpace                     : 220.62 GB
UnoptimizedSize               : 722.68 GB
SavedSpace                    : 502.22 GB
SavingsRate                   : 73 %
MinimuFileAgeDays             : 5
MinimumFileSize               : 32768
NoCompress                    : False
ExcludeFolder                 : {\avi}
ExcludeFileType               :
NoCompressionFileType         : {aac, aif, aiff, asf...}
ChunkRedundancyThreshold      : 100
Verify                        : False
```

By using Get-DedupMetadata, you can get detailed information about how deduplication processed files, which includes the number of chunks in the chunk store, the number of StreamMaps, and the number of hotspots. Hotspots are the most frequently referenced chunks. Enter the following command:

```
Get-DedupMetadata | fl
```

You see output similar to the following for each volume that uses deduplication:

```
Volume                         : I:
VolumeId                       : \\?\Volume{}\
StoreId                        : { }
DataChunkCount                 : 4082133
DataContainerCount             : 192
DataChunkAverageSize           : 58.21 KB
DataChunkMedianSize            : 0 B
DataStoreUncompactedFreespace  : 0 B
StreamMapChunkCount            : 36424
StreamMapContainerCount        : 18
StreamMapAverageDataChunkCount :
StreamMapMedianDataChunkCount  :
StreamMapMaxDataChunkCount     :
HotspotChunkCount              : 12422
HotspotContainerCount          : 1
HotspotMedianReferenceCount    :
CorruptionLogEntryCount        : 0
TotalChunkStoreSize            : 182.5 GB
```

Finally, you can use Get-DedupSchedule to examine the deduplication schedule. As shown here, the output depicts the start time of regular optimization tasks and garbage collection and scrubbing:

```
Enabled   Type               StartTime   Days            Name
-------   ----               ---------   ----            ----
True      Optimization                                   BackgroundOptimization
True      Optimization       1:45 AM     {Sunday, Monday... ThroughputOptimization
True      Optimization       9:00 AM     {Sunday, Monday... ThroughputOptimization-2
True      GarbageCollection  2:45 AM     Saturday        WeeklyGarbageCollection
True      Scrubbing          3:45 AM     Saturday        WeeklyScrubbing
```

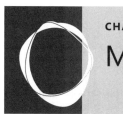

CHAPTER 18

Managing file sharing

Sharing files means that you allow users to access files from across the network. The most basic way to share files is to create a shared folder and make it accessible to users through a mapped network drive. In most cases, you don't want everyone with access to the network to be able to read, modify, or delete the shared files. Therefore, when you share files, the permissions on the shared folder and the local access permissions are very important in granting appropriate access and restricting access to files when necessary. File sharing and file security go hand in hand. You don't want to share files indiscriminately, and to help safeguard important data, you can configure auditing. Auditing enables you to track who accessed files and what they did.

Typically, you use file sharing with Volume Shadow Copy Service (VSS). This service offers two important features:

- **Shadow copying of files in shared folders.** You use this feature to configure volumes so that shadow copies of files in shared folders are created automatically at specific intervals during the day. This enables you to go back and look at earlier versions of files stored in shared folders. You can use these earlier versions to recover deleted, incorrectly modified, or overwritten files. You can also compare versions of files to see what changes were made over time.

- **Shadow copying of open or locked files for backups.** With this feature, you can use backup programs, such as Windows Backup, to back up files that are open or locked. This means you can perform a backup when applications are using the files and do not have to worry about backups failing because files are in use. Backup programs must implement the VSS application programming interface (API).

These features are independent of each other. You do not need to enable shadow copying of a volume to be able to back up open or locked files on a volume. Although Resilient File System (ReFS) provides a highly reliable file system, only NTFS volumes support shadow copies. Therefore, if you create shares on ReFS volumes, users won't be able to go back to previous versions of files and folders stored in shares.

File-sharing essentials

File sharing is one of the most fundamental features of a file server, and file servers running Microsoft Windows Server 2012 R2 have many file-sharing features. The basic component that makes file sharing possible is the Server service, which is responsible for sharing file and printer resources over the network.

Understanding file-sharing models

Windows Server 2012 R2 supports two file-sharing models: standard file sharing and public folder sharing. Standard file sharing allows remote users to access network resources, such as files, folders, and drives. When you share a folder or a drive, you make all its files and subfolders available to a specified set of users. Standard file sharing also is referred to as *in-place file sharing* because you don't need to move files from their current location.

You can enable standard file sharing on disks formatted with extended FAT (exFAT), FAT, FAT32, NTFS, or ReFS. One set of permissions applies to disks formatted with exFAT, FAT, or FAT32. These permissions are called *share permissions*. Two sets of permissions apply to disks formatted with NTFS or ReFS: *NTFS permissions* (also referred to as *access permissions*) and *share permissions*. Having two sets of permissions enables you to determine precisely who has access to shared files and the level of access assigned. With either access permissions or share permissions, you do not need to move the files you are sharing.

With public folder sharing, you share files just by copying or moving files to a computer's folder. Public files are available to anyone who logs on to a computer locally regardless of whether that person has a standard user account or an administrator user account on the computer. You can also grant network access to the Public folder. If you do this, however, there are no access restrictions. The Public folder and its contents are open to everyone who can access the computer over the local network.

When you copy or move files to the Public folder, access permissions are changed to match those of the Public folder. Some permissions are added as well. When a computer is part of a workgroup, you can add password protection to the Public folder. Separate password protection isn't needed in a domain. In a domain, only domain users can access Public folder data.

Inside OUT

Public folder sharing

Public folder sharing enables users with network access to view and manage public files. When you enable public folder sharing without password protection, the implicit Everyone group is granted Full Control permissions to public files and public folders. This allows anyone, including network users, to open, change, create, and delete public files.

When you enable public folder sharing with password protection, the implicit Interactive group is granted Read, Read & Execute, Write, and Modify permissions to public files and public folders. This allows anyone logged on locally to open, change, create, and delete public files. Users with network access who have the password can do the same.

Windows Server 2012 R2 can use either or both sharing models at any time. However, standard file sharing offers more security and better protection than public folder sharing, and increasing security is essential to protecting your organization's data.

Compound identities, claims-based access controls, and central access policies provide additional layers of security. Windows Server 2012 R2 enables administrators to assign claims-based access controls to file and folder resources on NTFS and ReFS volumes. Users are granted access to files and folder resources, either directly with access permissions and share permissions or indirectly with claims-based access controls and central access policies.

Enabling file sharing

You can configure the basic file-sharing settings for a server by using Advanced Sharing Settings. Separate options are provided for public folder sharing on the All Networks panel, and the status of public folder sharing is listed as On or Off, as shown in Figure 18-1.

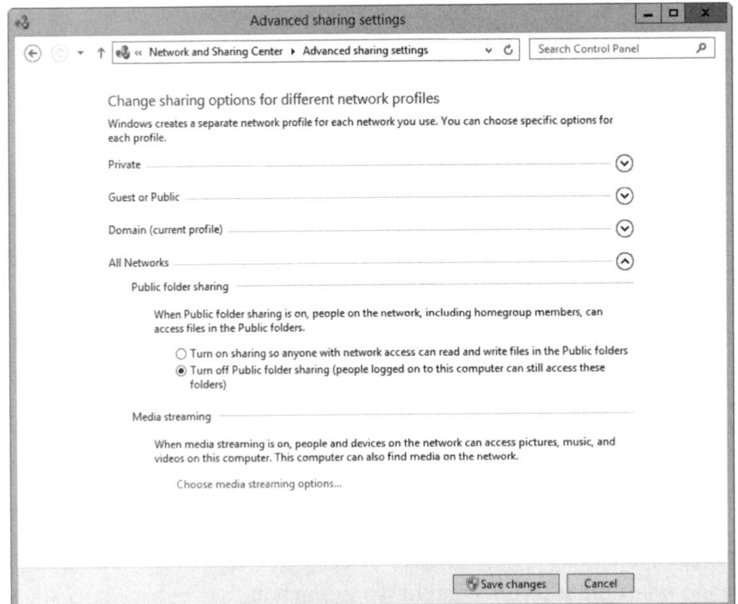

Figure 18-1 Configure basic file-sharing options.

To open the Advanced Sharing Settings page in Control Panel, tap or click View Network Status And Tasks under the Network And Internet heading and then tap or click Change Advanced Sharing Settings. Public folder sharing options control access to a computer's Public folder. To configure public folder sharing, expand the All Networks panel by tapping or clicking the related Expand button. Choose one of the following options and then tap or click Save Changes:

- **Turn On Sharing So Anyone With Network Access Can Read And Write Files.** Enables public folder sharing by granting access to the Public folder and all public data to anyone who can access the computer over the network. Keep in mind, however, that Windows Firewall settings might prevent external access.

- **Turn Off Public Folder Sharing.** Disables public folder sharing, preventing network access to the Public folder. Anyone who logs on locally to your computer can still access the Public folder and its files.

In a workgroup setting, you can manage password-protected sharing on the All Networks panel. You use password-protected sharing to restrict access so that only people with a user account and password on your computer can access shared resources. Select either Turn On Password Protected Sharing to enable password-protected sharing or Turn Off Password Protected Sharing to disable password-protected sharing and then tap or click Save Changes.

Using and finding shares

You share file resources over the network by creating a shared folder to which users can map as a network drive. For example, if the D:\Data directory on a computer is used to store user data, you might want to share this folder as UserData. This would enable users to map to it using a drive letter on their machines, such as X. After the drive is mapped, users can access it in File Explorer or by using other tools just as they would a local drive on their computer.

All shared folders have a share name and a folder path. The share name is the name of the shared folder. The folder path is the complete path to the folder on the server. In the previous example, the share name is UserData and the associated folder path is D:\Data. After you share a folder, it is available to users automatically. All they have to know to map to the shared folder is the name of the server on which the folder is located and the share name.

Whether you are working with Windows 8.1 or Windows Server 2012 R2, you can map network drives in the same way. When you open File Explorer, the This PC node should be opened by default. If you have an open Explorer window and This PC is not the selected node, tap or click the leftmost option button in the address list and then tap or click This PC. Next, tap or click the Map Network Drive button on the Computer panel and then tap or click Map Network Drive. This opens the Map Network Drive dialog box shown in Figure 18-2.

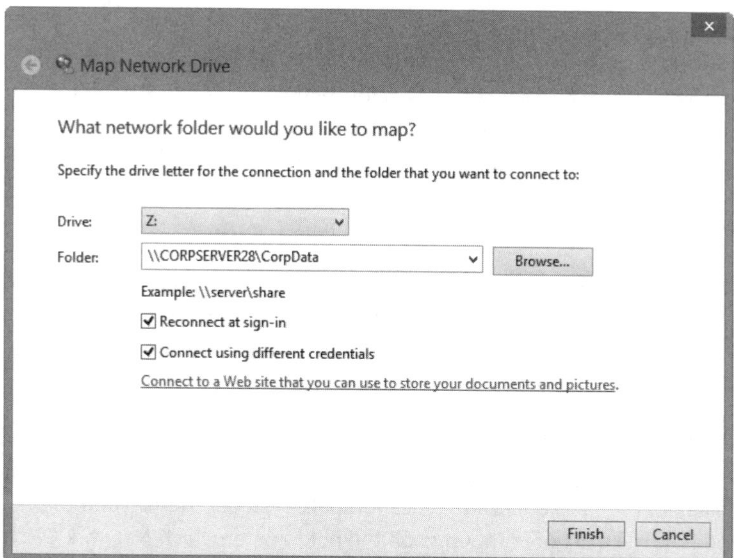

Figure 18-2 Open the Map Network Drive dialog box.

You use the Drive field to select a free drive letter to use and the Folder field to enter the path to the network share. You use the Universal Naming Convention (UNC) path to the share. For example, to access a server called CORPSVR02 and a shared folder called CorpData, you type **\\CorpSvr02\CorpData**. If you don't know the name of the share, you can tap or click the Browse button to the right of the Folder field. In the Browse For Folder dialog box, computers with shared folders are listed by name. When you expand the name of a computer in a workgroup or a domain, as shown in Figure 18-3, you see a list of shared folders. Select the shared folder you want to work with and then tap or click OK.

Figure 18-3 The Browse For Folder dialog box shows computers with shared folders.

By default, Windows automatically reconnects mapped network drives at logon. Clear the Reconnect At Sign-In check box if you only want to map the network drive for the current user session. Tap or click Finish. If the currently logged-on user doesn't have appropriate access permissions for the share, select Connect Using Different Credentials and then tap or click Finish. After you tap or click Finish, you can enter the user name and password of the account with which you want to connect to the shared folder.

As shown in Figure 18-4, enter the user name. To specify the domain, you can enter the name in Domain\Username format, such as **Cpandl\Williams**. Before tapping or clicking OK, select Remember My Credentials if you want the credentials to be saved. Otherwise, you need to provide credentials in the future.

Domain users can browse the network by using Network Explorer to find shares that have been made available, as shown in Figure 18-5. You can open Network Explorer from File Explorer. In File Explorer, tap or click the location path selection button and then tap or click Network. You now see a list of computers on the network for which Network Discovery is enabled. When you double-tap or double-click a computer entry, any publicly shared resources on that computer are listed, and you can connect to them just by double-tapping or double-clicking the associated folder.

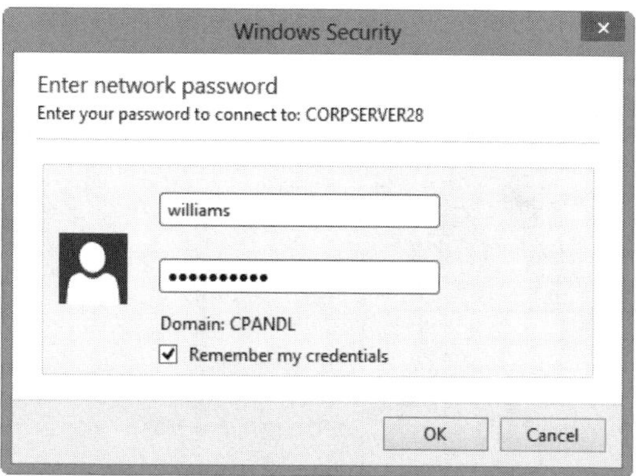

Figure 18-4 Open the Windows Security dialog box.

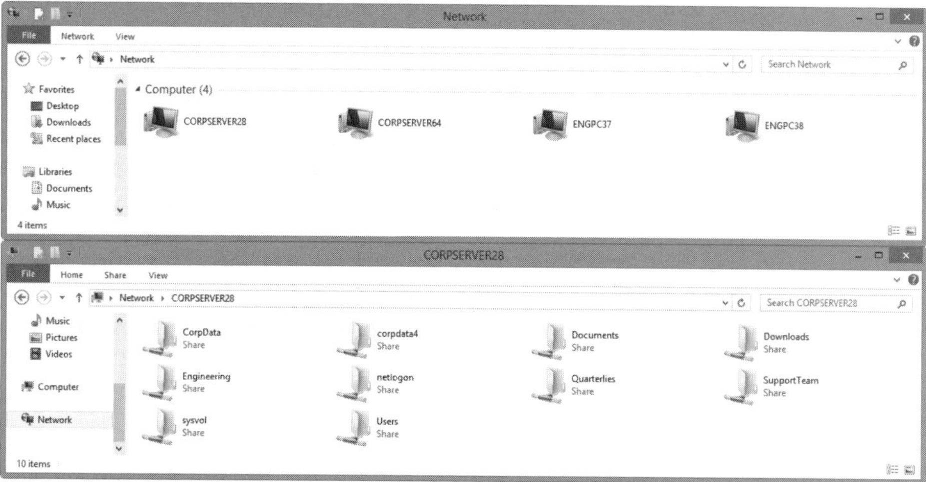

Figure 18-5 Network Explorer shows shares available on the network.

To make it easier for users to find shared folders, you can also publish information about shares in Active Directory.

When you publish shared resources, users can use Network Explorer to find them, and administrators can find them by using Active Directory Users And Computers. The procedures are similar regardless of which tool you are using. An example of how you can find shared folders follows.

1. In Network Explorer, tap or click Search Active Directory on the Network panel or, in Active Directory Users And Computers, press and hold or right-click the domain name in the left pane and tap or click Find.

2. As shown in Figure 18-6, in the Find list, choose Shared Folders.

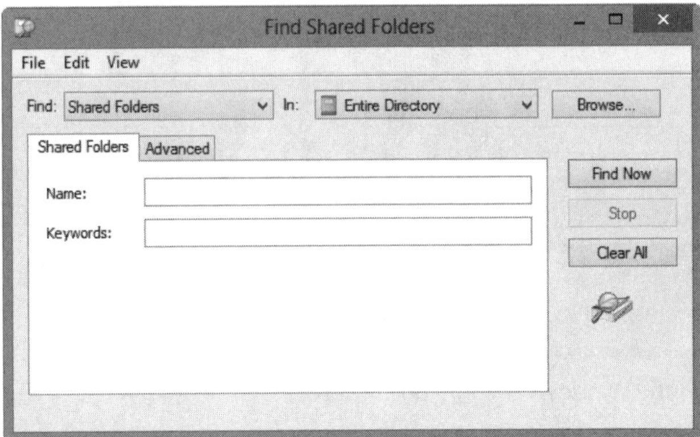

Figure 18-6 Use the Find Shared Folders dialog box to find shared resources such as folders and printers.

3. In the Name field, type the name of the folder you want to find and then tap or click Find Now. If you know part of the folder name, you can use the asterisk (*) to match partial names. For example, if you know that the folder name ends with the word "data," you could type ***data** to search for all folder names that end with the word "data."

4. In the Search Results area, you see a list of shared folders that match your search criteria, as shown in Figure 18-7. Press and hold or right-click any of the shared folders to display a shortcut menu. You can then open the shared folder, map a network drive to the folder, and access the share's properties.

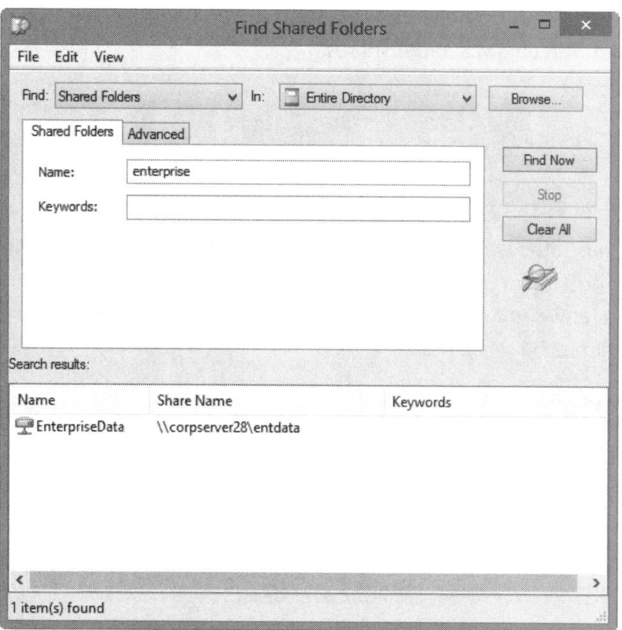

Figure 18-7 Review the list of shared folders in the Find Shared Folders dialog box.

Use keywords for searches

Shared folders can have associated keywords, and you can use these keywords instead of name values. Unlike names, partial keyword values are matched automatically. For example, if you know that the keyword "Engineering" is associated with the folder, you could enter eng in the Keywords box and then tap or click Find Now.

You can use keywords to refine searches as well. For example, if you know that the folder name ends with "data" and the keyword "Engineering" is associated with it, you could enter *data as the name and eng as the keyword for your search.

As an administrator, you can use Computer Management and Server Manager to work with shares. You also can view current shares on a computer by typing **net share** at a command prompt or by typing **get-smbshare** at a Windows PowerShell prompt. Computer Management, net share, and get-smbshare display information about Server Message Block (SMB)–based shares, including standard SMB folder shares, hidden SMB folder shares (those ending with the $ suffix), and SMB folders shared using distributed file system (DFS). Server Manager displays information about standard SMB folder shares, SMB folders shared using

DFS, and folders shared using network file system (NFS). Server Manager does not display information about hidden SMB folder shares.

Inside OUT

Connecting quickly to shares

As an administrator, you likely know the name of shares you want to work with. If your current logon account has appropriate permissions, you can connect directly to a special share or any standard share just by typing the UNC path for the share in the File Explorer address box. The basic syntax is:

```
\\ServerName\ShareName
```

where *ServerName* is the Domain Name System (DNS) name or IP address of the server, and *ShareName* is the name of the share. In the following example, you connect to the C$ share on FileServer34:

```
\\FileServer34\C$
```

Navigating SMB versions

SMB is the primary file sharing protocol that Windows operating systems use. As Windows itself has changed over the years, so has SMB. To allow for version and feature changes, SMB was designed to enable clients and servers to negotiate and then use the highest version supported by both the client attempting to connect an SMB share and the server hosting the share.

The current version of SMB is version 3.02, which Windows 8.1 and Windows Server 2012 R2 support. Thus, when a computer running Windows 8.1 connects to an SMB share hosted on a server running Windows Server 2012 R2, SMB 3.02 is the version used for the SMB session.

The earliest implementation of SMB was called Common Internet File System (CIFS), which was introduced with Windows NT 4.0, followed by SMB 1.0, which all versions of Windows from Windows 2000 to Windows Server 2003 R2 use. Beginning with Windows 8.1 and Windows Server 2012 R2, support for CIFS and SMB 1.0 is an optional feature that must be enabled. Because CIFS and SMB 1.0 are outdated, perform poorly, and are less secure than their predecessors, SMB 1.0/CIFS File Sharing Support should not be enabled unless required. That said, if a computer running Windows 8.1 needs to connect to a server running an early Windows operating system, the computer must have the SMB 1.0/CIFS File Sharing Support feature enabled. In addition, if a computer running an early Windows operating system needs to connect to a server running Windows Server 2012 R2, the SMB 1.0/CIFS File Sharing Support feature must be enabled on the server.

Table 18-1 provides a summary of the current versions of SMB, the associated versions of Windows, and the major features introduced. You can enter **Get-SmbConnection** at an elevated, administrator Windows PowerShell prompt to determine the version of SMB a client has negotiated with a file server. In the command output, the version is listed in the Dialect column, as shown in the following sample output:

```
ServerName  ShareName   UserName          Credential        Dialect    NumOpens
----------  ---------   --------          ----------        -------    --------
Server36    IPC$        CPANDL\williams CPANDL\williams     3.02       0
Server36    PrimaryData CPANDL\williams CPANDL\williams     3.02       14
```

Table 18-1 Overview of current SMB versions

SMB Version	Windows Version	Features
SMB 2.0	Windows Vista SP1, Windows Server 2008	Increasing scalability and security, asynchronous operations, larger reads/writes, request compounding
SMB 2.1	Windows 7, Windows Server 2008 R2	Large maximum transmission unit (MTU) support, BranchCache support
SMB 3.0	Windows 8, Windows Server 2012	Enhancements for server clusters, BranchCache v2 support, SMB over Remote Direct Memory Access (RDMA), improved security
SMB 3.02	Windows 8.1, Windows Server 2012 R2	Improved performance for SMB over RDMA, additional scale-out options, Hyper-V live migration support

IMPORTANT

SMB 3.0 and SMB 3.02 brought many enhancements for performance, especially when you use clustered file servers. A key enhancement that doesn't rely on a special configuration is end-to-end encryption of SMB data, which eliminates the need to use Internet Protocol security (IPsec), specialized hardware, or wide area network (WAN) accelerators to protect data from eavesdropping. SMB encryption can be enabled on a per-share basis.

Hiding and controlling share access

Because there are times when you don't want everyone to see or know about a share, Windows Server also enables you to create hidden shares. Hidden shares are made available to users but are not listed in the normal file share lists or published in Active Directory. You can create hidden shares by adding the dollar sign ($) to the end of the share name. For example, if you want to share E:\DataDumps but don't want it to be displayed in the normal file share lists, you could name it Backup$ rather than Backup.

Hiding a share doesn't control access to the share, however. Access to shares is controlled using permissions. Two permission sets apply to shared folders: share permissions and local access permissions. Share permissions set the maximum allowable actions available within a shared folder. Access permissions assigned to the share's contents further constrain the actions users can perform. For example, share permissions can allow a user to access a folder, but access permissions might not allow that user to view or modify files.

Keep in mind that by default, when you create a share, everyone with access to the network has Read access to the share's contents.

NOTE

You also can hide shares by using access-based enumeration. This feature displays only the files and folders that a user has permissions to access. For more information, see "Creating shared folders in Server Manager" later in this chapter.

Special and administrative shares

In Windows Server 2012 R2, you'll find that several shares are created automatically. These shares are referred to as *special shares* or *default shares*. Most special shares are hidden because they are created for administrative purposes. Thus, they are also referred to as *administrative shares*.

The special shares that are available on a system depend on its configuration. This means a domain controller might have more special shares than a member server or that a server that handles network faxing might have shares that other systems don't.

C$, D$, E$, and other drive shares

All drives, except USB drives and CD/DVD-ROM drives, have special shares with access to the root of the drive. These shares are known as C$, D$, E$, and so on, and they are created to enable administrators to connect to a drive's root folder and perform administrative tasks. For example, if you map to C$, you are connecting to C:\ and have full access to this drive.

On workstations and servers, members of the Administrators or Backup Operators group can access drive shares. On domain controllers, members of the Server Operators group can also access drive shares.

NOTE

Windows allows you to delete drive shares. However, the next time you restart the computer or the Server service, the drive shares will be re-created.

ADMIN$

The ADMIN$ share is an administrative share for accessing the %SystemRoot% folder in which the operating system files reside. It is meant to be used for remote administration. For administrators working remotely with systems, it is a handy shortcut for directly accessing the operating system folder. Thus, rather than having to connect to C$ or D$ and then look for the operating system folder, which could be named Windows or just about anything else, you can connect directly to the right folder every time.

On workstations and servers, members of the Administrators or Backup Operators groups can access the ADMIN$ share. On domain controllers, members of the Server Operators group can also access the ADMIN$ share.

FAX$

The FAX$ share supports network faxes. By default, the special Everyone group has Read permissions on these shared folders. This means that anyone with access to the network can access this folder.

IPC$

The IPC$ share is an administrative share that supports named pipes, which are used for inter-process (or process-to-process) communications. Because named pipes can be redirected over the network to connect local and remote systems, they also enable remote administration and are what enable you to manage resources remotely.

NETLOGON

The NETLOGON share is used by domain controllers. It supports the Netlogon service, and this service uses it during the processing of logon requests. After users log on, Windows accesses their user profiles and, if applicable, any related logon scripts. Logon scripts contain actions that should be run automatically when users log on to help set up the work environment, perform housekeeping tasks, or complete any other task that must be routinely performed every time users log on.

PRINT$

The PRINT$ share supports printer sharing by providing access to printer drivers. Whenever you share a printer, the system puts the printer drivers in this share so that other computers can access them as needed.

SYSVOL

The SYSVOL share supports Active Directory. Domain controllers have this share and use it to store Active Directory data, including policies and scripts.

Accessing shares for administration

As Figure 18-8 shows, administrators can view information about existing shares on a computer, including the special shares, by using Computer Management. In Computer Management, expand System Tools, expand Shared Folders, and then select Shares.

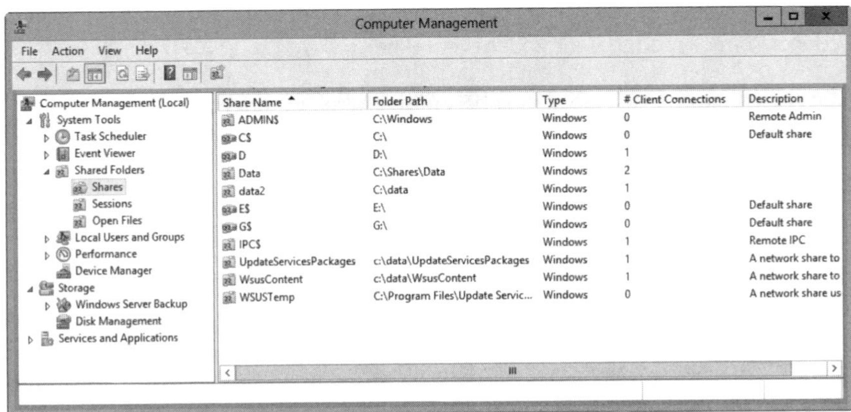

Figure 18-8 Use Computer Management to access shared folders.

If you want to work with shares on a remote computer, press and hold or right-click the Computer Management node in the left pane and select Connect To Another Computer. This opens the Select Computer dialog box. Select Another Computer and then type the computer name or Internet Protocol (IP) address of the computer you want to use. If you don't know the computer name or IP address, tap or click Browse to search for the computer you want to work with.

Creating and publishing shared folders

To create shares on a server running Windows Server 2012 R2, you must be a member of the Administrators or Server Operators group. You can create shares by using File Explorer, Computer Management, Server Manager, New-SmbShare, or Net Share from the command line. When deciding which option to use, keep the following in mind:

- File Explorer works well when you want to share folders on computers to which you are logged on. Because users who are not administrators typically share folders by using File Explorer, it's important to understand the quirks that come with this approach (and this also might help you more easily resolve related access issues).
- By using Computer Management, you can share the folders on the local computer and on any computer to which you can connect. You can configure share permissions and offline settings as well.

- Server Manager enables you to manage shared folders on any server added for management. You can provision all aspects of sharing, including access permissions, share permissions, encrypted data access, and offline settings for caching.
- With New-SmbShare, you can create shares by using Windows PowerShell. Type **get-help new-smbshare** at the Windows PowerShell prompt for details about using this cmdlet.
- By using Net Share, you can create shares from the command line or in scripts. Type **net share /?** at the command prompt for details about using this command.

After you create a share, you might want to publish it in Active Directory so that it is easier to find.

Creating shares by using File Explorer

By using File Explorer, you can share folders on the computer to which you are logged on. In File Explorer, press and hold or right-click the folder you want to share and then select Properties. In the folder's Properties dialog box, tap or click the Sharing tab to view the current sharing configuration (if any), as shown in Figure 18-9.

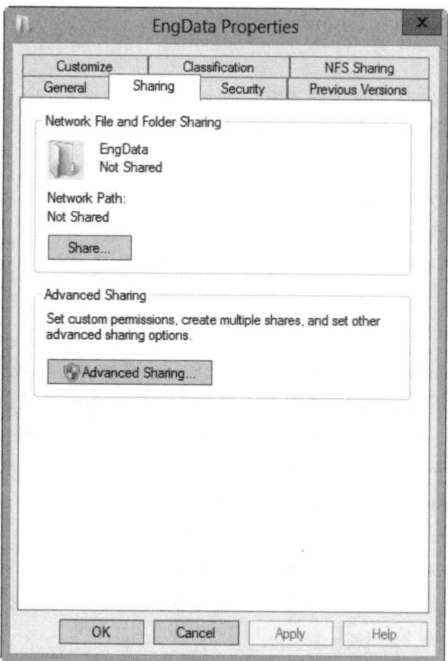

Figure 18-9 View the current sharing configuration.

Tap or click Share to open the File Sharing dialog box, as shown in Figure 18-10. Tap or click the selection arrow to the right of the text-entry field provided and then select Find People.

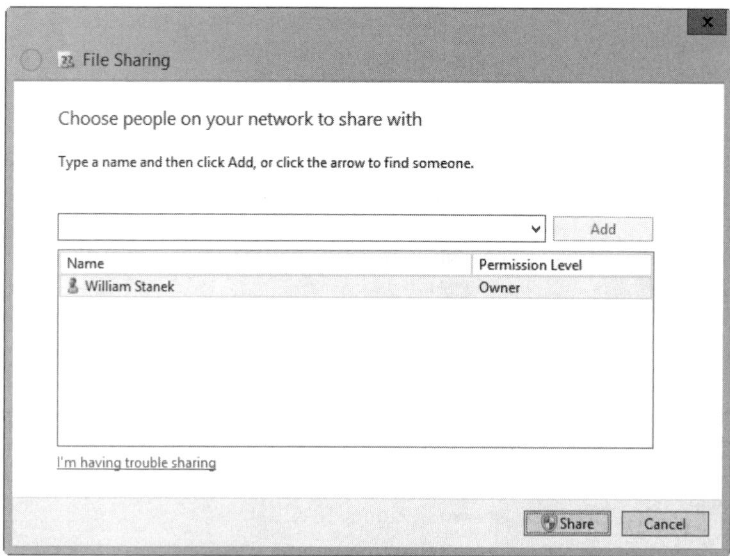

Figure 18-10 Configure sharing access and permissions.

In the Select Users Or Groups dialog box, shown in Figure 18-11, check the value of the From This Location field. In workgroups, computers always show only local accounts and groups. In domains, this field is changeable and set initially to the default (logon) domain of the currently logged-on user. If this isn't the location you want to use for selecting user and group accounts to work with, tap or click Locations to see a list of locations you can search, including the current domain, trusted domains, and other resources that you can access.

IMPORTANT

Another way to open the File Sharing dialog box is to press and hold or right-click a folder in File Explorer, tap or click Share With, and then tap or click Specific People. Contrary to what you might think, when you set permissions by using the File Sharing dialog box, you are configuring the underlying access permissions rather than share permissions. When you assign a user or group the Read permission level, the user or group is granted Read & Execute permissions on the folder. When you assign a user or group the Read/Write permission level, the user or group is granted Full Control permissions on the folder. The share permissions on the folder are set so that the Everyone and Administrators groups have Full Control.

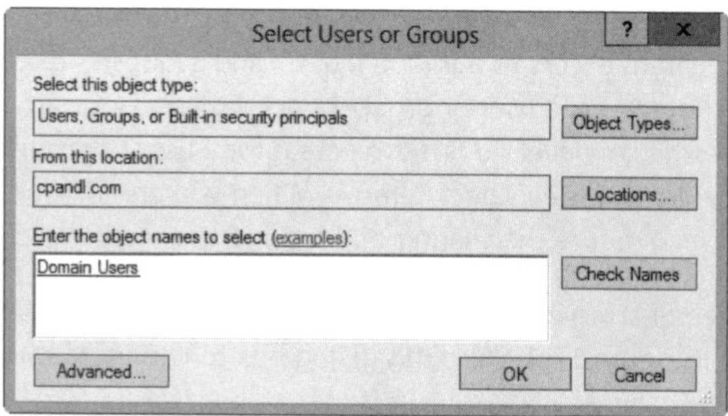

Figure 18-11 Choose users with whom to share the folder.

In the Enter The Object Names To Select field, type the name of a user or a group account previously defined in the selected or default domain. Be sure to reference the user account name rather than a user's full name. When entering multiple names, separate them with semicolons.

Tap or click Check Names. If a single match is found for each of your entries, the dialog box is automatically updated as appropriate and the entry is underlined. Otherwise, you see an additional dialog box. When no matches are found, you've either entered an incorrect name part or you're working with an incorrect location. Modify the name in the Name Not Found dialog box and try again or tap or click Locations to select a new location. When multiple matches are found, select the name or names you want to use in the Multiple Names Found dialog box and then tap or click OK.

When you tap or click OK, the users and groups are added to the Name list. You can then configure permissions for each user and group added by tapping or clicking an account name to display the Permission Level options and then choosing the appropriate permission level. The options for permission levels are as follows:

- **Read.** Grants the user or group Read & Execute permissions. These are access permissions.
- **Read/Write.** Grants the user or group Full Control permissions. These are access permissions.

Finally, tap or click Share to create the share. The top-level share permissions are set so that the Everyone and Administrators groups have Full Control. After Windows creates the share and makes it available for use, note the share name. This is the name by which the shared resource can be accessed. If you want to email a link to the shared resource to someone, tap or click E-mail. If an email application is not installed on the system from which you are sharing a folder, a dialog box will appear reporting this. If you want to copy a link to the shared resource to the Clipboard, tap or click Copy. Tap or click Done when you are finished. The share is immediately available for use.

If you tap or click the Share button on the Sharing tab when sharing is already configured, you can change share permissions. Grant access to additional users and groups as discussed previously. To change the permission level for a user or group, select the user or group in the Name list and then select the new permission level. To remove access for a user or group, select the user or group in the Name list and then select Remove. When you are finished making changes, tap or click Share to reconfigure the sharing options and then tap or click Done.

If you tap or click the Advanced Sharing button on the Sharing tab, you see the Advanced Sharing dialog box, as shown in Figure 18-12. Use this dialog box to configure top-level share permissions and offline caching.

Figure 18-12 You can configure different shares of the same folder with different names and permissions.

Use the options in the Advanced Sharing dialog box as follows:

- Tap or click Add to share the folder again, using a different name and a different set of access permissions. When you create multiple shares for the same folder, the Share Name box of the Sharing tab becomes a selection list that you use to select a share to work with and configure. After you select a share to work with, the options on the Sharing tab apply to that share only. You also have a Remove option, which you can use to remove the additional share.
- Tap or click Permissions to view and set the share permissions as discussed in "Managing share permissions" later in this chapter. Share permissions provide the top-level access controls to the share. By default, only users you specify have access to the share. This important security feature is designed to help ensure that permissions aren't given to users unless you grant them.

Inside OUT

Additional sharing options

If a folder hasn't been shared previously, you can use options in the Advanced Sharing dialog box to share it. To do so, select Share This Folder and then enter the share name or accept the default value (which is the name of the folder). At this point, you could tap or click OK to create the share. However, when you create a share in this way, the only group granted access by default is the Everyone group, which is granted Read access by default. Thus, instead of tapping or clicking OK at this point, tap or click Permissions and then use the options provided to set additional top-level share permissions.

After you set share permissions, you might want to configure the share for offline use. By default, the share is configured so that only files and programs that users specify are available for offline use. If the BranchCache For Network Files role service is installed on the file server, you might want to keep this setting but also enable BranchCache. To do this, tap or click Caching and then select Enable BranchCache to enable computers in a branch office to cache files that are downloaded from the shared folder and then securely share the files to other computers in the branch office.

Creating shares by using Computer Management

By using Computer Management, you can share the folders of any computer to which you can connect on the network. This is handy for when you are sitting at your desk and don't want to have to log on locally to share a server's folders. After you start Computer Management, you can connect to the computer you want to work with by pressing and holding or right-clicking Computer Management in the console tree and then selecting Connect To Another Computer. Use the Select Computer dialog box to choose the computer you want to work with. When you are finished, expand System Tools and Shared Folders and then select Shares to display the current shares on the system you are working with.

You can then create a shared folder by pressing and holding or right-clicking Shares and then selecting New Share. This starts the Create A Shared Folder Wizard. Tap or click Next to display the Folder Path page, as shown in Figure 18-13. In the Folder Path field, type the full path to the folder you want to share. If you don't know the full path or you want to share a new folder, tap or click Browse. You can now do the following:

- Use the Browse For Folder dialog box to locate and select the folder you want to share
- Select where you want to create a new folder, tap or click Make New Folder, type a name for the folder, and then press Enter

NOTE

You can start the Create A Shared Folder Wizard by typing shrpubw in the App Search box and pressing Enter.

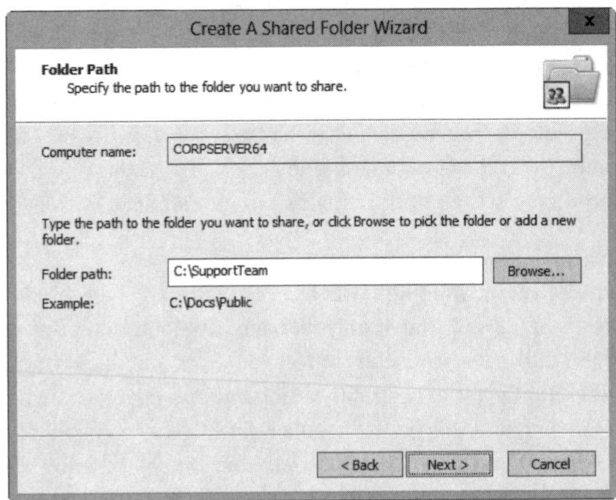

Figure 18-13 Specify the folder path or tap or click Browse to search for a folder to use.

Tap or click Next when you are ready to continue. In the Share Name field, type a name for the share, as shown in Figure 18-14. This is the name of the folder to which users will connect, and it must be unique on the computer you are working with. Share names can be up to 80 characters in length and can contain spaces. If you want to provide support for early Windows operating system clients, you should limit the share name to eight characters with a three-letter extension. If you want to hide the share from users (which means that they won't be able to see the shared resource when they try to browse to it in File Explorer or at the command line), type **$** as the last character of the share name. Keep in mind that you can hide shares only from normal users. If users have Administrator privileges, they can get a list of the shares.

Optionally, type a description of the share in the Description field. The description is displayed as comments when you view shares in Network Explorer and other Windows dialog boxes. Next, configure offline settings as appropriate.

By default, the share is configured so that only files and programs that users specify are available for offline use. Normally, this is the option you want to use because this option also enables users to take advantage of the new Always Offline feature. However, if you use this setting, you might also want to enable BranchCache. To do this, tap or click Change, select Enable BranchCache (as shown in Figure 18-15), and then tap or click OK. When the BranchCache For Network Files role service is installed on the file server, enabling BranchCache enables computers in a branch office to cache files that are downloaded from the shared folder and then securely share the files with other computers in the branch office.

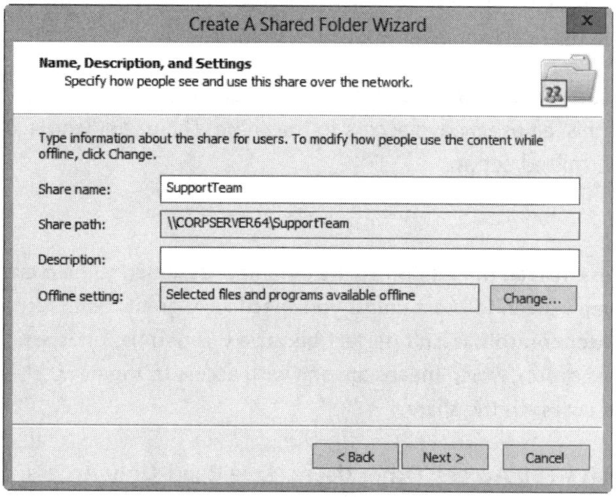

Figure 18-14 Set the share name and description.

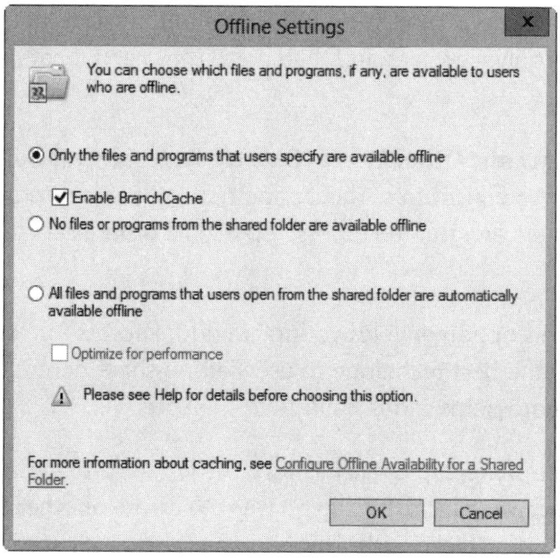

Figure 18-15 Configure the offline settings.

Alternatively, tap or click Change and then select All Files And Programs That Users Open From The Shared Folder Are Automatically Available Offline. With this setting, client computers automatically cache all files and programs that users open from the share. You can then also select Optimize For Performance to run cached program files from the local cache instead of from the shared folder on the server.

When you are ready to continue, tap or click Next to display the Shared Folder Permissions page, shown in Figure 18-16. The available options are as follows:

- **All Users Have Read-Only Access.** Grants the Read share permission to the Everyone group. Because of this, all users have access to the share. The underlying access permissions determine permitted actions.

  NOTE

  Granting Read access instead of Full Control by default is designed to help ensure that permissions aren't given to users unless you specifically grant them. Although it is a step toward better controls, it isn't perfect because this permission is assigned to the special Everyone group, which means anyone with access to the network—even Guests—have Read access to the share.

- **Administrators Have Full Access; Other Users Have Read-Only Access.** Grants the Full Control share permission to Administrators and the Read share permission to Everyone. This option gives administrators full access to the share and allows administrators to create, modify, and delete files and folders. On NTFS and ReFS volumes, it also gives administrators the right to change permissions and to take ownership of files and folders. Other users can only view files and read data. They can't create, modify, or delete files and folders.
- **Administrators Have Full Access; Other Users Have No Access.** Grants the Full Control share permission to Administrators. This option gives administrators full access to the share. Because no others are granted access, it prevents other users from accessing the share.
- **Customize Permissions.** This option enables you to configure access for specific users and groups, which is usually the best technique to use. Setting share permissions is discussed fully in "Managing share permissions" later in this chapter.

After you set up permissions on the share, tap or click Finish. The wizard displays a status report, which should state, "Sharing was successful." If you want to create another share, select the related check box before you tap or click Finish. This runs the Create A Shared Folder Wizard again.

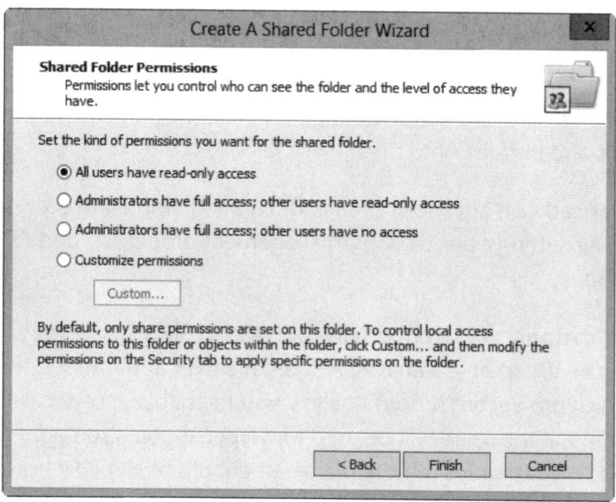

Figure 18-16 Set the share permissions.

Creating shared folders in Server Manager

In Server Manager, the Shares subnode of the File And Storage Services node shows existing shares for file servers that have been added for management. I recommend getting to know the options here and using Server Manager for creating and managing shares whenever possible.

As shown in Figure 18-17, the shares are listed in alphabetical order for each server. If you select a share, the Volume panel provides information about the underlying volume and the Quota panel displays information about File Server Resource Manager (FSRM) quotas.

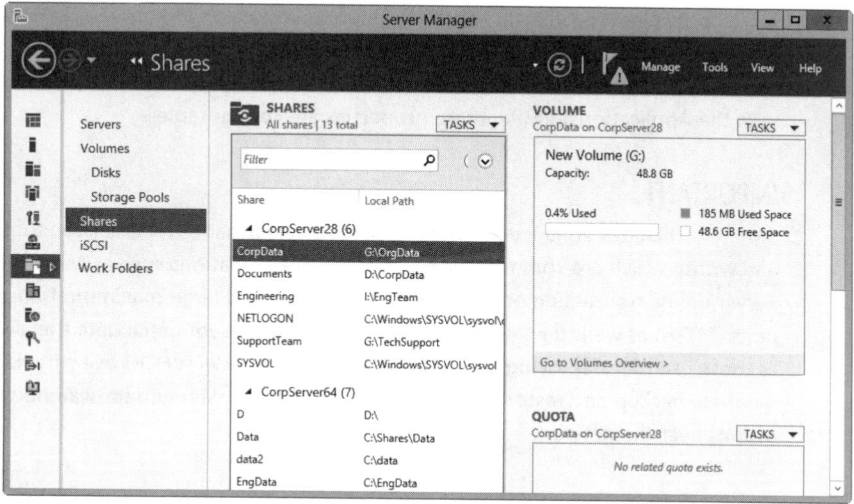

Figure 18-17 View currently configured shares.

On the Shares panel, tap or click Tasks and then tap or click New Share to start the New Share Wizard. The New Share Wizard has several file share profiles:

- **SMB Share - Quick.** A basic profile for creating SMB file shares that you can use to configure their settings and permissions.
- **SMB Share - Advanced.** An advanced profile for creating SMB file shares that you can use to configure their settings, permissions, management properties, and FSRM quota profile (if applicable).
- **SMB Share - Applications.** A custom profile for creating SMB file shares with settings appropriate for Hyper-V, certain databases, and other server applications. It's essentially the same as the quick profile, but it doesn't allow you to enable access-based enumeration or offline caching. If the share will be used for Hyper-V, you also might need to enable constrained delegation for remote management of the Hyper-V host.
- **NFS Share - Quick.** A basic profile for creating NFS file shares that you can use to configure their authentication settings, manage permissions for hosts, and manage permissions for users.
- **NFS Share - Advanced.** An advanced profile for creating NFS file shares that you can use to configure their authentication settings, manage permissions for hosts and users, add management properties, and assign an FSRM quota profile (if applicable).

NOTE

The differences between the file share profiles are fundamental. Whether you are working with SMB or NFS, the Advanced profiles enable you to add management properties and assign FSRM quota profiles; the Quick profiles don't. The Applications profile is the same as the Quick profile except that it disables access-based enumeration and offline caching in the wizard UI because you don't want to use these settings with server applications and certain databases. If you later edit the properties of a share created with the Applications profile, these properties are configurable.

IMPORTANT

SMB 3.02 includes enhancements that improve performance for small random reads and writes, which are common with server-based applications such as Microsoft SQL Server online transaction processing (OLTP). Packets use large maximum transmission units (MTUs) as well to enhance performance for large, sequential data transfers, such as those used for deploying and copying virtual hard disks (VHDs) over the network, database backup and restore over the network, and SQL Server data-warehouse transactions over the network.

Choose one of the available SMB share profiles and then tap or click Next. On the Select The Server And Path For This Share page, shown in Figure 18-18, select the server and volume on which you want the share to be created. Only file servers you've added for management are available.

NOTE

Server Manager creates the file share as a new folder in the \Shares directory on the selected volume by default. To change this, choose Type A Custom Path and then either type the desired share path, such as D:\Data, or click Browse to use the Select Folder dialog box to select the share path. If the folder path doesn't exist, the wizard will create folders as necessary.

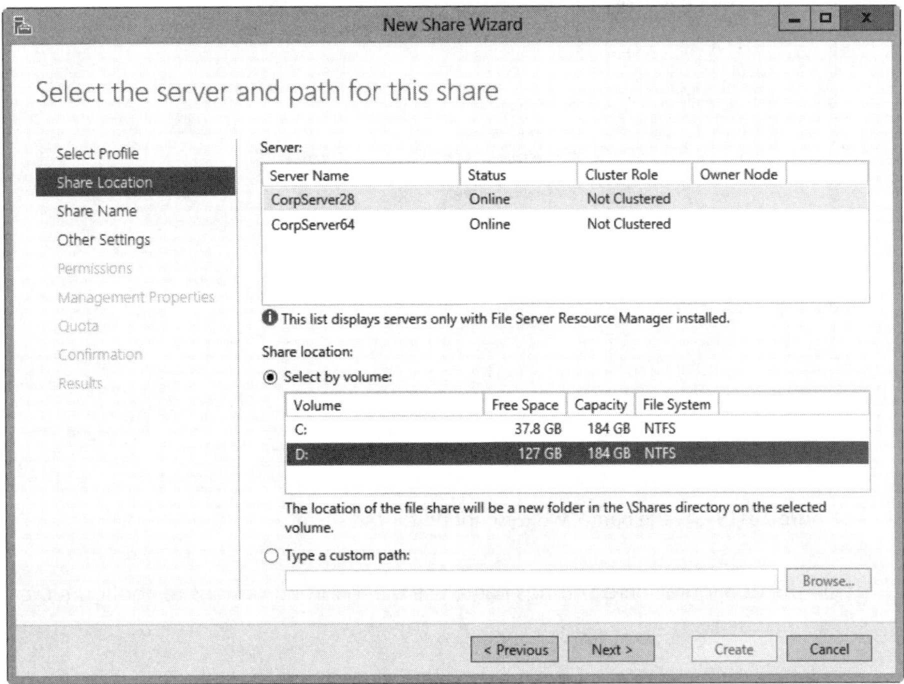

Figure 18-18 Set the location of the share.

Tap or click Next when you are ready to continue. On the Specify Share Name page, type a name for the share, as shown in Figure 18-19. This is the name of the folder to which users will connect. Note the local and remote paths to the share. These paths are set based on the share location and share name you specified. Keep in mind that share names must be unique for each system and that the wizard creates folders as necessary. For example, if the path is D:\

Shares\EngData and neither the Shares folder nor the EngData subfolder has been created, the wizard will create both folders to ensure that the share path is valid.

Optionally, type a description of the share in the Share Description text box. When you view shares on a particular computer, the description is displayed in Computer Management. When you are ready to continue, tap or click Next.

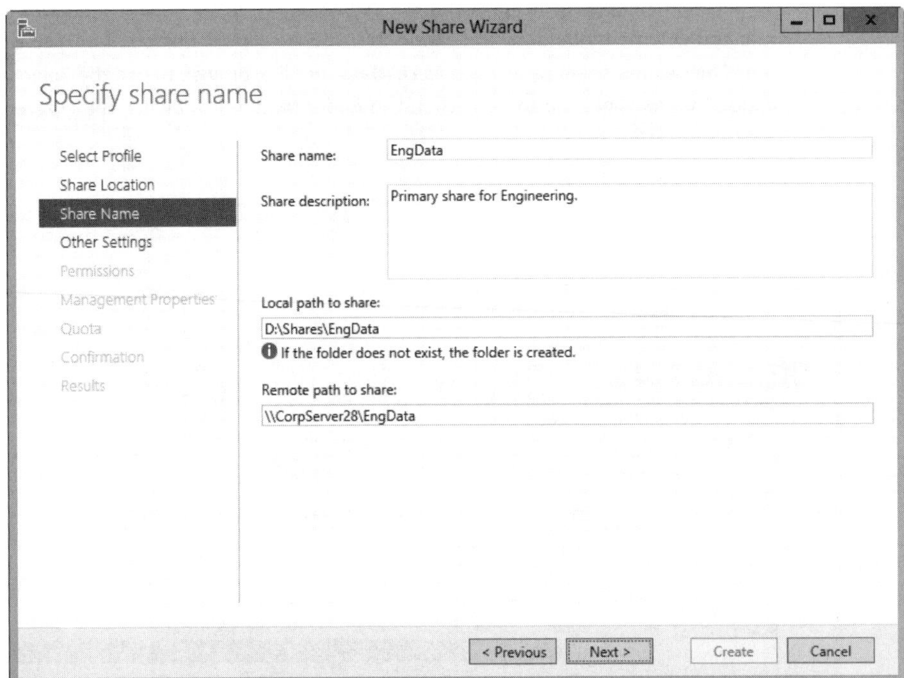

Figure 18-19 Set the name and description for the share.

On the Configure Share Settings page, use the following options to configure the way the share is used:

- **Enable Access-Based Enumeration.** With this setting, the wizard configures permissions so that when users browse the folder, only files and folders to which a user has been granted at least Read access are displayed. If a user doesn't have at least Read (or equivalent) permission for a file or folder within the shared folder, that file or folder is hidden from view. (This option is dimmed if you are creating an SMB share optimized for applications.)
- **Allow Caching Of Share.** With this setting, the wizard configures the share to cache only the files and programs that users specify for offline use. Although you can later

edit the share properties and change the offline files' availability settings, you normally want to select this option because it enables users to take advantage of the new Always Offline feature. Optionally, if the BranchCache For Network Files role service is installed on the file server, select Enable BranchCache to enable computers in a branch office to cache files that are downloaded from the shared folder and then securely share the files to other computers in the branch office. (This option is dimmed if you are creating an SMB share optimized for applications.)

- **Encrypt Data Access.** With this setting, the wizard configures the share to use SMB encryption, which protects file data from eavesdropping while it is being transferred over the network. This option is useful on untrusted networks.

Tap or click Next. On the Specify Permissions To Control Access page, shown in Figure 18-20, the default access permissions assigned to the share are listed. By default, the special Everyone group is granted the Full Control share permission and the underlying access permissions are as listed. To change the share, access, or both permissions, tap or click Customize Permissions and then use the Advanced Security Settings dialog box to configure the desired permissions. See "Configuring share permissions" later in the chapter for more information on setting permissions.

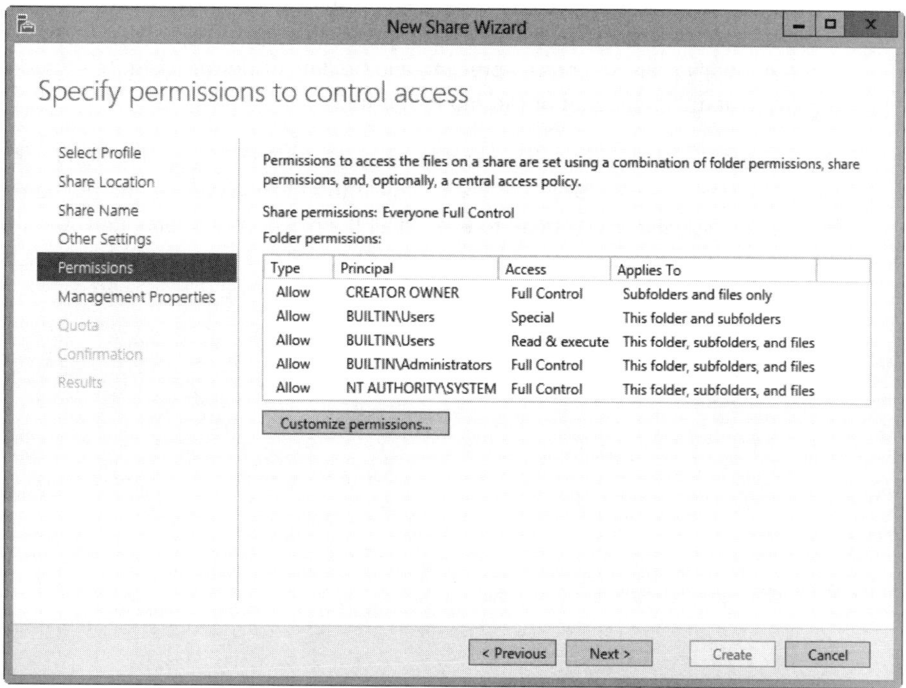

Figure 18-20 Review the default permissions and set other permissions as appropriate.

If you are using the advanced profile, do the following:

- Optionally, set the folder management properties and then tap or click Next. These properties specify the purpose of the folder and the type of data stored in it so that data-management policies, such as classification rules, can then use these properties.
- Optionally, apply a quota based on a template to the folder and then tap or click Next. You can select only quota templates that have already been created. For more information, see "Managing file-screen templates" in Chapter 20, "Managing file screening and storage reporting."

On the Confirm Selections page, review your selections. When you tap or click Create, the wizard creates the share, configures it, and sets permissions. The status should state, "The share was successfully created." If an error appears instead, note the error and take corrective action as appropriate before repeating this procedure to create the share. Tap or click Close.

Changing shared folder settings

When you create a share, you can configure many basic and advanced settings, including those for access-based enumeration, encrypted data access, offline settings for caching, and management properties. In Server Manager, the Shares subnode of the File And Storage Services node shows existing shares for file servers that have been added for management. You can modify share settings by pressing and holding or right-clicking the share you want to work with and then tapping or clicking Properties.

In the Properties dialog box, shown in Figure 18-21, you have several option panels that can be accessed by using controls in the left pane. Although you can expand the panels one by one, tap or click Show All instead to expand all the panels at the same time and then just scroll through the properties to review the settings. The available options are the same whether you used the basic, advanced, or applications profile to create the shared folder.

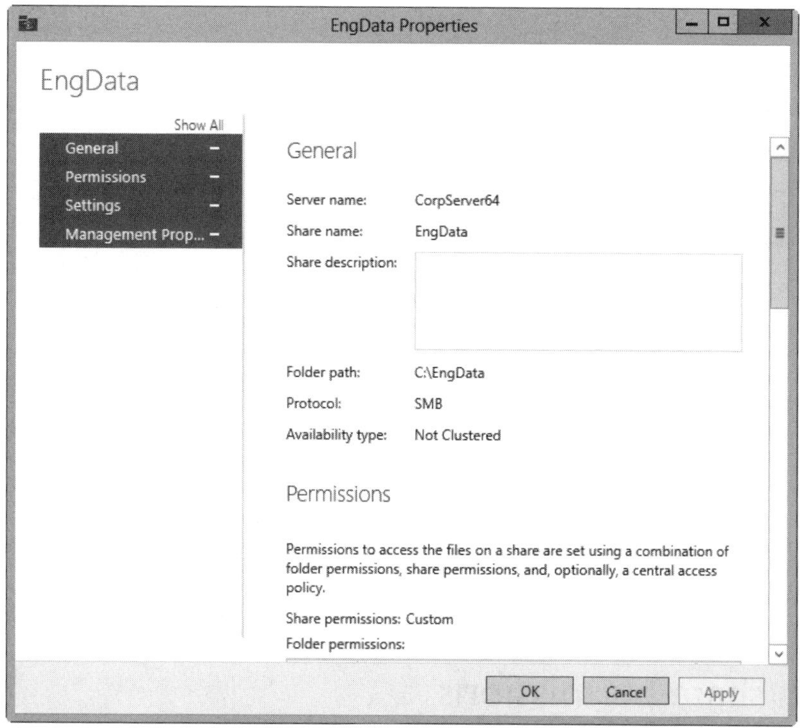

Figure 18-21 Review and modify the share settings.

Publishing shares in Active Directory

Sometimes, you also want to publish shares in Active Directory to make them easier to find. The quickest way to do this is to use Computer Management. After you start Computer Management and connect to the computer you want to work with, expand System Tools and Shared Folders and then select Shares to display the current shares on the system you are working with.

You can then publish a shared folder by pressing and holding or right-clicking the share in the details pane and then selecting Properties. In the share's Properties dialog box, tap or click the Publish tab, as shown in Figure 18-22. Finally, select the Publish This Share In Active Directory check box and then tap or click OK.

> NOTE
>
> **As discussed earlier in the chapter, in "Using and finding shares," search keywords can help users find shares. To add search keywords, tap or click Edit. In the Edit Keywords dialog box, enter a keyword and then tap or click Add. Repeat as necessary to add more keywords.**

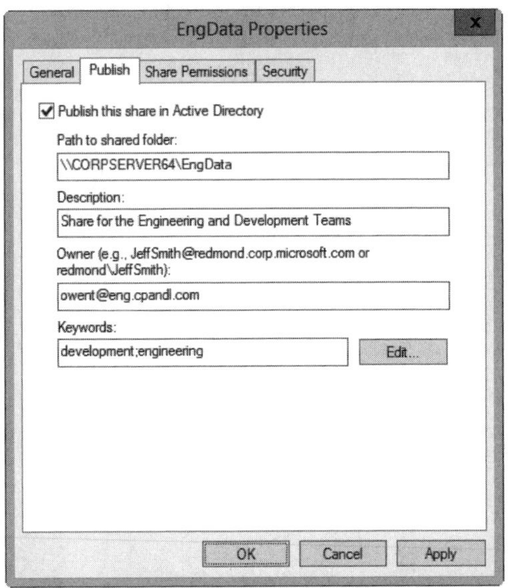

Figure 18-22 Publish the share in Active Directory.

Managing share permissions

As discussed previously, Windows Server 2012 R2 has two levels of permissions for shared folders: share permissions and access permissions. Share permissions are applied any time you access a file or folder over the network. These top-level permissions set the maximum allowable actions available within a shared folder. Although share permissions can get you in the door when you work remotely, the access permissions can further constrain access and the allowable actions.

When accessing files locally, only the access permissions are applied. However, when accessing files remotely, first the share permissions are applied and then the access permissions. In the case of file allocation table (FAT) volumes, the share permissions are the only permissions, and if a user has local access to the folder, she can perform any action.

Understanding share permissions

With shared folders, you use share permissions to set the maximum allowed access level. Share permissions are applied only when you access a folder remotely, and they can be used to grant access directly to users or implicitly through the groups to which users belong.

The available share permissions are as follows:

- **Full Control.** By granting this permission, users have Read and Change permissions and additional capabilities to change access permissions and take ownership of files and folders.
- **Change.** By granting this permission, users have Read permissions and the additional capability to create files and subfolders, modify files, change attributes on files and subfolders, and delete files and subfolders.
- **Read.** By granting this permission, you allow users to view file and subfolder names, access the subfolders of the share, read file data and attributes, and run program files.

If you have Read permissions on a share, the most you can do is perform read operations. If you have Change permissions on a share, the most you can do is perform read operations and change operations. If you have Full Control, you have full access. However, in any case, access permissions can further constrain access.

Permissions assigned to groups work like this: If a user is a member of a group that is granted share permissions, he also has those permissions. If a user is a member of multiple groups, the permissions are cumulative. This means that if one group of which the user is a member has Read access and another has additional access, she has additional access as well.

Inside OUT

Changes might be needed to enhance security

When you create a shared folder, default access permissions are assigned. Watch out, though, because the default in most cases is either to give Read access or Full Control to the special Everyone group, and both configurations allow Guests to access shares. This doesn't mean Guests can read files, however, because this is determined by the base-level access permissions. In most cases, it is more prudent to lock down access and grant permissions only to users who truly need access to a shared folder. If you really want to grant wide access to a shared folder, you might want to use the Domain Users group to do this rather than the Everyone group. In this case, you remove the Everyone group and add the Domain Users group. By using Domain Users, you require users to have a logon account to access the shared folder, which excludes Guests.

To override this behavior, you must specifically deny an access permission. Denying a permission is the trump card—it takes precedence and overrides permissions that have been granted. When you want to single out a user or group and deny it a permission, configure the share permissions to deny that permission specifically to the user or group. For example, if a user is a member of a group that has been granted Full Control over a share, but he should have only Read permissions, configure the share to deny Change permissions to that user.

Configuring share permissions

The easiest way to configure share permissions is to use Computer Management. After you start Computer Management, connect to the computer you want to work with by pressing and holding or right-clicking Computer Management in the console tree and then selecting Connect To Another Computer. Then use the Select Computer dialog box to choose the computer you want to work with. When you are finished, expand System Tools and Shared Folders and then select Shares to display the current shares on the system you are working with.

To view or manage the permissions of a share, press and hold or right-click the share and then select Properties. In the share Properties dialog box, tap or click the Share Permissions tab, as shown in Figure 18-23. You can now view the users and groups that have access to the share and the type of access they have.

In this example, members of the Domain Admins group have Full Control over the share and members of the Domain Users group have Change access. The Everyone group was removed to enhance security as discussed in the Inside Out "Changes might be needed to enhance security" sidebar earlier in the chapter.

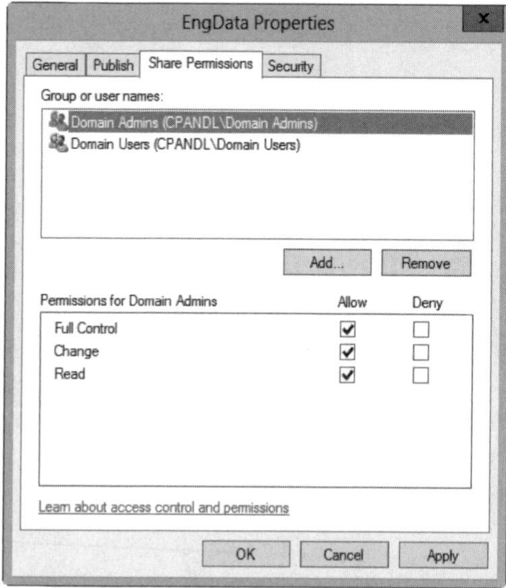

Figure 18-23 View or set share permissions.

You can grant or deny permission to access a share by following these steps:

1. In Computer Management, press and hold or right-click the share and then select Properties. In the share Properties dialog box, tap or click the Share Permissions tab.
2. On the Share Permissions tab, tap or click Add. This opens the Select Users, Computers, Service Accounts, Or Groups dialog box.
3. The Locations button enables you to access account names from other domains. Tap or click Locations to see a list of the current domains, trusted domains, and other resources that you can access. Because of transitive trusts, you can usually access all the domains in the domain tree or forest.
4. Type the name of a user or group account in the selected or default domain and then tap or click Check Names. The options available depend on the number of matches found, as follows:
   - When a single match is found, the dialog box is automatically updated as appropriate and the entry is underlined.
   - When no matches are found, you've either entered an incorrect name part or you're working with an incorrect location. Modify the name and try again or tap or click Locations to select a new location.
   - If multiple matches are found, select the name or names you want to use and then tap or click OK.
5. To add additional users or groups, type a semicolon (;) and then repeat this process.
6. When you tap or click OK, the users and groups are added to the Name list for the share.
7. Configure access permissions for each user and group added by selecting an account name and then allowing or denying access permissions. If a user or group should be granted access permissions, select the check box for the permission in the Allow column. If a user or group should be denied access permissions, select the check box for the permission in the Deny column.
8. When you're finished, tap or click OK.

NOTE

You can select the opposite permission to override an inherited permission. In addition, Deny normally overrides Allow. For example, you can explicitly deny permission to a user or group for a child folder or file. This permission is then denied to that user or group of users.

In Server Manager, the Shares subnode of the File And Storage Services node shows existing shares for file servers that have been added for management. Press and hold or right-click the share you want to work with and then tap or click Properties. In the Properties dialog box, tap or click Permissions in the left pane. You can now view the users and groups that have access to the share and the type of access they have.

To change share, folder, or both permissions, tap or click Customize Permissions and then select the Share tab in the Advanced Security Settings dialog box, as shown in Figure 18-24. Users or groups that already have access to the share are listed in the Permission Entries list. You can remove permissions for these users and groups by selecting the user or group you want to remove and then tapping or clicking Remove.

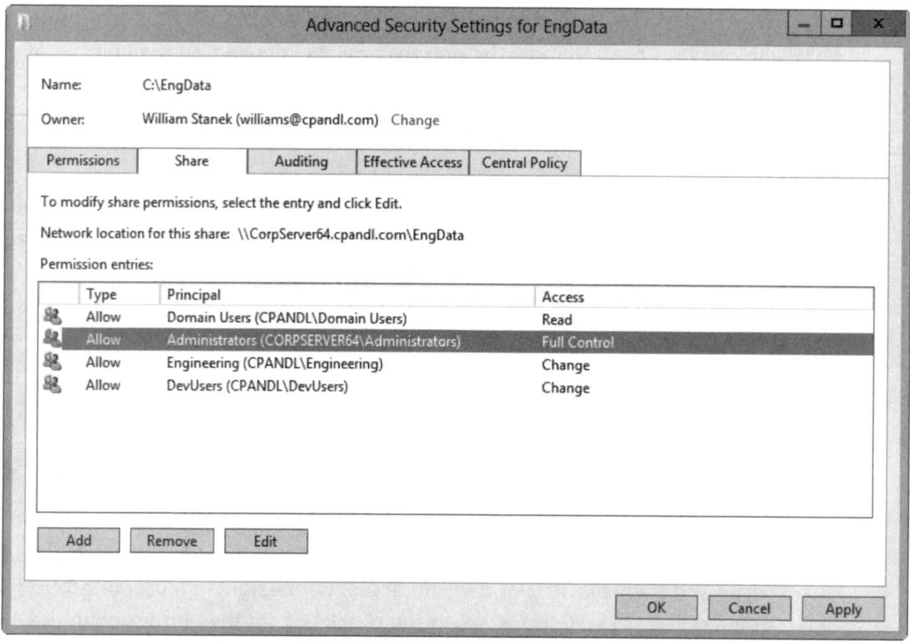

Figure 18-24 Use the Advanced Security Settings dialog box to manage share permissions.

You can change permissions for these users and groups by doing the following:

1. Select the user or group you want to change and then select Edit.
2. Allow or deny access permissions in the Permissions list box and then tap or click OK.

To add permissions for another user or group, follow these steps:

1. Tap or click Add to open the Permission Entry dialog box, shown in Figure 18-25. Next, tap or click Select A Principal to open the Select User, Computer, Service Account Or Group dialog box. Type the name of a user or a group account and then tap or click Check Names. Only one name can be entered at a time. Be sure to reference the user account name rather than the user's full name.

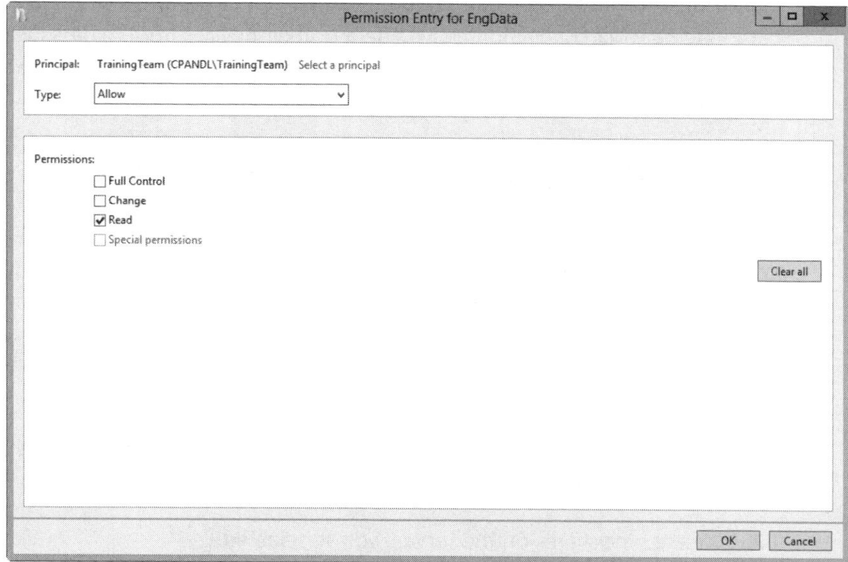

Figure 18-25 Add permissions entries to allow or deny access.

2. If a single match is found for each entry, the dialog box is automatically updated and the entry is underlined. Otherwise, you see an additional dialog box. If no matches are found, either you entered the name incorrectly or you're working with an incorrect location. Modify the name in the Name Not Found dialog box and try again or tap or click Locations to select a new location. When multiple matches are found, in the Multiple Names Found dialog box, select the name you want to use and then tap or click OK.

3. When you tap or click OK, the user or group is added as the Principal, and the Permission Entry dialog box is updated to show this.

4. Use the Type list to specify whether you are configuring allowed or denied permissions and then select the permissions you want to allow or deny.

5. Tap or click OK to return to the Advanced Security Settings dialog box. To assign additional security permissions for controlling access, see "Managing access permissions" in Chapter 19, "File security, access controls, and auditing."

Configuring synced sharing

Although standard file sharing requires a computer that is joined and connected to the enterprise domain, synced sharing does not. With sync shares, users can use an Internet or corporate network connection to sync data to their devices from folders located on enterprise servers. You implement synced sharing by using Work Folders, a feature that you can add to servers running Windows Server 2012 R2 or later.

Understanding Work Folders and sync shares

Work Folders use a client-server architecture. A Work Folders client is natively integrated into Windows 8.1, and clients for Windows 7, Apple iPad, and other devices are (or will become) available. You deploy Work Folders in the enterprise by performing these procedures:

1. Identify servers that you want to host sync shares and add the Work Folders role to these servers.
2. In Group Policy, enable discovery of Work Folders for the appropriate domains and organizational units.
3. Create sync shares on the servers you've selected.
4. Optionally, enable SMB access to sync shares.
5. Configure clients to access Work Folders.

Work Folders use a remote web gateway configured as part of the Internet Information Services (IIS) hostable web core. When users access a sync share through a URL provided by an administrator and configured in Group Policy, a user folder is created as a subfolder of the sync share and this subfolder is where the user's data is stored. The folder-naming format for the user-specific folder is set when you create a sync share. The folder can be named by using only the user alias portion of the user's logon name or the full logon name in alias@domain format. The format you choose primarily depends on the level of compatibility required. Using the full logon name eliminates potential conflicts when users from different domains have identical user aliases, but this format is not compatible with redirected folders.

To maintain compatibility with redirected folders, you should configure sync folders to use aliases. However, in enterprises with multiple domains, the drawback to this approach is that there could be conflicts between identical user aliases in different domains. Although the automatically configured permissions for a user folder would prevent davidw from the cpandl .com domain from accessing a user folder created for davidw from the adatum.com domain, the conflict would cause problems. If there were an existing folder for davidw from the cpandl .com domain, the server would not be able to create a user folder for davidw from the adatum.com domain.

Inside OUT

Work Folders might not be compatible with your existing infrastructure

Work Folders use the IIS hostable web core. If you deploy roles and features that require a full version of the Web Server (IIS) role, you might find that these roles and features or the Work Folders feature itself don't work together. A conflict can occur because the full version of the Web Server (IIS) role has a Default Web Site that uses port 80 for HTTP communications and port 443 for secure HTTP communications. For example, running Windows Server Essentials Experience and Work Folders on the same server requires a special configuration. Typically, you need to change the ports Windows Server Essentials Experience uses so they don't conflict with the ports Work Folders uses.

With Work Folders, you have several important configuration options. You can do the following:

- Encrypt files in Work Folders on client devices
- Require screens to lock automatically and require a password
- Enable SMB access to sync shares

Encryption is implemented using the Encrypting File System (EFS). EFS encrypts files with an enterprise encryption key rather than an encryption key generated by the client device. The enterprise encryption key is specific to the enterprise ID of the user (which by default is the primary SMTP address of the user). Having an enterprise encryption key that is separate from a client's standard encryption key is important to ensure that encrypted personal files and encrypted work files are managed separately.

When files are encrypted, administrators can use a selective wipe to remove enterprise files from a client device. The selective wipe simply removes the enterprise encryption key and thus renders the work files unreadable (without affecting any encrypted personal files). Because the work files remain encrypted, there's no need to delete the work files from the client device. That said, you could run Disk Optimizer on the drive where the work files were stored. During optimization, Disk Optimizer should then overwrite the sectors where the work files were stored. Selective wipe only works when you've enabled the encryption option on Work Folders.

Encryption is only one way to protect enterprise data. Another way to protect enterprise data is to configure client devices to lock screens and require a password for access, which ensures the following:

- A minimum password length of six characters
- A maximum password retry of 10
- A screen that automatically locks in 15 minutes or less

NOTE

If you enforce the use of automatic lock screens and passwords, any device that doesn't support these requirements is prevented from connecting to the Work Folder.

By default, sync shares are not available in the same way as standard file shares, and users can only access sync shares by using the Work Folders client. If you want to make sync shares available to users as standard file shares, you must enable SMB access. After you enable SMB access, users can access files stored in Work Folders by using syncing and by mapping network drives.

When a user makes changes to files in Work Folders, the changes might not be immediately apparent to others using the same Work Folders. For example, if a user deletes a file from a Work Folder using SMB, other users accessing the Work Folder might still see the file as available. This inconsistency can occur because, by default, clients only poll the sync server every 10 minutes for SMB changes. In addition, to minimize support issues related to Work Folders, you want to assure users that changes might not be immediately apparent; therefore, they need to be patient when waiting for changes to propagate.

Sync servers also use the Work Folders client to check periodically for changes users have made using SMB. The default polling interval is 5 minutes. When the server identifies changes, the server relays the changes the next time a client syncs. Following this, you can determine that it could take up to 15 minutes for a change made using SMB to propagate fully.

You can control how frequently the server checks for changes made locally on the server or through SMB by using the *–MinimumChangeDetectionMins* parameter of the Set-SyncServerSetting cmdlet. However, because the server must check the change information for each file stored in the sync share, you need to be careful that you don't configure a server to try to detect changes too frequently. A server that checks for changes too frequently can become overloaded. Remember, change detection uses more resources as the number of files stored in the sync share increases.

Deploying sync shares through Group Policy

To deploy Work Folders, you add the File And Storage Services\Work Folders role to a file server and then configure Work Folders by using Server Manager. Afterward, you can use policy settings to control related options such as the server to which users can connect remotely and access Work Folders.

Clients use secure encrypted communications to connect to work folders as long as the file servers hosting Work Folders have valid Secure Socket Layer (SSL) certificates. When a device initiates an SSL connection, the server sends the certificate to the client. The client evaluates the certificate and continues only if the certificate is valid and can be trusted. If you configure a connection to an exact URL, the client can connect directly to the specified server and synchronize data in Work Folders. The server's certificate must have a Common Name (CN) or a Subject Alternative Name (SAN) that matches the host header in the request. For example, if the client makes a request to https://server25.cpandl.com, the CN or SAN must be server25.cpandl.com.

In Group Policy, you specify the URL used within your organization for Work Folders discovery by using the Specify Work Folders Settings policy found under Administrative Templates policies for User Configuration\Windows Components\Work Folders. You control the connection to servers in one of two ways:

- By specifying the exact URL of a file server hosting the Work Folders for the user, such as https://server29.cpandl.com
- By specifying the URL used within your organization for Work Folders discovery, such as https://workfolders.cpandl.com

Any server configured with Work Folders acts as a discovery server by default. If you configure a discovery URL, a client connects to one of several servers and the email address of the user is used to discover which specific server hosts the Work Folders for the client. The client is then connected to this server. Each discovery server needs to have a certificate with multiple Subject Alternative Names (SANs), including the server name and the discovery name. For example, if a client makes a request to https://workfolders.cpandl.com and connects to FileServer83.cpandl.com, the server's certificate must have a CN or SAN of fileserver83.cpandl.com and a SAN of workfolders.cpandl.com.

If you want to configure Work Folders in Group Policy, use the following technique:

1. Access Group Policy for the system, site, domain, or OU you want to work with. Access the Work Folders node by using the Administrative Templates policies for User Configuration under Windows Components\Work Folders.
2. Double-tap or double-click Specify Work Folders Settings and then select Enabled (see Figure 18-26).

3. In the Work Folders URL text box, enter the URL of the file server that hosts the Work Folders for the user or the URL used within your organization for Work Folders discovery.

4. If you want to prevent users from changing settings when setting up Work Folders, select Force Automatic Setup. When you enforce setup, users cannot opt out of using Work Folders and are prevented from manually specifying the local folder in which Work Folders stores files.

5. Tap or click OK.

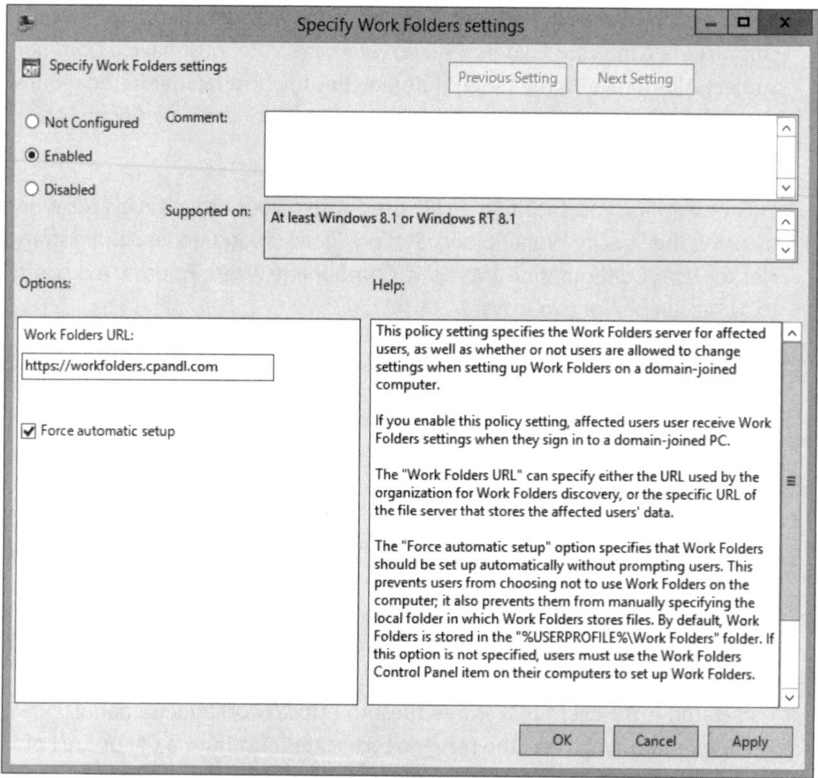

Figure 18-26 Enable Work Folders and then specify the URL to use for discovery.

To enable detailed logging of Work Folders, you can enable and configure the Audit Object Access policy setting for a Group Policy Object (GPO) processed by the server. You find this setting in Administrative Templates For Computer Configuration under Windows Settings \Security Settings\Local Policies\Audit Policies. After you enable Audit Object Access, add an audit entry for the specific folders you want to audit. In File Explorer, press and hold or right-click a folder you want to audit and then select Properties. In the Properties dialog box, on the Security tab, select Advanced. In the Advanced Security Settings dialog box, use the options on the Auditing tab to configure auditing.

Creating sync shares and enabling SMB access

You create a sync share to identify a local folder on a sync server that will be synchronized and accessible to domain users through the Work Folders client. Because sync shares are mapped to local paths on sync servers, I recommend creating any folders that you want to use before creating sync shares. This will make it easier to select the exact folders you want to work with.

To create a sync share, complete the following steps:

1. In Server Manager, select File And Storage Services and then select Work Folders. On the Work Folders panel, select Tasks and then select New Sync Share. This opens the New Sync Share Wizard. If the Before You Begin page is displayed, select Next.

2. On the Select The Server And Path page, shown in Figure 18-27, select the server you want to work with. Keep in mind that only servers that have the Work Folders role installed are available for selection.

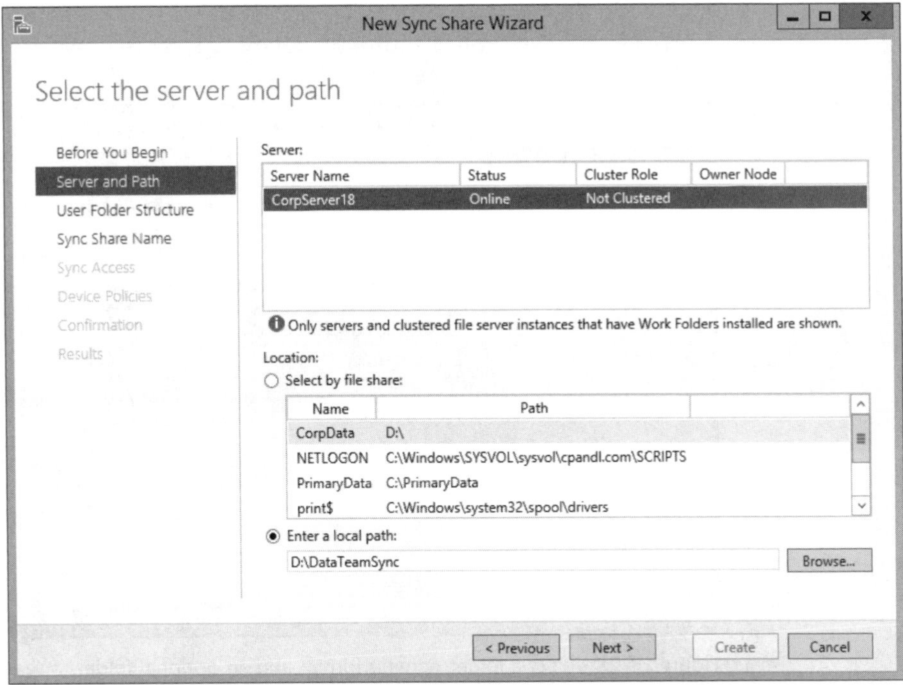

Figure 18-27 Specify the server and folder to use.

CHAPTER 18

3. When configuring sync shares, you have several options. You can do the following:
   - Add syncing to an existing file share by choosing Select By File Share and then selecting the file share that should also be synced
   - Add syncing to an existing local folder by choosing Enter A Local Path, selecting Browse, and then using the Select Folder dialog box to locate and choose the folder to sync
   - Add syncing to a new local folder by choosing Enter A Local Path and then entering the path to use
4. When you are ready to continue, tap or click Next. If you specified a new folder location, you are prompted to confirm whether you want to create this folder. Select OK to create the folder and continue.
5. On the Specify The Structure For User Folders page, shown in Figure 18-28, choose a folder-naming format for the subfolders where user data is stored. To use only the user alias portion of the user's logon name for naming user folders, choose User Alias. To use the full logon name for naming user folders, choose User alias@domain.

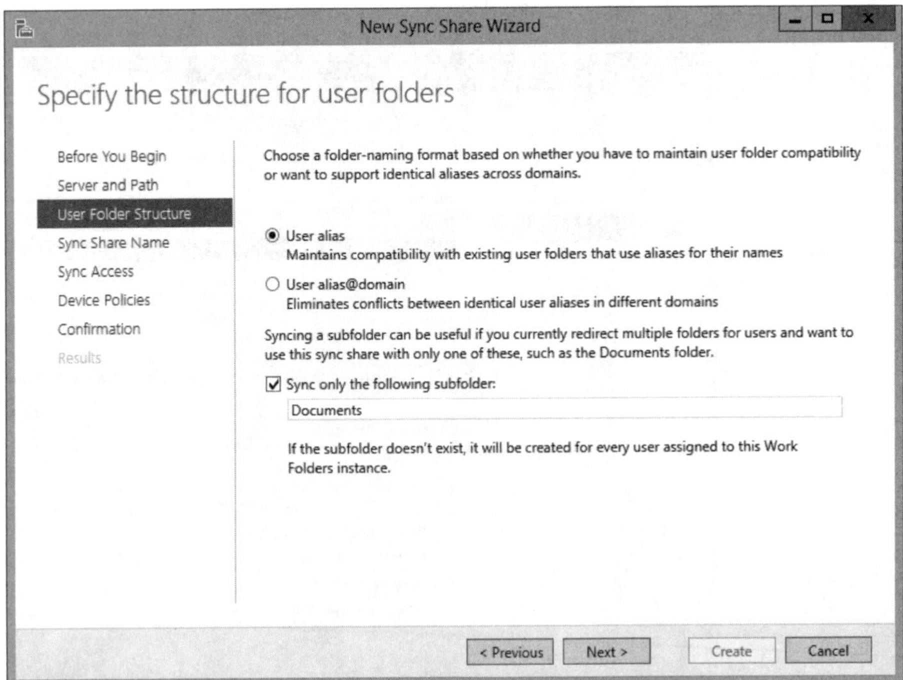

Figure 18-28 Select a folder-naming format and an optional folder to sync.

CHAPTER 18

6. By default, all folders and files stored under the user folder are synced automatically. If you'd prefer only a specific folder to be synced, select the Sync Only The Following Subfolder check box and then enter the name of the folder, such as Documents. Note that if the specified subfolder does not exist, it will be created for every user to whom this policy is applied. Select Next to continue.

7. On the Enter The Sync Share Name page, enter a share name and description before selecting Next to continue.

8. On the Grant Sync Access To Groups page, shown in Figure 18-29, use the options provided to specify the users and groups that should be able to access the sync share. To add a user or group, select Add and then use the Select User Or Group dialog box to specify the user or group that should have access to the sync share.

NOTE

Any users and groups you specify will be granted permissions on the base folder that allows the users and groups to create folders and access files in their folders. Specifically, Creator/Owner is granted Full Control on subfolders and files only. The users and groups are granted List Folder/Read Data, Create Folders/Append Data, Traverse Folder/Execute File, and Read/Write attributes on the base folder. Local System is granted Full Control of the base folder, subfolders, and files. Administrator is granted Read permissions on the base folder.

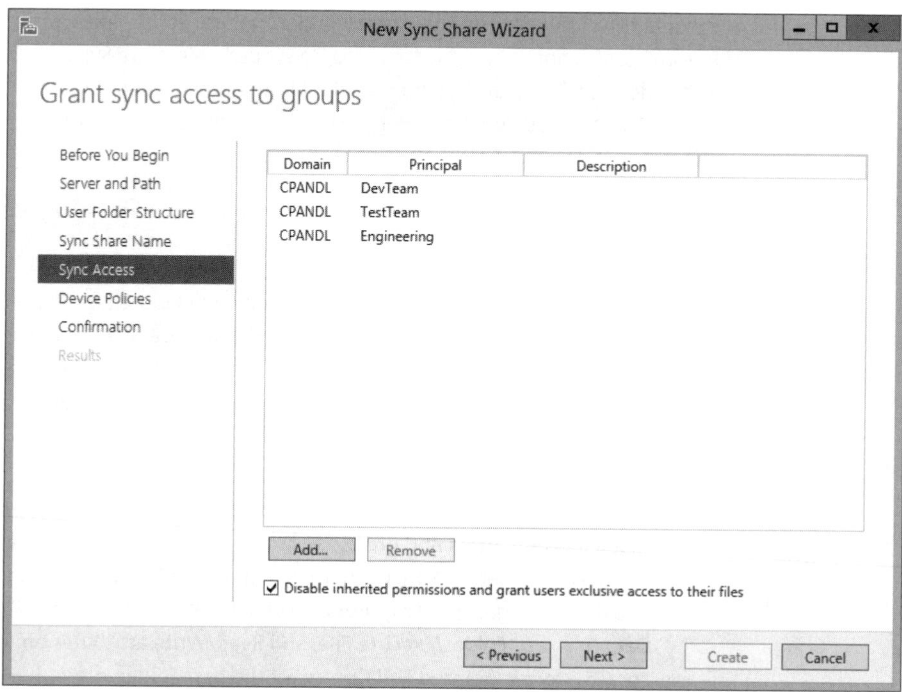

Figure 18-29 Specify the users and groups that should have access to the sync share.

By default, inherited permissions are disabled and users have exclusive access to their user folders. Because of this, only the user who stores a file has access to this file on the share.

9. If the base folder for the share has permissions that you want to be applied to user folders, such as those that would grant administrators access to user folders, clear the Disable Inherited Permissions check box. When you are ready to continue, tap or click Next.

10. On the Specify Device Policies page, you have two options. You can select Encrypt Work Folders to encrypt files in Work Folders on client devices. You can select Automatically Lock Screen And Require A Password to ensure that the screens on client devices lock automatically and require a password for access.

11. Tap or click Next to continue and then confirm your selections. Select Create to create the sync share. If the wizard is unable to create the sync share, you see an error; you need to note the error and take appropriate corrective action. A common error you might see occurs when the server hosts both Work Folders (which use the hostable web core) and the full Web Server (IIS) role. Before you can create sync shares, you need to

modify the ports used so they do not conflict or install Work Folders on a server that doesn't have the full Web Server (IIS) role.

If you did not select an existing file share during setup and want to enable the sync share for SMB access, open File Explorer. In File Explorer, press and hold or right-click the folder, select Share With, and then select Specific People. Finally, configure file sharing as discussed earlier in the chapter.

Accessing Work Folders on clients

Users with a domain user account can access Work Folders from a client device over the Internet or over the corporate network. You configure Work Folder Access for a user by completing the following steps:

1. In Control Panel, select System And Security and then select Work Folders. On the Manage Work Folders page, select Set Up Work Folders.
2. On the Enter Your Work Email Address page, enter the user email address, such as johng@cpandl.com, and then tap or click Next. If the client device is joined to the domain, you will not be prompted for the user's credentials. Otherwise, you are prompted for the user's credentials. After the user enters her credentials, you can select Remember My Credentials to store the user's credentials for future use and then tap or click OK to continue.
3. On the Introducing Work Folders page, note where the work files for the user will be stored. By default, work files are stored in a user profile subfolder called Work Folders. For example, the work files for JohnG would be stored under %SystemDrive%\Users\JohnG\WorkFolders. To store work files in another location, select Change and then use the options provided to specify a new save location for work files. When you are ready to continue, select Next.
4. On the Security Policies page, review the security policies that will be applied and then have the user select the I Accept These Policies On My PC check box. You cannot continue if you do not select this check box.
5. Select Set Up Work Folders to create Work Folders on the client device.

After you configure Work Folders for initial use on a client device, the user can access Work Folders in File Explorer. When a user opens File Explorer, the This PC node should be opened by default. If so, the user simply needs to double-tap or double-click Work Folders to view work files. If a user has an open File Explorer window and This PC is not the selected node, he simply needs to tap or click the leftmost option button in the address list and then tap or click This PC.

As the user works with files, the changes he makes trigger sync actions with the server. If the user doesn't change any files locally for an extended period of time, the client connects to the server every 10 minutes to determine whether there are changes to sync.

CHAPTER 19

File security, access controls, and auditing

Few aspects of the operating system are more important than file security, access controls, and auditing. These topics are so interconnected, in fact, that talking about one without talking about the others is difficult. File security and access controls protect important data on a server by restricting access. Auditing protects data by tracking who accessed files and folders and identifying the actions they performed.

Managing access permissions

You can think of access permissions as the base-level permissions—the permissions that are applied no matter what. For NTFS and Resilient File System (ReFS) volumes, you use access permissions and ownership to constrain actions further within the share and to share permissions. For file allocation table (FAT) volumes, share permissions provide the only access controls because FAT volumes have no file and folder permission capabilities.

Access permissions are much more complex than share permissions, and to understand fully how they can be used and applied, you must understand ownership and inheritance and the permissions that are available. Because Windows Server 2012 R2 adds new layers of security, access permissions now include basic permissions, claims-based permissions, and special permissions.

> **Inside OUT**
>
> ***Changes to basic file and folder attributes are sometimes necessary***
>
> **As administrators, we often forget about the basic file and folder attributes that can be assigned. However, basic file and folder attributes can affect access, so let's look at these attributes first and then look at the access permissions you can apply to NTFS and ReFS volumes.**

> **All files and folders have basic attributes regardless of whether you are working with FAT, NTFS, or ReFS. These attributes can be examined in File Explorer by pressing and holding or right-clicking the file or folder icon and then selecting Properties. Folder and file attributes include Hidden and Read-Only. Hidden determines whether the file is displayed in file listings. You can override this by telling File Explorer to display hidden files. On NTFS and ReFS volumes, the Read-Only attribute for folders is initially shown as unavailable. Here, this means the attribute is in a mixed state regardless of the current state of files in the folder. If you override the mixed state by selecting the Read-Only check box for a folder, all files in the folder will be read-only. If you override the mixed state and clear the Read-Only check box for a folder, all files in the folder will be writable.**

File and folder ownership

Before working with access permissions, you should understand the concept of ownership as it applies to files and folders. In Windows Server, the file or folder owner isn't necessarily the file's or folder's creator. Instead, the file or folder owner is the person who has direct control over the file or folder. File or folder owners can grant access permissions and give other users permission to take ownership of a file or folder.

The way ownership is assigned initially depends on where the file or folder is being created. By default, the user who created the file or folder is listed as the current owner. Ownership can be taken or transferred in several ways. Any administrator can take ownership. Any user or group with the Take Ownership permission can take ownership. Any user who has the right to Restore Files And Directories, such as a member of the Backup Operators group, can take ownership, and any current owner can transfer ownership to another user.

You can take ownership by using File Explorer or Server Manager. In File Explorer, press and hold or right-click the file or folder and then select Properties. On the Security tab of the Properties dialog box, open the Advanced Security Settings dialog box by tapping or clicking Advanced.

If a folder has been shared, you can change its ownership by using Server Manager. In Server Manager, the Shares subnode of the File And Storage Services node shows existing shares for file servers that have been added for management. Press and hold or right-click the share you want to work with and then tap or click Properties. In the Properties dialog box, tap or click the Permissions in the left pane. Tap or click Customize Permissions to open the Advanced Security Settings dialog box.

As shown in Figure 19-1, the current owner is listed on the Permissions tab. Tap or click Change. Use the options in the Select User, Computer, Service Account, Or Group dialog box to select the new owner. If you're taking ownership of a folder, you can take ownership of all subfolders and files within the folder by selecting Replace Owner On Subcontainers And Objects. Tap or click OK twice when you are finished.

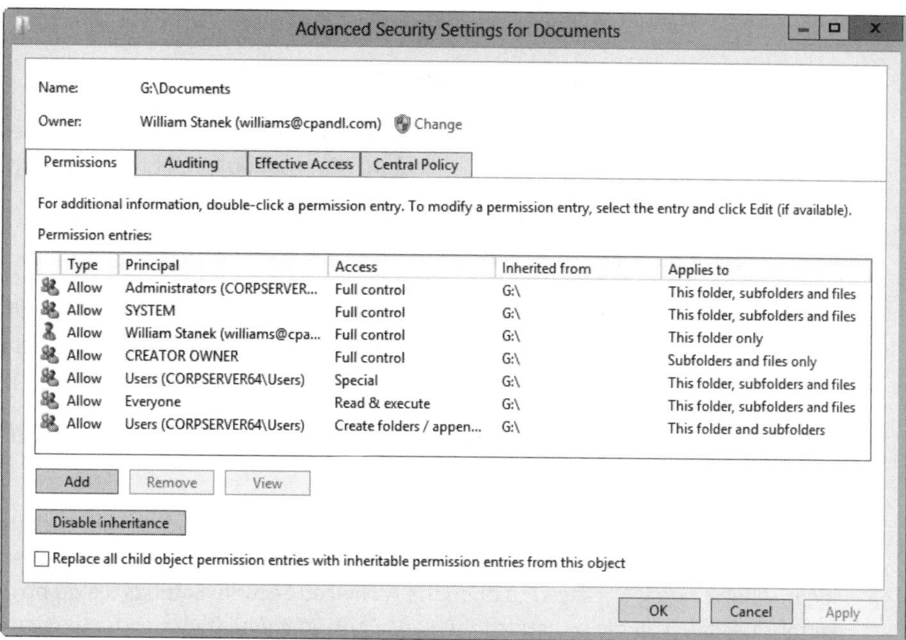

Figure 19-1 Take ownership by using the Permissions tab.

Permission inheritance for files and folders

By default, when you add a folder or file to an existing folder, the folder or file inherits the permissions of the existing folder. For example, if the Domain Users group has access to a folder and you add a file to this folder, members of the Domain Users group will be able to access the file. Inherited permissions are automatically assigned when files and folders are created.

When you assign new permissions to a folder, the permissions propagate down and are inherited by all subfolders and files in the folder and supplement or replace existing permissions. If you add permissions on a folder to allow a new group to access a folder, these permissions are applied to all subfolders and files in the folder, meaning the additional group is granted access. However, if you were to change the permissions on the folder so that, for instance, only members of the Engineering group could access the folder, these permissions would be applied to all subfolders and files in the folder—meaning only members of the Engineering group would have access to the folder, its subfolders, and its files.

Inheritance is automatic. If you do not want the permissions of subfolders and files within folders to supplement or replace existing permissions, you must override inheritance, starting with the top-level folder from which the permissions are inherited. A top-level folder is referred to as a *parent folder*. Files and folders below the parent folder are referred to as *child files and folders*. This is identical to the parent/child structure of objects in Active Directory.

Changing shaded permissions and stopping inheritance

If a permission you want to change is shaded, the file or folder is inheriting the permission from a parent folder. To change the permission, you must do one of the following:

- Access the parent folder and make the desired changes. These changes will then be inherited by child folders and files.
- Select the opposite permission to override the inherited permission if possible. In most cases, Deny overrides Allow, so if you explicitly deny permission to a user or group for a child folder or file, this permission should be denied to that user or group of users.
- Stop inheriting permissions from the parent folder and then copy or remove existing permissions as appropriate.

To stop inheriting permissions from a parent folder, press and hold or right-click the file or folder in File Explorer and then select Properties. On the Security tab of the Properties dialog box, tap or click Advanced to open the Advanced Security Settings dialog box. On the Permissions tab, you see a Disable Inheritance button if inheritance currently is enabled. When you tap or click Disable Inheritance, you can either convert the inherited permissions to explicit permissions or remove all inherited permissions and apply only the permissions that you explicitly set on the folder or file. (See Figure 19-2.)

IMPORTANT

If you remove the inherited permissions and no other permissions are assigned, everyone but the owner of the resource is denied access. This effectively locks out everyone except the owner of a folder or file. However, administrators still have the right to take ownership of the resource regardless of the permissions. Thus, if an administrator is locked out of a file or a folder and truly needs access, she can take ownership and then have unrestricted access.

If a folder has been shared, you can change its inheritance settings by using Server Manager. In Server Manager, the Shares subnode of the File And Storage Services node shows existing shares for file servers that have been added for management. Press and hold or right-click the share you want to work with and then tap or click Properties. In the Properties dialog box, tap or click the Permissions in the left pane. Tap or click Customize Permissions to open the Advanced Security Settings dialog box. After you tap or click Disable Inheritance, you can elect to convert the inherited permissions to explicit permissions or to remove all inherited permissions and apply only the permissions that you explicitly set on the folder or file. (See Figure 19-2.)

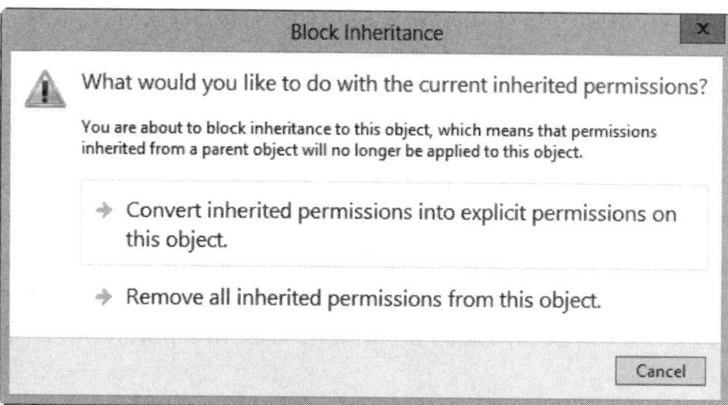

Figure 19-2 Block inheritance by converting or removing the inherited permissions.

Resetting and replacing permissions

Another way to manage permissions is to reset the permissions of subfolders and files within a folder, replacing their permissions with the current permissions assigned to the folder you are working with. In this way, subfolders and files get all inheritable permissions from the parent folder and all other explicitly defined permissions on the individual subfolders and files are removed.

To reset permissions for subfolders and files of a folder, open the Advanced Settings dialog box as discussed previously. Next, select Enable Inheritance. Optionally, before you tap or click OK, you can remove all explicitly defined permissions and enable propagation of inheritable permissions to any file or subfolder of the folder. To do this, select the Replace All Child Object Permission Entries check box and then tap or click Yes when prompted to confirm. (See Figure 19-3.)

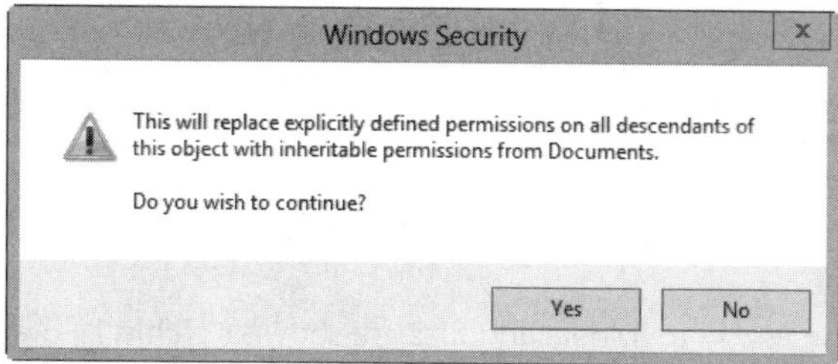

Figure 19-3 Confirm that you want to replace the existing permissions on subfolders and files.

Configuring access permissions

On NTFS and ReFS volumes, you can assign access permissions to files and folders. These permissions grant or deny access to users and groups. Keep in mind that if a permission has been explicitly denied, the deny setting will override any permission grant.

Basic permissions

In File Explorer, you can view basic permissions by pressing and holding or right-clicking the file or folder you want to work with, selecting Properties on the shortcut menu, and then, in the Properties dialog box, selecting the Security tab, as shown in Figure 19-4. The Group Or User Names list shows groups and users with assigned permissions. If you select a group or user in this list, the applicable permissions are shown in the Permissions For list. If permissions are unavailable, it means the permissions are inherited from a parent folder as discussed previously.

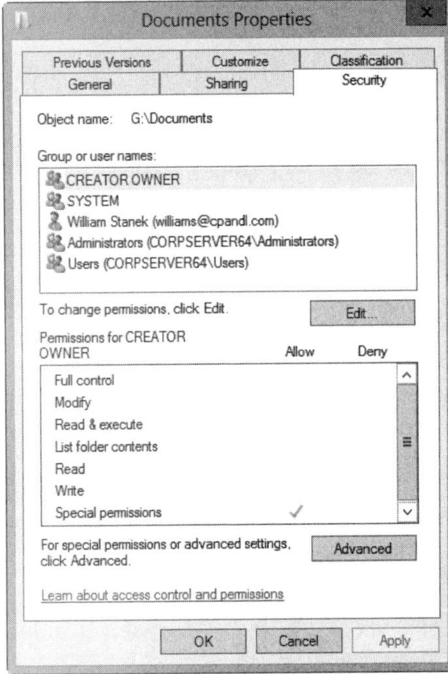

Figure 19-4 The Security tab shows the basic permissions assigned to each user or group.

The basic permissions you can assign to folders and files are shown in Table 19-1 and Table 19-2. These permissions are made up of multiple special permissions.

Table 19-1 Basic folder permissions

Permission	Description
Full Control	This permission permits reading, writing to, changing, and deleting files and subfolders. If a user has Full Control over a folder, she can delete files in the folder regardless of the permission on the files.
Modify	This permission permits reading and writing to files and subfolders, and it allows deletion of the folder.
List Folder Contents	This permission permits viewing and listing files and subfolders and executing files; it is inherited by folders only.
Read & Execute	This permission permits viewing and listing files and subfolders and executing files; it is inherited by files and folders.
Write	This permission permits adding files and subfolders.
Read	This permission permits viewing and listing files and subfolders.

Table 19-2 Basic file permissions

Permission	Description
Full Control	This permission permits reading, writing to, changing, and deleting the file.
Modify	This permission permits reading and writing to the file, and it allows deletion of the file.
Read & Execute	This permission permits viewing and accessing the file's contents and executing the file.
Write	This permission permits writing to a file. Giving a user permission to write to a file but not to delete it doesn't prevent the user from deleting the file's contents.
Read	This permission permits viewing or accessing the file's contents. Read is the only permission needed to run scripts. Read access is required to access a shortcut and its target.

You can set basic permissions for files and folders by following these steps:

1. In File Explorer, press and hold or right-click the file or folder you want to work with and select Properties. In the Properties dialog box, select the Security tab, as shown in Figure 19-4.
2. Tap or click Edit to display an editable version of the Security tab. Users or groups that already have access to the file or folder are listed in the Groups Or User Names list box. You can change permissions for these users and groups by selecting the user or group you want to change and then using the Permissions For list box to grant or deny access permissions.

3. To set access permissions for additional users, computers, or groups, tap or click Add. This opens the Select Users, Computers, Service Accounts, Or Groups dialog box.

4. The Locations button enables you to access account names from other domains. Tap or click Locations to see a list of the current domain, trusted domains, and other resources that you can access. Because of transitive trusts, you can usually access all the domains in the domain tree or forest.

5. Type the name of a user or group account in the selected or default domain and then tap or click Check Names. The options available depend on the number of matches found, as follows:
   - When a single match is found, the dialog box is automatically updated as appropriate and the entry is underlined.
   - When no matches are found, you've either entered an incorrect name part or you're working with an incorrect location. Modify the name and try again or tap or click Locations to select a new location.
   - If multiple matches are found, select the name or names you want to use and then tap or click OK.

6. To add additional users or groups, type a semicolon (;) and then repeat this process.

7. When you tap or click OK, the users and groups are added to the Group Or User Name list. Configure access permissions for each added user and group by selecting an account name and then allowing or denying access permissions. If a user or group should be granted access permissions, select the check box for the permission in the Allow column. If a user or group should be denied access permissions, select the check box for the permission in the Deny column.

8. When you're finished, tap or click OK.

Shared folders also have NTFS permissions. Use Server Manager to set basic NTFS permissions for shared folders by following these steps:

1. Press and hold or right-click the folder you want to work with and then tap or click Properties. This opens a Properties dialog box.

2. When you tap or click Permissions in the left pane, the current share permissions and NTFS permissions appear in the main pane.

3. Tap or click Customize Permissions to open the Advanced Security Settings dialog box with the Permissions tab selected. The available options include the following:
   - **Add.** Adds a user or group. Tap or click Add to open the Permission Entry dialog box, shown in Figure 19-5. Tap or click Select A Principal to open the Select User,

Computer, Service Account, Or Group dialog box. Type the name of a user or a group account and then tap or click Check Names. Be sure to reference the user account name rather than the user's full name. Only one name can be entered at a time.

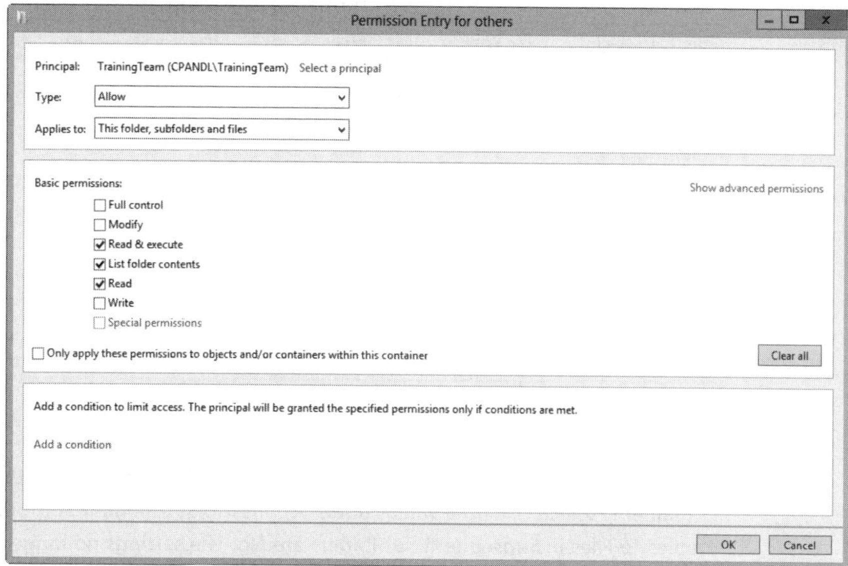

Figure 19-5 Use the Permission Entry dialog box to set basic permissions.

- **Edit.** Edits an existing user or group entry. Select the user or group whose permissions you want to modify and then tap or click Edit. The Permissions Entry dialog box shown in Figure 19-5 opens.
- **Remove.** Removes an existing user or group entry. Select the user or group whose permissions you want to remove and then tap or click Remove.

4. When you are editing permissions, you allow and deny special permissions separately. Therefore, if you want to both allow and deny special permissions, you need to configure the allowed permissions and then repeat this procedure, starting with step 1, to configure the denied permissions.

5. When finished, use the Applies To options shown in Table 19-3 to determine how and where these permissions are applied. If you want to prevent subfolders and files from inheriting these permissions, select Only Apply These Permissions To Objects And/Or Containers Within This Container. When you do this, all the related entries in Table 19-3 are No. This means the settings no longer apply to subsequent subfolders or to files in subsequent subfolders.

Table 19-3 Applies To permissions options

Applies to	Applies to Current Folder	Applies to Subfolders in the Current Folder	Applies to File in the Current Folder	Applies to Subsequent Subfolders	Applies to Files in Subsequent Subfolders
This folder only	Yes	No	No	No	No
This folder, subfolders, and files	Yes	Yes	Yes	Yes	Yes
This folder and subfolders	Yes	Yes	No	Yes	No
This folder and files	Yes	No	Yes	No	Yes
Subfolders and files only	No	Yes	Yes	Yes	Yes
Subfolders only	No	Yes	No	Yes	No
Files only	No	No	Yes	No	Yes

NOTE

When Only Apply These Permissions To Objects And/Or Containers Within This Container is selected, all the values under Applies To Subsequent Subfolders and Applies To Files In Subsequent Subfolders are No. The settings no longer apply to subsequent subfolders or to files in subsequent subfolders.

Special permissions

You can use either File Explorer or Server Manager to view special permissions. In Server Manager, press and hold or right-click the share you want to work with and then tap or click Properties. In the Properties dialog box, tap or click the Permissions in the left pane. Tap or click Customize Permissions to open the Advanced Security Settings dialog box.

In File Explorer, you can view special permissions by pressing and holding or right-clicking the file or folder you want to work with and selecting Properties on the shortcut menu. In the Properties dialog box, select the Security tab and then tap or click Advanced to open the Advanced Security Settings dialog box.

The available special permissions are as follows:

- **Traverse Folder/Execute File.** Traverse Folder enables you to access a folder directly even if you don't have explicit access to read the data it contains. Use Execute File to run an executable file.

- **List Folder/Read Data.** List Folder enables you to view file and folder names. Use Read Data to view the contents of a file.
- **Read Attributes.** Enables you to read the basic attributes of a file or folder. These attributes include Read-Only, Hidden, System, and Archive.
- **Read Extended Attributes.** Enables you to view the extended attributes (named data streams) associated with a file. As discussed in Chapter 15, "File system essentials," these include Summary fields—such as Title, Subject, and Author—and other types of data.
- **Create Files/Write Data.** Create Files enables you to put new files in a folder. Write Data enables you to overwrite existing data in a file (but not to add new data to an existing file because this is covered by Append Data).
- **Create Folders/Append Data.** Create Folders enables you to create subfolders within folders. Append Data enables you to add data to the end of an existing file (but not to overwrite existing data because this is covered by Write Data).
- **Write Attributes.** Enables you to change the basic attributes of a file or folder. These attributes include Read-Only, Hidden, System, and Archive.
- **Write Extended Attributes.** Enables you to change the extended attributes (named data streams) associated with a file. As discussed in Chapter 15, these include Summary fields—such as Title, Subject, and Author—and other types of data.
- **Delete Subfolders And Files.** Enables you to delete the contents of a folder. If you have this permission, you can delete the subfolders and files in a folder even if you don't specifically have Delete permission on the subfolder or file.
- **Delete.** Enables you to delete a file or folder. If a folder isn't empty and you don't have Delete permission for one of its files or subfolders, you won't be able to delete it. You can do this only if you have the Delete Subfolders And Files permission.
- **Read Permissions.** Enables you to read all basic and special permissions assigned to a file or folder.
- **Change Permissions.** Enables you to change basic and special permissions assigned to a file or folder.
- **Take Ownership.** Enables you to take ownership of a file or folder. By default, administrators can always take ownership of a file or folder and can grant this permission to others.

Table 19-4 and Table 19-5 show how special permissions are combined to make the basic permissions for files and folders. Because special permissions are combined to make the basic permissions, they are also referred to as *atomic permissions*.

Table 19-4 Special permissions for folders

Special Permissions	Full Control	Modify	Read & Execute	List Folder Contents	Read	Write
Traverse Folder/Execute File	X	X	X	X		
List Folder/Read Data	X	X	X	X	X	
Read Attributes	X	X	X	X	X	
Read Extended Attributes	X	X	X	X	X	
Create Files/Write Data	X	X				X
Create Folders/Append Data	X	X				X
Write Attributes	X	X				X
Write Extended Attributes	X	X				X
Delete Subfolders And Files	X					
Delete	X	X				
Read Permissions	X	X	X	X	X	X
Change Permissions	X					
Take Ownership	X					

Table 19-5 Special permissions for files

Special Permissions	Full Control	Modify	Read & Execute	Read	Write
Traverse Folder/Execute File	X	X	X		
List Folder/Read Data	X	X	X	X	
Read Attributes	X	X	X	X	
Read Extended Attributes	X	X	X	X	
Create Files/Write Data	X	X			X
Create Folders/Append Data	X	X			X
Write Attributes	X	X			X
Write Extended Attributes	X	X			X

Special Permissions	Full Control	Modify	Read & Execute	Read	Write
Delete Subfolders And Files	X				
Delete	X	X			
Read Permissions	X	X	X	X	X
Change Permissions	X				
Take Ownership	X				

You set special permissions for files and folders by using the Advanced Security Settings dialog box with the Permissions tab selected.

The options available include the following:

- **Add.** Adds a user or group. Tap or click Add to open the Permission Entry dialog box. Tap or click Select A Principal to open the Select User, Computer, Service Account, Or Group dialog box. Type the name of a user or a group account and then tap or click Check Names. Be sure to reference the user account name rather than the user's full name. Only one name can be entered at a time.
- **Edit.** Edits an existing user or group entry. Select the user or group whose permissions you want to modify and then tap or click Edit. This opens the Permissions Entry dialog box.
- **Remove.** Removes an existing user or group entry. Select the user or group whose permissions you want to remove and then tap or click Remove.

When you are editing permissions, only basic permissions are listed by default. Tap or click Show Advanced Permissions to display the special permissions, as shown in Figure 19-6. Use the Type list to specify whether you are configuring allowed or denied permissions and then select the permissions you want to allow or deny. If any permissions are dimmed (unavailable), they are inherited from a parent folder.

When finished, use the Applies To options shown in Table 19-3 to determine how and where these permissions are applied. If you want to prevent subfolders and files from inheriting these permissions, select Only Apply These Permissions To Objects And/Or Containers Within This Container. When you do this, all the related entries in Table 19-3 are No. This means the settings no longer apply to subsequent subfolders or to files in subsequent subfolders.

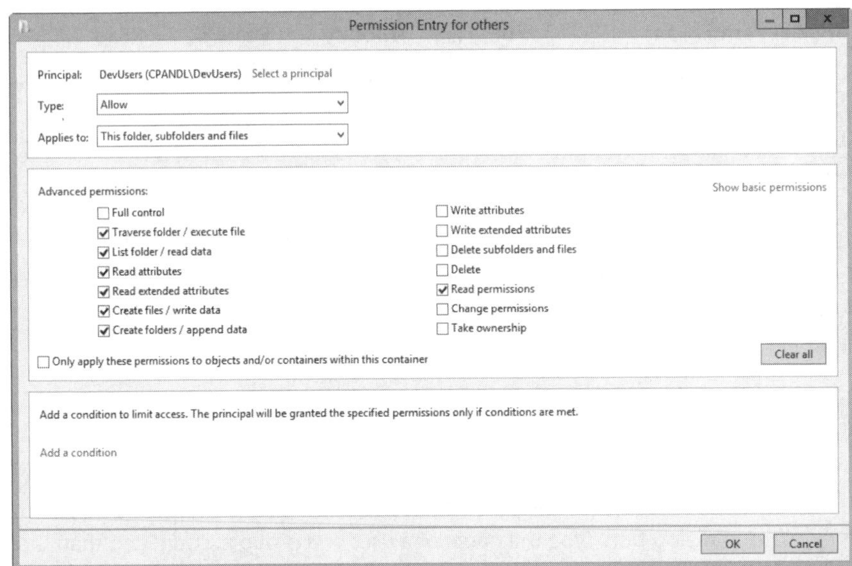

Figure 19-6 Use the Permission Entry dialog box to set special permissions.

Troubleshooting permissions

Navigating the complex maze of permissions can be daunting even for the best administrators. Sometimes it won't be clear how a particular permission set will be applied to a particular user or group. Sometimes even a minor change in permissions can have unintended consequences. Either way, you have a problem, and one of your first steps to resolving it should be to determine the effective permissions for the files or folders in question.

The effective permissions tell you exactly which permissions are in effect. For a user, the effective permissions are based on all the permissions the user has been granted or denied, no matter whether the permissions are applied explicitly or obtained from groups of which the user is a member. Similarly, for a group, the effective permissions are based on all the permissions the group has been granted or denied, no matter whether the permissions are applied explicitly or obtained from groups of which the group is a member.

> IMPORTANT
>
> **You must have appropriate permissions to view the effective permissions of any user or group. You also should remember that you cannot determine the effective permissions for implicit groups or special identities, such as Authenticated Users or Everyone. Furthermore, the effective permissions do not take into account permissions granted to a user because he is the Creator Owner.**

Cumulative permissions can be difficult to navigate because deny entries have precedence over allow entries. For example, if DevonP is a member of the Users, Engineering, DevUsers, and Managers groups, the effective permissions with respect to a particular file or folder are the cumulative set of permissions that DevonP has been explicitly assigned and the permissions assigned to the Users, Engineering, DevUsers, and Managers groups. If DevonP is a member of a group that is specifically denied a permission, he will be denied that permission, even if another group of which he is a member is allowed that permission.

User and device claims also have precedence. If you've configured claims-based policies and added a user claim that specifies that a user must or must not be a member of a particular group, that user claim can prevent access. Similarly, if there's a device claim that specifies that a user's computer must or must not be a member of a particular group, that device claim can prevent access.

You can use the Effective Access tab in the Advanced Security Settings dialog box to determine the effective permissions with regard to the related file or folder. On the Effective Access tab, use the options provided to determine the effective permissions for users, groups, and devices. Before you tap or click View Effective Access, keep the following in mind:

- If you only want to determine access for a particular user or user group, tap or click Select A User, type the name of the user or group, and then tap or click OK.
- If you only want to determine access for a particular device or device group, tap or click Select A Device, type the name of the device or device group, and then tap or click OK.
- If you want to determine access for a particular user or user group on a particular device or in a device group, specify both a user/user group and a device/device group.

As Figure 19-7 shows, the effective permissions for the specified user or group are displayed using the complete set of special permissions. If a user has Full Control over the selected resource, she has all the permissions. Otherwise, a subset of the permissions is selected, and you have to consider carefully whether the user or group has the appropriate permissions. Use Table 19-4, earlier in the chapter, to help you interpret the permissions. Any selected permissions have been granted to the user or group.

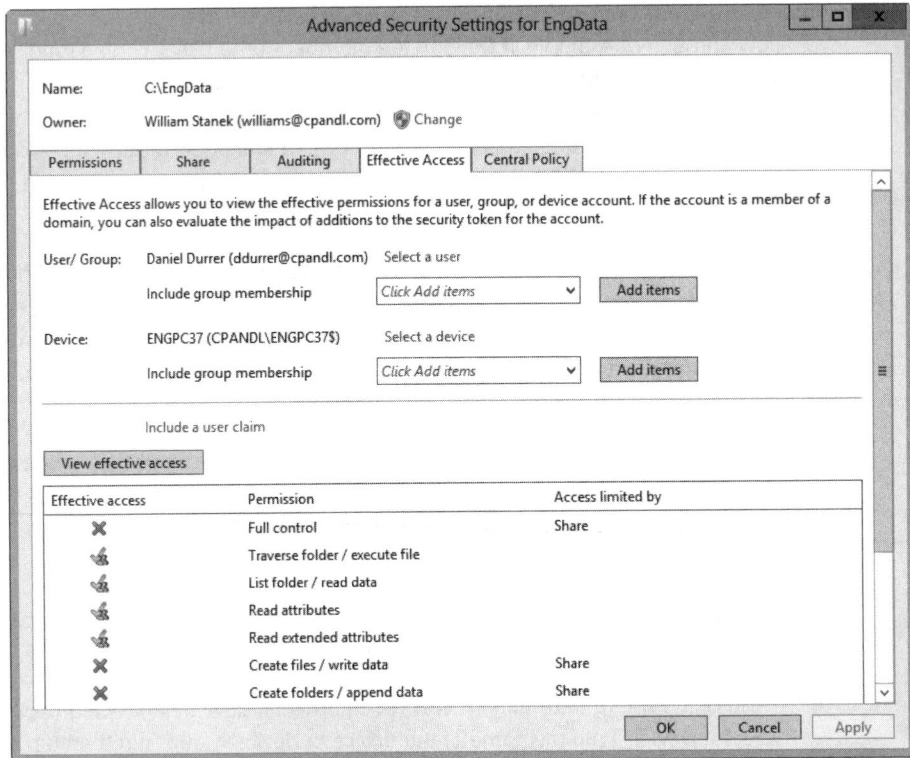

Figure 19-7 Determine effective access.

Managing file shares after configuration

Configuring shares can be a time-consuming process, especially if you are trying to troubleshoot why a particular user doesn't have access or set up a new server with the same file shares as a server you are decommissioning. Fortunately, there are some techniques to help you manage file shares, and the way they are implemented, better.

Net Share is a handy command-line tool for helping you track file-share and print-share permissions. You can use it to display a list of shares and who has access to them. If you redirect the output of Net Share, you can save the share-configuration and access information to a file, and this file can become a log that helps you track share changes over time.

To view a list of configured shares, type **net share** at the command prompt or **get-smbshare** at a Windows PowerShell prompt. The output of Net Share shows you the name of each share on the server, the location of the actual folder being shared, and any descriptions you've added. Here is an example of output from running the Net Share command:

```
Share name   Resource                        Remark

-------------------------------------------------------------
ADMIN$       C:\Windows                      Remote Admin
C$           C:\                             Default share
F$           F:\                             Default share
IPC$                                         Remote IPC
CorpData     C:\CorpData
CorpTech     F:\CorpTech
DevData      F:\DevData
EngData      C:\EngData
HRData       F:\HRData
Public       C:\Users\Public
UserData     C:\UserData
The command completed successfully.
```

The list of shares shown includes the file shares CorpData, CorpTech, EngData, Public, and others. Administrative shares created and managed by Windows are shown as well, including ADMIN$, IPC$, and any drive shares.

If you want to redirect the output to a file, you can do this by typing **net share > FileName.txt**, where *FileName.txt* is the name of the file to create and to which you want to write, such as:

```
net share > C:\logs\fileshares.txt
```

You can redirect the output from get-smbshare to a file as well:

```
get-smbshare > C:\logs\fileshares.txt
```

If you follow the Net Share command with the name of a configured share, you see the complete configuration details for the share, as shown in the following example:

```
Share name         EngData
Path               C:\EngData
Remark
Maximum users      No limit
Users
Caching            Manual caching of documents
Permission         CPANDL\Domain Admins, FULL
                   CPANDL\Domain Users, READ
                   CPANDL\EngineeringUsers, READ

The command completed successfully.
```

You can append the share configuration details to the previously created log file by using the append symbol (>>) instead of the standard redirect symbol (>), as shown in the following example:

```
net share corpdata >> C:\logs\fileshares.txt
```

Listing 19-1 shows the source of a command-line script that you could use to create a configuration log for the key shares on the computer. Although the path in the example is set to c:\logs\fileshares.txt, you can set any log path you want.

Listing 19-1 A sample share logging script

```
net share > C:\logs\fileshares.txt
net share c$ >> C:\logs\fileshares.txt
net share f$ >> C:\logs\fileshares.txt
net share corpdata >> C:\logs\fileshares.txt
net share corptech >> C:\logs\fileshares.txt
net share devdata >> C:\logs\fileshares.txt
net share engdata >> C:\logs\fileshares.txt
net share hrdata >> C:\logs\fileshares.txt
net share public >> C:\logs\fileshares.txt
net share userdata >> C:\logs\fileshares.txt
```

Managing claims-based access controls

Windows Server 2012 R2 adds Kerberos armoring, compound identities, and claims-based access controls to the standard access controls. Kerberos armoring improves domain security by allowing domain-joined clients and domain controllers to communicate over secure, encrypted channels. Compound identities incorporate not only the groups of which a user is a member but also user claims, device claims, and resource properties.

At their most basic, claims-based access controls enable you to define conditions that limit access as part of a resource's advanced security permissions. Typically, these conditions add device claims or user claims to the access controls. User claims identify users; device claims identify devices. For example, to access the CorpTech share, you might want to add a device claim to ensure that the computer being used to access a resource is a member of Tech Computers and add a user claim that ensures that the user is a member of the CorpUsers group.

Kerberos armoring, compound identities, and claims-based access controls can also work together as part of the extended authorization platform in Windows Server. This platform allows dynamic access to resources by using central access policies.

Understanding central access policies

With central access policies, you define central access rules in Active Directory and those rules are applied dynamically throughout the enterprise. Central access rules use conditional expressions that require you to determine the resource properties required for the policy, the claim types and security groups required for the policy, and the servers to which the policy should be applied.

Configuring central access policies is a multistep process that usually begins with defining the resource properties and claim types you'll use as part of your policies. Afterward, you create access rules based on the claim types and then you establish dynamic controls by adding the rules to the appropriate group policies. Thus, the process typically looks like this:

1. First, you create resource properties. Resource properties create property definitions for resources. For example, you might want to add Department and Country/Region properties to files so that you can control access dynamically by department and by country or region.
2. Next, you create claim types that use those properties. Claim types create claim definitions for resources. For example, you might want to create a user claim to add Department and Country/Region properties to User objects so that you can control access dynamically by department and by country or region.
3. After you create resource properties and claim types and determine where the policy should be applied, you create an access rule and then add it to a central access policy. Adding the rule to a policy makes it available for dynamic control.
4. Last, you apply the policy across file servers by using Group Policy.

Enabling dynamic controls and claims-based policy

Servers to which you want to apply dynamic controls must have the File And Storage Services role with the File Server, Storage Services, and File Server Resource Manager role services at a minimum. You need the File Server Resource Manager role service and the related tools to apply classification property definitions to folders.

Claims-based policy should be enabled for all domain controllers in a domain to ensure consistent application. A domain must have at least one Windows Server 2012 R2 domain controller, and file servers must run Windows Server 2012 R2. By default, domain controllers are placed in the Domain Controllers organizational unit (OU) and the Default Domain Controllers policy has the highest precedence among Group Policy Objects (GPOs) linked to the Domain Controllers OU.

If your organization uses this approach, claims-based policy must be enabled for the Default Domain Controllers policy. If your organization uses a different approach, you need to ensure that the GPO with the highest precedence for the appropriate OU has claims-based policy enabled and configured properly.

You enable claims-based policy by using the KDC Support For Claims, Compound Authentication Dynamic Access Control And Kerberos Armoring policy in the Administrative Templates policies for Computer Configuration under System\KDC. The policy must be configured to use a specific mode. The available modes are as follows:

- **Supported.** Domain controllers support claims, compound identities, and Kerberos armoring. Client computers that don't support Kerberos armoring can be authenticated.
- **Always Provide Claims.** Same as Supported, but domain controllers always return claims for accounts.
- **Fail Unarmored Authentication.** Specifies that Kerberos armoring is mandatory. Client computers that don't support Kerberos armoring cannot be authenticated.

You can then work with dynamic access controls in Active Directory Administrative Center. When you are working with the Dynamic Access Control node, I recommend using Tree View, as shown in Figure 19-8, rather than the List View. With Tree View, you see related subnodes in the left pane, and this will make it easier to configure central access policy.

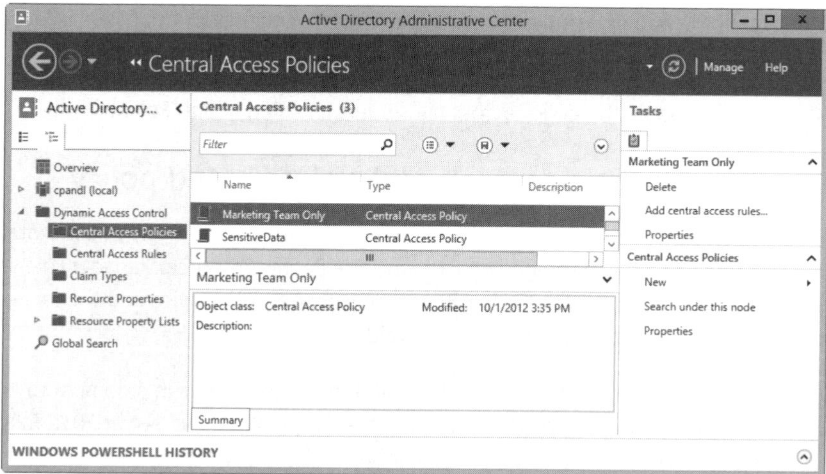

Figure 19-8 Use Active Directory Administrative Center to create and configure central access policies.

Defining central access policies

Central access policies don't replace traditional access controls. Instead, you use central access policies to enhance existing access controls by defining very precisely the specific attributes users and devices must have to access resources.

Before you can deploy central access policies, you need to perform the following tasks in Active Directory Administrative Center:

- Use the Claim Types node to create and manage claim types. For example, right-click in the Claim Types pane, click New, and then select Claim Type to start creating a new claim type.
- Use the Resource Properties node to create and manage resource properties. For example, right-click in the Resource Properties pane, click New, and then select Resource Property to start creating a new resource property. Resource properties are added as classification definition properties on file servers as well.
- Use the Central Access Rules node to create and manage central access rules. For example, right-click in the Central Access Rules pane, click New, and then select Central Access Rule to start creating a new access rule.
- Use the Central Access Policies node to create and manage central access policies. For example, right-click in the Central Access Policies pane, click New, and then select Central Access Policy to start creating a new access policy.

You can then complete the deployment by editing the highest-precedence GPO linked to the OU where you put file servers and enabling central access policies. To do this, follow these steps:

1. In Group Policy Management, open the GPO for editing. Navigate the Computer Configuration policies to Windows Settings\Security Settings\File System. When you select the Central Access Policy node in the left pane, any currently deployed central access policies are listed in the right pane, as shown in Figure 19-9.

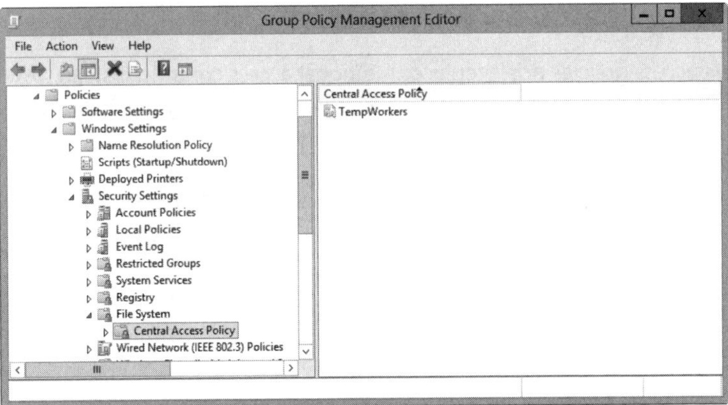

Figure 19-9 Access the policies in Group Policy.

2. Press and hold or right-click Central Access Policy and then tap or click Manage Central Access Policies. This opens the Central Access Policies Configuration dialog box.

3. In the Central Access Policies Configuration dialog box, shown in Figure 19-10, available policies are listed in the left pane and currently applied policies are listed in the right pane.

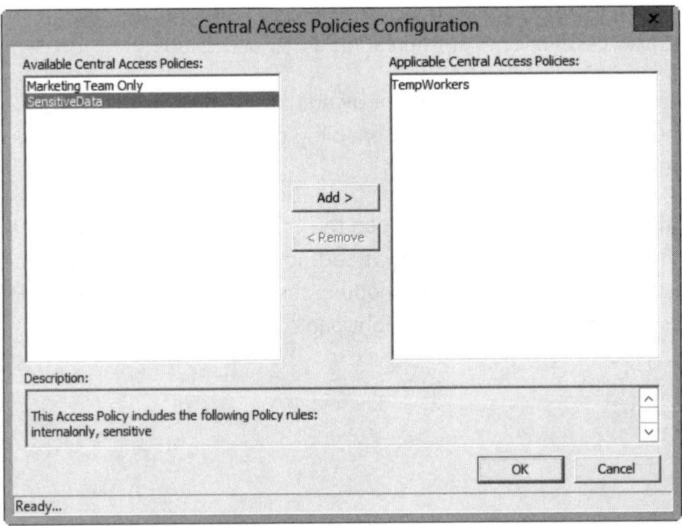

Figure 19-10 Use the Central Access Policies Configuration dialog box to add or remove policies.

4. To apply a policy, tap or click it in the left pane and then click Add. To remove a policy, tap or click it in the right pane and then click Remove.
5. Tap or click OK to apply any changes.

The dynamic controls are available as soon as the Group Policy changes take effect on your servers. You can speed the refresh along by entering **gpupdate /force** at an elevated command prompt.

After you enable central access policy and any time you update your classification property definitions, you need to wait for Global Resource Properties from Active Directory to refresh on your file servers as well. You can speed this along by opening an elevated Windows PowerShell prompt and entering **update-fsrmclassificationpropertydefinition**. Do this on each file server where you want to configure central access policies.

The deployment of central access policies isn't completed yet. You still need to edit the properties of each folder where you want a central access policy to apply and do the following:

1. Add the appropriate classification definitions on the folder's Classification tab. On the Classification tab, each resource property you created will be listed. Select each property in turn and then set its value as appropriate.
2. Enable the appropriate policy by using advanced security settings for the folder. On the Security tab, tap or click Advanced and then select the Central Policy tab. Any currently selected or applied policy is listed along with a description you can use to review the rules of that policy. When you tap or click Change, you can use the selection list provided to select a policy to apply or you can choose No Central Access Policy to stop using the policy. Tap or click OK.

You need to repeat this process for each top-level or other folder where you want to limit access. Files and folders within the selected folder inherit the access rule automatically unless you specify otherwise. For example, if you create an access rule called US Marketing Only and define Department and Country/Region resource definitions, you could edit a folder's properties, select the Classification tab, and use the available options to set Department to Marketing and Country/Region to US. Then you could apply the US Marketing Only policy by using the advanced security settings for the folder.

Auditing file and folder access

Access permissions only help protect data; they don't tell you who deleted important data or who was trying to access files and folders inappropriately. To track who accessed files and folders and what they did, you must configure auditing for file and folder access. Every comprehensive security strategy should include auditing. Auditing settings you configure are applied to specific computers through local computer policy and to multiple computers through Group Policy.

Because auditing policies are applied as part of computer configuration rather than of user configuration, they must be applied through GPOs that are applied to computer OUs. Therefore, if you want an auditing setting to be applied to specific file servers, you configure the auditing setting in a Group Policy Object linked to the appropriate resource OUs. If you want an auditing setting to be applied throughout a domain, you configure the auditing setting in a Group Policy Object linked to the domain, and the setting will apply to all computers in the domain.

Generally, when you want auditing settings to apply only to specified resources and groups of users, you modify the security settings of the relevant objects so that auditing is enabled for the security groups of which the users are members. For example, you could configure auditing on the CurrentProjects folder to track changes and deletions that members of the TempWorkers group make.

Windows Server supports basic auditing and advanced auditing. Basic auditing includes the settings under Windows Settings\Security Settings\Local Policies\Audit Policy. Advanced auditing includes the settings under Windows Settings\Security Settings\Advanced Audit Policy Configuration\Audit Policies. When you configure auditing, you use either basic or advanced auditing, not both. Advanced auditing can be applied to computers running Windows 7 or later and Windows Server 2008 R2 or later (and Windows Server 2008 and Windows Vista when logon scripts are used to apply advanced audit policy).

To track file and folder access, you must do the following:

- Enable either basic or advanced auditing.
- Specify which files and folders to audit or enable global object access auditing.
- Track audit events by monitoring the security logs or using a collection tool such as Audit Collection Services in System Center Operations Manager.

Keep in mind that global object access policy is designed to be used with advanced auditing. If you choose to use advanced auditing rather than basic auditing, you can prevent conflicts between basic and advanced settings by forcing Windows to ignore basic auditing settings. To do this, enable the Audit: Force Audit Policy security setting as appropriate in Group Policy. This security setting is under Windows Settings\Security Settings\Local Policies\Security Options.

Enabling basic auditing for files and folders

You configure basic auditing policies by using Group Policy or local security policy. Use Group Policy when you want to set auditing policies for an entire site, domain, or organizational unit. Local security policy settings apply to an individual workstation or server and can be overridden by Group Policy.

To enable basic auditing of files and folders for multiple computers through Group Policy, select Group Policy Management on the Tools menu in Server Manager. Next, press and hold or right-click the GPO you want to work with and then select Edit. In Group Policy Management Editor, expand Policies, Windows Settings, Security Settings, and Local Policies and then select Audit Policy, as shown in Figure 19-11.

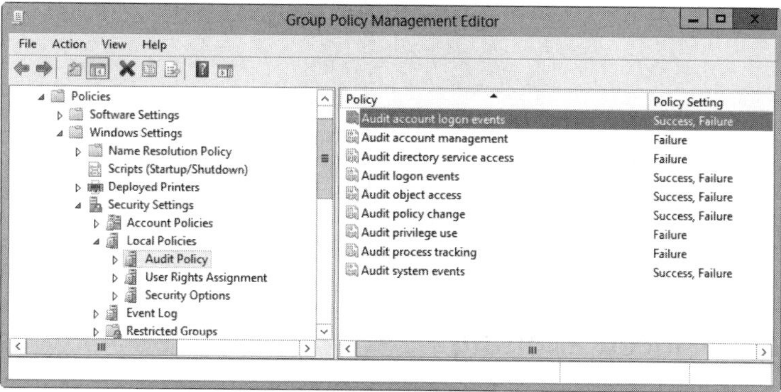

Figure 19-11 Access the basic auditing settings.

To enable basic auditing of files and folders for a specific computer, start the Local Security Policy tool by selecting the related option on the Tools menu in Server Manager. Expand Local Policies and then select Audit Policy.

Next, double-tap or double-click Audit Object Access. This opens the Audit Object Access Properties dialog box shown in Figure 19-12. In a domain, enable the policy for configuration by selecting Define These Policy Settings. Under Audit These Attempts, select the Success check box to log successful access attempts, the Failure check box to log failed access attempts, or both check boxes and then tap or click OK. This enables auditing, but it doesn't specify which objects should be audited. You do that by editing the properties of each object that you want to track, which can include files and folders, registry settings, and more.

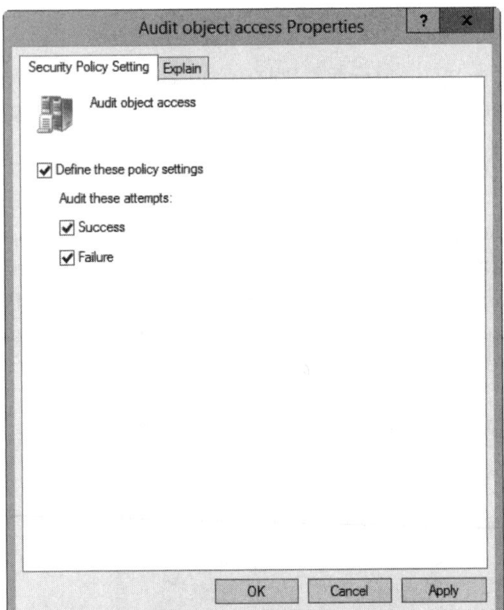

Figure 19-12 Configure auditing for object access.

Enabling advanced auditing

As with basic auditing, you configure advanced auditing policies by using Group Policy or local security policy. To enable advanced auditing of files and folders for multiple computers through Group Policy, select Group Policy Management on the Tools menu in Server Manager. Next, press and hold or right-click the GPO you want to work with and then select Edit. In Group Policy Management Editor, expand Policies, Windows Settings, Security Settings, Advanced Audit Policy Configuration, and Audit Policies and then select Object Access, as shown in Figure 19-13.

To enable auditing of files and folders for a specific computer, start the Local Security Policy tool by selecting the related option on the Tools menu in Server Manager. Expand Advanced Audit Policy Configuration and System Audit Policies - Local Group Policy Object and then select Object Access.

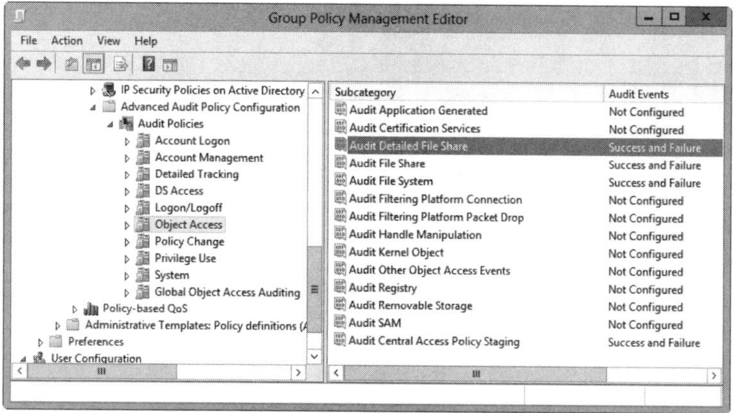

Figure 19-13 Access the advanced auditing settings.

With advanced auditing, identify specific types of object access to track by using the available options, which include the following:

- **Audit File Share.** Generates audit events whenever an attempt is made to access a shared folder. Because shared folders don't have system access control lists (SACLs), access to all shares on the system is audited (which includes network access to the SYSVOL on domain controllers). Only one audit event is recorded for any connection established between a client and a file share. To record events every time a file or folder on a share is accessed, use the Audit Detailed File Share policy.

- **Audit File System.** Generates audit events for objects when the type of access requested and the account making the request match the settings in SACLs set on the objects. For example, if a user tries to modify a file and is a member of a group for which you enabled auditing of success and failure Modify events, related audit events will be generated and recorded in the security log. An audit event is generated each time an account accesses a file system object with a matching SACL.

- **Audit Detailed File Share.** Generates audit events whenever an attempt is made to access a file or folder on a share. Because shared folders don't have SACLs, access to all shared files and folders on the system is audited. An audit event is recorded every time a file or folder on a share is accessed.

To configure these policies, double-tap or double-click a policy to open its Properties dialog box. As shown in Figure 19-14, select Configure The Following Audit Events and then select the Success check box to log successful access attempts, the Failure check box to log failed access attempts, or both check boxes and then tap or click OK. This enables auditing, but it doesn't specify which files and folders should be audited.

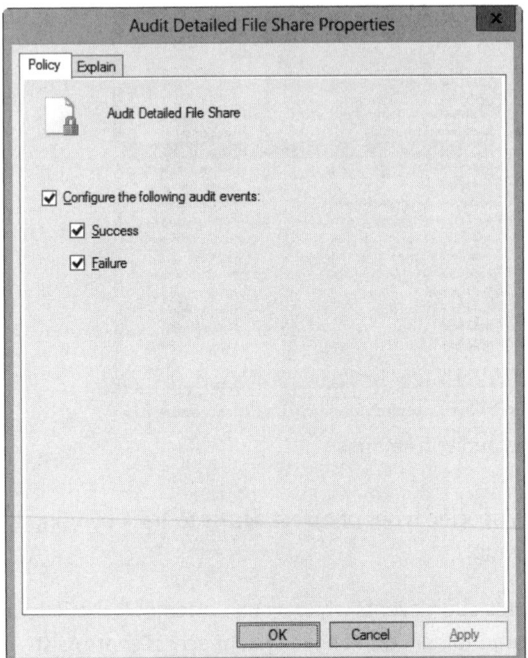

Figure 19-14 Configure auditing for a specific type of object access.

Next, ensure that advanced audit policy overrides basic audit policy. To do this, whenever you edit the Group Policy Objects and enable advanced audit policy, you must also enable the Audit: Force Audit Policy Subcategory Settings security setting. This security setting is under Windows Settings\Security Settings\Local Policies\Security Options.

In the Group Policy editor, double-tap or double-click the Audit: Force Audit Policy security setting to open its Properties dialog box. Select Define This Policy Setting and then select Enabled. Finally, tap or click OK.

Specifying files and folders to audit

After you enable the auditing of object access, you can set the level of auditing by either specifying which files and folders to audit or enabling global object access auditing. Auditing of individual folders and files enables you to control whether and how folder and file usage is tracked. Keep in mind that auditing is available only on NTFS and ReFS volumes. In addition, everything discussed about inheritance applies to files and folders as well—and this is a good thing. This enables you, for example, to audit access to every file or folder on a volume just by specifying that you want to audit the root folder of the volume.

You can use either File Explorer or Server Manager to view and configure auditing. In Server Manager, press and hold or right-click the share you want to work with and then tap or click Properties. In the Properties dialog box, tap or click the Permissions in the left pane. Tap or click Customize Permissions to open the Advanced Security Settings dialog box.

In File Explorer, you can view special permissions by pressing and holding or right-clicking the file or folder you want to work with and selecting Properties on the shortcut menu. In the Properties dialog box, select the Security tab and then tap or click Advanced to open the Advanced Security Settings dialog box.

In the Advanced Security Settings dialog box, tap or click the Auditing tab. You can now view and manage auditing settings by using the options shown in Figure 19-15.

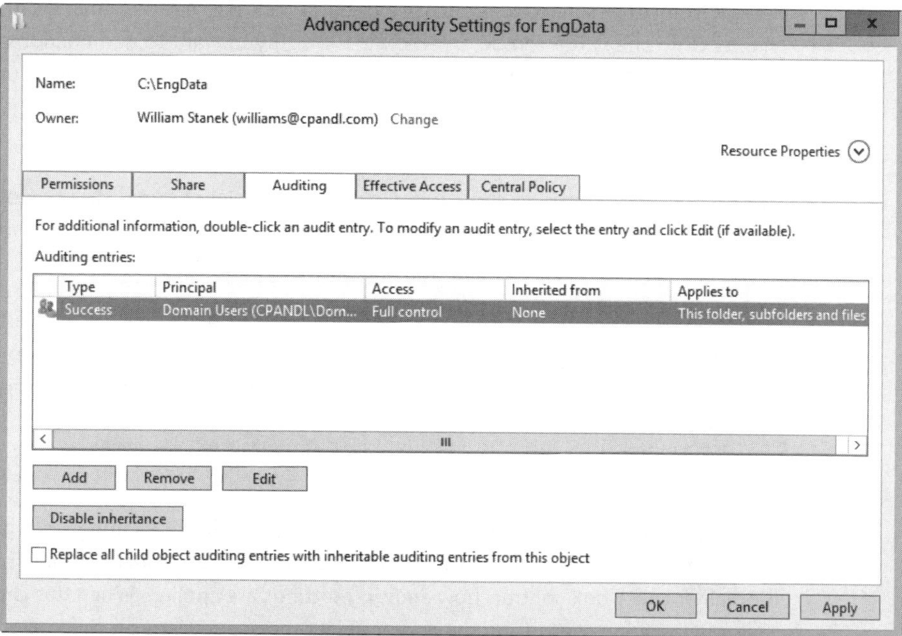

Figure 19-15 Specify the users and groups to which auditing should apply.

The Auditing Entries list shows the users, groups, or computers whose actions you want to audit. To remove an account, select the account in the Auditing Entries list and then tap or click Remove.

You can audit access related to basic permissions and special permissions as listed in Table 19-4 and Table 19-5, respectively. Keep in mind that basic permissions include multiple special permissions. Therefore, when you audit the Modify permission, this tracks access related to Traverse Folder/Execute File, List Folder/Read Data, Read Attributes, Read Extended Attributes, Create Files/Write Data, Create Folders/Append Data, Write Attributes, Write Extended Attributes, Delete, and Read permissions.

You can configure auditing for additional users, computers, or groups by following these steps:

1. Tap or click Add and then click Select A Principal to open the Select Users, Computers, Service Accounts, Or Groups dialog box.
2. Type the name of a user, computer, or group in the current domain and then tap or click Check Names. Be sure to reference the user account name rather than the user's full name. Only one name can be entered at a time. If you want to audit actions for all users, use the special Everyone group. Otherwise, select the specific user groups, users, or both that you want to audit.
3. Tap or click OK. The user and group are added, and the Principal and the Auditing Entry dialog box are updated to show this. Only basic permissions are listed by default. If you want to work with advanced permissions, tap or click Show Advanced Permissions to display the special permissions.
4. Optionally, use the Applies To list to specify at what level objects are audited. If you are working with a folder and want to replace the auditing entries on all child objects of this folder (and not on the folder itself), select Only Apply These Settings To Objects And/Or Containers Within This Container.

   NOTE

   The Applies To list enables you to specify where you want the auditing settings to apply. The Only Apply These Settings To Objects And/Or Containers Within This Container check box controls how auditing settings are applied. When this check box is selected, auditing settings on the parent object replace settings on child objects. When this check box is cleared, auditing settings on the parent object are merged with existing settings on child objects.

5. Use the Type list to specify whether you are configuring auditing for success, failure, or both and then specify which actions should be audited. Success logs successful events such as successful file reads. Failure logs failed events such as failed file deletions. The events you can audit are the same as the special permissions discussed previously, except that you can't audit the synchronizing of offline files and folders.

6. If you're using claims-based policies and want to limit the scope of the auditing entry, you can add claims-based conditions to the auditing entry. For example, if all corporate computers are members of the Approved Computers group, you might want to audit access closely by devices that aren't members of this group.
7. Tap or click OK. Repeat this process to audit other users, groups, or computers.

NOTE

Often, you'll want to track only failed actions. This way, you know if someone was trying to perform an action and failed. Keep in mind that a failed attempt doesn't always mean someone is trying to break into a file or folder. A user simply might have double-tapped or double-clicked a folder or file to which he didn't have access. In addition, some types of actions can cause multiple failed attempts to be logged even when the user performed the action only once. Regardless, as an administrator, you should check multiple failed attempts because of the possibility that someone is attempting to breach your system's defenses.

Instead of tracking access to specific files and folders, your business or compliance policies might require you to track specific types of access on sensitive computers. For example, you might need to track all access activity on servers containing sensitive data. To do this without having to configure SACLs, you can use global object access policy.

Global object access policy is designed to be used with advanced auditing and two object access areas:

- Audit File System, which must be enabled to track global access to files and folders
- Audit Registry, which must be enabled to track global access to the registry

After you enable file system auditing, registry auditing, or both, you can enable global access policy. Global access policy generates audit events for objects when the type of access requested and the account making the request match the settings in SACLs configured in the global access policy.

You configure global access policy by using Group Policy or local security policy. Follow these steps:

1. Open the GPO you want to work with for editing. Next, in Group Policy Management Editor, expand Policies, Windows Settings, Security Settings, Advanced Audit Policy Configuration, and Audit Policies and then select Global Object Access Auditing.
2. Double-tap or double-click the File System setting to open its Properties dialog box. Select Define This Policy Setting and then tap or click Configure. This opens the Advanced Security Settings For Global File SACL dialog box, shown in Figure 19-16.

3. In the Advanced Security Settings For Global File SACL dialog box, tap or click Add. Next, in the Auditing Entry dialog box, tap or click Select A Principal to open the Select User, Computer, Service Account Or Group dialog box. Type the name of the user, group, or computer to audit and then tap or click Check Names. Only one name can be entered at a time. Be sure to reference the user account name rather than the user's full name.

4. Use the Type list to specify whether you are tracking successful or failed access and then select the permissions you want to audit. If you want to track both successful and failed access, choose All as the type.

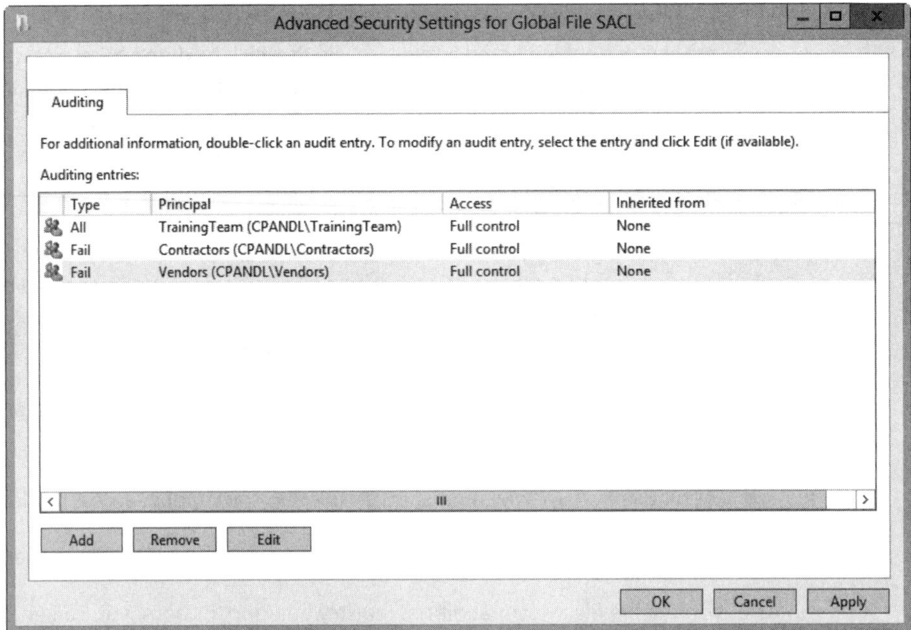

Figure 19-16 Specify the users and groups to which global auditing should apply.

Extending access policies to auditing

With Windows Server 2012 R2, you can extend claims-based access controls to auditing. Here, you create central audit policies that use claims and resource properties. The result is a more targeted and easier-to-manage auditing policy that can help you meet business and compliance requirements such as policies that do the following:

- Audit everyone who tries to access sensitive or confidential data but doesn't have a security clearance that would allow this

- Audit contractors and vendors when they try to access documents that aren't related to projects they are working on

Precise targeting helps limit the volume of collected data while focusing on the most relevant data. Although the auditing events are generated on a per-server basis, event collection and analysis tools, such as Audit Collection Services in System Center Operations Manager, make it possible to collect the events centrally and search through them in new ways.

The easiest way to extend claims-based access controls to auditing is to follow these steps:

1. Enable and configure central access policies as discussed in "Managing claims-based access controls" earlier in the chapter.
2. Enable either object access or global object access auditing as discussed in "Enabling advanced auditing" earlier in the chapter.
3. Use the claim types and resource properties you defined to help you fine-tune audit policy.

An example of extending claims-based access controls to auditing is shown in Figure 19-17. Here, you limit the auditing to members of the Contractors group who are outside a specified country or region and who don't have their Company property set as City Power.

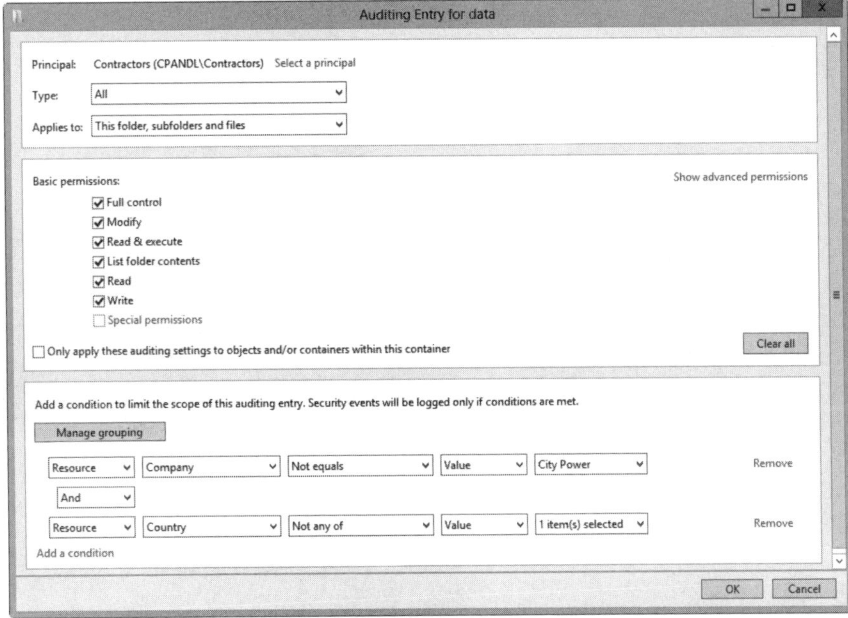

Figure 19-17 Use claims-based access controls to fine-tune auditing.

Monitoring the security logs

Any time files and folders that you've configured for auditing are accessed, the action is written to the system's Security log, where it's stored for your review. The Security log is accessible from Event Viewer. Successful actions can cause successful events, such as successful file reads, to be recorded. Failed actions can cause failed events, such as failed file deletions, to be recorded.

CHAPTER 20

Managing file screening and storage reporting

The Windows Server 2012 R2 operating system provides a robust environment for working with files and folders. For maximum control and flexibility, you'll usually format volumes with the NTFS file system. NTFS gives you many advanced options, including the option to configure file screening and storage reporting, which are available when you add the File Server Resource Manager role service to a server as part of the File Services role.

Understanding file screening and storage reporting

When you work with NTFS volumes, file screening is another tool you can use in your effort to keep networks safe from malicious programs and block unauthorized types of content. You can use file screening in conjunction with quotas and storage reports. By using file screening, you can monitor and block the use of certain types of files. You can configure file screening in one of two modes:

- **Active screening.** Does not allow users to save unauthorized files.
- **Passive screening.** Allows users to save unauthorized files but monitors or warns about using the files (or both).

You actively or passively screen files by defining a file screen. All file screens have a *file-screen path*, which is a folder that defines the base file path to which the screen is applied. Screening applies to the designated folder and all subfolders of the designated folder. The particulars of how screening works and what is screened are derived from a source template that defines the file screen's properties.

Windows Server 2012 R2 includes the file-screen templates listed in Table 20-1. By using File Server Resource Manager, you can easily define additional templates to use when you define file screens or you can set single-user, custom file-screen properties when defining the file screen.

Table 20-1 File-screen templates

File-Screen Template Name	Screening Type	File-Group Action
Block Audio And Video Files	Active	Block: Audio and Video Files
Block E-Mail Files	Active	Block: E-Mail Files
Block Executable Files	Active	Block: Executable Files
Block Image Files	Active	Block: Image Files
Monitor Executable And System Files	Passive	Warn: Executable Files, System Files

File-screen templates or custom properties define the following:

- Screening type: active or passive
- File groups to which screening is applied
- Notifications using email, an event log, a command, a report, or any combination of these

Table 20-2 lists the standard file groups for screening. Each file group has a predefined set of files to which it applies. You can modify the included file types and create additional file groups by using File Server Resource Manager.

Table 20-2 File-screen groups and the file types to which they apply

File Group	Applies To
Audio and video files	.aac, .aif, .aiff, .asf, .asx, .au, .avi, .flac, .m3u, .mid, .midi, .mov, .mp1, .mp2, .mp3, .mp4, .mpa, .mpe, .mpeg, .mpeg2, .mpeg3, .mpg, .ogg, .qt, .qtw, .ram, .rm, .rmi, .rmvb, .snd, .swf, .vob, .wav, .wax, .wma, .wmv, .wvx
Backup files	.bak, .bck, .bkf, .old
Compressed files	.ace, .arc, .arj, .bhx, .bz2, .cab, .gz, .gzip, .hpk, .hqx, .jar, .lha, .lzh, .lzx, .pak, .pit, .rar, .sea, .sit, .sqz, .tgz, .uu, .uue, .z, .zip, .zoo
Email files	.eml, .idx, .mbox, .mbx, .msg, .ost, .oft, .pab, .pst
Executable files	.bat, .cmd, .com, .cpl, .exe, .inf, .js, .jse, .msh, .msi, .msp, .ocx, .pif, .pl, .ps1, .scr, .vb, .vbs, .wsf, .wsh
Image files	.bmp, .dib, .eps, .gif, .img, .jfif, .jpe, .jpeg, .jpg, .pcx, .png, .ps, .psd, .raw, .rif, .spiff, .tif, .tiff

File Group	Applies To
Office files	.accdb, .accde, .accdr, .accdt, .adn, .adp, .doc, .docm, .docx, .dot, .dotm, .dotx, .grv, .gsa, .gta, .mad, .maf, .mda, .mdb, .mde, .mdf, .mdm, .mdt, .mdw, .mdz, .mpd, .mpp, .mpt, .obt, .odb, .one, .onepkg, .pot, .potm, .potx, .ppa, .ppam, .pps, .ppsm, .ppsx, .ppt, .pptn, .pptx, .pub, .pwz, .rqy, .rtf, .rwz, .sldm, .sldx, .slk, .thmx, .vdx, .vsd, .vsl, .vss, .vst, .vsu, .vsw, .vsx, .vtx, .wbk, .wri, .xla, .xlam, .xlb, .xlc, .xld, .xlk, .xll, .xlm, .xls, .xlsb, .xlsm, .xlsx, .xlt, .xltm, .xltx, .xlv, .xlw, .xsf, .xsn
System files	.acm, .dll, .ocx, .sys, .vxd
Temporary files	.temp, .tmp, ~*
Text files	.asc, .text, .txt
Webpage files	.asp, .aspx, .cgi, .css, .dhtml, .hta, .htm, .html, .mht, .php, .php3, .shtml, .url

Inside OUT

Exception paths

You also can configure exception paths to designate specifically allowed locations for saving blocked file types. You can use this feature to allow specific users to save blocked file types to designated locations or to allow all users to save blocked file types to designated locations. As an example, you might want to deter illegal downloading of music and movies within the organization by preventing users from saving audio and video files. However, if your organization has an audio/video department that needs to be able to save audio and video files, you can configure an exception to allow files to be saved in a folder accessible only to members of this department.

You can generate storage reports as part of quota and file-screening management. Table 20-3 provides a summary of the standard storage reports and their purposes. By using one of the standard storage reports, you can generate three general types of storage reports:

- **Incident reports.** Generated automatically when a user tries to save an unauthorized file or when a user exceeds a quota
- **Scheduled reports.** Generated periodically based on a scheduled report task
- **On-demand reports.** Generated manually upon request

Table 20-3 Standard storage reports

Report Name	Description
Duplicate Files	Lists files that appear to be duplicates based on the file size and last modification time. It helps reclaim wasted space resulting from duplication.
File Screening Audit	Lists file-screening audit events on the server for a specified period. It helps identify users and applications that violate screening policies. You can set report parameters to filter events based on the user and the minimum days since the screening event occurred.
Files By File Group	Lists files by file group, such as Compressed Files, Executable Files, or Office Files. It helps identify usage patterns and types of files that are using large amounts of disk space. You can set report parameters to include or exclude specific file groups.
Files By Owner	Lists files by users who own them. It helps identify users who use large amounts of disk space. You can set report parameters to include or exclude specific users and specific files by name pattern.
Files By Property	Lists files by a particular classification property. It helps track classification patterns and general usage of classification properties.
Folders By Property	Lists folders by a particular classification property. It helps track classification patterns and general usage of classification properties.
Large Files	Lists files that are of a specified size or larger. It helps identify file-classification usage patterns. You can set report parameters to generate a report about a specified classification property. You can include and exclude files only by name pattern.
Least Recently Accessed Files	Lists files that haven't been accessed recently. It helps identify files that you might be able to delete or archive. You can set report parameters to define what constitutes a least recently used file. By default, any file that hasn't been accessed in the past 90 days is considered a least recently used file. You can also include or exclude specific files by name pattern.
Most Recently Accessed Files	Lists files that have been accessed recently. It helps identify frequently used files. You can set report parameters to define what constitutes a most recently used file. By default, any file that has been accessed within the past seven days is considered a most recently used file. You can also include or exclude specific files by name pattern.
Quota Usage	Lists the quotas that exceed a minimum quota usage value. It helps identify file usage according to quotas. You can set report parameters to define the quotas that should be included according to the percentage of the quota limit used. For example, you might want to report when 75 percent of the quota limit has been reached.

You manage file screening and storage reporting by using the File Server Resource Manager console. This console is installed and available on the Tools menu in Server Manager when you add the File Server Resource Manager role service to the server as part of the File And Storage Services role. When you select the File Server Resource Manager node in the console, you see five additional nodes (as shown in Figure 20-1):

- **Quota Management.** Used to manage the quota features of Windows Server 2012 R2; discussed in Chapter 16, "Maintaining and optimizing storage"
- **File Screening Management.** Used to manage the file-screening features of Windows Server 2012 R2; discussed in this chapter
- **Storage Reports Management.** Used to manage the storage-reporting features of Windows Server 2012 R2; discussed in this chapter
- **Classification Management.** Used to manage the file-classification features of Windows Server 2012 R2
- **File Management Tasks.** Used to find subsets of files and then manage the files in some way

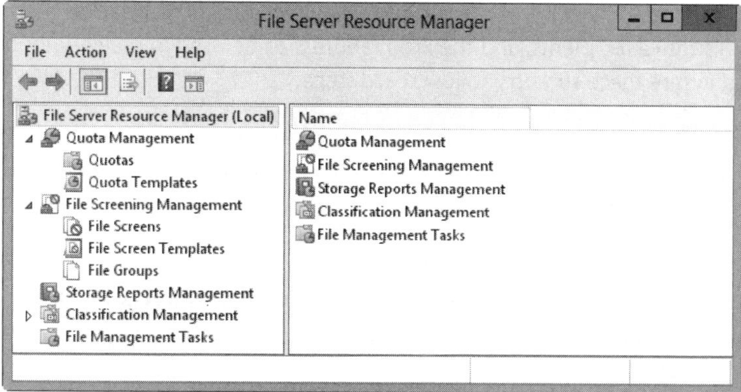

Figure 20-1 Use File Server Resource Manager to manage quotas, file screening, and storage reports.

Managing file screening and storage reporting

File-screening and storage-reporting management can be divided into the following key areas:

- **Global options.** Control global settings for file-server resources, including email notification, storage-report default parameters, report locations, file-screen auditing, and access-denied assistance

- **File groups.** Control the types of files to which screens are applied
- **File-screen templates.** Control screening properties (screening type: active or passive; file groups to which screening is applied; notifications: email, event log, or both)
- **File screens.** Control file paths that are screened
- **File-screen exceptions.** Control file paths that are screening exceptions
- **Report generation.** Controls whether and how storage reports are generated

The following sections discuss each of these management areas.

Managing global file-resource settings

You use global file-resource options to configure email notification, storage-report default parameters, report locations, and file-screen auditing. You should configure these global settings prior to configuring quotas, file screens, and storage reporting.

Configuring email notifications

Notifications and storage reports are emailed through a Simple Mail Transfer Protocol (SMTP) server. For this process to work, you must designate which organizational SMTP server to use, default administrative recipients, and the From address to be used in mailing notifications and reports. To configure these settings, follow these steps:

1. Open File Server Resource Manager. On the Action menu or in the Actions pane, tap or click Configure Options. This opens the File Server Resource Manager Options dialog box with the Email Notifications tab selected by default, as shown in Figure 20-2.
2. In the SMTP Server Name Or IP Address text box, type the fully qualified domain name of the organization's mail server, such as **MailServer48.cpandl.com**, or type the IP address of this server, such as **192.168.10.52**.

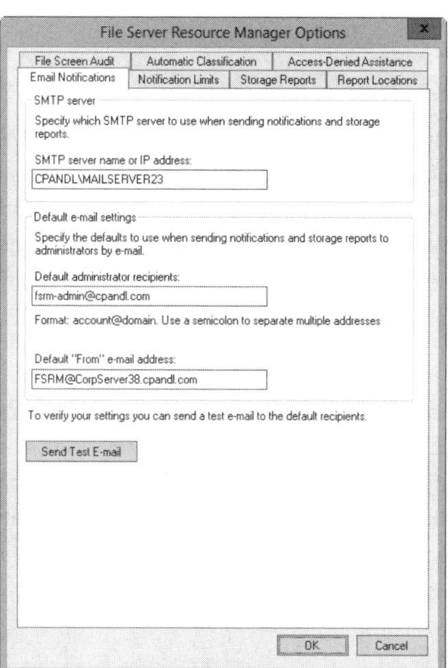

Figure 20-2 Set email notification and other global file-resource settings on the Email Notifications tab.

3. In the Default Administrator Recipients field, type the email address of the default administrator for notification, such as **filescreens@cpandl.com**. Typically, you want this to be a separate mailbox that is monitored by an administrator or a distribution group that goes to the specific administrators responsible for file-server resource management. You can also enter multiple email addresses. Be sure to separate each email address with a semicolon.

4. In the Default "From" E-Mail Address field, type the email address you want the server to use in the From field of notification messages. Remember, both users and administrators can receive notifications.

5. To test the settings, tap or click Send Test E-Mail. The test email message should be delivered to the default administrator recipients almost immediately. If it isn't, check to be sure that the email addresses used are valid and that the From email address is acceptable to the SMTP server as a valid sender.

6. Tap or click OK.

TROUBLESHOOTING

Resolving email notification problems

If you suspect a problem with notifications from File Server Resource Manager, the event logs are one of the first places you should look to resolve it. Events related to File Server Resource Manager can be found in the Application event log under the source SRMSVC. You also want to verify that the email options have been properly configured. Ensure that the SMTP server and default email recipients are valid. Next, send a test email message to confirm the email addresses and verify that the SMTP server is working as expected.

If email notifications are being sent but you aren't receiving as many notifications as you think you should, check the configuration of email notifications as discussed in the next section, "Configuring notification limits." Keep in mind that only one email notification is generated within the interval specified. Thus, whether a user attempts to save a blocked file or a file that exceeds a quota threshold one time or a hundred times in this interval, only one email message is generated.

Configuring notification limits

When a quota is exceeded or an unauthorized file is detected, File Server Resource Manager sends a notification to administrators by performing one or more of the following actions:

- Sending an email message to the user who attempted to save an unauthorized file, to a designated list of administrators, or to both
- Recording a warning message in the event logs
- Executing a command that performs administrative tasks under the LocalService, NetworkService, or LocalSystem account
- Generating one or more notification reports and optionally sending those reports to an authorized list of recipients

To reduce the number of notifications, you can set notification limits that specify a period of time that must elapse before a subsequent notification of the same type is raised for the same issue. The default notification limit for email notification, event log notification, command notification, and report notification is 60 minutes.

You can configure notification limits by following these steps:

1. Open File Server Resource Manager. On the Action menu or in the Actions pane, tap or click Configure Options.

2. In the File Server Resource Manager Options dialog box, tap or click the Notification Limits tab.

3. You can now configure limits for the following types of notifications:
   - **Email Notification.** Sets the interval between email notifications
   - **Event Log Notification.** Sets the interval between event-log notifications
   - **Command Notification.** Sets the interval between command notifications
   - **Report Notification.** Sets the interval between report notifications

4. Tap or click OK to save your settings.

Reviewing reports and configuring storage-report parameters

Each storage report has a default configuration you can review and modify by using File Server Resource Manager Options. Default parameter changes apply to all future incident reports and any existing report tasks that use the default configuration. You can override the default settings as necessary if you subsequently schedule a report task or generate a report on demand.

You can access the standard storage reports and change their default parameters by following these steps:

1. Open File Server Resource Manager. On the Action menu or in the Actions pane, tap or click Configure Options.

2. In the File Server Resource Manager Options dialog box, tap or click the Storage Reports tab.

3. To review a report's current settings, select the report name in the Reports list and then tap or click Review Reports.

4. To modify a report's default parameters, select the report name in the Reports list and then tap or click Edit Parameters. You can then modify the report parameters as necessary.

5. When you finish, tap or click Close or OK as appropriate.

Configuring report locations

By default, incident, scheduled, and on-demand reports are stored on the server on which notification is triggered in separate subfolders under %SystemDrive%\StorageReports. You can review or modify this configuration by following these steps:

1. Open File Server Resource Manager. On the Action menu or in the Actions pane, tap or click Configure Options.
2. In the File Server Resource Manager Options dialog box, tap or click the Report Locations tab.
3. The report folders currently in use are listed under Report Locations. To specify a different local folder for a particular report type, type a new folder path or tap or click Browse to search for the folder path you want to use.
4. Tap or click OK.

NOTE

You can use only local paths for report storage. Nonlocal folder paths are considered invalid.

TROUBLESHOOTING

Resolving problems with report generation

Occasionally, you might find that File Server Resource Manager fails to generate reports entirely and that the Application event logs contain little or no information that can help you resolve the problem. Here, errors or corruption on the volume where storage reports are being saved might be causing problems generating reports. If so, you can resolve the problem by running Chkdsk on the volume and then trying to generate the reports again.

Configuring file-screen auditing

By running a file screen auditing report, you can record file-screening activity in an auditing database for later review. This auditing data is tracked on a per-server basis, so the server on which the activity occurs is the one on which the activity is audited. To enable or disable file-screen auditing, follow these steps:

1. Open File Server Resource Manager. On the Action menu or in the Actions pane, tap or click Configure Options.
2. In the File Server Resource Manager Options dialog box, tap or click the File Screen Audit tab.
3. To enable auditing, select the Record File Screening Activity In Auditing Database check box.
4. To disable auditing, clear the Record File Screening Activity In Auditing Database check box.

5. Tap or click OK to save your settings.

Configuring classification

You use the classification rules and properties to classify files based on location, type, and content. Classification properties are values that you want to assign to files and folders. Classification rules assign classification properties to files. Each classification rule is used to assign a specific classification property to designated folders and their contents. Two types of properties can be created:

- **Local properties.** Properties defined on a specific server, using File Server Resource Manager
- **Global properties.** Properties defined in Active Directory, using Active Directory Administrative Center

Each classification rule you define has a specific scope. By default, classification rules apply to all files of any type within designated folders and their subfolders. You can limit the rule by assigning the rule to the lowest-level folders to which the rule should be applied. For example, rather than assigning the rule to a drive root, such as C:\, you could set the rule on the C:\Data, C:\Shares\Engineering, and C:\Reports folders. You can further limit the scope of the rule by applying it only to specific types of files, such as only user and group files.

The classification methods you can use include the following:

- **Folder Classifier.** Classifies files according to folder. When you use this classifier, every file in the designated folder (and in its subfolders) is assigned the classification property associated with the rule.
- **Content Classifier.** Classifies files according to search strings and regular expression patterns. When you use this classifier, any file containing all specified search strings and matching all specified regular expression patterns is assigned the classification property associated with the rule. The more complex your content classifier, the longer it takes to parse and assign the classification.
- **Windows PowerShell Classifier.** Classifies files by using Windows PowerShell scripts. Because scripts are entered directly as part of the classification parameters, you should test the scripts on a subset of data or a specific test set before applying.

Generally, classification rules are applied to files only when applications or file management tasks query their classification properties. Because processing classification rules at the time of a request might slow down performance, you typically want to classify files automatically beforehand. To do this, you create a schedule for automatic classification by using File Server Resource Manager.

Automatic classification can be scheduled to run weekly at a specific day and time, such as Sunday at 3:30 A.M., or monthly on a specific day of the month, such as the fifth day of every month.

Following this, you can configure classification by doing the following:

1. Create classification properties that you want to assign to files by using either File Server Resource Manager or Active Directory Administrative Center.
   - Create local properties in File Server Resource Manager. Under Classification Management, select Classification Properties to view currently defined properties. To create a local property, press and hold or right-click Classification Properties in the left pane, select Create Local Property, and then use the options provided to set the property type and value.
   - Create global properties in Active Directory Administrative Center. Under Dynamic Access Controls, select Resource Properties to view currently defined global properties and their enabled or disabled status. To create a global property, under Tasks, select New, select Resource Property, and then use the options provided to set the property type and value.
2. In File Server Resource Manager, create one or more classification rules for each classification property. Under Classification Management, select Classification Rules to view currently defined rules. To create a rule, press and hold or right-click Classification Rules in the left pane, select Create Classification Rule, and then use the options provided to define the rule.
3. In File Server Resource Manager, schedule automatic classification to pre-assign classification properties as appropriate. Under Classification Management, select Classification Rules and then select Configure Classification Schedule. You can now view the current classification schedule or define a new one.

Enabling access-denied assistance

In Group Policy, you can configure Access-Denied Assistance policies to help users determine who to contact if they have trouble accessing files. When you enable and configure Access-Denied Assistance policies, you can customize Access Denied errors with additional help text, links to help pages or documents, and an email address for requesting help.

To enable Access-Denied Assistance for all file types, configure Enable Access-Denied Assistance On Client For All File Types as Enabled and then customize Access Denied errors by enabling and configuring Customize Message For Access Denied Errors. As discussed in Chapter 19, "File security, access controls, and auditing," these policies are found in the Administrative Templates policies for Computer Configuration under System\Access-Denied Assistance.

When you add the File Server Resource Manager role to a file server, you can configure Access-Denied Assistance through File Server Resource Manager and then you can use its standard-message and request-assistance options to configure Access-Denied Assistance quickly. The standard assistance message is similar to the one shown in Figure 20-3. The standard message includes a clickable link to Microsoft Support. You can easily modify the standard message.

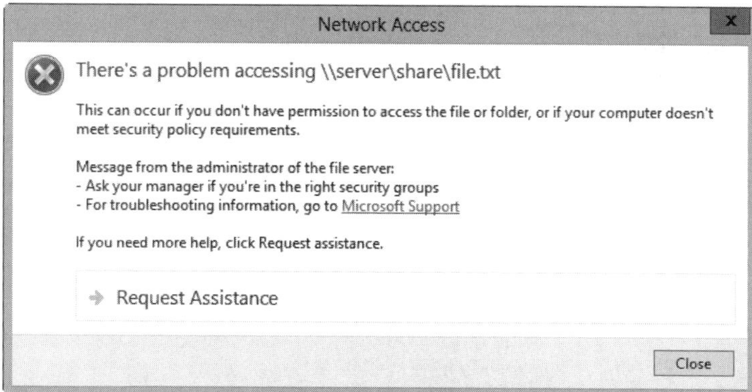

Figure 20-3 Set the default assistance message by using File Server Resource Manager.

To configure Access-Denied Assistance by using File Server Resource Manager, follow these steps:

1. Open File Server Resource Manager. On the Action menu or in the Actions pane, tap or click Configure Options.
2. In the File Server Resource Manager Options dialog box, tap or click the Access-Denied Assistance tab, as shown in Figure 20-4.
3. Select the Enable Access-Denied Assistance check box. You can modify the standard message by typing directly into the editable box provided on the Access-Denied Assistance tab. For example, you might want to replace the link to Microsoft Support with a link to your organization's help desk, as I've done here. When creating your message, keep the following in mind:
   - The message is standard text except for the *<a> </a>* tags. The begin and end anchor tags are the only acceptable HTML.
   - You can enter multiple anchor tags. Each *<a>* tag can have its own hypertext reference, and any text placed between the *<a>* tag and the *</a>* tag becomes a clickable hypertext link.

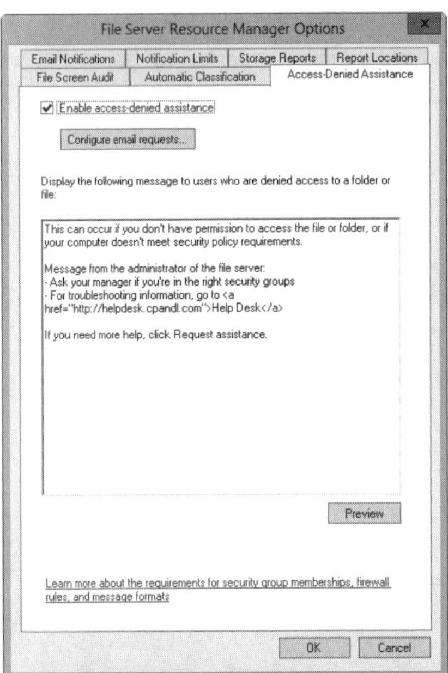

Figure 20-4 Customize the Access-Denied Assistance message for your organization.

4. If you want users to be able to request assistance by sending an email message to a predesignated administrator, tap or click Configure Email Requests and then select Enable Users To Request Assistance, as shown in Figure 20-5. Typically, you want to include user information (including user claims) and device state information (including device claims), which is why these options are selected by default.

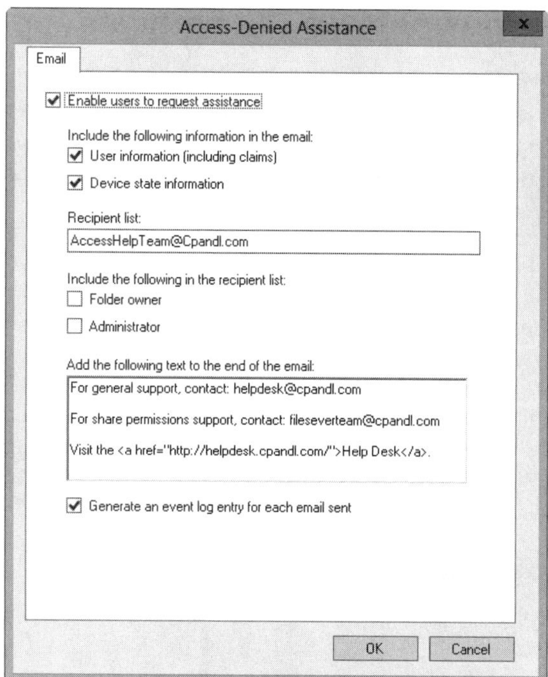

Figure 20-5 Customize the request assistance email requests.

5. In the Recipient List, enter a semicolon-separated list of recipients for the email request. However, rather than entering the email addresses of specific people, you might want to enter the email address for a distribution group. In this way, you can manage recipients by adding or removing group members rather than by editing the Access-Denied Assistance configuration.

6. By default, the email request also is sent to the folder owner and the Administrator account. If you have a specific team handling access assistance and you already provided the email address in the Recipient List, you might want to clear these options. Otherwise, accept the default selections.

7. Next, use the text box provided to customize the text added to the end of the email message. As before, this is standard text that can be modified as necessary and can include hypertext links.

8. By default, email requests are logged in the Application event log. If you don't want related events to be logged, clear the Generate An Event Log Entry For Each Email Sent check box.

9. Tap or click OK.

Managing the file groups to which screens are applied

You use file groups to designate sets of similar file types to which screening can be applied. In File Server Resource Manager, you can view the currently defined file-screening groups by expanding the File Server Resource Manager and File Screening Management nodes and then selecting File Groups. Table 20-2, shown previously, lists the default file groups and the included file types.

You can modify existing file groups by following these steps:

1. Open File Server Resource Manager. Expand the File Server Resource Manager and File Screening Management nodes and then select File Groups.
2. Currently defined file groups are listed along with included and excluded files.
3. To modify file-group properties, double-tap or double-click the file-group name. This opens a Properties dialog box similar to the one shown in Figure 20-6.

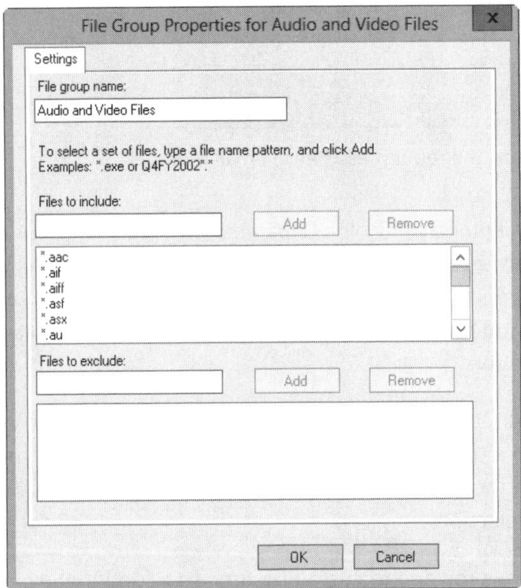

Figure 20-6 Include and exclude file types by modifying file-group properties.

4. In the Files To Include text box, type the file name extension of an additional file type to screen, such as **.pdf**, or the file name pattern, such as **Archive*.***. Tap or click Add. Repeat this step to specify other file types to screen.

5. In the Files To Exclude text box, type the file name extension of a file type to exclude from screening, such as **.doc**, or the file name pattern, such as **Report*.***. Tap or click Add. Repeat this step to specify other file types to exclude from screening.

6. Tap or click OK to save the changes.

You can specify additional file groups to screen by following these steps:

1. Open File Server Resource Manager. Expand the File Server Resource Manager and File Screening Management nodes and then select File Groups.

2. On the Action menu or in the Actions pane, tap or click Create File Group. This opens the Create File Group Properties dialog box.

3. In the File Group Name text box, type the name of the file group you're creating.

4. In the Files To Include text box, type the file name extension to screen, such as **.pdf**, or the file name pattern, such as **Archive*.***. Tap or click Add. Repeat this step to specify other file types to screen.

5. In the Files To Exclude text box, type the file name extension to exclude from screening, such as **.doc**, or the file name pattern, such as **Report*.***. Tap or click Add. Repeat this step to specify other file types to exclude from screening.

6. Tap or click OK to create the file group.

Managing file-screen templates

You use file-screen templates to define screening properties, including the screening type, the file groups to which a screen is applied, and notification. In File Server Resource Manager, you can view the currently defined file-screen templates by expanding the File Server Resource Manager and File Screening Management nodes and then selecting File Screen Templates. Table 20-1, shown previously, provides a summary of the default file-screen templates.

You can modify existing file-screen templates by following these steps:

1. Open File Server Resource Manager. Expand the File Server Resource Manager and File Screening Management nodes and then select File Screen Templates.

   Currently defined file-screen templates are listed by name, screening type, and file groups affected.

2. To modify file-screen template properties, double-tap or double-click the file-screen template name. This opens a Properties dialog box (shown in Figure 20-7).

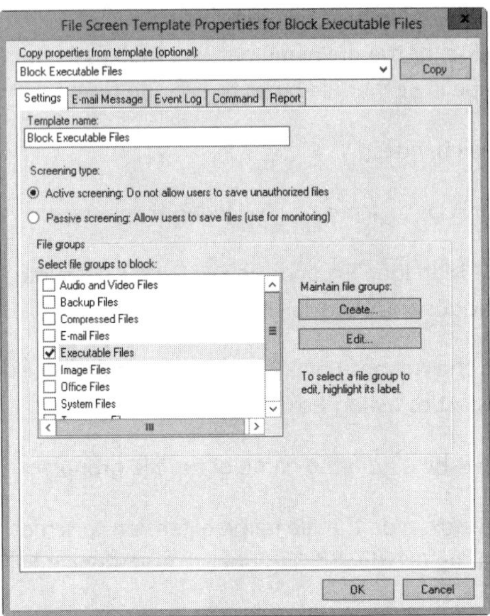

Figure 20-7 Use file-screen template properties to configure the screening type, the file groups to which a screen is applied, and notification.

3. On the Settings tab, you can set the template name, screen type, and file groups affected, using the controls provided.

4. On the E-Mail Message tab, you can configure the following notifications:

   - To notify an administrator when the file screen is triggered, select the Send E-Mail To The Following Administrators check box and then type the email address or addresses to use. Be sure to separate multiple email addresses with a semicolon. Use the **[Admin Email]** value to specify the default administrator as configured previously under the global options.
   - To notify users, select the Send E-Mail To The User Who Attempted To Save An Unauthorized File check box. In the Subject and Message Body text boxes, specify the contents of the user notification message. Table 20-4 lists available variables and their meanings.

5. On the Event Log tab, you can configure event logging. Select Send Warning To Event Log to enable logging and then specify the text of the log entry in the Log Entry field. Table 20-4 lists available variables and their meanings.

6. On the Report tab, select the Generate Reports check box to enable incident reporting and then select the check boxes for the types of reports you want to generate. Incident reports are stored under %SystemDrive%\StorageReports\Incident by default and can be sent to designated administrators and to the user who attempted to save an unauthorized file. Use the **[Admin Email]** value to specify the default administrator as configured previously under the global options.
7. Tap or click OK when you have finished modifying the template.

You can create a new file-screen template by following these steps:

1. Open File Server Resource Manager. Expand the File Screening Management node and then select File Screen Templates.
2. On the Action menu or in the Actions pane, tap or click Create File Screen Template. This opens the Create File Screen Template dialog box.
3. Follow steps 3 to 7 of the previous procedure.

Table 20-4 File-screen variables

Variable Name	Description
[Admin Email]	Inserts the email addresses of the administrators defined under the global options
[File Screen Path]	Inserts the local file path where the user attempted to save the file, such as C:\Data
[File Screen Remote Path]	Inserts the remote file path where the user attempted to save the file, such as \\server\share
[File Screen System Path]	Inserts the canonical file path where the user attempted to save the file, such as \\?\VolumeGUID
[Server Domain]	Inserts the domain of the server on which the notification occurred
[Server]	Inserts the server on which the notification occurred
[Source File Owner]	Inserts the user name of the owner of the unauthorized file
[Source File Owner Email]	Inserts the email address of the owner of the unauthorized file
[Source File Path]	Inserts the source path of the unauthorized file
[Source File Remote Paths]	For shared folders, inserts the source path in Universal Naming Convention (UNC) format, such as \\FileServer15\Data

Variable Name	Description
[Source Io Owner Email]	Inserts the email address of the user who caused the notification
[Source Io Owner]	Inserts the name of the user who caused the notification
[Source Process Id]	Inserts the process ID (PID) of the process that caused the notification
[Source Process Image]	Inserts the executable for the process that caused the notification
[Violated File Group]	Inserts the name of the file group in which the file type is defined as unauthorized

Creating file screens

You use file screens to designate file paths that are screened. In File Server Resource Manager, you can view current file screens by expanding the File Server Resource Manager and File Screening Management nodes and then selecting File Screens. Before you define file screens, you should specify file-screening groups and file-screen templates that you will use, as discussed in the "Managing the file groups to which screens are applied" and "Managing file-screen templates" sections earlier in the chapter.

After you define the necessary file groups and file-screen templates, you can create a file screen by following these steps:

1. Open File Server Resource Manager. Expand the File Server Resource Manager and File Screening Management nodes and then select File Screens.
2. Tap or click Create File Screen on the Action menu or in the Actions pane.
3. In the Create File Screen dialog box, set the local computer path to screen by tapping or clicking Browse. In the Browse For Folder dialog box, select the path to screen, such as C:\Data.
4. In the Derive Properties selection list, choose the file-screen template that defines the screening properties you want to use.
5. Tap or click Create.

Defining file-screening exceptions

You use exception paths to designate folder locations where it's permitted to save blocked file types. Based on the NTFS permissions on the excepted file path, you can use this feature to allow specific users to save blocked file types to designated locations or to allow all users to save blocked file types to designated locations.

You can create a file-screen exception by following these steps:

1. Open File Server Resource Manager. Expand the File Server Resource Manager and File Screening Management nodes and then select File Screens.
2. Tap or click Create File Screen Exception on the Action menu or in the Actions pane.
3. In the Create File Screen Exception dialog box, set the local path to exclude from screening by tapping or clicking Browse. Then, in the Browse For Folder dialog box, select the path to exclude from screening, such as C:\Data\Images.
4. Select the file groups to exclude from screening on the designated path.
5. Tap or click OK.

Scheduling and generating storage reports

Incident reports are generated automatically when triggered, as defined in the Reports tab properties of a file-screen template. (For details, see "Understanding file screening and storage reporting" earlier in the chapter.) Scheduled and on-demand reports are configured separately. In File Server Resource Manager, you can view currently scheduled reports by expanding the File Server Resource Manager node and then selecting Storage Reports Management.

You can schedule reports on a per-volume or per-folder basis by following these steps:

1. Open File Server Resource Manager. Expand the File Server Resource Manager node and then select Storage Reports Management.
2. On the Action menu or in the Actions pane, tap or click Schedule A New Report Task. This opens the Storage Reports Task Properties dialog box, shown in Figure 20-8.

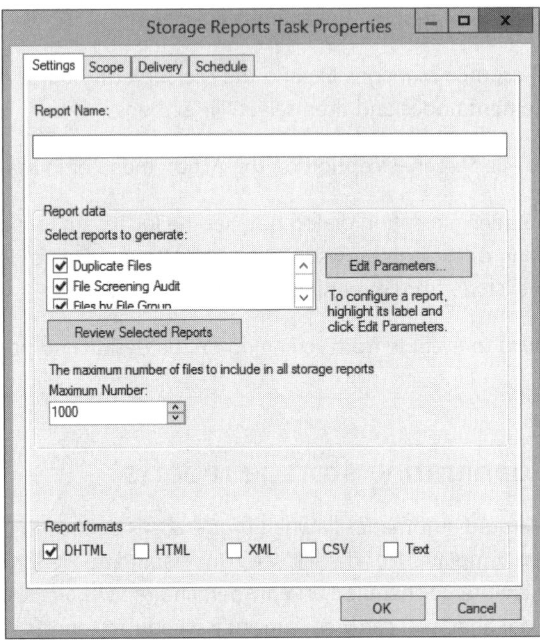

Figure 20-8 Schedule reports for delivery on a per-volume or per-folder basis.

3. On the Settings tab, type a descriptive name for the report, such as **Primary Share Storage Report**.
4. Under Report Data, select the types of reports to generate. Some of the reports have configurable parameters. If a report has configurable parameters, you can customize the report by selecting the report under Report Data and then tapping or clicking Edit Parameters.
5. By default, only the first 1000 files are included in storage reports. To specify a different maximum file value, enter the desired number in the Maximum Number combo box.
6. Under Report Formats, select the format for the report, such as Dynamic HTML (DHTML).
7. On the Scope tab, specify the general kinds of data to include by selecting the appropriate check boxes for the following:
   - **Application Files.** Data created by applications
   - **Backup And Archival Files.** Data created for backups and file archives

- **Group Files.** Data created and modified by multiple users rather than by a particular user
- **User Files.** Data created by specific users

8. On the Scope tab, tap or click Add. In the Browse For Folder dialog box, select the volume or folder on which you want to generate scheduled storage reports. Repeat these actions to add other volumes or folders.

   NOTE

   On clustered file servers, you can report only on volumes that belong to the same cluster resource group.

9. By default, Windows Server 2012 R2 stores scheduled storage reports as they're generated in the %SystemDrive%\StorageReports\Scheduled folder. If you also want to deliver reports by email to administrators, tap or click the Delivery tab and then select the Send Reports To The Following Administrators check box. Enter the email address or addresses to which reports should be delivered, being sure to separate each email address with a semicolon.
10. On the Schedule tab, use the options provided to define the run schedule for reporting. For example, you can run the reports weekly on a Monday at 4:30:00 A.M. or monthly on the last day of the month at 3:00:00 A.M.
11. Tap or click OK to schedule the report task.

You can generate an on-demand report by following these steps:

1. Open File Server Resource Manager. Expand the File Server Resource Manager node and then select Storage Reports Management.
2. On the Action menu or in the Actions pane, tap or click Generate Reports Now. This opens the Storage Reports Task Properties dialog box.
3. On the Settings tab, under Report Data, select the types of reports to generate.
4. Under Report Formats, select the format for the report, such as DHTML.
5. On the Scope tab, specify the general kinds of data to include by selecting the appropriate check boxes for Application Files, Group Files, Backup And Archival Files, and User Files.

6. On the Scope tab, tap or click Add. In the Browse For Folder dialog box, select the volume or folder on which you want to generate the on-demand storage reports. Repeat to add other volumes or folders.

7. Windows Server 2012 R2 stores on-demand storage reports in the %SystemDrive%\StorageReports\Interactive folder. If you also want to deliver reports by email to administrators, tap or click the Delivery tab and then select the Send Reports To The Following Administrators check box. Enter the email address or addresses to which reports should be delivered, being sure to separate each email address with a semicolon.

8. Tap or click OK. When prompted, specify whether to wait for the reports to be generated and then display them or to generate the reports in the background for later access. Tap or click OK.

Index

B

C

D

E

F

K

L

N

O

P

Q

R

U

W

X

Z

About the author

William R. Stanek (*http://www.williamstanek.com/*) has more than 20 years of hands-on experience with advanced programming and development. He is a leading technology expert, an award-winning author, and a pretty-darn-good instructional trainer. Over the years, his practical advice has helped millions of programmers, developers, and network engineers all over the world. William's 150th book was published in 2013, and more than 7.5 million people have read his many works.

William has been involved in the commercial Internet community since 1991. His core business and technology experience comes from more than 11 years of military service. He has substantial experience in developing server technology, encryption, and Internet solutions. He has written many technical white papers and training courses on a wide variety of topics. He frequently serves as a subject matter expert and consultant.

William has an MS with distinction in information systems and a BS in computer science, magna cum laude. He is proud to have served in the Persian Gulf War as a combat crewmember on an electronic warfare aircraft. He flew on numerous combat missions into Iraq and was awarded nine medals for his wartime service, including one of the United States of America's highest-flying honors, the Air Force Distinguished Flying Cross. Currently, he resides in the Pacific Northwest with his wife and children.

William recently rediscovered his love of the great outdoors. When he's not writing, he can be found hiking, biking, backpacking, traveling, or trekking in search of adventure with his family! In his spare time, William writes books for children, including *The Bugville Critters Explore the Solar System* and *The Bugville Critters Go on Vacation*.

Find William on Twitter at www.twitter.com/WilliamStanek and on Facebook at www.facebook.com/William.Stanek.Author.